WORKING ON THE SYSTEM

WORKING ON THE SYSTEM

A COMPREHENSIVE MANUAL
FOR CITIZEN ACCESS
TO FEDERAL AGENCIES

Edited by James R. Michael
with Ruth C. Fort

RALPH NADER'S CENTER
FOR STUDY OF RESPONSIVE LAW

BASIC BOOKS, INC., PUBLISHERS

NEW YORK

© 1974 by Center for Study of Responsive Law
Library of Congress Catalog Card Number: 73-81135
SBN: 465-09210-1
Manufactured in the United States of America
74 75 76 77 78   10 9 8 7 6 5 4 3 2 1

Contents

CHAPTER 4

ADMINISTRATIVE PROCEDURE: RULES OF THE GAME   65

CHAPTER 5

THE FEDERAL TRADE COMMISSION   85

CHAPTER 6

THE INTERSTATE COMMERCE COMMISSION   169

CHAPTER 10

CHAPTER 11

CHAPTER 12

CHAPTER 13

THE NATIONAL HIGHWAY TRAFFIC SAFETY
ADMINISTRATION

CHAPTER 14

CHAPTER 15

CHAPTER 16

CHAPTER 17

THE CONSUMER PRODUCT SAFETY COMMISSION

CHAPTER 18

ORGANIZING AND OTHER PROBLEMS: KEEPING GOING

Introduction

BY RALPH NADER

This is a guidebook and a handbook for citizen participation in the hitherto forbidden and foreboding territory known as the federal regulatory agencies. Draped in secrecy, steeped in bureaucratic labyrinths and surrounded by special interest lobbyists, these agencies are far removed from the processes of self-government. Yet their impacts on Americans everywhere are, by contrast, direct and serious. By their various regulatory authority over the food, drug, auto, utilities, energy, transportation, communications, pesticide and other industries, together with environmental policies, those agencies affect the health, safety, mobility, economics and thinking of citizens of all ages.

If citizens know more about them, what they do and don't do, and how people can exercise and broaden their rights to affect, initiate or stop their decisions, these regulatory agencies will be more responsive to the public interest. This is no longer just a hope, but has become an increasingly tested principle in the past few years. Reclaiming this portion of our government and developing the broader concerns of the citizenry requires knowledge, initiative and persistence.

This book is a product of the work and experience of the Center for Study of Responsive Law over the past several years. It is intended to provide, for the concerned layman as well as the professional, a usable guide to "working on the system" with a view toward greater justice through a more active citizenry.

Our experience indicates that a system of regulation, built up over many years and long neglected by Congress and the public, will not succumb to public participation and involvement without real citizen knowledge and understanding. The first step in this process is to know what these rarified regulatory agencies actually do and how their actions affect the lives of all Americans. In many instances, citizens experience the impacts, such as environmental depredation or unsafe products or consumer frauds, without knowing that regulatory agencies in fine marble buildings in Washington are supposed to be doing something to prevent these things from happening. One purpose of this book is to help fill that gap, to describe the activities of the agencies and the ways in which their behavior directly affects our health and well-being. But beyond knowing, this book is designed to encourage doing. That is, it is our intention to provide the tools, the basic building blocks of citizen action, so that citizen voices may be heard along with the imprecations of special interests. These tools are the laws and rules and regulations and procedures which govern access to the agencies and this book provides the reader with this information in useful detail. It also provides guidance and information on a vast array of data which the citizen will find invaluable—from names and addresses and telephone numbers of the people who administer the agencies to examples of petitions and other material used by citizens to gain entry into the federal regulatory system.

In the past several years, citizens have begun to reverse the national tide of helplessness and alienation by gaining small entries into the previously forbidden regulatory territory and in some cases in gaining small victories. This book details a variety of these specific examples with the hope that they will provide inspiration to ordinary people and groups in the country to go and do much more of the same. A description of some citizen activities will make this point clearer and more compelling.

In the summer of 1968, a group of six law and graduate students under my guidance began an inquiry into the Federal Trade Commission. The fifty-four year old FTC, housed in an architectural promontory at the juncture of Pennsylvania and Constitution Avenues, was supposed to be the government's chief consumer advocate. But, in fact, it was wallowing in a Rip Van Winkle-bureaucratic slumber, jolted awake periodically to succumb to the demands of a powerful corporation or trade association.

The students went to one office after another for interviews and information. For many old hands at the FTC, it was the first time they were interviewed by citizens asking what they were doing and why. They were accustomed to receiving, and lunching regularly with, corporate lawyers and business representatives. But this was different, a citizen-consumer study. The students outraged the then FTC Chairman, Paul Rand Dixon, by their repeated insistence on seeing reports, records, agreements with companies charged with illegal activity, and enforcement materials held from the public without justification.

As Chapter Five of this book makes clear, the way the FTC behaves affects millions of people, not just thousands of companies. Unfair business practices, deceptive advertisements, monopolistic or anti-competitive selling defrauds consumers of billions of dollars annually and frequently exposes them to avoidable health and safety hazards. The FTC is in charge of enforcing laws to prevent such abuses and to collect information and prepare studies about industry and commerce for longer range planning and prevention. Alas, for decades, political cronyism, sloth, and incompetence nourished a massive disinterest in law enforcement and a penchant for little charades of activity. Many of the Commissioners and higher agency officials stayed around for a few years for on-the-job training and then jumped into lucrative law firm practices or related opportunities in Washington.

During the sixties, the agency reached its lowest point under the Chairmanship of Paul Rand Dixon. In the book which came out of the students' research project (*The Nader Report on The Federal Trade Commission*, Random House, 1969), the authors documented the inert leadership which wafted like a somnolent plume over the 1,500 person agency and its eleven regional offices around the country. Slouched like a sorry sentinel by the cauldron of the marketplace frauds, the FTC would issue a few times a week its usual batch of "voluntary compliance" agreements or, more rarely, its "cease and desist" orders against the defendant companies. These mild moves took months, years or, on occasion, decades before being announced in such toothless form. While the FTC was thus trespassing on eternity with its administrative delays, the companies continued merrily to chalk up their ill-gotten gains which the agency was powerless to require them to return to the bilked consumers. Rather than asking Congress for authority to issue injunctions and assess money damages, the Commission preferred to continue its anemic way and order the culpable firms to "go and sin no more." Many of these firms simply changed their merchandising strategies and designed around the ban. And the entire cycle had to start all over again in its interminable way.

After the students' report came out in January 1969 urging many changes at the Commission, events moved with unaccustomed swiftness. The White House asked for and received from the American Bar Association a report that came to similar conclusions about the hapless state of the FTC as did the students. Congressional hearings and critical media commentary further showed the need for personnel and policy overhaul. A new chairman was installed by the President and under his successor, Miles Kirkpatrick, who took office in 1970, the FTC became somewhat more vigorous, more hardworking and more interested in consumer protection and antitrust enforcement.

That development was not the bedrock issue, important as it may have seemed. What was of greater consequence was the rise of public awareness over (1) the captive state of the FTC and other regulatory agencies to industrial and commercial interests and (2) the abysmal lack of citizen rights and representatives to intervene or challenge these agencies. The captive state phenomenon had long been chronicled in the legal and political science literature. But only in the past six years has the flagrant disregard, at times the chronic blockage, of citizen-consumer interests become understood popularly as the critical issue in seeking a responsive regulatory performance.

The story of the students and the FTC provides an example of how citizens can have an impact. This book is designed to give the reader the starting materials to learn about what the regulatory agencies are doing, how they are doing it, and guides to doing the same.

Here are some examples of what the law students learned about this process starting in late 1969. Using colorful acronyms such as SOUP (Students Opposing Unfair Practices), they began filing petitions for rule making or for intervening before FTC and other agency proceedings. This "learn by doing" legal education, initiated by Professor John Banzhaf III of George Washington University Law School, has jarred these agencies and helped illuminate the obstacles to citizen involvement before a wide public audience. Here is a sample:

—SOUP observed that the FTC would never require a company, after being ordered to "cease and desist" from continuing certain deceptive advertisements, to feature in its future ads a note for consumers as to its past deception. This is called an affirmative disclosure requirement. The students chose to intervene in a case involving the FTC against Campbell Soup regarding a deceptive soup ad on television. Their petition tried to chart a no-man's land because the FTC had never established any proceedings for citizens to intervene in a matter being negotiated between the agency and a company accused of a deceptive practice. They asked for the right to proceed *in forma pauperis* (that is, in poverty, so that they did not have to pay the exorbitant fees for printing briefs, copying documents, etc.), to obtain disclosure from the FTC files and to have an evidentiary hearing. Breaking new ground, the FTC granted them intervention rights, *in forma pauperis* status, some disclosure rights and an oral argument before the Commission. In addition, the Commission acknowledged for the first time its authority to order corrective advertising, even though it declined to order it in the Campbell Soup case.

In sum, the students did not achieve their objective of obtaining corrective advertising in Campbell Soup ads but won important rights of access to an FTC proceeding. Thus, other citizen groups can use and build on these rights in other cases before the Commission. Without SOUP's challenge, the FTC would have not had the occasion to respond.

—SMASH (Students Mobilizing on Auto Safety Hazards) was dismayed by the virtually worthless bumpers on automobiles in low-speed collisions. Walking speed (5 mph) bumps were costing motorists over a billion dollars a year in unnecessary damage repair bills. SMASH formally petitioned the National Highway Traffic Safety Administration to issue a performance standard for bumpers. The students wrote the performance standard they proposed and backed it up with much technical data from their engineering advisers. Their petition was one of several public moves which convinced Congress in 1972 to enact legislation requiring the NHTSA to issue bumper standards.

—STATIC (Student Taskforce Against Telecommunication Information Concealment) filed a petition asking the Federal Communications Commission to issue a rule requiring broadcast stations to present to the viewer or listener at regular intervals information about the station's obligations to the public. STATIC believed that few citizens were aware of these obligations or how they could go about enforcing them. Few Americans know that these stations come up for license renewal by the FCC every three years, that certain standards of fairness and completeness in their news coverage, time devoted to advertising, etc. must be met and that consumers now have the right to challenge these licenses or demand the right of reply when personally attacked on the station or urge counteradvertisements in certain controversial areas (as was the case before cigarette ads were taken off radio and TV).

—LABEL (Law Students' Association for Buyers' Education in Labeling) was another law student group which prepared a legal petition before the Food and Drug Administration, with detailed supporting materials, to require broader disclosure of ingredients on food and drink labels. FATS (Fight to Advertise the Truth about Saturates) were students who petitioned the FDA to issue a rule requiring disclosure of the fat content and type of fat of a number of food products. These actions led to a court declaration that FDA did have authority to require the disclosures LABEL wanted but FDA moved to ask for voluntary labeling by the companies as a start.

—FLITE (Future Lawyers Investigating Transportation Employment) intervened before the Civil Aeronautics Board urging that the Board examine an airline's minority hiring and promotion performance as a condition of approval of route changes, rate increases and other matters under CAB regulation. They submitted a brief citing federal law in support of their petition. The CAB issued a proposed rule similar to the one FLITE proposed and the government has taken legal action against minority employment discrimination by the airlines.

The above student projects are only a few of many such efforts in the past four years which have been directed toward the regulatory agencies. Recently established public interest consumer and environmental groups in Washington have initiated a wide range of legal actions relating to railroad passenger and freight service, pesticide regulation, food additives, meat and poultry inspection, air and water pollution, nuclear power plants, oil pipelines, timber cutting on U.S. forest lands, natural gas rate cases, interstate telephone rates, licensing of TV stations and hydroelectric projects, auto safety and recall policies, government secrecy and many others. The clubby world of the regulators and the regulated is being charted for reformation.

Here are some pertinent features which must be changed:

1. The agencies do very little to represent the interests of the unrepresented—namely the poor, the consumer, the tenant, the unborn. Even worse, these regulators erect procedural, economic and substantive obstacles to participation when these unrepresented on occasion receive the services of advocates for their cause. The U.S. Administrative Conference has sponsored studies in recent years which analyse this problem and suggest needed changes.

2. Congress does a very poor job of reviewing and monitoring the behavior of these agencies which it has created. Public hearings are infrequent and often shallow. At times, there is a very close relationship between the agency and the congressional committee, such as the Atomic Energy Commission and the Joint Committee on Atomic Energy, which precludes any arm's length evaluation on many basic issues. In addition, low budgets, weak staff and recruitment practices of these agencies are productive of situations which indenture the government to the industries it is supposed to be regulating.

3. There is a widespread absence of formal structures to represent consumer or broader public interests than those espoused and lobbied by the regulated industries. However, proposals to remedy this gap are gaining headway. Pending in Congress with substantial support is the

Consumer Protection Agency bill. This legislation would establish an independent consumer advocate office which would represent consumer interests before other federal agencies and in the courts. It would possess no regulatory power but would have the authority to participate in formal and informal proceedings of regulatory agencies to inject information and legal arguments which would advance consumer interests in health, safety, and economy.

Other proposals yet to be adopted include a recommendation in 1971 by an FCC staff group to establish a five-person Office of Public Counsel, which would be in, but not of, the FCC, to represent public interests in Commission proceedings. The group also suggested that special rules of procedure for public interest groups be adopted similar to the Model Rules of Citizen Participation (contained in this volume).

Public interest lawyers have discovered that the Federal Power Commission has the authority to employ attorneys for proper representation of the public interest in investigations made by it or proceedings before it. The Interstate Commerce Commission has comparable authority for railroad and motor carrier proceedings. Neither of these agencies are about to invoke such power unless they are pressured to do so by public interest groups.

This latter point, broadly applied, is cardinal to the thrust of this book. The more people who know their rights vis à vis these agencies, the more they will use them, which in turn expands these rights and remedies for others to use. What must be done quickly is to demystify these agencies and break the near-monopolistic access to their proceedings and inner forums which a handful of specialized Washington practitioners have on behalf of their corporate clients.

As the examples detailed in this book make clear, these are supposed to be agencies operating in behalf of the people of this country. Yet they are not receptive, responsive nor accountable to such people. What will change their priorities and policies is the development of a focused and knowledgeable constituency of citizens who work on these agencies regularly and relentlessly. This volume strives to provide the essential details about many of these agencies and charts the terrain for facilitating a citizen presence in the deliberation and promulgation of agency policies.

The current "energy crisis" is spawning a powerful new federal agency—one to oversee all energy matters. Known as the Federal Energy Office until approved by Congress when it will become the Federal Energy Administration, the power of this agency to affect the daily

lives of citizens is overwhelming. The agency will be able to: set the
temperature in every home by allocating heating oil; determine when
and where the public relaxes and vacations by rationing gasoline and jet
fuels; turn on and off lights by controlling electrical usage; and determine the cost of living by controlling petroleum prices. As a new
agency, the Federal Energy Office has not settled into a bureaucratic
slumber. It will become a more responsive public agency if the tactics
and materials in this guidebook are employed by an active citizenry.

The textual and reference materials of this volume are designed to be
mined to suit the purpose of the user—whether he or she be a lawyer,
an engaged citizen or a law student. At the minimum, for example, consumers can find out whom to complain to about what abuse. Such written complaints are not to be underestimated if they contain significant
information or if they total up to a "breakthrough" number. An example of the former category is the plea by the Food and Drug Administration to receive notice of harm done to consumers by cosmetics,
while the latter category piled up to such a mass at the ICC's moving
van regulations office that the Commission began to revamp its regulations. More intensively, the volume can be used by law students in
clinical education courses or projects. Finally, lawyers outside of Washington who are not specialists in these agency proceedings but who desire to represent consumer or environmental groups should find the
materials useful and time-saving.

It would strengthen the service function of any future editions of
this work were readers to send accounts* of their experiences—responses, failures, victories—with these regulatory agencies. The quantity
and quality of citizen efforts in these important arenas of national
decision-making will be enhanced if instructive experiences can be
cycled back to other readers.

Ralph Nader
February 1, 1974
Washington, D.C.

*Center for Study of Responsive Law
c/o Ruth Fort
P.O. Box 19367
Washington, D.C. 20036

Preface

BY JAMES R. MICHAEL

> *Before the Law stands a doorkeeper on guard. To this doorkeeper there comes a man from the country who begs for admittance to the Law. But the doorkeeper says that he cannot admit the man at the moment. The man, on reflection, asks if he will be allowed, then, to enter later. "It is possible," answers the doorkeeper, "but not at this moment." ... these are difficulties which the man from the country has not expected to meet; the Law, he thinks, should be accessible to every man and at all times. ...*
> —Franz Kafka, "Before the Law," from *Three Parables*

Don't make too much of it, but Franz Kafka was a career civil servant. Sooner or later, most people who deal with federal administrative agencies, including many who have never read a word written by Kafka, will describe the experience as "Kafkaesque." The term has passed into our language as a way of describing a common experience— wandering down endless corridors, referred from one official to another, told repeatedly that "the rules" forbid this and that, rebuffed by anonymous functionaries who, it seems, are never the people really in charge.

This book is designed to help you in some of your journeys through that world. As clearly as possible, it tells what federal agencies do, how they do it, and how you can affect what they do. Much of it is devoted to descriptions of how the agencies are organized and the procedures they use in going about their business. But one important attitude must be understood: The rules of administrative agencies are not neutral descriptions of the way things always happen, such as the "law" of gravity or the boiling point of water. They are tools to be used in

xxii   *Preface*

achieving objectives. For the agency, a decision to invoke rules as simple
as whether or not there is a charge for photocopying a document or
whether a deadline for filing a document is extended will depend on
who you are, and whether the charge or extension is convenient. Look
at rules in terms of the opportunities they present to you for action,
and also as potential obstacles which can be thrown in your way. Try
measuring the performance of government officials against the rules
they are supposed to follow. One of the greatest victories can be simply
to get the agencies to follow their own rules. True, once they are forced
to follow them for results which they don't intend, there will be a concerted effort to change the rules. But agencies may find that rules are
not all that easy to change. (See the description in Chapter 7 of how
the Federal Communications Commission tried and was turned down
by the courts.)

Although you will be concerned with a specific issue, it is worth
remembering that, whether you win or lose on that issue, your effort
can still have far-reaching consequences. The mere fact that an ordinary
citizen who does not represent some commercial interest has the
temerity to approach a federal agency may have a salutary effect on
agency employees. One outcome is the development of legal and quasi-
legal precedents regarding the treatment of consumers. This can range
from victories on legal issues involving long court fights, such as the
right of listener groups to intervene in television license proceedings
established in *United Church of Christ* v. *FCC* (see p. 259), to something
as informal as establishing your right to get a copy of the agency's telephone directory.

Even if it looks as though your efforts will have no chance of victory,
there is an educational value in trying. The education involved is the
agency's, the general public's, the industry's, and yours (the better to
fight the next time around). The agency's education will be furthered
because you will be raising questions which they simply have never
considered before in anything other than a ritualistic sense. Much consideration is given in administrative proceedings to the financial cost of
a proposed course of action for the regulated industry. Retooling costs,
loss of inventory, even the printing costs for correcting erroneous
information are regularly considered as reasons for delays or modification. No one is there to argue that there are also costs to consumers,
whether in physical injury or in the cumulating payment of a few cents
here and a few dollars there. Once such questions have been raised in a
proceeding, there may well be residual effects on other, similar proceedings. Staff members who have been reminded that there are people

out there may consider their welfare a little more the next time around, even if a citizen intervenor is not present. But don't depend unduly on the lasting value of a single example. Old habits die hard, and Washington lobbyists have seen reformers come and go.

Your efforts will also present an opportunity for educating the public on a point of view which is new to them. There is some intrinsic news value in your activity because, unfortunately, it is relatively rare. Like Dr. Johnson's comparison of a preaching woman to a dog walking on its hind legs, the marvel will be not so much that you do it well, but that you do it at all. This basic news value should be used carefully, since it offers an opportunity to communicate with many people who otherwise would never hear you.

The sight of a consumer group taking part in a regulatory agency proceeding will usually produce some predictable behavior on the part of the regulated industry. There will, of course, be editorials in the trade journals and speeches at trade association meetings denouncing "self-appointed" consumer representatives, and, at one point or another, you will probably be ritually accused of trying to undermine the free enterprise system. If your efforts are at all successful, the industry involved is likely to launch a public relations campaign, including a newly appointed vice president in charge of consumer relations and a series of advertisements on how much it cares about consumers and the environment. There also will be proposals for industry self-regulation as an alternative to action by the regulatory agency. As the Executive Director of the Federal Trade Commission noted in a speech to business representatives: "If businessmen believe that the commission and other government agencies are becoming more enforcement oriented, then we begin to hear the suggestion that self-regulation is a reasonable alternative to the time-consuming law suit." [Speech by Basil J. Mezines, FTC Executive Director, to American Society of Association Executives, Miami Beach, Florida, reported in *The Washington Post,* 24 August 1971, D6] Finally, and just possibly, the industry may reluctantly take steps to change the product or practice that has been questioned.

Just as important as the immediate result of a particular effort is its value in teaching you and others how the system works and how it can be dealt with. A great deal of the information on how regulatory agencies operate is buried in statutes and regulations, but much of it can only be learned through the process of actually dealing with the agencies. This book is an attempt to provide an introduction to that process, but there is no substitute for the kind of knowledge which comes from personal experience. In effect, you will be writing your own manual for future action as you begin the process of selecting an issue and dealing with an agency. The material you accumulate in your files and the knowledge compiled in your head will make steps which seem slow and tortuous the first time around much more routine in the future. Perhaps the most important lesson to be learned is the value of persistence and the necessity for persevering in the face of official indifference. That is the only way to avoid imitating the fate of the man from the country in the Kafka parable, who meekly accepted the doorkeeper's rebuff, and sat before the entrance to the Law for the rest of his life.

A Foreword on Boredom
and How to Avoid It
in Using This Book

The first rule in keeping from public attention important decisions which affect the entire public is to make them complicated; the second rule, which follows easily from the first, is to make them dull. This book deals with the step-by-step processes by which administrative agencies make such decisions, and it reflects their complexity; at times it commits the sin of tediousness for the sake of detail. There are no new charges or exposés, although the evaluation of agency efforts is often critical; there are no individual stories of human frailty and corruption to sympathize with or decry, since we are discussing a system which goes beyond mere personal corruption.

But there is a way to make the material in this book interesting, and that is not just to read it, but to *use* it. A clue can be found in the most grey and uninviting columns of daily newspapers, which are often pored over more intently than headlines—the classified ads and the stock market reports. While this book has more narrative continuity than those listings, a principle is worth remembering: If the information is vital to something you are doing, the format need not be a barrier; once you have embarked on a campaign in dealing with an agency, the material which now appears complicated and uninteresting will become, if not fascinating, at least worthy of attention. Then you will realize how much more you can add to it.

Acknowledgments

It would be an understatement to say that this book could not have been written without the assistance and cooperation of many people. The original conception was for public interest advocates who work on the federal agencies to set forth the information that is the basic tool of their trade, and to a large degree that conception has been honored. Chapter 10 on the Civil Aeronautics Board is the work of Reuben B. Robertson III, an attorney at the Center for Study of Responsive Law. Chapter 15 on air pollution control under the Environmental Protection Agency is based on a manuscript by John C. Esposito, co-author of *Vanishing Air* and a former consultant at the Center for Study of Responsive Law, Andrea M. Hricko, now at the Health Research Group in Washington, D.C., and attorney Clarence Ditlow. Chapter 11 on the Food and Drug Administration is largely based on a draft by James S. Turner, author of *The Chemical Feast*, and the work of attorney Judy Jackson. The chapter on the Federal Power Commission is a condensation of a draft by J. Shelby Bryan, now at the Harvard Business School, which drew on the research of Keith Roberts, an attorney currently working in San Francisco.

Chapter 7 on the Federal Communications Commission is largely based on materials prepared by Ralph M. Jennings, Communications Analyst with the Office of Communication, United Church of Christ; Marsha O'Bannon Prowitt, a Washington, D.C. communications consultant; Al Kramer, of the Citizens Communication Center in Washington, D.C.; and research by Drucilla Ramey, an attorney now working in San Francisco. Chapter 6 on the Interstate Commerce Commission and Chapter 8 on the Atomic Energy Commission were greatly facilitated by the research of two Oberlin College students, Deborah Gratz and William Byrd, as well as by Richard Sandler and attorneys Robert Fellmeth and Jon Rowe. Chapter 8 also draws upon materials on nuclear power plants prepared by the National Wildlife Federation. Chapter 5 on the Federal Trade Commission and Chapter 14 on the Internal Revenue Service are revisions of drafts prepared by two Georgetown University Law Center students, Robert Romano and Jerry Murphy. Attorney Mark Silbergeld assisted with Chapter 5 and attorney Tom Stanton assisted with Chapter 14. Chapter 13 on the National Highway Traffic Safety Administration is also based on the work of two Georgetown University law students, Collot Bruce and Bruce Meyerson. In addition, Dr. Carl Nash and Joan Claybrook provided added research assistance. The chapters on two new agencies—Chapter 17 on the Product Safety Commission and Chapter 16 on the Occupational Safety and Health Administration—were written respectively by attorney Judy Jackson and Andrea Hricko. Harrison Wellford provided useful information for Chapter 12 on the United States Department of Agriculture, and attorney Ron Plesser added recent developments to Chapter 3 on the Freedom of Information Act.

Valuable assistance was provided by the staff of the Administrative Conference of the United States, particularly by James Johnson. Models for many of the efforts suggested in this book have been provided, and sometimes anticipated, by the acronymically imaginative students of Professor John Banzhaf at the National Law Center of George Washington University, home of SOUP (Students Opposing Unfair Practices, Inc.), LABEL (Law Students Association for Buyers' Education in Labeling), and a host of other groups.

Many helpful suggestions were made by attorneys and others too numerous to mention who took time from their busy schedules to read portions of the manuscript. The manuscript was prepared by Connie Jo Smith, of the Center for Study of Responsive Law, who fueled the effort with optimism and created order from the apparent chaos of scrawled and stapled drafts. Ruth Fort of the Center coordinated the complexities of manuscript preparation. Without her patient and untiring efforts the manuscript would never have been completed. The project was made possible by a grant from the Carnegie Corporation, whose patience is as deserving of acknowledgment as their funds. And, of course, this book would never have been written had it not been for Ralph Nader.

—Center for Study of
Responsive Law
1974

WORKING
ON THE
SYSTEM

CHAPTER 1

FEDERAL AGENCIES
AND
U.S. CITIZENS

It must not be forgotten that it is especially dangerous to enslave men in the minor details of life. For my own part, I should be inclined to think freedom less necessary in great things than in little ones, if it were possible to be secure of the one without possessing the other.

Subjection in minor affairs breaks out every day, and it is felt by the whole community indiscriminately. It does not drive men to resistance, but it crosses them at every turn, till they are led to surrender the exercise of their will.

—Alexis de Tocqueville,
Democracy in America

Think of the federal government, and you are likely to think about the President, Congress, and maybe the Supreme Court. All of them have symbols which come readily to mind—the White House, the Capitol, the nine justices in black. You read about them in the newspapers, and you know, in a general way, what they do. But if you are moved to consider any of the regulatory agencies at all, you probably think of them only as the New Deal "alphabet soup" bureaucracies that use immense amounts of red tape in dealing with matters too specialized and complicated for any ordinary citizen to understand or care about. The duties of citizenship, it is normally assumed, are discharged by voting in elections, paying taxes, and occasionally doing a bit of work in a political campaign. Federal agencies are the province of experts who take care of technical matters in a nonpolitical way. They are remote from the lives of most people, it appears, and most people are content for the remoteness to be reciprocal.

The political concerns of most citizens are limited to the personalities of national campaigns, and to the processes and issues of local government. What they usually do not realize is that the distant and obscure processes of these agencies affect the basic way in which people live at least as much as the better known processes of national elections or local politics. They touch our lives daily in ways which are even more fundamental for being unpublicized and unnoticed. Consider a day in the life of a typical citizen.

A Day in a Citizen's Life:
How Federal Agencies Work on Him

Our typical citizen wakes up in the morning to the buzz of an electric clock, or perhaps to a clock-radio. He gives no more conscious thought to the electric power that wakes him than he gives to the rising of the sun, and a power reduction or blackout was, at least until a few years ago, viewed by most people with a mixture of alarm and incomprehension similar to their ancestors' reaction to a solar eclipse. To most people, electric power simply exists. Until the great eastern blackout of 1967, few questioned that electric power would continue to flow as a nearly free and dependable resource. And until it was pointed out by environmental activists, few thought to connect the power that flows from electrical outlets with dirty air and water. The name of the Federal Power Commission (FPC) will not come often to the average citizen's consciousness, but the power it regulates, and the costs of that power, enter his life every day.

One of the most significant effects of technology and science is that our lives are now fundamentally affected by processes which our unaided senses cannot even perceive, and our minds can barely comprehend. The most dramatic illustration of this in our time has been nuclear energy. As we have become aware of the environmental costs of producing power from fossil fuels, we have increasingly turned to nuclear energy as a "clean" power source. It is "clean" in the sense that we can perceive soot and smoke with our eyes and noses, but radioactivity is invisible without sensitive measuring devices. Similarly, we cannot sense the temperature of our water increasing a few degrees from the excess heat of a nuclear generating plant, and the connection to a shifting ecological balance is not immediately observable. While the shadow of the Bomb has been blamed for a great many things, the possibility of a nuclear "accident" from plants of our own making has not been widely raised until the past few years. If the average citizen learns that a nuclear plant is being built near him, his reaction is likely to be one of satisfaction that the source of public power is "clean," and confidence that the people who know about such things are taking all necessary precautions. It is unlikely to occur to him that the same agency, the Atomic Energy Commission (AEC), which is charged with insuring that such plants are physically safe and environmentally harmless, is also the agency charged with promoting the development and use of the nuclear plants which are now mushrooming around the country.

The power which flows into the average citizen's home not only runs the clock which wakes him, but also supplies the raw energy for the radio and television which provide him with the news which he believes and the entertainment which affects him more profoundly than he is likely to say or even know. The shows, sports, music, and public discussions of a country are fundamental elements of its culture—the way it sees the world, the way it sees itself, and what it does about those views. Television personalities have become a part of our lives in a way which used to be limited to relatives and trusted friends. The vital questions of who is granted the right to use the public airwaves, and for what they are used, are the responsibility of the Federal Communications Commission (FCC). The telephone which the typical citizen will use every day at home and in his office is part of a national communications system which is also regulated by the FCC. The efficiency of that system, the access of citizens to it, and many of the rates they must pay to use it, are also determined ultimately by the FCC.

As Mr. Average Citizen eats breakfast, the name of the Food and Drug Administration (FDA) is unlikely to come to mind. But that is the agency that determines how much of the "orange juice" he drinks is juice and how much is water. If he pops a pill to cheer him up, calm him down, or stop the queasiness from some undisclosed ingredient in his premixed breakfast, its effectiveness and safety also depend on how well the FDA has been doing another of its jobs. But if the queasiness results from his breakfast sausage being as much fat as meat, along with some extra unlisted ingredients from the floor of the packing plant, his complaint would be with the U.S. Department of Agriculture (USDA) rather than with the FDA. In one of those bureaucratic divisions of jurisdiction that owe more to history than logic, the Department of

Agriculture is in charge of the composition, purity, and labeling of food products which contain meat.

On an average day the average citizen will buy something. In all likelihood, he will choose the product on the basis of claims made for its safety and efficacy through advertising. If the product does not live up to its claims, the consumer may be disappointed, and try various methods of securing redress. But it is not too likely that he will think of the federal agency which is responsible, under a variety of statutes, for keeping the business world honest—the Federal Trade Commission (FTC). While the consumer may bridle at the imposition of a revenue tax by government, he is not likely to be aware of the unseen charges which he pays in the form of higher prices resulting from deceptive practices and market domination.

The consumer has some apparent freedom of choice in the products he buys, even if it is among products which are essentially the same but are heavily promoted on the basis of brand names and superficial distinctions of style. It is in the area of basic services and utilities, such as power and transportation, that he loses even that apparent freedom. Most of the food and consumer goods which he buys include in their prices the cost of transportation from somewhere else. That hidden price is largely determined by the transportation industry and approved by the Interstate Commerce Commission (ICC)—the oldest of the agencies. The ICC was formed to require fair dealing in providing transportation to farmers who were utterly dependent upon the railroads to get their goods to market, where they could be sold. Today's consumer is not subject to the same kind of economic threat which the railroads posed to farmers, but the invisible levies for transportation of goods are not made more equitable because they are less painful. The ICC touches the average consumer's life in other unseen ways, too. If he moves to another state, it will be under ICC rules at ICC rates. The very fact that he is likely to drive, take a bus, or fly if he is traveling between cities is attributable to the ICC's handling of its responsibility for rail passenger transportation. It was not until 1971 that the job was largely transferred to a new quasi-governmental corporation.

As a person gets into his car, he may buckle the seatbelt which is there because of safety standards issued by the National Highway Traffic Safety Administration (NHTSA). He may be dimly aware that Washington had something to do with the seatbelts, but it is unlikely that he would know about any of the other decisions made by that agency that will make it more or less likely that his trip will be interrupted by a crash.

If our hypothetical citizen travels by plane, he will come directly in contact with the regulations of the Civil Aeronautics Board (CAB). If the reservation "confirmed" by phone was not enough to guarantee him a seat, he may rail at the airline without being aware of the CAB rule which allows the practice. Whether he gets his money in such a situation, whether his baggage arrives, and, if he is handicapped, whether he is allowed to fly at all, are all determined by rules written at the CAB.

If our citizen exercises some rational caution in fastening his seatbelt, he may also have given up cigarette smoking when he learned about its hazards. But just as there are dangers built into automobiles that are beyond his control and up to the NHTSA and the manufacturer, there are pollutants in the very air he breathes that are equivalent to smoking a pack of cigarettes a day. And if he has little real choice in deciding whether or not to drive, he has no choice at all about breathing. The Environmental Protection Agency (EPA) is the federal agency responsible for controlling pollution of the air, along with other parts of man's environment.

Taxes, our citizen knows about. The Internal Revenue Service (IRS) intrudes itself into his consciousness at least once every year. He knows they make rules that determine how much he and others pay or do not pay, and he is dimly aware that there may be some way to appeal if he and the IRS disagree. But he probably has no idea of how those decisions are made, and assumes that whatever the IRS does is as inevitable as death.

A Tool Kit for Citizens:
How They Can Work on Federal Agencies

All of the preceding are examples of some of the ways in which the alphabetical jumble of federal agencies—the FPC, AEC, FCC, FDA, USDA, FTC, ICC, NHTSA, CAB, EPA, and IRS—will touch the life of an average person on an average day. The terms "citizen" and "consumer" have been used interchangeably because it is impossible for a citizen to choose not to be a consumer. The quality and quantity of the basic substances for life are increasingly determined by such agencies, and the level of marketplace justice which the consumer receives is largely dependent on the level of citizenship effort he exerts.

It is, of course, impossible for a single citizen to take an active part in the decision making processes of all the federal agencies which affect him. It would be difficult for one person, working part-time and alone, to have much impact on more than one of these agencies. But the efforts of one person can, if properly directed, have some impact. The cumulative effect of many people working alone can influence an agency, but the most effective form of citizen action is that carried out by an organization of concerned consumers. In addition to the pooling of personal and financial resources, such an effort provides the ingredient which is essential to counter the efforts of the well-organized and well-financed industry groups—continuity.

The material in this book is designed to provide some of the tools for consumers to use in gaining access to administrative agencies, working either alone or in groups. The basic tool provided is information about the agencies—what they do, where they are, how they are organized, and how they work. Also provided is information on where to go for more details and names of other groups which are concerned with the agencies involved. For all of the agencies we have attempted to provide a spectrum of possible actions, ranging from individual complaints to full-scale interventions in protracted trial-type hearings. Much of this material is immediately useful to laymen. For lawyers concerned with the more complex legal possibilities, references to statutes and cases are given for further research. Although citations to legal references are used for this purpose, the text, so far as possible, includes explanations of legal terms so that it may be read by laymen without serious difficulty. Lay readers may take some comfort in the knowledge that much of this material is also probably new to many lawyer readers, since the practice of law before administrative agencies is a relatively narrow specialty. Outside of their particular fields of interest, most lawyers are little more knowledgeable than laymen, except for their access to a library. Wherever possible, this book points out where to go in a law library, along with other sources of information.

One of the better-kept secrets of lawyers is the existence of "form books" which give samples of leases, wills, contracts, pleadings, and so on. Although the basic requirements for a legal document can be determined from statutes and regulations, lawyers are a cautious breed, and usually prefer to do it the way it was done once before by someone who won. It is to encourage citizen participation rather than to discourage innovation that we have included sample documents, such as petitions, as appendices to chapters on the agencies. Wherever possible these have been taken from documents actually filed with the agencies, with varying degrees of success. Although many of them have been revised slightly and retyped for publication, they are essentially the same as the papers that were filed.

But these are to be used as starting points for action, rather than fill-in-the-blank models. This book is a basic introductory manual for the concerned citizen, lawyer or not, who has only a general idea of what federal agencies do. If, after reading it, he decides to act on one of the suggestions and concentrate on an agency, he will soon need to go far beyond the material presented here.

The Way It Is with Federal Agencies:
Regulators and the Regulated Can Be Friends

Although conventional business rhetoric sometimes gives the impression that the federal regulatory agencies are the natural enemies of business, and that the captains of commerce long for the day when the Washington agencies wither or are withered away, the real world is a little different. Industry has learned all too well how to live with and even lean on those agencies in various ways. The partnership has been established, largely in the form predicted by a remarkably candid letter sent from the Attorney General to the president of a railroad company shortly after the creation of the ICC in 1887. The company president wanted the ICC abolished, but the Attorney General showed him a better way:

> The Commission, as its functions have been limited by the courts, is, and can be made, of great use to the railroads. It satisfies the popular clamor for a government supervision of the railroads, at the same time that that supervision is almost entirely nominal. Further, the older such a commission gets to be, the more inclined it will be found to take the business and railroad view of things. It thus becomes a sort of barrier between the railroad corporations and the people and a sort of a protection against hasty and crude legislation hostile to railroad interests. . . . The [better] part of wisdom is not to destroy the Commission, but to utilize it. [Robert Fellmeth, *Interstate Commerce Omission* (New York: Grossman Publishers, 1970), pp. xiv, xv]

The ICC is approaching its ninetieth birthday, and Attorney General Olney's prediction has been accurate. The other agencies have followed

in the tradition, and the youngest of the lot, the AEC, has been more
than ready "to take the business . . . view of things." But then the AEC
was pushed along by a statute that directed it to promote the industry
as well as to regulate it.

Some of the agencies—the AEC, CAB, FPC, FTC, and FCC—are "independent," like the ICC. That is to say that they are composed, at the top,
of a group of commissioners or members who, once appointed by the
President (and confirmed by the Senate), cannot be removed except
for good cause. This distinguishes them from other agencies—such as
the FDA, USDA, EPA, NHTSA, and IRS—which are within the Executive Branch, subject to Presidential direction, whose heads may be removed by the President at will. Changes in administrations affect the
independent agencies only indirectly, through the Presidential appointment power. Ever since the case of *Humphrey's Executor* v. *U.S.* [295
U.S. 602 (1935)] this independence has been recognized. In that case,
President Roosevelt asked for the resignation of an FTC Commissioner
whose economics did not quite fit the New Deal. Humphrey refused to
resign, and the Supreme Court upheld the principle, even if it no longer
did Humphrey himself any good.

It has become commonplace to say that the regulatory agencies have
become captives of the industries they regulate, but the judgment has
not been made false by becoming common. It is not through bribery
or treachery that agencies come to view the problems of industry more
sympathetically than they do those of consumers. The fundamental
problem is that the regulators see those who represent industry on a
near-daily basis, while consumer representatives are rarely seen. This
personal touch, carefully forged in hundreds of otherwise inconsequen-
tial conversations, leads people in the regulatory agencies to mention
things casually to industry representatives which they would refuse to
discuss with a consumer who "just walked in off the street." And it is
just such personal contact that leads agency men to accept the word of
their industry counterparts, and to appreciate the problems which any
proposed rule inevitably presents.

The Chairman of the Administrative Conference of the United
States, a sort of in-house government think tank that is supposed to
watch over all the agencies and make periodic suggestions about how
they could do their jobs better, described the process by repeating a
parable told by an anonymous former agency head:

A successful lawyer in Keokuk is appointed by the President to
serve on an independent regulatory agency or as an assistant

secretary of an executive department that exercises regulatory functions. A round of parties and neighborly acclaim surround the new appointee's departure from Keokuk. After the goodbyes, he arrives in Washington and assumes his role as a regulator, believing that he is really a pretty important guy. After all, he almost got elected to Congress from Iowa. But after a few weeks in Washington, he realizes that nobody has ever heard of him or cares much what he does—except for one group of very personable, reasonable, knowledgeable, delightful human beings who recognize his true worth. These friendly fellows—all lawyers and officials of the special interests that the agency deals with—provide him with information, views, and most important, love and affection. Except they bite hard when our regulator doesn't follow the light of their wisdom. The cumulative effect is to turn his head a bit. [Remarks by Roger C. Cramton at Administrative Process Symposium, Georgetown Law Center dedication, 17 September 1971]

The industry representative becomes a colleague, and it is only human nature to believe what colleagues say, and to view criticism of them with skepticism. As a former member of the FCC put it:

In time the vision of the larger and more distant public tends to grow dim and the members of the agency and its staff come, without realizing it, to see the public interest in terms of the few members of the public they see and know and quite often come to like. [Clifford Durr, quoted in *Washington Post* Potomac Magazine, 15 March 1970, p. 29]

For example, the dollars it will cost a textile company and the time it will take to convert to flame-retardant nightwear become the subjects of long conferences. The children in the burn wards are reduced at such conferences to remote statistical possibilities. They become remote because of an atmosphere which develops implying that these are all sincere men committed to the same goal, differing only on how to go about it. "Feasibility" is a word much used, and a common expression concerns whether a business "can live with" a particular regulation. It becomes almost a breach of etiquette for anyone to assert that a lower tolerance or a few months' delay means injury and suffering to people who are out there in the world beyond Washington. How many of them literally cannot live with a product standard or delay is not often mentioned.

It is to the raising of such questions concerning the individual that this book is dedicated. The process of government regulation now consists of a dialogue between the regulators and the regulated industries, and it is up to consumers to find out where it is going on so that they can add their own voices in order to protect their own welfare, which is supposedly the object of the whole process. And it is never too early to start. Consider this advice to industry given by two public relations men with much experience in Washington ways:

> . . .the time to build a communications path to the Federal Government is before you really need it. Often, businessmen come down to Washington when they are almost purple with apoplexy. A particular piece of legislation or an administrative ruling has been either passed or under consideration for weeks, months, or perhaps even a year. When it is about to be finalized—or even after it has been passed—the businessman shows up in Washington for a "last-ditch effort." He must necessarily be aggressive and antagonistic, in conflict with a policy or a program whose cement has virtually hardened. How much better for him if he makes himself known to people in government in advance, building an easy access and a ready communication with them before things reach a crisis stage in terms of any particular problem. [William Ruder and Raymond Nathan, *The Businessman's Guide to Washington* (Englewood Cliffs: Prentice-Hall, 1964), pp. 3-4]

How It Happened:
The Rise and Recline of a Bureaucratic Empire

How did the American citizen get to the point where so many of the vital decisions about how he lives are made by anonymous agencies he can't even find, let alone influence? It's a long way from the civics textbook model of a legislature composed of representatives who can be voted out, an executive to carry out the laws passed by the legislature, and a judiciary to settle legal disputes.

Part of the answer is that government became larger and more complex right along with commercial and social institutions. The relatively self-sufficient family farm is a thing of the past, and so is the small town in which a consumer can know personally the merchants he deals with, who personally produce much of what they sell. The Industrial

Revolution provided the model of large corporate structures, subsidized directly and indirectly by the federal government, which would convert natural resources into commercial products. As citizens became more and more removed from the sources of the things they needed for everyday life, they acquired a new and uneasy identity as consumers of the products of industry. Advertising grew up to lubricate the production chain by linking superficial product distinctions with deeply felt emotions.

With the end of the frontier, the average citizen became increasingly locked into the mechanism of the new corporate state. Market competition came to mean that a consumer could choose from a bewildering number of combinations within a small range: He could choose from thousands of optional automotive accessories, but it was very difficult for him to choose not to drive. It became literally inescapable that important decisions concerning the quality of such necessities as air and water would be made by corporations, subject to check only by parallel government structures.

The crash of the stock market in 1929 pointed out some of the defects of corporate America, and the need for new approaches. Administrative agencies were nothing new, and the ICC, established in 1887 to regulate the railroads in response to the Progressive movement, provided a model of sorts for governmental solutions to economic problems. The solution was appealing. Courts were oriented toward the solution of individual cases. Legislatures could not be expected to handle the combination of making rules and deciding cases which preceded the setting of rates and granting of licenses. Besides, many of the decisions involved familiarity with mountains of documents on technical matters in which expertise took years to develop. So the "alphabet soup" agencies of the New Deal were formed all over Washington.

Some independent commissions nearly constituted a new "fourth branch" of government (following the legislative, executive, and judicial), being as autonomous as was possible while subject to Presidential appointment and Congressional purse strings. Others were part of the Executive Branch, carrying out administration policy. All partook of a confidence in the ability of intelligence and expertise exerted in the public interest to produce regulatory solutions which would further that interest.

Not even the most independent of commissions was completely separated from Presidential and Congressional influence. The members of those bodies had to be selected somehow, and the source was almost always by choice of the President, usually with the advice and consent of the Senate. Also, it takes money to run agencies, and the money came from Congress. Presidential use of appointive power to pay off old political debts could doom an agency to years of lethargy. Congressional parsimony left agencies dependent on the regulated industries for the data which formed the basis for their decisions.

Statutory requirements limiting the number of members from one political party restrained one kind of partisanship, but could not block the most insidious kind of partisan from membership—the partisan of the industry to be regulated. The agencies were established in part because of a belief in the importance of expertise, and the only place to obtain such expertise frequently was by employment in the industry. The alternative was to learn about the subject in the lower echelons of an agency. But that kind of skill could be used more profitably in industry than in government service, and a pattern soon emerged of young men spending a few years in government while they learned the field, then turning to jobs in industry, where they could put their knowledge to use. Faced with that kind of career pattern, government personnel were quick to "understand the problems" of a given industry, since the "problems" would soon be their own. The pattern is not limited to lower level staff members in the agencies. While he was still head of the Federal Aviation Administration (FAA), Najeeb Halaby was recruited by Pan American Airlines for a vice presidency paying $30,000 more than the FAA [*Wall Street Journal*, 5 October 1971, p. 37].

More subtle, but no less powerful, influences have also played a part. It is not just where the senior regulators came from and where the junior regulators are headed. Even more influential is the pervasiveness of contact between representatives of the regulated industry and the regulators. When President-elect Kennedy asked James Landis to write a report on administrative agencies, Landis summed up the importance of this continual contact between the regulators and the regulated in a phrase which has been quoted in nearly every book on administrative law since then:

> Irrespective of the absence of social contacts and the acceptance of undue hospitality, it is the daily machine-gun-like impact on both agency and its staff of industry representation that makes for industry orientation on the part of many honest and capable agency members as well as agency staffs. [James Landis, *Report on Regulatory Agencies to the President-Elect*, 1960]

The day-in, day-out presence of the Washington lawyers and government trade associations will, in the end, be your most formidable obstacle. They were there before you, and they are confident that they will be there after you. To be effective, you must be at least as persistent as you are zealous.

The Washington lawyer is the basic unit of industry representation in Washington, and he provides the model for similar nonlawyer representatives in consulting and public relations firms. In practice, they all do many of the same things, since the true Washington lawyer is unlikely to see the inside of a courtroom more than a few times between admittance to the bar and retirement. There are about 13,000 lawyers in Washington, and they move easily from government positions to private practice and back again. They are skilled advocates, and their skill is no less for being exerted in the office conference or administrative hearing instead of in a court. They know the way the agencies work, since they usually have worked there themselves, and they know who is working there at any given time. Their tools include the phone call, the business lunch, and the informal conference. Above all, they know what is in the works at an agency long before a proposal hits the fine print of the *Federal Register* (about which see p. 25). It is this kind of informal familiarity that makes them worth their substantial fees (up to $250 per hour for a partner in a "name" firm). Their value begins with information, with knowing just a little bit more about what is going on, just a little bit sooner.

An Inventory of Tools

Information about an agency is the basis for any kind of effective citizen access. Everything you need to know about administrative agencies is not in this book, and is not even available in many libraries. But, as much as possible, we have tried to provide specific references to the sources of the detailed information you will need. For every agency there are a few basic sources of further information: the statutes, the regulations, the cases, and the specialized publications dealing with agency and industry affairs.

The agency itself probably has most of the information you need to get started (beyond that which is available in a public or law school library). But getting that information is in itself one of the most important areas of citizen access. The basic rule to keep firmly in mind is that all government information is legally available to the public unless there is a specific statutory reason for withholding it. That is the law, specifically the Freedom of Information Act (FOIA) (5 U.S.C.

552), and you will find yourself explaining it to the agencies again and
again. There are problems with huge loopholes in the form of exemptions written into the Act, and there are too many agencies which think
of the Act as consisting of nothing but loopholes. It is a prime example
of a law which the government itself will not obey unless citizens prod
it into obedience.

Chapter 3 deals with the Act in more detail, but your basic rights are
simple, and the procedures for asserting them are, in the initial stages
at least, not very complicated. The Act established the policy of disclosure of government information and set forth nine exemptions to this
policy. Those exemptions are for material relating to: national defense
or foreign policy, internal agency matters, material specifically made
secret by other statutes, trade secrets and confidential information,
memoranda which would not be available in a lawsuit, personnel and
medical files, investigatory files, information on regulation of financial
institutions, and geological information about oil and gas wells [5 U.S.C.
552(b)(1)-(9)]. These exemptions are so vague that almost anything
can be placed within them, and you will find that attempts are usually
made to do so. The mental process of many people in administrative
agencies when confronted with a request for information is first to
consider which reason to give for withholding it.

The Act also requires all agencies to print their own regulations for
carrying out the Act. These have been published in the Code of Federal
Regulations (C.F.R.), and a first step in basic research on an agency
will be to look them up. The regulations vary widely. Some agencies
only restate the language of the Act, while others offer some fairly
specific descriptions of just what information is considered to fall
within the exempt categories.

The process for obtaining information is simple in its broad outlines.
You write a letter, citing the Act and the agency regulations, asking for
the information and identifying it as specifically as possible. If the information is not available, ask the agency to give the specific statutory
justification for withholding it. The agencies can, and usually will,
charge an exorbitant rate for searching their files and making photocopies. The Act establishes your right of access to the material for inspection as well as copying, so indicate in your first letter whether you
merely want to inspect the material, or want to have copies sent to
you. If you want copies sent, it is a good idea to ask for an advance
estimate of the copying costs.

Most agencies provide for at least one level of administrative appeal
within the agency if your request is turned down. This procedure is

described in the agency regulations. Writing the appeal letter may require a little more effort, if you present your arguments as to why the exemption claimed for the information does not apply. You may find it helpful to refer to some of the cases which have been decided by federal courts in upholding citizen access to information under the Act. But it is probably more efficient simply to say you are appealing the denial and save your legal argument until the agency head takes final action. You may want to indicate what you want the information for, but don't be misled into thinking that you must persuade the agency that you should have it because your cause is just. Another fundamental principle of the Act is that citizens have the right to information regardless of why they want it. On a practical level, it is important to remember that there are people and institutions to which agencies are more responsive than they are to most citizens. These include members of Congress and the press. If you can get even passing support for your request from such sources, it makes it a little less likely that you will have to resort to the next step, which is to take the agency to court.

Going to court to get the information is not as simple as writing a letter, but it is not beyond your resources. The Act provides that you can sue in the federal district court nearest to you, and that cases brought under the Act will be given priority. You will probably need legal assistance in taking this step, but don't let that rule out the possibility of taking legal action. (See Chap. 18 for some possible sources of legal help.) Remember that success in the early stages will be much more likely if you can convince the agency that you are willing and able to take them to court if they refuse.

One basic problem of dealing with administrative agencies is that they do many different kinds of things under many different procedures. They make rules which have the same effect as laws, they try cases between competing parties much as courts do, and they conduct investigations of all sorts. The basic requirements which they must follow in doing all of these things are in the Administrative Procedure Act (APA). Since one of the rules governing agencies has to do with public information, the FOIA is actually an amendment to the APA. The APA establishes very general standards which the agencies must follow when they are making rules or deciding cases. These are discussed in more detail in Chapter 4, but the basic requirements are two:

1. Before making a rule, agencies must give the public notice and provide an opportunity for them to express their views.

2. In deciding an individual case, the agency must give notice and opportunity for the individual to be heard.

Much of the "law" of administrative agencies has been written by the courts in the process of deciding disputes over the meaning of the general requirements of the APA. One of the most important areas of law developed by this process is that of "standing"—that is, who has the right to participate in an administrative proceeding between the agency and an individual (or, more likely, a company). The question of the standing of citizen groups to participate in administrative proceedings goes to the heart of citizen access, since the usual proceeding is theoretically between the agency and the industry over whether the industry is adequately serving the public. Until a few years ago, members of the public whose welfare was their very subject were usually kept out of such proceedings. But the trend is running the other way now, and the most notable case is probably one in which a court ruled that members of a station's television audience have the right to be heard in a hearing on whether the station has been operating in the public interest (see pp. 79 and 259).

This and other court-made rules on administrative procedure are discussed in more detail in Chapter 4. Much of the law which has been developed in this area consists of rulings on just how long you must negotiate with an agency before you can take it to court. Another large part of the law consists of cases describing what sort of justification provided by the agency for its action or inaction will stand up in court.

There are three basic avenues for citizen access to administrative agencies: You can complain about a specific practice about which you think the agency should do something; you can take part in the agency's rule making process, either by submitting comments on proposed rules or by proposing them yourself; or you can intervene in the process of deciding cases which will affect you. These three general possibilities range from the relative simplicity of a single letter to the complexity of daily appearances in a courtlike proceeding which can go on for years. But the significance of the results does not depend on the course of action you choose. The abolition of cigarette commercials from television started with a single letter. As a general matter, complaints require the least investment of time in specialized legal and technical research. Commenting on proposed rules requires a little more sophistication, since most important rules are hidden in the *Federal Register*, and their significance is often apparent only if you already know something about the subject. Proposing rules through petitions for rule making is a bit more complicated. Essentially, you are making a suggestion for a new law, and some sort of background data will be necessary if the agency is to adopt your proposal or anything like it. Intervening in hearings can range from filing a statement commenting on the proceedings to full participation as a party to the hearing.

The Agencies

Although this book does not attempt to describe each of the regulatory agencies, the ones that are covered will give an idea of the way in which all agencies function. Some of the introductory material may seem somewhat prosaic; listing the statutory responsibilities of an agency and describing the functions of its various bureaus is not the stuff of which page-turners are written. But it is necessary as background material for those who are not familiar with the jurisdictions of these agencies, and the limits of agency jurisdiction over an industry are not always so clear-cut as might first be assumed. For example, the choice of whether to turn to the FCC or the FTC with a complaint about deceptive television advertising has as much to do with recent history as it does with statutory jurisdiction. Right now, the short answer is that the FTC is more likely to take effective corrective action.

It is for this reason that each chapter includes basic introductory and historical material about the agency and the industry it regulates. This includes information on the statutes which give the agency its responsibilities and powers, and the regulations it has adopted to implement them. It also includes a description of the regulated industry, how it affects the public, and how it deals with the agency. Names of trade journals and associations are given, along with information on the key Congressional committees which can prod or protect an agency.

The structure and functioning of each agency are also described, and organization charts are given to guide you through the bureaucratic thicket. In some cases, the differences between bureaus in the same agency are so great that the people who work there almost literally speak different languages. For example, the concern at the FCC's Common Carrier Bureau with rates is closer to the proceedings of the FPC than it is to radio and television license proceedings at the FCC's Broadcast Bureau.

Following the basic descriptive material on each agency is the description of access opportunities. This is generally an outline of what has been done and what can be done with the agencies. Wherever possible we have used case histories of recent attempts by individual citizens and consumer groups in dealing with the agencies. These range from writing complaint letters to the FCC in order to force stations to give air time for response to personal attacks, to descriptions of interventions in proceedings against deceptive advertisers by the FTC, and rate making proceedings at the ICC.

Three basic criteria have been used in selecting the agencies to be described in detail: the breadth of impact of the agency on the national population, the degree of access to citizen action which has been presented in the past, and the potential for citizen access which is presented in the future. Using the first criterion, we have not covered those agencies which deal only with a limited segment of the population, no matter how pervasive that jurisdiction is. We have instead turned to those agencies that make decisions which affect the broad and basic subjects of power, pollution, trade, transportation, and communication.

Under the second criterion of past citizen access, we have selected agencies which have been receptive in some degree to citizen petitioners and intervenors. The past, in almost all of these cases, refers to the last ten years, when there has been a tendency for more and more people to wage unprecedented attempts at storming the bureaucratic citadels. The doors at some of the agencies, such as the FTC, have been opened more than those of others. The ICC has been notably unreceptive to such attempts. But the attempts have been and are being made.

The potential for future citizen access represents courses of action which seem possible but are as yet unrealized. In some cases there is a possibility of cross-fertilization between efforts that have been successful with one agency and appear likely to succeed with others. An example is the tactic of negotiated settlements between intervenors and licensees. This was first used at the FCC between community groups and television licensees on the issues of community service and equal employment opportunities. Recently it has also been used to achieve environmental safeguards in the licensing of nuclear power plants before the AEC. Stated simply, this amounts to a contract between a licensee and a citizens' group which has intervened in opposition to the granting of a license by the agency in question. In exchange for withdrawal of opposition by the citizen group, the licensee promises to provide environmental safeguards or to eliminate discrimination in employment. Another opportunity which will be presented in the next few years involves the relicensing of hydroelectric power plants by the FPC. Many of the hydroelectric plants in this country were first licensed in the 1920s for periods of about fifty years. These licenses are now coming up for renewal, and these proceedings offer considerable opportunity for the public to consider how this stewardship of a natural resource has been treated, as well as a chance to have a say in how this responsibility will be treated in the future.

Even if your interest lies with agencies which are not treated in detail here, this book will be useful. The material on freedom of information, administrative procedure, and the general information will help in dealing with any government agency. The basic approach presented can be used in developing access to any agency. All of them have procedures for handling complaints, making rules, and deciding cases. All of them provide basic information to the public in the form of somewhat self-serving annual reports, descriptions in the Government Organization Manual, and offices of public information. The basic charter for each agency is set forth in the statutes, which can be found in the U.S. Code (U.S.C.), and detailed regulations are published in the Code of Federal Regulations (C.F.R.). For every agency there is a structure of influence and access which resembles the pattern of those described in this book. The constituent industries, the specialized trade press, and the Congressional committees which oversee the agency's functioning play similar roles for all regulatory agencies. This book is to provide guidance for developing another constituency—one of concerned citizens to monitor each agency.

CHAPTER 2

INFORMATION AND
TOOLS
Getting Started

> *He who would do good to another must do it in minute particulars.*
>
> — William Blake,
> *Jerusalem*

The first step in working on an agency is selecting the agency and learning about it. Normally you will begin with a problem, rather than the name of a particular agency, and it is quite likely that you will find several agencies concerned with various aspects of the same problem. The division and overlapping of responsibilities may seem bewildering and illogical at first. On further investigation it may become less bewildering, but it is not likely to appear any more logical. The basic reason is that the agencies were not conceived as parts of a grand plan, but grew up individually in response to periodic waves of public and Congressional indignation. Justice Holmes' comment on understanding property law—that a page of history is worth a volume of logic—applies equally to federal administrative agencies.

Sources of Information about Agencies:
Official Sources

Chapter 1 gives an idea of the ways in which various federal agencies can affect your life. Descriptions of the jurisdictions for agencies covered in detail in this book will give more detailed information. But for a complete listing of all the agencies of the federal government, with very brief descriptions of what they do, you need a copy of the U.S. Government Organization Manual. This is revised annually, and is available from the Government Printing Office (G.P.O.) for $3.00 a copy (see p. 27 on how to order from the G.P.O.). This will provide you with some very elementary information on each agency, such as names of incumbent commissioners and senior staff members, the major divisions of the agencies, a mailing address, and one telephone number. It also includes a somewhat self-serving description of the agency's history, structure, and responsibilities. But don't be discouraged if you have trouble understanding what an agency is all about after reading a section of the manual. In 1969 the Administrative Conference of the United States took a look and found that the "narrative text submitted by some of the agencies is outdated, unrevealing, cumbersome, or otherwise deficient." But until it is "rewritten at a high level of competence," as the conference recommended, it's the only one you've got.

The Government Organization Manual will also give the legal citations to the statutes which the agency is responsible for enforcing and citations to the regulations which it has promulgated under the authority of the statutes. Copies of the statutes and regulations for each agency can be ordered from the G.P.O., but they can be expensive and must be kept up-to-date. Another method is to look up the sources in a law library. If you are not an attorney, you can find these references in the nearest law school library, and sometimes in a well-equipped public library.

The basic source of statutory authority for each agency is in the U.S. Code (U.S.C.). This is cited as ____ U.S.C. ____ . For example, the Federal Communications Commission (FCC) operates under the Communications Act of 1934, which is found at 15 U.S.C. 21 and 47 U.S.C. 35, 151-609. The Code is a multivolume set of all federal laws. The first number (before the U.S.C.) refers to the "title" of the statute (which may include several volumes), and the number after the U.S.C. refers to the section. The U.S. Code Annotated (cited as U.S.C. Ann.) includes summaries of significant cases interpreting the statute. Changes in the statute and recent cases are added in the form of "pocket parts," which are inserted in the back of each volume.

The regulations issued by each agency are collected in the Code of Federal Regulations (C.F.R.). This is another multivolume set which is periodically revised and reissued, and it is available from the G.P.O. or in law libraries. The rules of practice and procedure for each agency are contained in the C.F.R. sections cited in the Government Organization Manual, and can be purchased separately from the G.P.O.

Before agency regulations are collected in the C.F.R., they first appear in the *Federal Register* as part of the rule making process. The *Federal Register* is sort of a cross between a daily published bulletin for the entire federal government and the legal notices section of your local paper. Publication in the *Federal Register* satisfies any statutory requirements for notice to the public, even though the language of the notices is frequently incomprehensible to someone not acquainted with a particular issue. As Betty Furness said when she was Special Assistant for Consumer Affairs to President Johnson:

> . . . the consumer is in a poor position to attempt to comprehend the legal and technical language comprising the typical *Federal Register*. The consumer does not have the benefit of the professional advice available to industry through house counsel, trade associations, trade papers, Washington counsel, etc. In most cases he has neither the time nor the collateral library materials to allow him to keep track of developments. [Letter to Chairman of Administrative Conference of U.S., quoted in *Report of the Administrative Conference*, 20 November 1968]

The Administrative Conference adopted a recommendation of Ms. Furness, and proposed that a "consumer bulletin" be published, with clearly written versions of *Federal Register* notices concerning consumer interests. President Nixon later adopted the idea as part of his consumer message. In October 1969 he announced that he was asking his Special Assistant for Consumer Affairs, Virginia Knauer, to undertake

> . . . the preparation and publication, on a regular basis, of a new *Consumer Bulletin*. This publication will contain a selection of items which are of concern to consumers and which now appear in the daily government journal, *The Federal Register*. The material it presents, which will include notices of hearings, proposed and final rules and orders, and other useful information, will be translated from its technical form into language which is readily understandable by the layman.

It took a while. In April 1971 the Office of Consumer Affairs published the first issue of a four-page leaflet, *Consumer News*. The lead story, entitled "President Speaks for Consumers," was a summary of the President's second consumer legislation proposal. It was not until

February 1972 that the *Consumer Register* supplement was added to *Consumer News*, with some summaries of proposed rules which had appeared in the *Federal Register*. Despite the Administration bias, the *Consumer News* is worth getting. It costs $1.00 per year, and can be ordered from the G.P.O. But if you are seriously concerned about the details of administrative rule making, check the *Federal Register* regularly. The format has been improved somewhat, and scanning the table of contents is a fast way to keep abreast of what the agency you are concerned with is doing. It is available in many libraries, or you can order it for $25.00 a year from the G.P.O.

The next source of information about an agency is the agency itself, in the department set up to provide the public with everything it needs to know—the Public Information Office. The basic document of the Public Information Office is the agency's annual report. The report on an agency by the agency should be read with skepticism, but it can provide some details about the current programs and emphasis of the agency. The offices of public information also have bushels of pamphlets and brochures which are usually free, and frequently not worth much. The overall message communicated by the annual report and the information pamphlets is that there are some problems, but the agency is doing its best to solve them, and the appropriate role for the consumer is to be cautious in his consuming habits and watch out for unscrupulous merchants.

Another kind of information from the Public Information Office is the press release. These vary in quality and availability among the agencies, but they can be valuable. If your local newspaper does not carry much news about federal administrative actions, the agency press releases can be an important source of current information. They will usually be issued for all speeches by commission members and for significant decisions by the agency. Usually they will contain some commentary to place a particular decision or policy statement in perspective. But don't rely exclusively on the press releases for interpreting the significance of decisions. The trade press for the regulated industry will often have other ideas about what a ruling will mean, and the publications of consumer and environmental protection groups will have another view. Arrange to get on an agency's free mailing list for press releases. The agency will want to know what type of releases you are interested in, since in most instances the releases are categorized by their appeal to a particular segment of an industry.

The G.P.O. is an important source of books with valuable information at relatively low prices. The G.P.O. has about 25,000 different publications available. There is no single catalog which lists all of the publications for sale, but there are free price lists of publications in nearly fifty different subject areas. There is also a monthly catalog which lists all government publications issued during a given month. A year's subscription to the catalog costs $12.50. Several of the subject area price lists might be of use to you in gaining access to administrative proceedings, such as the ones on "law, rules, and regulations" and "government periodicals and subscription services," so the first step is to order a free list of all the subject areas, and then get the subject price lists which you think would be useful. Write the Superintendent of Documents, U.S. Government Printing Office, Washington, D.C. 20402.

When you decide what publications you want to order, you must either know the price and pay in advance by check or money order, or send a deposit of at least $25. If you establish a deposit account you can order by phone and charge purchases against your account number. Send a letter saying that you want to open a deposit account, and enclose a check for at least $25 payable to the Superintendent of Documents. In about two weeks you will get a deposit number and you can charge your orders. But placing orders by long distance telephone can be expensive. Just about any time you call the G.P.O. (202-541-3000) you will get a recorded announcement that the clerks are busy, and that you will have to wait. The wait can be a long one.

The Congressional Record has all kinds of trivia in its pages, partly because any member of Congress can have anything printed there without even reading it. But some of the material inserted is useful, and the Record is available in most libraries. You can order individual copies for 25 cents from the G.P.O., or subscribe (at $45 per year). Your Congressman has eight subscriptions to the Congressional Record which he may give free of charge to constituents. If he has not filled his quota, he will probably be willing to add you to his list.

One class of government document deserves special mention for its usefulness. The transcripts of hearings before Congressional committees and other materials submitted to committees are often printed in booklet form. These can be valuable compilations of material from many sources, including agency documents for which you would probably have to pay exorbitant photocopying costs to get them from the agencies. These are referred to as "committee prints," and are printed by the G.P.O. for Congressional committees. Sometimes, if the committee so decides, the print will be sold through the G.P.O., but more often the copies are available only through the committee.

Much of the law governing citizen access to federal agencies has been established through appeals to federal courts. In order to find judicial decisions in those cases, you will need to know a little bit about legal research. The opinions of federal courts are printed in several different series of volumes, depending on the court which hands down the opinion. The name of each series is expressed in abbreviated form, such as: F. Supp. for the Federal Supplement; F.2d for the Federal Reporter, 2d Series; and U.S. for the U.S. Supreme Court's official series of reports. Opinions in individual cases are cited with the number of the volume first, and the page number following the abbreviation. For example, 294 F.2d 575 would refer to an opinion found in volume 294 of the Federal Reporter, 2d Series, on page 575.

Most of the cases cited in this book were before federal courts, and most of the citations are to the Federal Supplement, the Federal Reporter, or the U.S. Supreme Court reports. This is just a bare introduction to the maze of reports and library tools which you will need to use if you deal with an agency and use legal materials. Many of these publications which report court decisions come from the West Publishing Company (50 West Kellogg Blvd., St. Paul, Minnesota 55102), and a booklet called *West's Law Finder* will serve as an introduction to using the series from that publisher. A detailed guide to legal source material is *Effective Legal Research* (Miles O. Price and Harry Bitner, New York: Little, Brown and Company, 1970).

Sources of Information about Agencies:
Unofficial Sources

The sources of information just described are official ones. That is, they are statements made by the government in the form of statutes, rules, announcements, investigations, or judicial decisions. There is another body of material which is not official, but which can be extremely useful in dealing with administrative agencies. The first group of these unofficial sources is a variety of guides and manuals published by private companies as aids to attorneys dealing with federal agencies. Although these are useful, most of them are extremely expensive. Because of the expense, it is best to find a library which subscribes to the service.

One of these manuals is West's *Federal Practice Manual*, published by the West Publishing Company. This is a seven-volume set of guides to federal regulatory agencies written for attorneys. It does not cover all of the agencies, and all agency functions are not described equally. The emphasis is on agency functions which may affect business clients, and on the appropriate steps for attorneys to take in advising and representing clients before those agencies. Rather than being a subscription service, which many of the other sources are, the West *Federal Practice Manual* is composed of articles written mostly by attorneys who practice before the agencies involved. The current edition was printed in 1970, so the information is fairly up-to-date. The most comprehensive legal reference work on administrative law is the five-volume *Administrative Law Treatise* by Professor Kenneth Culp Davis. It costs $90 and it also comes from West Publishing Company.

Another commercial publishing firm which produces legal guides for attorneys in various specialties is the Commerce Clearing House, known as CCH (4025 West Peterson Avenue, Chicago, Illinois 60646). CCH publishes dozens of specialized subscription reports which condense and analyze administrative and judicial rulings in specialized areas, most of them in a loose-leaf binder format. These include reports on *Trade Regulation*, *Aviation Law*, and the *Clean Air and Water News*, among many others.

Bureau of National Affairs, Inc., despite the official-sounding title, is a private publishing company which specializes in similar reports (1231 25th Street, N.W., Washington, D.C. 20037). Two of their services which can be useful are the *Antitrust and Trade Regulation Reporter* ($220 per year) and the *Environment Reporter* ($340 per year). If you are concerned with environmental protection, the *Environmental Law Reporter* published by the Environmental Law Institute offers a much less expensive service on current legal developments. It is available for $50 per year from Suite 614, 1346 Connecticut Avenue, N.W., Washington, D.C. 20036.

A recent single-volume digest of information on environmental protection is *Your Government and the Environment* (244 pages, $9.95, Output Systems, Inc., 2300 Ninth Street South, Arlington, Virginia 22204; Library of Congress Catalog Card No. 77-166183). The *Pike and Fischer Administrative Law* series is organized on the structure of the Administrative Procedure Act, and reports both agency and judicial decisions on administrative procedure. It costs $390 for volumes already published and $215 a year after that (2000 L Street, N.W., Washington, D.C. 20036). Pike and Fischer also publishes a series reporting decisions in communications law ($710 to start and $440 per year thereafter) entitled *Pike and Fischer Radio Regulation*.

A useful guide to all forms of legal citation is the booklet, *A Uni-*

form System of Citation, published by the Harvard Law Review Association (Gannett House, Cambridge, Massachusetts 02138). This booklet, referred to as the blue book despite the current edition's white cover, is used primarily as an editorial guide for law journals, but can also be useful in translating citation abbreviations.

In addition to the publications oriented primarily toward lawyers, there are dozens of specialized trade journals keeping a careful watch on the Washington agencies which regulate their respective industries. You probably will never see most of these publications for sale on a newsstand, and some of them are reluctant to include nonindustry people among their subscribers. If you can get to these newsletters and magazines you will find them extremely valuable in dealing with a given industry/agency complex. They are described separately in the chapters on agencies, but a glance at one publisher's list gives an idea of the titles. McGraw-Hill publishes about sixty such journals, including *Modern Nursing Home*, *Air & Water News*, *Washington Drug Letter*, and *Nucleonics Week*. A division of the same company, Standard & Poor's, is a useful source of information on corporations, especially in its *Register of Corporations, Directors, and Executives*.

Another category of publications is the Washington magazine or newsletter. One useful source is the *National Journal*, published by the Center for Political Research in Washington (1730 M Street, N.W., Washington, D.C. 20036). An expensive ($300 per year) weekly, it attempts to cover the entire federal government. Two newsletters which provide comprehensive coverage of Congress are the *Congressional Monitor* (a daily for $285 per year, from 201 Massachusetts Avenue, N.E., 20002) and the older *Congressional Quarterly* (a weekly which costs $400 per year, from 1735 K Street, N.W. 20006). A different sort of publication is the *Washington Monthly*, a journal of analysis and opinion ($10 per year from 1028 Connecticut Avenue., N.W. 20036).

West Publishing Company, which dominates the publishing of court opinions (and has even replaced official publications in some states) also has a Washington publication, the *U.S. Code Congressional and Administrative News*. Published semimonthly when Congress is in session, it summarizes Congressional action and prints all Presidential orders and administrative regulations. It is useful for checking the legislative history of a particular act, to see if the administrative regulations issued by an agency under the act's authority are what Congress intended in passing the law. Of course, the intent of Congress is often obscure, contradictory, or intentionally vague.

Congress and the Agencies

The fastest way to get to an administrative agency often is by going through Congress. Since the agencies all derive their basic powers from acts of Congress, they can also have those powers taken away by Congress. That is the fundamental basis for Congressional influence over the agencies, but the day-to-day relationship is based on other considerations which are also powerful. Congress has the power of purse and publicity over the agencies. Agencies live from year to year on appropriations, and an ambitious program can be doomed if there is no money for it. Congressional power to investigate can focus the spotlight of publicity on a dark corner of agency operations at just about any time, and the agencies know it. Trudging up Capitol Hill every year to ask for money is demeaning enough, in the opinion of some agencies; answering embarrassing questions about programs which have failed, or sometimes about programs which have succeeded too well, can make the experience even more painful.

Another source of Congressional influence on the composition of regulatory agencies is the statutory responsibility of the Senate to approve Presidential nominees to such bodies. The process is not unlike that of confirming nominees to the federal judiciary, and it involves many of the same factors of Senatorial courtesy to nominees who have the sponsorship of another Senator. Most nominations go through without a hitch, but the appearance of a nominee before a committee offers one of the few opportunities for searching examination of his attitudes and affiliations while he is still vulnerable to the most extreme kind of Congressional influence—it is, after all, still possible at that point that he won't get the job.

Once confirmed, a commissioner will appear again before a committee when the committee is considering legislation which will affect the agency's budget or its legislative power. The annual authorization hearings are the closest an agency gets to making a regular accounting to Congress. While budget requests are first channeled through the Office of Management and Budget, the requested funds can be cut drastically in Congress, or, if influential Congressmen feel that the agency should be encouraged to greater effort or rewarded for past accomplishments, increased.

Although agencies ultimately depend on Congress as a body for their money and existence, their direct relationship is to particular committees of that body. These are referred to as committees with "legislative oversight" of the agency involved. The term refers to the committee which has jurisdiction over legislation involving the agency, although it has been suggested that the term can sometimes be taken in its other, literal, meaning of forgetfulness. Relationships between agencies and their Congressional supervisors range from hostility and suspicion to mutual admiration.

The nature of the relationship, and sometimes even the existence of any oversight at all, is a mixture of law and politics. There are some committees about which every agency is concerned, such as the Appropriations and Government Operations Committees. Others, such as the Joint Committee on Atomic Energy, are almost exclusively concerned with a particular agency. Most legislative oversight is based on obvious committee jurisdiction, such as the concern of the House Committee on Interstate and Foreign Commerce and the Senate Commerce Committee with the Interstate Commerce Commission (ICC). Frequently this oversight responsibility is delegated to a subcommittee, such as the Surface Transportation Subcommittee of the Senate Commerce Committee, which conducts occasional oversight hearings on the ICC.

Politics in a more obvious form sometimes enters into the zeal of Congressional oversight. There is an informal process by which a member of Congress carves out an issue or area of concern for himself. This is more obvious in the case of new members than old ones, but it can happen at any stage. The issue is usually related to some specific connection between the Congressman and the issue, such as an industry within his state or the jurisdiction of a committee to which he happens to be assigned.

The process almost always involves introducing a bill and holding hearings on the issue, and sometimes includes a book on the subject by the Congressman. Representative Jamie Whitten, a Democrat from Mississippi, is Chairman of the House Appropriations Committee Subcommittee on Agriculture, and, as such, is a powerful force to be reckoned with by the Department of Agriculture. He has staked his claim on pesticides, and is firmly allied with the National Agricultural Chemical Association (NACA), the chemical pesticide industry's trade association. It was at the suggestion of the NACA president that Whitten consolidated his claim by writing a book, *That We May Live,* a pro-industry rebuttal to Rachel Carson's *Silent Spring.* And it was because of subsidies for sales of the book provided by three major pesticide companies that it was finally published.

However it comes about, the result of such alignment of interest is that all Congressmen are not equal in the eyes of a given agency. There are Representatives and Senators who are known as friends and enemies of agencies; there are members of Congress whose letters will be given respectful attention at the agency simply because they are Congressmen, and there are others who, because of power and interest, can get immediate action on their inquiries. Whatever the reason, the attention of an interested and influential Congressman can make the difference between a form reply to a consumer letter and something more. One example may illustrate the process. Stanley Cohen, a writer for *Advertising Age*, wrote a letter in early 1970 to the Civil Aeronautics Board (CAB), asking why there was not some notice to airplane passengers of the limitations on carriers' liability for loss of luggage and life. The letter languished in the CAB files until Senator Warren Magnuson of Washington sent a note asking what had become of Mr. Cohen's letter. The CAB promptly drafted some of the suggestions in the letter as proposals for rule making, placed them in the rule making docket, and told Senator Magnuson what had been done. Senator Magnuson is on the Senate Committee on Aeronautical and Space Sciences, is Chairman of the Senate Commerce Committee, and has a reputation as a consumer spokesman. Ultimately the CAB issued a formal regulation calling for more adequate disclosure of these liability limitations.

An inquiry from just about any Congressman will be treated with more attention than one which comes over the transom from a consumer who has no connection with the regulated industry, but it will receive even more attention if it comes from a Congressman with a special interest in the agency. A basic source for locating the formal sources of power and interest in Congress is the *Congressional Directory*, available for $4.00 from the Government Printing Office. This contains all current committee assignments, along with a wealth of other information on Congress. An informal description of the workings of Congress can be found in Mark J. Green, James M. Fallows, and David R. Zwick, *Who Runs Congress? The President, Big Business, or You?* (Bantam Books, 1972). For profiles on individual members of Congress write to Grossman Publishers Congress Project, P. O. Box 19281, Washington, D.C. 20036. Include $1.00 in payment for each profile.

Although regulatory commissions are theoretically independent and bipartisan, the political process is such that most appointees are sponsored by members of Congress. Once a commissioner is in office he is theoretically independent (if he is a member of one of the independent regulatory commissions, instead of an Executive branch agency). But it is understandable that such commissioners listen a little more carefully when they are called by the patrons who got them their jobs.

Talking to Agencies

When you decide to do something about a problem under the jurisdiction of a federal agency, it is understandable that you will think of writing, calling, or going to Washington. But sometimes you can save yourself considerable time and trouble by going to an office in your own area. Most of the agencies have regional offices, and these can often be of more immediate help than the Washington headquarters, especially if your problem is a local enforcement matter. The Federal Trade Commission (FTC) in particular, as a part of its recent conversion to activism, has authorized and encouraged its local offices to initiate some actions on their own (see Chap. 5). The chapters on individual agencies list local offices, but a fast way to find if there is a branch in your city is to check your telephone directory (under U.S. Government).

The usual rule in deciding where to go is to consider whether you want general information, help with a particular problem, or if you are intent on action that will affect the regulated industry nationally. If it is the latter, you will probably have to go to Washington, either in person or by mail, sooner or later. But much of the preliminary information-gathering can be done at a local office. In fact, you may even find local officials more accessible than their Washington superiors. The headquarters of an agency, or at least a branch which is of particular concern to you, may sometimes be nearer than you think. Although the headquarters of most agencies are located in the Washington, D.C., area, many important research facilities are outside of the District of Columbia. For example, the air pollution research center for the Environmental Protection Agency (EPA) is in Durham, North Carolina.

Gaining access to one of the federal regulatory agencies isn't a neat process. You will spend much time and effort trying to find out just what is going on and who is involved. But the federal government is continually in the process of reorganizing itself, which may be one reason why it is so glacially slow about getting on with its business. Because of this process, by the time you read this book some of the agencies may have changed their names and appearances. Much of your effort will be spent in the informal process of making telephone calls, talking to (or trying to get in to talk to) agency officials, and writing letters. This initial orientation stage can be done quickly, if you are lucky, but it cannot be skipped. It can also be time-consuming, expensive, and maddeningly frustrating. There are some characteristic responses by government agencies to inquisitive citizens that would almost certainly stay the same even if the federal government were reorganized into five-person cadres, and there are some tactics which can help you a little in saving time, money, and sanity in coping with these characteristics.

Your first impulse, once you have decided that you'd like to have a word with someone in a federal agency, will be to pick up the telephone. Like many impulses, it can cause you untold grief if you don't maintain a little rational control. First of all, get a specific idea of where you want to call before you start dialing, if you are calling from outside Washington. Under the best of circumstances you will spend a lot of time on the phone. If it's all going to be charged to your long-distance bill, you can deplete your treasury just finding out that you've been calling the wrong agency. Figuring out which agency you want to talk to, or at least narrowing the field, is the first step.

Once you have detected which agency concerns you, you have only begun. Frequently, if you dial the number listed for the agency in the Washington telephone directory or in the Government Organization Manual, the answer will be anonymous voice that says "Federal Government." Unless you have a specific person or office to talk to, this can be the beginning of your troubles. The operator will listen to you and then quickly switch you to another operator, who will listen to you and do the same thing, and so on, until you start getting testy. The operator who has your call at that point is likely to hang up.

There is a better way. Each agency has a telephone directory. They may deny it, but they all have some sort of list of their telephone numbers for use in the government phone system, and with a little figuring you can usually use those numbers to dial directly from outside. One way of gauging an agency's receptiveness to public access is to ask for a copy of their directory. The real public-be-damned officials will say that they have one, but not for public use. Others will be a little more subtle and say that they don't have one, or that they did (but it's out of print), or they will (when it's revised). Persist. If you can't get them to tell you their telephone numbers, how far do you think you will get in affecting their decision making?

Many of the directories are for sale at the G.P.O., and others are available directly from the agencies. Order one. A list of directories and the prices is in Appendix 2-A (p. 40).

Letter-writing is the tool most commonly used by citizens in dealing with federal regulatory agencies. It remains a fundamental and inescapable method no matter what other stages the citizen/agency relationship attains. Telephone conversations and meetings with agency officials

may make letters more, rather than less, necessary, if only to remind
the officials of exactly what they said. Even when the citizen resorts to
lawsuits in order to force public business into public view, he may find
it useful as well as polite to drop a line and let the prospective defendant
know what's about to happen. So here are a few guidelines on what to
include in this simple, inexpensive, but often effective tool for dealing
with bureaucracies.

First of all, type it. The typed, not the written, word is the accepted
medium of recorded communication in the bureaucratic world. It is
bad enough that government officials operate on the assumption that
the only people they should listen to in person or through the mail are
those who represent some kind—any kind—of organization. A person
who can't get or form an organization to supply him with a letterhead
is likely to be classified as a crank or a lone complainant, and one who
can't arrange for a typewriter fares worse.

In most cases, it is better to send your letter to the top of the
agency. If the agency has a specific consumer complaint-handling section it may be faster to send the letter directly there, but the delay of
a few days may be worth the possibility of the letter's gaining additional clout by its detour through the agency head's office. The mania
for filing and record-keeping in government can multiply the effect of
your letter, since each person who touches a letter usually must make
some kind of marks on paper about it. This can range from initialing
a routing slip to writing a memo, but for a moment your letter will
have touched his life.

It is also wise to send the letter to several addressees, and in most
cases to let them all know who is getting copies. The additional recipients (who usually get carbon copies, the "cc: ____" at the end of the
letter) should be selected carefully. Copies to a dozen or more people
may be so excessive as to be self-defeating; besides, the tenth carbon
is hard to read. The addressees should be people who are likely to check
on whether the agency has done anything about your letter. This
usually includes your own Congressman, who cares about you as a
voter and who pays people to take care of letters such as yours.
Another addressee in Congress should be someone on the committee
charged with legislative oversight of the agency. These are described
in chapters on individual agencies, and for agencies not covered in this
book the appropriate committees can usually be determined by consulting the Congressional Directory. Selecting the committee member
to whom you should write may require some careful newspaper reading in order to determine the Congressman's attitude toward the agency

For example, it would be nearly useless to suggest to Representative Chet Holifield, Vice Chairman of the Joint Committee on Atomic Energy, that the Atomic Energy Commission (AEC) is anything less than scrupulous about dangers from radioactivity. While sending a copy to a sworn enemy of the agency may prejudice your cause, especially if he is an opponent without power, it is better to choose someone who will follow the agency's handling of your case with a skeptical eye, rather than one who is a loyal friend of the bureau.

At least one copy should go to the press, and selecting the publication and reporter may be crucial. The trade press which covers the agency will usually be more interested than general publications. For example, *Broadcasting* covers everything of significance about the FCC, sometimes before it is officially announced by the agency itself. *Advertising Age* is interested in the FTC's activities regarding product claims, and *Nucleonics Week* covers the AEC. Newspapers such as *The New York Times*, the *Washington Post*, and *The Wall Street Journal* may also be interested. A list of reporters who regularly cover consumer affairs is in Appendix 2-B (p. 42). It is often also useful to send a copy to a consumer or citizen group which deals with the agency. Examples are the Center for Auto Safety, for the National Highway Traffic Safety Administration (NHTSA), and the Sierra Club or Friends of Earth for environmental effects of decisions by agencies such as the AEC and the Federal Power Commission (FPC). In addition, send a copy to the Office of Consumer Affairs, Executive Office of the President, Washington, D.C. 20506.

Although the content of the letter can be as varied as the industries regulated by the agencies, there are a few possible generalizations about how to present your message. One important aspect of a letter is its tone. At the risk of oversimplifying things, a letter should sound sane without being subservient. A citizen letter-writer is usually outraged, or at least extremely irritated, before he resorts to the typewriter. But if the letter is nothing but spluttering outrage, it is more likely to be dismissed as just another note from a nut by those who view citizen interest in the workings of government as automatically suspect. On the other hand, a self-effacing suggestion that the agency might look into a particular problem is likely to get nowhere. Nicholas Johnson, a former member of the FCC, has described what he calls "the law of effective reform." It is worth remembering while writing letters:

[In] order to get relief from legal institutions (Congress, courts, agencies) one must assert, first, the factual basis for the grievance and the specific parties involved; second, the legal principle that indicates relief is due (constitutional provision, statute, regulation, court or agency decision); and third, the precise remedy sought (new legislation or regulations, license revocation, fines or an order changing practices). [Nicholas Johnson, *How to Talk Back to Your Television Set* (Boston: Little, Brown, 1970), p. 188]

He then illustrates the "law of effective reform" by describing John Banzhaf's campaign for antismoking messages on television. There the factual basis was the hazard associated with cigarette-smoking and the encouragement of smoking by cigarette commercials, the legal principle was the FCC's "fairness doctrine," and the remedy sought was presentation of the other side of smoking by television stations.

Many of the same guidelines for making telephone calls and writing letters also apply in talking to agency people in person. Be as specific as you can in your questions, and be persistent. Read about the subject before you go in, and try to learn some of the jargon used by the specialists. For example, if you are dealing with the FTC, read the *Nader Report on the Federal Trade Commission* (New York: Grove Press, 1969) and the *Report of the American Bar Association Commission to Study the Federal Trade Commission* (Chicago: American Bar Association, 1969). If you are concerned about government programs in automobile safety, flammable fabrics, or hazardous substances, be familiar with the "Heffron Report," a critical report on government efforts in all these areas prepared for the National Commission on Product Safety (Federal Consumer Safety Legislation, $1.25 from G.P.O.). If you are going to the Interstate Commerce Commission, read *Interstate Commerce Omission* (Robert Fellmeth, $1.45, Grossman Publishers, New York). Try to learn some of the shortcomings and criticisms of the agency that never show up in its annual reports or in the Government Organizational Manual.

Begin by trying to get information about what the agency is doing before you ask the critical questions about why they aren't doing something else. Take notes during the interview, unless it appears to make the person being interviewed reticent or ill at ease. If you feel that you can get more information by putting away your pencil, summarize the conversation immediately afterward. A comment that may appear trivial in an early interview can later prove to be a major lead. Respect confidentiality if it is asked for.

All of this is to give you an idea of how to get started, where to look for information, and how to avoid wasting too much time at the beginning. Much of the information you need for a general orientation is available to the public. But once you begin to focus on a particular issue you are likely to run into problems. The information, you will be told, is "internal" or a "trade secret." These are some of the more customary excuses for refusing to disclose information to which you have a right under the Freedom of Information Act. They are attempts to invoke the exceptions which the Act made from the general rule of disclosure, which it supposedly established. How to use the Act, and how to keep the legal exceptions from being the rule in practice, is what the next chapter is about.

Agency Telephone Directory List

The telephone directories of the departments and agencies listed below are available from the Superintendent of Documents, U.S. Government Printing Office, Washington, DC 20402.

Department of Agriculture..........................$ .75

Department of Commerce............................. 5.00

Environmental Protection Agency.................... .70

Federal Telecommunications System
(includes Atomic Energy Commission)............. 3.50

Department of Health, Education, and
Welfare (includes Food and Drug
Administration)................................. 2.75

Department of the Interior........................ 1.00

Department of Labor (includes
Occupational Safety and Health
Administration)................................. .75

Department of Transportation (includes
National Highway Traffic Safety
Administration)................................. 3.25

Department of the Treasury (includes
Internal Revenue Service)....................... .40

U.S. House of Representatives..................... .80

U.S. Senate....................................... 2.75

Remittance payable to the Superintendent of Documents must accompany orders unless a charge account is established. Supplies of publications are limited, and prices are subject to change without advance notice.

Some telephone directories are not sold through GPO, but are available from other sources.

Civil Aeronautics Board
    Publications Office
    Civil Aeronautics Board, Room B-22
    1825 Connecticut Avenue, N.W.
    Washington, DC 20428 .... .50

Federal Communications Commission
　　　Keuffel & Esser Company
　　　1521 N. Danville Street
　　　Arlington, VA 22201 　..................... $2.50+
　　　　　　　　　　　　　　　　　　　　　　　State Tax

Federal Power Commission
　　　Office of Public Information
　　　Federal Power Commission
　　　825 N. Capitol Street, N.E.
　　　Washington, DC 20426 　...................... Free

Federal Trade Commission
　　　Publications Office, Room 130
　　　6th and Pennsylvania Avenue, N.W.
　　　Washington, DC 20580 　...................... Free

Interstate Commerce Commission
　　　Publications Office, Room 1349
　　　Interstate Commerce Commission
　　　12th and Constitution Avenue, N.W.
　　　Washington, DC 20423 　...................... Free

Consumer Press List

Stan Cohen
Advertising Age
995 National Press Bldg.
Washington, DC 20004

Associated Press
1300 Connecticut Ave., N.W.
Washington, DC 20036

Helen Kahn
Automotive News
525 National Press Bldg.
Washington, DC 20004

Booth Newspapers
515 National Press Bldg.
Washington, DC 20004

Peter Weaver
665 National Press Bldg.
Washington, DC 20004

Thomson Newspapers
1135 National Press Bldg.
Washington, DC 20004

United Press International
315 National Press Bldg.
Washington, DC 20004

Arthur Rowse
Consumer Newsweek
813 National Press Bldg.
Washington, DC 20004

U.S. News & World Report
2300 N Street, N.W.
Washington, DC 20037

Ron Shafer
Wall Street Journal
245 National Press Bldg.
Washington, DC 20004

Ann McFeatters
Scripps-Howard Newspaper
    Alliance
777 14th Street, N.W.
Washington, DC 20005

Sidney Margolius
74 Davis Road
Port Washington, NY 11050

National Observer
11501 Columbia Pike
Silver Spring, MD 20910

Time Magazine
888 16th Street, N.W.
Washington, DC 20006

Broadcasting Magazine
1735 De Sales Street, N.W.
Washington, DC 20036

Peter Gall
McGraw-Hill Publications
400 National Press Bldg.
Washington, DC 20004

Nation's Business
1615 H Street, N.W.
Washington, DC 20006

Newsday
621 National Press Bldg.
Washington, DC 20004

Jim Bishop
Newsweek
1750 Pennsylvania Ave.,N.W.
Washington, DC 20006

Newhouse National News
    Service
1750 Pennsylvania Ave., N.W.
Washington, DC 20006

Dick Wightman
Fairchild Publications
399 National Press Bldg.
Washington, DC 20004

Ray Galant
Food Chemical News
601 Warner Bldg.
Washington, DC 20004

Albert B. Kelley
Insurance Institute for
    Highway Safety
600 New Hampshire Ave., N.W.
Washington, DC 20037

Journal of Commerce
1325 E Street, N.W.
Washington, DC 20004

Paul Hencke
Kiplinger Letter
1729 H Street, N.W.
Washington, DC 20006

Jane Wilson
Of Consumer Interest
2201 Wilson Blvd.
Arlington, VA 22216

Media & Consumer
P.O.Box 1225
Radio City Station
New York, NY 10019

Gannett News
1281 National Press Bldg.
Washington, DC 20004

Hearst Newspapers
1701 Pennsylvania Ave., N.W.
Washington, DC 20006

CHAPTER 3

THE FREEDOM OF INFORMATION ACT

Let My People Know

> The Mayor: ...it is a matter of the greatest concern to me that your report [that the public baths were contaminated]...must be withheld for the good of the community. Later on, I shall bring up the matter for discussion, and we shall deal with it as best we can—discreetly. But nothing of this dangerous business—not a single word—must become known to the public.
>
> —Henrik Ibsen,
> An Enemy of the People,
> Act II

There is a common bond of bureaucracy that transcends the centuries and the oceans, and the words of Ibsen's fictional nineteenth century mayor would fit neatly in the mouths of many twentieth century civil servants. Part of the bond is the assumption that information which a public agency acquires becomes the property of agency personnel, to be disclosed only to those who can show a good reason for disclosure and who can be trusted not to make a fuss.

It was to combat this attitude and to establish the principle that government information *as a rule* is available to the public that the Freedom of Information Act (FOIA) was passed and signed into law in 1966. Lyndon Johnson chose the Fourth of July as the day for the ceremony, and he signed it "with a deep sense of pride that the United States is an open society in which the people's right to know is cherished and guarded." But so far this guarding of the people's right to know has been done mostly by some of the people themselves, rather than by the agencies subject to the Act, with occasional assistance from the federal courts.

The fundamental principle established by the Act is that information in the possession of federal agencies is to be made available to the public *unless* withholding it is specifically justified under one of the statutory exceptions to this rule of disclosure. It is essential to keep this basic rule in mind, because, in spite of the statute, most officials with whom you will come in contact will act on the assumption that government information is to be kept secret unless there is a specific reason for disclosing it. It is ironic that the law provides penalties for disclosure of trade secret-type information [18 U.S.C. 1905], but provides no penalty of any sort for the withholding of public information. Therefore, the law has created an impetus for the public official to withhold information. In light of this, you should challenge the decisions and actions of government officials and administrators whenever public access is questioned.

The official title of the FOIA is Public Law 89-487, an amendment to the Public Information Section of the Administrative Procedure Act (APA). The FOIA was later incorporated into the U.S. Code (by Public Law 90-23 of 5 June 1967) as Section 552 of Title 5. The Act itself is fairly brief, and the entire text is in Appendix 3-A (p. 60). It covers all federal agencies in the Executive Branch and independent commissions, but it does not apply to Congress, the courts, the District of Columbia and territories, or state and local governments.

Basically, the FOIA requires all federal agencies to make certain material, such as opinions in cases, policy statements, and administrative instructions which affect the public, available for public inspection and copying. "Identifiable records" that are requested are also to be made available unless they fall into one of the exempt categories. There are nine of these categories, which will be discussed later. Remember that these are exceptions to the general rule of disclosure, and even if parts of the records requested are exempt the agencies must make available those portions which are not exempt. Although the Act may *allow* an agency to withhold information in such categories, it does not necessarily require such withholding.

The major problem with the FOIA is that it hasn't been used by the press, citizens, or citizen groups to any appreciable extent. As a result, many administrators maintain the attitude of secrecy that they had prior to its adoption. The FOIA has many shortcomings, but it can be an effective tool if it is used. The more it is used, the more effective it will become.

How to Use the Act

The first step in getting information from an agency under the FOIA is to determine as specifically as you can what information you want. One reason for this is the Act's requirement that records requested be "identifiable"; another reason is to aid in determining which agency you will ask, since frequently you will begin the process with an idea of what information you want, and proceed from that to learning which agency has possession of it. Although the Act was passed to establish a uniform policy for information disclosure through the federal government, regulations which the agencies have adopted to implement it vary widely, and the ways in which they apply vary even more widely.

The FOIA requires every agency to publish its procedures for obtaining information. Since each has separate and sometimes different regulations, the various agencies' regulations should be consulted when you are considering submitting an information request. These regulations are available in the Code of Federal Regulations (C.F.R.) under the title assigned to that agency. The C.F.R. should be available at any library, law library, or most law offices. The citations for each agency's regulations are listed on page 23 of the United States Government Manual 1972-1973, which is available for $3.00 from the Government Printing Office (G.P.O.). This manual is a must for any activity concerning the federal government. If a set of the C.F.R. is not available, write the Public Information Office of the agency and ask for a copy of their Freedom of Information regulations. They usually respond quickly to this type of request.

In 1968 the House Committee on Government Operations compiled all of these regulations and published them in a Committee print entitled *Freedom of Information Act (Compilation and Analysis of Departmental Regulations Implementing 5 U.S.C. 552)*. This is available from the G.P.O. for $1.25 and includes other material interpreting the Act, such as the Attorney General's Memorandum, along with an index to all departmental regulations printed in the C.F.R. However, this publication is seriously out of date and should be used only in conjunction with the current C.F.R.

A booklet which you may find useful in getting information from government sources is *The Damned Information* (Washington Institute for Quality Education, 300 M Street, S.W., Washington, D.C. 20024, $3.75). This contains a sample letter requesting information, similar to the one in Appendix 3-B (p. 64), and a complaint filed in federal court to force an agency to produce records under the FOIA. One warning: If you bring an action, at least consult an attorney; do not depend on the form of court pleadings contained in this otherwise helpful pamphlet. It also includes summaries of state freedom of information statutes, and guidelines on how government statistical information can be used.

Another important source of material for use in getting information from government sources at both the state and federal levels is the Freedom of Information Center (Box 858, Columbia, Missouri 65201, 314-882-4856). Subscribing memberships are $7.50 per year, and include the bimonthly *FoI Digest,* two reports published each month, opinion papers, and periodic newsletters from the Washington representative. The Center has an extensive supply of papers on specialized subjects in freedom of information, most of which are written by graduate journalism students at the University of Missouri, and you may find one that applies to your specific situation. These include a summary of all cases decided under the FOIA. The Center's orientation is journalistic, rather than legal, and it does not involve itself in litigation under the FOIA.

A more recent and very useful publication on the FOIA is John Shattuck, *You're Entitled to Know: Your Rights Under the Freedom of Information Act* (American Civil Liberties Union, 22 E. 40th Street, New York, N.Y. 10016, February 1973, a 25 cent pamphlet).

The House Foreign Operations and Government Information Subcommittee of the Committee on Government Operations has conducted a detailed survey of the practices of federal agencies in applying the Act. Hearings were held in the spring of 1972, and the bound transcript of the hearings is a valuable resource for use in dealing with federal agencies. The bound transcript of the hearings is available from the G.P.O. Ask for *U.S. Government Information Policies and Practices: Problems of Congress in Obtaining Information from the Executive Branch* (Hearings before a Subcommittee of the Committee on Government Operations, House of Representatives, 92nd Congress, 2nd Session, May and June 1972). As a result of those hearings, the subcommittee issued a report on the Administration of the Freedom of Information Act, House Report 92-1419, which provides excellent insight into

problems presented with that administration (this report is now out
of print and is available only in libraries).

Although you will probably need to refer to the agency's regulations
if the information you are seeking is extensive or important, minor
inquiries can be handled informally over the telephone. This frequently
involves, or at least begins with, a call to the agency's Public Information Office. The information you want may be available in an agency
publication, or the Public Information Office may be able to direct
you to the department which has the information on file. But don't
depend on the agency PIO for the final word on which department
has the information, or on whether the agency has it at all. Sometimes
it may be more effective to get a copy of the agency telephone directory (see Appendix 2-A, p. 40), determine which department is
most likely to have the information, and call that department directly.
Some agencies have made specific provisions in their regulations for
accepting information requests by telephone [e.g., Civil Aeronautics
Board, 14 C.F.R. 310.6(a); Securities and Exchange Commission, 17
C.F.R. 200.80(d)].

But many agencies are unlikely to respond to informal telephone
requests, especially if the information is at all significant, and in most
cases it will probably be necessary to write at least one letter requesting
the information before you get anything. To write that letter, you will
need at least a passing acquaintance with the terms and loopholes of
the Act, and the way in which they have been applied.

These are the nine exemptions to the Act, and the type of information exempt under each. The FOIA does not apply to matters that
are:

1. Specifically required by Executive order to be kept secret in the
   interest of the national defense or foreign policy. The documents exempt under this section are those, like the Pentagon
   Papers, which are classified. Courts are most reluctant to
   release information if this exemption is at all relevant. This
   does not necessarily eliminate the availability of information in
   the possession of the Department of State or the Department
   of Defense. Material such as results of drug-testing done on GI's
   returning from overseas is not exempt under this provision.
2. Related solely to the internal personnel rules and practices of
   an agency. This exemption relates to rules of internal management and covers things such as employee parking and cafeteria
   regulations, as well as certain manuals that relate to manage-

ment and organization of particular agencies. Staff manuals instructing inspectors or agents how to perform their job are *not* exempt.

3. Specifically exempted from disclosure by statute. This exempts documents and information which are exempt from disclosure by other statutes. The most notable among these are those that relate to the Internal Revenue Service (IRS) and Social Security Administration. In those cases, information that relates to individual taxpayers and recipients or applicants under Social Security is exempt. The attempt of the Social Security Administration to exempt from disclosure survey reports compiled on the conditions present in nursing homes under Medicare is presently being challenged in court. Since the information obtained does not relate to applicants or recipients, it is hoped the courts will release the survey reports.

4. Trade secrets and commercial or financial information obtained from a person and privileged or confidential. Under this section it seems clear that confidential information which is not a trade secret and not financial or commercial is disclosable. Thus the agencies may withhold information only if it is either a trade secret or commercial or financial. This exemption applies only to information which is submitted to the government. Government-prepared documents can never be exempted under this section.

5. Inter-agency or intra-agency memoranda or letters which would not be available by law to a party other than an agency in litigation with an agency. This exemption is the one most widely used by the government, and they will attempt to use it in almost every situation. Opinions and policy recommendations are the traditional types of information which are included within this exemption. A memo from a staff person to a supervisor advising that a policy be formulated would be exempt. However, factual reports or analyses of facts are not included. Reports of inspectors or field personnel should not be exempt. This material might contain opinions, but if it can be determined that it is more factual analysis than policy recommendation, then it should be available.

6. Personnel and medical files and similar files the disclosure of which would constitute a clearly unwarranted invasion of personal privacy. This exemption is self-explanatory. It should be pointed out, however, that this is the only exemption that encourages a balancing of interests between disclosure and non-

disclosure. If this exemption is related to the information requested, then a brief explanation as to the need for the information should be made so that it can be determined that the disclosure of information would not be a clearly unwarranted invasion of personal privacy.

7. Investigatory files compiled for law enforcement purposes except to the extent available by law to a party other than an agency. Almost any information that a regulatory agency has can be considered an investigatory file. The courts have stated that only where there is an imminent prospect of a law enforcement proceeding being undertaken can the exemption be used. Thus, in cases where it can be shown that a law enforcement action against the particular factory is imminent, the inspection reports are exempt. Also, if the information is transmitted to the people being investigated, the information is no longer exempt.

8 and 9. These are special interest exemptions and are not relevant to most applications of the Act.

The extent to which these exemptions can be used as grounds for refusing public information requests will have to be determined largely by the courts through litigation. But, at a minimum, they offer some guidance as to what is and what is not available under the FOIA.

In writing a letter to the agency, identify the material you are asking for as specifically as possible, and be sure to indicate whether you wish to examine the records, or are asking for copies of the records to be sent to you. Even if you are fairly certain that you want copies, ask the agency to estimate the cost and let you know the amount before they actually copy and send the records. Copy and search fees are sometimes used as a barrier to access. If the agency demands thousands of dollars in search and copying fees, challenge that in court as an agency denial.

The Federal Advisory Committee Act, Public Law 92-463 (which became effective on 5 January 1973), provides "Except where prohibited by contractual agreements entered into prior to the effective date of this Act, agencies and advisory committees shall make available to any person, at actual cost of duplication, copies of transcripts of agency proceedings or advisory committee hearings" [Section 12(a)]. It used to be a common practice that, in order for a person to get transcripts of proceedings, he/she would have to buy them directly from the commercial reporting company that originally prepared them, at $.75 to $1.50 per page. This can no longer occur. Actual cost of duplication should not exceed 10 cents per page. Most of the existing contracts with commercial reporting companies should have expired or be close to expiration by the time this book is published.

The Federal Advisory Committee Act provides for public access to all Advisory Committee meetings, with some limitations. Notices are published in the *Federal Register* stating the time and place of these meetings. While this is a beneficial law, it has serious short-comings. *Like FOIA, it does not provide for access to any government body which cannot be called an "advisory committee" and it does not provide for the right of access to public officials, i.e., interviews.*

Your initial letter of request for information should be drafted in accordance with the agency's procedures for requesting information, referred to earlier. Usually this request should be addressed to the agency's operations head, either by name or title. Include citations to the FOIA and to the departmental regulations. Since delay is frequently used as an informal barrier, it may be useful to request a reply within seven working days. If more time is needed by the agency to process your request, they at least should send you some notice informing you of the date when either the information or a decision on your request will be made available. In your initial request ask for a final determination. However, procedures promulgated by the agencies sometimes include a system of internal agency appeals which you may have to go through if your initial letter is not responded to with a final determination. In order to deal with this system as quickly as possible, your letter should state that, if your request is denied, that denial be substantiated by a statement of the statutory exemption being claimed by the agency, and why it is applicable to your request. The agency should also accompany any refusals of information requests with an outline of the agency's appeal procedure.

While initial information requests will vary according to the agency involved, a general form to follow is set forth in Appendix 3-A (p. 60). If your first letter is rejected, the rejection will at least give some idea of the legal issues which will be involved in your administrative appeal and in possible subsequent litigation in court. In making an administrative appeal you need to be familiar with interpretations of the statutory exemptions, as well as some common tactics used by agencies to avoid disclosure of information.

What the Exceptions Mean:
The Attorney General's Memorandum(s)

Following passage of the FOIA, the Department of Justice published a memorandum interpreting the Act for the use of government agencies. This is available in booklet form for 25 cents from the G.P.O., and is also included in the committee print compilation of departmental regulations. The official title is the *Attorney General's Memorandum on the Public Information Section of the Administrative Procedure Act.* While it is somewhat restrictive and self-serving, and is not binding on courts in interpreting the Act, it serves as a starting point for legal research, and may be useful in persuading agencies to disclose information in some cases. As the Memorandum notes (on p. 27), most cases involving appeals to federal courts from agency refusals to disclose information would be handled by the Civil Division of the Department of Justice, and the official interpretation of the Act by Justice should at least be persuasive to the agencies.

The basic structure of the Memorandum is a comparison of the provisions of the FOIA with the much more restrictive provisions of the Public Information Section of the APA, which it amended. The Memorandum gives a fairly expansive reading to the statutory exemptions from the rule of disclosure. However, faced with the conundrum exempting "trade secrets and commercial or financial information obtained from a person and privileged or confidential," the Memorandum begins by saying, "The scope of this exemption is particularly difficult to determine. The terms used are general and undefined. Moreover, the sentence structure makes it susceptible of several readings, none of which is entirely satisfactory." After reviewing the somewhat contradictory legislative history of this section, the Memorandum reaches the following conclusion, which also falls somewhat short of precision:

> It seems obvious from these Committee reports that Congress neither intended to exempt all commercial and financial information on the one hand, nor to require disclosure of all other privileged or confidential information on the other. Agencies should seek to follow the Congressional intention as expressed in the Committee report.

The Justice Department circulated another memorandum on 8 December 1969 which will have a much more practical effect on whether you get your information than all of the complicated statutory interpretations in the earlier memorandum. Basically, the Department told agencies that they should be willing to give in to requests for information, even when they think they can justify withholding it under one of the exemptions, if the disclosure is necessary to avoid the risk of a court ruling against the government. If an agency goes to court and loses, the ruling can be used against other agencies in similar situations. But if the agency relents and allows the information to be made public before a court orders it to do so, only that particular information is lost. As the Memorandum put it:

> Although the legal basis for denying a particular request under the Act may seem quite strong to an agency at the time it elects finally to refuse access . . . the justification may appear considerably less strong when later viewed, in the context of adversary litigation, from the detached perspective of a court . . . and a possible adverse judicial decision may well have effects going beyond the operations and programs of the agency involved.

Because of this, the Department asked all agency general counsels to consult the Justice Department before making a final agency refusal that could be appealed to a federal court. This is why a request that may be scoffed at by lower level agency personnel will be treated quite differently at the highest agency level. It is also the reason why you should persist in your administrative appeals to get to the top level of the agency as quickly as possible.

Tactics of Evasion
and How to Overcome Them

You should be prepared for some of the common tactics used by agencies to frustrate requests for information. As a matter of practice, most agencies have a two-pronged information policy: one policy toward citizens, and another for the special interest groups that form the agency's regulatory constituency. A pattern of preferential disclosure of information to those regulated industries gives them access to government information and proceedings during the crucial early stages of agency decision making, before the public is officially given notice by publication in the *Federal Register*.

Some of the favorite exemptions used by agency personnel to avoid disclosing information to those who are not part of the agency's regulatory constituency are the exemptions for "internal communications," for information "given in confidence," and for material being compiled "for investigatory purposes." One particular tactic is for an agency to open an investigatory file for some possible future action, and to conceal information of all sorts just by dropping it in that file. For example, the Department of Labor has denied access to records of violations of the Walsh-Healey Act which are five, ten, and fifteen years old. That Act sets minimum wages and safety standards for companies doing more than $10,000 worth of business with the federal government, and the only sanction for such violations is a three-year ban from further government contracts. The information was thus withheld under the exemption long after the practical deadline for imposition of any sanctions under the Act.

Another technique is that of "contamination," the mixing of material which should be available to the public with other material which can be withheld under one of the statutory exemptions. The Department of Defense, for instance, has refused to disclose information on the quantity of oil being pumped from the bilges of Navy ships into the water. The justification given for withholding these data is that they would be included in a report containing operational data on military characteristics which would be classified and withheld under the national security exemption.

One tactic for avoiding disclosure is to delay the administrative procedures so that inquisitive citizens are exhausted long before their administrative remedies have run out. Since a citizen is required to go through all of the agency's administrative procedures for appeal before he can go into federal court to secure his right to the information, prolonging the administrative process can hold him off until his need for the information becomes moot, or his financial resources are exhausted. In dealing with this tactic, it is worth remembering that a labor case which did not involve the FOIA, *Deering Milliken, Inc.* v. *Johnston* [295 F.2d 856, 4th Cir. (1961)], generally supports the position that administrative agencies cannot, in effect, withhold statutory rights by unduly prolonging administrative proceedings. According to the ruling in that case, a citizen may not be required to exhaust all of the administrative remedies available if it would result in "fundamental unfairness," or where the agency clearly has acted beyond the scope of its statutory authority.

But if the information for which you are asking is significant, be prepared for delays followed by delays. For example, Consumer's Union waited for ten months to obtain a final determination on its request for information on hearing aids [Prices of Hearing Aids, Hearing before the Subcommittee on Antitrust and Monopoly of the Senate Committee on the Judiciary, pursuant to S. Res. 258, 87 Cong., 2nd Sess. 257-58 (1958); paragraphs 10-18 of plaintiff's complaint in *Consumer's Union* v. *Veterans Administration*, 301 F. Supp. 796 (S.D.N.Y. 1969)]. A government-sponsored survey at two agencies found that action on some information requests had been pending for several months while the legal basis and policy reasons for possible withholding were studied, and in one case the request had been submitted more than a year before [Donald A. Gianella, Professor of Law, Villanova University, "Uniform Implementation of the Freedom of Information Act," 23 *Administrative Law Review* 217 (May 1971)].

During an interview in the course of that study, one staff member of an agency admitted candidly that requests from prominent national and Washington law firms ordinarily receive faster attention than requests from out-of-town persons unknown to the agency [*Ibid.*, 23]. This admission indicates one possible tactic for prodding agencies into giving faster attention to requests for information by enlisting the support or at least the interest of people to whom the agency pays more attention. An example would be to send copies of your letters requesting information to carefully selected Congressmen and journalists (see p. 42).

Until some schedule is established for handling information requests, either by Congress or by the agencies themselves, such as the ten-day guideline adopted by the Defense Supply Agency [32 C.F.R. 1260.6(b)(3)], it may be useful to set a deadline of your own in your information request, giving a date by which you expect at least an initial reply to your letter. Current regulations of the Department of Transportation allow a person requesting information to get final action on an administrative appeal if the initial decision on his request has been unreasonably delayed [49 C.F.R. 7.71(b)]. Check the agency's regulations closely, and hold them to any self-imposed time period, such as the seven-day period which the Civil Aeronautics Board (CAB) has established for handling appeals on information requests [14 C.F.R. 310.9(d)].

Some other common agency tactics are to insist that the information not be indexed, so it cannot be identified and retrieved from the files (or from the computers), and, if pressed, to resort to exorbitant charges for searching and copying. Remember that the Act provides for *inspection* and copying, and you don't have to pay the photocopy charge just to look at something.

Remember that these barriers are essentially delaying devices, and they will be relied on less by the agency as you go through your administrative appeals and make it clear that you are ready and willing to go to court. Somewhere along the line you will probably be offered a compromise of sorts. This usually involves offering the information, or some of it, as a "favor," and it frequently includes stated or implied conditions. The condition may be for you to concede that you have no right to the information, that you won't tell how you got it, or that you won't use it to embarrass the agency. Often you must choose between getting some of the information as a favor when you need it, and getting the information as a matter of right after fighting your way through the administrative appeals. This dilemma provides one explanation why newspapers, which were thought to be the main beneficiaries of the Act, have been less than ardent about using it. Of the 200 or so suits filed under the statute, only about five have been brought by newspapers, and a survey of Associated Press managing editors in *Editor and Publisher* (26 June 1971) indicated that few working journalists even use the threat of the Act to get information. One reason is that most newspaper stories are written on deadlines which don't allow for administrative appeals, let alone litigation. Another is that journalists are often dependent on inside sources, and sources can dry up quickly if they are pushed too far.

Going to Court

If the agency turns down your administrative appeal, don't stop trying. The Act specifically provides

> . . . The district court of the United States in the district in which the complainant resides, or has his principal place of business, or in which the agency records are situated, has jurisdiction to enjoin the agency from withholding agency records, and to order the production of any agency records improperly withheld from the complainant. [5 U.S.C. 552(a)(3)]

So, if you are turned down, you can go straight to court, and in your own district if you don't feel like going to Washington. When you litigate to force the agency to produce information, your case won't be subject to the same delays as are many ordinary civil cases, since the Act also provides

. . . Except as to causes the court considers of greater importance,
proceedings before the district court, as authorized by this paragraph, take precedence on the docket over all other causes and
shall be assigned for hearing and trial at the earliest practicable
date and expedited in every way.

Some other statutes also can help when you go to court. 28 U.S.C.
1361 authorizes suits in the nature of mandamus (see below) to compel
government officials to perform a duty; 5 U.S.C. 555(b) requires an
agency "to conclude a matter" before it "within a reasonable time";
and 5 U.S.C. 706(1) authorizes a reviewing court to "compel agency
action unlawfully withheld or unreasonably delayed."

"Mandamus" is a court order to a government official to do something which is "ministerial," that is, in which he has no discretion. It is
especially appropriate as a remedy for forcing government officials to
produce information which clearly should be public. Even if there are
some legal questions to be decided in determining whether or not the
information qualifies for exemption, it is clear that mandamus can also
be used to force an official to exercise his discretion one way or another
another, rather than delaying it indefinitely [*National Anti-Vivisection
Society* v. *FCC*, 234 F. Supp. 696 (N.D.Ill. 1964); *Indiana and Michigan
Electric Co.* v. *FPC*, 224 F. Supp. 166 (N.D. Ind. 1963)].

The statutory requirement in 5 U.S.C. 555(b) that agencies act with
"reasonable dispatch" is the current version of the statutory provision
which was used in the Deering Milliken case referred to on page 55. In
effect, it means that even if the agency has not taken final action, it is
possible to get relief from a federal court if the agency's delay is equivalent to a "legal wrong." Along with Section 706(1), this means that
an agency cannot keep you standing in the administrative halls forever
and remain immune from judicial intervention to force the agency to
act.

But don't get involved in any of these legal arguments at lower
bureaucratic levels. Until you get to court, your problem won't be
what the law says, but what the agency does. Be prepared for delays
and evasions, and don't be diverted by them. Remember that the
agency will be much more willing to grant access to the information
when you have gone through the administrative appeals and it appears
that you are likely to go to court. It is up to the agency to justify withholding under one of the statutory exemptions, so don't commit yourself to a particular legal argument or an interpretation of the exemptions
until you have appealed to the top of the agency. That is where the

administrative decision on any important information will be made, and your goal should be to get there as quickly as possible once your initial request is refused.

The Center for Study of Responsive Law has established a Freedom of Information Clearinghouse that can provide experienced guidance concerning any of the matters discussed in this chapter. If you need assistance, write a detailed description of your Freedom of Information problem, attach relevant correspondence, and mail it to Freedom of Information Clearinghouse, P.O. Box 19367, Washington, D.C. 20036.

The Freedom of Information Act

THE FREEDOM OF INFORMATION ACT
(5 USC 552, Act of June 5, 1967, P.L. 90-23, 81 Stat. 54)

§ 552 Public Information; agency rules, opinions, orders, records, and proceedings

(a) Each agency shall make available to the public information as follows:

(1) Each agency shall separately state and currently publish in the Federal Register for the guidance of the public--

(A) descriptions of its central and field organization and the established places at which, the employees (and in the case of a uniformed service, the members) from whom, and the methods whereby, the public may obtain information, make submittals or requests, or obtain decisions;

(B) statements of the general course and method by which its functions are channeled and determined, including the nature and requirements of all formal and informal procedures available;

(C) rules of procedure, descriptions of forms available or the places at which forms may be obtained, and instructions as to the scope and contents of all papers, reports, or examinations;

(D) substantive rules of general applicability adopted as authorized by law, and statements of general applicability formulated and adopted by the agency; and

(E) each amendment, revision, or repeal of the foregoing. Except to the extent that a person has actual and timely notice of the terms thereof, a person may not in any manner be required to resort to, or be adversely affected by, a matter required to be published in the Federal Register and not so published. For the purpose of this paragraph, matter reasonably available to the class of persons affected thereby is deemed published in the Federal Register when incorporated by reference therein with the approval of the Director of the Federal Register.

(2) Each agency, in accordance with published rules, shall make available for public inspection and copying--

    (A) final opinions, including concurring and dissenting opinions, as well as orders, made in the adjudication of cases;

    (B) those statements of policy and interpretations which have been adopted by the agency and are not published in the Federal Register; and

    (C) administrative staff manuals and instructions to staff that affect a member of the public;

unless the materials are promptly published and copies offered for sale. To the extent required to prevent a clearly unwarranted invasion of personal privacy, an agency may delete identifying details when it makes available or publishes an opinion, statement of policy, interpretation, or staff manual or instruction. However, in each case the justification for the deletion shall be explained fully in writing. Each agency also shall maintain and make available for public inspection and copying a current index providing identifying information for the public as to any matter issued, adopted, or promulgated after July 4, 1967, and required by this paragraph to be made available or published. A final order, opinion, statement of policy, interpretation, or staff manual or instruction that affects a member of the public may be relied on, used, or cited as precedent by an agency against a party other than an agency only if--

    (i) it has been indexed and either made available or published as provided by this paragraph; or

    (ii) the party has actual and timely notice of the terms thereof.

(3) Except with respect to the records made available under paragraphs (1) and (2) of this subsection, each agency, on request for identifiable records made in accordance with published rules stating the time, place, fees to the extent authorized by statute, and procedure to be followed, shall make the records promptly available to any person. On complaint, the district court of the United States in the district in which the complainant resides, or has his principal place of business, or in which the agency records are situated, has jurisdiction to enjoin the agency from withholding agency records and to order

the production of any agency records improperly withheld
from the complainant. In such a case the court shall
determine the matter de novo and the burden is on the
agency to sustain its action. In the event of noncompliance with the order of the court, the district court may
punish for contempt the responsible employee, and in the
case of a uniformed service, the responsible member.
Except as to causes the court considers of greater importance, proceedings before the district court, as authorized by this paragraph, take precedence on the docket over
all other causes and shall be assigned for hearing and
trial at the earliest practicable date and expedited in
every way.

(4) Each agency having more than one member shall
maintain and make available for public inspection a
record of the final votes of each member in every agency
proceeding.

(b) This section does not apply to matters that are--

(1) specifically required by Executive order to be
kept secret in the interest of the national defense
or foreign policy;

(2) related solely to the internal personnel rules
and practices of an agency;

(3) specifically exempted from disclosure by
statute;

(4) trade secrets and commercial or financial information obtained from a person and privileged or
confidential;

(5) inter-agency or intra-agency memorandums or
letters which would not be available by law to a
party other than an agency in litigation with the
agency;

(6) personnel and medical files and similar files
the disclosure of which would constitute a clearly
unwarranted invasion of personal privacy;

(7) investigatory files compiled for law enforcement purposes except to the extent available by law
to a party other than an agency;

(8) contained in or related to examination, operating, or condition reports prepared by, on behalf of,

or for the use of an agency responsible for the regulation or supervision of financial institutions; or

(9) geological and geophysical information and
data, including maps, concerning wells.

(c) This section does not authorize withholding of
information or limit the availability of records to the
public, except as specifically stated in this section.
This section is not authority to withhold information
from Congress. Pub. L. 89-54, Sept. 6, 1966, 80 Stat.
383; Pub. L. 90-23, § 1, June 5, 1967, 81 Stat. 54.

Sample Freedom of Information Act Request Letter

                                        (your address)
                                        (date)

(name and address of agency public information officer)

Dear (name of officer):

        Pursuant to the Freedom of Information Act, 5 U.S.C.
552, and to the regulations of the _____
(name of agency or department)   , _____C.F.R.
_____(citation to departmental regulations,
which can be obtained from committee print index), I
hereby request access to (identify records requested in
as much detail as possible).

        If there is any charge for locating and copying this
material, please advise me of the estimated cost in
advance. I would appreciate a reply to this request by
_____ (date giving agency reasonable time to
process request--seven to ten days) If the request is
denied, please indicate which section of the Freedom of
Information Act is being relied on as legal basis for the
denial.

        Thank you for your prompt attention.

                                        Sincerely,

CHAPTER 4

ADMINISTRATIVE

PROCEDURE

Rules of the Game

The legal rules for the games which federal agencies play are contained in the Administrative Procedure Act (APA) [5 U.S.C. 551-59, 701-706, 1305, 3105, 3344, 4301, 5335, 5362, 7521]. The Act grew out of the proliferation of administrative agencies during the New Deal. It was passed in 1946, partly in response to criticism of the administrative process expressed by groups such as the American Bar Association and the 1937 President's Committee on Administrative Management, which said:

> Pressures and influences properly enough directed toward officers responsible for formulating and administering policy constitute an unwholesome atmosphere in which to adjudicate private rights. But the mixed duties of the commissions render escape from these subversive influences impossible. [President's Committee on Administrative Management, Report with Special Studies 39-40 (1937)]

Basically, the Act:
1. Sets out the essential requirements for administrative proceedings, such as rule making and adjudication [5 U.S.C. 553-55].
2. Requires agencies to furnish the public with information unless exempted under the Act or by another statute [5 U.S.C. 552].
3. Spells out the duties of administrative hearing examiners [5 U.S.C. 554, 556-57, 1305, 3105, 3344, 5362, 7521].
4. Describes requirements for administrative hearings when they are required by law, and sets limits on administrative powers [5 U.S.C. 556-58].
5. Establishes legal standards for judicial review of administrative action [5 U.S.C. 701-706].

The Freedom of Information Act (FOIA), described in the last chapter, is actually an amendment to the APA.

The APA won't tell you exactly how to deal with a particular agency. For that you will need to study the statutes involved, as well as the regulations of the agency. But the Act does set forth some of the basic requirements which all agencies are supposed to meet in making rules and deciding cases. Although the Act applies to all "agencies" of the government, exceptions are made for Congress, the courts, territorial governments, and the District of Columbia government.

Administrative agencies do a lot of things, but most of their formal functions can be described as either making rules or deciding cases. These are described in the APA as "rule making" and "adjudication." The difference is important, because if an agency is engaged in rule making, it usually must give at least some kind of advance notice to the public in general, and provide them with an opportunity to submit comments before the rule is issued. For adjudication, the agency must give notice to the individual involved and give him a hearing before deciding his case.

Rule Making

A "rule" is defined by Section 2(c) as "the whole or a part of an agency statement of general or particular applicability and future effect designed to implement, interpret, or prescribe law or policy to describe the organization, procedure, or practice requirements of an agency . . ." [5 U.S.C. 551(4)]. For example, a motor vehicle safety standard of the National Highway Transportation Safety Administration (NHTSA) is a "rule," since it applies generally to all cars sold in the United States. According to Section 2(d), "adjudication" is the process of formulating an order, which is defined as a "final disposition . . . of an agency in any matter other than rule making but including licensing" [5 U.S.C. 551(6)(7)]. Most of the adjudicatory proceedings with broad public impact involve license proceedings. In other words, adjudication is just about everything that isn't rule making.

The fundamental requirement for rule making set forth in Section 4(a) of the APA is for general notice of the proposed rule, and opportunity for public participation in rule making. Section 4(b) states:

> [g]eneral notice of proposed rule making shall be published in the *Federal Register*, unless persons subject thereto are named

and either personally served or otherwise have actual notice thereof in accordance with law. The notice shall include (1) a statement of the time, place, and nature of public rule making proceedings; (2) reference to the authority under which the rule is proposed; and (3) either the terms or substance of the proposed rule or description of the subjects and issues involved. [5 U.S.C. 553(b) (1970)]

If notice is not given, the rule is no good [*Hotch* v. *U.S.*, 212 F.2d 280, 284 (9th Cit. 1954)]. This requirement was established to allow people

> to express themselves in some informal manner prior to the issuance of rules and regulations, so that they will have been consulted before being faced with the accomplished fact of a regulation which they may not have anticipated or with reference to which they have not been consulted. This provision will make for good public relations on the part of administrative agencies. Wisely used and faithfully executed, as it must be, it should be of great aid to administrative agencies by affording them a simple statutory means of apprising the public of what they intend to do and affording the interested public a nonburdensome method of presenting its side of the case. [92 Cong. Rec. 5650 (1946)]

Of course, this requirement only gives you the right to comment on a rule before it is filed; it does not require that the agency pay any attention to what you say. Unless an agency's own statute provides for the right to present oral testimony, you don't have that right, because the APA doesn't require hearings for rule making.

But the comments you submit on a proposed rule will not completely disappear into the agency's file cabinets. They, along with other comments submitted, will be summarized, and the summary will be published along with the final rule adopted. This is in accordance with the provisions of Section 4(b) that "the agency shall incorporate in the rules adopted, a concise general statement of their basis and purpose" [5 U.S.C. 553(c) (Supp. V)].

Two general areas of administrative action are not subject to the provisions of Section 4 on rule making requirements. These are (a) military or foreign affairs functions, and (b) functions of agency management, personnel, contracts, loans, grants, benefits, or public property [5 U.S.C. 553(a)]. In addition to these exemptions, Section 4(a) offers another escape hatch for an agency which wishes to avoid giving public notice. That section provides that, unless notice or hearing is required by another statute, it is not required for "interpretative rules, general statements of policy, or rules of agency organization, procedure, or practice," or "when the agency for good cause finds (and incorporates the finding and a brief statement of reasons therefor in the rules issued) that notice and public procedure thereon are impracticable, unnecessary, or contrary to public interest" [5 U.S.C. 553(b) (Supp. V)]. The second part of this exception was relied on by the Atomic Energy Commission (AEC) in making its new procedures for licensing nuclear power plants effective immediately upon publication in the *Federal Register*. The "good cause" was that the U.S. Court of Appeals for the D.C. Circuit had ruled that the old procedures violated the National Environmental Policy Act.

There are two kinds of rule making, formal and informal. If a particular statute requires that a rule be made "on the record," it is referred to as formal rule making. Formal rules must be based on the record compiled in a hearing. One example of this is rule making under the Food, Drug and Cosmetics Act [21 U.S.C. 371].

Although formal rule making must be based on the record of such a hearing, the formal rule making process is not the same as an adjudication hearing. The initial and recommended decision of the hearing examiner, which is required in adjudication, may be omitted in formal rule making under Section 8(b). The requirement of Section 5 that, in adjudication, the person who investigates or prosecutes a case cannot participate in deciding it, does not apply in formal rule making [5 U.S.C. 553 (Supp. V)].

Section 4(c) requires that a "substantive rule" be published at least 30 days before it becomes effective, but the exceptions to this requirement are so broad that it has little effective meaning [5 U.S.C. 553(d) (Supp. V]. For example, advance notice is not required if it would defeat the purpose of the rule, or if immediate action is required to protect property.

The fundamental right to petition an agency to issue or change a rule is set forth in Section 4(d) [5 U.S.C. 553(e) (Supp. V)]. But the right is an empty one, since the agency is not required to do anything with the petition except to tell you if it is turned down. Although the legislative history indicates that the idea was for the agency to examine the petition promptly and thoroughly, there is no such specific requirement in the statute [S. Doc. No. 248, 79th Cong. 2d Sess. 260 (1946)].

Hearings and Hearing Examiners

When a formal hearing is required by the Administrative Procedure Act there are certain requirements for the hearing. These requirements are in Sections 7 and 8 of the APA, which are Sections 556 and 557 of Title 5 in the U.S. Code. First of all, hearing examiners must be qualified. The relative independence of hearing examiners is the closest the agencies come to a system of administrative courts, which is periodically suggested and rejected. According to Section 11 [5 U.S.C. 3105] each agency "shall appoint as many hearing examiners as are necessary for proceedings required to be conducted" under Sections 7 and 8 of the APA. They are to be assigned to cases in rotation and, most important, they may not perform duties inconsistent with their roles as hearing examiners. The Civil Service Commission determines their compensation, and only the Commission can remove them.

Hearing examiners are given many of the powers of judges by Section 7(b) [5 U.S.C. 556(c)]. They are authorized to:

1. Administer oaths and affirmations.
2. Issue subpoenas authorized by law.
3. Rule on offers of proof and receive relevant evidence.
4. Take depositions or have depositions taken.
5. Regulate the hearings.
6. Hold conferences to settle or simplify issues, if the parties consent.
7. Handle procedural requests.
8. Make or recommend decisions.
9. Take other action authorized by agency rules.

But hearing examiners are still a long way from being "administrative judges." It is the agency that makes the final decision, and the agency can diminish the examiner's authority considerably by allowing many appeals from the examiner's rulings during the proceeding.

One of the supposed advantages of administrative proceedings over courtroom litigation is that all those sticky rules of evidence can be ignored; Section 7(c) of the APA expresses this as law. "Any oral or documentary evidence may be received, but every agency shall as a matter of policy provide for the exclusion of irrelevant, immaterial, or unduly repetitious evidence . . ." [5 U.S.C. 556(d) (Supp. V)].

Basically, this means that the hearing examiner will listen to just about any kind of evidence, and objecting on the grounds of hearsay, for instance, will be useless. The closest the courts have come to requiring agencies to establish rules of evidence is in a few decisions holding that there must be at least some "substantial" evidence to support a decision, along with all the hearsay [*Gilmore* v. *U.S.*, 131 F. Supp. 581, 583 (N.D. Cal. 1955)].

You can still take your Constitutional rights of due process with you into the agency hearing room. A party to a hearing has the right to present evidence and to cross-examine opposing witnesses. But you do not have the right to bring your own stenographer into the proceedings. [*In re Neil,* 209 F. Supp. 76, 77 (S.D.W. Va.)]

After the hearing examiner has heard all the evidence, he makes either an initial or a recommended decision. But it's still pretty much up to the agency to decide the case. For one thing, the agency can take the decision out of the examiner's hands and require the record to be certified to it for decision, either in a particular case or in a whole class of cases. And if the hearing officer decides to make an initial decision rather than merely recommending a decision, the agency is just as free to reject his initial decision as if he had only recommended it.

Adjudication

The closest administrative proceedings come to being "judicial" is in adjudicative hearings, which are subject to Section 5 of the APA [5 U.S.C. 554 (Supp. V)]. This section is only applicable when adjudication is "required by statute to be determined on the record after opportunity for an agency hearing. . . ." First of all, Section 5(a) requires the agency to notify everyone who will be affected by the adjudication of the hearing's time and place, the statute involved, and the factual dispute which will be decided [5 U.S.C. 554(b) (Supp. V)]. Also under Section 5(a), the "convenience and necessity of the parties or their representatives" is to be considered in fixing the time and place of the hearings, and the agency's convenience is not supposed to outweigh that of the private parties [S. Doc. No. 248, 79th Cong. 2d Sess. 203].

Probably the most important limitation which the APA places on hearing examiners in adjudication is the separation-of-functions requirement of Section 5(c) [5 U.S.C. 554(d) (Supp. V.)]. This prohibits the hearing examiner from (a) consulting any person or party on an issue of fact unless everyone has a chance to participate, or (b) being subject to the supervision or direction of an agency employee who is performing investigative or prosecuting functions.

In appearing before an agency, a private party has the same right as the agency to secure a subpoena. Under Section 6(c), all you have to show is the "general relevance and reasonable scope of the evidence sought" [5 U.S.C. 555(d) (Supp. V)].

But the APA provides little hope of forcing agencies to decide things quickly. Although the Act gives courts the power to force an agency to act if there is unreasonable delay, or if action is unlawfully withheld [5 U.S.C. 706 (Supp. V)], the authority has not been exercised much. Section 6(a) was intended to insure that "[n]o agency should permit any person to suffer injurious consequences of unwarranted official delay" [S. Doc. No. 248, 79th Cong. 2d Sess. 264 (1946)] but the judicial interpretation is that you must show that such proceedings normally take less time or prove a dilatory attitude on the part of the agency [*FTC* v. *J. Weingarten, Inc.,* 336 F. 2d 687, 691 (5th Cir. 1964) *cert. denied,* 380 U.S. 908 (1964)].

Investigation and Enforcement

Administrative agencies usually have broad grants of power to conduct investigations, both for the purpose of accumulating data on which to base rules and as a preliminary step in enforcement proceedings. These powers present significant opportunities for agencies to carry out their statutory duties. The information which agencies have accumulated and which they have the power to gather can be extremely useful to the public if the accumulated data can be pried loose from agency files, and if the agencies can be persuaded to use their dormant powers. But all too often the information to be gathered is limited to questions approved by industry trade associations, and the data which have been accumulated are locked in the files. Investigatory files for possible enforcement proceedings also serve as convenient repositories for embarrassing bits of information, since they are exempt from public disclosure under the FOIA.

One massive roadblock to accumulation of information by administrative agencies has been the Business Advisory Council on Federal Reports, which advises the Office of Management and Budget (OMB). The Council originated in the days of rationing and strict wage-price controls during World War II. In response to complaints by small businessmen that they were being flooded with forms and questionnaires which often overlapped and duplicated each other, Congress enacted the Federal Reports Act of 1942, which gave the Bureau of the Budget (now the OMB) the job of coordinating the collection of information. The Bureau of the Budget then turned to industry, which established and financed what was then known as the Advisory Council on Federal Reports. The Council organizes industry advisory committees or panels which in turn advise the OMB. Under the Federal Reports Act, any questions to be sent by a federal agency to more than nine companies must first be cleared by the OMB.

An agency's proposed questionnaire is first sent by the agency to the OMB, which then lists the questionnaire on "birdwatcher sheets" sent to industry and trade association representatives. If the questionnaire contains embarrassing questions, the Council, on behalf of one or more of its industry advisory committees, swings into action and tells OMB that it wants a meeting. OMB usually complies, and the agency which drew up the questionnaire can forget for a long time, if not forever, about asking its troublesome questions.

For example, in 1964 the Public Health Service requested approval of a questionnaire designed to find out the composition, volume, and locations of water-contaminating industrial wastes. The members of an industry advisory committee and other industry spokesmen objected to the questions on the proposed voluntary questionnaire, charging, among other things, that it would be misleading, expensive to answer, and would reveal trade secrets. In 1968 the request was renewed, but the advisory committee objected again, and the survey again was not approved. Finally, after considerable attention from Congress and the press, a pilot survey of a few firms in each state was approved.

The original purpose of the system was to prevent duplication of effort by agencies, and to assist in statistical analysis. In practice the system effectively bars any agency from asking questions which industry does not want asked. Although approval by the Council or the advisory committees it organizes is not provided for by law, OMB effectively delegates its decision making to them. The meetings, which are now sometimes open to nonindustry observers, are fascinating demonstrations of government abdication to industry representatives, and include harangues and filibusters at least as spirited as anything on Capitol Hill. The result is likely to be a stalemate, with trade association representatives offering to meet privately with agency representatives to "iron out" the questionnaire. If industry objections have been satisfied (usually by amending the questionnaire), OMB will follow with approval of the questionnaire for distribution. If the industry is not satisfied, OMB approval is often delayed indefinitely—a diversionary tactic that is often fatal to an information-gathering program [see *Hearings on S. 3067 Before the Subcomm. on Government Operations*, 91st Cong. 2d Sess. (1970)].

The enforcement process carried out by regulatory agencies bears a theoretical resemblance to the system of criminal justice which is administered through courts to deal with crimes committed by individuals against other individuals. But the resemblance ends with the theory. First, regulatory agencies don't arrest companies. The process usually begins with a polite inquiry as to whether the company is doing something against the law, whether it knows that it is against the law, and if it is going to continue. If the company answers, the agency may take the next step of asking the company to stop breaking the law. At this stage, a process of informal negotiation usually begins. In the other criminal justice system this is called "plea-bargaining," but in the world of administrative law it is referred to as voluntary compliance. If this process breaks down, the agency may proceed to the stage of a formal adjudicatory hearing. These hearings are subject to the general adjudicatory requirements of Section 5 of the APA as well as the agency's own procedural rules. To a growing extent, they offer an opportunity for public interest groups to intervene and participate in the process (see description of the intervention of Students Opposing Unfair Practices in the Federal Trade Commission Firestone proceeding, in Chap. 5). But the most common resolution of an enforcement proceeding is the negotiation of a consent order. Under the terms of a consent order, the alleged offender promises never again to do what the agency charged, but denies ever having done it in the first place.

Licenses, Rates, and Mergers

Licensing is an administrative process with far-reaching consequences that is carried out by adjudicative proceedings. Basically, licensing is the method used to insure that public property or a government-granted monopoly will be used in the public interest. One of the best examples of licensing, and one which has obvious public impact, is in licensing renewals of radio and television broadcasting stations. The licensing process is adversarial, but only in the sense of competition between companies vying for a government-sanctioned monopoly. For example, broadcast licenses are subject to renewal proceedings every three years, but, until a few years ago, representatives of the listeners and viewers who were supposedly served by the incumbent licensees were resolutely barred from participating in license renewal proceedings. The only parties who were considered to have a legitimate interest in the proceedings were commercial competitors.

Another kind of administrative proceeding that affects everyone is rate making—the process of determining what prices will be paid in the interstate sale of power, gas, transportation, and other basic services and commodities. Rate making proceedings are now almost exclusively the concern of industries seeking approval of their proposed rates. One case before the Interstate Commerce Commission (ICC), involving the District of Columbia Ad Hoc Committee on Consumer Protection, represents the furthest advance of consumer group participation in rate cases. For the first time representatives of the consumers who ultimately would pay the price increase intervened in a proceeding to approve higher rates for vegetable shipments (see Chap. 6).

Enforcement of the antitrust laws presents another kind of administrative adjudication. Among independent regulatory agencies, the Federal Trade Commission (FTC) is responsible for administrative proceedings to enforce antitrust laws generally, although other agencies are obliged to give consideration to antitrust implications of their decisions. Merger enforcement at the FTC follows the standard procedure of issuing complaints and eventually obtaining consent orders after protracted administrative hearings. (As determined in the S & H Trading Stamp Case—see Chap. 5—antitrust violations under Section 5 of the FTC may also include practices which are not specifically made illegal in other antitrust statutes. The Antitrust Division of the Department of Justice is the other agency primarily responsible for direct enforcement of antimerger and other antitrust laws.)

Judicial Doctrines

Federal judges have been reluctant to exercise a broad-ranging and thorough review of administrative proceedings, if only from self-interest (to avoid being drawn into the morass of technical and seemingly interminable agency proceedings). As one law review note put it:

> The law of judicial review of administrative action has an inordinate number of hangups, which are respectfully labeled "doctrines" by the courts and commentators. Among these are the doctrines of primary jurisdiction, ripeness for review, exhaustion of remedies, standing to sue, and unreviewability. [41 *Colorado Law Review* at 96-97 (1969)]

This book is primarily concerned with the right of citizens to participate in the proceedings of federal regulatory agencies. However, the right to participate effectively, or sometimes to participate at all, has often required recourse to the federal courts. Nonlawyers must at least be aware of some of these traditional hangups, because the administrative agencies are aware of them and will make use of them in dealing with citizens, and because participation in administrative proceedings is more effective if the citizen-participant keeps in mind that he may ultimately have to tell his story to a federal judge in order to reach his goal.

Most of the pronouncements concerning the right of citizens to participate in administrative proceedings have been made by federal courts in considering cases involving citizens and administrative agencies, rather than by the enactment of statutes. The general principles of law which have been applied in developing these doctrines are set forth in the Constitution and in statutes governing the agencies.

The basic statutory provision regarding a citizen's "standing" to have courts review agency decisions is in the APA: "A person suffering legal wrong because of agency action, or adversely affected or aggrieved by agency action within the meaning of a relevant statute is entitled to judicial review thereof" [5 U.S.C. 702 (Supp. V)]. The general nature of these basic principles makes it necessary to turn to decisions in particular cases in order to get a more specific idea of the extent to which citizens have the right to raise questions about the conduct of administrative proceedings. Statutes governing individual agencies are no more specific than the APA. The language they use to describe those citizens who will have some right to participate involves such terms as "adversely affected" (FDA), "aggrieved" (SEC), "party in interest" (ICC), or one who has a "substantial interest" (CAB).

Before turning to some particular doctrines which have been developed by courts, a few words on the sources and structure of the applicable principles of law are necessary. First is the Constitution. The most significant single provision of the Constitution, in terms of citizen access, is the due process clause of the Fifth Amendment, which guarantees that no one is to "be deprived of life, liberty, or property without due process of law." All other sources of law ultimately must meet the standard of Constitutionality, which is determined by court interpretations. Congress creates and shapes administrative agencies by enacting statutes which define structure, duties, and procedures. For example, the Federal Communications Act created the Federal Communications Commission (FCC), and gave the FCC the power to grant or withhold radio and television licenses according to the "public interest, convenience and necessity." The Act also prescribed procedures to be followed and specified the right of "aggrieved persons" to appeal final agency decisions to the courts.

During the New Deal, some thought that Congress had abdicated its authority by creating administrative agencies and giving them broad powers to make rules which had the force of law. The Supreme Court once held that Congress had gone too far in delegating its authority, and declared the National Industrial Recovery Act to be unconstitutional [*Schechter Poultry Corp.* v. *U.S.*, 295 U.S. 495, 541-42 (1935)]. But that decision exists now mostly as a matter of history, and as the example of the outer limits imposed by the Constitution on the extent to which Congress can delegate its power to make law.

In addition to laws governing particular agencies, in 1946 Congress enacted the APA, which has already been described, to govern the procedures used by administrative agencies. The APA provides that administrative action taken under subsequent legislation must follow APA procedures unless APA specifies otherwise. An amendment to the APA, FOIA (see Chap. 3), establishes the right of citizens to find out what their government is doing, often the first step to participation in government decision making.

Agencies are given broad powers to make rules in order to carry out the purposes of the statute, and these rules are the next level of authority in the sources of law governing agency action. In descending order, the levels of authority for agencies are the Constitution, general statutes such as the APA, the statute under which the particular agency operates, and rules which have been made by the agency.

The particular statutes and rules for each agency have been set forth in the separate chapters on those agencies. But they still only tell you the principles which apply to efforts to gain access to administrative proceedings. The natural and appropriate step for you to take in figuring out just how far you are likely to get with your efforts is to discover how successful other citizens have been in similar cases. In most cases these stories have been written in the reports of federal courts, in decisions on cases of citizens who have gone first to agencies, with less than complete success, and then gone on to the courts. For purposes of this chapter it is not necessary to go into the jurisdictional details of when to go to which court. It is enough to note that some agency statutes provide specifically for appeal from a final decision by an administrative agency to a United States court of appeals (the federal courts just below the U.S. Supreme Court). In other circumstances citizens will frequently take their case to United States district courts (the trial courts of the federal system). If there is a challenge on the basis of Constitutionality, the case may go to a special three-judge panel, and appeals from such a panel would go directly to the U.S. Supreme Court.

In a 1950 case Justice Frankfurter expressed the traditional reluctance of federal courts to hear cases which deviated from the common law tradition of suits between individuals:

> Limitation on the "judicial Power of the United States" is expressed by the requirement that a litigant must have "standing to sue" or, more comprehensively, that a federal court may entertain a controversy only if it is "justiciable." Both characterizations mean that a court will not decide a question unless the nature of the action challenged, the kind of injury inflicted, and the relationship between the parties are such that a judicial determination is consonant with what was, generally speaking, the business of the Colonial courts and the courts of Westminster when the Constitution was framed. [*Joint Anit-Fascist Refugee Comm.* v. *McGrath*, 341 U.S. 123, 150 (1950) Frankfurter, J., concurring]

This limitation on judicial review is the first source of the body of law applicable to citizen participation—Article III of the Constitution.

It also represents a legal and judicial point of view which may be difficult for laymen to understand. It is, fundamentally, the emphasis on
continuity which finds its expression in solving new problems, whenever possible, the way old problems were solved. The most common
manifestation is the often exhaustive search for some past resolution
of a dispute which is similar in some way to the problem in question.
The very existence of administrative agencies came about through the
realization that neither the traditional judicial processes nor the legislative process could cope with problems of broad economic and social
policies and their application to particular cases. But the need for
continuity through precedent applies to administrative as well as
judicial proceedings, and citizens who wish to participate in agency
proceedings are well advised to be familiar with the efforts of other
citizens in similar cases before them, particularly if other citizens have
had recourse to the courts in ordering administrative agencies to grant
them access.

Much of the historical development of common law came about
through disputes over property, and from the use of state power in
protecting the interests of private parties. It is not surprising that the
"standing" of citizens before administrative agencies which was first
judicially recognized was based on property interests, such as the right
of a radio station owner to be protected against ruinous competition
[*Sanders Bros. Radio Station* v. *FCC*, 309 U.S. 470, 476-77 (1939)].
It was some time before courts began to accept the idea that anyone
asserting an injury other than economic from an administrative decision had a right to be heard. An "aggrieved" person with a "legal
interest" was usually defined as a person (either a natural person or a
corporation) who stood to lose money in some way. Only in recent
years have courts begun to recognize the right of those who represent
the general public, or significant segments of the public, to be heard
against injuries to interests other than economic. There are many
reasons for this. The growth and concentration of population have
brought us to consider as valuable many common needs which were
once so readily satisfied as to be unnoticed. Technology has enlarged
the impact of private actions, and we have become more aware of such
impact. It may be that our sensibilities have changed, and inequities
once tolerable are no longer so. The social costs of allowing and
encouraging unlimited efforts for economic growth have arguably
become so great that at least a hearing must be given to representatives
of other interests. Whatever the reason, it is now generally recognized
that groups of citizens with interests other than financial well-being

have a right to participate in the decision making of administrative
agencies. It is no longer sufficient, if it ever was, to assume that the
existence of an administrative agency will, in itself, insure protection
of the public interest.

There are two distinct but related matters in considering the role
of courts in citizen access to administrative proceedings: (1) standing
to secure judicial review of agency proceedings, and (2) standing to
participate in agency proceedings. This section focuses on the second
issue. A court may uphold the right of citizens to participate in an
administrative proceeding, and still refuse to rule on what the agency
actually did in the proceeding [*Public Serv. Comm'n.* v. *FPC*, 284
F.2d 200, 206-207 (D.C. Cir. 1960)]. However, standing to participate
in agency proceedings and standing to secure judicial review of agency
decisions are fundamentally similar, in that both involve a determination
of what interests are deserving of legal protection. In many cases which
uphold standing to participate in agency proceedings, a principal justification has been that access to the agency proceeding is necessary to preserve the party's right of appeal to the courts. For instance, in *National
Coal. Ass'n.* v. *FPC*, the court said "[w]e think it clear that any person
who would be 'aggrieved' by the Commission's order, such as a competitor, is also a person who has a right to intervene" [191 F.2d 462, 467
(D.C. Cir. 1951)]. And in *American Communications Ass'n* v. *United
States*, another court said, "[i]n National Coal, intervention was necessary to secure the right to review; here intervention is necessary in order
to make the right to review effective" [298 F.2d 648, 650 2d Cir. (1962)].

One of the best examples of judicial recognition of the right of
public representatives to participate in administrative agency proceedings is *Office of Communication of the United Church of Christ* v.
FCC [359 F. 2d 994 (D.C. Cir. 1966)]. The opinion is important
because it explicitly recognizes both the necessity for and the right of
representatives of a substantial segment of the population to participate
in an administrative proceeding which would not affect them financially. It explicitly rejects the notion that a government agency necessarily represents the public interest:

> The theory that the Commission can always effectively represent
> the listener interests in a renewal proceeding without the aid and
> participation of legitimate listener representatives fulfilling the
> role of private attorneys general . . . is no longer a valid assump-
> tion which stands up under the realities of actual experience. . . .
> [*Ibid.* at 1003-1004]

The significance of the opinion is heightened by the fact that it was written by Chief Justice Warren Burger shortly before he was appointed to the Supreme Court, while he was on the Court of Appeals for the District of Columbia Circuit. The opinion treats standing to secure access to administrative proceedings according to the same standards as standing to secure judicial review of administrative decisions [*Ibid.* at 1000, n. 8]. The citizens in that case were members of the black community, which constituted a sizable part of the audience of station WLBT, a television station which was blatantly discriminatory in its programing. The court recognized that the Federal Communications Act meant to include listeners as "parties in interest" under Section 309(d), indicating that citizens could intervene even though they might lack a direct economic commercial interest in the outcome.

Citizen groups which represent a significant public interest will have a good chance of persuading a federal court to order an administrative agency to allow them to participate in its proceedings. But participation which does not achieve its aim is not very impressive. The next thing for citizen groups to consider is the reception federal courts will give to their appeals after they have been allowed to participate in agency proceedings, but were not able to prevail. As already mentioned, sometimes courts will uphold the right of parties to participate in administrative proceedings, but will not review the substance of the administrative decision resulting from the proceeding. One traditional formulation of such judicial reluctance is that courts will not substitute their judgment for that of the administrative agency. This point of view is usually formulated in terms of separation of powers, under the theory that each branch of government has its own tasks and its own expertise, and no arm should encroach on the work of another.

So even when courts review agency decisions, they exercise considerable restraint on the extent of their review. They will review for jurisdiction, to make sure that the agency had a right to decide the question in the first place; for errors of law, to determine if the agency acted in conformity with its statutory authority; for procedural fairness, to ensure that the agency followed the procedures required by the Constitution, the APA, and its own statute and rules; and to determine whether the decision was "unreasonable or arbitrary." A finding that the agency's action was "unreasonable or arbitrary" is usually made only if there is no basis in the administrative record for such a decision. However, these formulations and limitations do not completely close the door to effective review of administrative proceedings. In *Office of Communication of the United Church of Christ v. FCC,* the subsequent review of the proceeding did not purport to decide the merits of the case, but held that the record was so bad that it could not support a reasoned decision. In short, the agency was held to the standard that its decision must have some support in the record. A common articulation of this standard is that an administrative agency's decision must be supported by "substantial evidence on the record as a whole."

Another doctrine of judicial reluctance to become involved in administrative proceedings is the requirement that there must be "exhaustion of remedies" before the courts will review decisions of administrative agencies. This doctrine is one of which citizen groups should be aware, since it provides a basic guideline for their participation in administrative proceedings. Briefly stated, the doctrine is that all of the possible remedies available within the administrative agency must be pursued and exhausted before the courts will even listen to complaints about the agency's decision. There are some exceptions to this doctrine. For example, you need not try every agency procedure first if the agency is clearly acting unconstitutionally or if the delay would cause irreparable harm. But generally, if there are avenues available within the agency, you should pursue them to the end before going into federal court. Premature trips to federal courts will be rebuffed on the ground that administrative remedies have not been exhausted.

A somewhat similar judicial doctrine is that an administrative agency's decision must be "ripe" before it can be reviewed by a court. This is similar to the common statement that only a "final order" of an administrative agency can be appealed to the courts. All of these doctrines are available to federal courts for limiting the scope of their review over decisions by administrative agencies, or for avoiding such review completely. Drafting an appeal to the courts which is likely to prevail in the face of these doctrines requires considerable legal expertise. Nonlawyers should know that these doctrines exist, and do their best to use every administrative remedy available to them in order to make the best possible administrative record to serve as a basis for an appeal.

Judicial Remedies

One of the most common situations in dealing with federal regulatory agencies is to find that government officials are simply not doing what the law requires them to do. Sometimes it is possible to obtain a court order forcing government employees to do their jobs. This requires going to a federal district court with an application for a writ of mandamus. "Mandamus" is an ancient common law writ which consists of an order to a government official to perform his duty. Prior to 1962, the only district court in the United States where federal government officials and agencies could be sued in this form of action was in the District of Columbia. But that year Congress provided that most suits against federal officers could also be brought in the district in which the citizen resided [28 U.S.C. 1391(e)].

The major obstacle in obtaining such an order is that it only applies to "ministerial" government acts. Basically, a "ministerial" act is one in which the government official has no discretion. This has been defined as "a positive command and so plainly prescribed as to be free from doubt" [*United States* v. *Walker*, 409 F.2d 477, 481 (9th Cir. 1969)]. But at the very least such an order could be used to force an administrative agency to abide by its own procedural rules in making determinations. One case supporting such use of mandamus is *Knoll Associates, Inc.* v. *Dixon* [232 F. Supp. 283 (S.D. N.Y. 1964)]. The ruling in that case indicated that a federal court was warranted in ordering corrective measures if an administrative agency's hearing examiner disregarded the Constitutional rights of a party or denied a fair and impartial hearing to the party [*Ibid.* at 285]. Thus, when the rules of an agency permit citizens to file petitions asking the agency to amend its rules, the rules will often explicitly state that the agency must act on the request within a specific or a "reasonable" time. A person whose petition was left to lie fallow for many months could then bring a mandamus action to compel the agency (actually the person obligated to act on the particular request) to either grant or deny the petition.* While the official has considerable discretion when acting on the request, he has none as to *whether* to act.

Mandamus is severely restricted as a remedy for citizens to use by its limitation to ministerial acts of government officials. A broader judicial remedy is an injunction, which can be an order by the court to an official either to perform an act or to refrain from performing illegal acts. This lends itself more readily to stopping officials from continuing courses of conduct which are not authorized by law. An injunction is a general form of relief which can be used in place of or in addition to damages. The real defendant in a suit brought by a citizen for an injunction against a government official is the govern-

---

*Even when the rules do not specify a time for a decision, a "reasonable time" will be implied, with the length of time depending on the circumstances.

ment itself. But the doctrine of sovereign immunity—that "the king can do no wrong"—persists, and such actions are theoretically brought against the person who holds the government office instead of the government itself.

Another theory has been formulated to compel government employees to perform their statutory duties. It is based on a literal interpretation of the frequently voiced sentiment that "a public office is a public trust." A "trust" between individuals is a specific kind of legal relationship, with clear and high standards of care owed by the trustee to the beneficiary. The fiduciary obligations which govern this relationship are applicable in a number of different situations. One application involves behavior by government officers indicating a conflict of interest [see "The Federal Conflict of Interest Statutes and the Fiduciary Principle," 14 *Vand. L. Rev.* 1485, 1486 (1961)].

The basic theory of this remedy is that when a public official assumes office, he enters into a fiduciary relationship with the public to carry out his legal duties, and becomes liable for a breach of trust in failing to carry out those duties. Application of the theory would entitle a member of the public, as a beneficiary, to sue the official for damages suffered by reason of his failure to honor his fiduciary obligations, or to obtain a court order commanding the official to perform his duties. There have been some applications of this theory to remedy corruption in public office as a method of "recapturing" the proceeds of such corruption [see Lenhoff, "Constructive Trust as a Remedy to Corruption in Public Office," 54 *Col. L. Rev.* 214 (1954)].

When a public official breaches his trust by failure to carry out his statutory duties, an appropriate remedy would be for him to remit a portion of his salary for the period during which the breach occurred.

One method of determining the scope of a federal official's duties is by reference to the official standards of conduct for government employees. These are promulgated by the agencies and are based on minimum requirements established by the Civil Service Commission. They are contained in Title 5, Part 735 of the C.F.R. Many of these criteria deal with actual or apparent conflicts of interest, but they also include general standards of behavior which would adversely affect public confidence in the government [5 C.F.R. 735.201(f)]. While the regulations adopted by the agencies and the standards promulgated by the Civil Service Commission do not provide for any system of enforcement through citizen complaints, they do serve as statements of the duties which all federal employees owe to the public. One effective method of encouraging the development of administrative procedures to enforce these duties might be through recourse to the courts. Another might be through legislative proposals to establish some system for hearing complaints brought by citizens against government officials for failure to live up to their obligations. As in many other instances, the most effective spur to agency action is often the prospect of proceedings by the courts or the legislature.

CHAPTER 5

THE FEDERAL TRADE COMMISSION

> Sidney: *(to his wife, who is elaborately coifed for a television commercial)... you're not going to tell them that you got your—(reading the label of a large golden elegantly lettered box) Golden Girl Curl by sitting in Mr. Lionel's for several hours, are you?*
>
> Iris: *No, Sid. ... I am going to tell all the little housewifies that I just rolled it up on Golden Girl Curl and rollers. ... They do not pay you one hundred dollars an hour for hauling hamburgers. ... They do pay it for pretending that there is some difference between Golden Girl Curl and Wonder Curl. ... They just send you to the hairdressers to play safe. They have to have everything just so when they tape things for television, Sidney ... they can't have your hair falling down from some ... crappy old home permanent just when they're ready to shoot. ... But it works some, Sid. ... Do you think the FTC would let them just put anything on the air like that?*
>
> —Lorraine Hansberry,
> *The Sign in Sidney Brustein's Window,*
> Act II, Scene 3

Advertising: Then and Now

The Federal Trade Commission (FTC) would, and did, and to some extent still does, let advertisers put all sorts of deceptive sales pitches on the air and in print. The main difference between today and 1964, when

Lorraine Hansberry wrote *The Sign in Sidney Brustein's Window*, is
that the new, improved FTC frequently takes action of some sort to
stop such advertising. In 1964, the agency was pathetic because everyone
assumed that the reference to the FTC did nothing.

If concerned citizens had not taken a close look at the FTC and told
the world just how large the gap was between the Commission's responsibilities and its performance, it might still be doing nothing. After public speculation as to whether the FTC should even continue to exist,
and following significant reorganization and reorientation, the FTC is,
at this moment, probably the most responsive of all the independent
regulatory agencies. Even so, it took a push from consumers for the Commission to examine the television huckstering that Iris thought the FTC
was watching all along.In the fall of 1971 the Commission held hearings
to consider, among other questions, ". . . whether technical aspects of the
preparation and production of television commercials may facilitate
deception." Following a rule making petition from consumer advocates
(see Appendix 5-B, p. 134), the FTC has required advertisers to
furnish documentation for their product claims. As a starter, automobile
manufacturers were asked to back up such boasts as "stops three times as
fast" with test data, and other manufacturing industries, such as toothpaste, television sets, detergents, tires, air conditioners, electric shavers,
and cold remedies, are being selected for periodic questioning. Many of
the documents which these advertisers have submitted to the FTC do not
substantiate their advertised claims. "Golden Girl Curl" still lives!

Where the FTC
and Its Powers Come From

The FTC began as an antitrust agency in 1914, with a mandate under
the Federal Trade Commission Act to define "unfair methods of competition." Its origins can be traced to the Industrial Commission created
by Congress in 1898, which, after four years of study, recommended a
federal bureau to collect information on corporations. In 1903 Congress
acted on the recommendation and created the Bureau of Corporations
as a part of what was then the Department of Commerce and Labor,
but the Bureau had no enforcement powers. The FTC was created in
1914, modeled on the Interstate Commerce Commission (ICC). Since
that time the FTC has accumulated a variety of statutory responsibilities and powers under more than a dozen acts of Congress.

The Federal Trade Commission Act of 1914 [15 U.S.C. 41 *et seq.*]

gives the Commission powers in two broad areas. First, Section 5 of the original Act gives the FTC the power to act against "unfair methods of competition in interstate commerce." Also, since 1938, the Wheeler-Lea Act has granted the Commission additional power to act against "unfair or deceptive practices in interstate commerce" which deceive consumers, even if they do not affect competition. Although this is necessarily more than a little vague, courts have generally acquiesced in the FTC's definition of what is "unfair or deceptive." The greatest limitation on the FTC, as far as the individual consumer is concerned, is that in most cases the Commission can't get his money back. The FTC can only take steps against the offending company to see that other consumers aren't cheated in the same way. The potential range of "deceptive practices" against which the FTC can act is as varied as the ingenuity of those businessmen who view consumers as spenders to be separated from their money for as little consideration as possible.

The FTC's stepped-up actions against claims for nationally advertised products have drawn heavy fire from both advertisers and broadcasters. This was heightened when, in 1972, the FTC recommended to the Federal Communications Commission (FCC) that broadcast media be required to offer some amount of free time each week to noncommercial parties for the purpose of airing "counteradvertisements." These would present views (opposed to those of the advertisers) on controversial public issues raised directly or indirectly in commercial advertisements —such as environmental issues raised by advertising for automobiles or detergents.

The agency is also being pulled in numerous directions by a variety of academic and consumer groups. Some want greater FTC help in correcting basically local credit, repair service, and sales frauds. Others want the FTC to continue the present focus on advertising content. Still others have stated that FTC should shift its attention primarily to industrial economic concentration, contending that actions which restored price competition in a variety of industries would produce greater economic benefit to consumers than current antifraud and advertising programs.

The Commission's primary instrument for carrying out its responsibility to stop such practices is its authority to order an offender to "cease and desist." If a company refuses to comply with such an order, the Justice Department is authorized by the statute to sue in federal court for penalties of $5,000 for each offense. A decision by the Commission that a cease and desist order is justified can be appealed to a U.S. Court of Appeals by parties against whom the order is issued. But it still is not clear whether a citizen who intervenes in such a proceeding can appeal a Commission decision not to issue a cease and desist order. A motion in December 1972 by three consumer organizations to intervene in the "Wonder Bread" case on appeal before the FTC Commissioners sought the opportunity to establish that right.

The Commission has power, under Section 12 of the FTC Act, to act against false or misleading advertising of food, drugs, curative devices, or cosmetics. In such cases the FTC can ask the courts to issue a preliminary injunction to stop the advertisement while it conducts an investigation. In February 1971 the FTC began to flex this virtually unused muscle, and asked a federal court to order Medi-hair International of Sacramento, California, to stop certain ads and sales practices during litigative proceedings. Less than a month later, the Commission again asked a federal court to enjoin Philip Morris' American Safety Razor Division from inserting Personna Razor Blades in Sunday newspaper advertising supplements, after reports that the blades were injuring young children and pets.

Section 12 also authorizes the Commission to ask the Justice Department to seek criminal penalties if violators are deliberately attempting to defraud the public or to market hazardous food, drug, or cosmetic products. Section 6 of the Act gives the Commission power to conduct investigations which may be used as preliminary steps to cease and desist orders under Sections 5 and 12; they may also serve as effective tools to inform consumers and warn manufacturers, as in the current investigation of advertising product claims.

The FTC was originally created to enforce the prohibitions of the Clayton Act [15 U.S.C. 12 *et seq.*] against a variety of anticompetitive and predatory trade practices. The Clayton Act was amended in 1936 by the Robinson-Patman Act [15 U.S.C. 13], which gives the Commission the power to protect small businesses by prohibiting discriminatory pricing, and to set quantity limits on certain commodities in areas where monopolistic tendencies appear. Numerous legal commentators believe that these statutes give the Commission conflicting jobs. They maintain that the FTC cannot enforce Robinson-Patman, which can effectively stabilize prices, and still pursue a policy of promoting maximum competition. Section 3 of the Clayton Act prohibits "tying contracts" and exclusive dealing contracts when they substantially lessen competition. Section 7 prohibits anticompetitive holding company arrangements, mergers, and consolidations, and Section 8 is directed against anticompetitive interlocking directorates.

The FTC has general responsibility for enforcement of the Clayton and Robinson-Patman Acts, except for regulated industries which are subject to antitrust scrutiny from other agencies by statute. For example, airlines are supposed to be watched by the Civil Aeronautics Board (CAB), banks by the Federal Reserve Board, and common carriers by the ICC. The primary enforcement tools used by the FTC are the cease and desist order and divestiture orders to companies to give up their subsidiaries.

The Consumer Credit Protection Act (Truth-in-Lending) and the Fair Credit Reporting Act [15 U.S.C. 1601 *et seq.*] are recent additions to the Commission's enforcement responsibilities. The Truth-in-Lending Act requires all merchants and financial institutions extending credit to a consumer to give the borrower information about the cost and repayment of credit. Also, if the borrower puts up his principal residence as collateral for credit, he can, during a three-day "cooling off" period, rescind the contract. The Fair Credit Reporting Act gives a consumer the right to know what information credit agencies report about him to creditors, employers, and insurers, to inspect his own credit file, and to correct inaccurate or incomplete information. It also provides some protection against reliance by credit agencies on stale information by requiring them to check all references more than three months old and not report information after seven years, except in special circumstances. Both acts are enforced by the FTC through cease and desist orders.

Willful violations of the Truth-in-Lending Act may be prosecuted by the Justice Department at the request of the FTC, and are subject to fines of up to $5,000, one year's imprisonment, or both. The Act also provides for civil suits by consumers who are injured by violations of the Act, regardless of intent. Consumers who win can also collect reasonable attorney fees as set by the court.

A detailed guide for legal action under provisions of the Truth-in-Lending Act is available from the National Consumer Law Center (Boston College Law School, Brighton, Massachusetts, 02135). The Fair Credit Reporting Act also permits consumers to sue, but only for damages and only under certain conditions.

The FTC is also charged with enforcing several statutes which require disclosures of specific information in labels and advertising (the Wool Products Labeling Act of 1939 [15 U.S.C. 68], the Fur Products Labeling Act [15 U.S.C. 69], the Textile Fiber Products Identification Act [15 U.S.C. 70], and the Flammable Fabrics Act [15 U.S.C. 1,191]. Flammable Fabrics Act enforcement has become the responsibility of the new Consumer Product Safety Commission [CPSC]. Under these Acts the FTC has the power to require registration of products involved, and can issue appropriate rules and regulations. It can also test and inspect the products and institute seizure and condemnation proceedings against those which fail. It has the power to promulgate cease and desist orders (with criminal penalties for willful offenders), and can ask federal courts for temporary injunctions pending issuance of cease and desist orders.

The FTC shares its enforcement responsibility for the Fair Packaging and Labeling Act [15 U.S.C. 1451] with the Food and Drug Administration (FDA). This includes monitoring of the packaging and labeling of all commodities other than foods, drugs, curative devices, and cosmetics. The FTC has the power to make rules and issue cease and desist orders.

The Public Health and Cigarette Smoking Act of 1969 [15 U.S.C. 1331] also gave the FTC responsibility for enforcing its provisions. However, Congress has acted twice to prohibit the Commission from issuing trade regulation rules which would require warnings in cigarette advertising. The first restriction was in 1964, when Congress banned any such action for four years, and the second was in 1969, when Congress extended the prohibition until 1 July 1971. The second prohibition also required the Commission to give Congress notice at least six months in advance of any proposed rule on cigarette advertising. At this time the FTC has submitted legislation asking Congress to extend cigarette legislation coverage to little cigars, while declining (at least temporarily) to act against little cigar television advertising.

Other miscellaneous statutes enforced by the FTC include parts of the Lanham Trademark Act of 1946 [15 U.S.C. 1051], the Packers and Stockyards Act of 1921 [7 U.S.C. 181], the Export Trade Act [15 U.S.C. 61], and the Insurance Regulation Act [15 U.S.C. 1011 *et seq.*].

Criticism and Reform

During its first fifty years, the FTC was studied thoroughly at least seven times, and all reports were unfavorable, criticizing the Commission's lack of priorities and planning, sluggish enforcement, and preoccupation with trivial cases. In the summer of 1968, a team of students under the direction of Ralph Nader also investigated the FTC. Their analysis, published in 1969, described the same failings as previous studies, and also criticized deficiencies in personnel, such as poor recruiting and blatantly political hiring, and compulsive secrecy with public information. In the wake of this report, President Nixon turned to the American Bar Association (ABA) for yet another study. After five months of study, an ABA panel report echoed the conclusions of the Nader report and called for a halt to analysis and a beginning of reform:

> ... this [ABA] Commission believes that it should be the last of the long series of committees and groups which have earnestly insisted that drastic changes were essential to recreate the FTC in its intended image. ... Further temporizing is indefensible. Notwithstanding the great potential of the FTC in the field of antitrust and consumer protection, if change does not occur, there will be no substantial purpose to be served by its continued existence. ... [Report of the American Bar Association Commission to Study the Federal Trade Commission (Chicago: American Bar Association, 1969), p. 3]

Under criticism from both Ralph Nader and the ABA, the FTC was on the ropes. Before the reports came out, the staff was divided into factions, and some Commissioners were not speaking to others. Something had to be done about this continuing source of embarrassment to the federal government. In January 1970 President Nixon appointed Caspar Weinberger, a San Francisco attorney with almost no experience in FTC matters, as Chairman of the Commission. Weinberger had some administrative qualifications, based on his experience as California's finance director, but the degree of his commitment to consumer protection was unknown.

Weinberger gave the Commission an organizational shaking up, and some results of that agitation are still visible. Operating bureaus were streamlined, the Office of Policy Planning and Evaluation was created to establish priorities for Commission activities, and field offices were given new emphasis through delegations of power and creation of new programs. An Advisory Council was appointed to review the Commission's Rules of Practice and Procedure and to advise on cutting down delays. Weinberger took the advice of the Nader Report and began to ease the time servers and political cronies from the Commission's staff.

Just when it looked as though the FTC was about to take on new life, Weinberger left in August 1970 for the newly created Office of Management and Budget (OMB). There was considerable apprehension that the Commission would lapse into its old ways: The chances of two dynamic chairmen in a row after fifty-five years of mediocrity were just not that good. His successor was viewed with little enthusiasm by some consumers. Ignoring consumer organizations, Nixon had appointed Miles Kirkpatrick, whose Philadelphia law firm had defended many corporate clients before the Commission. But Kirkpatrick also had chaired the Committee which wrote the ABA report. Two weeks after he was appointed he named Robert Pitofsky, Counsel for the ABA Commission, as Director of the Bureau of Consumer Protection. Pitofsky was the closest thing to a consumer activist the FTC had seen within its staff ranks in years. He was relatively young, a professor of trade regulation and antitrust law at New York University Law School, coauthor of a leading work on antitrust, and chairman of the ABA Antitrust Section's Consumer Protection Committee. During his two and one-half years as Director he pressed for more vigorous enforcement of Section 5, especially against deceptive advertising.

One of the most important additions to the staff was the man appointed by Caspar Weinberger to fix up the impression which the Commission displayed to the public—David Buswell, the new Public Information Director. Under Buswell, FTC press releases have gone from what some Commissioners have called a "dry" and "not terribly entertaining document" to news stories which are usually brisk and informative. During his first year the number of releases increased 25 percent.

In January 1973 Kirkpatrick announced his resignation in order to return to private practice in Philadelphia, and Pitofsky resumed his professorship at New York University Law School. The changes had not been unexpected, in view of reported White House dissatisfaction with the new activism at the FTC. President Nixon was reported in the advertising and broadcasting trade press to have criticized Kirkpatrick by name at a private meeting with broadcasting executives, and consumers as well as FTC staff hired by Kirkpatrick were dubious about the President's intentions for the FTC's future. In January 1973 Mr. Nixon nominated a White House aide, Lewis Engman, to the chairmanship. Engman had served as general counsel to Virginia Knauer's Office of Consumer Affairs, and then as assistant director of the President's Domestic Council under John Ehrlichman. Consumer organizations' suspicions were somewhat increased by appointment of a White House aide. Engman's background in economics and representation of medium-sized business firms during law practice in Grand Rapids, Michigan, however, indicated both the possibility of better use of economic planning at the FTC, and the possibility of a certain wariness about the prerogatives of giant corporations.

The old FTC's emphasis on voluntary compliance, often at the expense of effective law enforcement, has been supplanted by more aggressive regulation. Alleged violators are now almost always required to litigate if they will not sign a consent order which, if violated, can result in court-ordered fines. No such penalties were possible for violations of the "assurances of voluntary compliance" which were used through most of the 1960s.

Hundreds of old, but still pending, investigative files have been closed, and criteria established for time controls on pending and future investigations, to prevent another build-up of stale matters in the active file. Weinberger promised, "The Commission is receptive to novel and imaginative provisions in orders seeking to remedy alleged violations." His economic naiveté, however, upset some of the antitrust staff. Under Kirkpatrick (and Pitofsky), steps were taken to fulfill Weinberger's promise.

One of the most controversial innovations was corrective advertising, which ordered deceptive advertisers to make public confessions for one year in a substantial portion of their subsequent advertising. The bakers of Profile Bread, for instance, were required to inform consumers that their product had fewer calories per slice because it is sliced thinner. Profile sales dropped 20 percent during the year in which these advertisements were aired. At least five other complaints sought similar remedies, and one respondent (Standard Oil of California) ran a two-page advertisement in major newspapers denouncing the FTC action. The advertising and broadcasting industries were not happy about these innovations at the FTC. At the same time, some consumers questioned the economic benefits to be derived from some of the matters in which these innovations were activated. The Standard Oil of California case, for instance, involved a series of alleged misrepresentations, including one in which an impressive-looking county court house is represented as the company's headquarters. Questions arise as to how the cost of gasoline to consumers will be reduced or held down by changing such advertising practices, especially when there is no price competition among the major companies in this industry.

Other novel approaches involving advertising include requiring an explanation to limit the scope of potentially misleading advertising claims, such as for enzyme detergents; prohibiting the use of dangerous ingredients and claims made about them in advertising, such as mercury-impregnated toothbrushes; and shifting the burden of proof for unsubstantiated advertising claims to the manufacturer, such as the order requiring automobile advertisers to submit data to substantiate performance claims. Another proposed complaint would require a product to be removed from the market if consumers could not effectively be informed of its potential for danger.

New approaches do not necessarily spring from creative staff attorneys at the Commission. The idea of requiring advertisers to produce data to substantiate their claims came to the FTC in the form of a petition from consumer advocates in the fall of 1970 (see Appendix 5-B, p. 134); it surfaced in the form of a Commission announcement the next spring. The proposition that it is misleading to claim uniqueness for products which are identical with competing brands was proposed by Students Against Misleading Enterprise (SAME), a group of George Washington University law students, who noted such claims for aspirins and liquid chlorine bleach. The theory was also used in a complaint against ITT-Continental Baking, makers of Wonder Bread [Docket No. 8860].

The Commission has also taken tentative steps to require deceptive advertisers in exceptional cases to repair some of the damage they have done, as well as forcing them to cease and desist. In two cases the Commission has required refunds for customers who fell for deceptive advertising and lost money because of it. Windsor Distributing Company, a supplier of vending machines, was required to make refunds which it had collected on behalf of two purchasers of its vending machine routes, but which it had refused to pay to them [Docket No. 8873]. Universal Electronics Corp., a distributor of radio and television tube-testing machines, was required to make refunds to customers who had purchased franchised dealerships [Docket No. 8815]. Similar complaints proposed against the Coca-Cola Company and *Reader's Digest* for their practices in the conduct of promotional games would require the companies to pay those who would have won if the games had been run as advertised. The limits of FTC power to require refunds have not been established.

The Fairly New,
Somewhat Improved Federal Trade Commission

Weinberger's reorganization reduced FTC's Washington headquarters from six to three Bureaus (Competition, Consumer Protection, and Economics). At the top the Commission itself stays the same, as required by statute. It is composed of the Chairman and four Commissioners, each appointed by the President and approved by the Senate.

They serve staggered seven-year terms. No more than three can be of the same political party. (Lyndon Johnson managed to stay within the law while reducing the number of political opponents to zero—in addition to three Democrats, there were serving at the same time an independent, Philip Elman, and a Republican who had supported LBJ for re-election in 1964, Mary Gardiner Jones.) The Chairman is the chief administrative officer; the duties of this office include presiding over meetings of the Commission, and some voice over the operations of the staff. During the Chairmanship of Paul Rand Dixon, who ran the agency during the period criticized by the Nader and ABA reports, the Chairman summarily appointed top staff officials. Under Weinberger and Kirkpatrick, however, these appointments were subject to approval by vote of all five Commissioners. The present Commissioners are Dixon, Jones, Everette MacIntyre, David Dennison, Jr., and the Chairman, Lewis Engman.

The Bureau of Competition is responsible for the FTC's antitrust enforcement. Headed by Alan Ward, a former private practitioner of antitrust law, it has initiated some interesting cases (investigations of which preceded Ward's arrival). The Bureau was primarily responsible for issuance of a complaint, now being litigated before an Administrative Law Judge, which could be the most important antitrust case in many years. In January 1972 the FTC announced its intention to issue a complaint against the four largest manufacturers of cold breakfast cereal—Kellogg's, General Mills, General Foods, and the Quaker Oats Company. The complaint was widely regarded to allege, in effect, that it is illegal for a few firms to obtain and maintain such substantial shares of a market that the industry is no longer price competitive.

The remedy sought by the FTC against the cereal manufacturers would infuse price competition into the industry by creation of more firms through splitting of some of the respondents into more than one company, and by requiring respondents to license their brand names and formulas to all qualified applicants for a period of years. If the FTC obtained this kind of order, it would be one of the first real trust-busting cases (breaking up existing firms) in many years to result from a situation other than a merger.

Ward and Pitofsky, however, have denied that the complaint is based on a theory that concentration to a degree which stifles price competition is illegal. The staff has not received any indication from the Commissioners as to the theory on which the complaint is based—it cites many specific practices as well as the concentration of sellers in the cereal industry. No further complaints similar to the cereal case have

been announced by the FTC in more than a year since that one was
officially made known. The question of what theory underlies the complaint is important, because it can determine whether an order will be
issued which merely says "deconcentrate," or whether one will be issued
which also specifies "and don't reconcentrate." The extent to which the
trial staff proves or does not attempt to prove the anticompetitive
effect of each course of conduct described in the complaint may indicate whether the complaint really alleges that mere anticompetitive
degrees of concentration are illegal.

The Bureau of Competition is also responsible for a series of cases,
now being tried, against the nation's seven largest manufacturers of soft
drink syrup. In these cases the FTC is seeking to strike down the restrictive agreements between the manufacturers and their franchised bottlers
which prevent competition in the sale of any given brand of soft drink
by dividing the nation into exclusive territories for each brand [Docket
Nos. 8853-8859]. These cases have resulted in a massive lobbying effort
by the manufacturers and bottlers to obtain legislation which would
legitimize the restrictive agreements even before the FTC's litigation is
completed. The legislation was effectively "bottled up" in committee
during the 92d Congress by proconsumer members of Congress, but at
this writing it appears that a similar bill in the 93d Congress will have at
least fifty sponsors when it is introduced into the Senate. Ward has
testified that the territorial restrictions cost consumers at least one-
quarter of a billion dollars every year.

The Bureau of Economics is, in effect, the FTC's intelligence branch.
It conducts economic surveys and performs economic analyses both for
general information purposes and for use in litigation by the trial staff.
Dr. H. Michael Mann is the Bureau Director. One Bureau study caused
a sensation in the spring of 1972 when it was leaked while still in draft
form to Senator George S. McGovern, then seeking the Democratic
Presidential nomination. The study listed 100 manufacturing industries
which the Bureau found to realize higher than competitive returns in
their investment. From the figures contained in the study, it is possible
to compute the dollar amount of oligopoly profits which each listed
industry annually imposes on the economy. McGovern, with a copy of
the study draft in hand, called upon the Price Commission (Phase II was
then in effect) to grant no further price increases to companies in the
industries on the Bureau's list, and instead to take action to roll back
prices in those industries. This highlighted the relationship between the
FTC's role in preserving competition and the effect of oligopoly pricing
power upon price inflation. The FTC refused, however, to release the

study in the face of demands by Senator William Proxmire, stating that the figures could not be used to compute dollar amounts of monopoly overcharges in the manner used by McGovern. However, when Ward testified on the annual cost to the consumer of the soft drink industry's territorial restrictions, his estimate coincided almost exactly with the figure which would be derived from using the study as McGovern had done. And a speech by Mann himself prior to the leaking of the study indicated that the computation of oligopoly overcharges was appropriate. The study is potentially useful to citizens who want to seek FTC investigations related to industry practices regarding the pricing power of leading firms in the industry—because it gives the citizen a way of estimating for the FTC the competitive importance of taking significant actions in that industry. The study, with commentary on use of the Bureau's data, appears in Scanlon," 'The McGovern Papers': The FTC and Phase II," 5 *Antitrust Law & Economics Review* 19 (Spring 1972).

There are two main sources of information at the FTC: the Office of Public Information, and the Division of Legal and Public Records, in the Office of Secretary Charles A. Tobin. The Office of Public Information provides press releases, news briefings, speeches, and various other services. The Office of Charles Tobin, the Secretary, handles formal information such as correspondence, motions, briefs, hearing transcripts, and all the reams of paper which constitute "the public record" on which Commission action is based. The Division of Publications also offers various pamphlets and reports on activities of the Commission.

One of the important changes made in the FTC has been the increased power granted to the regional offices. Previously, these offices were primarily investigative branches for the Washington headquarters, but they now have considerable opportunity for independent activity. Each office is run by a Regional Director, who is now officially encouraged to act on his or her own initiative. If a case involving FTC jurisdiction (with the exception of corporate mergers) is primarily regional, a regional office is now authorized to institute its own investigation, issue its own subpoenas, prepare a proposed complaint, negotiate a consent order, and conduct its own hearings if a complaint is issued. But the important decision as to whether a complaint will be issued is still under the control of the Washington headquarters.

There are eleven regional offices, in Atlanta, Boston, Chicago, Cleveland, Kansas City, Los Angeles, New Orleans, New York, San Francisco, Seattle, and Washington, D.C. There are subsidiary field stations in St. Louis; Dallas; Charlotte, North Carolina; Portland, Oregon; Upper Darby, Pennsylvania; Denver; Miami; Buffalo; Detroit;

Phoenix; San Diego; Washington, D.C.; San Antonio; and Honolulu.

The field offices have taken their cue from the Washington head-quarters and started programs to improve public relations. One step has been to set up Consumer Advisory Boards, composed of legal aid groups, consumer representatives, trade associations, local and federal prosecutors, and postal officials. Advisory Boards have been established in Chicago and New Orleans, and others are planned for the other nine field offices. They hold meetings which are open to the public, and are supposed to help the FTC learn about consumer problems and their remedies in particular areas.

Another program which the FTC has helped to launch is the Consumer Protection Committee, which is designed to act as a multi-governmental, one-stop consumer complaint center. These Committees have been established in six cities (Chicago, Los Angeles, Detroit, San Francisco, Philadelphia, and Boston), and more are planned. They include representatives from all government agencies with consumer protection responsibilities. A typical membership list includes representatives of the FTC, the FDA, the U.S. Postal Inspector's office, the U.S. Attorney's office, the state attorney general, the local district attorney, the office of the mayor, the local weights and measures office, the local police, and the local consumer council. The purpose of the Consumer Protection Committees is to eliminate overlapping efforts, pool information, and coordinate the policies of various government enforcement agencies.

A new breed of FTC employee, the Consumer Protection Specialist, has been created to help the field offices do their job. The Consumer Protection Specialist is a paralegal professional with the job of carrying out investigative and public information work which does not really require an attorney or professional investigator. Although many of them are recent college graduates, others are "lateral entries" whose previous jobs have ranged from teaching to acting to Army Intelligence. The Consumer Protection Specialists are usually assigned to one of three areas: They act as investigators and counselors in carrying out provisions of the Truth-in-Lending Act; they carry out investigations and conduct surveys on compliance with the Flammable Fabrics and the Wool, Fur, and Textile Acts; and they are active in consumer education and public relations programs on the local level. The last function includes making speeches, conducting workshops, arranging spot announcements on local television and radio stations, developing mobile consumer units, and participating in panel discussions. The Washington office distributes monthly work portfolios, called *Here's Help*, which contain suggestions for local projects. Efforts are being made to develop "consumerism" courses in local high schools and colleges (which have been linked to "model cities" programs in Newark and Chicago) and to extend the consumer education program to non-English-speaking people.

The Consumer Advisory Boards and Consumer Protection Committees offer opportunities for citizen access to FTC activities on the local level. Inquiries and suggestions should be directed to the local offices or to the coordinator in Washington: Mr. John M. Lexcen, Federal Trade Commission, Washington, D.C. 20580.

Another important part of the FTC's new organization is the Office of Policy Planning and Evaluation, which has the job of looking a few months or years ahead and advising the Commission on areas which will need attention after current crises have been dealt with. This office, now headed by former Kirkpatrick confidant Caswell Hobles III, has developed a series of economic "bench marks" which, when matched against the data on a given industry and trade practice, are expected to give the FTC the capacity to rate all of the potential cases from which it must select its workload, in order of the money they predictably will save consumers.

Some regional offices have taken the new mandate of widespread community involvement seriously. In Cleveland, the new Regional Director sent staff members into low-income areas to conduct public hearings at churches and community centers and find out about consumer problems. The New York office has established a series of pilot programs in cooperation with local legal aid societies under which FTC staff members spend one or two days a week at neighborhood offices to hear complaints. The program includes two storefronts in Harlem and one in Bedford-Stuyvesant, as well as local offices in Newark, Monmouth County, and Ocean County, New Jersey.

The Seattle office gives one example of imaginative regional office activity. In a community with a high proportion of Indians on welfare, it held public hearings on the increase in prices which occurred regularly on the day the welfare checks were distributed. The hearings were held the day before a scheduled check distribution; the following day's prices did not include the usual price hikes.

The case-by-case approach to enforcement of consumer protection laws makes an example of the worst available offender in hopes that other potential offenders will be deterred. But it does not have the industry-wide effect of protecting the customers of a great number of sellers unless the deterrent is extremely effective—and that is very hard to measure. A useful weapon in the FTC arsenal, therefore, is the rule making proceeding. Instead of attacking a practice as illegal by suing one or a few companies engaged in it, the FTC holds hearings to determine whether the practice should be declared illegal. Once it is so ruled as a result of such a hearing, the FTC need only prove that a company has engaged in the practice in order to move against the company. It need not prove in each subsequent case that the practice was illegal. This lack of opportunity for companies to challenge the allegations of illegality—after they are caught—enhances the probability that the FTC can obtain a consent order instead of carrying on lengthy litigation. And it is believed to enhance voluntary compliance with the rule, both because the rule can be used to prove the illegality of the practice and because spelling out the illegality before litigation is started lets those who do not want to get involved in such a Section 5 violation know ahead of time to avoid the practice.

At the moment the FTC has suspended enforcement of trade regulation rules because of an injunction, issued by the U.S. District Court in D.C., against enforcement of its promulgated rule requiring posting of octane numbers on gasoline pumps. The case awaits a decision from the Court of Appeals, which may have spoken by the time you read this book. The issue is whether the FTC has the authority to define unfair and deceptive practices by trade regulation rule, rather than by litigation with individual companies on a case-by-case basis. Indications are that if the Court of Appeals ruling is favorable, the FTC will resume issuing and enforcing rules, notwithstanding at least another year of expected appeals and hearings on remand to the District Court. Congress is also expected to vote on whether this authority for the FTC to issue rules should be made crystal clear. One important role which consumer groups can play, in addition to submitting complaints which can result in specific enforcement actions, is to petition for trade regulation rules, such as the proposal to make advertisers back up their claims (see Appendix 5-B, p. 134. It is important to remember that the classic stance of the administrator is roughly in the middle of the competing claims made on him. He hears daily from industry and others that almost any step taken toward corporate law enforcement will harm companies, jobs, and possibly even Constitutional rights (e.g., a speech by Herb Klein, White House Director of Communications, Little Rock, Arkansas, 11 June 1971, charging that FTC proposals to make advertisers substantiate performance claims diminish freedom of speech; see *The New York Times*, 12 June 1971). It is up to the consumers who pay for lax law enforcement to encourage the Commission to carry out its statutory duties.

Getting Information from the FTC

In order to have some effect on what the FTC does in the future, you first need to find out what it is doing right now. The primary source for much of this information is the Office of Public Information at the Washington headquarters. Call or write the Office of Public Information or the Division of Legal and Public Records and ask to be sent a list of their publications. Some of these (such as the advertisers' substantiation data) must be purchased through the National Technical Information Service or (especially out-of-date economic reports) from the Government Printing Office (G.P.O.).

Although the orientation of the Office of Public Information (OPI) is toward providing prewritten stories for members of the press, releases are available to anyone. The basic product of the Office is the press release, and in the past two years or so the Office has been producing more and better releases. Stories are now written on just about anything that happens around the Commission. In particular, statements are released on all proposed complaints, all provisional consent orders, all hearings on proposed rule making (with texts of proposed rules attached), and all advisory opinions which the Commission decides to make public (including the letter requesting an advisory opinion, and the opinion itself). Statements are also released on all formal complaints and the answers to them, final orders, assurances of voluntary compliance, and witness lists for rule making hearings. Press releases are prepared for announcements of new policies, new programs, new personnel, FTC-related court actions, and speeches by Commissioners and members of the Washington staff. Back-dated press releases, as well as current ones, are often available.

Every Friday afternoon a calendar of FTC activities scheduled for the following week is issued. This includes a schedule of all hearings to be held during the week, along with dates of speeches and television appearances by senior staff members. Every two weeks a four-page news summary of all recent FTC activities is compiled and released. Every week a ten-page cross-section of news clippings on FTC matters from papers across the country, called *Paper Clips*, is put together for the use of FTC staff members. For consumers, a four-page bulletin called *Consumer Alert*, which highlights recent FTC consumer protection efforts, has recently been added to the publication list.

Speeches made by FTC staff members are summarized in press releases, and full copies are usually available either from the Office of Public Information or from the Legal and Public Records Division, another important source of information. Texts of financial and economic reports and industry guidelines can also be obtained from either source. Sometimes the texts of letters between members of Congress and the Commission are available from the Office of Public Information, but Congressional letters are only released upon authorization by the Congressmen involved, and they often want to release the letters from their own offices.

All of this material is free, if you're on the mailing list. To get on it, write a letter and ask that the mailing list application be sent to you. This is more than just a name, address, and zip code form. It asks what your field is, what products or services interest you, and what type of FTC action you want to know about.

All the materials issued by the Office of Public Information in Washington are also available in the field offices. Copies of items such as *Consumer Alert* and the news summary are fairly easy to get, but staff members and reporters have prior claim on copies of individual press releases, and it is probably better to get on the Washington mailing list if you want all of them. But don't neglect your local field office. Local and regional activities are covered by releases originating in the field offices, and each office issues about twenty to twenty-five press releases of its own every year. If an official Commission action is initiated by the field office, it will be announced in simultaneous releases from both the field office and the Washington Office of Public Information.

Watching the newspapers carefully is another way to keep up on what is happening at the FTC, since most major papers have one or two staff reporters who concentrate on consumer issues. These are also the people to whom you should send your press releases if you decide to participate in FTC proceedings. On the *Washington Post*, the reporters are Morton Mintz, Carole Shifrin, and Bill Jones. Some others are Stanley Cohen, Washington editor of *Advertising Age*, Hal Taylor of the Fairchild News Service and *Women's Wear Daily*, Philip Dougherty and John Morris of *The New York Times*, Ron Shafer of *The Wall Street Journal*, Bailey Morris of the *Washington Evening Star-Daily News*, and syndicated columnists Ann McFeatters, Peter Weaver, Sidney Margolius, Milton Moskowitz, and Bill Vaughn. A longer list of consumer writers can be found in Appendix 2-B (p. 42). The practice of most newspapers is to relegate consumer news to the "Women's" or "Style" section. In some places, however, FTC news may be scattered—traditional "consumer protection" news on the women's page, antitrust stories of less than headline importance in the business section, and unusually important actions, such as the cereal complaint, in the news section.

The other major source of information at the FTC is the Office of the Secretary. The material available there is not as easy to read as a press release, and most of it is not free, but it is official. The titles of two of the information sections of the Office of the Secretary describe roughly what sort of information they can offer: the Rules and Regulations Section and the Legal and Public Records Division. To find out exactly what material these sections have, order their free List of Publications. The Commission's practice is to handle requests for any free publications on the list at the Commission office, and to refer requests for "priced" publications to the G.P.O.

Basic material from the Legal and Public Records Division which you should have in dealing with the Commission includes the *Organization, Procedures, and Rules of Practice* manual, and the texts of statutes enforced by the Commission. There is another publication, called *Organization, Procedures, Rules of Practice, and Statutes*, which combines this material and costs less than $1.00. Some free material includes selected economic and scientific reports, such as the report on tar and nicotine content of smoke from 122 brands of cigarettes; rules and regulations under several of the statutes enforced by the Commission; industry guides; Quarterly Financial Report on manufacturing industries and corporations; and various "consumer bulletins," which are pamphlets on how to avoid common consumer pitfalls. The Legal and Public Records Division will also supply free single copies of the texts of all proposed complaints, initial decisions and final cease and desist orders (either adjudicated or consented to), all proposed and adopted trade regulation rules and trade practice rules, and recent speeches by senior staff members.

Information on the FTC is relatively inexpensive so long as you stick to material which has been printed and is either available free from the Commission or at a small charge from G.P.O. But some crucial parts of the "public record" are not printed, and are only made available for inspection and copying, as required by the Freedom of Information Act (FOIA). All of this material can be inspected and copied at the Washington office between 8:30 A.M. and 5:00 P.M., Monday through Friday. Some portions of the public record are also available during the same hours at the field offices. The "public record," as defined by the Commission in detail at 16 C.F.R. 4.9, includes much of the material which is available for free or for a small charge. This includes publications, press releases, annual reports, and other similar material. One of the reports available from G.P.O., *Federal Trade Commission Decisions*, is worth mentioning in particular. This is relatively expensive—about $7.50 for three to six months' worth. It includes initial decisions by hearing examiners, Commission decisions on formal adjudicative matters (with majority, concurring, and dissenting opinions), significant inter-locutory decisions, consent order decisions, and advisory opinions, with a current index. Portions of the public record which are not usually printed include papers filed in judicial proceedings by the Commission; all pleadings, motions, hearing transcripts, documents, exhibits, and other materials which constitute the record in a formal adjudicative pro-ceeding; transcripts of hearings on petitions for rule making and industry guides, and the written comments submitted on them; and other miscellaneous material, such as compliance reports.

If you know exactly what you are looking for, you can write and ask the Commission to make photocopies of the material and send them to you. This will cost you at least 20 cents a page. Unfortunately, if you are serious about getting information, you will probably have to come to Washington. Docket facilities at the field offices are not complete, and are usually maintained for the convenience of staff attorneys. In Washington, dockets are kept in room 130, on the left as you come through the Sixth Street entrance from Pennsylvania Avenue. If you already know the docket number of the case, ask the clerk to see the "skeleton" or case history cards for that case. This will give you a chronological summary of what has happened in the case and what documents have been filed concerning it. After looking this over, tell the desk clerk which of the documents you wish to inspect. If the case is currently in litigation, either in the courts or at the Commission, the docket may be in use. Otherwise, the clerk will produce the documents you want to look at and you can sit at one of the desks and read the pleadings, motions, briefs, or other material in the file. You may copy the material in longhand, but to photocopy it you will have to fill in a "Request for Photocopies," at the counter. Again, it will cost you 20 cents for a standard page.

The right of the public under the FOIA to get information from the FTC has improved somewhat. For example, the Nader study group was completely barred from inspecting the texts of advisory opinions and correspondence relating to them. Now these are usually available from the Office of Public Information. But not all advisory opinions are avail-able as a matter of right, since the Commission can withhold them if it decides that release would not be in the "public interest" [16 C.F.R. 1.4(a)].

The Commission's regulations implementing the FOIA are in the *Federal Register*, as required by the Act [38 F.R. 1730, hereinafter cited as F.R.]. If you submit a written request for copies or if you per-sonally ask the Commission to copy something for you, you usually will have to pay unless the information is contained in a publication prepared for general distribution. But the regulations permit the Commission to waive the copying fee if it finds it will be of general public interest and benefit to do so. No criteria are stated for measuring the requisite "public interest" finding. Written application should be made to the Secretary if you believe that you have good reason for waiver of copying fees [38 F.R. 1730, 4.8(c)].

Section 4.10 of the regulations describes the "confidential information" which the FTC believes it is not required to make available for public inspection and copying. The categories are very close to the specific exemptions set forth in the statute. Among them are:

1. Records related solely to internal personnel rules and practices, including administrative manuals and instructions to personnel.
2. Trade secrets and commercial or financial information obtained from a person and privileged or confidential assurances of confidentiality given by the Commission staff are not binding on the Commission.
3. Memos (either intra- or inter-agency) and other material which you couldn't subpoena if you were "in litigation with" the FTC, and official minutes of the deliberations of Commission meetings.
4. Personnel and medical files, "the disclosure of which would constitute a clearly unwarranted invasion of personal privacy."
5. Investigatory files which could not be reached by a subpoena, and all *in camera* (closed session) testimony at adjudicative proceedings. It is not clear whether the new rules intend to protect such files once an investigation is closed; such files have been partially disclosed in the past.
6. Other files made confidential by statute or Executive order from the President.

The "trade secrets" exemption is particularly convenient for keeping information secret.

The regulations also have a catchall category for "confidential information." As section 4.10(c) says, any information obtained by the Commission which is not clearly public is confidential. Just for emphasis, in case some FTC staff members get enthusiastic about public disclosure, the regulations include in Section 4.10(d) a reminder that the penalty for unauthorized disclosure, under Section 10 of the FTC Act, can be a year in jail and a $5,000 fine.

The FTC acknowledges that the statutory exemptions from disclosure don't *require* information to be withheld, but only allow it. Section 4.11 provides that the Commission can disclose information which it considers confidential, but you have to ask for it in writing, and tell why you want it and what you will use it for. When this is read in conjunction with the Commission's broad definition of "confidential" as everything which is not specifically public, it offers an opportunity for the FTC to resurrect the old requirement that members of the public must show "good cause" before they can get public information.

If you submit such a written request, it will be placed on the public record. The General Counsel's Office will review your motion and send a letter granting access if it is determined that access is required by the FOIA. If the determination is that the FOIA does not require disclosure, the matter will be submitted to the Commissioners for a decision. The decision by the Commission is a final agency action which can be appealed to federal court.

Access at the FTC

There are six basic points in FTC proceedings where consumers may have some impact:

1. Filing an application for complaint proceedings.
2. Commenting on proposed consent orders.
3. Intervening in FTC adjudication.
4. Petitioning for rule making.
5. Commenting on proposed rules.
6. Commenting on advisory opinions.

The effort involved can range from writing a letter to spending thousands of dollars and months or years of time in hearings. These methods are more fully described, with examples, later in the chapter, but the following is a brief summary of what they involve.

A fairly simple method is the application for complaint, which is a letter asking the FTC to take some action to correct a violation of any law enforced by the FTC. Anyone can file an application for complaint, and it doesn't have to follow a specific format [16 C.F.R. 2.2(a)(b)]. Although it may prod the FTC into action to stop the practice and protect others in the future, it usually will not do much good in terms of compensating you for any injury which you have suffered. There have been tentative efforts at including provisions for restitution in FTC final orders, that is, making the companies pay for some of the damage they've done, but in most cases you probably would have to go to court to get your money back. As the FTC increasingly uses economic bench marks to evaluate its potential caseload, it is less likely to act on complaints on many false advertisements, local practices, and frauds by small companies. Emphasis will increasingly fall on matters involving opportunities to have a lasting effect on practices costing the economy millions, or even billions, of dollars annually.

A second point of access is commenting on a proposed consent order. A consent order is the FTC's version of copping a plea in criminal court. The Commission doesn't want to go through a full-scale adjudication, because that delays the effective date of the order and uses valuable resources. The company doesn't want to go through a full-scale adjudication, because of the cost (especially if the practice isn't essential to maintaining its sales volume). So they talk. If the negotiations are successful, the result is a provisionally acceptable consent order in which the company promises not to do something any more without admitting that it ever did it. Although the negotiation of these orders is done in private, the FTC is now considering an application by a group of law students at George Washington University to intervene in consent negotiations. Many questions are unanswered as to the basis for such interventions, if they are permitted, the degree of participation intervenors would be permitted, and whether the FTC would pay the expenses of an indigent party seeking to intervene in consent negotiations.

Once a consent agreement is reached, it is made available to the public and accompanied by a press release. These can be obtained without charge at the Office of Public Information. Single copies of the text of proposed complaints are also available without charge at the Division of Legal and Public Records [16 C.F.R. 2.35]. After the negotiations are over, the proposed consent order is placed on the public record for thirty days, and comments are invited. Comments on proposed consent orders are supposed to be directed toward whether or not the order is "inappropriate, improper, or inadequate," with supporting data included [16 C.F.R. 2.33]. They should be sent to the Office of the Secretary in Washington, with the file number of the case included.

The next point of consumer access at the FTC is formal intervention in adjudicative proceedings. Adjudication is, roughly speaking, the equivalent of a trial held when the FTC and the company can't make a deal for a consent order. The intervention of Students Opposing

Unfair Practices (SOUP) is an example which will be described in some
detail later. One approach to intervention in such adjudications is to
keep track of the formal complaints which the Commission has issued,
and look for proceedings which will be worth the considerable investment of time, money, and energy which intervention involves. Formal
complaints are not covered by full press releases, but by memorandums
making reference to press releases for the proposed complaint [16
C.F.R. 2.35]. Copies of the full texts of formal complaints and memorandums are available free of charge at the Office of Public Information
or the Division of Legal and Public Records. The complaint will include
the date and place of the hearing, and a hearing cannot begin until at
least thirty days after the complaint has been issued. At present, citizen
intervention in formal adjudication is still in the experimental stages,
and the high watermark is the SOUP intervention in the Firestone case,
described later (see Appendix 5-C, p. 156).

The next point of access is rule making. The two ways to participate
in rule making are by initiating rule making by a petition, and commenting on a proposed rule.

Filing a petition for rule making, such as the petition on advertising
in Appendix 5-B (p. 134), in effect is proposing a law to govern
the way everyone in the industry will act in the future. If your complaint is directed only at a particular company, an application for complaint would be more effective. In submitting a proposed rule, make the
best argument you can, with references to supporting research. The
formal requirements are set forth at 16.C.F.R. 1.15.

Commenting on proposed rules is not too difficult. Watch the *Federal
Register*, in which notice of proposed rules must be published [16
C.F.R. 1.16(b)], *Consumer News* from the White House Consumer
Advisor (see p. 26 on how to subscribe), and *Consumer Alert* from the
FTC. All of these will tell you how much time you have to submit
comments, and where to send them. The Commission may also hold
hearings and conferences, or make economic studies about proposed
rules. A hearing on the proposed rule offers another opportunity to
make your comments in person.

Still another area of possible access to the FTC is the advisory
opinion. An advisory opinion is given by the Commission to a business
on the legality of something the business is planning to do. It is given
only if (a) it concerns a future course of action, and (b) the practice
is not presently under investigation by the FTC or any other government agency. Only some of the advisory opinions are made public
through press releases from the Office of Public Information, and there

is usually a lapse of up to three months between the time the advisory opinion is sent to the businessman and the press release. Public comments on such advisory opinions have only been expressly invited by the FTC on premerger clearances, but advisory opinions are subject to modifications if circumstances warrant [16 C.F.R. 1.3(b)], and citizen access could be expanded with relatively little expenditure of time and energy by reviewing opinions which are made public and submitting comments.

APPLICATION FOR COMPLAINT

An application for complaint is nothing more than a letter to the FTC suggesting that something is wrong, and that the Commission has a responsibility to do something about it. Anyone is permitted to file an application for complaint [16 C.F.R. 2.2(a)], and it doesn't have to be in any particular format [16 C.F.R. 2.2(b)]. However, two things must be involved and should be discussed in your letter: The company you are complaining about must be doing business in interstate commerce, and there must be a deceptive or unfair practice or unfair method of competition involved. The National Consumer Law Center at Boston Law School has listed five points which should be covered in a well-drawn application for complaint:

1. Include the name and address of the company you are complaining about. This should be accompanied by an explanation that the company is engaged in a significant amount of interstate commerce.
2. Attach copies of any documentary evidence involved, such as advertisements or letters.
3. Describe the facts as clearly and completely as you possibly can. This is the information that probably will be most important in the staff's deciding whether to investigate further or to send you a polite brush-off.
4. As much evidence as possible that other consumers have been victims of the same deceptive practice should be included. The greater the number of consumers victimized, the more likely it is that the Commission will take some action. If other consumers are willing to sign affidavits, the application will have even more impact. There is little likelihood that they will actually be called as witnesses in formal hearings, but it is possible that they will be interviewed if the FTC decides to conduct an investigation.
5. The application for complaint must be signed by the consumer or his attorney, with a return address provided.

Once you have your application for complaint typed, you have to decide whether to send it to Washington or to your local field office. The rule of thumb is to send it to Washington if it involves a nation-wide practice by a large company. That address is: Office of the Secretary, Correspondent Section, Federal Trade Commission, Washington, D.C. 20580. Since there is an internal arrangement for routing complaints to the appropriate office, this decision isn't crucial.

If the field office decides to do something about your complaint, the first step will be for an attorney or Consumer Protection Specialist to conduct a preliminary investigation. This will usually involve at least a letter or phone call to you, if not an interview. It will also involve some discussion with the business about which you have complained. If you fear reprisals, the FTC will usually keep your name confidential. However, the nature of some applications, such as those involving a specific service or product, may make your identity obvious. And you may even want to issue a press release of your own along with your application for complaint. After preliminary investigation, a field office may apply to the appropriate Bureau Director in Washington for permission to open a full-scale hearing on a local matter. If the practice is national in scope or concerns a corporate merger, it will be turned over to the Washington headquarters for investigation.

If the practice you are complaining about is national, and you send the application for complaint directly to Washington, it will go through a similar procedure. It is docketed at the Secretary's Office, after being read by a "consumer correspondence assistant" (a sort of all-purpose letter reader) who then sends it to the appropriate operating bureau. At the bureau the letter is screened by a legal adviser to see if the Commission has jurisdiction and whether the "public interest" is involved [16 C.F.R. 2.3]. As is the case with most other agencies, it usually helps if the complaint comes from a Congressman's office.

The next step is the important decision by the Commission whether to proceed with a full-scale nonadjudicative investigation. If a pile of applications for complaint about a particular company begins to build up, a Dun and Bradstreet rating of the company is obtained, and the decision on whether to proceed with the investigation is made by the investigating attorney, the Division Chief, and sometimes the Bureau Director. When Senator T. Kennedy's Subcommittee on Administrative Practice and Procedure asked the FTC what criteria it relied on in deciding whether to proceed at this stage, Commissioner McIntyre gave the following reply:

1. Does the practice complained of indicate that there is danger to the public health or safety?
2. What are the indicated number of consumers adversely affected?
3. Is there a particular segment of consumer population affected perhaps deserving a special degree of protection: the poor, the elderly, the retired?
4. What is the materiality of a deceptive statement in the context of the total promotional approach: did the statement, alone or substantially contributorily, actually constitute the real inducement to buy?
5. What is the nature of the deceptive practice: did it constitute an outright fraud or did it concern a worthwhile (albeit misrepresented) product or service?
6. What is the amount or degree of loss suffered by the consumer: is he out of pocket a few cents, or has he mortgaged his home with the potential of foreclosure?
7. What is the economic magnitude of the given industry engaging in a complained of practice?
8. Are there honest competitors to protect?
9. Is there a fair prospect of success if we litigate: is the alleged unfair practice reasonably clear-cut, or does it present a controversial scientific issue?
10. All factors considered, is the matter one to which we can commit manpower and other resources in light of current priorities? [*Responses to Questionnaire on Citizen Involvement and Responsive Agency Decision-Making*, Subcommittee on Administrative Practices and Procedure, Committee on the Judiciary, 91st Cong., 1st session]

If the FTC decides to proceed, an investigation is conducted. Occasionally an investigational hearing will be conducted to obtain testimony and evidence submitted under oath. Unfortunately, these hearings are generally closed to the public [16 C.F.R. 2.8].

Just how much access there may be in these full-scale investigations is difficult to say. The complainant may be called as a witness or asked to submit a deposition, but not necessarily [16 C.F.R. 2.9, 2.10]. Of course, as with preliminary investigations, additional information can always be volunteered by the complainant. If you volunteer such additional information, be sure to include enough details to identify the case, including the file number if one has been assigned.

On the basis of this investigation, the investigating attorney decides either to drop the case, to seek voluntary compliance, or to recommend issuance of a proposed complaint and attempt negotiation of a consent order. The Commission must concur in any of these proposed dispositions once a formal investigation has commenced. (This procedure was established after the staff, responding to a contact from White House adviser Sherman Adams, President Eisenhower's top aide, closed an investigation of a company owned by Adams' friend, Bernard Goldfine.)

COMMENTING ON PROPOSED CONSENT ORDERS

If, after a full-scale nonadjudicative investigation, the Commission feels that further action is required, the attorney handling the case will invite the company to enter into negotiations for a consent order to put an end to matters without formal adjudication. This is done by drawing up a proposed complaint which sets forth the alleged practice and the provisions of the cease and desist order which the staff attorney is seeking (free copies available from the Office of Public Information).

To date, there has been no citizen access during the negotiating process. (As previously mentioned, a petition to intervene in consent negotiations is now before the FTC.) The result, if the negotiations succeed, is a proposed consent order. If it is eventually approved, the consent order has the same force as a cease and desist order. It is, however, only for settlement purposes and does not constitute an admission of guilt by the business, being somewhat similar to a plea of "no contest" in a criminal action. A proposed consent order is placed on the public record for thirty days, and the public is invited to comment on it (copies of the proposed consent order and press release are available at the Division of Legal and Public Records and the Office of Public Information, respectively [FTC Rules, Sections 2.31-2.33]).

Once the proposed consent order is put on the public record, anyone may comment during the thirty-day period. You must direct your remarks to whether or not the order is "inappropriate, improper, or inadequate," and include supporting data (or arguments) to substantiate your comments [16 C.F.R. 2.33]. Send all comments on proposed consent orders to the Office of the Secretary, Federal Trade Commission, Washington, D.C. 20580, and be sure to include the file number of the case.

The most successful, or at least the most celebrated, action by a nonindustry group on a proposed consent order was the Campbell Soup case [Docket No. C-1741] in 1969. The FTC had accused Campbell and its advertiser of using clear glass marbles in advertising photographs to push the solids to the top and make the soup look richer. A consent order was provisionally accepted, under which Campbell and its advertiser promised to stop putting marbles in the soup while denying that they ever did. During the thirty-day period for comment in September and October 1969, a group of law students from George Washington University, supervised by their professor, John Banzhaf III, mounted their attack. Acting under the acronym SOUP, they chose to do more than merely comment on the proposed order. Instead, they filed motions to have the proposed order set aside on grounds of inadequate consumer protection, and to intervene in any further proceedings. They also filed motions to extend the period for comment, for limited *in forma pauperis* privileges—the right to file only one copy of each document instead of the required twenty—and for the right to see the FTC investigation files leading up to the consent order.

SOUP felt that taking the marbles out of the soup would not be enough to undo the damage to consumers convinced by the ads that the soup was richer than it was. In order to offset the impact on consumer buying habits of past deceptive ads, SOUP argued that Campbell should include a message in future ads that their old ads were misleading. In effect, SOUP was asking the Commission to conduct a limited evidentiary hearing on issues of audience scope, nature, and effect of the ads, as well as the media used to disseminate them. SOUP argued that since it had raised serious doubts as to the adequacy of the proposed order, the Commission should withdraw its provisional acceptance of the consent order and order a hearing at which SOUP would intervene as a party.

In November the Commission granted an indefinite extension of time for comment, granted SOUP's limited *in forma pauperis* request, and provided for oral argument on whether an evidentiary hearing was necessary and whether SOUP should be allowed to intervene. In early December 1969, Consumers Union and the Consumer Federation of America filed documents with the Commission verifying that SOUP was a bona fide representative of consumer interests and supporting SOUP's motions for hearing and for intervention. After the oral argument in February 1970, the Commission decided that the evidentiary hearing was unnecessary and that SOUP would therefore be left with nothing in which to intervene. The FTC allowed limited access to its file on Campbell and gave SOUP until 20 March to submit further written comments on whether the order was adequate [Letter from Commission to Aaron Handleman, president of SOUP, Inc., 24 February 1970].

SOUP then asked the Commission to reconsider the motions it had denied, filed a long brief on the inadequacy of the provisional order, and requested that its *in forma pauperis* privileges be expanded to include a free transcript of the oral argument.

On 25 May 1970, in a 3-2 decision (Commissioners Elman and Jones dissenting vigorously in separate opinions), the Commission denied all of the motions except the transcript request. It held that SOUP's "intervention" was sufficient for its purposes; that the FTC had better things to do than worry about marbles in soup advertisements; and, most important, that, since the public health and safety were not at stake, the order was officially accepted as proposed.

Exactly what SOUP accomplished in the Campbell case is difficult to determine. Essentially, SOUP was only allowed what the rules said it was entitled to all along: the right to submit written comments on the adequacy of the consent order. But in a larger sense, the Campbell Soup case had considerable impact. The Commission was put in direct confrontation with a group of consumers in addition to the usual industry attorneys. It is likely that the Campbell case, more than any other single factor, paved the way for SOUP's subsequent, partially successful intervention in the Firestone case [Docket No. 8818], to be discussed later. (See Appendix 5-C, p. 156). The full story of the Campbell case remains to be told. SOUP has appealed the FTC's decision to the U.S. Court of Appeals for District of Columbia Circuit [*SOUP, Inc.* v. *FTC*, No. 24,476]. Some of the issues on appeal are:

1. Whether the Commission should have held a hearing on the factual questions raised by SOUP before accepting the consent order as adequate to protect the public.
2. Whether the Commission should have held a formal adjudication when SOUP objected to the adequacy of the relief contained in the proposed order.
3. Whether intervention in FTC proceedings is discretionary with the Commission, or a matter of right.

On 27 July 1971, a three-judge panel denied SOUP's request to proceed *in forma pauperis* in its petition for review of the Commission's order. The ruling was based on financial statements for each member of SOUP which had been filed at the request of the Court of Appeals. Chief Judge Bazelon dissented from this order. By:

looking behind the corporation to the individuals it represents,

today's order may have the unfortunate effect of deterring the use
of corporations as vehicles for raising issues of great public importance . . . we may discourage non-indigent individuals from joining
corporations that intend to bring law suits on behalf of the public.
[Order, 27 July 1971, *SOUP, Inc.* v. *FTC*, No. 24,476]

SOUP then sought relief in the Supreme Court on issue of *in forma
pauperis*. The Supreme Court refused to grant *certiorari* and the case
returned to the Court of Appeals.

The issue of the Commission's authority to pay for the expense of at
least some "indigent" intervenors has been determined administratively
in the affirmative. In a letter to Chairman Kirkpatrick dated 24 July
1972, U.S. Comptroller General Elmer B. Staats ruled that the Commission can pay the expenses of an indigent respondent (against whom
a complaint has been issued). This was the precise issue before the Commission, which had issued a complaint against the American Chinchilla
Corporation; the company could not afford the costs of litigation but
wanted to contest the complaint. Staats' letter went further than the
matter directly at issue, however. He informed Kirkpatrick:

> Insofar as intervenors are concerned, Section 5(b) of the Federal
> Trade Commission Act, as amended, 15 U.S.C. 45(b) specifically
> authorizes the Commission to grant intervention "upon good cause
> shown." Thus, if the Commission determines it necessary to allow
> a person to intervene in order to properly dispose of a matter
> before it, the Commission has the authority to do so. As in the
> case of an indigent respondent, and for the same reasons, appropri-
> ated funds of the Commission would be available to assure proper
> case preparation. [Letter from U.S. Comptroller General Elmer B.
> Staats to FTC Chairman Miles W. Kirkpatrick, 24 July 1972;
> Comptroller's reference No. B-139703]

Staats' choice of words raises a potential problem. The statutory basis
for intervention is *good cause shown*, but Staats concludes that the
Commission may provide expenses if it *determines it necessary to allow
a person to intervene in order to properly dispose of a matter before it*.
The language of the latter phrase constitutes a requirement more restrictive than the statutory language. The "necessary party" doctrine on
which it appears to be based is appropriate in civil cases, and to some
extent in FTC cases, in determining whether intervention must be
granted to a commercial party which, if not named in the order, could

render the order ineffective, or whose legal rights would be affected without an opportunity for it to be heard. Such an instance arose in the previously mentioned cases against the soft drink syrup manufacturers, when certain franchised bottlers, through their trade associations, sought and were granted intervention.

The Commission, however, could well find "good cause" for granting intervention to citizens without commercial interests or basis other than legal necessity. Possession of evidence or expertise not otherwise involved in the case, or expressions indicating a view of the facts or of the remedy which could prove useful in analyzing and disposing of the matter, might well be "good cause."

Since the Comptroller's letter purports to rely on the words of the statute, his adoption of more restrictive language in elaborating on his conclusion should not preclude an indigent intervenor from moving for FTC payment of some or all expenses associated with intervention.

Public comment on proposed consent orders, such as the SOUP effort, is a crucial point of access for airing citizen views. The new philosophy of enforcement at FTC, which focuses on consent orders, is a movement away from reliance on voluntary compliance, tempered by realities of the budget which discourage extensive use of the formal adjudicative machinery. Even some of the "less enlightened" Dixon holdovers concede that access by citizens through their comments is helpful—a far cry from their opposition to formal intervention by consumers.

The thirty-day limit for comments does not leave much time for the average citizen to find out about the order and research and formulate a response. However, the announcement of the proposed complaint comes early enough to alert you to look for the consent order and to begin preliminary investigation. Also, negotiations are supposed to be tailored around a thirty-day limit [16 C.F.R. 2.34(a)], but they generally involve one or more fifteen- or thirty-day extensions because of requests by respondents. The FTC has in the last year greatly reduced the number of extensions granted, allowing them only when the respondent has already submitted a negotiable written settlement offer, and then only if there are "compelling reasons" to do so.

INTERVENTION IN FORMAL ADJUDICATIVE PROCEEDINGS

Intervening in an adjudicative proceeding isn't easy. At a minimum, it requires a lawyer, and the financial expense can drain a budget quickly. But it also represents an opportunity for citizen access at the most immediate level of agency law enforcement—the "trial" of an alleged offender.

When negotiations fail to produce a consent order, the Commission issues a complaint. The complaint cites the statute involved, includes a brief statement of the facts, and proposes an order [16 C.F.R. 3.11 (1-3)]. It also includes the date and place of the formal hearings, to be held at least thirty days later, which (as indicated above) are frequently postponed for one reason or another. Formal complaints are not covered by a full press release, but merely by a memorandum referring to the previous release issued with the proposed complaint [16 C.F.R. 2.35]. The memorandum does note whether the formal complaint is identical to the proposed complaint. Free copies are available of the formal complaint (at the Division of Legal and Public Records) and the memorandum (at the Office of Public Information).

Once the formal complaint has been issued, the respondent (the company involved) may file a motion for a more definite statement of the allegations (within ten days after issuance of the complaint) [16 C.F.R. 3.11(c)], or an answer to the allegations (generally within thirty days after the day the complaint was served) [16 C.F.R. 3.12]. The answer that is filed is usually summarized in a press release from the Office of Public Information. If you file a formal motion to intervene, do so as soon as possible after the respondent files an answer. The regulations don't provide a deadline for intervention, but the longer you wait, the less sympathy you'll evoke, and it's better to avoid accusations by those who are already parties to the proceeding that your delay has prejudiced their case. Since citizen intervention at this stage is still experimental, prompt interventions are most likely to be treated seriously.

The most successful consumer attempt at intervention in an adjudicative proceeding was by SOUP, in the Firestone case [Docket No. 8818]. The complaint charged that Firestone and its advertising agency had made unsubstantiated claims and used dangling comparatives (e.g., "Wide-Ovals stop your car 25% faster"—faster than what?) in advertising. SOUP sought all the rights of other parties. In October 1970 the Commission, in a 4 to 1 decision, let SOUP intervene to a limited extent. SOUP was *not* allowed to participate at all in determination of the basic issue of whether or not Firestone's ads were in fact deceptive. Instead, they were allowed to present "relevant, noncumulative" testimony, exhibits, charts, and other data on the issue of the adequacy of any proposed order. They were also allowed to subpoena records, call witnesses, submit briefs, and participate in oral argument on the adequacy of the proposed order.

Although SOUP originally asked for the final cease and desist order to include a provision requiring Firestone to place corrective information in *all* current advertising [*Firestone*, Amended Motion of SOUP,

Inc., to Intervene, etc., 1 September 1970, at 9] (see Appendix 5-C, p. 156), the demand was modified at the hearing. Instead, SOUP asked that any statement by the FTC to the effect that past ads had been found to be misleading and deceptive should be included in Firestone ads making claims about safety performance, stopping performance, and price comparisons of its tires. In addition, SOUP asked that Firestone customers who purchased tires when deceptive advertisements were run be notified of the FTC findings by mail at Firestone's expense. Finally, SOUP wanted Firestone to pay back customers so notified, if they swore that they bought the tires on the basis of Firestone's deceptive and misleading claims, and returned the tires [*Firestone*, Amended Motion of SOUP, Inc., to Intervene, etc., at 10].

The Commission made it clear that SOUP intervention was not to "be construed as a permanent or irreversible policy decision," and that intervention was allowed only because of the threat to public health and safety (which was absent in the Campbell case).

Section 5(b) of the FTC Act [15 U.S.C. 45(b)] provides that "Any person, partnership, or corporation may make application, and *upon good cause shown* may be allowed by the Commission to intervene and appear in said proceeding" (emphasis added). There are very few cases to tell what kind of "good cause" you have to show to intervene. But on the basis of the two SOUP cases (Campbell and Firestone) and the Kennecott Copper case [Docket No. 8765], a few observations can be made, in spite of the Commission's warning that their "exercise of the discretion on a question of intervention depends on an assessment of all the facts and circumstances of a particular case and each grant or denial will have minimal, if not nonexistent precedential value" [Firestone Opinion, at 3].

Your reasons should *not* be "generalized and unsupported" [*Firestone,* Answer by Complaint Counsel to Motion of SOUP, Inc., to Intervene, etc., 13 October 1970, at 2] or "imprecise and speculative" [*Firestone*, Respondent's Memorandum in Opposition to Motion for Intervention by SOUP, Inc., 18 August 1970]. The would-be intervenor should show that his interest and expertise in the matter is somehow unique [*Firestone*, Respondent's Memorandum in Opposition to Renewed Motion for Intervention by SOUP, Inc., 14 September 1970, at 2,3] and that he is a responsible citizen spokesman without a direct economic stake in the outcome of the case [Amended Motion of SOUP, Inc., to Intervene, etc., 1 September 1970, at 5-9]. Mere assertion that the proposed order is inadequate, and that you will present evidence leading to a more adequate order, is not enough. You must demonstrate why the proposed order is inadequate, propose an order with the clauses needed to correct the inadequacies, and provide a description of the scope of evidence you intend to present to support your argument [Amended Motion of SOUP, Inc., to Intervene, etc., 1 September 1970. at 5-10]. The evidence you introduce must be relevant, material, and involve substantial factual and legal issues [*Firestone,* Request of SOUP, Inc., to File an Interlocutory Appeal from the Denial of Its Amended Motion to Intervene, 25 September 1970, at 7; *Campbell Soup*, Docket No. C-1741, Opinion of the Commission, at 3; *Firestone Tire and Rubber Company*, Docket No. 8818, Opinion and Order Granting Limited Intervention, at 3].

The case itself is, according to the decision to date, supposed to be "an aggravated proceeding directly involving the health and safety of the public" [*Firestone,* Request of SOUP, Inc., for Leave to File an Interlocutory appeal from the Denial of Its Amended Motion to Intervene, 25 September 1970, at 7; see also *Firestone Tire and Rubber Company*, Docket No. 8818, Opinion and Order Granting Limited Intervention, at 4; *Campbell Soup*, Docket No. C-1741, Opinion of the Commission, at 6]. (Note the difference between the two SOUP cases: Misrepresenting the vegetable content of soup isn't a threat to public health and safety, as is misrepresentation of the stopping distance of an automobile tire.)

The Commission also expects evidence demonstrating that it is worth their while to let you intervene. Citizen intervention necessarily adds some complexity, and could broaden the issues somewhat. The FTC, on the other hand, theoretically wants to avoid prolonged litigation at all costs, and the Commission's question is whether your ability to contribute outweighs your potential for getting in the way [*Firestone Tire and Rubber Company*, at 3-4].

Your motion for leave to intervene as a formal party must comply with requirements of form. It must be typewritten (8-8 1/2" X 10 1/2-11"), or printed (7" X 10"), on good unglazed paper [Proc. 4.2(d)(1,3, 4)]. It must be served, in person or by first class mail, to the Office of the Secretary [Proc. 4.4(b)]. You must serve the Secretary with twenty copies, one signed by your attorney or, if you have no attorney, by yourself [Proc. 4.3(c), (e)]. If you qualify for *in forma pauperis* treatment you may be relieved of the twenty-copy requirement. The FTC allows corporations and unincorporated associations, upon proper certification, to be represented by officers [16 C.F.R. 4.1(a)(2)], although you should have an attorney once you reach the hearing stage. You must also serve each other party (or its attorney) with a copy of the motion, either in person or by mail.

At this point, you probably will want to combine your motion to intervene with a motion to proceed *in forma pauperis*, with expenses of participation to be paid by the FTC. The entire question of *in forma pauperis* treatment of participants in FTC proceedings is still an open one. As noted previously, the Comptroller General's opinion in *American Chinchilla* indicates both promise and some question as to when citizen intervenors can receive expenses from the FTC.

The initial motion to intervene should include a motion to disclose, to get as much information as possible about the respondents from the Commission. SOUP used such a motion with some success in both the Campbell and Firestone cases. But you should avoid going on a "fishing expedition" by presenting a well-documented, or at least well-developed, theory of the case *before* you move for disclosure. When you move for disclosure, you are *required* to show that the information you seek cannot be voluntarily obtained elsewhere, and you must be as specific as possible in describing the documents sought [16 C.F.R. 3.36]. But you may move for disclosure more than once, at any time in the discovery and hearing stages when you feel that information in the Commission's exclusive possession may be helpful to your case. Also, you can ask to take a deposition of an FTC official or employee [16 C.F.R. 3.36].

If your motion to intervene is granted, you will almost certainly need a lawyer. The pressure of the hearing itself and the intricate evidentiary problems that may arise will require the expertise of an experienced trial attorney.

After a limited period for amending and supplementing pleadings [16 C.F.R. 3.15], the parties and the FTC initiate *discovery*. Discovery is the preliminary exchange of information among parties by means of written questions (interrogatories), oral questioning (depositions), and inspection of documents, records, and files. The purpose is to accumulate and preserve evidence, and to sharpen (or sometimes broaden) the issues. Though some information may be provided voluntarily by the parties, most crucial evidence requires an order of the Administrative Law Judge. To get such an order, submit a written application in the form of a motion to the Judge. It must meet the formal specifications (paper size, quantity, service requirements, and so on) of the original motion to intervene.

An application to the Judge to order an oral deposition or written interrogatories must include a brief description of the efforts made so far to get the information voluntarily. He will approve it only if he's convinced that relevant evidence will otherwise be lost, or that the proceeding will not be unduly delayed, or that it's likely the same evidence will not be given by someone at the hearing [16 C.F.R. 3.33(a)]. You also must give the time, place, and expected subject matter of a deposition, the name and address of the proposed deponent (who need not be a party to the proceeding), the name of the person who will conduct it, and a request for any necessary subpoenas [16 C.F.R. 3.33(b)].

Not less than five days after an application is approved, the deposition will take place, if there is no attempt by another party or the proposed deponent to modify the order [16 C.F.R. 3.33(d)]. At the deposition all parties have the right to cross-examine the deponent. A transcript of the proceedings is kept. Two copies go to the party who applied for the deposition and one copy goes to each of the other parties [16 C.F.R. 3.33(e)].

If the deposition is to preserve evidence for use at the hearing, the deponent must read and sign it upon request of the party who wants to use the deposition [16 C.F.R. 3.33(f)(1)]. It can be used against any party who was present when it was taken if the deponent is unavailable at the time of the hearing [16 C.F.R. 3.33(f)(2)].

Discovery also includes requests for admissions, either as to the genuineness of documents or the truth of any allegations. Such a request is made in writing and served in person or by mail upon a party. A copy is also filed with the Secretary. If a request for an admission is not responded to within ten days by a sworn specific denial or refusal based on privilege or irrelevance, it is considered to be admitted [16 C.F.R. 3.31].

Subpoenas can be issued at any time during the process. At this time the FTC must rely on the Justice Department for enforcement, although legislation to permit the FTC to enforce subpoenas itself is under consideration. Application for subpoenas to require someone to appear for a deposition or to produce certain documents must be made in writing to the hearing examiner [16 C.F.R. 3.34]. An application for a subpoena to produce certain documents (subpoena *duces tecum*) [16 C.F.R. 3.34(b)] is similar to an application for an order allowing access to a respondent's files [16 C.F.R. 3.32]. Both must be made in writing to the hearing examiner, and must describe the material you are after; both can be defeated if the information is privileged or otherwise confidential.

If the hearing examiner refuses your application for discovery, you can appeal to the Commission, but you must appeal within five days of the ruling, and must state your appeal in fewer than thirty pages [16 C.F.R. 3.35(b), 3.36(d)].

The next step is a prehearing conference, which will be called by the Administrative Law Judge. Its purpose is to narrow and focus the issues, amend the pleadings if necessary, and streamline and organize the evidence gathered so that the hearing will go faster [16 C.F.R. 3.21(a)]. It

is usually not open to the public [16 C.F.R. 3.21(c)]. When the prehearing conference is over the Judge issues an important order which
controls the subsequent proceedings [16 C.F.R. 3.21(d)]. Whether evidence to be used at the hearing is relevant depends on what the order
says the issues are; whether a witness may appear or a document be used
at the hearing depends on the witness and document lists in the order.
Give the prehearing conference as much attention as the hearing itself.

The Judge may decide all or part of a case without even waiting for
the hearing by granting a summary decision or partial summary decision.
A motion for summary decision can be made at any time after issuance
of the complaint (although the FTC attorney must wait thirty days),
but not within twenty days before the hearing date. In practice, this
almost never is granted [16 C.F.R. 3.24(a)(1)]. The idea is to allow the
Judge to eliminate trumped-up issues and proceed with the rest of the
case (partial summary decision) [16 C.F.R. 3.24(a)(5)], or to halt the
proceedings completely and enter an initial decision on the merits of the
entire case (total summary decision) [16 C.F.R. 3.24(a)(2)].

After the discovery and prehearing conference comes the hearing.
Remember that intervention is *not* an "all or nothing" proposition, since
the hearing examiner can, within the scope of the Commission's order
to permit intervention, limit intervention as he sees fit [16 C.F.R. 3.14].
The hearing will convene on the day and at the place indicated in the
complaint. Most hearings are held in Washington at 414 11th Street,
N.W. (also called the "Star Building" or "the 1101 Building," after
its Pennsylvania Avenue address), on the seventh floor, or at 1111 Constitution Avenue, N.W., in Courtroom 1 of the Tax Court. If a field
office has handled a case virtually from the beginning, and if it appears
more convenient for the attorneys and witnesses involved, the hearing
may be held at the field office, or in a local U.S. courthouse, federal
office building, or post office building.

The hearing is open to the public [16 C.F.R. 3.41(a)], and is
announced every Friday in the Office of Public Information's schedule
of events. It resembles a civil trial before a court with respect to the
rights of the parties in general [16 C.F.R. 3.41(c)] and evidentiary rules
[16 C.F.R. 3.41(d), 3.43]. It is important to remember that an Administrative Law Judge acts as a courtroom judge in many ways. He is selected
by the Director of Administrative Law Judges [16 C.F.R. 3.42(b)]
and he runs the entire hearing [16 C.F.R. 3.42(f)]. In addition to his
powers to rule on various prehearing motions already mentioned, the
examiner has the power to impose sanctions on attorneys for misconduct, which can include suspension or temporary disbarment from FTC

proceedings. Such action is rarely taken, but the threat remains, and attorneys who do not regularly practice before the Commission should be aware of it. The attorney has the right to appeal to the Commission, but he must do so within five days of the order and in a brief of fewer than thirty pages [16 C.F.R. 3.42(d)]. A Judge may hold in contempt anyone who fails to obey a valid order made by him [16 C.F.R. 3.42(h)].

It is possible to challenge an Administrative Law Judge for cause, that is, to ask for his removal on the ground that he is prejudiced against your case. You can file such a motion, supported by an affidavit, with the Commission at any time. The Commission allows the Judge ten days to disqualify himself and, if he refuses to do so, it will either decide the issue itself or designate another Judge to hold a hearing on the matter [16 C.F.R. 3.42(g)(2)]. But it's probably better not to try for such removal unless you have an overwhelmingly good reason—and even then you should be cautious. If the reason is so good, you can use it on a subsequent appeal.

The hearing itself is stenographically recorded, and copies of the transcript are available at astronomical rates [16 C.F.R. 3.44]. This is where the *in forma pauperis* status becomes important economically. Without a transcript to refer to by page, cross-examination and preparation of an appeal are severely restricted.

At the hearing the Judge may hear some evidence *in camera*, that is, out of hearing of all but the parties, the witnesses involved, and the reporter. Such evidence will be kept secret from the public, but remains part of the record for use by the parties, the Judge, and the Commission for purposes of the hearing and any subsequent appeal [16 C.F.R. 3.45]. The party that wants *in camera* treatment must have a substantial reason, such as exclusion of a customer list from the public record, even though the evidence may be relevant and not sufficiently confidential to warrant its total exclusion. Although *in camera* treatment of evidence won't affect your case, it will hinder future citizen attempts to gain a full understanding of the case from reading the public record.

After all of the evidence has been presented, you can submit proposed findings of fact, conclusions of law, and an initial order—in short, your idea of how the Judge ought to decide the case, with a supporting argument making references to the record [16 C.F.R. 3.46]. Unless he decides to reopen the proceeding to hear more evidence [Proc. 3.51(d)], the Judge then considers the various proposed findings and orders, as well as the evidence, and decides the case. Usually he issues an initial decision within ninety days after the close of the submission of evidence.

This becomes the final decision of the Commission thirty days later if no party has appealed [16 C.F.R. 3.51(a)]. The decision must include all essential findings of fact and conclusions of law upon which the order is based.

If you lose, you have ten days to file notice of appeal [16 C.F.R. 3.52(a)], unless the Commission decides on its own that the decision should be appealed [16 C.F.R. 3.53]. The appeal itself, in the form of a brief, must be in the hands of the Secretary within thirty days after the initial decision. The brief is limited to sixty pages [16 C.F.R. 3.52(e)]. The notice telling the Commission you want to appeal (called "noting an appeal") and the appeal itself must be submitted in twenty-five copies each (unless you are proceeding *in forma pauperis*), one of which must be signed by your attorney or by yourself [16 C.F.R. 4.2(c)].

If the other side loses and appeals, you have thirty days from the time it files its brief to file one of your own [16 C.F.R. 3.52(c)]. If it wants to rebut the arguments in your answering brief, it has a week to do so [16 C.F.R. 3.52(d)]. After all the briefs are in, the Commission presides at oral argument [16 C.F.R. 3.52(f)], which is nearly always held in Washington, and enters final judgment. On some occasions it may decide without hearing arguments. If you lose an appeal, you have twenty days to petition the Commission to reconsider their decision, but you can't reargue the same issues with the same arguments [16 C.F.R. 3.55]. The alternative at this stage is to appeal the Commission's order to the Court of Appeals, which has jurisdiction over all final orders of the FTC. The Commission can still decide to reopen the case if you have only filed your notice of appeal to the court [16 C.F.R. 3.72(a)]. But if you have already filed the FTC transcript in court, the Commission may not reopen its own case. You may appeal to the U.S. Court of Appeals in the District of Columbia. It is not clear whether an intervenor can also, as can a respondent, appeal to the U.S. Court of Appeals in the Circuit where you maintain legal residence (either personally or as an organization).

RULE MAKING

Participating in FTC adjudication takes a lawyer, lots of time and effort, and can cost quite a bit of money. It is useful primarily in cases which can serve as important precedents to dissuade other potential offenders. But participating in FTC rule making is a more direct way of dealing with a widespread deceptive practice. In effect, when the Commission makes rules, it is making laws which will govern all businesses in interstate commerce. There are two general ways you can have something to say in this process: One is to propose a rule, through a petition for rule making; the other is to express your opinions on a rule which the FTC is considering.

Submitting a petition for rule making is usually harder than just commenting on a proposed rule, because you are doing some of the Commission's work for it. The first step is to focus on a particular industry-wide deceptive practice. If there already is a law prohibiting this practice, especially if it is in the form of a specific trade regulation, the way to proceed is through an application for complaint, already described. If the practice is not specifically prohibited, consider submitting a rule making petition. But don't use this action against a lone offender. If a furniture dealer in your town uses deceptive payment books to induce unintentional defaults by credit customers, and then makes quick repossessions, he may be subject to a complaint proceeding. But if many credit merchants are doing it, trade regulation rule is the appropriate approach.

So you start with a problem—a practice being used by many companies throughout the industry, which involves interstate commerce. The first step is field research, careful accumulation and documentation of examples of the abuse. The petition in Appendix 5-B (p. 134) was directed at unsubstantiated claims made by advertisers, and the basic research involved weeks of monitoring television commercials and writing letters to advertisers in an attempt to determine what, if any, justification there was to back up their advertising claims. This step does not require any particular legal expertise, but it does take diligence and resourcefulness. The more specific examples you present, the more difficult it will be to pass off your petition as a gripe about isolated unethical acts.

The next step is legal research. This basically involves finding legal authorities of all sorts to support your proposed rule. The fundamental authority is usually the Commission's statutory mandate to act against deceptive practices, but that is only the first step. Other trade regulation rules directed at similar practices, enforcement proceedings against individual offenders for the same sort of deception which you have found to be industry-wide, and testimony before Congressional committees are just a few of the other possible sources. The regulations merely say that there must be "reasonable grounds" for the petition, and that is what you are providing. The field research should provide substantial evidence that the practice you are complaining about is both deceptive and widespread. The legal authorities are to support your argument that the Commission has a statutory duty to do something about the practice.

The FTC, under a recent Supreme Court decision, can find a practice unfair (and thus in violation of Section 5 of the FTC Act) if it is injurious to the public and violates any established body of public policy (whether or not found in another statute) [*Sperry Hutchinson Trading Co. v. Federal Trade Commission* (1971)].

The rule which you propose can be a simple prohibition of the practice, or it can require some affirmative action. The petition on unsubstantiated advertising claims is an example of the kind of affirmative action the Commission could require in order to stop a deceptive practice. It would simply require advertisers who make claims based on "scientific" studies to disclose those studies on request. The formal requirements for a rule making petition are not complicated. It must be in writing, it must include your version of the proposed rule, and it must be sent to the Office of the Secretary [16 C.F.R. 1.15]. But once the FTC gets the product of all your labors, it is not required to do anything with it. The Commission can approach rule making through hearings, conferences, economic studies, or a combination of all three [16 C.F.R. 1.16(a)], or it can refuse to act on a petition. In the case of the Nader-Cowan petition on advertising claims, the Commission did not treat it as a proposed rule. Instead, the FTC announced some months later that it would use its investigative powers to require selected industries to provide the Commission with the same sort of information to substantiate product claims which the rule proposed by the petition would have required.

COMMENTING ON PROPOSED RULES

If the Commission does decide to begin the process of rule making, either on the basis of a petition from the outside or a proposal initiated by the FTC staff, it must give notice to the public and provide an opportunity for them to express their opinions of the proposed rule. This presents another, and much simpler, method of participating in FTC rule making—commenting on proposed rules. All rule making proceedings are announced in the *Federal Register*, and press releases on proposed rules are available through the Office of Public Information. These describe the proposed rule, tell where to send comments and how long you have to send them, and give the time and place of any public hearings to be held on the proposal. Important rule making hearings are often held, sometimes in cities other than Washington. Public hearings have been given considerable emphasis by the Commission recently, and they provide a relatively simple and cheap method of making your views known.

One recent rule making proposal which was the subject of hearings in New York and Washington was a proposal to restrict the "holder in due course" legal doctrine that is a basic ingredient in many different consumer frauds. As it now stands, the doctrine makes it possible for a salesman to sell defective products or services which he can't perform and get away with your money. You buy a television set, or sign a health club contract, and put your name on a promissory note which obligates you to make periodic payments. The promissory note is then "sold" to a finance company or bank. After that the finance company or bank which bought the note has the right to your money when the payments are due, regardless of whether the television set works or the health club folds, if it was, in good faith, unaware of the seller's unlawful practices. You can sue the person with whom you made the original deal, if you can afford a lawsuit and if you can find him, but that doesn't affect your legal responsibility to keep making the payments to the company that bought the note, called a "holder in due course."

The proposed FTC rule would change this, so that you wouldn't have to pay unless you got what you bargained for in the first place. Responsibility for performance would go along with the note, instead of stopping when the note is sold to a bank or finance company. It would no longer be possible for the bank or finance company to demand payment from you for merchandise that didn't work or services which were never performed. The rule would give notice of this to potential "buyers" of a promissory note by requiring a statement on the face of it that legitimate consumer claims would still apply. The rule would also prohibit retailers from putting in notes clauses by which consumers waive this new right.

The Commission held hearings in Washington and New York, and published an article in the April 1971 issue of *Consumer Alert* (Vol. 1, No. 3) telling consumers how to take part in the hearings. The following excerpt from the article gives an idea of how to go about preparing for such a hearing.

How to "Speak Up" on the Rule

There are various ways that consumer organizations, individual consumers, businessmen, and others who are interested can participate in an FTC trade regulation rule proceeding: by testifying at a public hearing on the proposed rule, by filing a statement in advance of the hearing, by testifying *and* filing an advance statement, or by mailing in comments. In most cases, private consumers do not testify at Commission hearings but are represented by an appropriate advocate—a consumer organization, for instance, whose job it is to look after their best interests. The Commission takes all comments, statements, and testimony from the public into consideration before drafting and issuing the final version of a rule.

Originally, a single hearing was to be held on the Commission's proposed rule concerning consumer installment sales. This hearing was and still is scheduled for May 10, 11 at the FTC building in Washington, D.C. An additional hearing has been set, meanwhile, for June 7, 8 at FTC Offices in the Federal Building in New York City.

Anyone making arrangements to testify at the Washington hearing and/or filing a statement in advance should do so with the Assistant Director, Division of Industry Guidance, FTC, Washington, D.C. 20580 by May 5. Those filing statements for the New York hearing and/or planning to testify there should contact Mr. Myron Shapiro, FTC Offices, Federal Building, 25 Federal Plaza, New York City 10007 by June 1. Other hearings may be scheduled.

Written comments on the rule will be received by the Commission through June 1. They should be sent to the Assistant Director of Industry Guidance in Washington.

Only one copy of written comments or an advance statement need be submitted if it is two pages or less. If the text runs longer, 20 copies should be filed.

If and when you file comments, a statement, or a request to testify, give a brief description of yourself and why you are interested in the proceeding and—if you are going to testify—approximately how long your presentation will take. If you represent a business or organization, give its name, your title and function, and the knowledge or experience from which you speak.

For your reference in preparing to participate, copies of the full text of the proposed rule—"Preservation of Buyers' Claims and Defenses in Consumer Installment Sales"—are available from the FTC's Division of Legal and Public Records in Washington.

In testifying at a trade regulation rule hearing, you can use notes or an outline, speak extemporaneously, or read from a full text. (If you have filed an advance statement, you can just follow it if you wish.) Visual aids are welcome, provided the necessary props or equipment have been arranged for. Before speaking, you can obtain texts of other presentations to be given at the hearing. These are available at or near the hearing room. Glancing through them may bring to mind additional points you would like to make.

What to Say in Speaking Up

An FTC rule making proceeding is not an invitation to register consumer complaints. What the Commission *is* looking for is evidence to support or refute the need for the proposed rule, as well as sound recommendations for improving it.

Case histories recounting consumer problems and steps taken to solve them are especially helpful. A good case history on an installment note matter would include name and address of the person involved, a short description of his household, when the problem occurred, and the type of installment purchase. The description of what happened should answer questions like these:

- Was the consumer sufficiently knowledgeable—by education or experience—to understand what kind of obligation he signed and what the legal effects on him would be if it were sold to a third party?
- If he wasn't, when did he realize he had to pay someone besides the seller?
- Did he take the matter to court? If not, did he pay because he was told he had no legal alternative?
- Did the note the consumer signed contain any waivers of his rights to make claims against the seller?

Finally, of course, the Commission would want to know the outcome of any court action. Did the consumer have to pay off the note, and, if so, for what legal reasons?

Some states have passed laws similar to the proposed FTC rule. The Commission would like to know how successful these laws have been in curbing consumer problems and what hardships, if any, the legislation has caused retailers or consumers.

Data from individuals or organizations well-acquainted with these laws is extremely important. If possible, it should be supported by reliable studies and statistics and it should answer questions like these:

- Does the legislation forbid agreements causing the consumer to lose any legal rights he has to make a claim against the retailer or noteholder? Does it prevent them on all types of installment transactions or just some?
- Is credit more expensive or less expensive to obtain than it was before the legislation was passed?
- Is it more difficult now for retailers to sell their customers'

promissory notes to banks or finance companies? In other
words, are tighter standards being imposed on retailers by
financial institutions now that they share responsibility for
the product or service claims of the retailers?

Public participation in the current installment proceeding is not
only invited, it is essential. The FTC needs as much pertinent evidence as possible if it is to accomplish the purpose underlying its
rule making procedure to develop guide lines that are fair to business
while affording maximum protection to the nation's consumers.

The Office of Public Information also has prepared guidelines for presenting testimony. There are two things which might be added to the
FTC's guidelines. It is helpful to find out who else is going to appear;
you can learn this by getting the "Public Hearing Witness List" from the
Office of Public Information a few days before the hearing. Also, if you
want to add something to a statement you made at the hearing, you
have twenty-four hours afterward to write it down and get it into the
record [16 C.F.R. 1.16(c)].

After a hearing, all of the information submitted is collected, and the
presiding official reviews it, ponders for a while, and comes up with a
"final" rule which is sent to the Commissioners. It's not really final after
the Commission announces it, because it isn't effective for another
thirty days, and you can submit comments during that period if you
don't (or do) like the rule [16 C.F.R. 1.16(d)(e)]. As mentioned before,
the Commission isn't required to hold hearings, and a proposed rule may
just be published in the *Federal Register* with an invitation for comments. Significant proposed rules are also usually covered by press releases and in *Consumer Alert*, but it's still a good idea to scan the *Register* regularly. When comments are invited on proposed rules, prepare
them in the same way you would prepare oral testimony, but write
them down and send them to the Commission.

COMMENTING ON ADVISORY OPINIONS

It would be convenient for the average citizen if he could get a written opinion from the police department telling him whether something
he is thinking about doing is legal, but it doesn't work that way. However, it does work that way for businesses seeking the advice of the FTC
on whether something they plan to do will be considered legal by the
Commission. These "advisory opinions" haven't been available to the
public in the past, and not all of them are yet published. But those that

are made public present an opportunity for telling the FTC what you think of the advice it is handing out.

Advisory opinions will not be issued to businesses for something that is already being done; the practice must involve some future course of action, and must not be one which is being investigated for possible violation of some law, either by the FTC or by any other government agency. The business must submit a written request for the opinion, describing what it wants to do as completely as possible. The Commission may require a meeting between the applicant and the FTC staff to discuss the proposal, and it may also ask for more information [16 C.F.R. 1.2]. The FTC may or may not then provide a written advisory opinion [16 C.F.R. 1.3].

Some, but not all, of the opinions are made public. The Commission will only give public notice if it finds that it is in "the public interest" [16 C.F.R. 1.4(a)]. Premerger clearances, advisory opinions on the antitrust consequences of a merger between two companies, are a special kind of advisory opinion, and the oral communications about a premerger clearance must be summarized in writing. Public comment on these clearances is expressly invited [16 C.F.R. 1.4(b)].

But most advisory opinions involve mundane business questions such as proper labeling or the legality of a proposed promotional scheme. Some of these are made public through press releases from the Office of Public Information. Although public comment is not expressly invited on these advisory opinions, there is nothing to keep you from exercising your right to say what you think of them. Advisory opinions are not final rulings, and they can be modified if necessary [16 C.F.R. 1.3(b)].

So watch the press releases for announcements of recent advisory opinions, and let the Secretary of the Commission know what you think. This is one kind of public notice that doesn't go in the *Federal Register*, and the press releases are issued from a month to three months after the advisory opinion has been sent to the business, so act quickly when you see an opinion which you think should be challenged.

Conclusion

As federal regulatory agencies go, the FTC is relatively responsive to citizen access. Compared to the Commission of a few years ago, it is obviously improved. But it is important to remember that change at the FTC came about only after public criticism; left to its own devices, it probably would never have changed. The changes that have been made do not have a life of their own, and can easily degenerate into feeble gestures if they are not encouraged and prodded from the outside.

Working on the FTC can be as varied as your particular interests and as intensive as your resources will allow. Information about what the Commission is doing is available once an action is taken or proposed, and if you do not have a specific project already in mind, a way to start is to get on the mailing list and watch for a proposal or hearing that coincides with your interests or abilities. If you are in a city with a Consumer Advisory Board, you might start by talking to Board members, or perhaps even by getting on the Board yourself. Writing and submitting comments on proposed rules is one way to warm up for more intensive participation later, and can familiarize you with the research tools available.

The FTC's jurisdiction over unlawful trade practices in interstate commerce makes it the obvious agency to use in dealing with the more blatant commercial abuses. Those deceptive practices which have been emphasized in this chapter lend themselves particularly well to citizen action. But the Commission also has significant responsibilities in antitrust enforcement (which it shares with the Department of Justice) that are important in dealing with fundamental illegalities less obvious to the average consumer. This chapter's emphasis on the Commission's responsibilities to act against deceptive practices is not meant to deny the importance of vigorous antitrust enforcement, and the necessity for consumer action in that field. As the Commission's planning techniques are implemented, emphasis may shift heavily toward the antitrust area. The points of access which have been described are also available for citizen participation in antitrust enforcement proceedings, although the substantive legal issues involved in antitrust proceedings make it necessary to have some legal and economic expertise.

Although the FTC has changed its course, it needs continuing citizen surveillance and participation to stay on that course. One expression of this change came in a speech by Michael Vitale, formerly one of the FTC veterans with the least interest in an active Commission with consumer participation, and now Regional Director for the Washington, D.C., area field office.

> As long as there's a drive for the almighty dollar, there will be people competing for it who don't much care how they come by it. The day will never come when the consumer can afford to sit back and assume he's being taken care of. [*The Christian Science Monitor*, 11 February 1971]

Organization Chart of the Federal Trade Commission

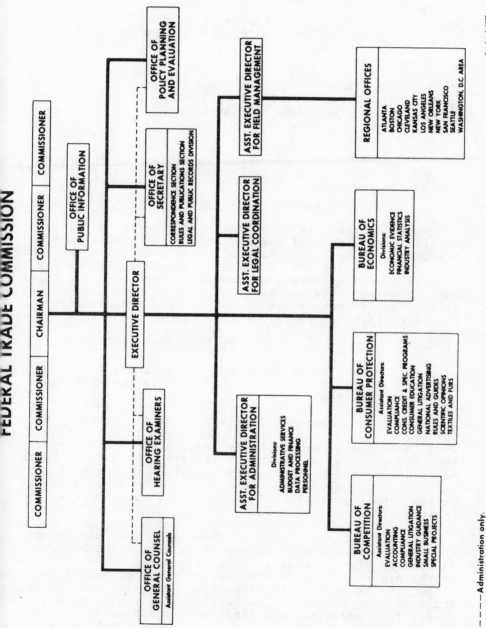

FEDERAL TRADE COMMISSION

October 1, 1971

COMMISSIONER · COMMISSIONER · COMMISSIONER · CHAIRMAN · COMMISSIONER · COMMISSIONER

OFFICE OF PUBLIC INFORMATION

OFFICE OF POLICY PLANNING AND EVALUATION

OFFICE OF SECRETARY
CORRESPONDENCE SECTION
RULES AND PUBLICATIONS SECTION
LEGAL AND PUBLIC RECORDS DIVISION

EXECUTIVE DIRECTOR

OFFICE OF HEARING EXAMINERS

OFFICE OF GENERAL COUNSEL
Assistant General Counsels

ASST. EXECUTIVE DIRECTOR FOR FIELD MANAGEMENT

ASST. EXECUTIVE DIRECTOR FOR LEGAL COORDINATION

ASST. EXECUTIVE DIRECTOR FOR ADMINISTRATION
Divisions:
ADMINISTRATIVE SERVICES
BUDGET AND FINANCE
DATA PROCESSING
PERSONNEL

REGIONAL OFFICES
ATLANTA
BOSTON
CHICAGO
CLEVELAND
KANSAS CITY
LOS ANGELES
NEW ORLEANS
NEW YORK
SAN FRANCISCO
SEATTLE
WASHINGTON, D.C. AREA

BUREAU OF ECONOMICS
Divisions:
ECONOMIC EVIDENCE
FINANCIAL STATISTICS
INDUSTRY ANALYSIS

BUREAU OF CONSUMER PROTECTION
Assistant Directors:
EVALUATION
COMPLIANCE
CONS. CREDIT & SPEC. PROGRAMS
CONSUMER EDUCATION
GENERAL LITIGATION
NATIONAL ADVERTISING
RULES AND GUIDES
SCIENTIFIC OPINIONS
TEXTILES AND FURS

BUREAU OF COMPETITION
Assistant Directors:
EVALUATION
ACCOUNTING
COMPLIANCE
GENERAL LITIGATION
INDUSTRY GUIDANCE
SMALL BUSINESS
SPECIAL PROJECTS

- - - - Administration only.

Nader-Adams Rule Making Petition

UNITED STATES OF AMERICA
BEFORE THE FEDERAL TRADE COMMISSION

RALPH NADER, AILEEN ADAMS, CONSUMER
ASSOCIATION OF THE DISTRICT OF COLUMBIA,
FEDERATION OF HOMEMAKERS, Petitioners

PETITION FOR TRADE REGULATION RULE PROCEEDING
AND ISSUANCE OF ENFORCEMENT POLICIES

Jurisdiction and Subject Matter

This petition is brought pursuant to the provisions of
Section 5, et seq., of the Federal Trade Commission Act, 15
U.S.C. 45, et seq., and Federal Trade Commission Procedures
and Rules of Practice, 16 C.F.R. 1.12, 1.15, requesting the
Commission to initiate a proceeding to promulgate a trade
regulation rule and to issue enforcement policies for the
elimination of unfair and deceptive acts and practices in
the advertising of goods and services in commerce.

The Petitioners

Petitioners Ralph Nader and Aileen Adams are consumers
who are exposed to misleading and deceptive advertising
claims in commerce.

Petitioner Consumer Association of the District of
Columbia has approximately 200 members. It has during the
last three years been actively involved in a variety of
consumer matters, including publicizing the sale of rotten
meats in supermarkets, testifying before the Federal Trade
Commission concerning the Association's study of Safeway
prices, and representing its members in complaints to
department and other kinds of stores.

Petitioner Federation of Homemakers is a nationwide
non-profit organization of consumers with 5,000 members in
46 states. The Federation is incorporated under the laws
of the District of Columbia, where it was organized in
1959. The Federation has long been active in protecting
the rights of consumers, especially with regard to baby
foods, food additives and other food substances.

Study of Advertising

Beginning in December, 1969, two researchers with the
Center for Study of Responsive Law (including Petitioner
Aileen Adams) tape-recorded and wrote descriptions of
hundreds of commercials telecast by the four commercial
stations in the District of Columbia. During the same
period they taped approximately 50 radio commercials and
clipped from newspapers and popular magazines those advertisements which seemed to make inflated statements or
claimed to be based upon clinical evidence. The researchers also requested and received from the Federal Trade
Commission copies of advertisements for tires, automobiles,
cereals, mouthwashes, toothpaste, and other products.

Letters were sent by Petitioners Ralph Nader and
Aileen Adams to 58 companies inquiring about 68 promotional claims. The inquiries, which were addressed to the
presidents of the companies, requested information that
would help to ascertain: (1) the extent to which data
substantiating advertising claims is available to the
public; (2) the willingness of corporations to clarify
vague promotional statements; (3) the availability to the
public of information about competitive brands to which
manufacturers allude in their advertisements; (4) the explanation why documentation was not provided (if it was
not); (5) the suggested recourse available to consumers
interested in substantiating advertising claims; and, (6)
the availability of sales figures and advertising expenditures.

To determine the availability and quality of clinical
evidence substantiating promotional claims, Petitioners
Adams and Nader asked companies to provide details and
conclusions of their test data. These companies included
Beecham Inc., which asserts that studies of a "major
dental clinic" show that its dentifrice, Macleans, gets
teeth "whitest" (App. pp. 32-34)[1]; Bristol-Meyers, which
assures viewers that "a study of hospital patients showed:
two Excedrin more effective in the relief of pain than
twice as many aspirin" (App. pp. 195-198); Lewis-Howe,

---

[1]The attached appendix reproduces copies of all in-
quiries sent to the companies by Petitioners Adams and
Nader and of all responses sent to them by the companies.
[Appendix not reprinted here.]

which states that "tests at a famous college" have shown
that Tums "neutralizes excess acid in a matter of seconds"
(App. pp. 157-159); and, the Block Drug Company, which
claims that "Nytol dissolves twice as fast as the other
leading sleep tablets" (App. pp. 35-37).

Other advertisements make claims for products without
explaining how the claimed qualities of the product produce the benefits suggested. For example, the Warner-
Lambert Company stresses Listerine's ability to kill "germs
by the millions" (App. pp. 51-55), and Richardson-Merrell
Inc. asserts that Lavoris "scrubs your breath clean" (App.
pp. 172-176). Both advertisements attempt to convince
consumers of the potency of the two products but do not
explain whether or how the killing of bacteria and the
"scrubbing" of one's breath substantially eliminates mouth
odor. Petitioners Adams and Nader sought information from
these companies clarifying these and other claims.

Petitioners Adams and Nader also sought information
concerning advertisements which included vague and unclear
statements. Several unclear statements involved the use
of dangling comparatives--implied comparisons for which the
basis of the comparison is not revealed. The Firestone
Tire and Rubber Company was asked to clarify its advertisement saying that its new "78" goes "thousands and thousands
more miles than you'd ever expect" (App. pp. 9-11).
Similarly, information was sought from the Dow Chemical
Company which assures the housewife that its oven cleaner
has "thirty-three percent more power" (App. pp. 99-102).
General Motors was asked to clarify its statement that the
Toronado's engine has "worry-free performance thousands of
miles longer" (App. pp. 12-13). Armour and Company, which
tells viewers that Armour bacon "gives you a little more
because it shrinks a little less," was asked to substantiate and clarify its claim (App. pp. 3-6).

These companies and others were asked to reveal
evidence supporting the implications of their state-
ments--for example, the number of miles the Firestone
Company was suggesting, how Dow had determined that its
oven cleaner had thirty-three percent more power, the
number of miles General Motors claims that the Toronado's
engine will last. Further, the manufacturers were asked
the basis of their comparisons--for example, General Motors
was asked to indicate what other automobile gave less
worry-free performance than Toronado, and Armour was asked
to supply the tests comparing its bacon with other brands.

Nine companies, whose advertisements implied extensive comparative product testing, were asked to provide
studies which compared their product to the products
alluded to in their claim, and to identify by brand name
the products to which their product was being compared.
The Clorox Company, for example, asserts that "Clorox gets
out stains that enzyme detergents leave in . . . and gets
out stains and dirt the presoaks leave in" (App. pp. 61-
68). The General Foods Corporation assures viewers that
its detergent Enzyme la France "whitens and brightens
better than bleach . . . and removes stains faster than
presoaks" (App. pp. 38-41). Procter and Gamble states that
"Biz soaks out a lot of stains you can't wash or bleach
out" (App. pp. 42-50). Ford, which claimed that Torino
was "the lowest priced hardtop in its class," was asked to
name both the automobiles considered to be in Torino's
class, and the average amount a consumer spends to buy a
brand new Torino with accessories (App. pp. 181-184).
The Standard Oil Company was asked to elaborate on its
statement that Esso Extra has "more smoothness ingredients
than most other gasolines" by naming the gasolines which
comprised "most other gasolines" and to provide data derived from comparative testing substantiating its claim
(App. pp. 133-135).

Letters were also sent to competing manufacturers
whose advertising promotes "product differentiation" by
attempting to distinguish physically identical items
through persuading buyers that one product is superior to
other brands. The over-the-counter analgesic industry
currently under investigation by the Commission spends
millions of dollars differentiating between nearly identical products. In an article entitled "A Comparative
Study of 5 Proprietary Analgesic Compounds" published in
the Journal of the American Medical Association (December
29, 1962), Dr. Thomas DeKornfeld and his associates
described their study of analgesics. After comparing the
pain-relieving ability of Anacin, Bayer, Bufferin, Excedrin, St. Joseph's Aspirin and a placebo, they concluded
that within the limits of generalization permitted by the
population studied, there are no important differences
among the compounds studied in rapidity of onset, degree,
or duration of analgesia. Confirming these findings in a
telephone conversation with Petitioner Adams on December
7, 1970, Dr. DeKornfeld stressed that "there was no statistically significant difference between the brands tested"--

that any small differences which appear are likely to be
due to chance and not due to any difference between the
efficacy of the compounds.[1]

Nevertheless, Bristol-Meyers spent approximately
$9,000,000 in 1969 promoting Excedrin, and is now asserting
that "two Excedrin [are] more effective in the relief of
pain than twice as many aspirin tablets" (App. pp. 195-
198). The Whitehall Laboratories Division of American
Home Products, which spent $25,000,000 in 1969 for Anacin
advertisements, implies that its tablet is the most effective of the analgesics because "two Anacin contain more
of the specific pain relievers doctors recommend most than
four of the other leading extra strength tablets" (App.
pp. 177-180). Sterling Drug spent more than $22,000,000
in 1969 trying to convince the public of Bayer's superior-
ity, "Bayer Aspirin is the best pain reliever on earth"
(App. pp. 166-171). Letters to these three companies,
which collectively spent more than $56,000,000 in 1969 to
distinguish between substantially homogeneous products,
asked them to provide their comparative studies of analgesic effects.

Petitioners Adams and Nader asked a number of
companies which manufacture products whose safety has been
questioned by reliable scientific data to supply evidence
that their product is safe for its intended use. Thus

---

[1]In a recent interview aired on the Nader Report
(December 2, 1970, 9:30 P.M., Channel 26), Dr. DeKornfeld
criticized Bristol-Meyers' use of a clinical study showing
Excedrin to be more effective than aspirin:

I would say that the claims made for
Excedrin show only one side of the story.
It shows the conclusions of one study and
completely omits any mention of the fact
that other studies have not been able to
show this difference and it is quite possible that the repetition of the study on
which these present claims are based would
also be unable to show this difference or
certainly a difference of this magnitude.
And all conclusions drawn from single
studies have to be taken with a great deal
of caution and we can accept the results
as valid only if they are supported by
additional investigation.

Procter and Gamble, Colgate Palmolive and the General
Foods Company were all asked to provide their testing
data showing that detergents with enzymes are safe. Researchers have reported in leading British and American
medical journals that enzyme detergents cause allergic
reactions such as severe dermatitis and asthma. See,
e.g., Ducksbury, C. F. J., et al., "Contact Dermatitis
in Home Helps Following the Use of Enzyme Detergents,"
British Medical Journal, February 28, 1970, p. 537;
Lowell, Francis C., "Antigenic Dusts and Respiratory
Disease," The New England Journal of Medicine, October 30,
1969, p. 1012; Flindt, M. L. H., "Pulmonary Disease Due to
Inhalation of Derivatives of Bacillus Subtilis Containing
Proteolytic Enzyme," The Lancet, June 14, 1969, p. 1177.

Beecham Inc., makers of Macleans toothpaste, and the
Colgate-Palmolive Company, makers of Ultra Brite, were
asked to provide tests showing that their dentifrices with
abrasives do not harmfully wear away the teeth of some
users. The Wall Street Journal reported that two members
of Indiana's Department of Preventive Dentistry found that
new dentifrices with whiteners contain such strong abrasives that they may harmfully wear away the teeth of some
people. Sept. 30, 1968, p. 1. The Council on Dental
Therapeutics has found ("Abrasive Toothpastes," Washington
Post, December 1, 1970, p. B1):

> Cementum and dentin are much softer
> tissues and even more susceptible to
> loss due to abrasion. Ordinarily
> these tissues are protected by the
> enamel . . . but individuals with
> exposed cementum, dentin and the soft
> restorative materials may lose signi-
> ficant amounts of tooth substance . . .
> when the more abrasive dentifrices are
> used routinely.

A few letters were sent to companies asking them to
clarify advertising testimonials by providing evidence
that one man's experience is a common phenomena among
users. The Goodyear Tire and Rubber Company was asked to
provide such evidence to substantiate the claim by Mr.
Allen that "I've had Polyglas tires for approximately two
years, and I've had about 35,000 miles on them" (App. pp.
74-79). Procter and Gamble was asked to substantiate a

woman's claim that her daughter "fries practically grease free with Crisco Oil." The woman showed french fries that were fried in one cup of Crisco Oil and claimed that all of the grease "comes back except one tablespoon" (App. pp. 46-50).

The responses received by Petitioners Adams and Nader can be organized into ten categories:

(1) sixteen companies sent no response whatsoever (App. pp. 1-31);

(2) six companies refused to substantiate their claims to consumers contending it was sufficient to do so to the appropriate government agency (App. pp. 32-60);

(3) four answers included cursory descriptions of company tests rather than detailed scientific data (App. pp. 61-90);

(4) fifteen companies purported to clarify vague and misleading statements in their advertisements (App. pp. 91-145);

(5) eight letters contained personal assurances by company presidents or other representatives that promotional claims were truthful representations of product quality rather than providing the scientific data requested (App. pp. 146-180);

(6) one company response retracted an advertising claim (App. pp. 181-184);

(7) two companies offered to send representatives to discuss their advertising campaigns (one later retracted the offer by telephone) (App. pp. 185-188);

(8) one letter indicated future correspondence would be forthcoming (no subsequent correspondence was ever received) (App. pp. 189-191);

(9) one company completely refused to cooperate (App. pp. 192-194);

(10) three responses included clinical studies,
the value of which was dubious (App. pp.
195-203).

For example, James H. Howe, President of the Lewis-
Howe Company, wrote one of the eight letters giving
assurances that advertising was truthful. He replied to
a request for a copy of the test "at a famous college"
which showed Tums to neutralize excess acid in a "matter
of seconds" with the following remarks (App. pp. 157-159):

We want to assure you that we have avoided
"the use of exaggerated or unprovable claims"
in our advertising and have based all the
claims we have made on good evidence and
advice. In fact, we pride ourselves on the
high standards we adhere to in all aspects
of our business.

Mr. Howe not only omitted the requested scientific data,
but also failed to indicate his reason for not providing
it.

Similarly, David J. Fitzgibbons, President of the
Sterling Drug Company, sent no details or conclusions of
comparative analgesic studies to substantiate claims that
Bayer Aspirin "is the best pain reliever on earth."
Instead he replied (App. pp. 166-171):

Please be assured that we share your
concern with the importance of providing
the public as well as the medical profession with accurate and truthful
information in advertising. The policy
of our company is, and always has been,
the accomplishment of this goal.

When he was asked again in a second letter for scientific
data, his response was similarly evasive.

Alfred L. Plant, President of the Block Drug Company,
was asked to document advertisements for Nytol tablets and
Tegrin Medicated Shampoo. He explained his unwillingness
to provide the information by noting that advertising
undergoes rigorous scrutiny by the company's legal and
technical departments, advertising agencies, television

networks, radio, other media, and various governmental
agencies, and "none of these overseers would permit . . .
advertising claims which are exaggerated or unprovable"
(App. pp. 35-37).

The J. B. Williams Company, manufacturer of Geritol,
was asked twice to provide clinical evidence verifying
claims made for Proslim, a diet wafer. A magazine advertisement asserted that "average weight loss [with Proslim]
was nearly five pounds the very first week [and] doctors
report pounds and inches lost in 7 days." The Company was
requested to provide such information as the names of the
doctors reporting the success of Proslim, tests comparing
the weight loss of people taking Proslim (plus the prescribed diet) with the weight loss of subjects taking the
prescribed diet alone, and a full explanation of the test
from which the "five pound average loss" was based. To
discourage further questioning, Mr. Roger A. Schultz,
Vice President Law, replied in his second letter (App.
pp. 56-60):

> Your original letter contains requests
> for such detailed scientific and medical
> information as to indicate a substantial
> lack of confidence in our product and our
> company. We would like to suggest that
> you consult your physician and develop
> alternate methods of reducing your weight.

Three companies provided cursory descriptions of
their test procedures. The Ralston-Purina Company, for
example, was asked to describe in detail the test upon
which they based their claim that Meat Plus is "so good
dogs chose it six to one in a recent test over the leading
competitive variety." Mr. J. E. Corbin, Director of the
Purina Pet Care Center, sent the following reply (App.
pp. 80-87):

> That test was conducted, under my direction,
> in July, 1968, at the Purina Pet Care Center,
> Gray Summit, Missouri. In this test, in-
> volving a statistically projectable sample
> of dogs of various sizes, ages, and popular
> breeds, Purina Meat Plus Beef and Meat By-
> Products, the variety featured in our adver-
> tising was tested against Alpo Beef and Meat
> By-Products, the leading competitive variety,
> in accordance with standard testing procedures.
> The dogs demonstrated a six to one preference
> for Meat Plus.

Since Mr. Corbin's explanation lacked significant information, for example, the number of dogs that were tested and the circumstances under which the experiment was conducted, he was requested to provide more comprehensive information about the test. In his response, Mr. Corbin indicated that the research and techniques utilized in the test had to remain confidential.

The Ralston-Purina correspondence was sent to Robert E. Hunsicker, the President of the Allen Products Company, which produces Alpo Beef. He was asked if he believed the testing procedure of his competitor to be a reliable method to determine the preference of dogs for food. Mr. James G. Schmoyer, Vice President for Research Quality Control, replied, "It is Allen Products Company's policy not to engage in disputes with our competitors" (App. pp. 88-90).

Other manufacturers, like R. B. Shetterly, President of the Clorox Company, were asked to comment on the claims of competitors which seemed to conflict with their advertisements. Responding as did the others, Mr. Shetterly indicated that the policy of his company was "not to comment on copy claims of other manufacturers" (App. pp. 61-68).

Of the nine companies asked to identify the specific products compared to their product in advertisements, only Ralston-Purina would even mention the other brand name (App. pp. 80-90).

Howard J. Morgens, President of Procter and Gamble, stated that the kind of information requested--such as scientific substantiation of advertising claims and test data concerning product safety--was only supplied to authorized government agencies (App. pp. 42-50):

> Since the [Federal Trade] Commission has been assigned by statute the responsibility for reviewing our advertising claims, we feel that our obligation in this respect must be to continue to respond fully and cooperatively to the designated agency of government, and that any duplication of this effort with private groups could hardly be expected to provide additional protection of the public interest.

Similarly, A. E. Larkin, Jr., President of General Foods
Corporation, said that he "would have no reluctance to
supply testing information to any duly authorized regulatory body with its attendant administrative safeguards"
(App. pp. 38-41). He would not, however, supply the
details and conclusions of tests to the public.

Advertising Claims Which Are Misleading or Unsubstantiated by Reliable Evidence Constitute a Deceptive and Unfair Trade Practice

The American consumer is faced with a virtually hope-
less situation. He buys hundreds of different items in
hundreds of different lines of products. In making each
purchase he must decide which products to buy and then
what brand to buy. He must distinguish between brands
which on their face seem completely or substantially
identical--like gasoline, or paint, or milk--or whose
differences are too complex for laymen to readily under-
stand--like the internal workings of an automobile engine.
He must weigh price, effectiveness, taste, warranty, ease
of repair, consistency with or contribution to health, and
many other factors. Advertising is supposed to supply the
consumer with the vital information he needs to choose
between competing products and brands.

Advertising should also provide a means by which
businessmen are encouraged to compete. The company which
provides the best product at the lowest price can truth-
fully describe its products to consumers and thereby
increase its volume and profits. Advertising, it is therefore said, is vital to a free enterprise system based upon
vigorous, effective competition.

In fact, however, as Americans know from their experience as consumers, and as the study of petitioners
Adams and Nader confirmed, advertising does not foster
effective competition. Advertisers do not supply the
consumer with information which would allow him to make
an intelligent choice between products and low prices.
Advertisers make vague claims which give consumers no real
understanding of the products' performance, invoke
clinical tests with little scientific basis to substantiate claims, and otherwise deliberately mislead and con-
fuse the consumer.

At the very least, manufacturers do not provide facts needed for the consumer to make informed market choices. Instead, many buyers are ingeniously induced by misleading claims to buy an inferior product or a similar product at a higher price. Competition in the marketplace is rapidly being reduced to competition in advertising as businessmen spend more and more money on inflated or deceptive advertising claims rather than improving products or lowering prices. The result is both the exploitation of the consumer and the undermining of serious, meaningful competition.

The Federal Trade Commission has the authority to compel advertisers to provide more information to the public. Under the Federal Trade Commission Act, an advertisement is deceptive if it creates in the mind of the average consumer an impression which has the capacity to be misleading. A violation exists when there is a capacity to deceive (Montgomery Ward & Co. v. FTC, 379 F.2d 666, 669 (C.A. 7, 1967); Feil v. FTC, 285 F.2d 285 F.2d 879, 896 (C.A. 9, 1960); Gulf Oil Corporation v. FTC, 150 F.2d 106, 109 (C.A. 5, 1945)), measured by the "net impression it [the advertisement] is likely to make on the general populace" (National Bakers Services, Inc. v. FTC, 329 F.2d 365, 367 (C.A. 7, 1967))]. As stated in National Bakers Services, supra, at 367, "Deception may be by innuendo rather than outright false statements." Statements susceptible of both a misleading and a truthful interpretation will be construed against the advertiser. Country Tweeds, Inc. v. FTC, 326 F.2d, 144, 148 (C.A. 2, 1964); Murray Space Shoe Corp. v. FTC, 304 F.2d 270, 272 (C.A. 2, 1962).

The research of petitioners Adams and Nader documents that manufacturers frequently make advertising claims which are either unsubstantiated or for which the manufacturers refuse to make available, upon request, the substantiating evidence they allegedly possess. The resulting deception takes several forms:

1. The most obviously deceptive practice occurs when a manufacturer implies that a claim made in advertising its product is directly substantiated by adequate clinical testing but no such evidence exists.

2. Advertising which seeks to promote product differentiation between products which are substantially identical is false and deceptive unless the manufacturer

can validate that advertising through clinical proof available to full public scrutiny. An example of such an advertising claim is the Sterling Drug Company's claim that "Bayer Aspirin is the best pain reliever on earth." Clinical evidence refutes that assertion.

3. When a manufacturer makes a claim for a product without explaining how the asserted quality of the product produces the benefits suggested by the advertisement, that claim is deceptive unless the manufacturer can demonstrate the relationship between the asserted qualities of the product and the benefits suggested to result from them. The advertising of Richardson-Merrell Inc., which asserts that its Lavoris mouthwash "scrubs your breath clean" is an example of this deception.

4. Since a testimonial statement implies that all buyers of that product can expect the same performance characteristics under the same conditions of use as the testifier or under normal conditions of use if the conditions are unstated in the commercial, use of a testimonial is deceptive unless adequate scientific or statistical data shows that general use of the product under the same conditions or under normal conditions will produce similar results. The results and methodology of the statistical surveys must be made available to public inspection. A testimonial is deceptive if, for example, the experience of the woman who claims that her daughter "fries practically grease free with Crisco Oil" and that all of the grease "comes back except one tablespoon" when she French fries potatoes cannot be duplicated by the average housewife preparing French fries with Crisco Oil. Similarly a commercial like the one for the Schick Chromium Blade in which 17 people get a close, comfortable shave with one blade is deceptive if the result in the commercial differs materially from the experience of buyers using the blade 17 times at normal intervals, and that fact is not disclosed. The Commission has recently indicated its concern over such advertising claims by challenging endorsements by well-known racing car drivers in advertisements for toy racing car and track sets. In the Matter of Mattel, Inc., File No. 702 3426, Determination to Issue Complaint, November 25, 1970; In the Matter of Topper Corp., File No. 712 3021, Determination to Issue Complaint, November 25, 1970.

5. When an advertiser uses a "dangling comparative" --"33% more power," "lasts thousands of miles longer"-- it is impossible to determine what is being compared, and it is impossible to determine whether that comparison is substantiated by reliable evidence. The Commission has recently instituted proceedings seeking relief against this deception. In the Matter of the Firestone Tire & Rubber Co., File No. 682-3381, Determination to Issue Complaint, December 1, 1969.

6. Manufacturers do not supply consumers with the names of those products with which they have compared their product by using such phrases as "the leading brand" or "other brands." Therefore, consumers can neither evaluate the differences between unknown brand name products and the one being promoted nor evaluate the promotional claims being made. The Commission has recognized that such advertising claims are unfair and deceptive unless the manufacturer has substantiated them with comparative product testing, and is willing to identify the products involved in that comparison. In the Matter of American Brands, Inc., Docket No. 8799, Determination to Issue Complaint, September 29, 1969.

The failure to substantiate advertising claims with reliable information is clearly a violation of the Federal Trade Commission Act. As noted by Assistant to the Director of the Bureau of Deceptive Practices, Leslie V. Dix, speaking before the Broadcast Advertising Producers Society of America, on March 9, 1970:

> When [a manufacturer] advertises his
> claims for the efficacy of the product,
> he is clearly conveying to the viewer
> that the claims are supported by
> laboratory tests. When such supportive
> evidence is lacking the public is de-
> ceived. This constitutes a violation
> of the FTC Act . . . . Needless to add,
> the Federal Trade Commission Act con-
> tains the authority for the Commission
> to order proofs of such advertising
> claims.

The Commission has repeatedly taken the position that the Act is violated if the businessman fails to substantiate his advertising claims before making such representations to the public, with adequate, thorough and well-

controlled scientific tests, the results of which are in
writing and available for inspection. See In the Matter
of Bishop Industries, Inc., Docket No. C-1724, Decision
and Order, April 10, 1970; In the Matter of Charles
Pfizer and Co., File No. 702-3131, Determination to Issue
Complaint, April 16, 1970; In the Matter of Firestone Tire
& Rubber Co., Determination to Issue Complaint, April 16,
1970; In the Matter of Firestone Tire and Rubber Co.,
File No. 682-3381, Determination to Issue Complaint,
December 1, 1969; Proposed Guides for Advertising Over-
the-Counter Drugs, Guide 3(e).

In In the Matter of Heinz W. Kirchner, 63 FTC 1282
(1963), affirmed 337 F.2d 751 (C.A. 9, 1964), the Commission expressly stated:

> . . . an advertiser is under a duty,
> before he makes any representations
> which, if false, could cause injury
> to the health or personal safety of
> the user of the advertised product, to
> make reasonable inquiry into the truth
> or falsity of the representation. He
> should have in his possession such
> information as would satisfy a rea-
> sonable and prudent businessman,
> acting in good faith, that such rep-
> resentation was true. To make a
> representation of this sort, without
> such minimum substantiation, is to
> demonstrate a reckless disregard for
> human health and safety, and is clearly
> an unfair and deceptive practice. That
> this is so is evident from basic prin-
> ciples governing the law of false and
> misleading representations. [emphasis added]

Where there is no danger of personal injury, the injury to
the consumer is, of course, less severe. But the consumer
is also entitled to protection against deception which
harms or has the capacity to harm him financially.

Even when the advertiser does not make express claims
concerning a product, there are situations where the advertiser must have adequate scientific data available. By
placing a product on the market, a manufacturer impliedly
represents that its normal intended use does not pose a
health or safety hazard to the individual user or an

environmental, health, safety, or other hazard to the
public in general. The manufacturer must, therefore, have
in his possession information that would support a reasonable determination that his implied representation is true.
Beyond this, however, when a substantial controversy exists
as to the safety or other harm to the individual user of a
product in its normal intended use (for example, enzyme
detergents), or as to the safety or other harm to the general public indirectly affected by the product's use (for
example, leaded gasoline), the continued advertising and
sale of the product, which implies that it is not a hazard,
is itself an unfair and deceptive trade practice until the
product can be demonstrated to be nonhazardous. At the
very least, the manufacturer should be required to warn
the consumer of the possible danger to himself or to the
public at large inherent in the product's use. See J. B.
Williams v. FTC, 381 F.2d 884 (C.A. 6, 1967); Ward Laboratories, Inc. v. FTC, 276 F.2d 952 (C.A. 2, 1960); Keele
Hair and Scalp Specialists, Inc. v. FTC, 275 F.2d 18 (C.A.
5, 1960); Kerran v. FTC, 265 F.2d 246 (C.A. 10, 1959).
See also Helene Curtis Industries, Inc. v. Pruitt, 385
F.2d 841 (C.A. 5, 1967); Petition for Trade Regulation Rule
Proceeding Concerning Enzyme Detergents, File No. 692-
3393, filed with the F.T.C., June 12, 1970.

Advertisers should not only have scientific data
supporting their explicit and implicit claims, but this
data should be available to the public. The research of
petitioners Adams and Nader indicates that manufacturers
almost invariably refuse to provide such information to
consumers and frequently attempt to justify their refusal
by asserting that their only obligation is to provide such
information to the Federal Trade Commission. In his letter
to Mr. Ralph Nader of March 16, 1970, former Chairman
Caspar Weinberger stated: "it is not the intention of the
Commission in instituting an investigation concerning any
advertising claim, that the company being investigated
should on that account consider itself relieved of an
obligation to respond to consumer inquiries about the claim
in question." It follows, a fortiori, that advertisers
may not hide behind the FTC in refusing to provide information when no FTC investigation has even started.

Proposed Federal Trade Commission Action

As the study of petitioners Adams and Nader demonstrates, much of the advertising in the media is blatantly or subtly deceptive. The Commission, working on a

case-by-case basis, has not been able to deal effectively
with this continuing and serious problem. If the Commission is to enforce the Act effectively against advertisers who make misleading or vague claims or claims which
are not supported by substantiating evidence, it is
essential that the Commission develop new enforcement
procedures.

Petitioners submit that the Commission should promulgate a trade regulation rule requiring national
advertisers to make their scientific information available, at the time they make their claims, to the Commission
and, through the Commission, to the public; and requiring
all other advertisers to make their scientific information
available to either the Commission or the public.

The study of petitioners Adams and Nader makes clear
that most advertisers will not voluntarily disclose to the
public the information which purports to support their
claims. Such information will only be disclosed if legally
required. We submit that the Commission should adopt such
a requirement in order to assist consumers in obtaining the
information necessary for informed, rational choices in
today's market. The disclosure of the information requested would further assist consumers and consumer organizations in obtaining information needed to register informed complaints with the Commission, helping it to enforce the Federal Trade Commission Act to deter dishonest
advertisers.

There are several reasons for this proposal:

First, public disclosure can directly assist consumers in making intelligent choices in buying goods.
Individuals and consumer organizations will have the
opportunity to obtain important information they could not
otherwise acquire. They will then be in a position to
publicize this information in order to assist the entire
public.

Second, a requirement making this information available
to the public would also promote competition by helping
to protect honest businessmen from unfair methods of
competition. Manufacturers who make the effort to test
their products adequately prior to making advertising
claims are presently placed at an unfair competitive

disadvantage since unscrupulous advertisers are able to hide the basis for their claims. All advertisers are encouraged to exaggerate the claims they make because of the unlikelihood that any legal or economic consequences will attach. The likelihood of public disclosure that claims made by advertisers are not supported by reliable evidence would have a significant deterrent effect when combined with the increased possibility of legal action by the Commission or by consumer groups.

Third, public disclosure is necessary if the Commission is to carry out its responsibilities effectively to prevent deceptive and unfair advertising. As the Commission is well aware, it does not have the necessary manpower or sufficient funds to police adequately all the claims made by advertisers for their products. If data is made available to the public, interested consumers and consumer organizations will be in a far better position to aid the Commission in enforcing the Act.

The Commission clearly has the authority to compel such public disclosure. Under Section 6(g) of the Act, 15 U.S.C. 46(g), the Commission has the power to issue trade regulation rules designed to prevent deceptive and unfair practices. The exercise of this power to supplement enforcement under Section 5(b) has been explicitly upheld by the courts. See United States v. Morton Salt Co., 338 U.S. 632 (1950); Hunt Foods & Industries, Inc. v. FTC, 286 F.2d 803 (C.A. 9, 1961); Prima Products, Inc. v. FTC, 209 F.2d 405 (C.A. 2, 1954). As we have seen above, misleading, vague and unsubstantiated advertising claims constitute deceptive and unfair trade practices. Under Section 6(g), the Commission may properly issue a trade regulation rule requiring public disclosure of information purportedly supporting advertising claims as a means of enforcing the Act's proscription of such practices.

Furthermore, the Commission has the authority to require public disclosure on the ground that failure to provide information to substantiate claims at the request of consumers is itself an unfair trade practice in violation of Section 5 of the Act. When an advertiser makes a claim and refuses to make public supporting information, this is unfair to the consumer who is seeking more facts. The only remedy for this unfairness is public disclosure. See Atlantic Refining Co. v. FTC, 381 U.S. 357 (1965);

FTC v. Colgate Palmolive Co., 380 U.S. 374 (1965); FTC
v. Cement Institute, 333 U.S. 683 (1948); Jacobs Seigel
Co. v. FTC, 327 U.S. 608 (1946). See also FTC Trade
Regulations Rule for the Prevention of Unfair or Deceptive Advertising and Labeling of Cigarettes in Relation
to Health Hazards of Smoking, Accompanying Statement of
Basis and Purpose of Rule, June 1964.

Regulations requiring manufacturers to make information supporting their advertising claims available to the
public should be designed to impose the minimum burden on
honest businessmen. We therefore suggest that national
advertisers be required to submit information supporting
their claims to the Commission where it would be available
for inspection or reproduction, at a reasonable fee, to
the public. Other businessmen should be allowed either to
provide, within a reasonable period of time, the substantiating evidence upon request from any member of the
public or, if the number of requests becomes too numerous,
to supply the information to the Commission which would
make it available to the public. This requirement would
not impose on businessmen an obligation to conduct any
additional tests or do anything else to substantiate their
claims beyond that which is already required under present
law--the requirement to be truthful and not to deceive or
mislead consumers.

Finally, we urge that the Commission immediately
adopt, under its powers under Section 5 of the Act,
several enforcement policies concerning --

1) dangling comparatives;

2) testimonials in which individuals
    make representations about a product
    which are not accurate when the pro-
    duct is normally used in the manner
    stated, or are not accurate under
    normal use.

These policies will make clear to businessmen what should
be, and is, clear under existing law--that such advertising
is deceptive and unfair.

For the reasons outlined above, petitioners urge that
the Commission:

A. Trade Regulation Rule

1. Adopt the following procedures:

    (a) Hold hearings on the proposed regula-
         tion within 60 days;

    (b) Permit petitioners to participate in
         these hearings with all the rights of
         formal parties.

2. Issue, on the basis of these procedures, the
    following trade regulation rule --

    (a) It is a deceptive and unfair trade
         practice for any person, partnership,
         or corporation, its officers, agents,
         representatives, and employees, directly
         or through any corporate or other device,
         in connection with the advertising of
         any consumer products on two or more
         television or radio stations or in two
         or more newspapers separated by more than
         100 miles or in any magazine or other
         written publication, ten percent of whose
         distribution is in more than three
         states --

         (i) to make, directly or by implica-
         tion, any statement or representation
         regarding the safety, performance, or
         effectiveness of such products or com-
         paring such product to other products
         (including through testimonials) unless
         such statement or representation has been
         fully and completely substantiated by
         competent scientific tests, or

         (ii) to advertise any product con-
         cerning which there is any reasonable
         doubt that it poses a health or safety
         hazard to the individual user or an
         environmental, health, safety or other
         hazard to the general public unless com-
         petent scientific tests show that no real
         hazard exists;

and these tests (1) are in writing, and (2) are sent in advance of advertising to the Federal Trade Commission where they will be made available to the public.

(b)   It is a deceptive and unfair trade practice for any person, partnership, or corporation, its officers, agents, representatives and employees, directly or through any corporate or other device, in connection with any advertising not within subsection (a) above or any offering for sale, sale, or distribution of any consumer products --

(i)   to make directly or by implication, any statement or representation regarding the safety performance or effectiveness of such products or comparing such product to other products (including through testimonials) unless such statement or representation has been fully and completely substantiated by competent scientific tests, or

(ii) to advertise any product concerning which there is any reasonable doubt that it poses a health or safety hazard to the individual user or an environmental, health, safety or other hazard to the general public unless competent scientific tests show that no such hazard exists;

and these tests and surveys (1) are in writing, and (2) are made available to any member of the public within a reasonable period of time upon request or are submitted to the Federal Trade Commission where they will be made available to the public.

B.   Enforcement Policy

Adopt as soon as possible the following enforcement policies:

The Federal Trade Commission deems it a deceptive and unfair trade practice for any person, partnership, or corporation, its officers, agents, representatives, and employees, directly or through any corporate or other device, in connection with the advertising, offering for sale, sale, or distribution of any consumer products:

a. To make any comparison unless the basis of the comparison is clearly and specifically stated in the advertising, unless the company makes available to both the FTC and consumers the exact other products compared, and unless the comparison is based on identical conditions of use;

b. To make use of any individual's testimonial statement if such testimonial makes, directly or by implication, any statement or representation regarding the safety, performance or effectiveness of such products as used by the individual or anyone else unless adequate scientific data shows:

    (i) if the conditions of use are stated, the general use of the product under the same conditions will produce similar results; or

    (ii) if the conditions of use are not stated, general use of the product under normal conditions will produce similar results.

All these actions are clearly illegal under Section 5 of the Federal Trade Commission Act. The Commission intends to enforce the Act vigorously, and particularly with regard to national advertisers, against these deceptive and unfair practices.

Respectfully submitted,

Of Counsel:

Bruce J. Terris
2008 Hillyer Place, N.W.
Washington, D.C.

Attorney for Petitioners

Geoffrey Cowan
2008 Hillyer Place, N.W.
Washington, D.C.

Amended Motion of SOUP to Intervene and Proceed *in forma pauperis*

UNITED STATES OF AMERICA
BEFORE THE FEDERAL TRADE COMMISSION

In the Matter of	)
	)
THE FIRESTONE TIRE & RUBBER COMPANY,	) DOCKET NO. 8818
a corporation.	)

AMENDED MOTION OF SOUP, INC. TO INTERVENE,
FOR LEAVE TO PROCEED IN FORMA PAUPERIS,
AND FOR DISCLOSURE

Students Opposing Unfair Practices, Inc., a corporation (hereinafter "SOUP, Inc."), respectfully moves the Hearing Examiner to intervene in this proceeding and to participate as a full party, with all the rights of parties. In addition, SOUP, Inc. respectfully requests that it be granted leave to proceed in forma pauperis, that it be given disclosure of certain specified documents in the Commission's files, and that it be afforded a reasonable opportunity to reply to the points raised in any answers opposing this motion.

The major substantive difference between this motion and the original motion of SOUP, Inc. to intervene is that this motion sets out in concrete and specific detail the reasons why SOUP, Inc. has good cause to intervene in this proceeding.[1]

---

[1]The original motion of SOUP, Inc. to intervene, filed July 29, 1970, was "denied in all respects" on the sole ground that it "failed to show good cause" in support thereof. Order of August 21, 1970.

Complaint counsel had argued in his answer that our showing of good cause was "generalized and unsupported." Similarly, Respondent had argued in its answer that our good cause showing was "imprecise and speculative." The order denying the original motion of SOUP, Inc. to intervene did not set out any basis or reasons why "good cause" had not been shown.

The remainder of this motion is divided into five parts, as follows: (1) This amended motion to intervene is properly before the Hearing Examiner; (2) SOUP, Inc. has good cause within the meaning of Section 5(b) of the FTC Act to intervene in this proceeding; (3) SOUP, Inc. should be granted leave to proceed in forma pauperis; (4) SOUP, Inc. has a right to disclosure and reproduction of certain documents and materials in the Commission's files; and (5) SOUP, Inc. should be granted a reasonable opportunity to reply to the points raised in any answer opposing this motion.

I.   This Amended Motion to Intervene is
     Properly Before the Hearing Examiner.

Section 3.15(a) of the Commission's Rules of Practice for Adjudicative Proceedings provides that the Hearing Examiner, in his sound discretion, may receive amended pleadings. That section, in pertinent part, states:

> "If and whenever determination of
> a controversy on the merits will
> be facilitated thereby, the hearing
> examiner may, upon such conditions
> as are necessary to avoid prejudicing
> the public interest and the rights of
> parties, allow appropriate amendments
> to pleadings. . . ."

This creates a two-part test for the acceptability of amended pleadings: (A) whether this motion is an "appropriate" amendment, and (B) whether the intervention of SOUP, Inc. will facilitate determination of this controversy on the merits. If both of these parts are satisfied, the Hearing Examiner should grant SOUP, Inc. intervention taking a third point into consideration: (C) whether this motion will prejudice the rights of the parties or the public interest.

A.   This Motion is an "Appropriate" Amendment. This motion is substantially similar to the original motion of SOUP, Inc. to intervene. The major substantive difference between the two motions is that this one sets out in concrete and specific detail the reasons why SOUP, Inc. has good cause to intervene. The original motion was "denied in all respects" by the Hearing Examiner on the sole ground that it "failed to show good cause" in support thereof. The order denying our original motion did not set out the "reasons or basis" why SOUP, Inc. had not shown good cause, as seemingly required by Section 8(c)(A)

of the Administrative Procedure Act (5 U.S.C. § 557(c)(A)).
Since this motion addresses and cures the single technical
defect of our previous motion, we cannot conceive of a
more "appropriate" amended pleading. In Part II, immediately below, this motion sets out the specific reasons
why the proposed order is inadequate to protect the public
interest, the specific additional clauses the final order
must contain to adequately protect the public interest,
and the precise evidence SOUP, Inc. will introduce to
justify inclusion of these additional clauses. At this
point, we reasonably believe that there will be no overlapping of our evidence with the evidence submitted by
complaint counsel, in the event that Respondent contests
the allegations of the complaint.

  B. The Intervention of SOUP, Inc. will Facilitate
Determination of this Controversy on the Merits. SOUP,
Inc. recognizes that its intervention will "complicate"
these proceedings. If Respondent contests the complaint,
and a hearing takes place, the participation of SOUP, Inc.
will prolong the hearing. Similarly, if Respondent
elects not to contest the complaint, the substantial
factual issues SOUP, Inc. raises in this motion require a
limited hearing. Therefore, if the term "facilitates" in
Section 3.15(a) is synonomous with "shortens," SOUP, Inc.
cannot intervene. However, a determination on the merits
is not facilitated if an order is entered which is inadequate to protect the public interest simply to shorten
and simplify the proceeding. The Hearing Examiner has a
duty to consider evidence and proposed clauses which relate directly to the adequacy of this order to protect
the health and safety of the public (see below). In
addition, a number of factors indicate that our participation will not unduly burden this proceeding: We have
specified the exact evidence we desire to introduce; we
have specified the exact additional clauses in the final
order which this evidence requires; the Hearing Examiner
may regulate our participation at the pre-hearing conference; and, finally, repetitious evidence may be curtailed by the Hearing Examiner during the hearing. When
these factors, together with the substantial questions of
fact, law, policy, and discretion we raise are balanced
against the added complexity our intervention will create,
surely our participation will facilitate the determination
of this controversy on the merits.

  C. This Motion Does Not Prejudice the Rights of the
Parties or the Public Interest.

  The original motion of SOUP, Inc. to intervene did
not prejudice the rights of the parties or of the public

interest. This amendment is substantially identical with
our previous motion, the main difference is that this
motion goes into greater detail. This motion, therefore,
could not prejudice the parties or the public interest.
If anything, this motion is less prejudicial because all
parties know exactly what the scope of our participation
will be, whereas our previous motion was somewhat generalized. Furthermore, how can the public interest be prejudiced by our intervention when our participation is to
insure that the resultant order adequately protects that
same public interest?

It might be argued that the "lateness" of this motion
is prejudicial. This is clearly erroneous: This motion
was filed within a reasonable time after the denial of our
original motion, and all parties have a reasonable time
prior to the hearing in which to reply. Respondent has
not even filed his answers to the complaint as yet.[2]

II. SOUP, Inc. has "Good Cause" Within the
     Meaning of Section 5(b) of the FTC Act
     to Intervene in this Proceeding.

Section 5(b) of the Federal Trade Commission Act, 15
U.S.C. § 45(b), provides in pertinent part:

> "Any person, partnership, or
> corporation may make application,
> and upon good cause shown may be
> allowed by the Commission to
> intervene and appear in said pro-
> ceeding by counsel or in person."

Section 3.14 of the Commission's Rules of Practice
of Adjudicative Proceedings, 16 CFR § 3.14, sets forth
the procedure by which a prospective intervenor can make
his showing of good cause:

> "Any individual, partnership, un-
> incorporated association, or cor-
> poration desiring to intervene in
> an adjudicative proceeding shall
> make written application in the
> form of a motion setting forth
> the basis therefor."

---

[2]Complaint counsel, in his answers to our original
motion, even suggested that our motion was "premature."
Answer filed August 13, 1970, at page 2.

As "good cause" to intervene in this proceeding, SOUP,
Inc. sets forth the following:

A. This is an aggravated case directly involving the
public health and safety. A substantial number of consumers who purchased Respondent's tires under the erroneous and mistaken belief that Respondent's tires are safer
than they in fact are, still retain this belief while
these tires remain on their vehicles. These deceived
purchasers are a serious danger to the health and safety
of other drivers, passengers, pedestrians, and themselves.
If this proposition is true, that as a factual matter many
deceived consumers of Firestone tires do rely on the deceptive statements in the advertisements after purchasing
Firestone tires, then one of the direct residual effects
of Respondent's deceptions has been, and will continue to
be until said deceptions are counteracted, collision-
caused property damage, personal injury, and loss of life.
SOUP, Inc. desires to introduce evidence, as set forth
below, showing these residual effects of Respondent's
deception.

Any additional time and complexity caused by SOUP,
Inc.'s intervention in this proceeding is outweighed by
the duty of the Federal Trade Commission to insure that
the health and safety of drivers, passengers and pedestrians are adequately protected by the cease-and-desist
order in this case. The proposed final order contains no
provisions to counteract the above residual effects of
Respondent's deceptive advertisements. Suggested below
are a number of clauses which, when included in the final
cease-and-desist order, would adequately protect the
public interest.

B. SOUP, Inc. is a responsible representative of
the consumers' interests. It is a non-profit organization, incorporated in the District of Columbia, whose main
purpose is to assist the Federal Trade Commission in
vigorously and creatively stopping and counteracting misleading and deceptive acts or practices. SOUP, Inc. is
composed of law students dedicated to advancing the public
interest, and no member of SOUP, Inc. has any private or
commercial interest in this proceeding. In addition, our
past involvement insures that we will responsibly and
adequately represent the consumers' interests. In a
previous proceeding, Commissioner Jones graciously said
that our participation presented "a graphic illustration
of the responsibility and high quality of the substantive
contribution which members of the public are in a position
to make to the work of federal agencies." In the Matter

of <u>Campbell Soup Company,</u> Dkt. No. C-1714, final order of May 25, 1970 (Separate statement).[3]

In addition, both Consumers Union and Consumers Federation of America have recognized SOUP, Inc. as a responsible consumer representative. See, <u>Campbell Soup</u>, <u>supra</u>, Brief submitted by Consumers Union on December 5, 1969; Consumer Federation of America's letter to former Chairman Dixon on December 4, 1969.

Respondent, in its answer to our original motion to intervene at page 5, stated:

> "SOUP's purported representation
> of consumers is unnecessary unless
> it is established that Complaint
> Counsel and the Commission are un-
> able or unwilling to discharge their
> acknowledged responsibility to
> consumers."

Complaint counsel seems to be suggesting a similar point when he states in this answer at page 3:

> "Good cause is not established by
> suggestions that . . . complaint
> counsel may not . . . adequately
> discharge his duty to protect the
> public interest."[4]

---

[3]Commissioner Jones has also stated that the right of citizens to directly intervene in Commission proceedings "is essential in order to ensure the responsiveness of the Commission to the problems of consumers as consumers see them and to make available to the Commission the viewpoints and ideas of consumers as to the types of remedies which should be directed and other like matters. Moreover, I am also convinced that consumers have a legal right to intervene in Commission proceedings and that in time, if the Commission does not act voluntarily, it will be directed by by the Court to grant intervention to consumers in proper cases." Paper delivered by Commissioner Jones before the Biennial World Conference of the INTERNATIONAL ORGANIZATION OF CONSUMER AFFAIRS in Baden/Vienna, Austria, released by the Commission on June 29, 1970, at pages 19-20.

[4]Complaint counsel also suggests that SOUP, Inc. should funnel any ideas we may have through complaint counsel's office. This is a reasonable alternative, but

(continued on following page)

First of all, we have not said, and do not believe,
that complaint counsel has failed to discharge his duty.
The order which is proposed is similar to many orders used
recently by the Commission in deceptive practices cases.
However, as Chairman Weinberger recently stated, this is a
period of radical reappraisal of Commission orders and the
scope of Commission statutory authority.[5] An order which
was considered adequate to protect the public interest
yesterday will not necessarily be considered adequate
tomorrow. SOUP, Inc. carefully distinguishes between the
proposed order, which is inadequate to protect the public
interest, and complaint counsel, who we do not dispute is
sincerely and conscientiously endeavoring to adequately
protect the public interest.

(continued from preceding page)

it is not the system created by Congress for citizen participation in adjudications. Congress provided that the proper procedure was for the person to himself intervene. FTC
Act § 5(b), 15 U.S.C. § 45(b). This does not mean that
complaint counsel and SOUP, Inc. must conflict with each
other. SOUP, Inc. earnestly desires to work with and
assist in any way possible complaint counsel in this proceeding. Both complaint counsel and SOUP, Inc. are endeavoring to advance the public interest, and should work
together, not at cross-purposes.

[5]Chairman Weinberger, in a letter to Senator Edward
Kennedy, Chairman of the Subcommittee on Administrative
Practice and Procedure, dated July 22, 1970, and released
by the Commission on August 13, 1970, made the following
comments on this recent radical reappraisal of Commission
orders and the scope of the Commission's statutory
authority:

> "We have been examining closely the
> contours of our laws to see how they
> should be interpreted in ways most
> applicable to modern market practices."
> Letter, at 7.

> "We have encouraged the staff to make
> recommendations to us which will probe
> the frontiers of our statutes, so that
> in today's market of ever more complica-
> ted products and ever more complicated
> ways of promoting and distributing these
> products the Commission may continue to
> fulfill what Learned Hand called its duty

(continued on following page)

Moreover, judicial decisions clearly do not stand for the principle stated by Respondent at page 5 that "SOUP's purported representation of consumers is unnecessary unless it is established that complaint counsel and the Commission are unable or unwilling to discharge their acknowledged responsibility to consumers." The proper test is whether consumers are within the zone of interest sought to be protected by the statute in question (the FTC Act); if we are, we have a right to participate in decisions concerning our interests. Office of Communication of United Church of Christ v. FCC, 359 F.2d 994 (U.S. App. D.C. 1966); Scenic Hudson Preservation Conference v. FPC 354 F.2d 608 (2d Cir. 1965).[6]

_____

(continued from preceding page)

> 'to discover and make explicit those un-
> expressed standards of fair dealing which
> the conscience of the community may pro-
> gressively develop.'" Letter, at 1-2.

> "Among the most important of the re-
> sources, given to us by the Congress,
> which must be efficiently employed, are
> our statutes.

> "In the past six months while I have
> been at the Commission, we have en-
> couraged the staff, and we have tried
> ourselves at the Commission level, to
> make the most use of the statutes which
> describe our powers. Typical of this
> attitude is a Commission directive to
> the staff stating that 'the Commission
> is receptive to novel and imaginative
> provisions in orders seeking to remedy
> alleged unlawful practices' and urging
> the staff 'to include such provisions
> in orders for future submissions to the
> Commission recommending issuance of
> complaints.'" Letter, at 5-6.

[6]See, also, Citizens Committee for the Hudson Valley v. Volpe, 425 F.2d 97 (2d Cir. 1970); Crowther v. Seaborg, 312 F. Supp. 1205 (D. Colo. 1970) and cases cited therein.

It must be remembered that all members of SOUP, Inc. are consumers, and therefore, affected by deceptive advertising. In addition, each member of SOUP, Inc. risks personal and property damage due to drivers who believe the tires on their cars (made by Respondent) are safer than they in fact are. Finally, one member of SOUP, Inc., Ivan Vance White, had seen the deceptive advertisements by Firestone and was motivated into purchasing Firestone tires (which are presently on his car) because of the safety features advertised.[7]

C. SOUP, Inc. will introduce evidence on the following points, which evidence will not be introduced by complaint counsel,[8] and the Hearing Examiner would therefore not otherwise receive it:

(1) A significant number of deceived purchasers of Firestone tires who are still using these tires on their motor vehicles, are still erroneously informed as to the safety of their tires.

(2) This erroneous belief enhances the possibility of collisions and other accidents, resulting in property damage, personal injury, and loss of life.

(3) This residual effect of Respondent's deceptions will remain until the purchasers of Firestone tires are informed that the tires are not as safe as they suppose.

(4) Many purchasers of Firestone tires would not have purchased those tires if they were honestly informed as to their safety.

(5) Tests by government agencies, including the National Highway Safety Bureau, and tests by other reputable organizations have shown that Firestone tires have failed minimum safety requirements.

---

[7]See attached affidavit by Mr. White, marked Exhibit "A," which is incorporated by reference and made a part hereof. [Not reprinted here.]

[8]If SOUP, Inc. has wrongly assumed that complaint counsel will not introduce evidence on these points, complaint counsel may so indicate at the pre-hearing conference, and the Hearing Examiner can rule out SOUP, Inc.'s identical evidence.

D. The final cease-and-desist order in this proceeding will not adequately protect the public interest unless it requires Respondent to:

(1) Inform, in its current advertisements, those consumers who were deceived by past advertisements, that Firestone has been found guilty of violating the FTC Act by deceptively advertising the safety of Respondent's tires.

(2) Inform personally, by certified mail or otherwise, all purchasers of Firestone tires during the time period such deceptive advertisements were run and for an equal time period thereafter, that Firestone has been found guilty of violating the FTC Act by deceptively advertising the safety of Respondent's tires. (See brief for SOUP, Inc. requesting the Commission to withdraw its proposed consent order dated March 20, 1970, In the Matter of Campbell Soup Co., Docket No. C-1741 at 19, for an example of possible phrasing.)

(3) Make immediate restitution to those purchasers so notified who will sign an affidavit stating that they would not have purchased Respondent's tires if they had not been deceived concerning the safety of such tires, by returning such tires to the original selling dealer, when convenient, or to any authorized Firestone dealer when inconvenient. (See McDonald's Corp., File No. 692 3074, and The Coca-Cola Co., File No. 702 3014, where the proposed orders contain similar requirements.)

(4) Require numbers (1), (2), and (3) supra, for any future deceptive advertisements.

E. We emphatically are not going outside the allegations of the complaint. The substantial and material questions of fact, law, policy, and discretion we raise are based upon, and only upon, the allegations of deception contained in the complaint. Given those allegations, and the residual effects of Respondent's deception, additional facts are necessary in order to see whether additional corrective clauses are necessary in the cease-and-desist order.

F. SOUP, Inc. has set out above the precise reasons why this proposed order is inadequate to protect the public interest, the precise clauses which must be added to adequately protect the public interest, and the precise

nature of the evidence we desire to introduce (the prehearing conference will specify this in greater detail).
Considering the aggravated nature of this case, involving
the health and safety of the public, this is sufficient
to establish good cause.[9]

> III.   SOUP, Inc. Should Be Granted Leave
>   to Proceed In Forma Pauperis.

SOUP, Inc. respectfully requests that it be allowed
to proceed in forma pauperis in this proceeding, since
SOUP, Inc. has no funds at present. The important immediate effect this would have would be to allow us to file
only one copy of future papers, the Commission itself ,
making the additional copies. SOUP, Inc. was allowed to
proceed in forma pauperis by the Commissioners in
Campbell Soup, supra.

> IV.   SOUP, Inc. Has a Right to Disclosure
>   and Reproduction of Certain Documents
>   and Materials in the Commission's Files.

SOUP, Inc. respectfully requests to examine the
following documents in the Commission's files, pursuant
to §§ 4.8-4.11 of the Commission's Rules, and § 3 of the
APA, 5 U.S.C. § 552:

> A.   All Firestone ads (television, radio, newspaper,
>   magazine, etc.) which represent, directly or
>   by implication, that the tires are safe or free
>   from defects.
>
> B.   All tests, findings, or other similar factual
>   data or material relevant to the safety of
>   Firestone tires by the National Highway Safety
>   Bureau and any other public or private testing
>   organization.
>
> C.   All other material compiled in the preliminary
>   stages of this proceeding relevant to the safety
>   of Firestone tires.

See, Campbell Soup Co., supra, letter to Mr. Aaron Handleman
of February 24, 1970, granting partial disclosure. See,
also, Bristol-Myers Co. v. FTC, 424 F.2d 935 (U.S. App. D.
C. 1970); Grumman Aircraft Engineering Corp. v. Renegotia-
tion Board, 425 F.2d 578 (U.S. App. D.C. 1970).

---

[9]See Campbell Soup Co., supra, Brief for SOUP, Inc.
in Support of Intervention and Hearing at 1-20. That brief
and all other papers in the Campbell Soup Co. file are incorporated by reference and made a part hereof.
[Not reprinted here.]

V. SOUP, Inc. Should be Granted a Reasonable
Opportunity to Reply to the Points Raised
in Any Answer Opposing this Motion.

Because of the substantial danger to public health
and safety involved in this proceeding, it is submitted
that SOUP, Inc. should be given a reasonable opportunity
to reply to any answer opposing this motion. Such a reply
is within the discretion of the Hearing Examiner as provided in § 3.22(c) of the Commission's Rules of Practice
for Adjudicative Proceedings. Permitting such a reply
here will better enable the Hearing Examiner to determine
whether SOUP, Inc. should be permitted to intervene in
this proceeding and will avoid any further delay.

Respectfully submitted,

Peter Harwood Meyers
Member-Representative for
    SOUP, Inc.
Apt. J-1017
1021 Arlington Blvd.
Arlington, Virginia 22209

Ivan Vance White, Jr.
Member-Representative for
    SOUP, Inc.
Apt. 40
4089 S. Four Mile Run Drive
Arlington, Virginia 22204

Dated: September 1, 1970

CERTIFICATE OF SERVICE

I hereby certify that a copy of the foregoing amended motion of SOUP, Inc. to intervene, for leave to proceed in forma pauperis and for disclosure was sent by mail, first class, postage prepaid, to the Firestone Tire and Rubber Company, through its attorney, Thomas A. Gottschalk, 2900 Prudential Plaza, Chicago, Illinois 60601, this _____ day of _____, 1970.

Peter Harwood Meyers
Member-Representative for
   SOUP, Inc.

CHAPTER 6

THE INTERSTATE
COMMERCE COMMISSION

> *It [the Interstate Commerce Commission]
> satisfies the popular clamor for a government
> supervision of the railroads, at the same time
> that that supervision is almost entirely nomi-
> nal. Further, the older such a commission gets
> to be, the more inclined it will be found to
> take the business and railroad view of things.
> It thus becomes a sort of barrier between the
> railroad corporations and the people and a
> sort of protection against hasty and crude
> legislation hostile to railroad interests. . . .The
> part of wisdom is not to destroy the Com-
> mission, but to utilize it.*
>
> —Letter from United States Attorney General
> Richard Olney to Charles E. Perkins, President
> of the Chicago, Burlington and Quincy Rail-
> road, 28 December 1892 [Robert Fellmeth,
> Interstate Commerce Omission (New York:
> Grossman Publishers, 1970), pp. xiv, xv].

Introduction

Things have worked out pretty much as Attorney General Olney said
they would when he dissuaded his railroad friend from trying to do away
with the Interstate Commerce Commission (ICC). Events have even
come full circle. Trucks, buses, household movers, pipelines, and barges
have joined the railroads under the Commission wing. While the Commission looks out for these industries generally, the railroads often feel
they get less attention than the others.

So today, when reformers demand that the ICC be abolished, and
that free-market forces be allowed wider play in transportation, it is the
truckers et al. who snap back with charges of "Communism" and "hippie/
radic/lib," while the railroads are of a mixed mind. Attorney General
Olney's prediction has come true; only the details are not exactly as he
foresaw.

Bill Hernandez calls up his local railway station to find out when the next train leaves for Chicago. The 100-mile trip by train should be much more pleasant than traveling by auto or plane, and just as fast, since the tracks go right into the center of the city. But he can't make a reservation, no travel agency can help since railroads ignore them, there is no advertising, and the railroad official puts him on hold for thirty minutes.

When he does go to the station, Hernandez notices that the train is forty minutes late, the cars are thirty years old, and the heating in the cars has broken down in ten-degree weather. Hernandez can't help but wonder if the railroads are not trying to downgrade passenger service in order to discourage passengers and thus justify complete discontinuance of the runs before the ICC. Why do the railroads not want to carry passengers if there is a possible market? Why do they allow the kind of treatment that saw one train stop and strand its passengers in the middle of its run in a tiny Midwestern town within minutes after winning permission from the ICC to discontinue that run? Hernandez knows that the railroads now have enormous monopoly power in the transportation of freight—and no competition from autos or planes—but is not the ICC supposed to set standards for passenger service, pass on discontinuance requests for runs not covered by AMTRAK, and curb excess profits where the railroads have been given monopoly power?

Jake Hastings called up the moving van firm with the largest ad in the New York Yellow Pages. He needed to move the belongings in his house to California within one month. He was told it would cost $400, but they couldn't come for six weeks. He called another firm, which couldn't come for two months. The first firm eventually got the job, but it was three weeks late in picking up, one month late in arriving, some belongings were missing, and two favorite lamps were smashed.

The total cost was $430. Hastings had the $400 of the estimate in cash, but not the extra $30. The movers refused to unload until they received $430 in cash. Hastings borrowed the money and paid. A carefully packed formal set of dinnerware had been opened, and someone had actually eaten a meal on some of the dishes—leaving an encrustation of dried tomato or chili sauce. The movers refused to pay for the lamps or for a lost mattress, or to move some books they had left in New York. Hastings wants to know how all this comes about, and what he can do. He writes to the ICC, which grants his moving firm the authority to operate the New York-California route and which prevents other firms from competing. They send back a polite letter denying jurisdiction in the matter.

Although about 20 cents out of every consumer dollar is spent on transportation, few Americans think of the ICC unless they catch a daily ride on one of the few halting passenger trains left, or contemplate the ordeal of an average household move. Like many other federal regulatory agencies, the impact of the ICC is pervasive but hidden.

Abuses of the transportation monopoly and the dereliction of government are not hidden from public scrutiny because of any deliberate conspiracy. The secrecy comes instead from sheer complexity.

The major effect on efficiency, prices, and the environment, although massive, is indirect. Because ICC proceedings have become so esoteric, few outside the transportation industry even follow them, let alone comprehend them. It is difficult at first for the uninitiated to even remember that a shipper is the one who sends things (such as a manufacturer shipping widgets or a homeowner moving his furniture), while a carrier is a railroad, trucking company, or barge line which charges for carrying those things. Nevertheless, there *are* ways the public can make itself heard at the ICC. They have just begun to be used.

ICC History:
The ICC and How It Grew

Federal regulation of interstate commerce is rooted in Article I, Section 8, of the Constitution, authorizing Congress "to regulate commerce with foreign nations, and among the several states." The Populist movement in the late nineteenth century prodded Congress into exercising this power. After investigating the railroad industry, exposing discriminatory freight rates and passenger fares, it passed the "Act to Regulate Commerce" [49 U.S.C. 1, later called the Interstate Commerce Act].

Initially, the ICC was under the Secretary of the Interior. In those early days the Commission was only concerned with transportation by rail or a combination of rail and water. Its main job was to make the railroads publish their fares, refrain from discriminating against particular localities or groups of customers, use lawful management, and charge rates that were "reasonable and just." As the country grew, so did the ICC. It became a permanent agency, no longer responsible to the Secretary of Interior, and expanded from five to seven commissioners. The commissioners were—and still are—appointed by the President and approved by the Senate; only four of them could be members of the same political party. The President could not veto Commission decisions.

Today there are eleven commissioners, with a maximum of six from the same political party. The President appoints the chairman.

The jurisdiction of the Commission has grown through over 200 amendments deposited on the original Interstate Commerce Act by periodic waves of public indignation. The Elkins Act of 1903 required carriers to file and adhere to tariffs, and prohibited carriers from favoring a particular shipper. For example, a carrier must offer similar services at the same price to all customers, and can't charge one shipper lower rates than it does another. It must justify differences in rates by "some cost or value or competitive distinction." (Defining which services are alike, and so must be offered at the same price to all shippers, has provided the ICC with a continuing source of controversy and transportation attorneys with a continuing source of income.) The Elkins Act also banned secret agreements for unpublished rebates.

In 1906 Theodore Roosevelt signed the Hepburn Act, a major amendment which gave the ICC authority to establish maximum railroad rates. In the late 1890s the United States Supreme Court had ruled that the Commission had the right to disapprove rates, but not the power to set acceptable rates. The Hepburn Act clarified the resulting vagueness somewhat, and granted the Commission the "direct power to determine and prescribe just and reasonable . . . regulations or practices for the future, upon complaint." Another amendment, the 1910 Mann-Elkins Act, gave the ICC the power to stop or suspend proposed rates while it investigated them. Today it uses this power while holding a hearing on challenges by shippers, consumer groups, or others. The Panama Canal Act of 1912 barred railroads from operating water lines if such activity would decrease competition, and gave the Commission power to set rates and routes for joint rail-water shipping. The 1917 Esch Car Service Act gave the ICC the power to determine the fairness of freight car service rules and to make such rules on its own.

During World War I the federal government temporarily took over the railroads, and after the war Congress passed the Transportation Act of 1920, broadening ICC authority. The new powers included authority to regulate commerce within a state as well as between states "when necessary to remove discrimination against interstate commerce"; to prescribe *minimum* as well as maximum rates; and to require that the establishment or discontinuance of railroad or transportation routes be justified by "public convenience and necessity." The Commission then began a plan to create a national railroad network based on the smaller competing railroads, and attempted to fix railroad rates to guarantee a 6 percent return on investment.

In 1935, Congress, recognizing that much cargo which previously had gone by rail was being transported by trucks, brought motor carriers under ICC jurisdiction. The Motor Carrier Act of 1935 (now Part II of the Interstate Commerce Act) authorized the ICC to regulate motor carriers of people and freight, as it already regulated rail carriers. The Commission could determine who could participate in interstate trucking, and what their tariffs and routes would be.

The Transportation Act of 1940 gave the ICC its third major area of transportation jurisdiction, over "coastal, inter-coastal, and inland water carriers." Until that time, in keeping with its origin, the ICC focus had been on protecting shippers from unfair charges. But with its new responsibility for domestic water transportation as well as motor carriers and railroads, the Commission began to regulate competition between the different *modes* of transportation as well as between the carriers and their customers. It drew up a "National Transportation Policy" and abandoned the national rail network project. It also granted special exemption for trucks carrying agricultural goods and barges transporting "bulk commodities" such as ore, coal, or grain. (Actually, these rates are now lower than rates charged by ICC regulated carriers.)

By 1940 the ICC had accumulated most of its present authority to forbid rate cuts, fix specific rates, and shield certain industry-proposed mergers from antitrust action. It had also entrenched its outlook in two major premises. The first was that a large railroad is a sound railroad; thus the ICC policy of promoting mergers. The second was a fear of what it terms "destructive competition."

In 1942, Part IV of the Interstate Commerce Act brought freight forwarders under ICC jurisdiction. In 1947 Congress passed the Reed Bullwinkle Act over the veto of President Truman. It legalized organized price fixing in the transportation industries. Specifically, it allowed truck, barge, and railroad companies to unite in "rate bureaus" for agreeing on rates they would charge. Such price fixing previously had been a violation of antitrust laws. Now, however, the carriers needed only to file such rates (in "tariffs") with the ICC to make them legal. In theory, the Commission only approves those tariffs which advance the interests of the National Transportation Policy. In practice, however, all are automatically approved unless someone protests. Critics contend that only occasional carriers and a few large shippers are able to protest, and that they usually do so merely to stop a rate reduction they do not want to compete against.

The Transportation Act of 1958 authorized the ICC to let railroads discontinue individual passenger trains if the Commission found that the unprofitable line would threaten the existence of the railroad's remaining passenger or freight service. The railroads were eager to bring their less profitable passenger lines to the ICC for burial, including many which were failing mainly because of deliberate company practices. And the ICC obliged, so that today passenger trains are nearly as rare as the buffalo which the original process of railroad building threatened with extinction. Another section of the 1958 Transportation Act alloted indirect subsidies to the railroads by providing Uncle Sam-guaranteed low-interest commercial loans.

In 1965 and 1966, the Interstate Commerce Act was again amended to enable the Commission to enter into agreements with the states for joint enforcement of motor carrier laws and regulations. Also in 1966, a major structural revision was enacted. The National Transportation Policy, which since 1940 had guided the ICC's words if not its actions, was largely stripped from the Commission and entrusted to the new cabinet level Department of Transportation (DOT). The DOT took over broad powers, including the ICC's former authority to establish and enforce railroad, trucking, and pipeline safety standards, and control over the transportation of hazardous or dangerous goods by any mode.

After all this Congressional cutting and pasting of power, it can be hard to remember what agency or level of government regulates what kind of transportation. State governments regulate transportation within their boundaries which does not affect interstate commerce. (Urban mass transit is under the DOT.) But all interstate rail transportation is subject to ICC regulation, except for safety, now under DOT, and intercity passenger service, now under the National Rail Passenger Corporation (Amtrak). The ICC's jurisdiction extends to ground commercial travel between Mexico and the United States, and between Canada and the United States.

Most of the trucking industry is regulated by the ICC, with the important exception of interstate trucks carrying many agricultural products. Also exempt are: truckers engaged in private operations not selling transportation to the public; school buses; taxicabs; hotel buses; motor vehicles of agricultural cooperative associations; and vehicles transporting livestock, fish, and most nonmanufactured agricultural commodities. "Contract" carriers, serving a limited number of shippers, are under less stringent regulations. The Federal Highway Administration has jurisdiction over construction and maintenance of federal highways used by truckers.

The ICC's control over waterways is limited to domestic shipping (inland and coastal), and interstate water carriers carrying liquid and some dry bulk commodities are exempt. Ocean shipping is under the Federal Maritime Commission and the Maritime Administration in the Department of Commerce. The Army Corps of Engineers develops harbors, the U.S. Coast Guard is responsible for water carrier safety.

The ICC still has its original jurisdiction over oil pipelines, but the Federal Power Commission (FPC) regulates pipeline transportation of natural and artificial gas.

The ICC's power to regulate can be viewed in three parts: *operating rights, rates,* and *finance.* Nine of the eleven commissioners have been grouped into three divisions corresponding to this breakdown, allegedly to dispatch commission business more efficiently. The Chairman, George M. Stafford, and Vice Chairman, W. Donald Brewer, do not serve on any of the divisions.

A transportation firm must have ICC permission to operate as a common carrier if regulated by the ICC. The ICC issues "certificates of public convenience and necessity" or "permits" giving a truck, bus, water carrier, or freight forwarding firm the right to do business.

Economists such as Ann Friedlander, James Nelson, and Thomas Moore argue pursuasively that this operating rights regulation spawns enormous inefficiency, excess costs, and misallocation of resources. In the trucking industry, for example, critics point out that firms are given the authority to carry only specific commodities from specific points along specific routes. Hence, one trucker has the authority to carry all flexible hose from Dubuque to Indianapolis, but another has the right to carry only *rubber* hose between the same two points. A third may have the right to carry all hose from Dubuque all the way through to Miami, but may not use a freeway which is available to the other two. The resultant mass of rules and regulations means that the ICC fritters away its resources settling petty disputes between carriers, each one desiring his own transportation fiefdom free from competition.

All of the legal hassling, lack of competition, and waste of half-empty trucks or roundabout routes add up to tremendous inefficiency and consumer costs, according to economists and critics.

Other critics point out the agency's unwillingness to make carriers serve the public in return for freeing them from competition. Hence, the ICC rarely suspends or revokes operating rights even when carriers fail to pay damage claims, are late or undependable, violate safety, environmental, or service standards or regulations, or bribe shippers. Despite the glaring need to crack down on such problems with its only potent weapon—suspension or revocation of operating rights privileges—the ICC has used this power only four times since 1935.

On the contrary, critics contend that when a new firm applies for operating rights the ICC will not even listen to its claims to offer lower rates, better service, or more efficiency than existing firms. The ICC will normally let the new firm compete only if the already entrenched firm cannot carry existing traffic, and is not willing to equip itself to do so.

Construction or abandonment of railroad lines also comes under "operating authority." Critics here contend that railroads have been allowed to abandon communities and impose "external" costs on those settling and investing there. Other critics add that the agency has allowed railroads to downgrade passenger service to show lower "passenger demand" and win permission to discontinue service.

Operating rights issues are decided by Division One, comprised at this moment of commissioners Rupert L. Murphy, Robert C. Gresham, and Alfred T. MacFarland.

The Commission settles disputes over rates between competing modes of transportation, shippers, and receivers of freight. It determines the supply, movement, and control of railroad equipment such as boxcars, and it has authority to prevent what it calls "destructive competition," rebating, and unlawful discrimination in rate structures. Under certain conditions, it can direct the way railroads handle and move traffic.

Critics contend that the ICC does not monitor "rate bureaus," the assemblies of carriers which collusively set rates. They argue that the legal power of the rate bureaus prevents anyone from charging less than these collectively set rates.

Economists believe that the "minimum rate floors" set by carriers in their bureaus and enforced by the ICC protect inefficient firms and prevent healthy price competition. They argue that when each mode of transport sets rates as a group there is enormous rate discrimination. For example, water carriers set rates three times as high where there is no railroad competition than where there is such competition, and railroads do the same to the water carriers. Trucks reap great profits on short runs, where they have lowest costs, so they can cut rates below cost and drive railroads out of business on longer runs, where railroads have a cost advantage. (Rather than drive a railroad literally out of business, this usually means undercutting its business by convincing new firms to relocate away from tracks and near freeways.) This sort of game results in discrimination by weight, region, distance, commodity, and mode. The total result is inefficiency and waste, higher costs and inflation, and misallocation of resources. Consumer critics argue that the ICC has failed in its duty to monitor maximum rates, to prevent both discrimination and excess profits. The agency accepts industry cost figures on faith, asking few questions. It has allowed virtually every rate increase the carriers have requested.

Small shippers argue that there is subtle violation of the Elkins Act which the ICC ignores. They point to specially equipped freight cars which only big auto firms can use, special weight agreements, credit extensions, and many other discriminative favors which benefit the big shippers.

Farmers have long argued that the agency has yet to solve the boxcar shortage problem, though it has plagued many of them for almost 100 years. The railroads do not have enough plain, unequipped boxcars to carry Midwestern harvests to market during peak periods. Hence, farmers must resort to other means of transport at greater cost, or let a crop rot. Meanwhile, thousands of railroad cars sit around empty at the instant disposal of General Motors, Ford, and other large shippers.

Rates and practices is Division Two of the Commission, and consists at present of Virginia Mae Brown, Dale W. Hardin, and A. Daniel O'Neal.

The ICC approves or disapproves the sale of common carrier companies, and issuance of their securities. Mergers, consolidations, and acquisitions of control over such companies are also subject to ICC approval. The Commission sets accounting rules and administers laws governing railroad bankruptcy.

Critics contend that the ICC has failed to find out who actually owns these regulated firms, that it has routinely approved both interlocking directorships and rail, truck, and other mergers without hesitation or caution. The result, they hold, is a bloated, concentrated, and uncompetitive transportation industry controlled by unknown people.

Economists contend that the agency has ignored the conglomerate takeover of carriers, even though these giant combinations are often also involved in shipping and other modes of transportation as well. The agency has developed no comprehensive policy beyond a single staff report.

Congressional critics have asserted that ICC laxity regarding accounting and bankruptcy has already cost shippers and taxpayers dearly in the collapse of the giant Penn Central Railroad. The government had to bail out this recently merged railroad after the revelation of extraordinary mismanagement and waste by railroad executives, including two former Interstate Commerce Commissioners.

Division Three, currently made up of Kenneth H. Tuggle, Willard Deason, and Chester M. Wiggin, has the job of overseeing the financial health and merger activities of regulated carriers.

In describing its own regulatory authority, the ICC emphasizes the self-imposed limits on its regulation. It stresses the freedom of transportation companies to determine their rates, to merge with or buy control of other carriers, and their independent determination of the number, size, and type of carriers they use. As the General Counsel, Fritz R. Kahn, has proudly said, "We play a passive role, because we believe our statutory function is to respond to carrier excesses" [*National Journal,* 18 April 1970, p. 839]. The Commission rarely acts on its own to carry out its regulatory authority; rather, it reacts to applications and protests which originate almost entirely in the transportation industry. For example, of approximately 200,000 tariffs (which set forth the products to be shipped, the distance, and price) filed each year, the Commission suspends or investigates fewer than 2,250. And it does so almost exclusively after protest by competing carriers.

Structure: How the ICC Works

At present the ICC, illustrated in the chart in Appendix 6-A (p. 210), consists basically of five offices and five bureaus. There is a director at the head of each, who supervises section chiefs under him. The offices handle *functions* that cut across all the ICC work. The bureaus work only in a particular *subject* area.

The Offices are those of Secretary, Proceedings, General Counsel, Managing Director, and Hearings. The Office of the Secretary records, files, and tells the public about ICC policy decisions and rulings. In this office is the Section of Dockets and Service. If you ask at the Public Information Office for information beyond its scope, they will refer you to the Secretary. This is where to go for ICC notices, reports, orders, and dockets.

The Office of Proceedings processes formal cases involving rates and operating rights. Within this office are the Sections of Operating Rights, Rates, and Finance. These sections write the Commission's final reports and recommendations in cases brought before it. The Office of Hearings includes the 105 Administrative Law Judges (formerly called Examiners) who conduct most of the ICC's public hearings. These judges make decisions that are crucial to citizen access, and they are required by the Administrative Procedure Act (APA) to be independent of the Commission.

The Office of the General Counsel is the ICC's lawyer. The General Counsel gives legal advice to the Commission and defends Commission orders which are challenged in court. The Office of the Managing Director is the ICC housekeeper. It has charge of money, personnel, and supplies.

The ICC's Bureaus are Accounts, Economics, Operations, Enforcement, and Traffic. The Bureau of Accounts audits the books of regulated companies, to make sure they comply with Commission regulations. The Bureau of Economics does economic research and analysis. It conducts transportation studies, and reports to the Commission on how ICC decisions may affect the economy in general, and the economic status of carriers, shippers, and consumers in particular.

The Bureau of Operations is the Commission "cop." It is supposed to uncover violations of the Interstate Commerce Act and of the Commission's regulations. Field agents from this bureau investigate whether carriers are obeying economic or service rules. Their reports go first to the Section Chiefs in Washington, and from there to the Bureau of Enforcement for possible prosecution.

If the Bureau of Operations is the Commission cop, the Bureau of Enforcement is the District Attorney. It decides what actions, if any, to take against violations of the Interstate Commerce Act and the Commission's rules. It can make "deals" or "settlements" with carriers who break the law. The Bureau of Enforcement consists mostly of attorneys, who sometimes appear in ICC proceedings to put forth "facts and issues in the public interest." Whenever people complain that the public has no voice at the ICC, the Commission answers by saying that the Bureau of Enforcement handles that job.

The Bureau of Traffic examines and judges rates filed with the Commission. If the bureau finds that rates are unjust, unreasonable, or illegal, it can suspend them pending a complete investigation.

The Commission has six regional offices, each headed by a Regional Manager (see Appendix 6-D, p. 254, for a listing of the regional headquarters and field offices). In practice, personnel at these regional offices spend about half of their time on such paperwork as processing complaints and applications for temporary authority. District supervisors report to the regional managers on activities within their district. In addition, there are about twenty-five district supervisors who act as roving, full-time investigators. They deal primarily with motor, water, and freight-forwarder regulation. A rate and tariff expert is assigned to each regional office.

The compliance survey is one method used by field officers to determine whether motor carriers are violating ICC regulations. In such a survey, the field officers examine the bills of lading, freight bills, C.O.D. registers, and routings—in short, the business records—of the carriers. Violations can be detected if the carrier has kept accurate records. But many breaches of ICC regulations cannot be discovered this way. Consider such examples as using misleading commodity labels, ignoring restrictions on what the carrier can carry, serving unauthorized areas, household moving violations (low estimates, overcharging), and truck safety violations (hours of work, equipment breakdown).

Suppose you run a plumbing supply company and think a competitor is getting a special deal on his trucking rates. Or suppose you think a household mover has overcharged you or hasn't obeyed the Commission's special regulations. You gather as much information about the problem as you can, and submit a complaint to the ICC. (Perhaps you send copies to both the Commission's field office and Washington headquarters, and to your Congressman and Senators as well.)

What happens then? Briefly, the complaint goes down through the Commission's chain of command to a field investigator, who is supposed to check it out thoroughly. The investigator writes a report which then goes back up the chain of command. If the investigator's Bureau of Operations is satisfied that the report is complete, it goes to the Bureau of Enforcement, which makes the final decision on what action, if any, to take.

The Commission has various ways of dealing with violators. Which one it uses depends on the law and the agency's resources, priorities, and whims. Often a phone call, letter, or comment over lunch, suggesting that the offense cease, is the only action taken. Going one step further, the ICC can ask a court to *order* the offender to halt an illegal action.

Why should the Commission have to go to court to get a violator to stop doing something that is already illegal? That is how the law was written, and it is much easier than getting a court to punish the offender. To do that, the Commission has to prove that an offense was "knowing and willful." In addition, once the Commission has a court order stopping the violation, the penalties for future misdeeds are severe.

In theory, the Commission carries a heavy stick. Criminal violations of the Interstate Commerce Act, for example, are subject to fines of $5,000 for each day of the offense. Discriminating in rates, fares, or charges can subject a carrier to two years in prison. Violators of the Elkins Act ban on favoring certain shippers can subject a carrier to fines of from $1,000 to $2,000 per offense, or to two years in prison. One of the Commission's most powerful—and least used—weapons is its authority to suspend or take away a carrier's license to operate.

But the Commission's performance has fallen far short of its mandate. When it uncovers a violation, "informal warnings" are all too frequent. Fines are generally so small that breaking the transportation laws remains good business. Imprisonment is a punishment on the statute books, but the ICC is too timid to ask for this penalty and courts are squeamish about putting businessmen in prison. Only four times since 1935 has the Commission used its most effective enforcement weapon, the power to suspend or revoke a carrier's license to operate.

This enforcement lethargy is just an offshoot of the Commission's sedate view of its function. Passively waiting for applications, complaints, and protests, instead of acting on its own, is rooted in the Commission's mentality. Since most of these requests come from the Commission's industry clientele—both carriers and shippers—there is a dearth of action to protect the public at large.

The Interstate Commerce Act and You: What Your Rights Are and How You Can Stand Up for Them

The Interstate Commerce Act can be a dense jungle even to lawyers, let alone to the lay public. A main reason the public has been so cut off from the ICC is that the Commission has retreated into a shell of legal jargon and Byzantine procedures. If we could cut away these encrustations, and restore the broad principles of equity and justice the ICC was meant to uphold, the public could gain a larger voice. We could have a healthier, more competitive, and responsive transportation system, and legislators would see more clearly how the Act itself needs reform. As a first step in that direction, here is a general summary of what the ICC is supposed to do and how the public can have a voice. This summary won't tell you exactly what your rights are in a specific case or how to enforce them. But it should suggest to you whether your claim or grievance is valid, and whether further legal research or consultation is in order.

1. What does the Interstate Commerce Act require of "carriers" (trains, buses, trucks, barges, and "freight forwarders")?
   a. With a few exceptions, they must have a permit from the ICC, and obey the terms of that permit.
   b. They must make their services available to all, equally and without discrimination.
   c. They must file their rates with the ICC and adhere to these rates at all times.
   d. They must collect their charges promptly, and they may grant credit only as the Commission's regulations allow.
   e. They must get ICC approval before they merge or buy control of one another.

2. What are the duties and rights of people ("shippers") who *use* the services of these carriers?
   a. They must use only carriers that have ICC permits, when the law requires such permits.
   b. They must pay the rate that the carrier has on file with the ICC, within the time the Commission's credit regulations allow.
   c. They must *not* seek special treatment, either as to service or rates.
   d. They have a *right* to receive the same service, at the same rate, as all other shippers like themselves.

3. What can the ICC do to enforce these duties and rights? The Commission has a very broad range of powers to enforce the Interstate Commerce Act. In some or all cases it can take a violator to court (itself or through the Attorney General) to seek:
   a. A criminal prosecution.
   b. A "civil" fine or penalty.
   c. An order to stop the illegal practice.

The Commission can itself suspend or revoke a carrier's permit to do business. It can also reach out-of-court "settlements" with violators, and issue its own orders to stop illegal practices. (If the Commission does suspend or revoke a permit, or issue a cease and desist order, the violator may of course appeal the action in court.)

4. What can the public do to enforce and protect its rights under the Interstate Commerce Act?

a. You can *report* violations of the Interstate Commerce Act to the Commission Chairman. You can report, for example, a household mover or a bus company that has treated you unfairly, or has violated specific ICC regulations. Here are some pointers for getting action:

   (1) Spell out *exactly* what the carrier did.

   (2) If you can, name specifically the law or regulation you think has been violated. (The Commission has a special booklet on the rights of household-moving customers. Send for it. It is entitled *Summary of Information for Shippers of Household Goods,* available from G.P.O. for 20 cents.)

   (3) Send a copy of your complaint to your Senators, Congressmen, and to a consumer action group, and keep them informed on what the Commission does.

   (4) Keep pressing for action. Don't let the Commission get away with saying it can't do anything. Its powers are broad enough so that when it feels enough heat it can do *something* to help.

b. More specifically, you can demand that the ICC suspend or revoke a carrier's permit to operate. The Commission has broad power to do this when carriers disobey the law or Commission regulations, or otherwise abuse the public. If the Commission used this power more often, the public would get better service and the Commission would get fewer complaints.

c. In some cases, you can go directly to federal court to make a carrier cease violations that are harming you.

d. When the Commission takes enforcement action against a carrier, you, the person whose rights were violated, do not necessarily gain. The carrier just gets punished. There *are* ways, however, that persons harmed by violations of the Interstate Commerce Act can recover their loss. For example, the Commission can make a carrier compensate a customer ("shipper") for any charges that were unjust, unreasonable, or which discriminated against that customer. Such compensation is called "reparation." The Commission can also make carriers pay back overcharges.

> The Commission could do much more than it now does to require carriers to compensate customers for losses and damages. For example, when customers of household goods-movers have to spend hundreds of dollars on hotel bills because the mover was two weeks late, the mover should bear at least some of the expense. Similarly, the Commission's regulations for the settling of loss and damage claims, and for carrier liability, are sad examples of the regulatory process used for industry convenience. More customer protection in such cases would be worthwhile goals for consumer and public interest groups.

Regulated Industries, Consumers, and ICC Regulars

The ICC regards the transportation industry as its real constituency largely because there are actually three industries—motor, rail, and water carriers—competing vigorously for its attention. And it hears little from anyone else. All of these carriers and the freight forwarders have aggressive trade associations in Washington: the American Trucking Association, Inc., the Association of American Railroads, the American Waterways Operators, Inc., and the Freight Forwarders Institute. Usually the competition is between the railroads and the water carriers, but the motor carriers are also at odds with the railroads in some cases.*

The American Trucking Association, Inc. (ATA), illustrates how the trade associations work. The ATA provides everything for its members, from group life insurance and standard employment application forms to a "Safety Service"—a troupe of trained dogs to carry the ATA message to grade schools. Its magazine, *Transport Topics,* provides current information on everything at the ICC which affects trucking ($15 per year from 1616 P Street, N.W., Washington, D.C. 20036). The intensive ATA public relations program includes a weekly radio program called "Guest Conductor," on a Washington station. For the program the ATA invites a Congressman or "key government official" to select his favorite music and tell the listening audience why he likes it. In the ATA's words, the program then "is transcribed and presented to these guests

*If preference for a particular industry on the part of ICC commissioners can be measured by the jobs to which they retire, railroads appear to have an edge. Out of twelve commissioners who left the ICC between 1958 and 1970, four turned to the railroads for jobs, more than any other single industry [*CPR National Journal,* 18 April 1970, p. 831].

in a handsome leather album as a memento of their 'Guest Conductor' participation." (The Association of American Railroads is no stranger to using the airwaves for public relations either, having hired a former astronaut to do commercials for the industry.)

Commercial shippers who have to pay the ICC-approved rates to carriers are also a powerful voice at the ICC. Frequently these commercial shippers are the Commission's idea of "consumers." Carriers have to prove to the ICC that proposed rates are "just and reasonable," and the shippers' lobby sometimes challenges them. The National Industrial Traffic League is the largest national shipper group, representing about 1,800 companies. The Small Shipments Association is another group. Individual industries also frequently intervene through their trade associations to oppose rate increases for their commodities. Two examples are the National Grain Trades Council, representing grain shippers, and the Midwest Coal Producers Institute, Inc. *Traffic World,* which costs about $140 a year, is a publication which railroads and shippers use to keep track of pending rate increases.

Public input at the ICC is small but growing. Before Amtrak took over passenger trains, a group was established to represent people who ride, or would like to be able to ride, trains. The National Association of Railroad Passengers (NARP) (417 New Jersey Avenue, S.E., Washington, D.C. 20003) challenged discontinuances of railroad passenger service and argued that the ICC had authority to regulate service on passenger trains. NARP still speaks actively and effectively for the interests of railroad passengers and on behalf of a balanced transportation system in Congress, court actions, and through state and federal agencies.

NARP has sought to intervene in the Penn Central bankruptcy case on behalf of the public, to make sure the bankruptcy court takes account of the public need for railroad service, and doesn't simply let creditors strip away the company's assets. NARP has also been pushing for better commuter rail service in major urban areas, and has been watchdogging the Amtrak effort to revive passenger trains. The group won a landmark legal victory in January 1973 when its right to bring suit in federal court to enjoin discontinuation of railroad passenger service under the Amtrak Act [45 U.S.C. 501 *et seq.*] was upheld by the U.S. Court of Appeals [*Potomac Passengers Assn.* v. *Chesapeake and Ohio Railway Com.,* D.C. Cir., Nos. 71-1321 and 71-1546 (January 5, 1973)]. NARP issues a monthly newsletter, available to subscribers at a membership rate of $10 a year.

Another nonindustry group dealing with the ICC is the Ad Hoc Committee on Consumer Protection (AHCCP). Formed in 1963, it is a coalition of Washington, D.C., groups, including the NAACP, the ADA, the Office of Urban Affairs of the Archdiocese of Washington, and the Council of Churches. AHCCP was the first consumer organization to intervene in a freight rate case. In that case, described in detail later (see p. 200), it challenged a proposed rate increase on vegetables from the West Coast.

One must have ICC approval before he can represent another—i.e., "practice"—before it. Lawyers in good standing get this approval automatically; they need only register in the way the Commission's regulations prescribe. Nonlawyers can practice, too, but only if the Commission decides they are "possessed of the necessary legal and technical qualifications" and are "otherwise competent to advise and assist in presentation of matters before the Commission" (49 C.F.R. § 1100.8(b)).

Whether a nonlawyer can practice before the ICC rests entirely on the Commission's judgment. The nonlawyer must submit an application and a certificate signed by at least three current practitioners (ICC regulations set out the form for each). The Commission may require further information from these sponsors. If the Commission turns down an applicant, the regulations give him the right to a hearing.

All who practice before the ICC—both lawyers and nonlawyers—must obey the Code of Ethics for Practitioners before the ICC which appears as Appendix A to the General Rules of Practice. (The General Rules of Practice is available from the Government Printing Office for $1.25.) If they do not, the Commission can suspend or revoke their right to practice.

But the Commission has been less than vigorous in enforcing its impressive Code, at least where influential practitioners are concerned. An example is the case of former Commissioner Charles A. Webb. During Webb's term in office, the Commission had been involved in a series of enforcement actions against the Safeway Trails bus company for serious safety violations. Like so many other Commissioners, Webb stepped right from his ICC post to a top job with an industry he once regulated—in his case, the National Association of Motor Bus Owners (NAMBO). As NAMBO President, he personally intervened in the later stages of the enforcement actions against Safeway Trails. An associate of Ralph Nader pointed out to ICC Chairman George Stafford that Webb's stepping into a matter in which he had been involved as a Commissioner appeared to violate Section 40 of the Canons of Ethics (as well as the Code of Ethics of the American Bar Association and the Federal Conflict of Interest Laws).

Predictably, the Commission grasped for an excuse to do nothing. Pretending that Mr. Webb's alleged impropriety was one of the matters still before the Commission in the pending Safeway Trails case (it wasn't), Chairman Stafford pleaded helplessness. "I am neither disposed nor permitted to respond to your views as to the merits of the issues under consideration or your allegations as to the improprieties made to the Commission," Stafford replied in typical, obfuscatory officialese.

The Code of Ethics for Practitioners before the ICC (49 C.F.R. 1100 Appendix A) has some interesting provisions. One (No. 28) warns against communications with the press that are likely to "inflame" the public or "stir up possible hostility toward the Commission. . . ." Another provision advises practitioners to avoid charges which "undervalue" their services (No. 14). The practitioners are scrupulous about this, and experienced transportation attorneys get upwards of $45 an hour, and often $75 an hour or more if they win. A typical hearing day costs $300 in attorneys' fees, plus expenses. A full hearing can swiftly pile up hundreds of thousands of dollars in fees for the practitioners, a fact which may help account for the incredibly slow pace of proceedings before the ICC, where a case may drag on for ten years or more. (Indeed, the delay and incompetence of ICC regulatory proceedings has been found by Congressional investigators to have been a major factor in the financial collapse of the Penn Central Railroad shortly after the merger creating the new company was approved. The approval took six years.) [See, e.g., *The Penn Central and Other Railroads,* Staff Report to Senate Committee on Congress, 92d Cong., 2d sess., pp. 316-325 (December 1972].

The National Association of Regulatory Utility Commissioners (NARUC) has a Directory of Consultants, many of whom serve as expert witnesses in ICC proceedings. But they are almost as expensive as attorneys, and the experts' fees in an average rate case are about $4,000 to $5,000.

There is more written by and about the ICC than most people have the interest or time to read. As one ICC official said to a consumer group that wanted prepared rate changes to be published in the *Federal Register,* Commission rate schedules read like a telephone book, except that most would find a telephone book easier to follow. Nevertheless, you have to know where to look in the masses of ICC paper in order to find out what the Commission is doing.

The *Interstate Commerce Acts Annotated* is a multivolume text of the entire Interstate Commerce Act. It includes brief digests of court decisions interpreting various sections. The Government Printing Office

(G.P.O.) publishes and sells this set, supplemented every month by the *Advance Bulletin of Interstate Commerce Act Annotated*. Of course, the Interstate Commerce Act also appears in the *U.S. Code Annotated*, available at law and many public libraries.

The Code of Federal Regulations (C.F.R.) sets out the details of the ICC's organization and the regulations the Commission has adopted for carrying out the act. Title 49 of the C.F.R., dealing with transportation, is divided into three parts (available from the G.P.O. separately):

1. Parts 1000-1199: General, Enforcement, Rules of Practice, Special Procedures. Order number GS 4.108:49 (1000-1199) $2.75.
2. Parts 1200-1299: Uniform System of Accounts, Destruction of Records, Report, Valuation. Order Number GS 4.108:49 (1200-1299) $3.
3. Parts 1300-end: Tariff and Credit Regulations. Order number GS 4.108: 49 (1300-end) $2.

The ICC's General Rules of Practice can be purchased alone from G.P.O. for $1. This is a loose-leaf collection of the Commission's rules for formal proceedings, with recent amendments. The Commission's Annual Reports, which contain a listing of ICC publications along with economic and financial statistics, are also available from G.P.O. for $1 per copy.

Formal notices of proposed rules (but not rates), such as those governing household movers, are published in the *Federal Register*. Press releases on Commission decisions, reports, and public statements are available from the Office of Public Information of the Interstate at the Washington headquarters (12th and Constitution, N.W., Washington, D.C. 20423). You can request to be placed on the permanent mailing list. You can also get a free ICC telephone directory from this office. Press releases are available in the Reference Issuance Rooms in the Washington headquarters. Docket files—complete records of all cases— are kept in room 1221. You can examine them in person at any time during business hours, 8:30 A.M. to 5:00 P.M. Monday through Friday, but you may not remove them from the room. The Commission still expects the public to pay 25 cents per page for copying,* even though commercial copiers can make a profit by charging 5 cents per page or less. Docket files are not kept at field offices, but are available for inspection and copying at the regional offices (listed in Appendix 6-D,

---

*The rate may be changed under the 1973 Federal Advisory Commission law. See Chapter 3.

p. 254. The Status Branch in the Office of the Secretary can tell you what has happened to a particular case in which you are interested.

In March and April all ICC-regulated carriers must submit reports to the Commission. The public can inspect these Annual Reports in the Public Reference Room. Among other things, the Annual Reports give facts and statistics about the railroad and trucking industries, oil pipelines, express companies, rate bureaus, and other areas of the industry. They also disclose how much the companies spend on legal help beyond their own staffs of lawyers. Monthly and quarterly carrier reports on wages, commodities, and other statistics are also available. Photocopies of these reports can be ordered for 25 cents a page from Publications, Room 1349, Interstate Commerce Commission, Washington, D.C., 20423.

You can also get free copies of all Commission orders, reports, recent decisions, certifications, and notices from the Office of the Secretary in Washington, or from regional offices. Tariffs published by ICC-regulated carriers may be examined in the Tariff Room at the Washington headquarters. Hearings are usually announced by press releases from the Office of Public Information. These give the date and location, and are usually sent to the financial editors of newspapers in the areas where the hearings are being held. You can get more detailed information about hearings either by contacting the field offices or by telephoning the Hearing Room Clerk in Washington (202-343-6246, extension 319).

The ICC's Annual Report, recounting the major activities for the year and including information on such subjects as budget and legislative recommendations, is available from the G.P.O.

Freedom of Information at the ICC

Like the other government agencies, the ICC was required by the Freedom of Information Act (FOIA) [5 U.S.C. 552] to publish in the *Federal Register* its regulations spelling out how it would apply the Act's policy of public disclosure of government information (32 Fed. Reg. 9020 1967, 1000.10). Many agencies issued regulations which just repeated the exemptions to the Act, but not the ICC. Briefly the ICC isn't going to publish its decisions in the *Federal Register* because it says there are too many of them and they are too complicated. Thus, if you want to find out exactly what the Commission is doing, you usually have to go to Washington to look it up. As the Commission put it:

> Because . . . statements of policy and interpretations of general
> applicability are scattered throughout the more than 320,000 pages
> in over 400 volumes of Commission reports and because such poli-
> cies and interpretations must be revised or repealed from time to
> time as required by changing technology and economic conditions,
> it is not feasible, and is wholly impractical, to state them separately
> and publish them in the *Federal Register*. Further, to be fully
> understood, such statements of general policy of interpretations of
> general applicability must be read in context of the Commission's
> reports where they are explained, revised, or repealed in relation
> to the factual situations to which they are applicable. [32 Fed.
> Reg. 9020, 1967, 1000.10]

The Commission did say that general policy statements or interpretations would appear in the *Interstate Commerce Acts Annotated* and can
be found interspersed amid the thousands of individual case reports, classified into three series of ICC reports: the ICC Reports (I.C.C.), the
Motor Carrier Cases (M.C.C.), or the Valuation Reports (Val. R.). Cases
which are not considered important enough for these publications are
called "no print reports and orders." These are distributed only to the
parties involved and to the press. If you want to look at them you have
to know the docket number, title, and subject matter of the case. Then
you can look it up in the Section of Reference Services of the Commission in Washington, or write to the Secretary for copies.

Section 1001.0 of the Commission's regulations reveals just what
files and records the Commission now opens for inspection in Washington. These include tariffs and rate schedules, carrier reports, annual
reports, and other data, all docket files (including pleadings, depositions, exhibits, transcripts, and other detailed case information), certain
enforcement records, and the ICC Administration Manual. Some information is also available at the Commission's regional and field offices.
The addresses of these offices are in Appendix 6-D (p. 254).
Address requests for information to the Secretary of the ICC. If he
turns you down, you must appeal to the Chairman of the Commission
before you can go to court (49 C.F.R. 1001.4).

Working on the ICC

Just because the ICC provides a forum where transportation companies
can divide up the market and fix prices doesn't mean that these activities always go peacefully. Despite the Commission's distaste for "cut-

throat competition," on occasion common carriers have been known to compete with one another. When they do, the fight usually ends up before the Commission, with consumers unrepresented. These disputes usually fall into one of three categories, which correspond to the three Commission divisions:

1. Operating rights cases, usually involving disagreements between carriers over what company has the right to haul what goods in a particular area.
2. Rate cases, which are disagreements between carriers or different modes of transportation over commodities to be carried and prices to be charged.
3. Finance cases, which usually involve disputes over the buying and selling of transportation companies, with the Commission either approving or vetoing purchases or mergers.

When such a corporate contestant comes complaining to the ICC, an official called an Administrative Law Judge gets it first. He decides whether the case needs full-scale treatment, in the formal docket, or whether it can be settled informally through the modified procedure. (About 75 percent of all ICC cases are so handled.) If the case gets onto formal docket, an Administrative Law Judge handles it. If the modified procedure is used, it goes to the Office of Proceedings. The division which has jurisdiction over the subject matter may then rule on it immediately, or an Administrative Law Judge may issue a preliminary report. If there is a preliminary report, the parties may protest or disagree either with "statements of law or matters of fact." If there are no such objections to the report, it becomes effective as law. If there are objections, the division which has jurisdiction rules on them. Unsatisfied parties may appeal to the division involved, or, if a question of "general transportation importance" is at stake, it may be appealed to the full Commission.

Under the modified procedure, attorneys in the Section of Opinions take the first crack at the case. Their recommendation goes to the Review Board of the division involved. After this judgment, the case may be appealed just as under the formal procedure.

The above may give some idea of what the ICC does and how to find out more about it. But it is very difficult for anyone to have a say at the Commission unless he represents one of the regulated industries. The ICC believes that one of the two industry parties to any given dis-

pute represents the public, or that it will fill this role itself in its decision. For the rare case in which the Commission concedes that the public's interest might not coincide with that of one of the industry parties,
it feels its Bureau of Enforcement would intervene as a "public interest
party," in order to "develop the facts." The Commission is hostile
toward further public input. As one commissioner said, "It is not the
ICC's job to go out and solicit complaints from the public, or to let
them know of the Commission's existence."

Due largely to public outrage, this attitude has begun to thaw. As a
gesture toward the public, the Commission now attempts to inform
some consumer groups of proposed rules and orders. Official policy now
states that

> in the general public interest, in addition to the petitioning carriers
> and persons who filed replies to this petition . . . all state governors,
> and all the federal, state, county, and city offices charged with
> consumer protection, and all known voluntary consumer organi-
> zations . . . should be notified of the filing of the petition and have
> an opportunity to participate.

To find out about proposed ICC rules and regulations that may affect
you, write to the Office of the Secretary, the Interstate Commerce
Commission, Washington, D.C., 20423, and ask to be put on the mailing list for notice of *all* rule making proceedings. While you're at it, you
can ask for a copy of the Commission's rules for taking part in these
proceedings, in case you want to comment.

The simplest way to affect ICC actions is to express your views on
proposed rules. Although the ICC doesn't publish proposed *rates* (see
vegetable rate case below), it does publish for comment most *rules* it
may enact. Like all other agencies subject to the APA, the ICC gives
notice to the public through the *Federal Register*. Reading the *Register*
is the only way to be absolutely sure of catching notices of proposed
rules (and even then the rules may be written so ponderously that their
meaning is hidden). There *are* other ways, however, of keeping up with
new developments. *Consumer News*, from the White House Office of
Consumer Affairs, sometimes reports significant ICC proposals. And
trade magazines such as *Transport Topics* and *Traffic World* are quick
to pick up anything which would affect industry.

An example of the public's difficulties in trying to get a word in at
ICC rule makings occurred in the spring of 1971. Household moving is
one ICC-regulated industry with an immediate impact on most Ameri-

cans. The ICC gets thousands of complaints about interstate movers every year, and even after a recent flurry of versions, the rules governing the movers are another sad case of industry's convenience put above the public's.

One household-moving abuse which most consumers know little about is called "bumping"—increasing the scale weight of a shipment. It is the household-moving equivalent of the butcher's thumb on the scales. And a heavy thumb it is. In 1964 a study by the Comptroller General of the United States found that the Department of Defense was paying five million dollars every year to household movers for moving tons of things that weren't there. Well over half (65.5 percent) of the shipments observed weighed less than the movers claimed, and the average overcharge was for 365 pounds.

In November 1970 Reuben B. Robertson III, an attorney consultant at the Center for Study of Responsive Law, wrote to the Commission, prompted by a consumer complaint letter, and asked about a Commission rule related to bumping. The movers, it seems, were charging customers for reweighing shipments even when the reweighing revealed the mover's original weight was false. Robertson also asked about procedures for changing the regulations if existing ones allowed such charges for reweighing. The Commission's reply gave no hint it might consider new rules on the subject.

The following March, Robertson heard that the Commission was indeed considering making new rules on the subject. But when he called the ICC and asked for notice of such action, all he received was a standard information pamphlet on weighing shipments of household goods. Still later Robertson learned that, back in February, the ICC had initiated a rule making proceeding to amend Section 1056.6(d) of the regulations, dealing with reweighing shipments [49 C.F.R. 1056.6(d)].

The Commission's notice of proposed rule making had required anyone who wished to participate to file, within a month, a formal "statement of intention to participate." This is an ICC complication of the normal administrative rule making process, in which a notice appears in the *Federal Register* simply setting forth the text of the proposed rule and asking for comments during a stated period, usually thirty or sixty days. Unlike the practice of other agencies, the ICC procedures in most rule making cases pile step after step onto the process, immensely increasing the burdens of public participation. After all of the "statements of intention" are in, those who do submit comments must then send copies to all the other "parties" designated by the Commission who have filed statements. It is like a full-blown "rule making on a record," in that there are "parties" to the proceeding. But instead of having a hearing, "parties" to ICC rule making just send copies of documents to one another. This means that citizens wishing to participate by submitting comments on a proposed rule may be required to mail copies to hundreds of other companies and organizations.

In its notice of proposed rule making on reweighing household shipments, the ICC took a small and halting step toward what it considered to be representing the public interest. It mailed copies to the governors and public utility commissions of all the states and directed its Bureau of Enforcement to participate. Apparently the Commission thought that this step was enough to make sure the thousands of American families who entrust their possessions to household movers every year would have a voice. Robertson was allowed to file comments only by special leave after he protested strongly against the Commission's procedures.

Ultimately the Commission did tighten up to some degree its rules concerning reweigh charges, although not to the extent urged by Robertson and other consumer advocates who argued that accepting any fraudulent or negligent overcharge by a mover was inequitable.

Commenting on proposed rules is a way to react to what someone else, usually the Commission, thinks should be done about a problem. But it is primarily a defensive tactic—a way to combat harmful or halfway proposals. A first step toward improving things is to submit your own solution to the Commission through a petition for rule making.

Just as with the other agencies, a rule making petition to the ICC takes some skill and much effort to prepare. Because of the legal and procedural aspects, it helps if you are an attorney, or have the help of one. The Administrative Procedure Act (5 U.S.C. 553e) requires every agency to "give any interested person the right to petition for the issuance, amendment, or appeal of a rule." The ICC's requirements for a rule making petition appear in Rules 15 through 22 of the ICC's General Rules of Practice (49 C.F.R. 1100.15 *et seq.*). While any person can file, the Commission has accorded itself, through its regulations, "final" say over whether or not to hold a proceeding. Just because the Commission says a ruling is final, however, does not make it so, and unsuccessful petitioners can always challenge the Commission's decision in court.

A proposed rule can cover almost anything under ICC jurisdiction. Since the Commission takes such a timid view of its own authority, its first reaction to proposed rules is often that it can't do the sort of thing requested. The latent ICC authority to regulate household moving companies is one example, and the Commission's reluctance to act against discriminatory hiring by licensed carriers is another.*

The rule making petition to ban smoking on buses in Appendix 6-B (p. 211) illustrates an appeal to the ICC to take action on a common nuisance—both in ordinary and in legal language—that is well within the Commission's jurisdiction. The ICC's reaction to this petition shows how it can freeze even a simple proposal through compromise and delay. The original petition was filed in January 1970. After publishing it in the *Federal Register* and receiving comments, the ICC issued an order in August of that year for a hearing, which was held in October. After the hearing there were more briefs and delay. In November 1971, over a year after the hearings and almost two years after the original petition, the Commission issued a compromise order for interstate bus companies to restrict smokers to the rear 20 percent of their buses. The rule was to take effect in January 1972, but it didn't. NAMBO asked the Commission to reconsider its decision, and to suspend the order in the meantime. So two years after the filing of this relatively simple petition to deal with a nuisance clearly within the ICC's jurisdiction, the issue was still mired in the ICC's "due process."

Finally, in March 1972, the Commission turned down the NAMBO request. NAMBO promptly appealed to the U.S. Disrtict Court, where the matter still sat in January 1973.

Commissioner Stafford has cited the following current rule making and appeal proceedings as evidence of consumer concern:**

1. *Ex parte* No. MC-1 (Sub-No. 3), *Payment of Rates and Charges of Motor Carriers—Credit Regulations—Household Goods.*
2. *Ex parte* No. MC-85, *Transportation of "Waste" Products for Reuse and Recycling.*
3. *Ex parte* No. MC-86, Implementation of Public Law 91-375, *Postal Reorganization Act (Motor Carrier Licensing Provisions.*
4. *Ex parte* No. MC-5 (Sub-No. 1), *Broken Security for Protection of the Public.*
5. *Ex parte* No. MC-19 (Sub-No. 7), *Practices of Motor Common*

---

*In late 1972-early 1973 the Commission stepped up enforcement of its household moving regulations, partly and temporarily suspending the operations of major companies like Aero-Mayflower, Red-Ball, and Allied. But the rules are still so weighted in the movers' favor, given the bargaining position of the movers and their customers, that even more alert enforcement doesn't give the public much.

**Ex parte means the matter is not a simple dispute between two or more parties, but that the Commission itself is thinking of enacting new and general regulations. The number is the docket number; it is how you look up the matter at the ICC.

Carriers of Household Goods (prohibition against carriers participating in local and joint rates at different levels for transportation between same points in same direction.

6. *Ex parte* No. MC-19 (Sub-No. 12), *In the Matter of Modification of Part 1056—General Rules and Regulations of Motor Carriers of Household Goods.*

7. *Ex parte* No. MC-19 (Sub-No. 14), *Practices of Motor Common Carriers of Household Goods—Reweighing of Shipments.*

8. *Ex parte* No. MC-19 (Sub-No. 15), *Practices of Motor Common Carriers of Household Goods (Reservation of Vehicle Space by Shippers).*

9. *Ex parte* No. MC-78, *Vehicles Employed Solely in Transporting School Children and Teachers.*

10. *Ex parte* No. MC-82, *Proposed New Procedures in Motor Carrier Revenue Proceedings.*

11. *Ex parte* No. 263, *Rules, Regulations, and Practices of Regulated Carriers with Respect to Processing of Loss and Damage Claims.*

12. *Ex parte* No. 55 (Sub-No. 4), Implementation of P.L. 91-190, *National Environmental Policy Act of 1969 and Related Requirements.*

13. *Ex parte* No. MC-19 (Sub-No. 18), *Household Goods Carriers' Bureau Declaratory Order—Certain Procedures with Respect to Releasing the Value of Household Goods Shipments.*

14. *Ex parte* No. 278, *Equal Opportunity in Surface Transportation.*

15. *Ex parte* No. 272, *Investigation into Limitations of Carrier Service on C.O.D. and Freight-Collect Shipments.*

16. *Ex parte* No. 55 (Sub-No. 3), *General Rules of Practice—Discovery Rules.*

17. *Ex parte* No. MC-C-6,748, *Smoking by Passengers and Operating Personnel on Interstate Buses.*

18. *Ex parte* No. MC-C-7,255, *Petition for Rule-Making Proceeding Relative to Employment Practices of Motor Carriers.*

19. *Ex parte* No. MC-C-6,829, *Limitation of Free Baggage Allowance—Greyhound Lines—Petition for Investigation.*

20. *Ex parte* No. 35343, *Dept. of Defense* v. *Gulf, Mobile, and Ohio R.R. Co., et al.*

21. *Ex parte* No. 269, *Adequacy of Service Regulations under the RR Passenger Service Act of 1970.*

22. *Ex parte* No. 277, *Adequacy and Safety of Passenger Service.*

Although the scope of these proceedings is narrow, there is opportunity to comment and to support other petitioners.

Any submission to the ICC by a citizen, including comments and rule making petitions, must comply with the formal specifications for pleadings which are set forth in the Commission's "Rules of Practice" regulations [49 C.F.R. Part 1100]. If there is confusion about what rules are applicable or how they are interpreted, you are entitled to obtain information about procedure and instructions supplementing the rules by writing to the Secretary of the Commission in Washington, D.C. [49 C.F.R. 1100.3].

The Commission's formal specifications may not seem unduly burdensome when applied to large trucking companies, railroads, or industrial associations which are frequent participants in its proceedings. But when enforced against individual citizens who seek the opportunity to be heard or to request rule making action by the government, they are onerous indeed, and the Commission has been notoriously obdurate in its refusal to modify them so as to encourage or permit effective citizen participation in rule making.

Rules 15 and 16, for example, set forth typographical specifications and the requirement that multiple copies be provided to the Commission, usually an original and fifteen copies [49 C.F.R. 1100.15 and 16]. All pleadings must be printed or typed (double-spaced) on "opaque, unglazed, durable paper not exceeding 8½ by 11 inches." They are to be bound on the left-hand side, with ample margins on each side. Moreover, any pleading over fifty pages long, including cover pages, indices, and appendices, *must* be printed. Rule 15 warns that "failure to observe these specifications will result in rejection."

In the summer of 1972 the ICC, at the urging of the DOT, initiated another rule making proceeding concerning household movers, to consider the need for further consumer protection rules in that industry *Ex parte* No. MC-19 (Sub-No. 19). Grace Polk Stern, a Maryland housewife, was aware of many of the problems in this industry and intended to file comments on the need for the proposed regulations, until she learned of the burdensome pleading rules that would apply. As a result, she filed a motion before the Commission on behalf of herself and all other individual members of the public for a waiver of the requirements of these rules as regards individual citizens. Even this motion, of course, had to comply with the rules in question. Based on the standard copying charges at the ICC, Ms. Stern computed that a householder wishing to file a four-page comment would have to spend $16 to $19 on copying charges alone. She wrote:

Clearly, in such a situation, only those persons willing and able to make such an expenditure can participate, or be expected to participate, in this proceeding. Many members of the public could not afford to do so. The American public at large ought not to be priced out of a proceeding initiated and designed for its protection.

Nevertheless, the Commission remained unmoved. Commissioner Murphy, to whom the case was assigned, rejected the Stern petition, claiming that waiver of the typing and copying requirements would place a terrible burden on the Commission and that "there has been no persuasive showing at this time that movant or any other potential party to this proceeding is unwilling or unable adequately to represent the public interest . . . ."

Ms. Stern, however, was not willing to give up. She filed an appeal to the Commission and argued:

A refusal by the Commission to waive obscure and burdensome procedural requirements as to individual members of the public who would be interested in expressing their views in a proceeding initiated and designed for their protection can only serve to raise doubts as to the Commissions' interest in correcting abuses in this field. Rather, it would seem incumbent on the Commission in proceedings of this nature to seek out ways to encourage public participation so that a full and balanced record can be made and the Commission can have the basis for taking such corrective action as may be found to be desirable or necessary.

Meanwhile, she made sure that the Senate and House Commerce Committees and newspaper reporters covering the ICC were aware of the foolish position taken by the Commission, and several calls from Committee staff members and articles in the Washington papers ridiculing the ICC's practice helped to heighten the agency's sensitivity to the issue [see, *e.g.*, Stephen M. Aug, "Consumers Lose ICC Round," *Washington Star-News*, November 7, 1972]. Finally, the agency reluctantly gave in, and agreed to waive Rules 15 and 16 for that particular proceeding. While the ruling does not extend to any other cases, it does serve as precedent for other citizens seeking similar considerations in future proceedings.

Another of the Commission's burdensome procedural specifications is Rule 22 [49 C.F.R. 1100.22]. This generally requires every pleading

filed with the Commission to include a certificate of service vouching
that a copy of the document has been simultaneously sent, in person
or by first class mail, to every other "party" to the proceedings. In rule
making proceedings, the parties may include every company or person
who has filed a "statement of intention to participate."

The burden this can create is illustrated by a recent case that arose
when the Commission, under pressure from civil rights advocates, initiated a rule making proceeding to consider the problems of equal employment opportunities in trucking and other ICC-regulated industries
[Equal Opportunity in Surface Transportation, *ex parte* 278]. An associate of Ralph Nader petitioned for waiver of the cross-service burdens
of Rule 22, which would require that any citizen or public interest
group wishing to file comments in this important proceeding would
have to duplicate and mail or deliver copies to over 100 companies and
trade associations in addition to the multiple copies required to be
given to the Commission itself under Rule 16. As the motion noted:

> This proceeding is of special significance and interest to many
> individual citizens and civic organizations which have never before
> participated before the ICC. For the most part, such citizens and
> groups have extremely limited means and resources available for
> participation in such proceedings, and are at a serious disadvant-
> age with respect to the costs of such participation, since they are
> unable to pass these costs back to consumers as the regulated
> carriers normally do. [Motion of Reuben B. Robertson III for
> Relief from Requirement for Service of Documents on Parties,
> ICC *ex parte* 278]

Chairman Stafford, to whom the matter had been referred, turned a
deaf ear to the motion and its underlying rationale, ruling that "mov-
ants have failed to present any facts or evidence to support their assertion that certain unidentified parties to this proceeding do not have the
means and resources necessary to their meaningful participation herein"
[Order dated 6 October 1971, ICC *ex parte* 278]. On appeal in this
case, the full Commission, bolstered by the strong opposition of a
number of truckers and industry organizations to any liberalization of
the rules that might benefit the equal employment advocates, endorsed
Stafford's ruling completely, refusing to alleviate the costly requirements of Rule 22. The Commission based its decision on the grounds
that there was no proof that any person or group which desired to par-

ticipate in the proceeding was too poor to be able and willing to duplicate and mail the hundreds of copies required for industry parties, and
that if any relief were granted in this case "this Commission's extremely
limited staff and budgetary resources would not be able to meet the
additional burdens that would be placed upon them. . ." [Commission
Order dated 29 November 1971, *ex parte* 278]. Thus, while refusing to
recognize the limited resources available to civil rights and public interest advocates (and individual citizens), the ICC somehow concluded that
its own alleged poverty was so great that waiver of the rules could not
be permitted, although it never explained how such a waiver would result in any additional burden on it at all. (It wouldn't.)

While the cross-service requirement does not apply in every rule
making case (only where the initial "statement of intention to participate" procedure is used and listed parties may file "reply" comments),
this episode does give an insight into the ICC's adamant insensitivity to
the problems and burdens of citizen participation, and its irrational
hostility to public interest and civil rights proponents.

Participating in ICC rule making procedures is hard enough, but when
combined with a fight against an ICC rate increase it becomes a gauntlet
only the wealthy and well-represented can run. The experience of one
consumer group that tried to stop the constant increase in freight rates
for lettuce, melons, and other fresh vegetables gives some idea of what
you can expect if you venture into an ICC rate making battle. The
group was the AHCCP, mentioned earlier in this chapter.

When the Committee entered the 1969 railroad freight rate case, it
was the first time that real members of the public had raised their voices
in an ICC rate proceeding. They stepped in to oppose increases of from
3 to 21 percent in rates for shipping agricultural products from the
west to the east coast. Their reasoning: If the supermarkets had to pay
more for crates of lettuce, consumers would soon pay more for each
head. The group, represented by D.C. attorneys Jacob P. Billig and
Benny L. Kass, also argued that western shippers had agreed to the new
rates in return for unpublished rebates prohibited by the Elkins Act.

One of the AHCCP's moves was to ask the Commission, informally,
to publish all rate change proposals. It argued:

> As a general rule, the consumer does not become aware of pro-
> posed rate increases for a long time. In fact, by the time he does
> become aware of them they are in all likelihood no longer "pro-
> posed" but rather "in effect" . . . he becomes aware of all pro-
> posed rate increases via the diminishing contents of his pocket-
> book, ex post facto.

When this informal request failed, the Committee formally petitioned the Commission to begin a rule making proceeding to require publication of such rate increases.

Specifically, the AHCCP proposal would have required that "every proposed rate increase filed with the Interstate Commerce Commission will be published in the *Federal Register* with separate designations for their effects upon: (1) carrier's income; (2) shipper's costs; and (3) ultimate consumer price. And that such designations be readily determinable upon reasonable inspection by the Commission and the public." The AHCCP only submitted an original and two copies of its petition for *Federal Register* notice of rate increases. The ICC turned it down, citing its Rule 16 requiring fifteen copies of every petition submitted.

The Committee also filed a petition to proceed *in forma pauperis.* If granted, this would have relieved them of transcript and duplication expenses, and possibly attorney's fees. The ICC's Rules of Practice make no provision for *in forma pauperis* status, so the Committee based its petition on Section 17 (3) of the Interstate Commerce Act, which directs the Commission "to conduct its proceedings in such manner as will best conduce to the ends of justice and to conform its rules, as nearly as may be, to those of the courts of the United States." Since this section referred the ICC to the Federal Rules of Civil Procedure, the Committee cited in particular 28 U.S.C. 1915, which empowers a federal court to authorize litigation "without prepayment of fees and costs or security therefor, by a person who makes affidavit that he is unable to pay such costs or give security therefor."

The AHCCP drafted and signed such an affidavit, pointing out that it was "represented without fee by a volunteer attorney and law students; that the Ad Hoc Committee on Consumer Protection is a nonprofit public service association organized for the benefit of Washington area consumers; that the Committee has no assets or funds and that all matters performed by or on behalf of the Committee are on a volunteer basis." While the ICC expressed disapproval of this request through informal letters to the Committee, it never formally accepted or rejected it. The ICC doesn't have to do anything with such a petition, and it didn't. The petition still rests somewhere in the ICC files.

In the vegetable case the Committee had also requested a free transcript of the hearing. The ICC hearing examiner turned them down, but kindly referred them to the company which prepares the transcripts for the ICC. The company said it would sell them one for 85 cents per page, plus $2 a day delivery charge for each day the hearing continued. The hearing examiner also told them that they could, of course, inspect the transcript in the Commission offices. Only slightly daunted, the

AHCCP then suggested that if they could look at copies of the transcript at the ICC office, they should be allowed to photocopy the transcript for the same exhorbitant 30 cents per page fee the Commission charges for other Commission documents. Once again they were turned down, on the ground that the hearing transcript was not a "public record" under the FOIA. In rejecting the simple request to photocopy the transcript, the Commission showed whose interests it put first:

> Of overriding importance is the matter of our contract with a private company, CSA Reporting Company, which acts as the official reporter of the Commission and which makes its money from the sale of copies of the transcript to interested persons. Our contractual relationship with CSA is such that we cannot issue free copies without jeopardizing the reporting services required by the Commission.

At the ICC, even reporting companies come ahead of the public.

The efforts of the AHCCP in the vegetable case served mainly to show the ICC that there really were consumers out there affected by ICC decisions, and to show anyone who was watching that the ICC would nevertheless continue business as usual. The Committee lost each issue it raised. The rates went into effect as proposed, and a subsequent court appeal failed (although the court did allow the AHCCP to proceed *in forma pauperis* in the appeal). The petition to the ICC to proceed *in forma pauperis* was inconclusive generally, and the attempt to get a free transcript, or at least to photocopy the transcript at the regular ICC rate, fell flat. Commission silence froze the petition to have proposed rates published. But the AHCCP's efforts at least put the Commission on notice that its cozy tête-à-tête with the transportation industry would not continue, and that the broader public was determined to have a say. It was a beginning.

Two sections of the Interstate Commerce Act authorize the Commission to pay legal fees of needy parties before it. Under 49 U.S.C. 16(11) the Commission can provide attorneys to represent consumer groups in proceedings regarding railroads, and 49 U.S.C. 305 (j) provides similar authority to furnish legal representation in motor carrier proceedings. The first section states that

> The commission may employ such attorneys as it finds necessary for proper legal aid and service of the Commission or its members in the conduct of their work or for *proper representation of the*

> *public interest in investigations made by it or cases or proceedings
> pending before it* whether at the Commission's own instance or
> upon complaint. . .and the expenses of such employment shall be
> paid out of the appropriation for the Commission. (emphasis
> added)

Given its reticence where the public interest is concerned, it is not
surprising that it has *never* used this authority to provide legal representation for consumer groups at its "own instance." But it probably hasn't
used its authority to provide such legal representation "upon complaint" simply because, to date, no consumer group has made such
complaint.

Alternative Channels

Although the transportation lobbies are generous campaign funders and
skilled lobbyists, consumers may get action from Congress, too, if the
issue can gain publicity. In addition, the Commission often gives much
better treatment to letters Congressmen send to it than it gives to complaints it gets directly from the public.

If hearings and legislation could arise from your complaint, contact
the staff of either the Surface Transportation Subcommittee of the
Senate Commerce Committee or the Subcommittee on Transportation
and Aeronautics of the House Interstate and Foreign Commerce Committee. Senate Subcommittee Chairman Vance Hartke has become
increasingly active in overseeing the ICC. His small but sympathetic
subcommittee staff will read with interest letters with proposed legislation, complaint, and ideas.

One of the advantages of the fragmented authority over transportation is that one agency may disagree with another and fight its actions.
Such conflict, if not squelched by the President or the Office of Management and Budget (OMB), can open the political process to public
view and pressure. The Civil Aeronautics Board (CAB), the DOT, and
to a limited extent the Departments of Agriculture, Justice, and
Defense, may provide allies or information about the ICC. Economists
in particular are critical of the ICC, and may testify on your behalf or
provide other help.

Aiding those struggling to make the public voice heard within the
ICC, whether by letter of encouragement, legal assistance, or otherwise,

is another way to get the ICC activated. For example, when ICC special agent Frank Lawrence sought to press bribery charges against a leading freight forwarder, the ICC's managing director tried to have him fired for "incompetence" after nine years of service. It turned out that this managing director was often found at the firm's cocktail and yacht parties, had been offered a job by the firm's trade association, and informed the firm of the doings of rival freight forwarders, and so on. When the agent obtained free legal counsel from the Nader organization and decided to display the agency's linen in public by contesting his firing, the agency backed down and kept him. The managing director resigned shortly thereafter.

A similar case was that of former ICC hearing examiner Bernard J. Hasson, Jr. In late 1969 and early 1970 there was increasing public outrage over the Commission's fraternization with the transportation industry. To appease its critics, the Commission needed to make a show of cracking down. One target was Hasson, whom the Commission dismissed for such deeds as accepting "meals, cocktails, and entertainment" from the truckers involved in a particular West Coast hearing, and for spending certain evenings with a "lady friend."

Hasson shot back that the Commission was making a scapegoat of him. "Volumes of sworn testimony before several Congressional committees disclosed," his legal defense stated, "that (his) conduct was, at worst, the same and in most cases far less serious than the conduct of other ICC personnel, hearing examiners, and commissioners." Hasson sought to subpoena witnesses to prove this charge, including all the current commissioners, two former ones, and eight newspaper reporters.

As an example, Hasson pointed to a custom, "quaintly called the 'Pocatello rule,'" which had grown among attorneys and hearing examiners in West Coast ICC hearings. Under this "Pocatello rule," the attorney who submitted the fiftieth or one-hundredth exhibit in a drawn-out case would that evening have to buy a round of drinks for all who had attended the day's hearings. Hasson's defense did not prevail, but his revelations were educational.

With a few exceptions, ICC commissioners have been people of very ordinary ability and drive, with little or no background in transportation.* Thus they have been vulnerable to the pomp and glitter of being

---

*The newest ICC Commissioner, A. Daniel O'Neal, has been the lawyer on the Senate Transportation subcommittee and is expected to become the most knowledgeable and consumer-minded commissioner at the agency.

a commissioner, and this has helped give rise to the "Puerto Rico Effect," sometimes called the "Bahamas Phenomena."

This effect, discovered long ago by alert industry lobbyists, is one of the ways the ICC's clientele "acculturates" new commissioners and keeps them in the fold. They invite the commissioners to industry shindigs in attractive climes, treat them with studied esteem, and honor them with rapt attention when they address the gatherings. They present them with awards, treat them to standing ovations, and reprint their speeches and every utterance in trade publications. The healthy tension between regulators and regulated softens, and the more sordid forms of influence, like bribes, become for the most part unnecessary.

In the short run, the public cannot do much about commissioners' needs for acceptance and acclaim (given present methods of selecting them). But it can, and should, begin to harness the "Puerto Rico Effect" in more constructive directions. When consumer and public interest groups hold conferences, for example, they should invite a commissioner to come and speak. While the chance of getting one to do so, and the strength of the effect itself, may increase geometrically with proximity to San Juan, Honolulu, Geneva, and other such transportation meccas, the commissioners have been known to sally forth to industry audiences in less exotic places.

If a commissioner attends, and has to speak to your problem, he or she may get an inkling of your point of view. Sensing your support, this commissioner might even gain the courage to buck the industry at some time.

It will take many dedicated hands to gain real reform of the agency, or to replace it with another. Some citizens may wish to join in this effort. The first need is to create a competent agency which can advance the public interest in transportation, provide an effective forum for customers as well as carriers and commercial shippers, and carry out the laws and intent of Congress. This may well mean bringing the regulation of all transportation under a single agency, to replace the ridiculous, industry-serving fragmentation of authority we have now.

The second need is to bring the transportation laws themselves up-to-date.

While these are long-run goals, there are clear, simple steps the public can insist on now to make the current setup work better. Consider, for example, the commissioners. Critics contend that the present Commission consists almost entirely of officials who know nothing about economics, transportation, law, or regulation, but who are generally political hacks. And critics also claim that the atmosphere of regulation, from informal industry "advisory committees" to the worldwide banquet circuit, fosters a lack of objectivity. Finally, the lack of checks on financial holdings and future jobs of agency officials is cause for concern. Ten of the past twelve commissioners leaving the ICC have assumed high-paying jobs with the transportation industry.

Citizens can pressure the Congressional committees referred to above to refuse to confirm unqualified commissioners. Citizens can demand broad interpretation of bans on *ex parte* contact to prevent private communications between commissioners and parties to matters before the Commission. Citizens can demand passage of a law to require high agency officials to divest all nonpersonal assets into blind trusts while they stay in office. They can also push for a rule that would prevent commissioners from taking a job with the industry they regulated for at least five years after they leave government employ.

The ICC is among the most remote of all the independent federal agencies. This is due in part to the staggering complexity of rate making, in part to the decades of interbreeding with the transportation industries, and in part to the dead weight of tradition and habit at the oldest regulatory agency. One resolute citizen, however, a Sheperdstown, West Virginia, woman named Mavis Kennedy, has shown that the public *can* make its point. When the Baltimore and Ohio (B&O) Railroad decided to cut commuter service between Washington, D.C., and Harpers Ferry, West Virginia—service on which she and others depended—Ms. Kennedy decided to try, as an average citizen, to do something about it. Her persistent trail led her through a maze of government agencies to the ICC. There she made a gallant effort to navigate the Commission's procedures and get it to act.

Appendix 6-C (p. 223) sets out Ms. Kennedy's experience in her own words. After she wrote and filed a complaint with the ICC, the B&O's legal department cranked out a 100-page reply. Undaunted, Ms. Kennedy came back with a 20-page rebuttal which also appears in the appendix. She did deal with the B&O's legal arguments and factual assertions, but her main focus was the kind of information that the ICC hears all too seldom. As she put it:

> Throughout its voluminous response, Defendant frequently states, in proper legal parlance, "NOW COMES B&O" . . .denying, asserting, requesting, but not once, in all its verbiage, does B&O come to grips with the reality of the 14-hour and longer workday forced upon people who geared their lives (some for more than 20 years) to a commuter service that, until May 1, 1971, offered at

least minimal options for getting to and from their homes and jobs by train.

Mavis Kennedy did not succeed at the ICC. But she made her point both there and to the many officials with whom she came in contact. The regulators, especially those at the ICC, may be a bit more aware of the millions of people "out there" like Mavis Kennedy; people who don't have the money or the lawyers to appear before them, but who have very important interests at stake. And even railroads like the B&O may be a bit less cavalier about dropping passenger service, and about the way they treat their passengers.

In fact, the signs are pointing towards more concern for the general public. The Commission has been under increasing attack for some time. Back in 1962, the Doyle Report urged that the ICC be merged with the other federal transportation-regulating bodies into a single, streamlined agency. Eight years later, a Ralph Nader-led study, *The Interstate Commerce Omission,* reached the same conclusion. The Nader study sparked a fresh wave of criticism which even the Commission, in its elephantine torpor, could not ignore. Bills to abolish the ICC and bring our transportation laws up-to-date appeared in both the House and the Senate, and were supported by Republicans and Democrats alike. The President's Ash Commission on Executive Reorganization, the Council of Economic Advisors, and Departments of Transportation, Justice, and Agriculture have all come out for drastic revisions in the regulation of transportation.

In short, the Commission itself may be on the line, and the prospect of oblivion has given it a mild sense of urgency sadly lacking since the sheen wore off its original mission back in the early 1900s.

Unusual efforts may result. The recent wave of enforcement in the household-moving area is one sign. So is a sudden concern, at least at the public relations level, for "consumers" and the "public interest." A series of *Public Advisory Bulletins* have appeared, with such titles as *Householder's Guides to Accurate Weights* (#1), *Arranging Transportation for Small Shipments: Shippers' Rights, Remedies and Alternatives* (#2), *People on the Move* (#3), and *Lost and Damaged Household Goods—Prevention and Recovery* (#4). There is a new pamphlet called *Summary of Information for Shippers of Household Goods.* (Even in this quasi-Renaissance the Commission remains hypnotized by the language of the Interstate Commerce Act; hence customers are still "shippers.") While the Commission still may not be much help in such matters, at least now its easier to find out what it won't do.

Even the Commission's Annual Report reflects new gestures toward a public interest mission. Once a dreary chronicle of "carriers," "shippers," "modes," and "proceedings," the 1972 Report puts "Protecting the Consumer" right up front after the Introduction. There is a chapter called "Development of Policy" and even a section on "The Environment."

While the Interstate Commerce Act—which is the Commission's raison d'etre—may become more obsolete every day, and while habit and inertia may still paralyze the agency even when it means well, the new grasping after "relevance" can only improve things for the public. And it can become self-re-enforcing. The more public input there is, the more thought and attention the Commission has to give to its problems. Nor should people underestimate the sincere good intentions of many in the Commission's rank and file. Mediocrity at the very top and creaking obsolescence one and two steps down have tended to stifle action. But with enough public urging and support, the many frustrated but dedicated civil servants lower down may begin to carry more weight.

As with the other agencies, the easiest thing to do is to file comments on proposed rules, file complaints, and petition for rules on your own. Some areas of ICC jurisdiction have been the subject of rule making petitions, such as a lengthy petition on discriminatory employment practices by regulated carriers, filed by Reuben B. Robertson III and Eileen Schneider of the Center for Study of Responsive Law. Another area ripe for such a petition is the ICC's regulation of household movers. One possible approach would be to single out the worst offenders among the movers and petition for revocation of their ICC operating authority. If the ICC were responsive to the thousands of complaint letters it gets annually, it would have taken such action on its own years ago. The Department of Defense pays for thousands of household moves by servicemen and their families every year, and it presumably knows who are the worst offenders among movers. A possible course of action for a consumer group would be to try to get such information from the ICC (using the Freedom of Information Act, if necessary) or the Department of Defense, or from sources such as Consumer's Union, and take appropriate steps to see that the ICC takes action.

Carrying out the transportation laws has become complex and expensive, and frustrations of the AHCCP illustrate the difficulties awaiting a consumer group that tries to intervene in such proceedings. But a future ICC, if sufficiently revitalized, might make such efforts easier, or even encourage them. Ultimately, the answer for much of the ICC's lassitude must be, as the *Interstate Commerce Omission* report concluded, less regulation, more competition, and a single agency to oversee all the modes of transportation. But that, too, will require organized efforts by consumers who pay the costs of the present system. Such pressure, if increased, will force a breakthrough for change.

Organization Chart of the Interstate Commerce Commission

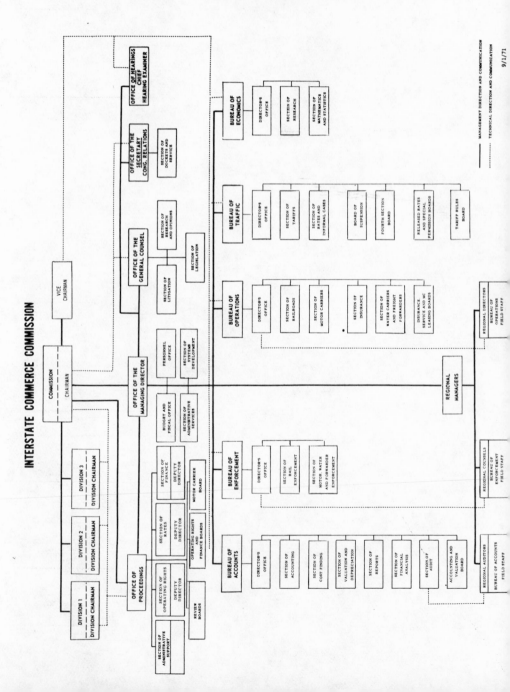

Petition for Rule Making

Ralph Nader,   :
      :
          Petitioner   :
      :

PETITION FOR RULEMAKING

Petitioner requests the Commission to establish a rule of general applicability for passenger motor carriers in interstate commerce, and to amend all certificates of convenience and necessity held by such carriers, to prohibit the smoking of cigars, cigarettes and pipes, by passengers or operating personnel, on all passenger carrying motor buses.

The authority of the Commission is found in the Interstate Commerce Act, part II, 49 U.S.C. 304(a)(1), which empowers the Commission to make "reasonable requirements with respect to continuous and <u>adequate</u> service," and 49 U.S.C. 308, which empowers the Commission to place conditions on certificates of convenience and necessity to carry out requirements established under 49 U.S.C. 304(a)(1).

Section 304(a)(3a) of Title 49 U.S.C., more particularly empowers the Commission to make "reasonable requirements with respect to comfort of passengers" for carriers of migrant workers, and under this authority the Commission has promulgated regulations respecting meal and rest stops, and protection from cold.   49 C.F.R. 198.4(h), 198.5(g).

This petition invokes the Commission's authority to provide for the adequacy of service and its specific authority, with respect to migrant workers, to provide for the comfort of passengers.   It is petitioner's premise that the adequacy of service includes provision for the health and comfort of passengers on buses, not merely the frequency of stops and of journeys.

A parallel petition is being filed with the Department of Transportation, the transferee of the Commission's regulatory authority over safety matters.

Petitioner is an adult male who frequently travels by interstate bus and who does not smoke.   The memorandum summarizing accepted scientific findings about the health hazards of inhalation of tobacco smoke establishes that smoking in buses creates a serious health hazard to petitioner and all other non-smoking bus riders.

William A. Dobrovir
2005 L Street, N.W.
Washington, DC 20036

Attorney for Petitioner

Memorandum

The Inhalation of Smoke as a Hazard
to the Health of Non-smokers

Tobacco is an herb containing cellulosic products, starches, proteins, sugars, alkaloids, pectic substances, hydrocarbon, phenols, fatty acids, isoprenoids, sterols and inorganic minerals. When burned it creates a smoke consisting of a heterogeneous mixture of gases, uncondensed vapors and liquid particulate matter. The Advisory Committee to the Surgeon General's Report on Smoking and Health (1964) states that cigarette smoke contains the following major ingredients (Ibid.):

MAJOR CLASSES OF COMPOUNDS IN THE PARTICULATE
PHASE OF CIGARETTE SMOKE

Class	Percent in particulate* phase	Number of compounds	Toxic action on lung
Acids.....................	7.7 - 12.8	25	Some irritant
Glycerol, glycol, alcohols..	5.3 - 8.3	18	Possible irritation
Aldehydes and ketones.......	8.5	21	Some irritant
Aliphatic hydrocarbons......	4.9	64	Some irritant
Aromatic hydrocarbons.......	0.44	81	Some carcinogenic
Phenols...................	1.0 - 3.8	45	Irritant
	66 %	254	and possibly cocarcinogenic

* Water 27%

SOME GASES FOUND IN CIGARETTE SMOKE

Compound	Concentration (ppm)	Safe level for industrial exposure*	Toxic action on lung
Carbon Monoxide	42,000	100	Unknown
Carbon Dioxide	92,000	---	None
Methane, ethane, propane, butane, etc.	87,000	500	None
Acetylene, ethylene, propylene, etc.	31,000	5,000	None
Formaldehyde	30	5	Irritant
Acetaldehyde	3,200	200	Irritant
Acrolein	150	0.5	Irritant
Methanol	700	---	Irritant
Acetone	1,100	200	Irritant
Methyl ethyl ketone	500	250	Irritant
Ammonia	300	150	Irritant
Nitrogen Dioxide	250	5	Irritant
Methyl Nitrite	200	---	Unknown
Hydrogen Sulfide	40	20	Irritant
Hydrogen Cyanide	1,600	10	Respiratory enzyme poison
Methyl Chloride	1,200	100	Unknown

* The values listed refer to time-weighted average concentrations for a normal work day.

The Surgeon General's Report made the following findings

with respect to the health dangers of cigarette smoking:

> The mortality ratio for male cigarette smokers
> compared with non-smokers for all causes of death
> taken together, is 1.68, representing a total
> death rate nearly 70 percent higher than for non-
> smokers. (This ratio includes death rates for
> diseases not listed in the table as well as for
> the 14 disease categories shown.) (p. 28)
>
> Expressed in percentage-form, this is equivalent
> to a statement that for coronary artery disease,
> the leading cause of death in this country, the
> death rate is 70 percent higher for cigarette
> smokers. For chronic bronchitis and emphysema,
> which are among the leading causes of severe dis-
> ability, the death rate for cigarette smokers is
> 500 percent higher than for non-smokers. For lung
> cancer, the most frequent site of cancer in men,
> the death rate is nearly 1,000 percent higher.
> (p. 29)
>
> Cigarette smoking is causally related to lung
> cancer in men; the magnitude of the effect of
> cigarette smoking far outweighs all other factors.
> The data for women, though less extensive, point
> in the same direction. (p. 31)
>
>   xxx
>
> Cigarette smoking is the most important of the
> causes of chronic bronchitis in the United States,
> and increases the risk of dying from chronic
> bronchitis and emphysema. (p. 31)
>
>   xxx
>
> The death rate for smokers of cigarettes only, who
> were smoking at the time of entry into the particular
> prospective study, is about 70 percent higher than
> that for non-smokers. The death rates increase with
> the amount smoked. (p. 35)
>
>   xxx
>
> Cigarette smoking is the most important of the causes
> of bronchitis in the United States, and increases
> the risk of dying from chronic bronchitis. (p. 38)
>
> Cough, sputum production, or the two combined are
> consistently more frequent among cigarette smokers
> than among non-smokers. (p. 38)

xxx

In view of the continuing and mounting evidence from many
sources, it is the judgment of the Committee that cigarette
smoking contributes substantially to mortality from
certain specific diseases and to the overall death rate.
(p. 31)

xxx

On the basis of prolonged study and evaluation of many
lines of converging evidence, the Committee makes the
following judging:

> Cigarette smoking is a health hazard of sufficient
> importance in the United States to warrant appro-
> priate remedial action.

These conclusions were expanded by the 1968 Supplement to

the 1967 Public Health Service Review of the Health Conse-

quences of Smoking (p. 3):

> Previous findings reported in 1967 indicate that
> cigarette smoking is associated with an increase
> in overall mortality and morbidity and leads to a
> substantial excess of deaths in those people who
> smoke. In addition, evidence herein presented
> shows that life expectancy among young men is
> reduced by an average of 8 years in "heavy" cigarette
> smokers, those who smoke over two packs a day,
> and an average of 4 years in "light" cigarette
> smokers, those who smoke less than one-half packs
> per day.

xxx

> Because of the increasing convergency of epidemio-
> logical and physiological findings relating cigarette
> smoking to coronary heart disease, it is con-
> cluded that cigarette smoking can contribute to the
> development of cardiovascular disease and particular-
> ly to death from coronary heart disease.

It is the inhalation of tobacco smoke which causes

the health hazards of smoking and one need not be a smoker

to suffer the ill effects of smoking--if one is exposed to

and inhales tobacco smoke.

> Tobacco smoke contains a large number and a wide
> variety of compounds which may result in complex
> and multiple pathophysiological effects on the
> various tissues and organ systems. [1969 Supplement
> to the 1967 Public Health Service Review of the
> Health Consequences of Smoking (p. 6)]

In animal experimental studies, the animal presumably

is not a smoker; animals are exposed to the inhalation of

tobacco smoke much as a person in a confined space--a room

or a vehicle, for example--is involuntarily exposed to

smoke inhalation. The 1967 Public Health Service Review

of the Health Consequences of Smoking at 106 reported a

study that reflects the type, if not the quantity of ex-

posure to smoke experienced by persons enclosed in a con-

fined space in which tobacco smoking occurs:

> Results of two experimental studies relating
> smoke inhalation to lung parenchymal changes in
> dogs have been published in the last 3 years.
> Hernandez and his coworkers (39) used 23 healthy
> greyhounds retired from racing. Eight served as
> controls and 15 were exposed to high concentrations
> of cigarette smoke for 30-45 minutes twice daily
> in wooden inhalation chambers. Seven animals were
> exposed for approximately 5 months and the remaining
> eight were sacrificed after almost 15 months of
> smoke inhalation. Disruption of the lung parenchyma
> was assessed macroscopically by comparison with pre-
> selected standards graded in severity from 0 to 3.
> Assessment was made without knowledge of the source
> of the lung specimen. Lung damage among dogs that
> were exposed longer showed significantly greater
> disruption of the lung parenchyma.

The tobacco smoke to which the non-smoker is exposed

while in a confined space is of three types. First is the

smoke which comes from the front of the cigarettes, pipe

or cigar which is not even taken into the mouth of the

smoker and which is not filtered through the cigar, pipe or cigarette. This is the most toxic smoke--more toxic even than the smoke used in the majority of the studies upon which the Surgeon General's Reports were based. See Scassellatti-Sforzolini, Non-Smokers Share Carcinogenic Risk While Breathing Air Among Smokers, Medical Tribune (December 4, 1967). A second class of smoke is that which is drawn through the pipe, cigar or cigarette into the mouth of the smoker but which is not inhaled. Some portion, but far from all of the harmful elements in the smoke are left in the smoker's mouth. The 1964 Surgeon General's Report (p. 264) concluded that the exhaled smoke contained 33 - 66% by weight of the tars which were included in the original smoke. The third type of smoke is that which is inhaled by the smoker and then exhaled. In this case 10 - 20% of the particles of the smoke are released into the air when the smoke is exhaled (1967 Surgeon General's Report, p. 264) and an unknown portion of the gas contained in the original smoke is released into the air, a fact demonstrable even to laymen who see and breathe the smoke exhaled by others.

The scientific evidence clearly demonstrates that even small quantities of such tobacco smoke (and thus small quantities of the particles and gases in tobacco smoke) are hazardous to health. For instance, the 1968 Supplement to the 1967 Public Health Service Review of the Health Consequences of Smoking reported (p. 69-70):

Most surveys have been of adults, but Holland, et al. (26) reported the findings of an investigation of smoking and respiratory symptoms among more than 10,000 school children, age eleven or more, in England. The survey was conducted in 1965 and repeated in 1966. Cigarette smokers (at least one cigarette per week) more frequently reported symptoms of cough and phlegm production than non-smokers and the prevalence of symptoms increased with increases in the amount smoked. Children who smoked one year but did not smoke in the subsequent year had a lower frequency of symptoms in the second year.

Three other scientific studies have uncovered a direct correlation between illness and disease symptoms and the exposure of non-smokers to an environment in which others smoke. The conclusions of two of these studies were summarized in Volume 65, No. 1 of the Medical Journal of the West Virginia State Medical Association (p. 22):

Children living with an adult who smokes were sick more frequently than youngsters who live in homes of nonsmokers, reports a research team headed by Dr. Paul D. Cameron, Assistant Professor of Psychology at Wayne State University, Detroit.

Doctor Cameron's survey revealed that children exposed to tobacco smoke have respiratory diseases about twice as frequently as those in nonsmoking families.

In addition, the study found that the more smoke the youngsters were exposed to, the greater their chances of becoming ill. A similar study conducted in Denver two years ago came to the same conclusions. The more recent survey of 727 Detroit families takes the findings a step further. It discounts the effects of air pollution on the subjects.

Air pollution is recognized as being harmful to the respiratory systems of children. Detroit ranks as the ninth smoggiest city in the United States, while Denver comes in far down the list, at 27th.

Thus, according to Doctor Cameron, his surveys show
that background pollution does not mask the effects
of tobacco smoke on the young. In other words,
smoking parents cannot say that the air is so dirty
that their smoking will not make any difference to
the health of their children.

In a third study, reported in Volume 66, Number 1 (p.

42) of the Utah Issue (January, 1969) of the Rocky Moun-

tain Medical Journal, the following factors were dis-

covered (p. 45):

An initial control group of non-smokers showed
an unexplained low incidence of spirals. This
group was excluded because inquiry revealed a
history in every instance of working in offices
where there was exposure to second-hand environmental cigarette smoke. This observation clearly
identifies an important new problem. How much
health hazard does prolonged exposure and heavy
concentration of second-hand cigarette smoke represent for non-smokers? The incidence of spirals
suggests bronchial disease and infection could
result. There are other implications which need
study. (Emphasis added)

These studies confirm that the health hazards present

in tobacco smoke affect the individual who inhales the

smoke whether or not the inhalation occurs as a result of

the individual smoking or as a result of someone else

smoking.

The studies discussed above dealt with the disease

hazards from smoke inhalation by otherwise healthy

persons. Smoke directly aggravates the illness of persons

already suffering from diseases like chronic sinusitis,

asthma, hay fever, an allergy to smoke, chronic bronchitis,

emphysema, and other chronic lung diseases. The National

Health Survey which ended in June, 1967, gave the follow-

ing breakdown for lung disease in the United States:

Chronic bronchitis..........................400,000

Emphysema...................................726,000

Chronic sinusitus........................16,818,000

Asthma or hay fever......................16,099,000

Total....................34,000,000

An authority on allergic disease has written:

> The truly unfortunate patient is the one who
> develops severe asthma when he enters a smoke-
> filled room. It seems that cigars or pipe smoke
> will usually aggravate the asthmatic more than the
> cigarette smoke. We see many asthmatics who
> develop severe asthma from even one cigarette in a
> room or just by smelling the ashes in an ash tray.
> These are the patients who can be likened to the
> man living in Dante's Inferno where there is no
> escape from burnt fingers. Unfortunately, the
> non-allergic population has no understanding of
> what they do to their asthmatic members of the family
> when they smoke in their presence. (Caplin, The
> Allergic Asthmatic, 1968)

Testing has disclosed that "the problem of clinical hyper-

sensitivity to tobacco smoke is assuming greater importance

in atopic (allergic) patients, who do not smoke themselves,

but who are exposed to smoke either at school, office,

or home." The results of the testing showed definite

allergic symptoms in these patients when exposed to

tobacco smoke. With treatment, and avoidance of smoke,

the symptoms disappeared. (Zussman, Atopic Symptoms

Caused by Tobacco Hypersensitivity, 61 Southern Medical

Journal, 1175, 1968.)

CONCLUSION

The health hazards to non-smokers from the presence of tobacco smoke in a confined environment like that of a long distance bus--however well-ventilated--are obvious and well documented. The best, most obvious--and quite without cost to the carriers--is to prohibit tobacco smoking in interstate buses.

Complaint: *Mavis Kennedy v. Baltimore and Ohio Railroad*

BEFORE THE INTERSTATE COMMERCE COMMISSION

COMPLAINT

MAVIS KENNEDY

V.

BALTIMORE AND OHIO RAILROAD

The complaint of the above-named complainant respectfully shows:

I.   That the complainant is a resident of Shepherdstown, West Virginia, who commutes to and from the District of Columbia as a means of earning her livelihood.

II.   That the defendant above named is a railroad carrier engaged, among other things, in the passenger commuter service business between points in the States of West Virginia and Maryland and the District of Columbia and, as such, is subject to the provisions of the Interstate Commerce Act. '

III. That since May 1, 1971, the defendant has been engaged in gross and flagrant violation of Section 13a (1) of the Interstate Commerce Act resulting in continuing hardship and damage for the complainant and other West Virginia and Maryland residents.

This complaint maintains--

1.   That the Baltimore and Ohio Railroad (hereinafter referred to as the B&O) did on May 1, 1971, unlawfully eliminate passenger commuter service between Martinsburg, West Virginia, and Washington, D.C., and intermediate points on eastbound Train 34 which is scheduled to depart Martinsburg for Washington at 7:28 each morning,

2.   That the B&O, on May 1, 1971, also did eliminate passenger commuter service on westbound Train 5 departing Washington at 4:40 p.m., thus removing reasonable return service for riders of eastbound Train 52 that departs Martinsburg at 5:50 a.m. and was continuing to operate as of the filing of this complaint,

3.   That B&O did further eliminate passenger commuter service between Martinsburg and Washington on eastbound Trains 6, 8, and 12, on westbound Trains 17, 33, 35, and 11-7, to such extent as may be determined by the Commission through examination of B&O passenger records,

4.   That this elimination of passenger commuter service was accomplished simply by failure to operate the trains on or after May 1, 1971.

5.   And that this discontinuance of passenger commuter service was done without proper notification to the Commission required under Section 13a (1) of the Interstate Commerce Act; without payment of the fee for filing notice of discontinuance of commuter service required by Part 1002.2 (D) (17); without discontinuance hearings and without consent of the Commission and, in fact, in the face of an advisory letter of April 12, 1971, from the Commission's deputy director of the Office of Proceedings in charge of the section of finance stating that "there is a question" as to whether Train 34 and certain other trains named in the letter "provide commuter or other short-haul passenger service in metropolitan and suburban areas and may be excluded from the cited section" (401(a)(1) of P. L. 91-518, the Rail Passenger Service Act of 1970). The letter raises the issue that discontinuance of these trains under that section of the Act "may be unlawful."

IV.   By "passenger commuter service" this complaint refers to service as defined by the Commission in Finance Docket No. 26200 served on February 17, 1971, <u>Penn Central Transportation Company Discontinuance or Change in Service of 22 Trains between Boston, Mass., and Providence, R.I.</u>:

" . . . it is our considered opinion that, viewing as a whole the nature of the 'commuter and other short-haul service' exclusion as that term is used in section 102(5) (A) of the Rail Passenger Service Act of 1970, it would likely include some or all of the following features to be so considered:

(1)   The passenger service is primarily being used by patrons traveling on a regular basis either within a metropolitan area or between a metropolitan area and its suburbs;

(2) The service is usually characterized
by operations performed at morning and evening
peak periods of travel;

(3) The service usually honors commutation
or multiple-ride tickets at a fare reduced below the ordinary coach fare and carries the
majority of its patrons on such a reduced fare
basis;

(4) The service makes several stops at
short intervals either within a zone or along
the entire route;

(5) The equipment used may consist of
little more than ordinary coaches;

(6) The service should not extend more than
100 miles at the most, except in rare instances;
although service over shorter distances may not
be commuter or short haul within the meaning of
the exclusion."

V.   The passenger commuter service provided by B&O between Washington, D.C., and Martinsburg, West Virginia, prior to May 1, 1971, on Train 34 and certain
other trains referred to by number above met all six
tests of the Commission's definition, to wit:
morning and afternoon service into and out of a
metropolitan area with intermediate stops (Harpers
Ferry, Brunswick, Gaithersburg, Rockville, Silver
Spring); a total distance of 73 miles between Martinsburg and Washington; generally, coaches clearly intended for short-haul travel (limited restroom
facilities, no food or beverage service in most
cases); and, of special significance, trains arriving
and departing Washington with more than half of the
passengers carrying bonafide, special-rate commuter
tickets, as an examination of B&O records and/or
testimony of B&O train conductors under oath will
show.

VI.   Trains 17, 5, 33, 35, 11-7, 34, 6, 8, and 12 were
discontinued between Martinsburg and Washington, D.C.,
simultaneous with the elimination of these same
numbered trains between Cumberland and Washington,
Chicago and Washington, Cincinnati and Washington,
and other points under provision of the Rail Passenger Service Act of 1970. However, this Act,
(popularly called Railpax), in Section 102(5) (A),
expressly excludes "commuter and other short-haul"
service from its purview. As the Commission notes in
Finance Docket 26200, " . . . this legislation
created a railroad passenger corporation authorized
to own, manage, operate, or contract for the operation of 'intercity trains' later to be designated....

Railpax excluded from its coverage and kept within
our purview 'commuter and other short-haul service
in metropolitan and suburban areas' . . . . "

It is important to note that the Railpax law, in
designating which portion of rail passenger transportation was to be removed from the purview of the
Commission and which was to be·left untouched,
expressly differentiates between intercity and
commuter service, rather than between intercity and
commuter trains:

> " 'Intercity rail passenger service'
> means all rail passenger service other
> than (A) commuter and other short-haul
> service in metropolitan and surburban
> areas, usually characterized by reduced
> fare, multiple-ride and commutation
> tickets and by morning and peak period
> operations . . . ." (Section 102(5)(A),
> emphasis supplied.)

Discontinuance provisions of the Railpax Act simply
do not apply to commuter service. They apply only to
that portion of train service that is not commuter.
The law could not be plainer on that point. Prior to
May 1, 1971, some trains served a dual function, providing along certain portions of the run bonafide
commuter service meeting the essential tests set
forth in the Boston-Providence case, and providing
intercity service along other portions of the run.
Although there is nothing in the Railpax Act that can
be construed to allow discontinuance of the commuter
portion of passenger service, the B&O on May 1, 1971,
abandoned commuter service in every instance where
this service was provided by a train that also provided, however incidentally, some service that might
be regarded as non-commuter. In several of the
trains abandoned by the B&O, the only departure from
the Commission's criteria for commuter service was
that the trains continued 73 miles beyond Martinsburg, or 46 miles beyond the 100 mile criteria set
by the Commission. The Commission itself has stated
that the 100-mile limit might be exceeded "in rare
instances."

It would reveal an irresponsible attitude, contemptu-
ous of the Commission, the Congress and the public,
for the B&O to contend that a bonafide commuter run,
meeting all six criteria set forth by the Commission
in Finance Docket 26200, could be eliminated under

the guise of the Railpax Act merely because the train
happened to travel beyond the 100-mile limit after
providing commuter service.

The true test must be whether any particular run
carried a substantial percentage of commuter passengers and was a substantial element in the overall
viability of the commuter operation. To wantonly
abandon nine trains, as the B&O has done, leaving
Martinsburg and Harpers Ferry commuters one train
each way and a gruelling 14-hour day from departure
to return, is to undermine the commuter service altogether.

VII. We are dealing here with a railroad company that
clearly does not wish to retain even the rag-tag
remains of a once flourishing commuter service, let
alone offer and promote a convenient, comfortable
and modern service.

The larger issues of ecology and environment, of
unemployment and poverty, of housing, of quality of
life for the elderly, all are inextricably involved
in this matter of public transportation. In the case
at hand, we have commuters, including the complainant,
faced with such disruption of service as to pose a
direct threat to maintenance of their present homes
or present means of livelihood. The B&O's contemptu-
ous treatment of the residents of West Virginia,
Maryland, and the District of Columbia, who not only
depend upon, but, indeed, genuinely wish to support
a stabilized system of low-cost, public transport
as an alternative to the domination of the automobile
over our countryside and our lives, demonstrates a
disregard for the public welfare that invites regulatory scrutiny of the closest kind.

VIII. That the Commission clearly recognizes its responsibility and jurisdiction over passenger commuter
service is further evidenced by its action in the
Boston-Providence case where it held that certain
trains provided " 'commuter and other short-haul'
service within the contemplation of section 102(5)(A)
of the Rail Passenger Service Act of 1970"; and that
their proposed discontinuance "continues to be within
the jurisdiction of section 13a (1) of the Interstate
Commerce Act." In its order issued May 7, 1971,
Finance Docket 26633, instituting an investigation to
determine whether service performed by certain trains
of the Penn Central Railroad operating between New

York City and Chatham, New York, fall within the
jurisdiction of section 13a(1), the Commission
again demonstrates its responsibility to determine
and advise (in this instance the United States
District Court for the Eastern District of Pennsylvania) "whether the service performed by said trains
constitutes intercity rail passenger service within
the meaning of Section 102(5) of the Rail Passenger
Service Act of 1970, P.L. 91-518."

Exactly the same issues and principles apply here.
The B&O Railroad has eliminated a portion of its
passenger commuter service between Washington, D.C.,
and Martinsburg, West Virginia, without proper
notice and legal procedure and in defiance of the
Commission and the public. To contend otherwise
in the face of the fact that commuter service was
abandoned without benefit of the type of hearing
triggered by proper notice would be to impute to the
Commission substantive error or malfeasance.

Indeed, the B&O misled the Commission in a letter
of March 26, 1971, addressed to the Secretary of the
Commission and signed by the B&O's "general attorney,"
falsely invoking the Railpax Act. Submitted in
response to amendments to existing rules and regulations governing proposed discontinuances of train
service established by the Commission (Ex Parte No.
217), service date March 15, 1971, the B&O letter
states:

> "As counsel for the Baltimore and Ohio
> Railroad Company, it is my opinion that
> the trains to be discontinued May 1,
> 1971, by this company as described on
> the attached Notice are 'intercity'
> passenger trains subject to Railpax and
> are not excepted therefrom by Section
> 102(5) of the Rail Passenger Service
> Act of 1970 (P.L. 91-518)."

A more accurate description of service provided by
these trains appeared in an April 27, 1971, article
in The Washington Post that reported " . . . 600
suburban commuters . . . use the Potomac Valley
service into Washington every morning. . . . " The
article observed that "Having only a diesel and one
car, Train No. 34 is not exactly a monument to the
glory of passenger service, but, on a recent trip,
50 of the car's 68 seats were filled by the time

it reached Washington. <u>More important, 26 of those</u>
<u>seats were filled by passengers holding regular</u>
<u>commuter tickets . . . ."</u> (Emphasis supplied)

IX. By reason of the facts stated in the foregoing para-
     graphs, complainant prays that the B&O be ordered
     to restore Train 34 or similar service from Martins-
     burg to Washington, D.C., forthwith; that it be
     ordered also to restore Train 5 or similar service
     from Washington in order to provide a reasonable
     return time for passengers taking eastbound Train 52
     which continues in operation; that it be ordered
     also to restore Trains 6, 8, 12, 17, 33, 35, and 11-7
     between Washington, D.C., and Martinsburg, West
     Virginia, unless and until it can be shown in a
     hearing that these trains did not provide bonafide
     commuter service within the Commission's definition;
     and that B&O be put on notice that any and all
     commuter service so restored cannot be eliminated
     except under proper Section 13a(1) discontinuance
     procedure; and that in the event these trains are
     extended at some future time to provide intercity
     service on behalf of The National Railway Passenger
     Corporation and said service is later withdrawn,
     the commuter service between Martinsburg and
     Washington will remain under the jurisdiction of the
     Commission, and that discontinuance proceedings can
     only be instituted through procedures specified in
     13a(1) of the Interstate Commerce Act.

     The complainant prays for damages to the extent the
     Commission deems just compensation for devaluation
     of weekly commuter tickets caused by the elimination
     since May 1, 1971, of optional departure times in the
     morning and evening and the elimination of all
     Saturday and Sunday service.

     The complainant also prays for damages of $100 per
     day to begin the date of the filing of this com-
     plaint and to continue until Train 34 and other
     reasonable commuter service is restored, in

compensation for the threat to her livelihood,
the extra risk and extra time consumed in road
travel, the additional expenses incurred, and other
general aggravation caused by the B&O's elimination
of certain passenger commuter service without due
process of law.

Complainant further prays that the Commission fine
the B&O for its illegal actions such sum as is appropriate in the public interest for each day starting
May 1, 1971, until Train 34 and other reasonable
service is restored.

Dated at _____, 19_____.

_____
Complainant's signature

P.O. Box 604, Shepherdstown,
West Virginia 25443
Post Office Address

VERIFICATION

State of_____

County of _____

_____ being duly sworn deposes
and says: that she is the complainant in the above-entitled proceeding; that she has read the foregoing complaint, and knows the contents thereof; that the same are
true as stated, except as to matters and things if any,
stated on information and belief, and that as to those
matters and things, she believes them to be true.

_____

Subscribed in my presence, and sworn to before me, by the
affiant above named, this _____ day of _____, 19___.

_____

Commission expires_____

BEFORE THE INTERSTATE COMMERCE COMMISSION

MAVIS KENNEDY,   )
)
                Complainant   )
)   FINANCE DOCKET
        v.   )   NO. 26689
)
THE BALTIMORE AND OHIO RAILROAD COMPANY)
)
                Defendant   )

REPLY OF COMPLAINANT TO DEFENDANT'S STATEMENT
OF FACTS AND ARGUMENT SUBMITTED IN RESPONSE
TO CHARGES STATED IN THE COMPLAINT AND TO
DEFENDANT'S MOTION TO DISMISS AND
MEMORANDUM IN SUPPORT THEREOF

DUE DATE: September 24, 1971

Throughout its voluminous response, Defendant frequently states, in proper legal parlance, "NOW COMES B. & O"....denying, asserting, requesting, but not once, in all its verbiage, does B. & O. come to grips with the reality of the 14-hour and longer workday forced upon people who geared their lives (some for more than 20 years) to a commuter service that, until May 1, 1971, offered at least minimal options for getting to and from their homes and jobs by train.

Now, with winter approaching, the many who have had to substitute their automobiles because they could not endure the hardship and uncertainties of a train schedule offering only one train in each direction each weekday, or who drive longer distances to board trains in Brunswick, Md. (32 miles from Martinsburg, 18 from Shepherdstown), will have their lives further complicated by ice and snow. Already, some have moved into the city or given up their jobs. Others, who are trying to decide what to do, urgently need an early decision by the Commission. Some, still hoping for restoration of service, are burdened with the additional expense of a room or apartment in the city. I know of one father of several children who sees them only on weekends. A young woman can no longer live at home with her parents. One resident of Jefferson County, even if willing to accept the long hours, can't use the schedule offered, because his job requires evening work and there is no longer an evening train. He now must stay in a hotel four nights each week, driving into the city on Monday and returning Friday evening. Others, among them Capitol Hill employees, regularly used the now abandoned weekend service.

I do not claim to know personally all of the commuters dependent on train service in the Martinsburg-Washington corridor, but I know enough of them to be able to tell the Commission something of the general makeup of the group. In the main section of this response, with considerable help from a friend and fellow commuter, I will refute in detail Defendant's statement of facts and argument.

First, however, I believe the Commission is entitled to know more facts about the people who urgently need the commuter and short-haul service knowingly eliminated by the Defendant nearly four months ago. It is the human element in these proceedings that warrants the compassionate consideration of the Commission and immediate restoration of a viable commuter service.

Defendant's attempt to persuade the Commission that the new AMTRAK train that leaves Washington at 4:45 p.m. on weekdays compensates for commuter service formerly provided by B. & O. Train 5, which left the city at 4:40, clearly demonstrates that B. & O. is ignorant or insensitive or both when it comes to the people hurt by abandonment of its public service responsibilities.

True, the departure time is appropriate for those
whose workday begins at 8 a.m. or earlier and ends at 4
p.m. or thereabout. But the AMTRAK train, providing a
useful and much desired intercity service for otherwise
isolated parts of Maryland and West Virginia, does not
accept commuter tickets. This means that commuters from
Martinsburg who paid approximately $60 per month for
commuter tickets before May 1, 1971, would have to pay
nearly $160 per month to ride a commuter train into the
city and the AMTRAK train home.

Perhaps the Defendant has conjured up an image of
the commuter as banker or high salaried account executive
from Westchester County to whom $160 is a minor consider-
ation. But the people who catch Train 52, the 5:50 a.m.
out of Martinsburg, and come aboard at other stops along
the way, arriving in Washington at 7:35 a.m., do not lunch
at Sans Souci. They are largely the brown paper bag set
on their way to work as mechanics, stenographers, domes-
tics, draftsmen, maintenance personnel, waitresses, and
department store clerks. They are not, for the most part,
people who sit around all day purportedly thinking about,
and actually filling pages with, for example, words about
the need for more studies of studies on mass transportation, cutting traffic congestion and air pollution, and
preserving the natural environment. In other words, many
of them work on their feet. They desperately need a return time approximating that offered by the new AMTRAK
train, but they cannot afford to buy both commuter tickets for getting to work and full fare for going home. Nor
can they easily afford to buy their dinner in the city
while wating for the only return, Train 51 retained by
B. & O. after May 1, 1971, which departs at 6:15 p.m.

Other commuters and short-haul passengers in the
upper Martinsburg-Washington corridor, including those
who depended on the now abandoned service of Train 34,
which departed Martinsburg at 7:28 a.m., and Train 6, departing at 8:17 a.m., and who used corresponding return
service, are workers with similar jobs assigned to various
shifts, congressional aides, secretaries, businessmen,
government agency employees, journalists, and other writers, a few professors at Washington colleges and univer-
sities--very few, if indeed any, who could be termed
wealthy or "well-to-do" or any of the other euphemisms
for income that keeps up with or ahead of "outgo."

In addition to those who have been commuting from the
Martinsburg/Harpers Ferry area for many years--at one time
enjoying almost hourly service--are more recent residents
responsible for the burgeoning population of West Virginia's Eastern Panhandle and adjoining parts of Virginia and
Maryland. Young families unable to afford the high cost
of renting or buying homes with yards and space for a
garden in the District are better able to afford them
further out in the Martinsburg-Washington corridor. Single

women also find it easier to buy less expensive property
and to obtain mortgages in the periphery of the metropolitan area.

Commuter tickets and reduced fare for multiple rides
are essential not only for regular Martinsburg-Washington
passengers going to work, but also for patients at Newton
D. Baker Veterans Hospital near Martinsburg who frequently visit Washington, and for visitors to the hospital.

Short-haul passengers, other than commuters, include
school children taken by their teachers to visit their
nation's Capitol and college students who supplement limited local library facilities by using educational resources in the city. Shoppers, patients in need of special medical practitioners and treatment, travelers continuing on to other parts of the country who must make
plane and train connections in Washington, college students attending institutions in Washington and elsewhere
also depended upon the trains illegally terminated by the
Defendant.

We are racially heterogeneous, much more so in the
westernmost parts of the corridor than in suburbs border-
ing the city. We are, in a sense, Appalachia and the
South merging with the mainstream. Statistics categorize
ours as a "depressed" area. But our sources of livelihood in the city help us strengthen our community economy; the goods and services we purchase in the city make
the benefit mutual. The tourism that train transportation promotes to our home counties, particularly to Harpers Ferry in Jefferson County, enriches Washington tourism.

Our regional and national leaders seek ways to aid
Appalachia; Complainant maintains that good public transportation is essential to the success of all other efforts to promote employment.

We also hear much about putting an end to divisive-
ness in this country, and hopes for making the Washington
area a model of cooperation. Complainant believes that
efficient, moderately-priced public transportation available between city and countryside is not only the most
obvious way to bring people together, but one of the best.

Defendant's illegal abandonment of commuter and
short-haul service in the Martinsburg-Washington corridor
is, thus, demonstrably a burden on commerce and a detri-
ment to social progress of the region. Immediate restoration of service is imperative to prevent compounding
harm already done.

Defendant calls these people and their transportation needs "incidental." Complainant believes the Commission will see them as important and, indeed, will deem

the restoration of viable commuter service in the Martinsburg-Washington corridor as a vital "convenience and
public necessity."

Point by point examination and refutation of Defendant's argument follow, but I plead with the Commission
to keep clearly in mind the human needs represented by
this Complaint.

The Commission's jurisdiction in this matter--the
Defendant's primary claim for dismissal--will be discussed in the final section of this submission and in
separate arguments submitted by other interested parties.

FURTHER ARGUMENT OF COMPLAINANT IN RESPONSE
TO REPLY AND ARGUMENT OF THE B. & O.

Complainant has read the voluminous material filed
by the B. & O. Sept. 9, 1971, in response to her Complaint filed with the ICC June 23, 1971 (Attachment 1),
and her further statement filed August 9, 1971 (Attachment 2). It is apparent that Defendant has misrepresented certain facts and distorted the issues in this proceeding in order to come to its various conclusions as
this reply will show.

1.   B. & O. in the first sentence of its letter of transmittal to Secretary Oswald misrepresents the nature of
this Complaint by alleging that the Complaint concerns
itself with elimination of trains which "afforded some
incidental 'commuter and other short-haul service'"
[emphasis added] between Washington, D.C., and Martinsburg, West Virginia. This Complaint, as has been and
will be further shown, is only remotely concerned with
the question of "incidental" commuter and short-haul
service.

2.   On page 3 of its REPLY and again on page 8, Defendant notes that AMTRAK on Sept. 7, 1971, inaugurated certain elements of service between Washington, Silver
Spring, Harpers Ferry, Martinsburg and points to the West.
This AMTRAK service is only of peripheral interest in
this proceeding since it refuses to accept commuter tickets, is subject to withdrawal by AMTRAK without public recourse, and is subject also to future schedule changes by
AMTRAK to better accommodate western points on the route
now reached after midnight. Prior to May 1, 1971, a
number of commuters were dependent on midafternoon return
service on Train 33 or early peak hour return service on
Train 5. Since May 1, 1971, these commuters from Harpers
Ferry and Martinsburg have had either to stop commuting
by train or to wait until 6:15 p.m. for return service,

forcing them into a 14-hour commuter day at great physical hardship. The new 4:45 p.m. AMTRAK train provides
them with a Hobson's choice of service, since they are
required to pay $16.25 a week (Harpers Ferry) or $22.50 a
week (Martinsburg) on top of their commuter fare in order
to use it.

On sheets 21 and 22 of its Philadelphia-New York decision (F.D. 26634), the Commission notes that it has repeatedly taken cognizance of the fact that commuter fares
are "an essential item" in the budget or cost of living
of the person traveling to or from work.

Perhaps AMTRAK and B. & O. could work out an accom-
modation on commuter tickets once the ICC has established,
through this proceeding, that the responsibility for providing the service rests with B. & O., not AMTRAK, and
must be continued by B. & O. subject to Section 13(a)
discontinuance procedures if the AMTRAK trains are later
withdrawn. But B. & O. cannot expect AMTRAK to shoulder
its commuter obligations.

3.   In its statement of "Issues Involved" on page 3 of
its REPLY, the B. & O. again stresses the myth of "incidental service," by stating that the issue raised in this
proceeding is whether Congress intended to exempt "all
incidental commuter or other short-haul service" [empha-
sis added] from discontinuance by virtue of the Railpax
law.

This Complaint is not directed, as the B. & O. would
like to pretend, against abandonment of commuter service
which was somehow merely incidental to the function of the
train along some random segment of rail corridor. Rather,
it is directed against the unlawful abandonment of key
elements of Potomac Valley commuter and other short-haul
service specifically in the corridor between Washington
and Martinsburg, where the railroad itself had utilized
the trains in its commuter service and sold and honored
commuter tickets accordingly, where the trains involved
either served primarily as commuter and short-haul trains
or contributed so substantially to the viability of the
commuter and short-haul service as to impair the service
by their abandonment, where the abandonment of the trains
left passengers with no reasonable alternative service,
and where the railroad itself decided arbitrarily which
elements of commuter and other short-haul service it would
abandon and which elements it would retain, without reference to any regulatory body.

4.   On page 3 of its REPLY, B. & O. further lists as an
"issue" the question of whether the nine trains involved
in the proceeding were intercity rail passenger trains or
[emphasis added] "'commuter and other short-haul' service
trains." This assertion of an "either-or" classification
of trains does not state the issue; it begs the issue. As
was stated in the Complaint, some trains served a dual

function, providing along certain portions of the run bonafide commuter service meeting the essential tests set forth in the Boston-Providence case (F.D. 26200), and providing intercity service along other portions of the run. As will be shown at greater length later, the segmenting of functions of the same train is supported by the language of the Railpax law, by the conclusions of the ICC in its jurisdictional determinations relating to commuter service since that law was enacted, and by the B. & O. itself in publication and dissemination to the public of separate schedules for separate services of the same trains prior to the unlawful abandonments on May 1, 1971.

5.   On page 7 of its REPLY, and again on page 14, B. & O. so grossly distorts the Complaint as to set up a "straw man" argument. Complainant nowhere contends, as the B. & O. says she contends, that if a B. & O. train "incidentally transports one commuter" [emphasis in original] between Washington and Martinsburg, that only the intercity portion of said train's operation can be discontinued under the Rail Passenger Service Act of 1970.

    B. & O., having set up this straw man, goes on to say, on page 15, that such a construction "could negate the discontinuance of any portion of an intercity passenger train." [emphasis in original]

    Since the B. & O. gives so much weight to its "one commuter" spectre, let us respond to it. In the first place, the question could not come up along any portion of an intercity passenger run. It could only arise, under the provisions of the Railpax law, along a portion of the run on which the railroad, prior to the discontinuance, had operated "commuter and other short-haul service in metropolitan and suburban areas, usually characterized by reduced fare, multiple-ride and commutation tickets and by morning and peak period operations."

    Elsewhere along the run, the "one commuter" has had it, by virtue of legislation duly enacted by Congress and signed by the President which denies the public any recourse (other than changing the law) to actions of the railway companies or AMTRAK. This is a central feature of the AMTRAK law.

    However, public recourse is left untouched in regard to commuter and other short-haul service as defined in the Railpax law. B. & O. makes light of its "one commuter," but suppose this "one commuter" lost his job or had to give up his home, or is forced upon dangerous icy roads with little sleep as a result of the elimination of his train service? Does the B. & O. suggest that it can deprive a man of his home or his job, or force upon him hazards to his health without due process of law? Under the law the B. & O.'s "one commuter" still has recourse either to the ICC or to the Courts, and recent cases show

the Courts will turn to the ICC for a determination in
any event. The ICC is bound to weigh all the factors,
including the functions of the train in question, whether
the "one commuter" is left with any alternative service,
whether (if damages are claimed) the railroad was acting
in good faith or simply attempting to slide out of a public service obligation, etc., and reach a conclusion in
accordance with its understanding of the law. Thus the
"one commuter" will have been accorded due process, which
is as much as Claimant can ask in this or any proceeding.

Four of the trains eliminated May 1, 1971, are portrayed as having relatively small percentages of commuter
ridership on page 5 of Mr. Howes' accompanying affidavit.
Complainant knows one commuter who regularly used inbound
morning Train 6. Since its elimination he, like a number
of others not party to this Complaint, has largely given
up the trains and found supplemental housing in Washington
while awaiting the outcome of this proceeding. Perhaps he
will be provided viable alternative service with the restoration of Train 34. But what of the commuters who used
Train 11-7 (morning outbound) Train 8 (late afternoon inbound) and Train 12 (midevening inbound)?   These constitute a group of trains that provided reverse direction and
evening service in the Washington-Martinsburg corridor and
for which B. & O. has supplied no alternative.

6. On page 7 of its REPLY, par. (c), B. & O. makes an
assertion that seems central to its entire argument in
this proceeding. It states baldly that "B. & O. retained
all of its commuter service" [emphasis in original] when
it dropped a number of trains May 1, 1971. The importance
to the B. & O. of this assertion that it retained all
commuter service is that unless it can be sustained, that
is, unless the B. & O. can demonstrate that every one of
the nine trains in question was properly discontinued its
entire case unravels: its basis of differentiation between the trains it kept and the trains it dropped, namely, that all nine of the trains dropped were ones that
ran west beyond Martinsburg after providing service
through the Washington-Martinsburg commuter corridor and
hence were "intercity trains" is totally eroded; its denial that trains can be segmented as to types of service
becomes untenable; and it is exposed to extensive restoration orders and imposition of fines and damages by the
ICC for unlawful abandonment of service.

It should be patently obvious from the facts developed in the original Complaint and subsequent submissions,
even including the facts submitted by B. & O., that the
railroad did indeed drop major elements of commuter service on May 1, 1971. Later, Complainant hopes to demonstrate this even to the satisfaction of Commissioners who
dissented in the Philadelphia-New York discontinuance
case (F.D. 26634).

7.   On pages 15 and 16 and elsewhere, B. & O. makes much
reference to its interpretations of Congressional intent
in passage of the Railpax law. It would seem appropriate
to submit these comments from Rep. Harley Staggers who
introduced the bill in the House:

> Surely it was not the intention of Congress
> in establishing Railpax to abolish rail ser-
> vice. What we had in mind was to improve
> it.... Congressional Record, March 25,
> 1971, p. H 2045.
>
> I have had literally thousands of complaints
> from people along the B. & O. and from other
> Congressmen.
>
> Congress usually gets the blame, but I feel
> the fault lies with the railroads' management
> who are primarily interested in dropping as
> many passenger trains as possible....
>
> If I had thought it was going to turn out
> like this, I would never have worked so hard
> to get this legislation through the House....
> Congressional Record, March 23, 1971, p. H 1859.

On page 16 of its argument, B. & O. would have it that
Complainant based her emphasis on the word "service" on
"Isolated quotations from the Congressional Record or the
wordage in Section 102(5)." [emphasis added] Complainant denies that she made any isolated quotations from
Section 102(5). She quoted the pertinent portion of the
section in full, noting that the law plainly differentiates between intercity service and commuter and other
short-haul service, rather than between intercity trains
and commuter and other short-haul trains. This wording
of the law allows for recognition of the dual function of
some trains and the segmenting of functions of trains
along different sections of their runs. In its New York-
Chatham decision (F.D. 26633) the Commission took significant cognizance of the distinction between the "upper portion" and "lower portion" of the route (sheet 6). In
Harrisburg-Philadelphia (F.D. 26632) the Commission found
"back-to-back commuter operations joined at Lancaster"
(sheet 28). In Philadelphia-New York (F.D. 26634) the
Commission found a series of services overlapping. Thus
B. & O.'s preoccupation with its characterization of the
nine trains eliminated May 1, 1971, as "intercity trains"
is of scant help in illuminating the issues in this proceeding, since they were also commuter and other short-
haul trains. B. & O.'s contention on page 17 that these
trains cannot be segmented would no doubt be warmly em-
braced by the residents of Cumberland, Md., and other
points west in the event the ICC orders service restored.
In point of fact, the argument against segmentation falls
on its face in a restoration proceeding, which is the case

here. The ICC can order restoration only in the commuter
and other short-haul area. It cannot extend the service
beyond that area. In other words, it must segment the
trains. This is allowed by the language of Section
102(5).

8.   B. & O. states on page 16 that recent decisions of
the ICC supports its contention that a carrier may discontinue an "intercity passenger train" even though the
train "may incidentally transport over segments of its
entire run some commuter or short-haul traffic."

     Examination of the decision cited by B. & O. reveals
a rather different construction. Chairman Stafford, on
sheet 6 of the New York-Chatham decision (F.D. 26633), in
which the service at issue was ruled intercity, takes
pains to point out that "...the railroad intends to offer
additional service from Dover Plains if the trains involved here are discontinued even if MTA does not take
over on the theory that it would be supplementing the service over the lower portion of the route which it considers to be commuter to make up for the loss of the trains
involved here by those who have been utilizing the same
trains for only the southern portion of the route."
[emphasis added]

     In the instant proceeding B. & O. has not provided
any alternative service for any of the trains it eliminated May 1, 1971. Complainant is simply asking in this
proceeding that the ICC order the B. & O. to do in the
Washington-Martinsburg corridor what the Penn Central
assured the Commission it would do in the Dover-New York
corridor, without which assurance the Commission could
not have reached the finding it did. Likewise, in the
Philadelphia-New York decision (F.D. 26634) cited by B.
& O., in which four trains were ruled to provide intercity service, Commissioner Bush notes that commuter riders of these trains "can be accommodated on the 200-
series trains" (which were ruled to be commuter and short
haul), and further, that the State of New Jersey had
submitted no evidence as to the commuter nature of the
four trains and was not asking for their restoration
(sheets 14, 23, 24). [emphasis added]

9.   Contrary to B. & O.'s assertions on pages 19 through
23, the service eliminated May 1, 1971, did possess the
six features the Commission listed in the Penn Central
decision (F.D. 26200) as likely to occur in "commuter and
other short-haul service" excluded by Section 102(5)(A):

        (a) The distance covered between Washington
        and Martinsburg was 73 miles, well within the
        100 mile guideline.

        (b) The equipment on Trains 17, 33, 34, and
        35 consisted of old coaches, presumably util-
        ized because of the "operating restrictions"

cited by the B. & O. on page 19 which Defendant says precluded it from using Budd RDC
units on the portion of the run beyond Martinsburg. Some of the Budd equipment on the
portions of service retained in operation by
B. & O. to date is newer and more comfortable
than the old coaches on Trains 17, 33, 34,
and 35, and features 2-2 reclining seating.
Only three of the nine trains eliminated--5,
6 and 11-7--carried equipment to accommodate
passengers for long-haul travel, so the "ordinary coach" test was met in most instances
and the wording of B. & O.'s statement on
page 19 is deceptive in this regard. A few
of the trains did offer food service but so
do some of the trains preserved as commuter
in F.D. 26634 (sheet 7).

(The type of seating is, of course, irrelevant
to the passengers who find standing room only
day after day as far out as Rockville, often
in a baggage compartment. B. & O. seems determined to avoid carrying enough coaches to
accommodate and enhance its service. On Train
34, for example, B. & O. failed to provide a
stop at Gaithersburg, refused to bring the
train into Washington by 9 a.m. and put on one
of its largest coaches (a 68-seater) and still
could not provide seating for the growing
commuter traffic. At the last Presidential in-
auguration, B. & O. crammed some 165 people into this 68-seater rather than provide adequate
extra units--just one more example of the railroads indifference to its public service obligation.)

(c) An examination of B. & O.'s published
schedule for Potomac Valley Service prior to
May 1, 1971, shows 20 stops along the 73 mile
route, for an average distance of 3.8 miles between stops. The distance between stops made
by individual trains within this corridor varied
between 3.3 miles for Trains 37 and 38 (kept in
service), 3.5 miles and 3.8 miles for Trains 39
and 40 (kept in service), 12.2 miles for Trains
51 and 52 (kept in service), 12.2 miles for
Train 17 (eliminated May 1, 1971), 15 miles for
Trains 33, 34, and 35 (eliminated May 1, 1971),
and 24 miles for Trains 5, 6, and 8 (eliminated
May 1, 1971). It can readily be seen that there
is negligible or zero difference between the
number of stops made by Trains 51 and 52, which
the B. & O. continues to operate and 17, 33, 34,
and 35, which it illegally abandoned, and its
attempts to demonstrate a difference in sheets
20 and 21 and subsequent attachments therefore
fail.

The Commission recognized in its Philadelphia-
New York decision (F.D. 26634), sheets 12, and
19, that each train involved in a commuter and
short-haul service may not stop at each station and in fact of the trains adjudged commuter and short-haul in this decision those
making the most stops averaged nine miles between stops and those making the least stops
averaged 30 miles between stops.

Hence the service in the instant proceeding
meets the fourth test of the "commuter" formula as well if not better than the service adjudged commuter in the Philadelphia-New York
decision.

(d) Defendant concedes on sheet 21 that all
nine trains in question honored commuter and
reduced fare tickets. Defendant further concedes that Train 34 "averaged about 60% of its
patronage on reduced fares." Elsewhere in its
ARGUMENT (sheet 23) B. & O. makes a point of
its contention that commutation fares were
honored on its trains "only as far west as Martinsburg." One would expect, therefore, that
B. & O. would acknowledge the obvious fact that
commuter use in the Martinsburg-Washington corridor was the primary function of this train.
But no, Defendant asserts the "primary purpose"
and "central mission" was to provide through
service between Cumberland and Washington. The
facts submitted by B. & O. alone show that such
through service was only a secondary function
of this train.

B. & O. goes on to state that the majority of
the revenue of Train 34 was derived from other
than reduced fare and commuter tickets. (The
commuter and other reduced fare revenue is
stated as 37% of Train 34's total revenues on
sheet 5 of Mr. Howes' accompanying affidavit.)
The B. & O. attempts, by its juxtaposition of
sentences, to imply that the remainder of revenues was generated by through service between
Cumberland and Washington. But the evidence
for this is to be found nowhere in more than 40
pages of documentation. The reason no such documentation was submitted, it is fair to conclude,
is because it would show that the bulk of the remaining revenue was generated from other short-
haul patrons traveling on a regular basis in the
Washington-Martinsburg corridor.

This was the train, along with the later and
often undependable Train 6, used by persons
traveling to Washington for shopping, business

at government agencies, etc., since it
arrived at 9:12 a.m. and was obviously
preferable to the earlier Train 52 which
required in Martinsburg setting the alarm
at 4:40 or 5 a.m. It was a popular train
among commuter and other short-haul passengers alike. The same general usage pattern
prevailed on the abandoned Train 17 (midevening outbound daily) Train 33 (midafternoon outbound Monday through Friday) and 35
(midday outbound weekends and holidays).
Their primary passenger use was in the
Martinsburg-Washington corridor in commuter
and other short-haul service.

Curiously, B. & O. supplies no passenger or
revenue figures for the Washington-Martinsburg segment of these trains as against the
Martinsburg-Cumberland segment, or comparison
of commuter versus non-commuter usage within
these segments, although such figures would
be the only ones remotely germane to the
question of "primary purpose" or "central
mission" bandied about on sheets 22 and 23.
The truth is, as B. & O. full well knows,
that Trains 17, 33, 34, and 35 were integral
units of a group of trains whose "central
mission" and primary function was to provide commuter and other short-haul service
between Washington, D.C., and its suburbs.
(This "central mission" was described to the
Commission at the time some of the trains in
dispute were put into service--see REPLY of
Potomac Passenger Association.) The group
includes the six trains B. & O. has kept in
service to date. Trains in this group--those
retained and those abandoned--are indistinguishable in primary function. The percentage of commuter use for the group overall is
extremely high. The mere fact that these
four trains also provided a secondary through
service beyond Martinsburg to Cumberland in
no way detracts from their status as commuter
and other short-haul service trains in the
Martinsburg-Washington corridor.

Train 5, which left Union Station at 4:40 p.m.
and continued on to Chicago, was also an integral part of this group at least Mondays
through Fridays. On page 5 of his affidavit,
Mr. Howes asserts that this train had 22.9%
commuter ridership. This in an incredibly
high percentage considering that the Washington-Martinsburg corridor constitutes only 10
percent of the run. It is even more impressive when one considers that the non-commuter

percentage was made up not only of passengers
boarding in Washington but also of persons
who got on and off the train at various
points all the way to Chicago. The figure
enlarges further in actual terms Mondays
through Fridays since this is when most of
the commuter travel occurred. Mr. Howes' figure is an average spread over 7 days. The
point here is that within the Washington-Martinsburg corridor, commuter and short-haul
passenger usage of Train 5 vied in importance
with long-haul passenger usage (again B. & O.
fails to supply pertinent statistics). Train
5 was a dual purpose train, so used by the
passengers and by B. & O., and for which B. &
O. has since provided no alternative service.
Taking these various trains together as a
group, the third element of the commuter formula is abundantly satisfied. It should be
noted that in table after table of statistics,
B. & O. also fails to shed any light on the
passenger use of Trains 6, 8, 11-7, and 12 in
the Washington-Martinsburg corridor. These
trains provided offpeak and reverse direction
service, and on weekends were vital to the important short-haul transport of visitors to
Harpers Ferry. This weekend service to Harpers Ferry will be subject to removal without
public recourse if it is allowed to remain dependent solely on AMTRAK.

(e) B. & O.'s attempt on page 22 to cast doubt
on the fact that Trains 34 arriving in Silver
Spring at 8:47 a.m. and Washington at 9:12 a.m.,
and Train 5, departing Washington at 4:40 p.m.
and Silver Spring at 4:45 p.m. were engaged in
peak-period travel illustrates the desperation
of their argument. As for the other trains
mentioned, suffice to note that the Commission
has recognized in its previous decisions that
not all elements of the commuter and short-haul
service need occur at peak periods. Thus, Defendant's denial that the second element of
commuter service has been satisfied is without
merit.

(f) There is no dispute over geographic boundaries in this proceeding. Defendant has characterized Harpers Ferry and Martinsburg as suburbs
in previous proceedings before this Commission
and the first test is met.

10. On page 24, B. & O. says there is "no contention"
that Defendant violated the notice requirements of Section
13a(1), and therefore no basis for awarding damages. Complainant noted in her original filing June 23, 1971 (page

2, par. 5 of the Complaint), that B. & O. had failed to provide proper notification and pay the required fee for notice of discontinuance of commuter service.

11. In the affidavit submitted by Mr. Howes, the Commission is misled by the statement (page 2) that prior to May 1, 1971, the B. & O.'s Washington-West Virginia service was comprised of two services, one of which was an intercity service operating as far west as Chicago and the other of which was a commuter service consisting of six trains operating as far west as Brunswick and/or Martinsburg.

B. & O.'s service prior to May 1, 1971, did indeed consist of two services, and one was a service operating to intercity points to the West, but the other was the B. & O.'s "Potomac Valley Service" between Washington and Cumberland which was presented as such in separate schedules which were printed and distributed to passengers and which listed the commuter fares. This Potomac Valley Service consisted of the six trains which the B. & O. now calls commuter along with the other trains, some of them in peak hour service, which the B. & O. has now abandoned.

It is with the restoration of abandoned elements of B. & O.'s Potomac Valley Service in the Martinsburg-Washington commuter corridor that this Complaint is concerned.

THE ISSUE OF JURISDICTION:
COMPLAINANT'S MEMORANDUM OF REBUTTAL
TO DEFENDANT'S MOTION TO DISMISS

The preceding, and most comprehensive, section of
this response is addressed in part to the question raised
by the Defendant about the Commission's "jurisdiction to
determine whether particular passenger train service is
within the exception contained in Section 102(5) of the
Rail Passenger Service Act."

Furthermore, Complainant has been informed that two
participants supporting her Complaint intend to research
laws and litigation that establish the Commission's jurisdiction and to submit their findings in separate documents
as part of their response to the Defendant's Motion to
Dismiss on jurisdictional grounds.

Believing that the Commission is, of course, the best
authority on matters of its own jurisdiction, and that
Complainant's and Participants' substantiation of the
agency's right to rule in the case at hand is necessary
only to comply procedurally; Complainant, nevertheless,
suggests that an informal private citizens-eye-view of B.
& O.'s challenge to the Commission may be helpful.

Certainly it does not take legal training or other
expertise to see that Defendant's basis for charging lack
of jurisdiction strains the process of ordinary logic.
Defendant states: "No provision of the Interstate Commerce Act authorizes the ICC to determine whether particular train service is within the exception contained in
Section 102(5) of the Rail Passenger Service Act. The
language in the exception is not found anywhere in the
Interstate Commerce Act." How could there be such provision or language when the ICC Act predates the Railpax
Act by many years?

Complainant finds this B. & O. observation akin to
the kind of inverted logic that would have weekday visitors arriving in Harpers Ferry via AMTRAK Train 5 (page
12, par. 4 of Defendant's Statement of Facts and Argument) at 5:50 p.m., "departing eastward from Harpers
Ferry via Train 8 at 3:45 p.m." • Are visitors expected to
depart Harpers Ferry two hours before they arrive? Or
are they expected to see Harpers Ferry after the National
Park Service exhibits are closed for the day and leave
before they open in the morning? Or wait nearly 24 hours
for the next train back to the city?

Of similar logic is B. & O.'s emphatic denial that
there has been no weekend train service to Harpers Ferry
(page 9 and 19, item (d)) since May 1, 1971. (The Complaint and supporting statements were filed before in-
auguration of AMTRAK intercity service on September 7.)

Defendant says "Weekend visitors can use Trains 51
and 52." In other words, B. & O. offers Harpers Ferry
visitors a chance to get there on the last train one week
and to return on the first train of the next week. (Arrive Friday evening about 7:30 p.m.; leave Monday morning
on the 6:18 a.m.) Never mind that most of the visitors
to Harpers Ferry come for the day; that overnight accommodations are limited, and that families with school-age
children, or organized groups of children supervised by
adults (typical Harpers Ferry visitors), cannot or would
not want to pay for meals for two days and rooms for
three nights in order to get in a few hours of sightsee-
ing. Equating one-shot, special weekend trains with regular weekend service for Harpers Ferry visitors and commuters and other short-haul passengers who go into the
city to work, shop, or for other purposes, is another
desperate, hence irrational, attempt of the Defendant to
claim credit for service where none exists.

Conjuring up imaginary service to passengers is bad
enough, but attempting with similar abracadabra, to dispose of the Interstate Commerce Commission's jurisdiction
and authority to determine jurisdiction over commuter and
short-haul train service is defiant of the law and the
Congress that created it. There is only one reason why
the Defendant would go to such lengths to challenge the
Commission's authority: Defendant fears the exercise of
that authority in the resolution of this Complaint.

The heart of Defendant's jurisdictional argument
appears to be stated on page 6: "Thus the regulatory
scheme of the Rail Passenger Service Act is one of narrowly limited functions both for the ICC and the Courts.
Regulation by the Commission and the Courts was severely
limited as a matter of Congressional policy."

What Defendant pretends not to understand is that
the severe limitations placed on ICC and the Courts by
the Railpax law apply expressly and solely to intercity
service. Commuter and short-haul service is expressly
exempted from these severe limitations by section
102(5)(a).

What B. & O. really means by "severe limitations" is
the denial of public recourse in the matter of removal of
train service. The 1970 Railpax Act is extraordinary
legislation which strips away public recourse in order to
allow the administrators of AMTRAK and the Department of
Transportation to establish a national rail passenger
system which in their eyes best serves the interests of

the nation overall without having the aims of the system
thwarted by public clamor in individual localities.

In enacting this extraordinary legislation, Congress
recognized the need to protect and shield commuter and
short-haul service, where local interests determine the
scope of such service and where public recourse must of
necessity be preserved. The law in respect to regulation
of commuter and short-haul service was thus left un-
touched--and all the laws governing ICC regulation of all
train service prior to enactment of the Railpax law were
left in force for commuter and short haul.

Defendant's citation of Congress of Railway Unions
v. Hodgson, 326 F. Supp. 78-79 (D.D.C. April 30, 1971)
"for discussion of the issue of 'standing to sue' under
said Section 307(a)" illustrates their failure to comprehend the utterly different legal situation surrounding
intercity service as compared to commuter and other short-
haul service as a result of enactment of the Railway Passenger Service Act of 1970. Complainant is not bringing
action under 307(a), which relates to intercity service.
This complaint is concerned with a violation of portions
of the Interstate Commerce Act unaffected by the Railpax
law. Note Section 307(b):

"Nothing contained in this section shall be construed as relieving any person of any punishment, liability, or sanction which may be imposed otherwise than under this Act." (emphasis added)

Note also the last sentence of Section 201 of the
Railpax law, which expressly recognizes the separate
character of Section 13a proceedings:

"The exclusion of a particular route, train, or service from the basic system shall not be deemed to create
a presumption that the route, train, or service is not
required by public convenience and necessity in any proceeding under Section 13a of the Interstate Commerce Act
(49 U.S.C. 13a). (Emphasis added--note that the 1970
Railpax law here recognizes the distinction between
"train" and "service.")

Now comes the B. & O. contending that the ICC has
narrowly limited powers in the area of commuter and other
short-haul service and that perforce it should throw out
all its post--AMTRAK decisions where its jurisdiction was
exercised; that the Courts have little to say about the
matter either, and the public has nowhere to turn for
protection against unlawful acts by carriers engaged in
commuter and other short-haul service.

B. & O.'s memorandum is tantamount to an assertion
that its commuter service is not subject to public regulation and that the only body qualified to determine

whether Section 102(5) applies to particular train service
is the Board of Directors of the B. & O. Defendant certainly does not list any other person or agency that it
considers so qualified.

Complainant submits otherwise. The Interstate Commerce Commission has the mandate to make determinations
and adjudicate complaints relating to rail service untouched by the 1970 Railpax Act, and the Defendant's motion to dismiss is without merit.

Indeed, the Commission needs to make determinations
of service in order to know when and where its mandate
must be exercised.

I do not know how often in the past the ICC has dealt
with complaints centered around abandonment of service,
but I can only ask how often in the past has a carrier
abandoned service without obtaining or even seeking the
permission of any regulatory body?

*   *   *   *

Perhaps the Commission is interested in knowing how
someone initially unfamiliar with the ICC, the Railpax
law, the phrase "discontinuance procedure," and other
elements important to this Complaint decided the Commission was my hope for help.

The last week in May, 1971, I returned to the Washington area from a two-month assignment in western states
and discovered my trains were gone--trains I had used
nearly every weekday in March. My work is such that I
sometimes go into the city every day for a period of time,
then work at home for awhile; but I must be able to get in
on short notice and be able, also, to return. I moved to
Shepherdstown, West Virginia, more than three years ago
motivated to a large degree by the convenience of getting
into the city by train. I do not consider my driving
skills adequate for freeways, beltways, and city traffic
and have never driven into Washington. There is no bus
service in my area. In other words, without train service, I cannot live where I now live.

I had heard rumors that our train service might be
affected by the new national railroad passenger system,
but I did not believe them. I did not believe that B. &
O. could cut out commuter service and expect to get away
with it. And with people on peak hour trains standing in
the aisles by the time we reached Washington, I could not
imagine they would want to try.

I did not react to loss of my trains calmly. Frankly, I was furious--outraged by the spectacle of a large

company apparently thumbing its nose at little people. I
also felt deceived. This was supposed to be a new age of
"corporate responsibility," of new business and government concern for the consumer. How empty all this sounded when related to B. & O.'s action and the inaction or
inability of any government agency at any level to prevent it. The worst part, except for actually losing the
trains, was the way anger at first tended to dissolve into helplessness.

But by the time my son came home from college for
the summer and had to wait 24 hours for a train to Harpers Ferry, I was determined to do something; to take some
form of action.

As a total non-joiner, I do not belong to any organization so this had to be direct <u>individual</u> action. I
could not afford to engage an attorney, nor did I feel
this should be necessary in order to secure another
party's compliance with the law.

The first step was to seek information; to learn
what could be done to get service restored. And as cyn-
ical as some foregoing comments may sound, I really did
believe there must be a better, more responsible way to
run a railroad, and that someone with the power to do so,
would want to help.

Capitol Hill was the first stop in my search for information.

I requested from my Congressman's office copies of
hearing transcripts, committee reports, statements from
the <u>Congressional Record</u> pertinent to the Railpax bill,
and copies of the actual law. I was interested in my
Congressman's own views of what was happening as expressed to me personally, and in what was a matter of
public record. As Chairman of the House Committee on
Interstate and Foreign Commerce, his opinions were especially relevant. With some degree of determination on
my part, an assistant agreed to ask him to see me. The
interview was brief, but pleasant and satisfactory. I
left his office with a clear impression that he was unhappy with the way Railpax legislation was working out to
date and that he felt "they are trying to get around the
intent of Congress." My impression as to whom he meant
by "they" was not so clear, nor did I think he had quite
decided where the fault lay--perhaps with AMTRAK, perhaps
with the carriers, probably with a combination of involved parties. But the information he supplied was
vital--Congress was unhappy about the trains, so what was
happening was not the will of Congress.

Congressional action, amendments, new legislation--
was not, however, the kind of direct action that could
bring about immediate restoration of commuter service in

the Martinsburg-Washington corridor; in any case, Congress had expressed its will in regard to commuter service.

After a visit to the office of the Speaker of the House, in whose home state I had first read some of the editorial commentary of Railpax, I inquired as to the actual whereabouts of AMTRAK.

At the administrative headquarters in L'Enfant Plaza, AMTRAK had all the signs of a new organization, including a receptionist intensely interested in her new job, who saw her role as one of helping visitors and not necessarily protecting the staff from all but VIP interruptions. Indeed, I found that even my refusal to be satisfied with conversation with the P.R. man's secretary and then with the P.R. man himself ruffled no feathers. Insisting that I could only learn what I had to know from a policymaking board member, I was granted a most courteous, serious and comprehensive interview by a board member who is also the director of operations.

And although AMTRAK was and, perhaps, still is one of the most popular whipping boys around, I did not see how it could be faulted for problems with local commuter service. Nor did I see, given its assignment and its resources, that helping to solve these problems was properly a concern of AMTRAK.

The search for information about a source of help continued at the Departments of Transportation, Justice, and Commerce.

I trod miles of elegant carpeting and saw innumerable gorgeous outer offices at DOT on two different occasions. I was never treated discourteously; in fact, quite graciously, I was directed from office to office. One executive spent a sizeable amount of time telling me how everyone, including the Secretary, was working very hard. Another person, reached after half-a-dozen reroutings, gave me a number to call for an appointment the following week. But I had neither time nor resources to continue on this circuitous route for information.

At the Justice Department, I was treated with extreme rudeness by a receptionist and a guard. The latter, posted at the second entrance I tried to enter, would not even let me speak to a receptionist. All I was requesting at this point was an opportunity to find out with whom I should discuss this matter, and to telephone from the lobby for an appointment. My new view of myself as intrepid researcher shattered and, alas, reduced to tears by the degree of personal rudeness to which I was subjected, I was ordered to go to an outside phone (there was only one pay station in the area) in order to call in for an appointment "and then we'll check to see if we'll let you in lady." At that point, I did not even know to whom to place the call.

Rather late one afternoon, I arrived at ICC. I asked the guard who was in charge of railroads. He said I should probably try the seventh floor. We looked together in a building directory and decided that the Railroad Service Board sounded a logical place to begin.

My reception there was just fine. The gentleman to whom I introduced myself and explained my quest for information answered a number of questions, then called in two others to explain further the workings of the Commission. In response to my questions, I was supplied with copies of public documents (for the first time I learned there was something called a Finance Docket) and procedural forms. My inquiries were respectfully considered and given thoughtful answers. As to what I should actually do to engage the Commission's assistance in getting commuter service restored, I was told direct advice would not be proper.

Included with the materials given to me at ICC was a copy of the Commission's <u>General Rules of Practice Pertaining to the Filing of Formal Complaints</u>. Although most of the rules had to do with freight, rates, tariffs, transit points, etc., reference was made to "transportation of property or passengers."

After studying all of the material collected from the various individuals and agencies mentioned, and after reviewing my notes on the personal conversations, I concluded that my proper recourse as a private citizen was through the Interstate Commerce Commission. [From Reply of Complainant to Defendant's Statement, Kennedy v. B&O Railroad Co., Finance Docket No. 26689, pp. 17-20.]

                                   Respectfully submitted,

Dated at _____ 19_____ .

                              /s/   MAVIS KENNEDY
                              Complainant's signature

                              P.O. Box 604, Shepherdstown,
                              West Virginia 25443
                              Post Office Address

                        VERIFICATION

STATE OF_____

CITY/COUNTY OF_____

_____ being duly sworn deposes and
says: that she is the Complainant in the above-entitled

proceeding; that she has read the foregoing Complaint,
and knows the contents thereof; that the same are true as
stated, except as to matters and things if any, stated on
information and belief, and that as to those matters and
things, she believes them to be true.

_____

Subscribed in my presence, and sworn to before me, by the
affiant above named, this _____ day of _____,
19_____ .

_____

My Commission Expires: _____

ICC Field Office Locations

AL	2121 8th Avenue, N Birmingham 35203 205 325 3781	ID	455 Federal Bldg. Boise 83702 208 342 2711 EX. 2505
AK	G-31 Federal Bldg. Anchorage 99510 907 272 3922	IL	219 S. Dearborn Street Chicago 60604 312 353 6124
AZ	3427 Federal Bldg. Phoenix 85025 602 261 3834		325 West Adams Street Springfield 62704 217 525 4075
CA	7708 Federal Bldg. Los Angeles 90012 213 688 4008	IN	345 West Wayne Street Fort Wayne 46802 219 422 6131
CO	2022 Federal Bldg. Denver 80202 303 837 3162		Century Bldg. Indianapolis 46204 317 633 7465
CT	324 U.S. Post Office Hartford 06101 203 244 2560	IA	677 Federal Bldg. Des Moines 50309 515 284 4416
DC	ICC Bldg. Washington 20423 202 343 1100 EX. 7671	KS	234 Federal Bldg. Topeka 66603 913 234 8661 EX. 266
FL	288 Federal Bldg. Jacksonville 32202 904 791 2551		501 Petroleum Bldg. Wichita 67202 316 267 6311 EX. 209
	105 Cox Bldg. Miami 33155 305 350 5551	KY	222 Bakhaus Bldg. Lexington 40505 606 252 2312
GA	1252 W. Peachtree,N.W. Atlanta 30309 404 526 5371		

KY   426 U.S. Post Office
     Louisville 40202
     502 582 5167

LA   T-4009 Federal Bldg.
     New Orleans 70113
     504 527 6101

ME   305 U.S. Post Office
     Portland 04112
     207 775 3131

MD   814-B Federal Bldg.
     Baltimore 21201
     301 962 2560

MA   Kennedy Bldg.
     Government Center
     Boston 02203
     617 223 2372

     338-342 Federal Bldg.
     Springfield 01103
     413 781 2420

MI   10 Witherill Street
     Detroit 48226
     313 226 7245

     225 Federal Bldg.
     Lansing 48933
     517 372 1910
     EX. 568

MN   448 Federal Bldg.
     Minneapolis 55401
     612 725 2326

MS   145 East Amite Bldg.
     Jackson 39201
     601 948 7821

MO   1100 Federal Bldg.
     Kansas City 64106
     816 374 5561

     210 N. 12th Street
     St. Louis 63101
     314 622 4103

MT   U.S. Post Office
     Billings 59101
     406 245 6711
     EX. 6261

NE   320 Federal Bldg.
     Lincoln 68508
     402 475 3395

     711 Federal Bldg.
     Omaha 68102
     402 221 4644

NV   203 Federal Bldg.
     Carson City 89701
     702 882 2085

NH   424 Federal Bldg.
     Concord 03301
     603 224 1887

NM   10515 U.S. Courthouse
     Albuquerque 87101
     505 843 2241

NJ   902 Federal Bldg.
     Newark 07102
     201 645 3550

     204 Carroll Bldg.
     Trenton 08608
     609 599 3511

NY   518 New Federal Bldg.
     Albany 12207
     518 472 2273

     518 Federal Bldg.
     Buffalo 14203
     716 842 2008

     26 Federal Plaza
     New York 10007
     212 264 1072

     104 O'Donnell Bldg.
     Syracuse 13202
     315 473 3440

NC   BSR Bldg., Suite 417
     Charlotte 28202
     704 372 0711

     624 Federal Bldg.
     Raleigh 27611
     919 755 4650

ND   Federal Bldg.
     Fargo 58102
     701 237 5771
     EX. 5285

OH   5514-B Federal Bldg.   TN   1808 West End Bldg.
      Cincinnati 45202   Nashville 37202
      513 684 2975   615 749 5391

      181 Federal Bldg.   TX   1012 Herring Plaza
      Cleveland 44199   Amarillo 79101
      216 522 4000   806 376 2138

      255 Federal Bldg.   1100 Commerce Street
      Columbus 43215   Dallas 75202
      614 469 5620   214 749 3691

      5234 Federal Bldg.   9A27 Fritz Garland Lanham
      Toledo 43604   Federal Bldg.
      419 259 7486   Fort Worth 76102
                                          817 334 2794
OK   240 Old Post Office
      Oklahoma City 73102   8610 Federal Bldg.
      405 231 4496   Houston 77002
                                          713 226 4241
OR   450 Multnomah Bldg.
      Portland 97204   301 Broadway Bldg.
      503 226 3361   San Antonio 78205
                                          512 225 5511
PA   508 Federal Bldg.   EX. 4318
      Harrisburg 17108
      717 782 4437   UT   5239 Federal Bldg.
                                          Salt Lake City 84111
      1518 Walnut Street   801 524 5680
      Philadelphia 19102
      215 597 4449   VT   52 State Street
                                          Montpelier 05602
      2111 Federal Bldg.   802 223 6001
      Pittsburgh 15222
      412 644 2930   VA   10-502 Federal Bldg.
                                          Richmond 23240
      309 U.S. Post Office   703 782 2541
      Scranton 18503
      717 344 7111   5104 F. B. Thomas Bldg.
                                          Roanoke 24011
RI   187 Westminster Street   703 343 1581
      Providence 02903
      401 528 4306   WA   6130 Arcade Bldg.
                                          Seattle 98101
SC   300 Columbia Bldg.   206 442 5421
      Columbia 29201
      803 253 8371   WV   3108 Federal Bldg.
                                          Charleston 25301
SD   369 Federal Bldg.   304 343 6181
      Pierre 57501
      605 224 2812   416 Old Post Office Bldg.
                                          Wheeling 26003
TN   933 Federal Bldg.   304 232 6960
      Memphis 38103
      901 534 3437

WI   139 West Wilson Street
      Madison 53703
      608 256 4441

      135 West Wells Street
      Milwaukee 53203
      414 224 3183

WY   1006 Federal Bldg.
      Casper 82601
      307 265 5550
      EX. 3243

CHAPTER 7

THE FEDERAL COMMUNICATIONS COMMISSION

> *Individual citizens and the communities they compose owe a duty to themselves and their peers to take an active interest in the scope and quality of the television service* which stations and networks provide and which, undoubtedly, has a *vast impact on their lives and the lives of their children.* Nor need the public feel that in taking a hand in broadcasting they are unduly interfering in the private business affairs of others. On the contrary, *their interest in television programming is direct* and their responsibilities important. *They are the owners* of the channels of television—indeed, of all broadcasting.
>
> —FCC, *Television Network Program Procurement,* H.R. Rep. No. 281, 88th Cong., 1st Sess. 20, quoted, with emphasis added, in *Office of Communication of United Church of Christ* v. *FCC,* 359 F. 2d 994, 1000 (D.C. Cir. 1966)

Introduction

The Federal Communications Commission (FCC) first made the statement quoted above, but it was in 1963, and the Commission was talking to Congress in generalities, and without the italics for emphasis. The statement was thrown back at the FCC with emphasis in 1966, and it was in a very specific order from the U.S. Court of Appeals for the District of Columbia Circuit for the Commission to listen to representatives of a predominantly black community protesting the license renewal of a blatantly racist television station. The emphasis was added by Judge Warren Burger, who is now Chief Justice of the United States. He went on to add a few words of his own.

The theory that the Commission can always effectively represent the listener interests in a renewal proceeding without the aid and participation of legitimate listener representatives fulfilling the role of private attorneys general is one of those assumptions we collectively try to work with so long as they are reasonably adequate. When it becomes clear, as it does to us now, that it is no longer a valid assumption which stands up under the realities of actual experience, neither we nor the Commission can continue to rely on it.

If a starting point for the phenomenon of public participation in federal administrative agencies had to be picked, it would probably be when the residents of Jackson, Mississippi, decided to do something about station WLBT. They had some help from the Office of Communication of the United Church of Christ, and the first decision in that case is usually called the United Church of Christ decision. There were later decisions and appeals, but that was where it started, when people began to talk back to the broadcasters.

It was appropriate for citizen action to start with the communications industry and the federal agency that is supposed to regulate it, since the industry has a pervasive impact on all our lives. Television, radio, and the telephone touch all of us continually, and they affect the way we communicate with each other in fundamental ways. Ninety-five percent of all American homes have television receivers, and in the average home the set is on for five and three-quarters hours every day; there is at least one operating radio set for every person in the United States, without including the 74 million car radios; 89 percent of all American households have telephones. We are only beginning to understand the effect that this continual electronic assault on our senses has on the way we think and act. It starts with the realization that the power to determine what we hear and see of the world beyond our immediate senses is often the power to determine what we do about that world. The success of television advertising in persuading us to spend and vote is just an example of how this power can be used.

The communications industry regulated by the FCC ranges from small radio stations to one of the largest corporations in the world—American Telephone & Telegraph (AT&T). For purposes of regulation it is divided into two areas—broadcasting and "common carriers" (primary telephone service), and the two major bureaus covered in this chapter will be the Broadcast Bureau and the Common Carrier Bureau. The other Bureaus, which will not be covered, are the Safety and Special Services Bureau, which regulates radio broadcasters such as ham operators, the

Field Engineering Bureau, which is concerned with technical regulations, and the Cable Television Bureau.

FCC History

The FCC's authority to regulate radio and television is based on one basic fact and a policy decision about that fact. There is a limit on the number of audio and video signals which can be transmitted at the same time. Instead of letting the airwaves turn into an electronic battleground of competing signals, Congress decided that broadcasters who use this public property should be licensed. Congressman (later Senator) Wallace H. White, Jr. said it pretty well in 1926:

> We have reached the definite conclusion that the right of all our people to enjoy this means of communication [radio] can be preserved only by the repudiation of the idea . . . that anyone who will, may transmit, and by the assertion in its stead of the doctrine that the right of the public to service is superior to the right of any individual to use the ether. . . . [In debates leading to enactment of the 1927 Radio Act, 67 Cong. R. 5479, 12 March 1926]

It took several years of experience to establish that access to the airwaves could not be unlimited. Marconi transmitted the first radio signals in 1895, but it wasn't until after World War I that broadcasters began in earnest to transmit entertainment to the public and commercials for advertisers. Understandably, many people were eager to get in on the act, and by 1925 the electromagnetic stage was jammed. Under the Radio Act of 1912, the Secretary of Commerce could license stations and operators, but could not limit broadcast time and power. In the words of the FCC's Broadcast Primer, this "caused bedlam on the air." As a first step in bringing order to that bedlam, Congress passed the Dill-White Radio Act of 1927, which created the Federal Radio Commission. The major function of the Radio Commission was to straighten things out and keep the broadcasters from stepping on each other's wavelengths. There were already too many broadcasters, and 150 of the 732 licensees were ordered out.

The Communications Act of 1934 (47 U.S.C. 151 *et seq.*) established the FCC in its present form of seven commissioners, to regulate all interstate and foreign communication by wire and radio, including telephone, telegraph, and broadcast. The commissioners are appointed by the President, with approval by the Senate, for seven-year terms, and one of them is designated as Chairman by the President. Not more than four of the commissioners may be members of the same political party.

These are the commissioners in office at this time. Their terms expire at the end of June in the years indicated.

Dean Burch, Chairman (Republican)	1976
Benjamin L. Hooks (Democrat)	1979
H. Rex Lee (Democrat)	1975
Robert E. Lee (Republican)	1974
Charlotte Reid (Republican)	1978
Richard E. Wiley (Republican)	1977

To give some idea of the underlying sympathies of the commissioners, a recent study showed that 20 percent of the members appointed from 1934 through 1972 came from jobs in the communications and newspaper industries [Ross D. Eckert, "Spectrum Allocation and Regulatory Incentives," *Proceedings of Office of Telecommunications Policy Conference on Communications Policy Research,* Washington, D.C.: Office of Telecommunications Policy, Executive Office of the President, 1972, p. 104, Table 1]. Even more astonishing is the fact that twenty-three of the thirty commissioners who have left office for reasons other than ill health or retirement have gone into jobs with regulated firms.

The Commission's utter insensitivity to the need to preserve some semblance of propriety in terms of the members' and staff's possible future employment interests is vividly demonstrated by a recent case. One of the applicants for a valuable broadcasting license was disturbed when he overheard a competing applicant quietly discussing with the Commission's staff attorney whether he would "be interested in joining our firm as a trial attorney." The FCC's Review Board, to which the matter was referred for decision, determined that the incident was not in "good taste," but could not be deemed legally improper because the invitation was too amorphous and vague to be considered a definite offer of employment [FCC 72R-, Memorandum Opinion and Order of the Review Board, released December 15, 1972, Docket No. 19, 122]. This sense of laxness has characterized the Commission's attitudes toward its public responsibilities essentially since its establishment as an independent agency.

Forces outside the Commission have considerable influence. In

Congress, Senator John O. Pastore (D.–R.I.) watches the Commission from his seat as chairman of the Senate Commerce Committee's Subcommittee on Communications. When the FCC refused to renew the television license of WHDH in Boston in 1969, Pastore leaped to the defense of the broadcasting industry by introducing a bill which would have required the Commission to find a licensee unfit before it could consider any competing applications. The FCC was sufficiently intimidated to adopt an administrative policy that did nearly the same thing. But another outside force came into play, and in response to a suit brought by a public interest group, the Court of Appeals for the District of Columbia Circuit ruled that the Commission's new policy violated the Federal Communications Act [*Citizens Communications Center et al.* v. *Federal Communications Commission*, 447 F.2d 1201 (1971)].

Public interest groups such as the United Church of Christ's Office of Communications, the Citizens Communications Center, which challenged the FCC's license renewal policy, and the Stern Community Law Firm are relatively new and important influences on the Commission. Although they all have limited funds and staff, they can serve as sources of technical and legal assistance to your efforts.

On the industry side, the National Association of Broadcasters (NAB) is a powerful voice. *Broadcasting* magazine ($14 per year from 1735 DeSales Street, N.W., Washington, D.C., 20036) is a vital source of information which often has an inside line into what the Commission is about to do, and which usually supports the NAB. The National Cable Television Association is the spokesman for industry in that field of enormous potential for public welfare and private profit.

Under the Nixon Administration, the White House has taken an active interest in communications. The White House Office of Telecommunications Policy headed by Clay Whitehead has become the Administration's voice on communications matters and the chief weathervane of Presidential pleasure or displeasure with the electronic media.

FCC Structure, Functions, and Access Opportunities

Opposing renewal of a broadcaster's license, as the residents of Jackson, Mississippi, did, is probably one of the best-known examples of citizen access at the FCC, but it is not the only opportunity, and not the place to start. The fairness doctrine of the FCC presents other opportunities for citizen action that are only beginning to be realized. The range of possible complaints against programing that is "unfair," and the range of possible remedies, is only as limited as broadcasters' ability to abuse their public trust and your own resourcefulness in challenging them. The Personal Attack Rules which the FCC has adopted under the Fairness Doctrine spell out the remedies you may utilize if you are subject to a broadcast personal attack. Although the Commission has authority to act against commercials that are too loud, too frequent, and deceptive, it has taken only hesitant steps in that direction. The longest steps—requiring broadcast of messages about adverse effects of cigarette smoking and acceptance of advertising on controversial subjects—have been taken because citizens with no financial interests at stake were forcing them to act. Not all of the opportunities for citizen action have to do with what broadcasters send out over the air. Broadcasters are subject to regulations requiring them to eliminate discrimination in employment, and the annual reports which they are required to publish can give you an idea of how much progress is being made. Like other federal agencies, the FCC has authority to adopt rules which have the force of law, and the regulations on discrimination in employment by broadcasters are one example of how this power can be used. Another example of how the rule making process can be used is the petition for rule making on children's television filed by Action on Children's Television (ACT), which has already forced broadcasters into making some concessions and is still pending before the Commission.

In dealing with broadcasters, you can use a variety of techniques alone or in combinations, depending on the issues and your resources. The usual approach in working on a problem that is limited to a single station is to organize a group of citizens, do the necessary research and monitoring, get some legal assistance, negotiate with the station, and send whatever is necessary to the FCC. The last step may be as simple as writing a letter or as complicated as filing a petition to deny a station's license. When a problem is more widespread than a single station, you should at least consider asking the FCC to adopt rules to deal with it.

The Common Carrier Bureau, which is concerned primarily with telephone communication, also offers some opportunities for public access. As a practical matter, the opportunities are limited because most direct contacts between telephone companies and the public are primarily regulated by the state utility commissions, rather than by the FCC, and because the Commission is outweighed and awed by the size of the Bell Telephone System which it is supposed to regulate. But there are opportunities for complaining about various abuses by the telephone company, and determined consumer groups could have some impact by intervening in the Commission's proceedings on interstate telephone rates.

Cable Television (CATV) is a hybrid in many ways. It is part broadcast and part wire communications, and it is regulated by both the FCC and local communities. Its potential ranges from getting a sharper television picture to transforming our lives by placing vast resources at our electronic fingertips. The opportunities for public access are now primarily at the level of community planning. In the past, CATV was utilized to connect isolated rural areas to regular television. However, in the next ten years, CATV will be in a majority of American households, including most urban centers. It is important that communities educate themselves. There is presently a good opportunity to participate in public hearings on a local basis. Issues to be settled include who will own and operate CATV, and to what uses CATV will be put.

Some of the access opportunities to be described are relatively simple. Others are complicated legal proceedings that will require organizing, fund raising, and expert help. But the gaining of access starts when you decide to do something, and the first step in doing something is getting information.

The most basic source of information about broadcasting is the television set in your home. One useful tactic in dealing with broadcasters is to organize systematic monitoring of their programs and compare the results with the promises they make in applying for license renewals. But you also need to know the rules and decisions of the FCC, as well as what is written about and by broadcasters.

The official opinions of the FCC are in bound reports known as "Federal Communications Commission Reports," which are cited in legal style, with the volume first and the page number after the title. They are now in a second series, so a sample opinion cited as 4 FCC 2d 504 would refer to the fourth volume in the second series, page 504. You can find them in law school libraries, or subscribe from the Government Printing Office (G.P.O.). The Code of Federal Regulations (C.F.R.), which is also available from the G.P.O., includes the administrative regulations of the Commission, as well as those of other agencies. The FCC regulations are in Title 47 of the Code (47 C.F.R. 0-99), and Volumes I and III of the FCC Rules and Regulations are the ones related to broadcasting. Volume I describes the Commission's organization and sets forth the rules for filing complaints and petitions. Volume III has the rules which apply to commercial and noncommercial radio and television broadcasting. New FCC rules and policies are published in the *Federal Register* along with those of all the other agencies. (The Pike and Fischer Radio Regulation Service contains FCC decisions, court opinions on communications, and Commission rules and regulations. The service is a private publication that is often cited as a source for Commission decisions [for example, a case would be cited as _____ RR____]. It can be useful if you can refer to it in a law school library, but, at $710 for the first year, it's too expensive for most citizen groups.)

By far the most helpful information put out by the FCC for citizens interested in broadcasting cases is its *Broadcasting Procedural Manual,* issued in late 1972. This layman's guide to the complexities of the agency's procedures is written in clear language and is an invaluable resource for participation by consumers.

The FCC's Annual Report is available at the end of each fiscal year from the G.P.O., and you can also get revised editions of the Communications Act of 1934 from G.P.O. A list of current FCC publications, called "Administration Bulletin No. 1," is available from the Office Services Division, Office of the Executive Director, FCC. The FCC Office of Reports and Information can supply copies of most Commission decisions and policy statements free of charge (if you don't ask for too many). These are some of the basic materials which are free from the FCC:

1. *What You Should Know About the FCC*
2. *How to Apply for a Broadcast Station*
3. *Broadcast Primer*
4. *1960 Programming Statement* (FCC 60-970)
5. *Fairness Doctrine* (FCC 64-611)
6. *Use of Broadcast Facilities by Candidates for Public Office* (FCC 66-386)
7. *Rules on Personal Attacks and Political Editorials* (FCC Rules 73.123 *et seq.*)
8. *Statement of Policy Concerning Loud Commercials* (FCC 65-618)
9. *FCC Rules on Equal Employment Opportunities* (FCC Rules 73.125 *et seq.*)
10. *Policy Statement on Comparative Hearings Involving Regular Renewal Applicants* (FCC 70-62)
11. *Primer on Ascertainment of Community Problems by Broadcast Applicants*

12. "AM-FM Broadcast Financial Data" (annual report)
13. "Television Broadcast Financial Data" (annual report)
14. "Newspaper and Broadcast Station Crossownership Report" (annual report)

Press releases and public notices are also available, but they must be picked up in person at the Office of Reports and Information. If you can't make it to Washington every day, there are mailing services (such as the Chittenden Press Service, 1067 National Press Building) which will pick up the releases and mail them to you for about $15 a month.

Some detailed studies of television ownership and performance are also found in the published decisions and opinions of the Commission, particularly in separate opinions issued by former Commissioner Nicholas Johnson. These include "Broadcasting in America and the FCC's License Renewal Process: An Oklahoma Case Study" [14 FCC 2d.1], "New York State License Renewals" [18 FCC 2d 268, 269, 322], and "District of Columbia, Maryland, Virginia, and West Virgina Broadcast License Renewals" [21 FCC 2d 35]. Johnson's *How to Talk Back to Your Television Set* (New York: Bantam, 1970, 95 cents) is a very good basic text, and has an extensive bibliography.

The Office of Communication of the United Church of Christ (289 Park Avenue South, New York, New York, 10010), which has actively participated as a public interest advocate in a number of FCC proceedings, has published several immensely helpful books and pamphlets on citizen involvement at the Commission which are available free or at nominal cost. These include *Racial Justice in Broadcasting* (free). *A Guide to Understanding Broadcast License Applications* ($1), *How to Protect Citizen Rights in Television and Radio* (free), and *Guide to Citizen Action in Radio and Television* (free). Soon to be published is a handbook for lawyers, *Representing the Audience in Broadcast Proceedings*, by Robert Bennett, Esq. The Citizens Communications Center (1812 N. Street, N.W., Washington, D.C. 20036, 202-296-4238) has prepared a *Primer on Citizens' Access to the Federal Communications Commission* and will provide one copy free, multiple copies at reproduction cost. A pamphlet published by the Institute for American Democracy, Inc. (Suite 101, 1330 Massachusetts Avenue, N.W., Washington, D.C. 20005) is entitled *How to Combat Air Pollution—A Manual on the FCC's Fairness Doctrine* (50 cents). A subscription to *Broadcasting* magazine may also be helpful.

In the CATV area, a useful manual is *Cable Television in the Cities: Community Control, Public Access, and Minority Ownership*, edited by

Charles Tate ($3.95). Another useful handbook on CATV for local officials is *The Wired City* by Theodore Ledbetter, Jr., and Gilbert Mendelson ($2.95). They can be ordered from the Cable Television Information Center, 2100 M Street, N.W., Washington, D.C. 20037.

The Office of Communication of the United Church of Christ has published two excellent guides on CATV entitled *Cable Television: A Guide for Citizen Action* by Monroe Price and John Wicklein (Philadelphia, Pa.: Pilgrim Press, 1972, $2.95) and *A Short Course* (12 pp., free, available from the Office of Communication). Proposed FCC standards and governing rules and regulations are being promulgated at this time. Although technical and sometimes confusing, you should acquaint yourself with them. Copies may be obtained from the FCC or the Superintendent of Documents, Government Printing Office, Washington, D.C., 20402, at nominal costs. A copy of the FCC Cable Television Report and Order and Reconsideration, February 1972, plus comments by the Commissioners, may also be obtained from the G.P.O. for $1.75.

Radio and television broadcasters are given exclusive licenses by the FCC to use assigned frequencies for three-year periods. At the end of the three-year period the license comes up for renewal, and the licensee stands on his record and his promises in applying for the next term. The license is renewed if the Commission finds that renewal is in "the public interest." For most licensees, especially those with profitable VHF television (channels 2-13) licenses, this is a license to make more money from public property.

Although renewal time is when licensees are most vulnerable to charges that they have neglected their public responsibilities, you can't wait until the end of the three-year period before presenting your case. You may be able to get the station to correct its deficiencies before then, for one thing. For another, the FCC

> . . .does not condone the practice of community groups waiting until long after an application for renewal of license has been filed before raising any complaints they may have concerning a station's policies or program practices. . . . The practice of waiting until long after a renewal application is filed before seeking correction of alleged past derelictions of a licensee (which it has been given no prior opportunity to consider) is disruptive of the Commission's processes. [WSM, Inc., *et al.*, 24 FCC 2d 561, at 563-4]

This can be interpreted as a large-scale version of a common experience in dealing with bureaucracies—if you get to the right window with your complaint, it's always closing time, and it's your fault for not starting sooner. When you have a complaint about a broadcaster, take it to the station and the FCC at once. Even if no corrective action is taken at that time, all complaints received by the FCC about a particular station are placed in the official public file on that station and may be brought up again when the station's license is up for renewal. Citizens who are interested in protesting the conduct or operations of a broadcaster should, if possible, examine the public file to see what other complaints may have been filed that would lead to helpful information or allies.

The Broadcast Bureau is not supposed to determine the content of what is broadcast, but there are several huge exceptions to this rule, and those exceptions are the basis for much of this chapter. First of all, the Bureau is not supposed to act as a censor, but broadcasters, like publishers, have found that the First Amendment doesn't really mean that *anything* can be said in print or over the air. The prohibition on broadcasting obscenity has been applied to sex rather than violence, and the culprits have mostly been ham radio operators and a few FM radio stations. The networks which originate most television programing are sufficiently wary of offending any sizable segment of their viewing audiences to make what is omitted from broadcasting as much of a problem as the offensiveness of what is sent over the airwaves.

This brings us to the two major exceptions to the rule that the FCC doesn't determine the content of broadcasting that will concern you. First, the licensee must operate his station "in the public interest"; second, he must be fair. Obviously, these statements fall a little short of precision. The FCC has attempted to spell out what the public interest and fairness are, but the real process of definition is just beginning. That process will depend largely on citizen action. The FCC has no systematic program for actually monitoring what is broadcast, and it's up to viewers to give the Commission an idea of what stations licensed to operate in the public interest are putting into the air. Defining what is and is not "in the public interest" or "fair" must be an adversary process between broadcasters, who are unlikely to admit to being against the public interest or unfair, and consumers, who know what they see and hear.

The fairness doctrine is not a single act of Congress or a single decision by the FCC. It developed out of a series of decisions, and is based on the assumption that a licensee using public property should not be allowed to limit that use to presentation of a single point of view. Most of the development of the doctrine has been in the form of decisions by the Commission and by the courts in individual cases. When the Radio Commission had to choose between licensees, it chose those who had been in business longest, *unless* the senior broadcaster had used its station for presentation of a single point of view.

The Sixth Annual Report of the FCC in 1940 stated, ". . . the stations are required to furnish well-rounded rather than one-sided discussions of public questions," and in the 1941 case of Mayflower Broadcasting [8 FCC 333] the Commission said that ". . . the broadcaster cannot be an advocate." This was thought to prohibit any editorializing by broadcasters until the FCC issued its Report on Editorializing in 1949. In that Report, the Commission emphasized that fairness was not the same thing as avoiding controversy to the point of dullness.

> . . . the licensee's obligation to serve the public interest can[not] be met merely through the adoption of a general policy of not refusing to broadcast opposing views when a demand is made of the station for broadcast time . . . it is evident that broadcast licensees have an affirmative duty generally to encourage and implement the broadcast of all sides of controversial public issues over their facilities, over and beyond their obligation to make available on demand opportunities for the expression of opposing views. It is clear that any approximation of fairness in the presentation of any controversy will be difficult if not impossible of achievement unless the licensee plays a conscious and positive role in bringing about balanced presentation of the opposing viewpoint.

The most specific expression of Congressional intent on the fairness doctrine was a sort of backhanded reference in the law authorizing the 1960 election debates. The bill suspending the broadcast time requirement for all candidates stated that nothing in the exemption from equal-time requirements would relieve broadcasters of the obligation otherwise "to afford reasonable opportunity for the discussion of conflicting views on issues of public importance."

That "obligation" is a shorthand definition of the basic fairness doctrine. The FCC's own statement of the fairness doctrine, along with digests of some of the more significant cases up to 1964, is contained in "Applicability of the Fairness Doctrine in the Handling of Controversial Issues of Public Importance." This is available on request from the FCC, or you can look it up in the *Federal Register* at 29 Fed. Reg. 145, 25 July 1964. The Commission is currently engaged in a comprehensive review of the doctrine [Obligations of Broadcast Licensees

Under the Fairness Doctrine, 35 Fed. Reg. 7820] and the rules may have changed by the time you read this.

Many broadcasters seem to feel that their obligations under the fairness doctrine are discharged if their programing is so patently inoffensive that no one is sufficiently offended to object. This may have some validity in fact, but not in law. A licensee has a clear duty to broadcast discussions of "controversial issues of public importance," and to allow presentation of all points of view. Fairness complaints almost always involve attempts by listeners to respond to a broadcast which they believe to be unfair, but the doctrine is much broader than that, and the remedy is not limited to a few minutes of air time to present another view. The refusal by a broadcaster to transmit either (or any) side of a "controversial issue of public importance" is part of his record when his license is up for renewal. The remedy at renewal time can include refusal by the Commission to renew the license, or a negotiated truce in which the broadcaster promises to change his ways. But, as mentioned earlier, you must start objecting when the broadcasts are made instead of waiting until renewal time.

The fairness doctrine does not require that *equal* time be given to all points of view on an issue. That term is usually used, although incorrectly, for the special rules on broadcasts by political candidates. It does require that the licensee's overall programming afford a reasonable opportunity for the discussion of conflicting views on issues of public importance. The licensee is allowed to limit the use of the airwaves to "responsible" spokesmen, and he has considerable leeway in deciding who is responsible. But *everything* that is broadcast is required to meet the test of fairness. The special rules in cases of personal attack and political broadcasts are specific applications of this general fairness requirement.

At one time it was thought that the fairness requirements did not include commercials, but one giant exception has been made by the FCC regarding cigarette commercials. That exception was made on the basis of a petition filed by a New York lawyer named John Banzhaf. The case went on to court [*Banzhaf* v. *FCC*, 405 F. 2d 1082], with the Commission and the court saying that even if antismoking spots were required, cigarettes are an extraordinary product, and the principle should never be applied to commercials for any other product. Cigarette advertising eventually was banned from the airwaves by Congress as of January, 1971 [Public Law 91-222, Section 2, 15 U.S.C. 1335]. Despite all the judicial and administrative pronouncements that cigarettes are different from any other dangerous product, it is possible that the fairness doctrine will require countercommercials "on other products" [*Friends of the Earth* v. *FCC*, 449 F. 2d 1164].

The FCC has authority to act against other abuses in commercials, but so far it has taken little action. The Commission only requires broadcasters to indicate on their license renewal forms how many minutes per hour of broadcast time they intend to make available for commercials. No objections are made by the FCC to proposals by television broadcasters to spend sixteen minutes out of an hour for commercials, or by radio broadcasters to spend eighteen minutes out of every hour. One simple technique for monitoring a broadcaster's performance is to compare the proposed commercial time in his last application for license renewal with the actual commercial time being broadcast.

The FCC has taken some steps to deal with loud commercials, in making a *Statement of Policy Concerning Loud Commercials.* If you are concerned about loud commercials, get a free copy of that statement, which describes a system for referring complaints about loud commercials. Basically, your complaint should go to both the station and the FCC, with the date and time of the commercial, the sponsor, and the station's call letters.

Broadcasters are also responsible, in theory, for false and deceptive advertising. But in the past the FCC has refused to take action on complaints against licensees for broadcasting such commercials, unless the offending ads involve some controversial public issue and therefore can be dealt with under the fairness doctrine rules, which are discussed in detail below. Outside of those cases, the most effective thing to do about false and misleading advertising under the present circumstances is to send complaints to the broadcaster and the Commission on a regular basis, and present the broadcaster's record when his license is up for renewal. The Federal Trade Commission (FTC) also has the power to stop companies from deceptive advertising, and in the last few years it has shown considerably more interest in taking effective action. To fight a deceptive advertising campaign, the best starting point is to file a complaint with the FTC (see Chap. 5). One possible approach which has not been thoroughly explored is to ask the FTC, upon a finding that broadcast advertising is misleading, to petition the FCC to order the offending ads off the air. By the same token, the Office of Consumer Affairs in the Department of Health, Education, and Welfare could also participate in this manner as a public advocate in broadcasting, but it has not done so in the past.

The first step in combating broadcasting which you think is unfair is literally prosaic—write a letter. The first letter goes to the station which made the offending broadcast. It should be sent to the local station, not to the network, since individual stations, rather than networks, are licensed and regulated by the FCC. The letter should contain specific information about the public issue involved, the date and time of the broadcast, and the reasons for your belief that only one side of the issue has been presented. It is also useful to suggest "responsible" spokesmen who could present contrasting viewpoints to achieve fairness. One thing to remember in writing such a long letter is that it may be just the opening skirmish in a hard battle, and it often is important to take careful steps just for the record. You may feel that it is futile to complain to a particular station, or that it is a waste of time to participate in sometimes lengthy negotiations with licensees. But if every reasonable alternative has not been tried it is quite possible that the FCC (or perhaps the courts) will send you back to start all over again. So don't be intimidated, but make haste carefully.

One thing to be careful about is using the magic words, "controversial issue of public importance." It may seem ritualistic, but it is important to use just that phrase in describing the subject of the broadcast. By doing so, you invoke a whole list of FCC and judicial decisions on the broadcaster's duty to present conflicting points of view on such issues. You must also back up your use of the label by presenting arguments as to why the particular issue is both controversial and of public importance. Broadcasters and the Commission are capable of some pretty close reasoning on this question. For example, the Commission ruled in 1970 that while the war in Indochina might be considered controversial, recruiting the forces to fight it was not [FCC 70-595 (46924), letter to Mr. Donald A. Jelinek, 70-596 (46925), letter to Mr. Albert A. Kramer, 70-597 (46926), letter to Mr. Alan F. Neckritz, all of 4 June 1970), *Green* v. *FCC,* 447 F. 2d 323 (1971)].

Many stations do not keep recordings of their broadcasts, and it is useful, if you can afford it, to make a tape of the offending broadcasts, or at least to prepare careful summaries. If the station does not offer a reasonable opportunity to a responsible spokesman to present the other point of view, the next step is to write another letter, this one to the Secretary, Federal Communications Commission, Washington, D.C., 20554.

The letter should restate all of the details of the broadcast which were in your original letter to the station. Describe your communications with the station and your efforts to get the station to broadcast contrasting views, then give your reasons for concluding that the station's offers (if any) have been inadequate. The qualifications of persons suggested to present opposing views should be described to establish them as "responsible spokesmen."

The FCC's first step will be to refer the complaint back to the broadcaster and ask for his response. If there is no serious factual discrepancy between your account and the broadcaster's response, the FCC staff will then evaluate the actions taken by the station to determine whether they satisfy the fairness doctrine. If the requirements of the doctrine are not satisfied, the staff will notify the station and ask what steps will be taken.

There are several sanctions which the Commission can impose on broadcasters who violate the fairness doctrine. Fines may be imposed, or the agency can go to court to get a cease and desist order. But an order from the Commission is usually all that is needed. The problem lies in getting the FCC to issue the order. The Commission can also revoke a license, refuse to renew it, or grant a short-term renewal conditioned on correction of violations. There's much more you need to know to prepare for license renewal proceedings, but before that there is a specific application of the fairness doctrine called the personal attack rules, which you may need if you take on the broadcasters.

The personal attack rules are based on the fairness doctrine. Basically, these rules [47 C.F.R. 73.123, .300, .1598] require any station which broadcasts an attack on a person or group to notify the person or group attacked and offer air time for a response. There are hitches and exceptions to this general definition, but they are relatively minor, and their extent hasn't been fully spelled out through application in particular cases. A "personal attack" is an attack on an individual's or group's honesty, character, or integrity. For the rules to be applied, the attack must be in connection with our old friend—a "controversial issue of public importance." If a personal attack is made, you have a right to reply, even if there's factual basis for the attack. The exceptions for bona fide newscasts, interviews, attacks on foreign groups, and on-the-spot news coverage do not exempt editorials broadcast during newscasts or documentaries.

The personal attack rules don't apply to attacks made by political candidates or their spokesmen on other political candidates. The "equal time" law concerning political candidates specifies that if a broadcaster furnishes broadcast time to one candidate, he must provide an equal opportunity for other candidates at an equivalent price [47 U.S.C. 151-52, 315]. The set of rules on broadcast access by political candidates won't be covered in this book, but if you are running for office they will be of tremendous importance to you. They can be obtained by writing to the FCC Office of Reports and Information and asking for *Use of Broadcast Facilities by Candidates for Public Office* (FCC 66-386).

The first step in proceeding under the personal attack rules against a station which has broadcast an attack on you or a group to which you belong is to find out about the broadcast. Of course it's the broadcaster's obligation to notify you of such an attack, but his definition of personal attack may be more limited than yours, or the FCC's, or the Supreme Court's. Another problem in learning when and where personal attacks have been broadcast is that many attacks are made on syndicated programs. There is no requirement that the syndicator notify the target of an attack, or even that the syndicator supply, upon request, a list of stations broadcasting a particular attack. If you learn from other sources that an attack against you has been broadcast, let the broadcaster know, and ask him how he intends to comply with the personal attack rules. A sample letter would be something like this:

Station XYZ

Dear Sir:

I have learned that on (program name), which you broadcast on (date) at about (time), a personal attack was made on (you or your organization). Please inform me of the arrangements which you are making to provide (you or your group) with a tape or summary of the attack, and to furnish an opportunity to broadcast a reply to this attack.

Send the letter by registered mail and wait for the response. Remember that the personal attack rules are not satisfied merely by an offer to *sell* you air time. It is not enough for a station to reply, as one did to a complaint by a man accused of Communist associations, merely by sending a "rate card" listing the station's charges for air time. If you are not offered a satisfactory opportunity to broadcast a response to the attack, your next step is to write the FCC. The letter should contain all of the details concerning the attack which were in your initial letter to the station. You should also include a brief explanation of how the attack was made in connection with a "controversial issue of public importance," along with a description of any offers made by the station and why you consider them to be unsatisfactory.

As with fairness complaints, the FCC will first ask the station for its side of the story. If the broadcaster's reply is unsatisfactory, the Commission may order it to provide free broadcast time for your response. If the station doesn't comply, the Commission can issue an order or impose a fine, although it has never done so. If relief is not obtained by going to the FCC, the next step is to go to court. That has been done once by a man who went all the way to the U.S. Supreme Court—but won. You might not have to go that far. But even if you decide not to go to court over your complaint, your efforts are not necessarily in vain. As mentioned earlier, station licenses are renewed every three years, and licensees are supposed to stand on their records at renewal time. Your personal attack complaint is a part of that record. A file of unresolved complaints under the personal attack rules or the fairness doctrine can determine whether, how long, and under what conditions the broadcaster's license is renewed.

The commercials that are broadcast are frequent and loud reminders that broadcasters see their licenses primarily as a source of income. But messages that are not broadcast are the other side of the same phenomenon. Until recently, paid messages were limited by almost all stations to advertisements to sell products and services; attempts to buy time to present persuasive messages on public issues other than election campaigns were routinely rejected. "Public interest" spots were limited to noncontroversial appeals for support of the Boy Scouts or similar organizations, aired during graveyard viewing hours when nobody else wanted to buy time, and served up to the FCC as proud examples.

In 1969 the Business Executives' Move for Vietnam Peace repeatedly tried to buy time from station WTOP, in Washington, D.C., for an antiwar message. The station refused, relying on its "long established policy of refusing to sell spot announcement time to individuals or groups to set forth views on controversial issues." The group filed suit in federal court, and in August 1971 the U.S. Court of Appeals for the District of Columbia Circuit ruled that it was unconstitutional for a station to accept commercial advertising and refuse to accept any paid public issue announcements [*Business Executives' Move for Vietnam Peace* v. *FCC,* 450 F. 2d 642 (1971)]. Unfortunately, the ruling was overturned in May 1973 by the Supreme Court which decided that there is neither a First Amendment right nor a statutory right to buy radio or television time.

Although broadcast time is expensive, it is a powerful means of influencing public opinion. That is why large corporations rely heavily on television and radio advertising not only to sell products, but also to persuade people that industry is doing the very best it can to protect the environment and generally be a good corporate citizen. One approach you might consider would be to prepare to acquire a short radio or television message on a public issue, such as pollution control, and submit it to the station to run without charge as a public interest message. If it is bland enough to be approved by the Advertising Council (825 Third Avenue, New York, N.Y. 10022), it has a better chance of being accepted by the broadcaster as a public service message.

Broadcasters have no obligation to let a particular person have air time or to provide time free to respond to advertising. Under the fairness doctrine, stations are obligated only to present the other side to the institutional corporate advertising they run if an issue of public controversy is involved. The station has wide discretion in choosing the context, persons, and format for the presentation of opposing viewpoints, and only where it can't find a competing viewpoint to be presented on a paid basis is it obligated to make the time available free. If your message is rejected, you can file a fairness complaint, and the FCC will determine whether the station has exercised its discretion in good faith; or, if you can afford it, you can ask the station to sell you air time for the same message. Remember that the court's decision that the station could not flatly refuse to accept paid public interest messages was based on the Constitution, not on the fairness doctrine, so buying time doesn't necessarily make your fairness complaint invalid. The Businessmen's Educational Fund (1330 Massachusetts Avenue, N.W., Washington, D.C. 20005, 202-737-3408), the Stern Community Law Firm (2005 L Street, N.W., Washington, D.C. 20036, 202-659-8132), and an affiliated group, Stern Concern (260 South Beverly Drive, Beverly Hills, California 90212, 213-275-0135) have prepared various countercommercial messages, and might be of assistance in getting access to air time or the technical preparation of messages.

Television and radio broadcasters operate under licenses to use public property—the airwaves—for periods of three years. They use these licenses to make money and to serve the public. At the end of every three years they must apply for renewal of their licenses, and renewal depends on how well they have carried out their public service responsibilities. The possibility of not having a license renewed, or having it renewed only for a limited period, is the ultimate sanction that backs up most of the methods of citizen participation suggested in this chapter.

Not all of the stations in the United States come up for renewal at the same time. The renewal dates are staggered according to states, and a list of the states with the license renewal dates for their stations is available from the Office of Public Information. The file of complaints which the station has received is only one indication of how well it has performed during the license period. An even more important standard by which to measure the station's performance is the requirement that broadcasters actively involve the listening and viewing public in planning their programing. That is a positive duty, and not just a matter of responding to complaints from the public. To find out what this requires in detail, get the FCC's free *Primer on Ascertainment of Community Problems by Broadcast Licensees.*

Basically, the licensee is required to survey the listening and viewing public, and to consult with community leaders to find out what sort of programing the community needs. In the application for renewal, the licensee must give specific information about what it has done. By looking at Section IV of the license renewal application, the Statement of Program Service, you can tell:

1. The methods which the broadcaster used to survey the community.
2. What the broadcaster considers to be the community which it serves.
3. The leaders and organizations in the community which were consulted.
4. What the licensee believes are the needs and interests of the public which it will serve.
5. The programs broadcast and planned for broadcast to meet those needs.
6. The procedures which the broadcaster uses to consider complaints and suggestions from the public.

That section of the renewal application also has a detailed description of the broadcaster's past programing. Section VI of the application for renewal is the licensee's report on its equal employment program, and, starting in 1971, licensees have had to file annual reports listing their minority group employees by number and job category.

A rough checklist for evaluating a station's performance (developed by the Office of Communication of the United Church of Christ) is a good place to start in taking a critical look at a broadcaster:

1. Does the station make a serious effort to consult with representatives of community groups about the kind of programming it is providing and how it might improve its service?
2. Does the station present a balanced program schedule, offering

programs in each of the fourteen areas enumerated by the FCC as representing local needs?

3. Does the station program discussion of controversial issues that are important to the community? Does this programming give opposing points of view the opportunity to be heard or does it give voice to only one point of view? Are members of minority groups included in discussions of community issues? Are news and documentary programs biased toward one viewpoint or a limited number of viewpoints?

4. Do announcers or guests of the station attack individuals or groups? Does the station feature "call-in" programs on which anonymous callers are allowed to make attacks on individuals or organizations? If such attacks are made, does the station offer those attacked an immediate opportunity to reply?

5. How much time does the station devote to public service broadcasting for nonprofit organizations within the community? Are these programs aired during hours when people are likely to be viewing or listening or are they on the air at a time when people are in bed, at meals, or in church? Are the programs aimed at a variety of audiences, or are they directed at a particular segment of the community?

6. Are the interests, tastes, needs, and desires of minority groups, such as blacks and Chicanos, adequately served? For example, do blacks receive treatment equal to that accorded to whites? Do they appear regularly on the station on all types of programs at all times of day? Are racial issues and the affairs of the black community dealt with fairly and objectively? Do black leaders have regular access to the station to present their views? Are the lives and problems of blacks portrayed to the whole community with depth and meaning? [Ralph M. Jennings, *How to Protect Citizens' Rights in Television and Radio* (New York: Office of Communication of the United Church of Christ, 1969)]

The fourteen areas of programing referred to in the second area of evaluation are taken from *Report and State of Policy re: en banc Programming Inquiry* (FCC 60-970), 25 F.R. 7291:

1. Opportunity for local expression
2. Development and use of local talent
3. Programs for children
4. Religious programs

   5. Educational programs
   6. Public Affairs programs
   7. Editorialization by licensees
   8. Political broadcasts
   9. Agricultural programs
  10. News programs
  11. Weather and market reports
  12. Sports programs
  13. Service to minority groups
  14. Entertainment programs

Broadcasters are not required to have any particular percentage of their programing in any of these areas, but they usually should have at least some programing from each area.

Before 1966, the FCC considered license renewal proceedings as industry disputes, and ordinary citizens were excluded from the process. But that was the year of the first United Church of Christ decision, which held that spokesmen for groups representing listeners and viewers had standing to challenge license renewals, even if they didn't have an economic interest.

In 1964, the Office of Communications of the United Church of Christ had aided local citizens in asking the FCC to refuse renewal of the licenses for two Jackson, Mississippi, television stations (WJTV and WLBT). Forty-five percent of the audience for these two stations were black people who had been consistently discriminated against by devices such as refusal to broadcast any coverage of civil rights activities. The FCC refused to listen to the group, on the grounds that they did not have "standing," and refused to hold a hearing on whether the licenses should be renewed. The U.S. Court of Appeals for the District of Columbia Circuit reversed the FCC, holding that groups representing listeners and viewers have standing to challenge license renewals. Grudgingly, the FCC held a public hearing in Jackson, Mississippi, as ordered by the court, but over-ruled the church group and renewed the license. The challengers went to court again. In a blistering opinion written by Judge (now Chief Justice) Warren Burger, the court criticized the hearing examiner's "curious neutrality-in-favor of the licensee," and reversed the Commission again.

It was bad enough for most broadcasters, who had come to view renewal time as a triennial ritual, that they had to put up with public intervenors. But that same year an FCC hearing examiner refused to renew the license of a Boston television station, and awarded it to a competing applicant. The NAB stormed up Capitol Hill and had a bill introduced which would have required the Commission to find that a license should not be renewed before it could even consider a competing application. The proposal was described as being roughly similar to a law that would prohibit anyone from running against a Congressman unless the incumbent had been impeached. With one eye on Congress, the FCC adopted a *Policy Statement on Comparative Hearings Involving Regular Renewal Applicants* that would have had about the same effect as the pending bill. But, as previously mentioned, the Court of Appeals ruled in 1971 that the policy statement was illegal.

The effect of this decision was to reopen for citizen participation a door that had been partially closed. But remember that using this legal remedy to force substantial changes in the policies of a broadcaster takes much more organization, legal expertise, and continued effort than a single fairness complaint.

The first step, before you begin discussions with the broadcaster or consider legal action, is to form an organization. The discussion in Chapter 18 may be useful in this step, but there is one qualification. Since your standing depends largely on your representing the community, you should try to include representatives of as many community organizations as possible. At times this may reduce your flexibility and freedom of action, but it is essential for this purpose. The free pamphlets from the Office of Communication of the United Church of Christ are very useful for informing people of their rights and assisting in organizing a coalition.

You will need some legal assistance once your organization is formed, long before you take any legal action. This is partly because you will need legal advice in negotiating with the station and in such routine matters as forming a corporation. But you will also need the assistance of attorneys who are willing to study some communications law and handle the necessary FCC proceedings if you decide to take that step. National public interest groups such as the Citizens Communications Center, the Office of Communication of the United Church of Christ, the Stern Community Law Firm, and the Media Access Project may provide some assistance, but as a practical matter most of the work will have to be done by you and your attorneys. Much of your bargaining power in negotiation with a station depends on your ability to take legal action if it becomes necessary.

The next step is investigation and monitoring. Examine the licensee's last application for renewal, and compare it with performance since then. Evaluate the licensee's employment practices and consultation

with the community as well as the quality of his programing. Inspect
the records which each licensee is required to make available to the public. Remember that it is not up to community organizations to go
begging to the licensee for an opportunity to be heard. The FCC
imposes a positive obligation on the part of a licensee to find out the
community needs which he is required to serve. He must consult with a
representative range of community leaders, and his application for
renewal must describe how he did this. He must include in his application for renewal all significant suggestions he has received, even if he
doesn't intend to use them in his programing. He must describe how he
intends to use his programing, if the license is renewed, to meet the
community needs he has learned about.

All of these requirements offer opportunities for you to see how
well the broadcaster serves the community. Make your own community
surveys, and then make some concrete suggestions concerning how the
station can better serve the community. If the licensee hasn't consulted
with community groups, ask him why.

There are several ways of checking the station's past performance.
One useful information source is the programing log for a composite
week that is compiled when the licensee applies for renewal. The Commission chooses seven days at random from the previous three years.
The licensee must state the hours and percentage of total air time
spent on these categories: news, public affairs, and all other programs
other than sports and entertainment. The broadcaster must also describe
a typical week of programing which is planned if the license is renewed.
The amount of time devoted to commercials in the composite week
must be specified, and the licensee must tell the maximum amount of
time to be spent on commercials in the future. *All* of this information
is available at the station.

Applicants and licensees are required by Rule 1.526 [47 C.F.R.
1.526] to provide copies of their applications for public inspection at
the studios or another local designated location. Copies are also on file
and available for public inspection at the FCC offices in Washington.
An invaluable guide to this material is the United Church of Christ's
Guide to Understanding Broadcast License Applications.

Take a look at what is actually broadcast. One of the most time-consuming jobs is the day-in, day-out, systematic monitoring of programs.
It does not take technical training, and it can yield surprising results,
especially when actual programing is compared with promises made at
the last renewal proceeding.

Monitoring a station's programing takes careful planning to be useful.

The Office of Communication of the United Church of Christ has developed considerable expertise in such planning, and the observer's report form in Appendix 7-A (p. 304) is an example of how monitoring can be reported. Remember that the purpose of monitoring is to develop objective data on programing which can be used to compare a station's performance with its promises and with the performances of other stations. To get an idea of what this involves, get copies of other evaluation systems and use them to design your own plan for monitoring. One evaluation is a comparative analysis of television stations' performances in New York and New Jersey by FCC Commissioners Johnson and Cox. It is contained in a separate statement in the report on Renewal of Standard Broadcast and Television Licenses, 18 FCC 2d 268, 269. A detailed comparison of television broadcasters in a regional area is included in *Television Today: The End of Communication and the Death of Community,* a report of the Institute for Policy Studies, which is available from Communication Service Corp., 1333 Connecticut Avenue, N.W., Washington, D.C. 20036, for $6.50 ($10 for hardcover).

A plan for monitoring a station's performance can include any standards which you can devise to determine how well a station is serving the community in comparison with other stations, with its own promises, and with the needs of the community. Find out what percentage of broadcast time (or prime time) is devoted to locally originated programing, news or public affairs, local or regional news, public service announcements, children's programs, and so on—the categories are limited only by your interests and imagination. Once you have developed a plan for monitoring and accumulated your data, use them to compare your station's performance with its programing proposals and with the programing of other stations in the same geographic area or in similar communities. The Institute for Policy Studies developed a numerical rating system for comparing the performance of stations in the same geographic area.

Decisions made by licensees concerning the people they hire to do the broadcasting can be as important as what is broadcast. Since 1969 the FCC has required broadcasters to take steps against discrimination in employment, and many groups have focused their efforts as much on this issue as on the content of broadcasting. The regulations are in Part 73, Chapter 1 of Title 47 in the C.F.R. In 1970 the Commission adopted a rule requiring all radio and television stations with five or more employees to include a report on their equal employment opportunity practices in their applications for license renewal. This information is in Section VI of the renewal application, which has three parts: a description of the plan which the licensee has undertaken to ensure equal opportunity; the specific practices of the licensee in carrying out the plan; and a description of any complaints about discrimination filed with the station, and the disposition of the complaints. Since 1971 broadcasters have been required to file annual employment reports, called Form 395s, which give the number of minority group employees and their job classifications. These reports must be filed by 31 May of each year, and are available in the public files of the broadcasters for seven years.

Once you have accumulated data on the station's performance, establish specific objectives and decide on their priorities. These will depend on the needs of your community and on the broadcaster's performance. Your goals may range from minority employment to children's television programing. Once you have formulated your objectives, decide on the techniques you will use to achieve them.

Your efforts are not necessarily limited to fairness complaints and contesting license renewals. Like other agencies, the FCC has authority to make rules, and a successful rule making proposal may have an impact on broadcasting which goes far beyond a single station. The simplest method of participating in rule making is to submit comments on proposed rules when they are published in the *Federal Register*. If possible, you should submit fourteen copies of such comments to the address given in the notice.

A more difficult method is to submit a petition of your own for rule making. For example, the rules on equal employment were initiated by a petition of the United Church of Christ. Another petition with great impact was one submitted by ACT, a group of Boston area mothers concerned about the quality of children's television programs and the influence of commercials on their children. ACT has now grown far beyond its origin as a group of five concerned mothers who objected to cutting "Captain Kangaroo" from an hour to half an hour. They now have legal counsel and other expert support, many affiliated groups, and a program of negotiation with networks which has won concessions. Their original proposal called for a minimum of fourteen hours of commercial-free children's programing to be carried by all broadcasters every week, and a ban on selling of products by performers on children's programs. The FCC published the petition as a notice of proposed rule making, which prompted an unprecedented flood of consumer mail. As one writer put it: "ACT's demands came in the form of a legal petition for rule making—not scrawled on the scented, pastel stationery often associated with housewives' complaints to federal agencies—which is, perhaps, one reason the FCC chose not to ignore them."

Another petition, which is in Appendix 7-B (p. 309), was filed by a group of George Washington University Law School students who called themselves the Student Task-force Against Telecommunications Concealment (STATIC). The petition was for a rule to require licensees to broadcast information, similar to that contained in this chapter, on citizen rights in broadcasting. The Commission then published a proposed rule of its own (Docket No. 19,153) which would require licensees to make periodic broadcasts informing people that the airwaves are public property to be used by licensees in the public interest. The STATIC petition was treated by the FCC as a comment on the Commission's subsequent proposal. The FCC's proposed rule prompted a flood of industry comments, and the matter is still pending.

Petitions for rule making suffer from one fundamental defect: The Commission can ignore them completely. But if they are combined with other techniques, such as negotiation with broadcasters, they can have some impact. If the broadcasting practice which concerns you is widespread, you should consider filing a rule making petition. It can also serve as a vehicle for coordinating your efforts with those of similar groups in other areas.

A broadcaster's willingness to consult with the community about the kind of broadcasting it needs, to provide equal opportunity in employment, and to listen to complaints, may well be merely a response to legal obligations, but the willingness is reinforced by the realization that failure to carry out those obligations can result in the loss of the ticket to make money—the broadcasting license. The broadcaster's fear of possibly losing this enormously profitable license is the basic sanction that lies behind the other techniques of citizen access.

Although the following tools are used primarily when broadcasters apply for renewal of their licenses, similar objections can be raised at other times. The sale of a broadcast station must be approved by the FCC, and the procedure is roughly similar to a license renewal. There are two particular reasons why the sale of a station can be significant to the public. First, a sale is often accompanied by a marked change in the station's programing. A common pattern is for a station which provides programing for a specialized audience, such as classical music, jazz, or programs for a particular ethnic group, to be sold and converted to more generalized programing which will deliver a larger audience for advertisers. Second, the FCC is committed to preference for diversity in ownership of broadcasting facilities, and sales of stations are frequently made to media conglomerates which control other broadcast stations and publications. So the sale of a station usually involves a change in programing which affects a sizable audience, and raises an issue of ownership diversity.

But the most common and predictable opportunity for public participation is when the license is up for renewal every three years. The simplest method is to file an "Informal Objection" to renewal under Rule 1.587 [47 C.F.R. 1.587]. This is not subject to the filing deadlines for a "Petition to Deny." It can be filed any time prior to Commission action on the broadcaster's application, and it can hold up Commission action on the application. It is a useful device for raising questions about the licensee's performance without launching a full-scale legal action. There is no particular format for an Informal Objection, but it's a good idea to follow roughly the pattern of a Petition to Deny, with specific factual allegations and information supporting the charges.

A Petition to Deny is a formal request under Rule 1.580 [47 C.F.R. 1.580] for the Commission to deny the renewal (or station construction or license transfer) which the licensee seeks. The Petition to Deny can only be filed within a specific period. Licenses for all stations within a state expire every three years on the same day, and the stations file for renewal ninety days before the date of expiration. You cannot file a Petition to Deny the renewal until ninety days before the expiration date, and your petition must be filed before the last month of the license period begins, so you must file within a two-month period. The Petition to Deny must be served on the broadcaster, who has ten days to file his opposition. You then have five days to reply. Extensions of these time limits are often granted if "good cause" can be shown.

Start your petition with an explanation of the representative nature of your group to justify your "standing" to participate. The charges you make about the broadcaster will follow your explanation of why your group is a "party of interest." These "allegations of fact" should be as specific as possible, and be backed up by affidavits. For example, the Petition to Deny the license of station WMAL-TV (Washington, D.C.) included affidavits from leaders of Washington's black community that they had not been consulted by the station in its efforts to ascertain community needs. Charges about programing or employment should be backed up with the results of program monitoring and statistics on minority groups in the area. If the Commission finds that your petition hasn't raised a "substantial and material question of fact," it may grant the application and issue a statement of its reasons without holding a hearing. If that happens, you probably will have to go to court to get a hearing. But if the FCC decides that you have raised substantial questions, it will schedule a hearing, which will probably be held in your area if you ask for it.

Your petition will be treated much more favorably if you have already presented your objections to the broadcaster and tried to negotiate a solution. Start as early as possible—no later than three months before a license expires. (Remember that a Petition to Deny must be filed by a month before the expiration date.) If negotiations are stalled, prepare a draft Petition to Deny or an Informal Objection. If the broadcaster is willing to make specific changes, get them in writing and make sure they are included in the application for renewal. For example, a group in Texarkana, Arkansas, challenged a license renewal and then withdrew their petition in exchange for reforms by the broadcaster. The policy statement was broadcast on prime time and included in the renewal application of the licensee. To insure that the policy would amount to more than a statement of good intentions, the agreement provided that any variance from the policy would be a failure to operate in accordance with the station's license. As such, deviations from the new policy would be grounds to refuse renewal of the license.

If you decide to file a Petition to Deny, you will need legal assistance from attorneys who have experience in communications law. The most efficient way to accomplish this is for local volunteer attorneys to work with the few national groups which can provide guidance and expertise. The Citizens Communication Center and the Office of Communication of the United Church of Christ are the two main sources of assistance for such efforts. Some other public interest groups in Washington, such as the Stern Community Law Firm and the Center for Law and Social Policy, have handled some FCC cases, and some of the public interest firms listed in Appendix 18-D of Chapter 18 (see p. 931) might be of some help.

If you enter the license renewal process, you will need all the help you can get, because you will be up against well-paid attorneys who are specialists in communications law. As the Chairman of the FCC put it in 1969, in a response to a questionnaire on citizen participation from the Subcommittee on Administrative Practice and Procedure of the Senate Judiciary Committee: "In most cases, the principal input is by parties having a financial interest in the outcome of the proceeding and resources sufficient to retain competent professional assistance, and by the staff of the Commission as repesentatives of the public."

While some law firms are willing to provide assistance without charge for public interest groups, don't expect such legal assistance from communications attorneys. In 1971 an FCC staff task force examined in great depth the difficulties and burdens on public interest and community groups seeking to participate in FCC proceedings. Among other things, the Policy Review Committee surveyed fifteen of the major law firms practicing before the Commission, in order to learn where groups with no financial interest at stake might get legal assistance to participate in FCC proceedings. Of the firms contacted, only two—Arnold and Porter, and Arent, Fox, Kintner, Plotkin, and Kahn—stated unqualifiedly that they would be willing to represent public groups against a broadcast station in Commission proceedings, in the absence of some mandate requiring all communications firms to represent such groups. Three firms flatly refused, and the others placed conditions on their responses "such as to make it doubtful whether a case could be found which they would be willing to handle." As the committee stated in its confidential report to the Commission:

> The problem is one of client relations and credibility as a representative of broadcast interests. A broadcaster-client, it seems, would find it difficult to understand why an attorney he trusted to handle his interests in Commission proceedings would represent a public interest group attacking the interests of another broadcaster, particularly if the client might be susceptible to criticism or attack on the same or similar grounds. This would particularly be so where such assistance was rendered voluntarily and without a fee and where substantial fees were paid by broadcasters for similar services. Vigorous representation of a public interest group, possibly establishing precedent damaging to the broadcaster-client, in short, would tend to damage the attorney's credibility as a representative of the client's interests.

The Commission had already rejected one possible solution, that of allowing provisions in settlement agreements for reimbursement of legal expenses [KCMC, Inc., 25 FCC 2d 603]. The Policy Review Committee concluded its hard-hitting report with a strong recommendation for the immediate establishment of a five-man Office of Public Counsel in the FCC (but separated functionally from other offices and bureaus) to represent and assist public interest groups in Commission proceedings. It also suggested that special rules of procedure for public interest groups be adopted. Despite the urgent need for improving the Commission's procedures and facilitating public interest representations, the Policy Review Committee's recommendations have been ignored and forgotten inside the agency.

The Common Carrier Bureau of the FCC is principally concerned with regulating one giant company—AT&T. Comparing the resources of the regulator and the regulated makes it understandable, if not defensible, that the Commission threw up its bureaucratic hands in late 1971 and said that an investigation of AT&T would be more than it could handle. The Commission later modified its statement and began an inquiry of sorts, but the fundamental disparity remains. AT&T's yearly toll call revenues alone are more than 6,000 times the Bureau's total budget. AT&T is more like a country than a company, with functional, rather than geographic, boundaries. In 1969 its assets totaled almost $44 billion, which was slightly less than the gross national product for the entire continent of Africa. The boundaries of the Bell System, of which AT&T is the parent company, are the outer limits of its horizontal and vertical monopoly over common carrier communications products and services.

The Common Carrier Bureau is occupied with the structure of the Bell System, the limits on what it can do, and what it can charge. Long-distance telephone rates are the most visible subject of regulation for the average consumer. But one thing must be remembered—the Common Carrier Bureau regulates interstate common carrier communications. Section 152 of the Communications Act [47 U.S.C. 152] explicitly bars the FCC from regulating the *intra*state affairs of the Bell System. Many consumer complaints about services and rates are not handled by the FCC because they concern matters that are subject to regulation by state officials.

The Common Carrier Bureau came into being as a result of the Communications Act of 1934, which created the FCC and directed it to regulate "interstate and foreign commerce in communication by wire and radio so as to make available . . . to all people of the United States a rapid, efficient, Nation-wide, and worldwide wire and radio communication service with adequate facilities at reasonable charges." The Bureau now has about 150 employees spread over its six divisions.

The Domestic Rates Division has about seventy employees who oversee the activities of all domestic communications common carriers. The Bell System is a common carrier in the sense that it is selling a transportation service—the interstate and foreign transportation of information by electronic media. As a common carrier, AT&T is required by the Communications Act to furnish service upon reasonable request [Section 201(a)], to limit its charges, classifications, and regulations to those which are "just and reasonable" [Section 201(b)], and to refrain from "undue or unreasonable" discrimination [Section 202(a)]. The Act also requires common carriers to file information concerning their

activities with the Commission. The information which is most important to the average consumer is that contained in "tariff" filings. A tariff is not limited to a proposed charge for services. It also includes
classifications, regulations, and practices which go beyond rates. Other
information which must be filed by common carriers includes applications for approval of proposed construction, acquisition, discontinuance
or curtailment of services, and mergers.

Since many of the tariffs to be approved by the Commission are concerned with how much profit the common carrier is allowed to make
from its investment, much of the Domestic Rate Division's time is spent
in determining the accounting methods to be used. This division also
handles most consumer complaints about telephone and telegraph services.

The Domestic Common Carrier Radio Division exists because common carrier communication is not limited to conversations transmitted
over wires. In most cases, an interstate telephone conversation will be
transmitted over at least part of its journey by way of very high frequency radio waves. Seventy percent of all long-distance circuit mileage
is by microwave radio. Other information, such as facsimile, data, and
television signals, is also transmitted by microwave, and some inroads
have recently been made into AT&T's monopoly of interstate microwave
transmission. All applicants who propose to provide such microwave
service must obtain permission from the Commission and file annual
reports.

The International and Satellite Division is responsible for administration of the Communications Satellite Act of 1962 and regulation of
American-based international communications carriers. The Domestic
Services and Facilities Division serves primarily to pass on applications
for new facilities and acquisitions. The Economic Studies Division was
formed in 1966. Its five economists are mostly engaged in research on
long-range economic principles of common carrier regulation. The Field
Operations Division has two field offices, in New York and St. Louis,
which inspect common carrier facilities.

The average consumer is most likely to consider recourse to a regulatory agency when the regulated industry curtails the service provided.
In the case of common carrier communications, this occurs when the
telephone subscriber finds that his phone is dead, or only functioning
intermittently. At the outset, remember that many complaints about
telephone service may be rejected by the FCC as intrastate communications matters which are left to state regulation. In such a case, your recourse is usually limited to the state regulatory commission. But there

are signs that the FCC may not take such a restrictive view of its authority in the future. The Chief of the Common Carrier Bureau has requested and received monthly reports from AT&T on telephone service in twenty-five areas. This information may provide the basis for future action by the Commission concerning the quality of telephone service, especially if consumers take an active interest.

But we are now concerned with the courses of action available at the FCC for the individual consumer who finds himself holding a dead telephone. The first step is to contact the local telephone company (if you can find another working phone, this can be via a telephone call). If service is not quickly restored, begin the process of writing letters. The first letter should be to the local phone company, and it should include:

1. Name, address, telephone number, and past contacts with the company, such as date of installation.
2. Any notice received from the company concerning disconnection, and a demand for any justification of the disconnection by statute or company regulation.
3. Rebuttal of any reasons already given by the company for disconnection, and a demand for renewal of service and compensation for any injuries suffered because of the disconnection.

The next step, if the company does not restore service, is to contact a regulatory agency. Since general telephone service may be used for either inter- or intrastate calls, this step may involve contacting either your state regulatory agency or the FCC [47 U.S.C. 152].

The Communications Act gives the FCC jurisdiction over complaints submitted by "any person . . . or State commission" concerning interstate or foreign activities of a common carrier. The FCC rules (found in 47 C.F.R.) provide two basic avenues of approach: the informal and formal complaint. The major initial consideration in deciding to file an informal or formal complaint is whether you want monetary damages. If you do, a formal complaint is required [Rule 1.723].

An informal complaint under Rule 1.716 must be in writing, addressed to the Chief, Common Carrier Bureau, Federal Communications Commission, Washington, D.C., 20554. The complaint should include:

1. The names and addresses of the complaining person and the common carrier.
2. A complete and well-documented statement of the facts of the

dispute, "tending to show that such carrier did or omitted to do
anything in contravention of the Communications Act.
3. An indication of the remedy which you are seeking.

Any complaint about the quality of domestic telephone service, such as
dial tone delays, installation delays, or deprivation of service will be
handled by the Domestic Services and Facilities Division of the Common Carrier Bureau. Other complaints are handled by the Legal and
Tariff Branch of the Domestic Rates Division. Until recently, the volume of complaints has been low, probably because the public was not
aware of the FCC's power in this area, and to whom specific complaints
should be sent.

When the complaint is received, a copy must be sent to the carrier
with a request that the carrier either "satisfy the complaint or advise the
Commission of its refusal or inability to do so" [Rule 1.717]. Normally, the carrier is given thirty days to reply. A letter is sent to the
person who submitted the complaint, advising him that the carrier has
been notified. After the carrier responds to the complaint, a letter is
sent to the complaining person with a copy of the carrier's reply. Even
if the carrier decides to satisfy the complaint, it must notify the Commission [Rule 1.713]. If the complaint is not satisfied, the next step is
usually to file a formal complaint. This must be done within six months
[Rule 1.718]. Frequently, the Commission will recommend filing a formal complaint, and will send instructions to the consumer.

There are several important differences between formal and informal
complaints. As already mentioned, informal complaints cannot include
claims for damages, while formal complaints can. Informal complaints don't
challenge the *validity* of a company's rule or regulation, but charge that the
company has *abused* the rule or regulation in practice. Formal complaints
can challenge the legality of a rule, and can result in retraction of a rule
found to be illegal. Formal complaints must be ruled on by the Commission, while informal complaints normally do not reach the Commission.

The form and content of formal complaints are governed by specific
Rules 1.721-1.734. To understand the implications of filing an informal
or formal complaint, and the considerations which go into taking subsequent steps, consider the case of a man we will call Mr. K.

In 1967 K's telephone company demanded a large deposit from him,
and orally threatened to disconnect his phone if he did not comply.
The reason given by the company was that his mother, who lived with
him, owed money to the telephone company. He refused to make the
deposit, and his telephone was disconnected. He made several unsuc-

cessful requests for the company to restore telephone service. Instead of going to the state regulatory commission, he first went to the state courts, where he lost. He then filed an informal complaint with the FCC. The complaint was referred to the telephone company, which refused to restore service. The Common Carrier Bureau then suggested to Mr. K that he file a formal complaint, which he did.

He could have framed his complaint as narrowly or widely as he chose. He could have challenged merely the company's admitted violation of its own rule requiring written notice prior to disconnection. This might have resulted only in temporary reconnection of his phone, however, and the deposit demand would have gone unchallenged. He could have challenged the deposit demand as a violation of the Communications Act, or he could have challenged the rules which authorized the deposit as illegal.

He decided to challenge the legality of the deposit demand, and, framing his complaint in the required form set out in Rule 1.721, he sent an original and nineteen copies to the Secretary, Federal Communications Commission, Washington, D.C., 20554, pursuant to Rule 1.729. In the complaint he alleged that the company had acted in violation of two sections of the Communications Act [Sections 202(a) and 201(a)]. Section 202(a) states that "It shall be unlawful for any common carrier to make any unjust or unreasonable discrimination in charges, practices, classifications, regulations, facilities or services . . . directly or indirectly. . . ." As required by Rule 1.726, he specifically alleged that the company's demand for a deposit based on his mother's debt was an "unreasonably discriminatory practice." Section 201(a) states that "It shall be the duty of every common carrier (under the Act) . . . to furnish such communication service upon reasonable request therefor . . .," and he alleged that the company's refusal to provide him with telephone service was a violation of the section.

He asked for restoration of service, and also for compensatory and punitive damages. Section 206 of the Communications Act states: "In case any common carrier shall do . . . any act, matter or thing in this chapter prohibited or declared to be unlawful . . . such common carrier shall be liable to the person . . . injured thereby for the full amount of damages sustained in consequence of any violation . . . together with a reasonable counsel or attorney's fee. . . ." He specifically documented the injury he sustained because of the company's actions, and he stated that he had no court action pending (because Section 207 says that damages may be sought by complaint to the Commission or by suit in federal district court, but not both).

Several other provisions of the regulations regarding damage claims
might be useful, although they were not relied on in this case. Two or
more complainants may join in one complaint "if their respective causes
of action are against the same defendant and concern substantially the
same alleged violation of the Communications Act, and substantially the
same facts." This means there is a potential for class-action claims [Rule
1.725(a)]. Even if damages are not requested in the original complaint,
a supplemental complaint can be filed after the Commission has made a
finding on the first complaint. Thus, if Mr. K had not requested
damages, but the Commission had found that the company violated the
Communications Act, he could have filed a supplemental complaint
seeking damages (subject to the one-year limit of the statute of limitations) [Rules 1.723(a)(10)(b), 1.727(b); and Section 415(b) of the
Communications Act].

He could also have asked the Commission to invoke section 202(c) of
the Act, which says that "Any carrier who knowingly violates the provision of this section [discussed above] shall forfeit to the United States
the sum of $500 for each such offense and $25 for each and every day
of the continuance of such offense." The Commission could have
instituted civil court proceedings against the company. Mr. K's telephone had been illegally disconnected for a year and a half, and the
Common Carrier Bureau had repeatedly written the company about its
violations. Thus, the company could have been threatened with a forfeiture of close to $14,000, and the Bureau reminded the company of this
possibility.

All complaints must include an affidavit attesting to the truth of the
statements contained in the complaint, signed by the complainant and
notarized. Complaints should include any special requests, such as a
request for waiver of the requirement for twenty copies. You can also
ask for the attorney's fees to be awarded in the event that the Commission awards damages under Section 206. The section allows such fees to
be awarded in a court proceeding, and it could be extended to administrative hearings.

When a formal complaint is filed, the Common Carrier Bureau sends
a copy to the carrier and asks for a response, just as it does with informal complaints. The carrier has several alternatives. It may file an answer, under Rule 1.730, answering the charges and presenting its defenses, and under Rule 1.731(b) it may ask for clarification of the allegations. It may include with its answer a motion to dismiss the complaint
"because of lack of legal sufficiency appearing on the face of such complaint" [1.731(a)], or, under 1.713, the carrier may actually satisfy the

complaint. In Mr. K's case, the telephone company submitted an answer and a motion to dismiss the complaint, claiming, among other things, that Mr. K had no standing to complain and that the FCC has no jurisdiction.

When all of the pleadings and motions are in, the Commission, usually acting on the Bureau's recommendation, decides whether or not to hold an evidentiary hearing, under Section 208 and Rule 1.1. This decision takes the form of a "Memorandum Opinion and Order," published in the *Federal Register.* If the Commission refuses to hold a hearing, the complainant may file a "petition for reconsideration." Any petition for reconsideration of a Commission decision should be filed within thirty days. It should be no longer than twenty-five pages, and should include "findings of fact and/or conclusions of law (in the decision) which petitioner believes to be erroneous. . . ."

In the case of Mr. K, the Commission decided to hold a hearing. In its order the Commission noted that the request for punitive as well as compensatory damages was novel, but that "There appears to be no provision in the Act that prohibits us from awarding punitive damages where justified by the evidence." Although the Commission set the case for hearing, Mr. K chose to settle the matter informally. The company had offered to negotiate a settlement soon after the formal complaint was filed, and the prospect of punitive damages may have provided an additional incentive for the company to settle. A Joint Motion for Termination of Formal Complaint Proceedings was filed by the company and Mr. K. In exchange for a promise to drop the complaint and not bring any future action, the company paid $200 and restored service without requiring a deposit.

Complaints to the FCC can sometimes make the telephone company surprisingly responsive, even if letters to the company and the state regulatory commission have had no effect. For example, informal complaints to the FCC about billing matters are usually quite effective in prodding a recalcitrant company to drop an unjust or unreasonable long-distance charge. This can include ordinary mistakes which the company has refused to rectify, such as that unknown call to Mexico that appeared on your bill. The most common instance of unfair billing is telephone company action on "third party" charges. These are charges on a bill for calls made by some other person from some place other than your phone. For example, if someone makes a long-distance call from a pay phone and charges it to your number, it's a "third party" charge, and the company can't disconnect your phone for your refusal to pay for such an unauthorized call. An informal complaint will usually impel prompt FCC action. But if an informal complaint does not produce satisfaction, you may file a formal complaint for damages.

As seen in the case of Mr. K, companies sometimes demand deposits illegally, or in amounts which are illegal. The FCC has issued rules that limit deposit demands to twice the estimated monthly interstate charge [Tariff No. 263] and set uniform standards for credit ratings. State commissions also set limits on deposits for *intra*state service, so complaints alleging violation of deposit rules may be sent to the state agency or to the FCC.

Telephone company rules require investigation of consumer complaints about obscene or harassing calls, if the identity of the caller can be determined. If the company does not investigate, complaints to the FCC can be effective in encouraging the company to take action. The Communications Act provides criminal penalties for such calls [47 U.S.C. 223]. Telephone company rules also require investigation of alleged wiretapping, and prohibit eavesdropping by telephone company personnel. The FCC is authorized to enforce this prohibition under Section 605.

One recently concluded case [Complaint of Mrs. Martha Tranquilla against Mississippi Telephone and Communications, Inc., *et al.*; Docket No. 19,271] illustrates some telephone company abuses against which the FCC will take action. Briefly, the subscriber alleged that the company had charged her for long-distance calls she did not make, and that it had sent her a disconnection notice for a bill which she had paid, among other problems. In ordering a formal investigation [FCC 71-668, released 29 June 1971], the Commission noticed a few other peculiarities in the telephone company's behavior. The Company had aroused the FCC's ire by making no response at all to the Commission's requests for information. The Commission took a close look at the case and found, among other things, that the company: apparently imposed an illegal penalty charge for late payment on interstate calls, which is not part of the AT&T tariff; billed a call to the subscriber from a city which the Commission could not even find on a map; and previously had disconnected the subscriber's phone for refusal to pay the federal excise tax on her phone bill. The last action can be significant to those who refuse to pay the excise tax as a gesture of protest. In its order for a formal investigation, the Commission said

> . . . it was determined that while the tax is charged on the customer's bill, the Internal Revenue Service does not hold the telephone company responsible for the amount, but upon notification

of the refusal by the telephone company, will proceed directly against the subscriber. (See IRS Procedural Rules § 601.403(c)(2)) In this situation it cannot be considered that the tax is a "sum due the telephone company," within the meaning of Section 2.4.3 of American Telephone and Telegraph Company's Tariff F.C.C. No. 263 which provides for disconnection of service upon non-payment. Therefore, a serious question is raised as to whether the disconnection was not a denial of interstate telephone service in violation of the tariff and therefore of Section 203(e)(3).

The situation was a serious one for the telephone company, since the rules [Section 202] provide for a penalty of up to $500 and $25 per day. It would also subject the company to possible civil liability to the subscriber, under Section 206, which provides that any telephone company which ". . . shall omit to do any act . . . in this chapter required to be done . . . shall be liable to the person or persons injured thereby for the full amount of damages sustained in consequence. . . together with a reasonable counsel or attorney's fee. . . ."

In May 1972 an initial decision by the hearing examiner, Ernest Nash, was released in favor of the telephone company. He ruled that there was no harassment of the subscriber and that the telephone company's discontinuance of phone service was the result of a misconception by the company. The matter did not end there, however. The Common Carrier Bureau disagreed with this decision and filed an appeal to the FCC Review Board, asking, among other things, for a forfeiture to be imposed on the telephone company for disconnection of the subscriber's phone. The decision of the Review Board, released in November 1972, largely vindicated the position of the Bureau and the subscriber. Finding that the company's imposition of unauthorized late charges and its disconnection of service for refusal to pay the federal excise tax were violations of the Federal Communications Act, the Review Board fined the telephone company $3,325 and ordered the late payment penalties to be refunded to all subscribers from whom they had been collected [FCC 72R-346, Decision of Review Board, released 29 November 1972].

Every time you cut short an interstate long-distance call by saying "this is costing money," you are talking about rates regulated by the Federal Communications Commission. The problem is that regulation by the FCC is largely a process of informal negotiation with AT&T known as "continuous surveillance," or lengthy hearings pitting an underfunded FCC staff against the world's biggest company. In this process the Commission is so outweighed by the gigantic AT&T, parent company of the Bell System, that it does little more than occasionally question some AT&T figures. For a detailed and highly readable account of the difficulties experienced in trying to regulate AT&T, Joseph Goulden's *Monopoly* (New York: Pocket Books, 1970, 95 cents) is an excellent starting point. While rate making is complex and requires considerable economic expertise, it presents an unused and valuable opportunity for a consumer organization to participate as a representative of telephone users in the process of setting what amounts to an unofficial tax.

The latest hearing and continuous surveillance proceedings were initiated by Commission order in 1965. At that time the Commission laid down the procedures to be followed. A limit of 7 to 7.5 percent on AT&T's rate of return on its investment was set after the first hearing in these proceedings in 1967, but that rate of return has been consistently exceeded in recent years. Then in 1969 there was a "continuous surveillance" proceedings in which Bell met in private with the FCC Commissioners. Some FCC staff were permitted to act as consumer advocates as an experiment. The experiment met with little success. The advocates were not permitted to call their own witnesses or to request material from AT&T (other than that which had already been submitted prior to the hearing). Their cross-examination was limited in scope and time, and they were unable even to obtain three-year investment forecasts from AT&T.

The only outsiders allowed to sit in on the continuous surveillance process are representatives of the National Association of Regulatory and Utilities Commissioners (NARUC). This group represents the state commissions (which exist in every state but Texas) responsible for *intra*state regulation of the telephone system. Transcripts of such proceedings were made available to the public later, and the results of these negotiations were released in a public notice—permitting Bell to earn around 8 percent on overall investments.

In the period 1970-1973 the FCC conducted a new rate-of-return proceeding on AT&T and has permitted a rate of return up to 9 percent, with the understanding that when Bell earns more than that, the FCC will not act immediately to cut Bell back to the allowed rate. In this hearing the Commission again set up part of its staff to act as consumer advocates, and then proceeded to all but ignore them. Several public interest groups also intervened in this proceeding, but most of the work for the consumer was done by the FCC trial staff.

One possible method of citizen participation in rate making is through challenges to common carrier tariffs [47 U.S.C. 203]. Section

203 of the Communications Act requires common carriers to file with the Bureau all of their rules, regulations, rates, classifications, and practices. If these tariffs are not challenged within thirty days of filing, they automatically have the force of law. Under Section 204, only the Commission may suspend the effective date of a tariff, pending a hearing of its legality, but this suspension can only be for a maximum of three months. When ordering a hearing on a rate increase which has gone into effect, the Commission may order the carrier to keep account of all revenues collected by reason of the increase. If the increase is ultimately found to be illegal, the Commission may order refunds.

Rule 1.773 allows any person to petition for the suspension of a newly filed tariff. Such a petition for suspension should include a specific reference to the FCC tariff number and the particular tariff in question. This information is available from the Chief of the Domestic Rates Division, Common Carrier Bureau. It should also contain a statement "indicating in what respects the protested tariff schedule is considered unlawful." Sections 201 and 202 of the Communications Act provide the statutory basis for such a challenge. Section 201 states that "any charge, practice, classification, or regulation that is unjust or unreasonable is declared to be unlawful," and Section 202 makes unlawful any "unjust or unreasonable discrimination" in charges, practices, or classifications.

The rules now allow only sixteen days for filing a petition to suspend after the date of the tariff filing, although a telegram sent to the FCC and the carrier may serve to meet the deadline in emergencies. An original and fourteen copies of the petition normally must be filed with the FCC, and copies must be served on the carrier and the Chief of the Common Carrier Bureau. The first problem in meeting this brief deadline is to find out about the tariff filing. Rule 61.72 requires that all tariff filings must be made available for public inspection at the FCC office and in a number of telephone offices throughout the country, and, although it is not required to, the FCC Office of Information usually issues an information bulletin on important tariff filings. Rules have been proposed which would allow thirty days for filing petitions to suspend, require carriers to inform customers of some proposed tariffs, and require carriers to notify the Commission of the steps taken to inform customers.

After receiving a petition for suspension of a tariff, the Chief of the Common Carrier Bureau makes a recommendation to the Commission as to whether or not to set the case for hearing. If the petition is denied, a "petition for reconsideration" under Rule 1.106(d) can be filed. Such a petition should be filed within thirty days after notice of the decision not to hold an evidentiary hearing. It should be not more than twenty-five pages long, and include "findings of fact and/or conclusions of law" believed to be erroneous, any additional findings of facts and conclusions that should be made, and the form of relief desired.

If the Commission decides to order a hearing, either in response to a petition or on its own initiative, it will be announced in a Public Order. Consumers may participate in such a hearing either as "public witnesses" or by intervening as parties. Under Rule 1.225, anyone who wishes to appear before the Commission may be allowed to appear as a public witness. Send a written request to the Secretary of the Commission, and if you are allowed to appear you will be notified of a date and time to present testimony. Public witnesses need only show that their testimony is "relevant, material, and competent." This participation does not require an attorney, and the Common Carrier Bureau counsel will provide some assistance. Such an appearance at least offers an opportunity to be heard by the Commission in its consideration of rates. However, your freedom of participation is limited; a public witness has no right to cross-examine other witnesses, and cannot appeal the decision made at the hearing.

Intervention in a hearing as a party provides a much greater opportunity for effective access to the rate making proceeding, but it is much more costly in terms of time, money, and effort. Hearing procedures are complex, and under Rule 1.351 the Federal Rules of Civil Procedure which are followed in federal courts govern the proceedings. Legal assistance is a necessity for intervention as a party in hearings. To intervene as a party, a petition to intervene must be filed under Rule 1.223 within thirty days after publication of the Hearing Order in the *Federal Register*. It should include:

1. The basis of the group's interest in the proceedings (telephone consumers should have standing to intervene in hearings on rate proceedings, just as representatives of listening audiences have standing in broadcast license proceedings).
2. How participation would "assist the Commission in the determination of the issues in question."
3. An affidavit to the truth of all the allegations in the petition.

The Hearing Examiner rules on the petition for intervention. If it is denied, you have five days to appeal the denial to the Commision under Rule 1.115. The appeal is called an "Application for Review," and it should be less than ten pages long.

If the Hearing Examiner, or the Commission on appeal, allows you to intervene, you have full rights to participate as a party. Under Rules 1.311-1.340, a party can participate in prehearing depositions and discovery. This includes the right to serve other parties with written "interrogatories" under Rule 1.316, as well as questioning other parties orally under 1.315. A party may also request the presiding officer to order any other party to produce for inspection or copying "any designated documents, papers, books . . . not privileged," which are considered relevant to the issues in question, under Rule 1.325. The hearing officer may enforce informal requests by subpoena under Rules 1.331-1.340.

Within fifteen days of the original Hearing Order, any party may file a motion to "enlarge, change, or delete issues," under Rule 1.229. A vital stage for participation is the prehearing conference held under Rule 1.248. At the prehearing the issues to be decided by the hearing are defined.

When the hearing begins, each party presents its case through witnesses and exhibits. After presentations by all of the parties, each party files a detailed analysis of its finding of fact under Rule 1.264, and the Hearing Examiner issues his decision. Appeals from this decision must be made within thirty days under Rule 1.276. The appeal may be to the Commission or to a Review Board, if the Commission has delegated its review function to such a board under Rule 1.271.

An alternative route for consumer action is the filing of a formal complaint against a communications common carrier subject to FCC regulation, charging violation of the Communications Act, the provisions of a carrier's tariff, or Commission rule or policy. These filings are described in Sections 1.711-1.740 of the Commission rules. A feature of formal complaints is the opportunity for the complainant to recover damages.

Occasionally the FCC can be persuaded to look into a matter that appears to concern only local telephone service under regulation by a state commission. If a consumer can convince the FCC that what appears to be a state matter in reality involves the quality of interstate service, then the FCC may assert jurisdiction and give the consumer a better opportunity than he would get on the state level.

Public access to the proceedings of the Common Carrier Bureau is a different matter from Broadcast Bureau proceedings, as you may have gathered. When it comes to individual complaints about deposits, illegal termination of service, and so on, the Bureau may be of some assistance in persuading the telephone company not to come down on you quite so hard. But that possibility requires that your complaint involve inter-

state telephone communications, and that you have the good luck to
have your complaint selected for attention by the overloaded FCC staff.
Otherwise your recourse must be to your state regulatory commission—
which is likely to be responsible for regulating all of the public utilities
in the state, and incapable of handling any of them. [See "State Utility
Commissions," Senate Document No. 56, 2 November 1967, prepared
for Subcommittee on Intergovernmental Relations, Senate Government
Operations Committee, by Vic Reinemer, executive secretary to Sen.
Lee Metcalf.]

Access to FCC regulation of the Bell System on a larger scale is a
quantum jump from making individual complaints. There is a crying
need for representation of telephone subscribers before the FCC in the
process of setting rates, not only because the process determines
long-distance charges directly, but also because state regulatory commissions often follow the FCC's lead. But such representation will have
to be a well-organized, continuing effort with a professional staff of
attorneys and economists. There are few if any opportunities for access
to the FCC's regulation of AT&T by small community groups; their
efforts would probably be better directed toward dealing with their
state commissions. Even an attempt to force the Bell System to implement nondiscriminatory employment policies took the efforts of the
Equal Employment Opportunity Commission (EEOC). (Their report,
A Unique Competence, is available free from the EEOC's AT&T Task
Force, 1800 G Street, N.W., Washington, D.C., 20503.) The need for
some national effort by telephone subscribers to counter the massive
presence of AT&T at the FCC is great and growing.

The FCC is often held up as an example of what citizen access to
federal agencies is about. After all, that was where John Banzhaf sent
his letter to get antismoking messages on television, and that was the
forum for the black people of Jackson, Mississippi, to challenge the
"whites only" broadcasting of their television station. The existence of
the FCC and the fact that it has something to do with the major leisure
activity of most Americans does not require the explanation needed by
other agencies and their functions. Sometimes this leads to an erroneous
assumption that access to the FCC does not require the same kind of
effort that is necessary for participation at other agencies. While it is
true that individual letters of complaint can have an effect, the letter
that John Banzhaf wrote had to be reinforced by lawsuits before it was
effective. And, as already described, the viewers of station WLBT had
legal help from the Office of Communications of the United Church of
Christ. They serve as examples of what can be accomplished by initia-

tive, organization, and perseverance, but the effort required for such efforts should not be underestimated.

Citizen involvement in communications goes far beyond the formal procedures of the FCC. Even participation in the license renewal proceedings which are at the heart of the Commission's regulation of broadcasting requires considerable organization and negotiation in the community if it is to be effective. Still, the possibilities for reform through citizen activism in the licensing process are so substantial that broadcasters, with the Nixon Administration's assistance, have been pushing hard for legislative change to extend license duration to five years, and thus avoid the threat of citizen opposition to their lucrative operations every three years. The process of participation in vital decisions about cable television is still almost entirely at the local level, deciding what franchises will be granted by municipal governments. And effective regulation of the telephone system will require efforts with state level regulatory commissions as much as with the FCC's Common Carrier Bureau.

It would be ironic if the basis for strengthening communities turned out to be a shared sense of frustration with the homogeneous blandness of our common electronic world. As one judge put it in the process of ruling that a station could not refuse to sell time for messages on public issues:

> All too often in our society one particular ideology—that of passivity, acceptance of things as they are, and exhaltation of commercial values—is simply taken for granted, assumed to be a non-ideology, and allowed to choke out all the rest [*Business Executives' Move for Vietnam Peace* v. *FCC*, 450 F. 2d 642 (1971)].

United Church of Christ
Observer's Report Form

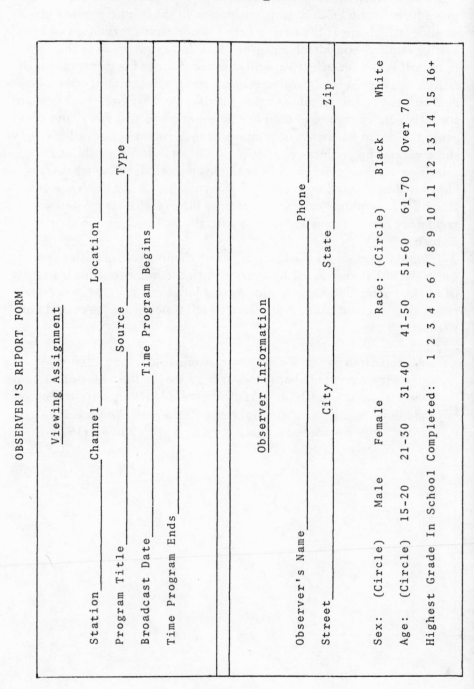

OBSERVER'S REPORT FORM

Viewing Assignment

Station _____ Channel _____ Source _____ Location _____ Type _____

Program Title _____

Broadcast Date _____ Time Program Begins _____

Time Program Ends _____

Observer Information

Observer's Name _____ Phone _____

Street _____ City _____ State _____ Zip _____

Sex: (Circle) Male Female Race: (Circle) Black White

Age: (Circle) 15-20 21-30 31-40 41-50 51-60 61-70 Over 70

Highest Grade In School Completed: 1 2 3 4 5 6 7 8 9 10 11 12 13 14 15 16+

Description

DIRECTIONS: Complete this box while you watch the assigned program. Be objective and accurate. Describe each incident where a racial issue is treated or where a black person appears. Pay close attention to the visual as well as the sound portion of the program. Note the length of each incident.

Item No.	Time	Description

When program is over turn to next page.

OBSERVER'S REPORT FORM

After the program is over answer the following questions. Here we seek your thoughtful reactions to what you have seen. Be sure you explain your answers.

1. If racial issues were discussed, were they treated fairly?
    Yes _____ No _____ Don't Know _____ Explain below.

2. If blacks appeared, were they accorded the same treatment as whites?
    Yes _____ No _____ Don't Know _____ Explain below.

3. Do you feel that this program adequately treated the interests of the black community? Yes _____ No _____ Don't Know _____ Explain below.

4. How could this program have better served the black community?

5. If you have further comments about this program, please give them in the space below.

INSTRUCTIONS FOR COMPLETING OBSERVER'S REPORT FORM

Before beginning your television observation, please read these instructions carefully and examine the Observer's Report Form. You should also read the other
materials you have been given: the pamphlet, HOW TO PROTECT CITIZEN RIGHTS IN
TELEVISION AND RADIO, and the mimeographed sheets titled "Television Observing:
A Statement of Purpose" and "A Television Program Service: What Are Its Elements."

You will report all information concerning each program you view on an Observer's
Report Form.

It is easiest to do observing if you will sit in a comfortable chair with a table
either in front of you or at your immediate side on which to write on the report
form. Be sure to have several pencils at hand, or if you use a pen have a spare
in case you run out of ink. Also, be sure to have a good electric clock or watch
on which the minutes are clearly marked and which has a sweep second hand. Timing
is very important, so be sure you have the correct time.

Completing the Form

1. Your Assignment. The upper box marked "Viewing Assignment" has been
filled in for you. This is the program you are to watch.

2. Observer Information. Directly below your assignment is a box in which
we ask some important questions about you. We ask your name, address, and phone
number in case we need more information on the program you viewed. We also ask
your age, sex, education and race. This information will be used statistically
to see if differences in people have any effect on the way they react to a
program.

3. Description. This is for you to describe the program. Be sure to report
each instance when a racial issue is discussed or when a black person appears.
Number each incident you describe in the "Item No." column. Using your watch or
clock, carefully note the length of each incident and mark the "Time" column. If
no black person appears or there is no treatment of race, please note that fact.

Describe the program objectively and accurately. Tell it so that someone else will know exactly what happened. Remember, your opportunity to react to the incidents will come after the program is over. First report what you see and hear.

4. Your Reactions. When the program is over, you have an opportunity to present your reactions to what you have seen. Answer each of the first three questions by checking one of the choices and then explain the reason for your opinion. (If you offer specific comments on any of the incidents under "Description," note its number in your response.) Question four gives you the chance to tell how a program of the type you have just seen could better serve the needs of black people. If you have further comments which do not fit into the other questions, place them under question five.

Returning Your Forms

At the end of each week of observing, place your completed forms in one of the envelopes provided and mail them immediately.

STATIC Rule Making Petition

Before the

Federal Communications Commission

Washington, D. C.

IN RE Public Rights in   )
)
the Broadcasting Media   )   RM-1737
)
)
)
)
)
)
)
)

Petition for Rulemaking   January 8, 1971

I.   Pursuant to 5 USC Section 553, the statutory authority,
and 47 CFR Section 1, 40(a), the Commission authority,
STATIC, Student Task-force Against Telecommunication Information Concealment, a group of students from George Washington University Law School, as members of the general
public, respectfully requests that the Commission adopt as
part of their Rules and Regulations requirements for licensees designed to give the public effective notice of their
rights vis-a-vis the licensees as established by statute,
administrative policies and decisions, and judiciary review
decisions.

II.   Summary of the Problem
      The Federal Communications Act of 1934 was passed in
part in recognition that the electronic mass media should

serve the public. The Act empowered the Federal Communications Commission to regulate the use of the frequency spectrum. The rights of the public to complete coverage of controversial subjects and to inoffensive and factual transmission of news were included in the statutory language.[1] Correlatively, the licensee, as a condition of being granted the license to broadcast, has the duty to serve the public interest by respecting these rights.

The duties the licensee owes the public have been further delineated since 1934 through administrative policy statements and judicial review. The licensee's programming, it is now recognized, must be balanced and fair, and

> That the licensee responsibility is to
> be exercised in the interest of, and as
> a trustee for the public at large.[2]

Furthermore, the public has standing at Commission hearings. Nonetheless, the public is not made aware of their rights, and they are unable to fully protect their interests. The duties of the licensee must include informing the public of its rights through the media. Otherwise, the statutory rights of the public serve merely to protect the licensees from competition. They will not insure that the interests of the public be served.

The Commission does not have the resources to effectively monitor and identify the licensees who violate the public trust. In the thirty-six years of existence, the

Commission has expanded the personnel in its broadcast bureau three-fold, while the number of licensed stations has increased ten-fold. The Commission requires the licensee to ascertain the community needs and program accordingly. In this way the licensees satisfy their statutory requirement of public service. The Commission cannot independently evaluate each community's needs, and should not depend solely on the licensee's evaluation of its own performance.

Therefore, as a mode of elucidating the public interest the Commission should invite the licensee to open direct avenues of communication with the public.

III. Proposed Solution

In order to actualize the statutory intent and purpose it is necessary that the licensees be required to inform the public of its rights and of the duties owed by the licensees. In order to effectively administer the Act, and present Commission policy, the Commission should adopt our petition for rulemaking which would require the licensees to give effective notice to the public of its rights.

IV. The Rationale of the Present System

The original Federal Radio Commission (1927) and the succeeding Federal Communications Commission (1934) were

created in response to two problems involving the allocation of the frequency spectrum: the prevention of technical interference and the choice of who is to operate upon
the limited number of frequencies.[3] The allocating mechanism adopted by Congress was licensing.

The problem of preventing technical interference was
easily solved. The FCC limited the number of licenses to
transmit and regulated their power and frequency transmission.

The second problem was more intractable. The
Commission is instructed to grant or renew a license "if
in public interest, convenience, or necessity."[4] This
language was taken from public utility legislation and
lacked any definite criteria for the Commission.

The relationship between the broadcast industry and
the public is special and unique. The FCC could not issue
licenses on a first come basis and depend upon competition
to protect the public interest. The major theorem of the
competitive model is that the interaction of buyers and
sellers insures the interest of each one is maximized.
However, in commercial broadcasting, the licensees are the
sellers and the advertisers are the buyers. Therefore,
the public interest is not directly considered if the
broadcasting industry is unregulated.

Moreover, the technically limited frequency spectrum
created an oligopolistic industry structure which

necessitates regulation. However, regulating the profits
of the licensee as if he were a common carrier or public
utility was quickly rejected. It was felt that this type
of regulation would in no way protect the public interest.

On the other hand if the public was merely a third
party beneficiary of a contract between the owner of the
broadcast station and its advertisers who pay to broadcast, the public would not have any rights cognizable in
a judiciary forum. This is not the case.

Thus, the vague language of the statute considering
the "public interest" must involve a special kind of
regulation. One side argued for precise legislative
standards for licenses while the other side advocated
permitting administrative discretion.[5] The statutory
language permits administrative discretion.

The FCC enabling legislation, subsequent FCC policy
statements and decisions, and judicial review decisions
have better defined the role of the public and formalized
the relation among the parties of interest.

V.   The Rights of the Public

Numerous conflicting policies and actions can be
rationalized under the rubric of public interest. Nonetheless, some definite meaning to "serving the public
interest" has been acquired, since the Federal

Communications Act of 1934, through administrative policy
decisions and judicial review.

The statutory language explicitly defined three
aspects of what would serve or insure the public interest:
the airways were to be fully utilized;[6] controversial
subjects were to be covered completely;[7] offensive and
unfactual transmission of news was prohibited.[8]

The function of the FCC is not only to issue and
renew licenses, but as importantly to insure that the
public interest is considered by the licensee. To those
who argued that we should "regard the Commission as a kind
of traffic officer, policing the wave lengths to prevent
stations from interfering with each other," Mr. Justice
Frankfurter answered:

> But the Act does not restrict the Commission
> merely to supervision of traffic. It puts
> upon the Commission the burden of determining
> the composition of that traffic. The facili-
> ties of radio are not large enough to accommo-
> date all who wish to use them. Methods must
> be devised for choosing from among the many
> who apply. And since Congress itself could
> not do this, it committed the task to the
> Commission.
>
> The Commission was, however, not left at large
> in performing this duty. The touchstone pro-
> vided by Congress was the "public interest,
> convenience or necessity."
>
> ...The facilities of radio are limited and
> therefore precious; they cannot be left to
> wasteful use without detriment to the public
> interest.... The Commission's licensing
> function cannot be discharged, therefore,
> merely by finding that there are no techno-
> logical objections to the granting of a

> license. If the criterion of "public
> interest" were limited to such matters,
> how could the Commission choose between
> two applicants for the same facilities,
> each of who is financially and techni-
> cally qualified to operate a station?
> Since the very inception of federal regu-
> lation of radio, comparative consideration
> as to the services to be rendered have
> governed the application of the standard
> of "public interest, convenience or
> necessity."[9]

In subsequent proceedings the Commission further
defined the statutory language. Full utilization of the
airways means in part that the public is to be protected
from over-commercialization.[10] The licensee's programming
must be balanced; thus, the Commission identified fourteen
areas in which the licensee must provide programming.
These areas include programming of religion, education,
politics, sports, entertainment, news, agriculture,
weather and public affairs, editorializing, service to
children and minority groups, opportunities for local expressions, and development and use of local talents.[11]
Recognizing the importance in a democracy of public
response to controversial issues, the Commission formulated
the Fairness Doctrine.[12]

The licensee's programming must be relevant to the
community. In Simmons v. F.C.C., 169 F.2d 670 (1948), the
D.C. Court of Appeals upheld an FCC ruling that a
licensee who makes no effort to structure its programs to
the particular needs of the community does not satisfy the

public service responsibility of a broadcast licensee.
A licensee must not only be cognizant of the community
needs, but his programming must reflect the various
interests of the community.[13]

In the Office of Communication of United Church of
Christ v. FCC, 359 F.2d 994, it was recognized that the
public does have standing before the FCC to enforce its
rights. Thus the court recognized the public as an active
participant in broadcasting. In order to make this participation more effective the public must be informed of
its rights.

Considering that the airways are public property
which the licensee is merely given permission to use at
nominal cost, the duties the licensee owes the public are
not oppressive. They do not even endanger the licensee's
monopoly profits.

VI. In Respect of the Rights of the Public

The rights of the public are essential in the mass
communication media industrial structure, and yet the
licensees appear to pay more lip service to the public's
needs and interest. To realize how true this statement
is, students of the mass communication media consider it
axiomatic that the present performance of licensees with
respect to public service can be improved.[14]

Thus, under the present system, the rights of the public are well documented and recognized, and yet there is no effective mechanism to insure that these rights are honored.

Unsurprisingly, the public has not acted vigorously to protect its own rights. In fact, most of the public is unaware of its rights.

> Most people believe that radio and television
> are like the weather. Bad weather exists.
> But it is no one's fault. Accordingly, nothing
> can be done about it. The same is widely
> believed to be true of radio and television.[15]

The public may also be apathetic to the duties the licensee owes them. Even if the people are apathetic, an opinion that no one has taken the trouble to verify, their apathy is no excuse for not informing them of their rights. Democracy is principled upon the proposition that the public has rights and has the freedom and information to exercise those rights. Rights of which the public has no knowledge are not rights at all.

VII.   The Trend Toward Active Public Participation

The broadcast license is issued by the FCC for a three year term. Upon expiration, the licensee is eligible to renew.[16] The statutory criterion for licensing is: "whether the public interest, convenience and necessity will be served by the granting of such application."[17]

Since the statutory language of licensing criterion is
vague, the Commission has had to develop its own operational criteria consonant with the statute.

As recently as ten years ago, the Commission's
criteria was criticized as confusing. The reason, Judge
Friendly argued, was that the Commission mistook evidentiary items for elements of policy. He sought to isolate
two main elements of policy: the community should have the
programming best adapted to its needs, and ownership of the
mass communications media should be diversified.[18] The
FCC officially adopted similar guidelines.[19] The evidentiary items such as local ownership, integrated ownership
management, and management participation in civic affairs
are supposed to relate to an applicant's ability to achieve
the policy goals.[20] For example, the local applicant was
considered better aware of the community needs, and
therefore more likely to be able to program in accordance
with those needs. It was even better if the local applicant participated in civic affairs, because that indicated an awareness and interest in the welfare of the
community. Furthermore, the full-time participation by
the applicant in the station's operation was of substantial importance because that enhanced the probability the
station would be responsive to public needs and demands.

The use of such propositions to develop evidentiary
items is understandable in hearings for new licenses. In

an application for a license, empirical evidence concerning
the relevance of the proposed programming to the community's needs is not available. However, in a license
renewal hearing, the public's evaluation of the licensee's
programming is readily available, is pertinent, and should
be ascertained.[21]

The 1970 Policy Statement directly addresses this
issue in the first step. In addressing this issue, the
Commission has neglected to create a mechanism by which it
can obtain an objective evaluation of the public's needs.
It must be remembered that the adversarial function within
the administrative system is different from that within
the courts. The Commission has two roles--advocate for
the public--and judge. The Commission cannot independently
assess the public's interest and needs, so it gives that
duty to the licensee. The licensee is required to complete
FCC Form 303 Sec. IV-B Part I which asks: "to state the
methods used...to ascertain the needs and interests of the
public served by the station (and to identify) representative groups, interests, and organizations which were consulted." To satisfy this requirement, a licensee need
simply talk to many important ("representative") people and
organizations in the community.[22] The applicant is also
asked to list typical programs which "have served public
needs and interest." Still missing is any well-defined
idea of what are the public needs and interests to be

served.   More blatantly missing is the use of any general
public response in order to ascertain the needs and
interests of that public.   Unsurprisingly, two commissioners concluded in 1968 that the licensee's local surveys
were useless.[23]   Nonetheless, in determining whether the
licensee's programming has been "substantially attuned,"
the Commission relies upon the licensee's own local
surveys.

It is unquestioned that the FCC lacks the resources
to properly police the licensees as the representative of
the public.   In 1969, the Commission's broadcast bureau
staff was only three times larger than when it began
operations.   That staff was responsible for more than
7500 operating broadcasting stations, an amount ten times
greater than the number of operating stations when the
Commission began operation.   Although the Act of 1934
provided for "any party in interest (to) file with the
Commission a petition to deny any application," the public
was not considered a party in interest until 1966.   Chief
Justice (then Judge) Warren Burger recognized that the
Commission lacked resources and that:

> The theory that the Commission can effec-
> tively represent the listener interest in
> a renewal proceeding...is no longer a
> valid assumption.

The remedy was to extend standing to intervene in license
proceedings to "responsible spokesmen for representative

groups in the listening community." It remains for the
public to protect its own interests in light of Chief
Justice Burger giving judicial recognition to the right of
the public to protect its rights.

The trend toward public participation in the mass
electronic media is not complete. The FCC requires the
licensees to consider the public interest in forming its
programming by consulting representative public groups.
It is our contention that the community's needs cannot be
ascertained adequately by delegating the duty to the
licensee. A more efficient means would be to give the
public the duty to protect its rights.

Therefore, we propose that the FCC adopt the following rules:

I. The licensee shall be required to provide a
specified period of time, to be determined by the FCC,
to broadcast informative, impartial and effective notice
to the public at large of its rights and the licensee's
duties under existing statutes and administrative policy
decisions. Such broadcasts shall be aired at intervals
specified by the FCC, but in no event less than once every
six months, and shall be made during the prime hours of
7:00 to 10:00 P.M.

II. Such broadcasts should be designed to impartially
and effectively inform the public at large of its rights

and licensee's duties including the following topics which
are not meant to be exhaustive.

    a)   The Fairness Doctrine including:

        1)   right to reply to controversial programs,
editorials, or opinions aired or expressed
by licensee.

    b)   right to reply to personal attacks made by persons
whose views have been broadcast by the individual
licensee. Such time being provided by such
licensee.

    c)   complete coverage of controversial subjects or
programs.

    d)   right to unoffensive and factual transmission of
news.

    e)   right to complaint either to station itself or
to the FCC concerning any and all grievances felt
by individual members of the community by licensee.

    f)   right to intervene in licensee renewal proceeding
including:

        1)   right to petition against granting of said
license.

        2)   right of complaint to licensee or FCC.

        3)   explanation of the requirements under Rule
1.580 concerning license renewal.

g) the licensee's duty to provide balanced pro-
    gramming in the interest of public spirit and
    taste without over-commercialization by such
    licensee's sponsors.

h) the licensee's duty to actively elicit public
    opinion concerning its overall operation.

i) activities of other groups contesting renewals.

In order to insure the public's right under the proposed rule we recommend that each individual licensee be
required to maintain a log of all responses made by the
public to said licensee concerning all aspects of the
licensee's performance as well as the action taken by the
licensee regarding such responses. The maintenance of
such a log would greatly facilitate the interaction
between the licensee and the community being served as
well as providing an effective aid in determining a
licensee's performance in regard to the license renewal
procedure. By having the individual licensee be responsible for maintaining a record of public response and actions
taken accordingly, a large portion of the burden of policing the broadcast frequencies would be handled by the public
at large, thereby reducing the role of the FCC in this
area.

Thus, we believe that the individual licensees and the
communities they serve, could through the operation of the

proposed rule reach a considerably higher level of mutual
discourse and cooperation while furthering broadcast
standards, community interest, and effective utilization
of the broadcast frequencies. This proposed rule will
also make Rule 1.580 more effective by giving the public
information upon which to make complaints.

We do not believe that this rule would be followed
by increased dependence of the public on the Commission
or an increased workload on the Commission's staff.
Rather, just the opposite will occur. This rule will
encourage critical monitoring and discourage frivolous
complaints by the public because the public will be aware
of what the licensee's duties are. Furthermore, this rule
will encourage the formation of responsible civil groups
which can open avenues of discourse with the licensee,
and when necessary, provide the means to make program
agreements like those in Rochester and Texarkana, bypassing
the Commission.

Unlike the Illinois committee,[24] the present petition
for rulemaking does not ask the licensee to delegate to an
outside organization the right to broadcast announcements.
It does not depend on the FCC finding license renewal a
controversial issue falling under the Fairness Doctrine
but rather follows the Commission's implicit suggestion
that the proper method through which to enlarge the

licensee's requirement for publication of information is
the rulemaking procedure.

Wherefore, these arguments considered, the Commission
is respectfully requested to issue an appropriate notice
of proposed rulemaking.

Respectfully submitted,

/s/
Howard Leslie Sribnick
Chairman STATIC
2121 H Street, N.W.
Washington, D.C. 20037

[1]47 U.S.C. 315a, 303(m)(1)(b).

[2]Office of Communication of the United Church of Christ v. FCC, 359 F.2d 994 (1966).

[3]Coase, Federal Communications Commission, 2 J. Law & Econ. 8 Oct. '59.

[4]47 U.S.C. 309(a).

[5]McDonald, Need for Standards in Selection of Licensees, 17 L.R. 61 Fall '64.

[6]47 U.S.C. 303.

[7]47 U.S.C. 315(a).

[8]47 U.S.C. 303(m)(1)(D).

[9]National Broadcasting Co. v. United States, 319 U.S. 190, 213, 215-17 (1954).

[10]317 FCC Annual Report 92 (1963).

[11]25 Federal Register 7291, 7295 (1960).

[12]In the Matter of Editorializing by Broadcast Licensees, Docket # 8516 13 FCC 1246 (1949) Sec. 3.

[13]Capital Broadcasting Co.

[14]Barrow, The Attainment of Balanced Program Service in Television, 52 Va. L. R. 633 (1966).

[15]Broadcasting in America and the FCC's License Renewal Process: An Oklahoma Case Study. A Statement by Commissioners Kenneth A. Cox and Nicholas Johnson, 14 FCC 2d1 (1968).

[16]47 U.S.C. 307.

[17]47 U.S.C. 309a.

[18]The Fed. Admin. Agencies, 1962, 57-9.

[19]1 FCC 2d 393, 1965.

[20]Ibid. p. 58.

[21]One reason the 1970 Policy Statement omits diversification of ownership as an item of policy is because
diversification is a surrogate measure of the likelihood
of diverse programming designed to meet the community
needs. In license renewal proceedings, direct evidence of
licensee's past record is available to evaluate whether
his programming was substantially attuned to the community
needs, and surrogate measures are not needed.

[22]WHDH: The FCC and Renewal Proceedings, 82 Harv.
L. Rev. 1693 (1963).

[23]14 FCC 2d 9.

[24]Federal Communications Commission reply to Illinois
Citizens' Committee for Broadcasting, FCC 70 1141 Oct.
21, 1970.

Comment to F.C.C.

re: Notice of Inquiry and Notice of Proposed Rule Making -
Docket No. 19153

by: STATIC

In its notice of inquiry and proposed rule making
(#19153) the commission notes Static's petition for rule
making and states that the commission will use Static's
proposals as comment on its own.

The members of Static feel that it is necessary to
comment in response to the F.C.C.'s proposals. Static's
petition made it clear that it was the purpose of our proposed rule to have the public informed not only as to the
public ownership of the airwaves but also what that ownership means. The right to protest to the broadcaster or to
the F.C.C. is of little value to the viewer without his
being educated as to such policies as the fairness doctrine, the right to complete coverage of news and controversial issues and the right not to be inundated with
commercials. Therefore, while the F.C.C.'s proposal is an
important first step, it is disappointing because it fails
to provide for the education of the public.

Finally, the right to protest will be of little value
unless the F.C.C. makes its procedures, especially the license renewal procedures, more responsive to public interveners.   Howard Sribnick
                                     /s/
                                     Chairman, Static
                                     May 3, 1971

Proposal for FCC Public Counsel

In April, 1971 the FCC's Policy Review Committee
focused on the serious problem of inadequate representation of public interest and consumer groups in Commission
proceedings. As a result the Committee made several
specific, far-reaching recommendations for immediate
action by the full Commission to alleviate these problems. The following excerpts of the Committee's confidential memorandum to the Commission set forth the most
important of these recommendations. They have never been
acted on.

FEDERAL COMMUNICATIONS COMMISSION
Washington, D.C.   62987

April 27, 1971

INTER-OFFICE MEMORANDUM

FOR: General Agenda

TO: The Commission (LIMITED DISTRIBUTION)

FROM: Chairman, Procedure Review Committee

SUBJECT: Measures to encourage and facilitate participa-
            tion by public interest groups in Commission
            proceedings.

RECOMMENDED
ACTION: See paragraph 26.

     1.   As the Commission will appreciate, substantial
and increasing efforts are being made by public interest
groups to participate actively in administrative proceedings. The Commission has repeatedly stated that it
encourages such participation, but has had to concede that
effective participation by such groups is rare and that
their inability to obtain expert professional assistance
is an important contributing factor. Former Chairman
Hyde's response to a questionnaire prepared by the Subcommittee on Administrative Practice and Procedure of the
Senate Judiciary Committee (March 1969) described the
situation as follows:

***More typically, however, the ordinary
citizen does not play a prominent role in
the decision-making process. Thus, though
citizens often write to the Commission to
complain or to express their views, though
formal proceedings may result, and though
the citizen would be welcome and would be
encouraged to participate, experience indicates that it is difficult for such
groups to gather the resources and knowledge required for full and effective participation. In most cases, the principal
input is by parties having a financial
interest in the outcome of the proceeding
and resources sufficient to retain competent professional assistance, and by the
staff of the Commission as representatives
of the public.

*   *   *   *   *

The quantity and quality of citizen input
could be increased by forging a connection
between concerned citizen groups and the
competent professional assistance required
for more effective participation.

The Procedure Review Committee has considered the citizen
participation problem as thus defined and sought a solution. We believe that citizen participation on a professional level is desirable, can be helpful and should be
encouraged and facilitated. We have inquired into the
problems faced by public interest groups and particularly
into the problems involved in obtaining (and furnishing)
the expert legal assistance required for effective participation. We have considered a number of possible solutions and endeavored to devise from among them an overall
plan for dealing with the problem. This memorandum is
divided into three parts: an outline of the problem; a
discussion of possible solutions; and the Committee's
recommendations.

The Problem

2. Public interest groups seeking effective participation in Commission proceedings are faced with a three-
fold problem. First, law firms with an established
communications practice are almost universally unwilling
to represent public interest groups against any broadcast
station. Secondly, most public interest groups lack the
resources to pay an attorney's fee or even to reimburse
the firm representing them for out-of-pocket expenses.

Third, public interest law firms active in the communications area are limited in number, in personnel and resources, a situation which is exacerbated by the inability
of their clients to pay a fee or to reimburse them for expenses, and are consequently unable to handle the current
demand for legal assistance or at least to turn out a
quality product in all of the matters with which they are
asked to deal. The end result is that the public interest
groups who do participate in Commission proceedings must
often do so without any (or without adequate) legal
assistance.

... ...

Possible Solutions

7. The Committee has considered a number of possible
ways in which adequate legal assistance could be made
available to public interest groups desiring to participate in Commission proceedings. None of the possibilities
is flawless. Several could be tried in combination. They
are discussed below.

8. Government-wide solution. One approach is to
defer action pending Congressional action on establishment
of a government-wide agency which would represent public
groups in administrative proceedings (e.g., the Public
Counsel Corporation, as proposed in S. 3434). It may be
that the problem of citizen participation will be resolved
for us in this way. However, it remains to be seen
whether such an agency will be established and, if so,
what functions and resources it will have. Whatever those
resources may be, they are certain to be spread thin in
their application to hundreds of agencies and matters of
public concern. Our feeling is that the Commission, while
watching developments in this area, should proceed on its
own toward a solution.

9. Financial assistance for firms who undertake pro
bono communications work. There are two groups (the
Citizens Communication Center and the United Church of
Christ) which have demonstrated their commitment to providing representation for public interest groups in
Commission proceedings. The work of the Center is limited
solely by its resources; and if these were increased, the
Center would be expanded and would undertake more work. We
know less about the resources of the Church; but it seems
probable that financial assistance would increase the
number of cases it underwrites. Measures such as those
discussed below would, in addition, encourage other public
interest law firms and firms operated for profit to undertake pro bono communications work. In some cases,

doubtlessly, such work could be undertaken only with such assistance. It is less certain, but possible, finally that financial assistance would lead to the establishment of new public interest communications firms. This would depend on a number of factors, including the extent to which the need for legal services was met by increased activity on the part of existing organizations. A number of possibilities are discussed below.

. . .   .

11. A second possibility would involve compensation to law firms for work done on behalf of public interest groups in Commission proceedings. Compensation should include reimbursement for out-of-pocket expenses, such as duplicating and transcript costs and travel to the place of hearing. It could be enlarged to include the payment of fees although this would raise administrative difficulties. Compensation would be paid to firms which operate for profit as well as public interest firms. Payments would be made only to attorneys, however, and would not be made directly to other individuals or groups, whether or not they were represented by attorneys. As this indicates, our objective is to bring participation by public interest groups up to a professional level, where it can be helpful to the Commission, and we would not encourage participation without professional assistance. It is desirable, in this respect, that the individual or group have to persuade an attorney that it has a meritorious case (a real grievance and an arguable position) before payments encouraging participation by that group become available.

. . .   .

15. The compensation approach has merit. The use of public interest law firms and non-communications firms operated for profit avoids actual or apparent conflict of interest problems associated with other possible approaches discussed below. While the sums involved are sizeable and open-ended, depending on what turns the proceeding takes, and while this might be considered a negative feature, we point out that the funds would be directly related to the work done by the firm and to the expenses incurred (and, if fees were paid, to the time expended). Reimbursement of expenses would substantially augment the resources of the public interest firm and do much to encourage pro bono communications work generally. Many of the expenses, moreover, follow directly from Commission actions or from its procedural rules. The Commission, for example, prescribes the number of copies of pleadings to be filed, and the number is far in excess of the four or five copies which are absolutely necessary. The recording contract

negotiated by the Commission provides that free copies
of the transcript will be furnished the Commission but
makes no provision for others unable to pay the substantial fees involved. The Commission designates the place
for hearing.

16. The obvious defect with any plan involving the
payment of money, of course, is that it may not be achievable. Should the Commission approve any such approach, we
believe it would be necessary to request a special appro-
priation and authority to make expenditures in the manner
described. We do not know whether the Congress would
respond favorably to such a request. Our collection of
fees could be a point in our favor. The pendency of
general consumer legislation indicates congressional concern with the problem, but the pendency of such legislation could work against favorable action on particular
measures proposed by the Commission. Whereas measures
relating specifically to Commission proceedings would be
the most effective in channelling public interest firms
into communications work, the Congress might see this as
moving such firms away from other areas (such as the
ecology) which are of pressing current concern. Favorable
action will in any event involve considerable delay. This
approach is not a solution to the short-range problem.

17. There are two alternative ways in which financial assistance could be made available to firms which
undertake pro bono communications work. The first en-
tails approval of settlement agreements in which licensees
reimburse law firms representing public interest groups
for the expenses incurred. Since this approach has been
expressly rejected by the Commission, KCMC, Inc., 25 FCC
2d 603 (1970), we do not pursue it further. Secondly, it
would be possible to adopt special procedures for public
interest groups which would minimize or eliminate certain
of the expenses incurred by law firms which represent them.
We could, for example, allow public interest firms to submit only the four or five copies of pleadings absolutely
required for our purposes. We could allow them to file
only one copy of pleadings and provide for Commission
duplication of copies it requires. We could provide for
duplication of copies required by public interest groups
for service on other parties to the proceeding. We could
reduce charges for use of the coin-operated copy machine
in the Public Reference Room from 25¢/page to 5¢, which
approximates the commercial rate. We could renegotiate
the recording contract to obtain one additional free copy
of the transcript for use by public interest firms where
such firms are participating in a proceeding. And so
forth. Some drawbacks would be associated with such

changes. Different rules for classes of parties would add
an undesirable element of complexity to our procedures.
The changes would entail costs for the Commission and would
burden its staff. The distribution of pleadings within the
Commission would be diminished or retarded. Delay in service, on the other hand, could be avoided by early submission of the pleading for copying. These are factors
which should be balanced against the increased representation for public interest groups which reduced expenses
would permit.

                . . .   .

        20. Office of Public Counsel. Thus far we have con-
sidered measures which would augment the resources of law
firms which are representing public interest groups and
would encourage firms not so engaged to enter into pro
bono communications work. A third alternative, considered
here, is for the Commission to establish an Office of
Public Counsel, which would furnish the needed legal
services directly. The nature and scale of such assistance are subject to considerable variation, in accordance
with the Commission's wishes. A number of possibilities
are considered below.

        21. A small Office of Public Counsel could furnish
useful but limited legal services. As we conceive of it,
such an Office would consist of one lawyer and one secretary and would be organizationally separate from other
bureaus and offices. It could be free to function in any
matter subject to the Commission's jurisdiction. Because
of its size and because public interest groups are most
active in matters relating to broadcasting, however, the
Office would function principally in broadcast matters.
. . . .

                . . .   .

        22. By augmenting the secretarial staff of the
Office, it would be possible to provide secretarial services to public interest law firms, including such matters
as typing and duplicating pleadings and filing and serving the same. The use of the Office staff and Commission
facilities (particularly duplicating), free of cost, would
be of very substantial benefit to such firms.

        23. A third possibility involves enlarging the legal
staff of the Office and fundamentally altering its responsibilities, so that the staff of attorneys would serve as
counsel for public interest groups in Commission proceedings. If such an Office were established, it should have

access to Commission facilities (such as duplicating machines) but should in other respects have the same status as a private law firm. It should not attend Commission meetings. Its access to Commission records should be subject to the Public Information Act. It should participate only as counsel for public interest groups, however, and not on its own as party to a Commission proceeding. It is not contemplated that the Office would prepare applications as counsel for public groups or that it would be authorized to appeal Commission decisions. Though the problem of credibility would be present here, as where a communication firm undertakes pro bono work ..., it would, we think, be present to a lesser degree.

24. The contribution which could be made by an Office of Public Counsel with these larger responsibilities would depend, of course, on the size of its staff. In our judgment, one experienced attorney and four young assistants could make a substantial contribution. Recent law school graduates would learn quickly, with expert guidance, and many would relish the opportunity for such experience. Younger attorneys on the Commission's staff could be rotated through the Office (perhaps for two-year tours of duty), and judging from complaints from younger members of the staff that they are not being properly utilized, would eagerly compete for positions in the Office.

25. We think this approach would not require enabling legislation or specific appropriations. The cost of the Office could be held down by the use of young attorneys. If the necessary funds could be diverted from other purposes, it should be possible to establish such an Office without delay. If funds are available, but limited, a beginning could be made with a partial working force and appropriations could be sought for subsequent expansion. In view of the present emphasis on consumer protection measures, we think that there is a good possibility of favorable action by the Congress on any necessary request for appropriations.

Recommendations

26. The Committee recommends that the following actions be taken:

(1) That the Commission establish a five-man Office of Public Counsel ...; that such an Office be established (on a limited basis, if necessary) with such funds as are available; and that it be assigned responsibility for

representation of public interest groups in Commission proceedings. (See paragraphs 23-25, <u>supra</u>.) Assuming the
availability of funds, we consider this the best short-term
way in which to provide representation for public groups.

(2) That the staff be directed to draft a letter,
for signature of the Chairman, requesting that the FCBA
develop a system for <u>pro bono</u> representation of public interest groups by communications law firms. (See para. 8,
<u>supra</u>.) A major effort by the bar could largely solve the
public participation problem. The question is whether the
bar would respond favorably to such a request. Most members of the Committee are not overly optimistic. Changes
in our procedures (recommendation 3) and compensation for
out-of-pocket expenses (recommendation 5) would aid us in
obtaining the bar's cooperation. In any event, we feel
the proposal should be made.

(3) That the staff be directed to draft special
rules of procedure for law firms representing public interest groups in Commission proceedings and to proceed
with other measures discussed above (at para. 17) designed
to minimize the expenses of such firms. This is the simplest and the most conventional of the several measures
proposed. It would substantially aid us in seeking the
cooperation of the communications bar.

(4) That the next budget contain a request for such
additional funds as may be needed to maintain an Office of
Public Counsel.

(5) That the next budget contain a request for funds
to be used in compensating law firms for out-of-pocket expenses incurred in representing public interest groups in
Commission proceedings. We do not recommend the payment
of fees. ... Whether the Congress would appropriate
funds for this purpose is doubtful. There is, however,
much to be said for this approach as a long-range solution to the problem, and we would like to see the Congress
given an opportunity to consider it.

                                        /s/
                                        Procedure Review Committee

CHAPTER 8

THE ATOMIC
ENERGY COMMISSION

> *... [A]ll this business about breeder reactors
> and nuclear energy is over my head. That
> was one of my poorest subjects, science....
> But it has always been fascinating to me
> because it seems to me that if a people are
> going to be a great people, we must always
> explore the unknown. We must never be
> afraid of it. That is why we have to go into
> space. That is why we should have built the
> SST. That is why, as far as that particular
> matter is concerned, in terms of nuclear
> power we must not be afraid. We must ex-
> plore it. We can't be sure what it is going to
> produce, but on the other hand, we know by
> exploring the unknown, we are going to grow
> and progress.... There is a wonderful story
> about Benjamin Franklin that illustrates my
> point on that score. A balloon was sent aloft,
> the first time that Americans at that time
> had seen a balloon, and somebody asked
> Franklin, "Of what possible use is that thing?"
> His answer was, "Of what possible use is a
> newborn babe?" So that is what we have
> here.*
>
> —President Richard M. Nixon,
> 26 September 1971, remarks while
> visiting Hanford, Washington,
> nuclear power project

Hiroshima and the Peaceful Atom

It wasn't exactly the best story for persuading people that the unknown
effects of nuclear energy would all be benign, with its echo of "Little
Boy"—the code name for the first atomic bomb dropped by the United
States. Ever since that nuclear device was exploded in the air over Hiroshima, followed shortly by the "Thin Man" that destroyed Nagasaki,
there have been assurances that the peaceful uses of atomic energy

337

would make up for it. And the Atomic Energy Commission (AEC), with its conflicting responsibilities for military and civilian applications of nuclear power, and for both promoting and regulating nuclear energy, has been the focus of all the hopes and fears evoked by the awesome potential of nuclear power.

The atomic bomb was developed under military control by the Manhattan Project, and a controversy quickly arose at the end of World War II as to whether control of this new and potent form of energy would continue in the military or be turned over to some civilian authority. In 1946 Congress decided the question by creating the AEC as an independent agency of five civilians to exercise both military and civilian responsibilities. The Atomic Energy Act [42 U.S.C. 2011] calls for: "the development, use, and control of atomic energy . . . to make the maximum contribution to the general welfare, subject at all times to the paramount objective of making the maximum contribution to the common defense and security," and "to promote world peace, improve the general welfare, increase the standard of living, and strengthen free competition in private enterprise." The Joint Committee on Atomic Energy (JCAE) was created by Congress to oversee the operation of the Commission.

From the beginning the AEC was a different kind of government agency. It directed military and civilian activities, operating many facilities itself and leasing others to private organizations. It was created to develop and promote an industry which did not then exist, and was given the power to regulate that industry once it came into being. This presented a fundamental dilemma which only now is being fully realized. When the AEC passes on the safety and desirability of a proposed nuclear power plant, it is, in effect, passing judgment on the product of its own twenty-five year effort. Security restrictions surrounding the development of nuclear energy have forced almost everyone working in the field of nuclear development to spend considerable time either working for the Commission or in close cooperation with it, making it extremely difficult to find experts who are both qualified to evaluate the effects of nuclear power and yet are outside the AEC's sphere of influence.

In 1954 Congress amended the Atomic Energy Act in an attempt to encourage development of a civilian nuclear industry under the supervision of the AEC. The amendments provided for "a program to encourage widespread participation in the development and utilization of atomic energy for peaceful purposes to the maximum extent consistent with the common defense and security and with the health and safety of the public." Specifically, they authorized the Commission to license private construction and ownership of atomic power plants and nuclear fuel, and allowed some private patents for civilian applications of nuclear energy.

The AEC ventured once into nuclear-powered commercial shipping. That effort, in conjunction with the Maritime Administration, resulted in a prototype ship, the NS (for Nuclear Ship) *Savannah*. The *Savannah* has been something of a white elephant for the Commission—too expensive to operate commercially and too well publicized to conceal. The Commission's major nonmilitary activity has been the researching, developing, licensing, and regulating of nuclear electric power plants. These plants have been built mostly through joint ventures of several private utility companies. Nuclear power plants have, so to speak, mushroomed throughout the country. In 1960 there was only one civilian nuclear power plant. There are now twenty-eight said to be in operation, and no less than 122 more are either planned or under construction. The primary opportunity for public participation in AEC proceedings is in the licensing of these plants (see Appendix 8-A, p. 360).

The rapid increase in the number of nuclear power plants is partly attributable to an enthusiasm at the AEC that is rare in government agencies. Unfortunately, the zeal is to promote the use of nuclear power, and it results in impatience with those who question the desirability and safety of such power. The source of this zeal has its roots in the years after World War II, when the AEC was seen as the vehicle of expiation for what the A-bombs, "Little Boy" and "Thin Man," had done. Even nuclear scientists who stoutly defended the use of atomic weapons were anxious to show that nuclear energy could do as much for people as it had done against the inhabitants of Hiroshima and Nagasaki. The missionary attitude continues, and a frequently heard expression is that nuclear power came along just in time, just as a growing population was demanding more power. Since the federal government has spent well over three-quarters of its energy research and development dollars attempting to bring nuclear power plants into service, it is little wonder that today the position of the nuclear advocates is somewhat strengthened by the sorry state of the coal- and oil-burning technologies. Alternatives do exist, however, both for clean-burning fossil fuel techniques, and for more desirable machines that utilize energy from the sun and from within the earth (called geothermal energy).

Up to a certain point, laymen with questions about nuclear power are treated with patient condescension and flooded with explanatory material. AEC staff members are accustomed to what they feel are irrational, if understandable, fears of radiation and nuclear accidents, and they are ready to explain them away. But if the questioners are not converted, and if they get in the way, they become

> . . . a lot of people going around the country spreading "scare talk" about nuclear power. Some of these people, whom I have called the "stirrer-uppers," like Larry Bogart, apparently make their living by creating controversy without regard to fact. Others are scientists who haven't done their homework or who insist on broadcasting their theories without first subjecting them to the review of their peers. [Former Commissioner James T. Ramey, "The Role of the Public in the Development and Regulation of Nuclear Power," Conference on Nuclear Power and the Environment, Madison, Wisconsin, 4 April 1970. The conference was published by the University of Wisconsin Press (Madison) in 1970]

If precautions are being taken by the experts in charge, why should you be concerned about what the AEC does? First, the people in charge are, in effect, judging their own work, and that can sometimes make for a less than critical evaluation. In addition, the biological effects of nuclear power plants are still largely a matter of estimation, and the possible consequences have caused a growing tide of concern about AEC-licensed power plants. Nuclear power necessarily involves radioactivity, and this raises questions which are not disposed of by the explanation that a power plant is not the same thing as a bomb. The possibility of a nuclear "incident" such as the one that occurred at the Enrico Fermi reactor at Lagoon Beach, Michigan, in October 1966, increases with the geometric proliferation of other reactors. The Fermi reactor experienced an accident believed by the Commission to be so unacceptable in its magnitude that it barely bordered on the type of event termed a "maximum credible accident." What happened was that the core of the nuclear reactor partially melted down!

Another basic problem of nuclear plants is that of seepage of radioactive material. A plant which has functioned for some time has more radioactivity stored in it than that found in a powerful nuclear bomb. The danger is not that the reactor will explode, releasing its radioactivity into the stratosphere, but rather that the seepage from a reactor can be trapped under a stable inversion layer and concentrated within a few hundred square miles in a truly frightening manner.

A 1957 study on *Theoretical Possibilities and Consequences of Major Accidents in Large Nuclear Plants* (the Brookhaven National Laboratory Report) [Available from the Government Printing Office, 1957, Catalog #Y3. At 7:22/WASH-7-40. Revised copy available soon from the Public Document Room of the AEC, 1717 H St., N.W., Washington, D.C. 20006] concluded that an accident in a major reactor could kill 3,400 people and injure 43,000 more. The report was reviewed and basically confirmed in 1965 and 1970 in letters from the former chairman of the Commission, Glenn Seaborg, to Congressman Holifield and Senator Gravel, respectively. Seaborg pointed out, however, that since the present generation of reactors are five times larger than those analyzed in the 1957 report, the spectre of damage from a maximum accident would be a good deal more severe.

The AEC's answer that they have had a good safety record with the few plants in operation is not sufficient to dispel qualms over the long-term effects of nuclear plants all over the continent. Outgoing Commission Chairman James Schlesinger, in safety hearings before the JCAE, 23 January 1973, pointed to the fact that then, as now, "we do not in this industry have sufficient statistical experience so that one can make these calculations." In other words, we simply don't know how likely it is that the holocaust mentioned by the Brookhaven Report will occur.

The skeptical eye of private industry viewed the possibility of nuclear "accidents" as a potential source of financially disastrous lawsuits, in view of the Brookhaven Report's estimate of seven billion dollars in possible property loss from one plant's "big accident." Industry reluctance to participate in such undertakings was alleviated when the AEC got Congress to pass a law providing private industry with government insurance against such lawsuits. The 1957 Price-Anderson amendment to the Atomic Energy Act [42 U.S.C. 2210] limits financial liability for claims over $560 million following a nuclear accident, and provides government insurance for $478 million of that possible liability.

Thus relieved of most potential liability for nuclear accidents, the companies building the plants have been less than painstaking about construction in their haste to get the plants finished, licensed, and on line. For example, the company building a nuclear power plant in Surry County, Virginia, chose to ignore persistent complaints from their welding supervisor, Mr. Carl Houston, that standards of the American Society of Mechanical Engineers were not being followed in welding the piping system. Because of the essential cooling function of the piping system in a nuclear plant, the charges had serious safety implications. But the welding supervisor was fired for his trouble. Six months later, however,

the AEC's chairman, then Glenn T. Seaborg, said ". . . the general validity of Mr. Houston's eight allegations was verified . . ." [*Washington
Post*, 19 August 1971, p. G-1]. A tragic addendum to this story occurred on 27 July 1972, when two employees at this plant were killed
by scalding steam which engulfed them in their work area. The AEC
later admitted, "The accident that has resulted in the death of two employees was caused by inadequate design of a secondary steam pipe
system" [AEC news release, 18 September 1972].

But public concern is not based only, or even primarily, on the
doomsday possibility of a nuclear power plant gone out of control.
There is also the steady emission of low-level radioactive effluents from
nuclear power plants, the cumulative effects of which will not be known
for generations. The debate over the adequacy of the AEC's limits on
radiation emissions and the Commission's practice of urging companies
to keep emissions "as low as practicable" within those limits has been
fierce, and a recapitulation of the arguments is beyond the scope of
this chapter. However, it is worth noting that two of the primary opponents of the AEC on this issue, Drs. John Gofman and Arthur Tamplin,
are long-time members in good standing of the nuclear technocratic
establishment, and that they came to their position in the course of re-
futing some claims about the effect of radioactive fallout on infant mortality.

Another source of public concern is the question of what will be done
with the leftovers from nuclear power plants. This presents a nightmar-
ish version of the country's general problem with solid waste disposal,
since nuclear wastes are loaded with deadly radioactivity that remains
toxic for thousands of years. With revelations of such events as the
recent spill of 115,000 gallons of high-level radioactive waste at Rich-
land, Washington, it is understandable that citizens in other states might
be uneasy about precautions in establishing dumping grounds for the
country's nuclear garbage. Although the piling up of nuclear wastes is
cause for concern, the opportunities for public participation are not as
clear as, and have been used less than, the procedures for licensing of
power plants.

Another silent and invisible by-product of nuclear power is heat. It
goes into rivers and lakes, and is known as "thermal pollution." Heat is
also a by-product of conventional fossil-fueled generating plants, but
there is a lot more of it from nuclear plants. The power plants are located near bodies of water because they must have this "free" natural
resource to cool their generating system. Water is taken from the river
or lake, run through the condenser to lower the temperature of the

"coolant" that is circulated and recirculated in the generator, and then sent back where it came from, several degrees hotter. Among other things, this kills fish and lowers the oxygen content of water. The primary aim of much citizen action is simply to get the utility companies to return the water at the same temperature it was when they got it.

Before getting into the structure and functions of the Commission itself, you should know about the relationship between the AEC and Congress's JCAE. A Congressional committee which exercises legislative oversight over an agency can be an ally for citizens who are concerned about the way the agency is doing its job, but it's not likely with the Joint Committee. The JCAE is composed of nine Representatives and nine Senators, and its relationship to the Commission is that of a proud parent. The records of hearings are a valuable source of background information, but it is unlikely that the Committee as presently constituted will cast a very critical eye on anything the AEC does. The current Chairman of the JCAE is Representative Melvin Price, and the Vice Chairman is Senator John Pastore. Former Commissioner James T. Ramey was Staff Director of the Joint Committee from 1956 until 1962, when he was appointed to the Commission. His term expired in June 1973.

The AEC and How It Works

At the top of the AEC structure are the five members of the Commission who are appointed by the President with Senate approval for five-year terms. The present Chairman, Dixy Lee Ray, was appointed in February 1973 to succeed James R. Schlesinger, who had been Chairman for almost two years. The other commissioners are Clarence E. Larson, whose first term expires in 1974; William O. Doub, whose first term expires in 1976; and William E. Kriegsman, whose first term expires in 1975; and William A. Anders, whose first term expires in 1978.

The Commission's job of development and regulation are carried out through the General Manager and the Director of Regulation. At present the General Manager is Robert E. Hollingsworth, and the Director of Regulation is L. Manning Muntzing.

The General Manager has six Assistant General Managers for special areas such as Research and Development. Each of the assistant managers supervises subordinate divisions. For example, an Assistant General Manager has jurisdiction over three divisions with which you might come in contact: Public Information, Industrial Participation, and the Office of Congressional Relations.

You probably will be most concerned with the licensing and regulatory functions under the Director of Regulation. Of the three major units under this Director, you are likely to find yourself dealing with the Directorate of Licensing.

If you participate in the licensing proceeding for a nuclear power project, it will be before an Atomic Safety and Licensing Board, which is a quasi-judicial board of two scientists and one lawyer. Another group which is of, but not in, the AEC is the Advisory Committee on Reactor Standards. This fifteen-member panel is charged by Congress with reviewing each license application. The fifteen members are appointed by the AEC for four-year terms [42 U.S.C. 2039]. The Directorate of Licensing was consolidated from two separate divisions in April 1972, and the seven divisions under the Director of Regulations were reorganized into the present three Directorates. The Directorate of Licensing will be the one you encounter in public hearings. This Directorate initially determines whether and where nuclear reactors will be built. It also determines what is to be done with radioactive material.

Information on the AEC

As an antidote to the unmitigated optimism about nuclear power in the official AEC publications, it would be a good idea to read some other points of view, such as those found in John W. Gofman and Arthur R. Tamplin, *Poisoned Power, The Case Against Nuclear Power Plants* (Emmaus, Pa.: Rodale Press, 1971) or Richard S. Lewis, *Nuclear Power Rebellion* (New York: The Viking Press, Inc., 1972). But the publications of the AEC are an essential source of information. A booklet entitled *Science Information Available from the Atomic Energy Commission* (TID-4550) will advise you about a number of publications that would be of value in your efforts (AEC, P.O. Box 62, Oak Ridge, Tennessee, 37830).

Nucleonics Week is the major trade publication, but it costs $295 a year (330 West 42 Street, New York, N.Y., 10036). If you are concerned about nuclear power plants, it is important to find out about them as early as possible in the planning stage, so send $3 for the semiannual revision of *Nuclear Reactors Built, Being Built, or Planned in the United States* (TID-8200), Clearinghouse for Federal Scientific and

Technical Information, 5285 Port Royal Road, Springfield, Virginia 22151. Ask the Public Information Office of the AEC to put you on a mailing list for its free weekly compilation of press releases. The press releases are indexed, and include the texts of many speeches and reports. Press releases from Senator Mike Gravel's office contain many reprints of reports on power from nuclear plants and other sources. They are free, so get on his mailing list.

After you have done some background reading, start studying the statutes and regulations under which the AEC operates. The statutes are in Title 42 of the U.S. Code (U.S.C.), starting at Section 2011. The regulations under which the AEC operates are located in three different places in the Code of Federal Regulations (C.F.R.): Title 10 C.F.R. Chapter 1, 41 C.F.R. Chapter 9, and 41 C.F.R. Chapter 109. The two chapters in Title 41 cover procurement regulations and property management regulations, so most of the C.F.R. references you will be using are in Title 10. But be particularly careful that the regulations you rely on are up-to-date. The AEC has been revising its rules in order to respond to objections and, in the case of the rules on the licensing of nuclear facilities, to comply with a court order.

The procedures for rule making at the AEC are in subpart H of Title 10, Chapter 1. Section 2.801 says that rule making may be initiated by the Commission on its own, by recommendation of another agency, or "on the petition of any other interested person." Under Section 2.802, such an "interested person's" petition is to be addressed to the Secretary, U.S. Atomic Energy Commission, Washington, D.C. 20545, Attention: Chief, Public Proceedings Branch. The petition should include a statement of the proposed regulation or amendment, or specify the regulation to be rescinded or amended, along with a supporting argument. A docket number will be assigned to the petition, which will be deposited in the Public Document Room. But there won't necessarily be a hearing, since Section 2.803 provides that a hearing will be held only if "the Commission deems it advisable." If the Commission finds "that sufficient reason exists," a notice of proposed rule making will be published in the *Federal Register*. Otherwise the petition will be denied and the Commission will notify the petitioner of the grounds for denial.

If the Commission finds a "sufficient reason," and publishes a notice of proposed rule making, that notice will include:

1. The terms or substance of the rule, or the subject and issues involved.

2. A statement that copies of comments submitted may be examined in the Public Document Room, and the manner and time within which members of the public may comment.
3. The authority for the regulation.
4. The time and place of the public hearing, if there is to be one.
5. If there is to be a hearing, the presiding officer and procedures for the hearing.
6. An explanatory statement.

This published notice, or service on all persons subject to the notice, must be made at least fifteen days prior to any hearing, unless the Commission states a "good cause" for a shorter period of notice. Section 2.805 provides that interested persons will have an opportunity to participate in rule making through "the submission of statements, information, opinions, and arguments" according to the procedures stated in the notice. Subsection (b) allows the Commission to "hold informal hearings at which interested persons may be heard, adopting procedures which in its judgment will best serve the purpose of the hearing."

Of course, the AEC not only is not required to hold hearings on a proposed rule, it doesn't even have to publish the rule in the *Federal Register* and ask for public comments before it becomes effective. Some of the most important rules ever adopted by the Commission—the revisions to the rules on licensing of nuclear facilities—were made effective without any period for public comment. The Administrative Procedure Act (APA), as described in Chapter 4, allows for rules to be made effective immediately upon publication if there is "good cause." The "good cause" in this case, in the AEC's opinion, was that the Court of Appeals had ruled that the old procedures were inadequate. In general, if a finding of good cause could be expected to accelerate the availability of a nuclear power plant, you should expect the Commission to so rule.

The AEC's Public Document Room is at 1717 H Street, N.W., Washington, D.C. 20006. Section 9.7 of the Commission's information regulations describes the material you can look at there, including comments on proposed rules, environmental impact statements for projects, final opinions and orders, statements of policy not published in the *Federal Register*, a record of votes in Commission proceedings, and an index to those records and to those available in the major operating field offices. Other records, such as the AEC Rules and Regulations, the AEC Manual, and instructions to AEC personnel that affect any member of the public, are available for public inspection at the major operating field offices. If a record is not available at the Public Document Room or at one of the major operating field offices, write to the Secretary, U.S. Atomic Energy Commission, Washington, D.C., 20545.

The charges for locating and reproducing copies of records are in Section 9.9. A self-service coin-operated machine (5 cents per page) is available in the Reading Room next to the Public Document Room. If you can provide your own paper for copying, you can use a Thermofax machine in the Public Document Room for 50 cents per hour. Microfilm can be copied for a charge of 10 cents per page. Copying machines in the field offices are subject to the same charges, when they are available. Search fees start at $5 per person per hour for clerical personnel. Deposits for search and copying fees must be paid in advance. For transcripts of testimony in AEC proceedings you have to pay the private reporting firm which transcribed the proceedings under contract with the AEC. There is no charge for locating records on file in the Public Document Room, and no charge is made for search or copying if "the General Manager, the Director of Regulation or their authorized representatives determine it to be appropriate in the interest of the AEC program."

Section 9.5 describes the records exempt from public disclosure. Most of these exemptions simply restate the exemptions set forth in the Freedom of Information Act (FOIA), followed by examples of specific kinds of information which the AEC feels are covered by these exemptions. For instance, subsection (4) says that "trade secrets and commercial or financial information obtained from a person and privileged or confidential" are not available, using the same grammatically ambiguous terms used in the statute. But the AEC goes on to set forth four specific examples in subsections (i) to (iii), which include "information received in confidence, such as trade secrets, inventions and discoveries, and proprietary data" and "technical reports and data . . . or other types of proprietary information which are generated or developed by the AEC or for the AEC under contract." The exemption of "personnel and medical files and similar files the disclosure of which would constitute a clearly unwarranted invasion of personal privacy" is set forth in subsection (6), and the AEC considers this exemption to cover "(i) files containing the names of individuals who have received exposure to radiation."

The AEC is different from other administrative agencies in that much of its information is restricted for "security" reasons. This information, known as "restricted data," is available primarily to AEC contractors under elaborate regulations set forth in 10 C.F.R. 10. These are the "criteria for determining eligibility for access to restricted data or defense information," including guidelines such as the dividing of derogatory information about people applying for such access into "category 'A' derogatory information" [10.11(a)], and "category 'B' derogatory information" [10.11(b)]. Category "A" includes cases in which the individual or his spouse has "knowingly established an association . . . with traitors, seditionists, anarchists, or revolutionists." Category "B" includes incidents in which a person "has abused trust, has been dishonest, or has engaged in infamous, immoral or notoriously disgraceful conduct without adequate evidence of reformation" [10.11(b)(8)]. It also includes information that a person has refused "upon the ground of constitutional privilege against self-incrimination, to testify before a Congressional Committee regarding charges of his alleged disloyalty or other misconduct."

Opportunities for Citizen Participation

Citizen participation at the AEC is not as easily tailored to the limitations of your resources as it is with some other agencies. Complaining will get you almost nowhere, and even to comment on proposed rules requires considerably more technical expertise than with other agencies. Perhaps the primary opportunity for you to participate in AEC proceedings is by intervention in licensing hearings. Even if you are doing this on a limited issue, such as water pollution, you will need a lawyer, technical assistance, and an organization of some sort to keep the effort going. If you are interested in the nuclear power program in general, then the rule making process might be the best way to go. Given limited technical, legal, and financial resources, rule making proceedings provide an opportunity to influence each and every power plant in a one-step process.

The procedure for participating in AEC rule making is much the same as for other agencies. Start by reading the existing regulations and generally educating yourself about how they work. Watch the *Federal Register* and get on the mailing list for AEC news releases. In addition to looking for announcements of proposed rules which are formally published for public comment, be on the alert for references to informal conferences with industry which are often used to hammer out proposed rules. For example, in 1971 the Commission was considering amendments to its regulation that licensees keep radioactive emissions "as low as practicable," within the maximum limits. As a part of the rule making process, the Commission met once with representatives of environmental protection groups. The meeting was held at a downtown Washington, D.C. office, and the press was invited. But the same proposals were also being considered in a series of closed meetings with industry representatives in the AEC's Maryland offices. The Commission was adamant about keeping the meetings closed, despite a written request and Congressional inquiries. It was not until late in the afternoon before the day of the final meeting in the series that the AEC reluctantly agreed to allow representatives of environmental protection groups and the press to attend.

Rule making generally has not been much used as a vehicle for citizen participation, either through commenting on proposed rules or submitting rule making petitions. A well-drawn petition might be effective, but it would be subject to the same fundamental blockade as all rule making petitions—there is nothing to require the agency to do anything significant with a petition. But as the stunning Calvert Cliffs decision (discussed later in the chapter) should indicate, the rule making route provides a powerful legal and political tool. Frame your petition for rule making on narrow procedural grounds. After being turned down promptly by the Commission, you have short-circuited an otherwise arduous process and can now go directly to court. Since the issue you would raise in court would be procedural, in this case whether the AEC had to consider environmental matters under the National Environmental Policy Act, the court is then freed to poke around the soft underbelly of the technical questions.

On 30 November 1971 the Commission announced that it would hold hearings as a part of rule making proceedings. The rules involved are on the issues of what "as low as practicable" should mean as a limit on radiation from power plants, and on the emergency core cooling system (ECCS) that is the final safety device to prevent catastrophic harm to the public in the event of a major nuclear power plant accident. Over fifty groups have intervened in those hearings thus far. The groups have organized under the name of Coalition of National Intervenors (CNI), and have been very active in both rule making hearings. The "as low as practicable" hearings adjourned 6 May 1972, to be reconvened sometime in 1973 after issuance of an environmental impact statement by AEC. The ECCS hearings continued throughout 1972. CNI has succeeded in reopening the controversy surrounding cooling systems, and testimony has revealed many internal doubts within the

AEC relating to the safety of the ECCS, which has never been tested. Despite the controversy, AEC has continued to license new reactors. But public pressure is beginning to crack the AEC's conventional position on the safety of these reactors.

Participating in the Licensing Process

Intervening in a licensing proceeding is a different story from rule making. The Commission was not particularly reluctant about public licensing hearings when they first began, although utility companies were unenthusiastic, because they were seen as another way to allay the public's irrational fears. But that was several years ago, and licensing hearings have since become an avenue by which citizen groups have blocked nuclear power projects, secured concessions from licensees, and, in the Calvert Cliffs case, overturned the AEC's whole system of environmental protection regulations. But before getting into how you can participate in a hearing, you need a general outline of the steps that a utility goes through in applying for a license.

Utilities begin traveling down the road to a particular nuclear plant many years before their decision ever surfaces at the AEC Public Documents Room in the form of an application for a construction permit. There are at least four prior moves they will make before filing for an application:

1. Projection of the electrical demand for the future.
2. Analysis of many possible sites for construction of the power plant.
3. Selection of one site.
4. Ordering of basic reactor components.

Citizens should try to get into the process at the earliest possible time, for the further down the road the utilities get, the harder it will be for you to influence a change in course. Some mechanisms for getting in early are:

1. Following *Nucleonics Week* to determine which utilities have actually ordered reactors from the manufacturers.
2. Organizing stockholder efforts to force the utility to make its plans freely available.

3. Going directly to the utility executives and asking their permission to become a part of their site and reactor selection process—perhaps by forming a citizens' advisory power plant committee.
4. Lobbying state and local environmental and land use planning agencies to request access to the utility's power plant plans.
5. Going to the state utility regulatory agency and asking them for the information they have—and suggesting that they get more if needed.
6. Participating in the power plant siting processes that exist in a few areas by virtue of enlightened state laws.

Of course, if the laws are not adequate, a citizen can always set up an organization to lobby the state legislature to pass new ones.

A number of years after the utility company has decided to build a "nuke," as the plants are commonly called, it applies for a construction permit from the Commission. The company must submit two reports with its application for a construction permit: a safety report and an environmental report. The safety report describes all of the precautions the company promises to take to reduce radiation hazards. The environmental report describes some of the impact which the plant will have on the environment, and compares it with the impact of other possible alternatives.

The AEC then prepares a preliminary safety evaluation and a draft environmental statement on the project which is made available for public comment. Then the Commission publishes a final detailed environmental statement, and the whole matter goes to the three-man Atomic Safety and Licensing Board.

Once you find out about a proposed plant, get the safety and environmental reports and examine them. But don't be limited to the statements that the AEC and the company applying for the license have worked out. Ask to see the background reports that support the conclusions in the statements, and tell the AEC that you want to see the correspondence with the applicant concerning provisions in the original application. It is important to begin pressing for this material as soon as possible, even if the Commission is reluctant to make it available. The FOIA is still largely untested (see Chapter 3), and it will be an uphill fight to get the AEC to release anything that it has not previously made public.

When you get to the hearing, you will have a much better chance to force the release of background reports, but by that time the hearing will be underway and you will have less opportunity to analyze the reports thoroughly.

In addition to analyzing the applicant's statements, getting expert help, and deciding which issues you want to concentrate on, you need this preliminary period to enlist as many allies as possible. Look for them in other government agencies—local, state, and federal. They all have special interests and concerns of their own which may coincide with yours. On the federal level, the Environmental Protection Agency (EPA) may be a valuable source of information, if not of assistance, on questions of radiation standards and thermal pollution. Your state and local governments should be concerned about possible consequences to inhabitants, particularly if the electricity to be produced is to be consumed primarily in another jurisdiction. During this period you will be forming an organization, putting together a technical and legal staff, and getting to know the representatives of the news media that will be covering the hearings when they begin. (See Chapter 18 for some general guidelines on organizing.)

On 28 July 1972 the Commission altered the ground rules for the entire intervention process, making it harder to gain recognition as an intervenor and more difficult to pursue a variety of issues once you have obtained recognition. In addition, the hearing board examiner has now been granted the power to consolidate the petitions of intervenors which, in his judgment, "raise substantially the same questions" or represent "substantially the same interest."

Of course we cannot adequately recount the rules here, nor can we anticipate the inevitable changes. Therefore, careful examination of Chapters 1 and 2 of Part 10 of the C.F.R. is a must. Since the ground rules do change so frequently, and new issues constantly crop up in the nuclear reactor safety and environmental areas, it would also be wise to call or write one of the lawyers listed in Appendix 18-D (p. 931) for advice on the most logical and timely issues on which to base your intervention.

By the time you have reached the point of filing a petition to intervene, you should have formed some kind of organization and made arrangements for technical and legal assistance. These resources will be tested when the hearing begins. As Irving Like, an attorney who has participated in such proceedings, describes it:

> . . . the limited resource litigator enters upon a David-Goliath type confrontation pitted against the utility, the AEC technical staff and the titans of American industry. Arrayed on their side are also

the huge complex of dependent trade associations, economic interest groups, public relations media, the scientific engineering and
technical resources of the AEC, its national laboratories and sponsored research, and the AEC's Congressional protectors. [*Multi-
Media Confrontation—the Environmentalists' Strategy for a "No
Win" Agency Proceeding*, paper presented at American Law
Institute-American Bar Association Environmental Law conference
at the Smithsonian Institution, 29 January 1971].

As Like pointed out, licensing hearings serve as an educational forum
as well as being an administrative hearing. The hearing will probably be
covered by local news media, especially if you have set up an effective
public information system. You are not perverting the hearing process
by emphasizing its function of informing the general public as well as
the three men on the board. The AEC has recognized this function in
viewing the hearings as a method of educating the public and allaying
their fears [Harold L. Price, AEC Director of Regulation, Joint Committee on Atomic Energy Hearings on Licensing and Regulation of
Nuclear Reactors, 90th Cong., 1st Sess., Part 1, p. 43].

This approach does not mean that you can neglect the technical adequacy of testimony or forego legal arguments that are difficult to understand. It does mean that you should prepare daily news releases
summarizing important points in the hearing, and be prepared to give
interviews. Learn the deadlines of local newspapers and television stations, timing significant presentations accordingly. The licensing of a
local nuclear power plant is usually a source of sufficient concern that
newspapers and television stations will take an editorial stand. Long
before the hearing process begins you should begin presenting your
case to local newspapers and television stations. You can be sure that
the utility company involved, and other commercial interests that stand
to profit from the plant, will try to rally support as early as possible in
the game.

In the hearing itself, use all of the resources available. Technical experts who would be reluctant to risk their jobs by testifying for you
may still be willing to examine the applicant's data and provide you
with questions to be used. Don't limit yourself to raising questions
about the presentations of the applicant. Ask the board to take official
notice of reports on the effects of nuclear power plants. Be alert for
opportunities to use demonstrative evidence, or to ask the Board to inspect the proposed plant site. Apply for subpoenas to compel testimony
by government scientists. The AEC's Rules of Practice have a provision

[10 C.F.R. 2.733] for technically qualified persons who are not lawyers to act as lay interrogators. This presents an opportunity for an articulate technical expert to participate directly, rather than being limited to testifying as a witness.

The entire licensing process is carried out within a framework of formal and informal proceedings. Present rules encourage such devices as prehearing conferences and telephone conversations to expedite the hearing process. At the formal construction license hearing, the company will first tell why the permit to begin construction should be granted. The intervenors can then cross-examine and present their questions and objections. The hearing is run like a trial, with opportunities to present witnesses and to cross-examine witnesses from the other side. If you intervene you are required to state specific contentions outlining your safety and environmental concerns. Only if you are making a limited appearance before the Board will objections of a general nature be permitted entry into the record.

The issues raised by an intervention should not be limited to consequences based on the assumption that the nuclear technology of the plant will operate exactly as predicted. Just because the prospective licensee has projected certain numerical values regarding radioactivity and thermal pollution is no guarantee that those values represent the way the plant will actually function. For instance, computation of radiation dosage involves many assumptions and meteorological variables. Computation of offsite radiation dosage is based on "engineered safeguards" which are assigned certain numerical values through a process of private negotiations between the power company and the AEC staff. Skillful cross-examination is necessary to establish exactly how these computations were determined. Cross-examination also provides an opportunity for raising other questions about the reliability of the proposed technology, such as quality control requirements.

The petition in Appendix 8-B (p. 362) was submitted by Mr. Robert Head to intervene in the licensing hearing for the Waterford nuclear power plant in Louisiana. This should provide an excellent model for your own petition. Prepared by Mr. David Comey of Businessmen for the Public Interest (Chicago), it sets forth in detail arguments on radiation hazards and environmental consequences which the petitioners raised at the hearing. Some of the objections in the petition, such as the inadequacy of the applicant's analysis of the maximum hypothetical accident (MHA), would have to be tailored to meet the particular plans developed for a proposed plant. Others, such as the legal and technical adequacy of the AEC's Standards for Protection Against Radiation, are more generally applicable.

Your role in a licensing proceeding is that of an adversary. You are there to raise questions and to present the other side, with a goal of insuring that adequate precautions are taken for environmental protection and safety. If one assumes that there are simple existing technological remedies to the tremendous problems of this technology, then the possibility exists of achieving a negotiated settlement rather than unremitting opposition all the way to the appellate court level. The negotiated settlement in Appendix 8-C (p. 411) is an example of how this can be accomplished. The basic principle is the one used by other groups in dealing with radio and television licensees before the Federal Communications Commission (FCC). A company that ordinarily would not even be willing to listen to citizen suggestions may be prepared to make concessions when those citizens band together and intervene in the licensing proceeding. The negotiated settlement is a method of making sure that those concessions are binding. In exchange for a commitment from the company to take certain steps, such as installing cooling towers, the intervenors agree to withdraw their petition. While this tactic may be effective in achieving certain limited goals, for success with it you must first organize and establish the credibility that you are capable of going all the way in the licensing proceeding.

Licensing History of Calvert Cliffs

For an idea of how the AEC's licensing process works, consider the case of the Calvert Cliffs nuclear power plant in Maryland. It was a project that the AEC now probably wishes had never been started. In January 1968 the Baltimore Gas & Electric Company filed an application to construct a nuclear plant on the Chesapeake Bay. The plant, composed of two identical nuclear reactors, was to be forty-six miles from Washington, D.C. Many residents of Calvert and Anne Arundel Counties were concerned, and some of the people, particularly those in Calvert County, acted. On 29 January 1968 the Calvert Civic Association passed the following resolution:

> RESOLVED, that the Calvert Civic Association is seriously concerned about the effect that a nuclear power plant would have in heating the waters of the Chesapeake Bay, damaging the landscape by power lines, and by exposing a small rural county to all of the environmental hazards of a large nuclear plant. We believe that the construction of this plant would be disastrous to a county in which

the future depends upon wise management of its natural resources
and the pursuit of environmental quality. We, therefore, resolve to
oppose any further development of this power plant at hearings
before the Maryland Department of Water Resources and the U.S.
Atomic Energy Commission and request to be heard before these
agencies when this issue is discussed.

While the application was being processed, citizens near the site of
the proposed plant organized the Chesapeake Environmental Protection
Association. Meanwhile, the utility company had filed ten amendments
to its application, mostly on minor technical aspects, and obtained permission from the Commission to begin construction of certain non-
nuclear components of the plant. It was not until over a year later, in
April 1969, that the AEC's Division of Reactor Licensing produced a
safety evaluation of the proposed plant. The Advisory Committee on
Reactor Safeguards had made their review public in March 1969. Both
found the plant to be substantially safe according to their standards.

The hearing process started on 28 March 1969 with the notice of a
hearing to be held on 12 May. The Chesapeake Environmental Protection Association had asked to be informed of any hearings, and the
Association filed a petition to intervene on the grounds that the proposed plant would have an adverse effect on the health and safety of
its members, through radiological and thermal pollution of the Chesapeake Bay. The government of neighboring Anne Arundel County also
petitioned to intervene. The hearing board, composed of Chairman
Arthur W. Murphy, Dr. A. Dixon Callahan, and Dr. Clarke Williams,
accepted the petitions, but ruled that thermal pollution could not be
discussed under AEC regulations then in effect.

On 29 April a prehearing conference was held. Four parties to the
case—the AEC Division of Reactor Licensing, Baltimore Gas & Electric
Company, the Chesapeake Environmental Protection Association, and
Anne Arundel County—took part. It was repeatedly stressed that thermal pollution could not be discussed as an issue at the hearing. The
hearing itself took place on 12 and 13 May. From the notice of hearing to the hearing itself only a month and a half elapsed. The intervenors
had been fortunate in getting scientists from Johns Hopkins University
to prepare a paper called *Effects of Nuclear Power Plants on the Chesapeake Bay from an Environmental and Public Health Point of View*
[Available for reading or xeroxing (not by mail) from the Documents
Room, AEC, 1717 H St., N.W., Washington, D.C. 20006].

The hearing opened with the applicant's statement which emphasized that thermal pollution would not be discussed, followed by the presentation of the Division of Reactor Licensing, which generally approved the position of the applicant. Then James Cawood of the Chesapeake Environmental Protection Association presented his case, which included the Johns Hopkins paper and personal testimony from several of the scientists who had written it. Cawood's presentation emphasized the lack of knowledge about long-term effects of low doses of radioactive material, particularly of tritium, a radioactive isotope of hydrogen which would be the largest single release from the plant. But the Board granted the construction permit on 30 June, basically ruling in favor of the "Proposed Findings of Fact and Conclusion of Law" submitted by Baltimore Gas & Electric Company.

In August 1970 the Commission upheld the decision of the Atomic Safety and Licensing Board decision. A short time later the Maryland State Department of Water Resources gave Baltimore Gas & Electric a permit to heat and use the water of the bay.

But the intervenors persevered. The Sierra Club and the National Wildlife Federation, who were joined by the Calvert Cliffs Coordinating Committee, filed suit in the U.S. Court of Appeals for the District of Columbia Circuit. The groups actually filed two suits, one attacking the AEC's decision to permit the Calvert Cliffs project to go ahead, and another generally attacking the AEC's implementation of the National Environmental Policy Act. In July 1971 the court's opinion was handed down [*Calvert Cliffs Coordinating Committee, et al.* v. *AEC*, 449 F.2d 1109 (D.C. Cir. 1971)]. Instead of ruling on the particular case of the Calvert Cliffs project, the court held that the AEC's entire process for licensing of nuclear plants had generally failed to carry out the policies of the National Environmental Policy Act. So the case which had begun as opposition to a particular project had direct effect on plants all over the country. The AEC estimates that at least sixty-three license applications involving ninety-one nuclear reactors will be affected. A little over a month after the decision, the AEC issued new regulations to comply with the ruling and made them effective immediately, without a period for preliminary public comment. Generally, the court required the AEC to:

1. Provide for independent review by licensing boards of the environmental impact statements prepared by the AEC staff.
2. Require new environmental impact statements for projects licensed after January 1970, when the National Environmental Policy Act became effective.

3. Evaluate environmental effects, such as thermal pollution, independently, rather than relying on certification by other government agencies that their environmental standards would be met.
4. Review the environmental impact of projects which received construction permits before the National Environmental Policy Act was effective, but which have not yet received operating licenses.

To put it more bluntly than the court did in the Calvert Cliffs opinion, the AEC has been breaking the law in licensing nuclear power plants since the National Environmental Policy Act went into effect. Because of this, your opportunities for access are no longer limited to the licensing proceedings for new plants; you now have some opportunities to have a say about the conditions of operation for plants that are farther along. But remember that this summary is only an introduction. If you decide to take advantage of these opportunities, get the revised regulations, which are contained in *Appendix D—Interim Statement of General Policy and Procedure: Implementation of the National Environmental Policy Act of 1969*, available from the AEC.

Conclusion

The attendent risks of the nuclear power program are enormous. We do not have to take these risks, because there are safe and clean alternatives—such as clean and abundant fossil fuel energy, plus bountiful solar and geothermal energy (for more information write to the Environmental Policy Center, 324 C Street, S.E., Washington, D.C., 20003). Therefore, proposals for nuclear installations will presumably arouse strong feelings in communities. This chapter is an introduction to some of the things you should know and can do about such proposals. If you decide to take action, you should at least notify groups which have had extensive experience in dealing with the AEC. Two of these are the Union of Concerned Scientists (P.O. 289, M.I.T. Branch Station, Cambridge, Mass. 02139) and the National Wildlife Federation (1412 16 Street, N.W., Washington, D.C. 20036). A supply of the Federation's pamphlet, *Nuclear Power Plants and You,* which provided much of the information for this chapter, can be a useful tool for informing people in your community. For lawyers who have developed expertise in AEC licensing proceedings, consult Appendix 18-D (p. 931).

When the AEC began its proceedings for rule making on the safety of ECCS for nuclear plants and the limits on radioactive releases from plants, it prompted most of the groups in the country who had been dealing with the Commission to join forces. The CNI is another step toward coordination of the many small groups who often become aware of plans which the nuclear power industry and the AEC have concerning their communities when it is almost too late. A look at the map of proposed nuclear reactors in Appendix 8-A (p. 360) and a semi-annual check with the list of proposed plants may reveal that the AEC is planning to put your community on its map, too.

Nuclear Power Reactors in the United States and Status Report

A E C
UNITED STATES
ATOMIC ENERGY COMMISSION
Washington, DC 20545

No.   R-32
Contact: James Lyman   FOR IMMEDIATE RELEASE
Tel.   (301) 973 3446 (Friday, January 26, 1973)

NOTE TO EDITORS AND CORRESPONDENTS:

Following is a brief status report on the U.S. civilian nuclear power program for the year 1972:

During the year, electric utilities made known plans for 40 nuclear power generating units with a total capacity of 42,474,000 kilowatts to be located at 24 power stations. In this period, the utilities ordered 35 reactors (28 for units announced during the year and 7 for units previously announced) with a total capacity of about 37,929,000 kilowatts.

In 1971, utilities made known plans for 29 nuclear power generating units with a total capacity of 29,693,000 kilowatts to be located at 17 power stations. Reactor suppliers were selected for 20 units with a total capacity of about 19,921,000 kilowatts.

Status of U.S. nuclear power generating units, as of December 31, 1972

		kilowatts
29	operable	14,683,000
55	being built	47,775,100
76	planned (reactors ordered)	79,999,000
160		142,457,100

Attached for your information is a map of the United States showing the location of all present and proposed civilian nuclear power generating units for which reactor suppliers have been selected.

Enclosure

NUCLEAR POWER REACTORS IN THE UNITED STATES

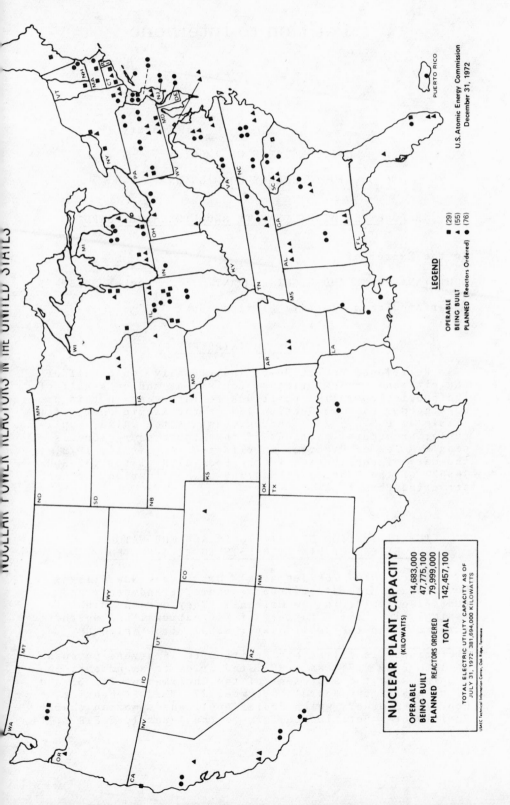

PUERTO RICO

U.S. Atomic Energy Commission
December 31, 1972

LEGEND

OPERABLE	■ (29)
BEING BUILT	▲ (55)
PLANNED (Reactors Ordered)	● (76)

NUCLEAR PLANT CAPACITY
(KILOWATTS)

OPERABLE		14,683,000
BEING BUILT		47,775,100
PLANNED	REACTORS ORDERED	79,999,000
	TOTAL	142,457,100

TOTAL ELECTRIC UTILITY CAPACITY AS OF
JULY 31, 1972: 381,694,000 KILOWATTS

USAEC Technical Information Center, Oak Ridge, Tennessee

Petition to Intervene

January 19, 1973

UNITED STATES OF AMERICA

ATOMIC ENERGY COMMISSION

BEFORE THE ATOMIC SAFETY AND LICENSING BOARD

In the Matter of   )
)
LOUISIANA POWER AND LIGHT COMPANY   )Docket No.50-382
)
Waterford Steam Electric Station, Unit 3)

PETITION TO INTERVENE

Petitioner Robert Head, individually, on behalf of the citizens of New Orleans, Louisiana, and on behalf of the public generally, petitions to intervene in this proceeding pursuant to Section 189 of the Atomic Energy Act (Title 42 U.S.C.§2239) and pursuant to the valid, applicable, procedural sections of the Atomic Energy Commission's Rules of Practice in effect on August 16, 1972, the date of publication in the Federal Register (37 F.R. 16562) of the "Notice of Hearing on Application for Construction Permit."*

I

IDENTIFICATION OF PETITIONER AND THE NATURE
AND EXTENT OF HIS INTERESTS TO BE AFFECTED

Robert Head resides at 617 Ursulines, New Orleans, Louisiana. His father, two brothers, grandmother and aunt also reside in New Orleans. They use the Mississippi River for a variety of recreational and aesthetic purposes, and the public water supply from which he

---

*Petitioner is filing his Petition to Intervene pursuant to 10 C.F.R. 2.714 as it existed prior to amendment, in keeping with the statement of the Chairman at Tr. 32 and ¶1 of p.5 of the Board's December 27, 1972 Prehearing Conference Order, which denied Applicant's motion that Petitioner's Petition conform to the later 10 C.F.R.2.714 (a).

derives his drinking water comes from the Mississippi
River. The city limit of New Orleans is 20 miles from
the proposed plant. Robert Head lives 25 miles from the
proposed plant and thus resides in a zone that would be
gravely contaminated by a major accident at Applicant's
facility. According to assumptions set forth in WASH-
740, Theoretical Possibilities and Consequences of Major
Accidents in Large Nuclear Power Plants (U.S. Atomic
Energy Commission, Washington, D.C., March 1957), Petitioner would be fatally injured upon the occurrence of
an accident at Applicant's plant similar to a Case III
accident described in the report. Therefore, his interests will be affected if the Commission issues a construction permit for Applicant's facility without a
thorough public hearing and resolution of the issues of
public health, safety and welfare, and the issue of environmental protection.

By seeking to intervene in this proceeding Petitioner Head endeavors to represent the interests of the
citizens residing within the area affected by the proposed plant. Pursuant to his right under the Atomic
Energy Act of 1954, Petitioner requests that he be permitted to fully participate in the hearing, including
that he be allowed to submit evidence and briefs, offer
argument, receive notice of hearing, be represented by
counsel, make appearances and fully and meaningfully
utilize discovery as provided by law.

Petitioner, as an interested member of the public,
petitions for full status as party to this proceeding
with all of the rights and privileges incident thereto.
Under 42 U.S.C. §2239, he should be permitted to intervene. That section of the Atomic Energy Act reads, in
pertinent part, as follows:

> "In any proceeding under this chapter,
> for the granting,...of any license...
> the Commission shall grant a hearing
> upon the request of any person whose
> interest may be affected by the pro-
> ceeding, and shall admit any such per-
> son as a party to such proceeding."

Although his interests are not primarily economic,
they are widely shared and are sufficient to qualify
Petitioner for the public role in AEC licensing proceedings envisioned by Congress. See Michigan Consolidated Gas Co. v. Federal Power Commission, 283 F.2d
214 at 224 (D.C.Cir. 1960). By law the interests of
the Petitioner are adequate for intervention, and essential to the administrative process:

> "[T]he trend of cases...has been toward
> recognizing that injuries other than
> economic harm are sufficient to bring

> a person within the meaning of the
> statutory language, and towards
> discarding the notion that an in-
> jury that is widely shared is ipso
> facto, not an injury sufficient to
> provide the basis for judicial re-
> view." Sierra Club v. Morton, 40
> U.S.L.W. 1397, 4401 (April 19, 1972)
> (cases collected).

Petitioner previously filed a Petition to Intervene
on September 12, 1972, in the form of a letter to the
Secretary of the Commission, in which the general subjects of emergency core cooling in the event of a loss-
of-coolant accident and radioactive releases were set
forth as matters the Petitioner wished placed in controversy in the construction permit hearing for Applicant's
proposed plant.

At the prehearing conference held on December 20,
1972, the Board heard argument on this Petition, and
entered an order on December 27, 1972, setting forth the
following:

> It appearing that there would be no
> significant prejudice to the appli-
> cant in view of the present status of
> the proceeding and particularly the
> fact that the safety evaluation of
> the regulatory staff, the report of
> the Advisory Committee on Reactor Safe-
> guards, and the final environmental
> statement of the regulatory staff were
> not available and would apparently not
> be issued in the immediate future, the
> Board granted Mr. Head thirty calendar
> days from December 20, 1972, the date
> of the prehearing conference, within
> which to obtain counsel and file an
> amended petition for leave to inter-
> vene. The Board's action was limited
> to the subject matter identified in
> the petition already filed by Mr. Head,
> and did not grant authority to inter-
> vene as to any other subjects. (pp.3-4)

Petitioner believes that the Board's Prehearing Conference Order is unduly restrictive and contrary to due
process. As the Board has noted in the above paragraph,
Petitioner did not have available to him at the time of
the prehearing conference any of the documents which are
statutorily required to be available before a hearing
can commence.* The Advisory Committee on Reactor Safe-

---

* Petitioner would like to note that Applicant is still
amending its PSAR even at this date; further analyses

guards has not yet written its report on this reactor,
and indeed did not hold its full review until late in the
day on January 12, 1972.

Petitioner did not receive from the Regulatory Staff
a copy of the Safety Evaluation until January 13, 1973.
A careful review of this document has revealed major
safety problems associated with the design of the Applicant's proposed plant that have a direct bearing not only
on the radiological matters in this proceeding but also
determinations with respect to environmental matters.
Therefore Petitioner is filing a Petition to Intervene
that goes beyond the two areas set forth in Petitioner's
earlier Petition of September 12, 1972, and believes
that there is good cause for so doing.

The matters raised in the instant Petition to Intervene are substantive issues pertaining to whether the
issuance of a permit for construction of the facility
will be inimical to the common defense and security or
to the health and safety of the public, and whether the
environmental review conducted by the Commission's Regulatory Staff pursuant to Appendix D of 10 C.F.R. Part 50
has been adequate and in compliance with the statutory
requirements of the National Environmental Policy Act
of 1969. Inasmuch as the Atomic Energy Act requires a
mandatory public hearing before a construction permit
may issue, and the Board has an obligation to make findings on all the five issues specified in the Notice of
Hearing, the contentions set forth in this Petition to
Intervene do not tender to the Board any issues beyond
those on which the Board is statutorily required to make
findings. In particular, Petitioner notes that pursuant
to the Notice of Hearing, the Board must independently
consider with respect to environmental matters the final
balance among conflicting factors contained in the record
of the proceeding with a view to determining the appropriate action to be taken, including whether the construction permit should be granted or denied. As set
forth in Section III hereinbelow, Petitioner contends
that the Safety Evaluation raises substantial doubt with
respect to whether this facility can be justified on any
cost-benefit analysis in view of the unresolved safety
items. Petitioner believes that on the basis of the
indeterminacies identified in the Safety Evaluation and
given specification in this Petition, the Board must find

---

on a number of safety items and responses to Staff questions are scheduled for submittal on February 1, 1973 and
successive dates throughout the spring of 1973. The
Staff, for its part, plans further Supplements to its
Safety Evaluation after review of outstanding unresolved
safety items. Petitioner fails to fathom the logic of
his being required to finalize his pleadings at a time
when the two principal parties to the matter have not
completed filing their case in chief.

in favor of an alternative to the construction of the
proposed facility and thus deny the application for a
construction permit.

Furthermore, the issues raised by the Staff's Safety
Evaluation were neither implicitly or explicitly apparent
from Applicant's Preliminary Safety Analysis Report, and
as will be set forth below in Section III of the Petition
to Intervene, they include issues on which the Draft Environmental Statement is silent or deficient. Therefore
Petitioner could not conceivably have made these contentions prior to having made a review of the Safety Evaluation.

Furthermore, Petitioner has only in the last two
weeks been able to secure the assistance of a consultant
to assist in specification of his contentions in a way
so as to be of assistance to the Board in evaluating the
Application and the Staff's review thereof.

Petitioner contends that in so filing this Petition
to Intervene, he has not prejudiced the interests of any
party in the proceeding inasmuch as the matter has not
yet been set down for hearing on a date certain, and
there is no way that any party to the proceeding could
have made decisions or commitments during the thirty days
after the prehearing conference that will be prejudiced
by admitting as matters in controversy the contentions
set forth in this Petition to Intervene.

Petitioner believes that the above is a sufficient
showing of good cause to entitle him to amend his Petition to Intervene, which is set forth below in reasonable
specificity so as to comply with 10 C.F.R. 2.714 and the
Board's December 27, 1972 Order.

II

FIRST PRELIMINARY STATEMENT OF CONTENTIONS
WITH RESPECT TO NUCLEAR SAFETY PROBLEMS AND
DEFECTS IN THE DESIGN OF THE FACILITY

Petitioner contests a negative finding by the Atomic
Safety and Licensing Board on the issue whether the
issuance of a permit for construction of the facility
will be inimical to the common defense and security or
to the health and safety of the public.

Petitioner further contests a positive finding on
whether the proposed facility can be constructed and
operated at the proposed location without undue risk to
the health and safety of the public.

Petitioner in addition contests a positive finding
on whether there is reasonable assurance that research
and development, which will be required to resolve the
safety questions associated with safety features or

components for the proposed facility, will in fact be
completed so these questions can be satisfactorily resolved at or before the latest date stated in the application for completion of construction of the proposed
facility.

Petitioner contends that the following General Design Criteria, set forth in Appendix A to Part 50 of the
Commission's Regulations, are not met and will not be met
by the present design of Applicant's plant, for the
reasons set forth below:

"Criterion 10--Reactor design.
The reactor core and associated coolant, control,
and protection systems shall be designed with
appropriate margin to assure that specified acceptable fuel design limits are not exceeded
during any condition of normal operation, including the effects of anticipated operational
occurrences."

"Criterion 12--Suppression of reactor power
oscillations.
The reactor core and associated coolant, control,
and protection systems shall be designed to
assure that power oscillations which can result
in conditions exceeding specified acceptable
fuel design limits are not possible or can be
reliably and readily detected and suppressed."

2.1 Petitioner contends that there is no acceptable
basis for the nuclear, thermal and hydraulic design of
the proposed Waterford Unit 3 core. Even the Staff has
recognized this fact in its Safety Evaluation, which is
riddled with caveats such as "In the event that the
information presented at the operating license stage is
not sufficient to demonstrate rigorously the acceptability of the design, suitable operating restrictions
can be imposed to limit operation to within known
acceptability limits" and "At this time we are unable to
reach a final conclusion as to the conservatism of the
proposed design limit peaking factors" and "In our detailed review of the application for an operating
license, we will consider the adequacy of design allow-
ances for analytical and measurement uncertainties, core
asymmetry, xenon redistribution, and control rod effects"
and "Additional data can reasonably be expected to be
available prior to the completion of the operating license review for the Waterford facility" and "The applicant has stated that estimates for engineering hot
channel factors will be further verified as manufacturing
data become available for fuel assemblies that will be
used in other CE-designed reactors...During the operating license review we can require the use of larger
factors if the proposed factors are not adequately justified." In short, LP&L is buying a $400,000,000 pig in
a poke. Petitioner contends that any issuance of a

construction permit for a reactor with so many unknowns would be a direct violation of the Atomic Energy Act.

2.2 Petitioner contends that there is no justification for reducing the engineering factor on hot channel heat flux and enthalpy rise to 1.03. Westinghouse has used an engineering factor of 1.10 in its Zion Station analyses, and Petitioner contends that a review of the testimony in RM-50-1 and the Palisades hearing shows that CE is even more incompetent than Westinghouse.

2.3 Petitioner contends that the proposal to use boron concentration adjustments to control xenon transients is entirely speculative, and part length rods will have to be used to control axial xenon oscillations. In order to sufficiently control for xenon, partial length rods with a worth of at least $2.0\%\Delta k/k$ will have to be used, which will result in power peaking at the top of the core. Together with gaps that will occur in the tops of fuel rods due to fuel densification, extreme local peaking will occur that will violate fuel integrity, and result in centerline temperatures over $5100°F$.

2.4 Petitioner contends that the proposed design of this core is unstable to azimuthal xenon, and if built, Applicant will have no way to detect azimuthal xenon oscillations before F_{xy}^N limits are exceeded.

2.5 Petitioner contends that because part length rods will have to be used to keep axial xenon oscillations from exceeding F_z^N limits, radial peaking factors of 1.8 or more should be used. There is no justification for the proposed radial peaking factor of 1.55.

2.6 Petitioner contends that there is also no justification for the axial peaking factor of 1.68 used by CE. Petitioner contends that an axial peaking factor of 1.8 must be used in view of the lack of confirmatory data from CE reactors in operation to date.

2.7 Petitioner contends that based on the above, the total heat flux factor should be 3.564 instead of the 2.68 proposed by CE, which would require a maximum linear power density far below the 18.5kW/ft proposed and result in a design power output far less than the 1165MWe currently being assumed (See Contentions 3.1 ff.).

2.8 Petitioner contends that the design of the fuel for Applicant's plant is defective in that it does not incorporate measures to prevent fuel densification. Fuel pellets will densify and shrink down within the fuel cladding, leaving empty spaces in the fuel rod. This will cause moderator changes and the local power generation will increase significantly in the region of the densified fuel. This will lead to rod burnup during steady-state operation, power oscillations that will cause departure from nucleate boiling, and will affect heat

transfer during blowdown after a LOCA. These increases
in power generation will significantly increase the
stress on the cladding and probably embrittle it such
that the clad would not be able to withstand the forces
during the blowdown phase of a loss-of-coolant accident.

2.9 Applicant and the Staff do not have enough information on fuel densification to justify granting a construction permit for the Waterford plant. The Staff and
Applicant have failed to perform parametric studies to
determine the rate and extent of densification for the
Waterford fuel, including a sensitivity analysis with
respect to creep-collapse time and differential pressure,
cladding temperature, cladding thickness, fission gas
production, initial flux, internal void volume changes,
and the solubility of the gases used to prepressurize the
fuel. Until such analyses and experiments have been completed, the Applicant should be required to perform all
accident analyses using the following conservative
assumptions (at the minimum): a maximum cladding temperature in a LOCA of 1800°F., plus the "Tentative Suggestions" contained in the Regulatory Staff's written
testimony of November 1972 in Docket No. Rm-50-1 concerning the present status of the Interim Acceptance Criteria. It should also be assumed "that axial gaps occur
immediately when the reactor is operated" (p. 70 of
Staff November 14, 1972 Technical Report) and "the gap
conductance should be evaluated assuming that cladding
creep does not contribute to gap closure" (op.cit.p.66).
On the other hand, one cannot rule out clad collapse
because of the high coolant pressure and high neutron
flux levels in the Waterford reactor:

> "Pressurization of fuel may not preclude
> collapse unless the amount of pressuriza-
> tion is determined from an analysis of
> operating conditions in the plant that
> will use the fuel." (op. cit. p. 47).

2.10 The Staff should require Applicant to supply it
with the computer cards or tapes containing the codes
used to calculate the results derived in these analyses
so that an independent verification can be performed by
a competent national laboratory or consultant.

2.11 The Staff has not evaluated the Combustion Engineering fuel densification analytical model to a degree
sufficient for the Waterford plant to be given a construction permit. The November 14, 1972 Technical Report
deals only with direct effects of fuel densification and
not secondary effects on such matters as ability to withstand mechanical effects on the reactor core during
blowdown in a LOCA, ability to retain a core geometry
amenable to cooling after a LOCA, and other important
safety considerations.

There must be a specific analysis made for the

Waterford core and reactor coolant system:

> "The effects of fuel densification cause
> the fuel rod to contain more stored
> energy, increase the linear heat genera-
> tion rate of the pellet, decrease the
> heat transfer capability of the fuel rod
> and create the potential for a local
> power spike in any fuel rod. To assess
> the safety implications of fuel densifi-
> cation, all of these effects must be
> evaluated for each reactor under all
> modes of reactor operation." (op.cit.
> p. 44; emphasis added).

2.12 Petitioner contends that the following General
Design Criterion, set forth in Appendix A to Part 50 of
the Commission's Regulations, is not met and will not be
met by the present design of Applicant's proposed plant,
for the reasons set forth below:

> Criterion 35--Emergency core cooling.
> A system to provide abundant emergency
> core cooling shall be provided. The
> system safety function shall be to trans-
> fer heat from the reactor core following
> any loss of coolant accident at a rate
> such that (1) fuel and clad damage that
> could interfere with continued effective
> core cooling is prevented and (2) clad
> metal-water reaction is limited to neg-
> ligible amounts.
>   Suitable redundancy in components
> and features, and suitable interconnect-
> ions, leak detection, isolation, and
> containment capabilities shall be pro-
> vided to assure that for onsite electri-
> cal power system operation (assuming off-
> site power is not available) and for
> offsite electrical power system opera-
> tion (assuming onsite power is not avail-
> able) the system safety function can be
> accomplished, assuming a single failure.

Petitioner further contends that the following
Interim Acceptance Criterion for Emergency Core Cooling
Systems for Light-Water Power Reactors is not met by
Applicant's proposed plant, for the reasons set forth
below:

> "On the basis of today's knowledge, the
> performance of the emergency core cool-
> ing system is judged to be acceptable
> if the calculated course of the loss-of-
> coolant accident is limited as follows:
> .....3. The clad temperature transient
> is terminated at a time when the core

geometry is still amenable to cooling,
and before the cladding is so embrittled
as to fail during or after quenching."

Applicant's proposed core design incorporates a
fuel lattice and grid spacers that will cause significant
pressure differentials between areas of the core to develop during a LOCA and cause radial flow during the injection of emergency core cooling water, thus bypassing
core hotspots and resulting in an irreversible core melt.
In addition, the design of the fuel lattice in Applicant's proposed core will cause significant Leidenfrost
migration, preventing the emergency core cooling water
from reaching hotspots and contributing to severe cladding embrittlement and core meltdown.

Petitioner further contends that the action of
Applicant's emergency core cooling system will accentuate
the adverse effects of a LOCA, because there will be extensive flow blockage in the core due to fuel rod swelling and bursting. There will be a flow blockage of
approximately 95 percent of the normal coolant flow
channels in approximately 80 percent of the core, which
will cause clad temperatures to rise into the autocata-
lytic region above 2800°F. within 15 seconds after the
onset of the loss-of-coolant accident. Even if the emergency core cooling system were to succeed in injecting
water into the core subsequent to this 15-second period,
irreversible core meltdown would have already begun, and
the injection of water would merely exacerbate the situation by fueling metal-water reactions.

This contention is not a challenge to the Interim
Acceptance Criteria, because it has been admitted by the
Regulatory Staff (11.4-7, Tr. 699, Docket No. RM-50-1)
that the flow blockage and embrittlement are not part of
the CE evaluation model for ECCS, so that in order to
determine whether Applicant's plant complies with the
Interim Acceptance Criteria, further calculations taking
flow blockage and embrittlement into consideration must
be made in order to ensure that the core retains a geometry amenable to cooling; in the case of the Waterford
core and ECCS, the latter criterion is not ensured and
therefore not met. Moreover, Chapter 20 of Exhibit 1113
in RM-50-1 (Testimony of the AEC Staff) notes a number
of parameters that must be considered to demonstrate
conformance with Interim Acceptance Criterion 3, none of
which have been calculated or demonstrated by the Applicant here.

2.13 Petitioner contends that the emergency core cooling
system for Applicant's plant is defective and cannot comply with the Interim Acceptance Criteria because it cannot overcome and mitigate the consequences of the rupture of several steam generator tubes during the course
of a LOCA. If several steam generator tubes rupture during the course of a LOCA, the emergency core cooling

water in Applicant's plant will be prevented from reflooding the core so as to avoid a fuel core meltdown.

This contention is not a challenge to the Interim
Acceptance Criteria for ECCS, since consideration of this
issue was explicitly ruled out of the ECCS Rule-Making
hearing by an Order of that Board:

> "This hearing will not concern itself
> with peripheral matters which are covered
> by other Commission criteria. These in-
> clude but are not limited to, such items
> as: postulated failure of steam generator
> tubes due to a LOCA." (February 29, 1972
> Board Order Re Schedule and Scope, Docket
> RM-50-1, pp. 8-9).

Thus this issue is ripe for litigation at the forthcoming
construction permit hearing.

Petitioner contends that such a rupture of the
steam generator tubes in the event of a LOCA is highly
probable, both because the steam generator tubes in Applicant's plant do not meet General Design Criterion 31
due to the traditional poor quality assurance of CE steam
generator tubes, and also because the feedwater deminer-
alizing in Applicant's plant is inadequate to ensure that
the steam generator tubes will not be subject to thin-
ning. Petition contends that the configuration of reactor coolant piping and steam generator tubing in Applicant's plant will cause waterhammer that will lead to
rupture of the steam generator tubes during the blowdown
phase of a LOCA, and thus prevent reflooding of the core.

2.14 Petitioner contends that in the event of a "hot
short," the motor operated isolation valve between the
accumulator tanks and the reactor coolant system will
fail in a closed position, thus preventing the emergency
core cooling water from being injected in the event of a
loss-of-coolant accident.

2.15 Petitioner contends that because Applicant's safety
injection system is not designed to ensure that the piping systems will be completely full of borated water at
all times, the rapid deceleration of this water when the
safety injection pumps are started will produce stresses
at pipe elbows and partially closed valves that will result in a rupture of the safety injection lines and prevent the emergency core cooling water from reaching the
reactor core.

2.16 Petitioner contends that no assurance exists to
guarantee the integrity of the safety injection lines
that are not protected by thermal sleeves where they connect to the reactor coolant system lines. The stress due
to thermal cycles of ECCS testing will weaken these lines

to the point that if waterhammer develops in the lines
during the ECC water injection, the lines will rupture
and prevent the water from reaching the reactor core.

2.17 Petitioner contends that the safety injection valve
control scheme that permits the reactor operator to mani-
pulate the valves so as to balance the flow through the
four injection lines after a loss-of-coolant accident is
so complicated and lacking in clear indications that
operator error is highly probable and will cause an exa-
cerbation of the accident rather than a mitigation of it.

2.18 Petitioner contends that it is unclear what the
capacity and pressure of the safety injection tanks will
be. At p. 6.2-2 of the Applicant's PSAR, it is stated
that the liquid volume will be 1100 ft.^{3} and the pressure
250 psig. The Staff Safety Evaluation says at p. 82 that
the liquid volume will be approximately 1500 ft.^{3} and the
pressure will be 600 psig. Regardless of which figure is
correct, Petitioner contends that there is insufficient
evidence that either of these pressures will be enough to
overcome the counterpressures resulting from steam binding in the core during injection.

2.19 Petitioner contends that Applicant has analyzed
only a small portion of the locations at which breaks can
occur in the reactor coolant pressure boundary, and there
is no assurance that the actual locations selected are
representative of the worst-case locations for this particular reactor coolant system.

2.20 Petitioner contends that the following General Design Criteria, set forth in Appendix A to Part 50 of the
Commission's Regulations, are not met and will not be met
by the present design of Applicant's plant, for reasons
set forth below:

> "Criterion 14--Reactor coolant pressure
> boundary. The reactor coolant pressure
> boundary shall be designed, fabricated,
> erected, and tested so as to have an ex-
> tremely low probability of abnormal
> leakage, of rapidly propagating failure,
> and of gross rupture."

> "Criterion 30--Quality of reactor coolant
> pressure boundary. Components which are
> part of the reactor coolant pressure
> boundary shall be designed, fabricated,
> erected, and tested to the highest qual-
> ity standards practical. Means shall be
> provided for detecting and, to the extent
> practical, identifying the location of
> the source of reactor coolant leakage."

"Criterion 31--Fracture prevention of reactor coolant pressure boundary. The
reactor coolant pressure boundary shall
be designed with sufficient margin to assure that when stressed under operating,
maintenance, testing, and postulated accident conditions (1) the boundary behaves
in a nonbrittle manner and (2) the probability of rapidly propagating fracture is
minimized. The design shall reflect consideration of service temperatures and
other conditions of the boundary material
under operating, maintenance, testing, and
postulated accident conditions and the uncertainties in determining (1) material
properties, (2) the effects of irradiation
on material properties, (3) residual,
steadystate and transient stresses, and
(4) size of flaws."

Petitioner contends that Applicant has failed to
analyze the most severe credible accident for this reactor, which is failure of the reactor pressure vessel.

The dimensions of the maximum credible accident are
set forth in Part 50 of the Commission's regulations,
Appendix A, where under definitions and explanations a
loss-of-coolant accident is defined as follows:

"Loss of coolant accidents. Loss of
coolant accidents mean those postulated
accidents that result from the loss of
reactor coolant at a rate in excess of
the capability of the reactor coolant
makeup system from breaks in the reactor
coolant pressure boundary, up to and
including a break equivalent in size to
the double-ended rupture of the largest
pipe of the reactor coolant system."

There is no basis for excluding a reactor pressure vessel
failure from the only definition of a loss-of-coolant
accident found in the regulations. The definition states
that a loss-of-coolant accident is a "break" in the reactor coolant pressure boundary equivalent in size to the
large double-ended rupture. The definiton does not state
that the break should be analyzed for a pipe break, but
rather any break which is equivalent in size to a break
of the largest pipe. Since the pressure vessel is part
of the reactor coolant pressure boundary, it is clear
that the analysis of a loss-of-coolant accident for Applicant's plant must include an analysis of a break
equivalent in size to the double-ended rupture of the hot
leg or any other portion of the reactor coolant pressure
boundary.

The above definition of a loss-of-coolant accident

does not exclude'pressure vessel failure but, rather,
includes pressure vessel failure. There is no other
regulation which prohibits analysis of reactor pressure
vessel failure and in line with the Commission's October
26, 1972 decision reversing the Atomic Safety and Licensing Appeal Board's September 27, 1972 decision in Indian
Point 2 (ALAB-71), the Applicant must analyze a rupture
of the reactor pressure vessel, and demonstrate why a
pressure vessel failure is not to be included in the analysis of a loss-of-coolant accident for this reactor.

Petitioner contends that a brittle fracture of this
reactor pressure vessel is a credible accident because of
stress corrosion, neutron irradiation embrittlement,
hydrogen embrittlement, shifts in the nil ductility transition temperature of the reactor pressure vessel, and
there is particular reason to believe that the thermal
shock during ECCS injection will cause a failure of this
vessel.

According to UKAEA reports of Irvine and Quirk, "The
Application of the Stress Concentration Theory of Fracture Mechanics to the Assessment of the Fast Fracture
Characteristics of Thick Walled Nuclear Pressure Vessels"
(August, 1971), a crack propagation in this vessel could
"only result in complete catastrophic destruction of the
reactor vessel." Monroe S. Wechsler's ORNL report entitled "The Radiation-Embrittlement of Pressure Vessel
Steels and the Safety of Nuclear Reactor Pressure Vessels"
indicates that a failure rate for U.S. reactor pressure
vessels, based on a recorded failure rate of British and
German non-nuclear pressure vessels, can be as high as
5×10^{-4} per vessel per year, which places this accident
close to the predicted loss-of-coolant accident rate of
1×10^{-3} per reactor per year postulated in the December
1972 draft of WASH-1250.

In addition, there are special considerations that
make it necessary that potential reactor pressure vessel
failure be considered for the Waterford plant. The vessel
has been fabricated by Combustion Engineering but does not
comply with the latest edition of Section III of the ASME
Boiler and Pressure Vessel Code. The quality control at
CE's Chattanooga facility is notoriously poor (see for
example Region II Compliance Reports CE 71/2 and CE 71/3).

Since Combustion Engineering strenuously opposes
subjecting its vessels to the rapid cooling that testing
of the safety injection system during hot functional tests
would engender, it is fairly obvious that despite their
protests to the contrary, CE does not believe that the
Waterford vessel would withstand a failure during operation of the emergency core cooling system.

2.21 Petitioner contends that the following General
Design Criteria, set forth in Appendix A to Part 50 of the
Commission's Regulations, are not met and will not be met

by the present design of Applicant's plant, for the reasons set forth below:

> "Criterion 16--Containment design. Reac-
> tor containment and associated systems
> shall be provided to establish an essen-
> tially leak-tight barrier against the un-
> controlled release of radioactivity to the
> environment and to assure that the contain-
> ment design conditions important to safety
> are not exceeded for as long as postulated
> accident conditions require."

> "Criterion 50--Containment design basis.
> The reactor containment structure, inclu-
> ding access openings, penetrations, and
> the containment heat removal system shall
> be designed so that the containment struc-
> ture and its internal compartments can
> accomodate, without exceeding the design
> leakage rate and, with sufficient margin,
> the calculated pressure and temperature
> conditions resulting from any loss-of-
> coolant accident. This margin shall re-
> flect consideration of (1) the effects of
> potential energy sources which have not
> been included in the determination of the
> peak conditions, such as energy in steam
> generators and energy from metal-water and
> other chemical reactions that may result
> from degraded emergency core cooling func-
> tioning, (2) the limited experience and
> experimental data available for defining
> accident phenomena and containment res-
> ponses, and (3) the conservatism of the
> calculational model and input parameters."

The containment pressure transient peak in the event
of a large-scale loss-of-coolant accident will be far in
excess of the design limit for the containment vessel
because significant energy sources have been overlooked
in the transient analyses done by the Applicant and Staff.

Because the amount of decay heat in the core will be
greater than the Applicant has assumed in his analysis of
a loss-of-coolant accident, the pressure transient in the
containment will be correspondingly higher. The standard
used, ANS-5.1, used heating rates in calculating the decay
heat that ignored such key factors as neutron absorption,
coupling systematics, and several generations of coupled
progeny. A best estimate of heat generated by accumulated
fission products during the first 1000 seconds following
a loss-of-coolant would be approximately 30 percent in
excess of ANS-5.1, and in keeping with the AEC's policy
of adding a 20 percent conservatism to the best available
estimate of the rate of decay heat generation, the proper
calculation for the Waterford reactor should be ANS-5.1

plus 56 percent.

2.22   Another significant source of energy adding to the
containment pressure transient in the event of a LOCA at
full power is safety injection water carried into the
steam generators and superheated from the secondary side
of the plant.   This additional energy source will raise
the containment pressure transient beyond the yield point
for the containment vessel.

2.23   A further significant energy source that has not
been considered in the analysis of the containment pressure transient is the stored thermal energy in the fuel
rods which will be greater than the amount assumed in
the Applicant's analysis.   First, the Applicant has
used a value of 97 watts per centimeter for the integral
of UO_2 conductivity from 32°F. to 3632°F.   Because of the
great indeterminacy of present assumptions for calculating stored thermal energy in a reactor core, it is only
prudent to use the more conservative value of 81 watts
per centimeter in analyses of the Waterford core.
Second, the Applicant has assumed diametral gap closure
between the fuel pellets and the cladding during operation of the Waterford reactor, despite Applicant's knowledge of the radial shrinkage of the fuel pellets due to
densification and the retardation of clad creepdown onto
the pellet due to initial pre-pressurization of the
Waterford fuel.   Third, Applicant has assumed that there
is uniform radial heat flow between the pellets and the
cladding, which is a highly unrealistic assumption in
view of asymmetries in pellet stack geometry that have
been observed in other operating reactors as the result
of fuel cracking.   Finally, Applicant's analysis under-
estimates the reduction of gap conductivity due to build-
up of fission product gases, so that a lower steady-
state gap h value should be used.   In his analysis, the
Applicant has failed to make a sensitivity analysis of
these parameters and generally uses gap conductance
values for which there is no adequate experimental or
analytical basis.

2.24   Petitioner further contends that in the event of
a main stream line break inside the containment upstream
of the flow limiting device, the pressure transient
inside the containment will exceed 52 psig, well over the
containment design pressure of 44 psig.   This will cause
the containment vessel to rupture and there is a reasonable probability that sections of falling containment
vessel plating will cause a LOCA.   This will result in a
massive release of radioactivity to the environment
through the breached containment.

2.25   Conversely, there is a significant probability that
a LOCA with a break occurring near the steam generator
will generate pipe whip and missiles that will sever the
steam generator supports, thus causing the steam generator to drop vertically and cause a break in the main

steam line inside the containment. The containment pressure transient from the LOCA, combined with the steam line break pressure transient, will far exceed the containment design limit and cause it to rupture.

2.26 Petitioner contends that the Applicant and the Staff have not made analyses of containment pressure-time responses out to a minimum of two hours post-LOCA for a spectrum of reactor coolant system breaks below 1.14 ft.^{2} and have no assurance that these do not represent the worst accident.

2.27 Petitioner contends that Applicant's criteria for physical separation of electrical cables for redundant safeguards systems do not meet the intent of General Design Criterion 24 or IEEE-279. Petitioner contends that at no point past the control room should any redundant cables be closer than five feet vertically and fifteen feet horizontally.

2.28 Petitioner contends that Applicant's proposed system of indicating bypassed or inoperative emergency safeguard trains is inadequate. If Applicant intends to operate this plant with one emergency safeguard train inoperative due to maintenance or repair, then there should be a total of three separate redundant safeguard trains (including three emergency diesel generators) so that a single failure in one of the operative safegaurd trains does not leave the plant with no safeguard system at all.

2.29 Petitioner contends that in the event of complete blockage of one core support plate flow hole, the departure from nuclear boiling ratio will be less than 1.0 at design power. If more than one flow hole is blocked, there will be widespread fuel rod melting and rupture.

2.30 Petitioner contends that Applicant's analyses for potential transportation accidents on the Mississippi River do not represent a complete listing. Applicant's Amendment 26 of November 1972 ignores two accidents, both of which would render the nuclear plant subject to severe accident conditions. One is the explosion of a barge fully loaded with liquid natural gas. The other is the rupture of a barge containing nerve gas.

2.31 The Staff should be required to make an analysis of the consequences of a direct impact on the containment building or the auxiliary building of a fully-loaded Boeing 747 aircraft. Such aircraft are scheduled to begin using New Orleans International Airport in April of 1973, and during the 40-year proposed life of Applicant's plant, even larger aircraft can be expected to be built and operated from the vicinity of the plant. Moisant Field and the Baton Rouge Airport are to be replaced by one regional airport that will be located within a few miles of Applicant's plant, and unless it can be shown that the

containment and safety-related equipment can be protected
against the impact of a 747 or its equivalent, the construction permit for this plant at the present site should
be denied.

2.32 Petitioner contends that the emergency plans in the
event of an accident releasing gross amounts of radiation
(Preliminary Safety Analysis Report, Vol. 3, Appendix 12)
are worthless. They are completely vague and inadequate.
For example, there is no discussion of the fact that there
are only two highways leading east out of New Orleans
away from the proposed plant. Petitioner further contends
that local officials have no experience or expertise in
evacuating this area.

2.33 Petitioner contends that the following General Design Criterion, set forth in Appendix A to Part 50 of the
Commission's Regulations, is not met and will not be met
by the present design of Applicant's plant, and thus the
issue is ripe at the construction permit hearing:

> "Criterion 60--Control of releases of
> radioactivity to the environment.
> The facility design shall include those
> means necessary to maintain control over
> the plant radioactive effluents, whether
> gaseous, liquid or solid, Appropriate
> holdup capacity shall be provided for re-
> tention of gaseous, liquid or solid efflu-
> ents, particularly where unfavorable en-
> vironmental conditions can be expected to
> require operational limitations upon the
> release of radioactive effluents to the
> environment. In all cases, the design for
> radioactivity control shall be justified
> on the basis of 10 CFR 20 requirements for
> normal operations and for any transient
> situation that might reasonably be anti-
> cipated to occur."

The analysis by the Applicant of the radiation doses
to the public from this proposed Plant are inadequate
because it contains no present estimated offsite radiation doses for operation with leaking fuel elements.
Since the operating histories of pressurized water reactors have shown that leaking fuel elements exist during
normal operation, there should be estimates in the PSAR
based on discharges from operating pressurized water
reactor plants, and indicate the potential population
doses from the operation of the Waterford Unit 3 considering leaking fuel conditions. There should also be a
more definitive statement of the risks to the public
resulting from the aforesaid potential offsite doses.

2.34 Applicant's PSAR indicates no commitment by the
Applicant to use the proposed Plant's radioactive treatment system to the full extent of its capacity and to

maintain radioactive waste effluents at as low a level as practicable, and the analyses of all radionuclides proposed to be released as effluents from the proposed Plant are incomplete and inadequate in that they do not adequately state internal and external offsite dose rates measured under both worst-case conditions and conditions which have occurred in the operation of other pressurized water reactors.

In light of the fact that the Atomic Energy Commission requires radioactive emissions to be as low as practicable, the Applicant's radioactive waste systems described in the PSAR are inadequate because they do not provide for essentially zero radioactive waste disposal units despite the fact that such systems are commercially available and are being installed on pressurized water reactors throughout the United States.

2.35 In view of Applicant's very poor record of pollution control at its other plants, which must be taken into consideration when considering the qualifications of the Applicant to construct and eventually operate Waterford Unit 3, Petitioner considers it likely that Applicant will exceed the radioactive limits imposed by the Commission for normal releases and not report them. Since the Commission's Division of Regulatory Operations makes no independent check of radioactive releases, but merely inspects Applicant's records, there is no assurance that Applicant will comply with the limits set forth in Part 20 of the Commission's Rules and Regulations.

2.36 Petitioner contends that analytical techniques alone are inadequate for reliable failure predictions. In particular, reliability estimates substantiated by failure tests should be available for each critical component in the plant operating system. These data should then be used to establish a "reliability tree" for both subsystem and system performance. This has not been done in the Applicant's Preliminary Safety Analysis Report. Furthermore subsystem results of each system under operating conditions of dynamic pressure, temperature and humidity should be reported. If these test results are obtained through scale model testing then the validity of these data should be demonstrated by correlation with tests on similar full scale systems. Such systems have not been reported in the Applicant's Preliminary Safety Analysis Report. Petitioner contends that such reliability testing is common practice in the aerospace industry in particular on manned space flight programs such as Gemini, Saturn 1B, Saturn V and Apollo and that the precautions taken to protect the lives of entire geographic regions should be at least as great as precautions to protect the lives of two or three flight crew members, yet Applicant has taken no such precautions.

2.37 Petitioner contends that in view of the indeterminacies of the design of the Waterford reactor, the lack

of experimental data to support the conclusion that engineered safeguard systems will operate as designed, and the
proximity of the site to the very large population of
New Orleans, to construct this reactor at this site would
be a direct violation of 10 C.F.R. Part 100:

> "The site criteria contained in this part
> apply primarily to reactors of a general
> type and design on which experience has
> been developed, but can also be applied
> to other reactor types. In particular,
> for reactors that are novel in design
> and unproven as prototypes or pilot plants,
> it is expected that these basic criteria
> will be applied in a manner that takes into
> account the lack of experience. In the
> application of these criteria which are
> deliberately flexible, the safeguards pro-
> vided--either site isolation or engineered
> features--should reflect the lack of cer-
> tainty that only experience can provide."
> ($100.2(b)).

Petitioner contends that the Waterford reactor is novel in
design and unproven as a prototype. The ability of its
emergency core cooling system to control a loss-of-coolant
accident has never been experimentally tested under scale
or even half-scale conditions. In addition to the above,
10 C.F.R. Part 100 also states:

> "Where very large cities are involved, a
> greater distance may be necessary because
> of total integrated population dose con-
> sideration." ($100.11(a)(3)).

> "For further guidance in developing the
> exclusion area, the low population zone,
> and the population center distance, refer-
> ence is made to Technical Information Doc-
> ument 14844."   (Footnote to Part 100.)

TID-14844 indicates (at p. 33) that the population center
distance for a reactor the size of Waterford should be
34.0 miles. The city of New Orleans is, according to the
Staff Environmental Statement, about 25 miles from the
site.

                    *   *   *

     In addition to the specific contentions made above,
Petitioner believes that Applicant's plant can be shown
to have failed to comply with other General Design Criteria for reasons which will be set forth when information
and documents not available in advance of the filing of
this petition to intervene, such as Combustion Engineering
so-called proprietary reports are produced in accordance
with pre-hearing discovery.

III

FIRST PRELIMINARY
STATEMENT OF CONTENTIONS WITH RESPECT
TO SIGNIFICANT ADVERSE EFFECTS OF THE
PROPOSED FACILITY ON THE ENVIRONMENT
AND COMPLIANCE WITH THE REQUIREMENTS
OF THE NATIONAL ENVIRONMENTAL POLICY ACT

Petitioner contests a positive finding by the Board
on the issue whether, in accordance with the requirements
of Appendix D of 10 C.F.R. Part 50, the construction permit should be issued. Petitioner additionally contests
any positive finding by the Board that the requirements
of section 102(2)(C) and (D) of the National Environmental Policy Act of 1969 and Appendix D of 10 C.F.R. Part
50 have been complied with in this proceeding. Petitioner contends that this Board must independently consider the final balance of the conflicting factors set
forth below and reach a determination that this construction permit should be denied.

3.1 Petitioner contends that in view of the nuclear
safety indeterminacies set forth in Contentions 2.1ff.,
all of the cost benefit calculations performed by the
Applicant and Staff for this plant have no meaning.
Petitioner contends that this plant, if built, could not
be safely operated at more than 80% of its rated power
level of 1165 MWe. Although there is no operating experience for reactors of this size at the present time,
reliability figures for reactors in the 500-800 MWe class
indicate a plant availability factor of approximately
60%. Assuming that this availability factor could be
raised to 70% by the time this plant were built, taking
into account the 80% power level would mean that over a
30 year period this plant would produce 5.74×10^9 kW-hr.
Using the Staff's estimated total present worth of this
plant (from Table XI-3 of the Draft Environmental Statement) of $579,000,000, this would mean the cost of the
electricity generated would be $1.1008710801/kW-hr. This
is 20.93% greater than the cost of electricity that would
be generated from a coal-fired 1165 MWe plant operating
at an 80% availability over 30 years: 8.2×10^9 kW-hr
divided into the Staff's estimated total present worth
for a coal-fired plant of $684,000,000 = $0.0834146341/
kW-hr.

3.2 Petitioner contends that the Staff's figure of
$579,000,000 total present worth for this plant is both
erroneously calculated and unrealistic. The Staff has
capitalized the 21.7 million dollars of annual operating
costs at a discount rate of 8.75% over a period of 30
years and arrived at a figure of $229,000,000. This is
an incorrect calculation: the correct figure is
$268,743,335.40, an amount 17.4% greater. Petitioner
contends that even this corrected figure is unrealistic,
since uranium fuel shortages being predicted by the AEC's

Division of Fuel and Materials make an annual 11% increase
in nuclear fuel price a realistic figure to use. Factor-
ing in this value for fuel, but keeping the Staff's value
for labor, maintenance and materials and insurance, gives
a capitalized annual operating cost over 30 years of
$431,614,406. This is 88.5% greater than the Staff's fig-
ure, and is far more realistic.

3.3 Petitioner contends that the Staff's estimated capital cost of $350,000,000 for this plant is erroneous and
too low. Based on the Staff's assumption that the plant
can operate at 1165 MWe, this works out to a $300/kW capi-
tal cost, considerably below the current contractual figures not only from CE but from Westinghouse and Babcock
and Wilcox. Petitioner contends that a more realistic
figure would be 30% greater, or $455,000,000, in view of
inflation and unresolved design problems, such as containment redesign, etc.

3.4 Petitioner further contends that the Draft Environmental Statement ignores in its calculation of the plant's
cost the inevitable costs that will result from licensing
delays. Applicant, according to a Federal Power Commission document of August 1972, estimates that a one year
delay of the Waterford plant will cost an additional capital amount of $27,845,000. Because of Board recesses,
Staff difficulties in completing necessary documents on an
expeditious schedule, Staff difficulties in finding and
producing documents sought on discovery, licensing proceedings have been taking reasonably long times to complete, both for construction permits and for operating
licenses. The Midland construction permit proceeding ran
more than two years before an initial decision was issued
by the Board, and the Shoreham proceeding has taken even
longer. It is perhaps not unrealistic to assume that a
construction permit hearing in the Waterford docket may
also take two years before a final order is issued, which
represents an additional capital cost to the plant (assuming Applicant's estimate is not fictitious) of $55,690,000.
Assuming two additional years beyond the initial decision
for judicial reversal and remand for de novo hearings,
the total construction permit delay would amount to $111,
380,000. Petitioner contends that it is also highly
likely that there will be a contested proceeding at the
operating license stage. Based on representations by
Applicant's attorneys that each day's delay of a plant
this size represents an additional cost of approximately
$125,000, this additional cost could be sizable. For ex-
ample, the operating license hearing in the case of Point
Beach Unit 2, a case Applicant's attorney is intimately
familiar with, has gone on for nearly two years without
issuance of a full power license. A two year delay in
securing an operating license would add $91,250,000 to the
capital cost of this plant (assuming that the $125,000
figure is also not a fiction). The total cost of these
delays adds up to $202,630,000, a sizable figure, but it
has been ignored by the Applicant and the Staff in their

cost-benefit analyses and comparisons with alternatives.

3.5 Petitioner further contends that Applicant's estimated cost of decommissioning the Waterford plant for
$1,900,000 is totally unrealistic. Assuming that a decom-
missioning at least as thorough as that being performed
at the Elk River plant is done at Waterford, the estimated
decommissioning cost will be approximately $45,000,000.
Petitioner contends that this figure must be incorporated
into the cost-benefit calculations for the Waterford
plant.

3.6 Petitioner contends that when all of the above costs
are put together in a realistic way, the Board cannot
possibly find in favor of a nuclear plant instead of a
coal-fired plant. Assuming a basic $455,000,000 capital
cost for the plant, $202,630,000 cost of licensing delays,
capitalized annual fuel and operating costs of $431,614,
406, and an 80% power level and 70% availability factor
over 30 years, plus a $45,000,000 decommissioning cost,
the electricity that would be generated by this nuclear
plant, if built, would cost $0.1976035551/kW-hr. or 136.9%
more than the electricity to be generated from an equivalent sized coal-fired plant.

3.7 Petitioner contends the $11,000,000 additional incre-
mental cost of a closed-cycle cooling pond cited in Table
XI-3 of the Draft Environmental Statement bears no reality
to the actual cost of constructing and operating such a
pond. Assuming reasonable diking costs and pumping factors, a 1500-acre cooling pond can be constructed and
operated for an incremental cost over open-cycle discharge
into the Mississippi River for less than $4.7 million.
This is not a high expense compared with the risks to
aquatic biota and the New Orleans drinking water supply
engendered by Applicant's proposed discharge into the
river.

3.8 Petitioner contends that the Staff's Environmental
Statement is insufficient because it fails to analyze the
environmental impact of accidents involving a breach of
containment and deposition of fission products in the
range from 2×10^7 Ci to 1×10^9 Ci. Presumably the Staff
is taking guidance from the September 1, 1971 Annex to
Appendix D which says of such accidents:

> "Their consequences could be severe.
> However, the probability of their occur-
> rence is so small that their environmen-
> tal risk is extremely low. Defense in
> depth (multiple physical barriers), qual-
> ity assurance for design, manufacture, and
> operation, continued surveillance and test-
> ing, and conservative design are all ap-
> plied to provide and maintain the required
> high degree of assurance that potential

> accidents in this class are, and will re-
> main, sufficiently remote in probability
> that the environmental risk is extremely
> low. For these reasons, it is not neces-   •
> sary to discuss such events in applicants'
> Environmental Reports."

Petitioner contends that this Annex has not been adopted
as a Commission regulation and therefore has no force.
Petitioner further contends that the language of it clearly applies only to applicant's Environmental Reports, and
does not absolve the Staff from fulfilling its duties
under the National Environmental Policy Act. Petitioner
furthermore challenges the truth of the quotation set
forth above. The defense in depth concept has never been
demonstrated to have any basis in fact, and the assertions
contained within the quotation concerning the low probability of major accidents are purely speculative and totally lacking in any evidentiary basis. Petitioner contends that the Commission has admitted its lack of knowledge by commissioning Professor Norman Rasmussen of MIT
to make a probability assessment of major reactor accidents. Petitioner notes that in its August 4, 1972 letter
to the Joint Committee on Atomic Energy, the Commission
said:

> "The present state of knowledge probably
> will not permit a complete analysis of
> low-probability accidents in nuclear
> plants with the precision that would be
> desirable."

> "It may turn out after further research
> that it is impossible to make such assess-
> ments with sufficient precision to be use-
> ful. In this event a longer term effort
> on the probabilities of accident-causing
> events would be required."

Petitioner contends that the probability of a Class 9
accident is in the range of 1×10^{-2} per reactor per year
to 1×10^{-3} per reactor per year. Therefore the Staff
should include environmental impact analyses of this class
of accidents in its Environmental Statement, and the failure to do so is a violation of the National Environmental
Policy Act.

3.9 Petitioner contends that Applicant's discharge to the
Mississippi River will affect an area far larger than contained in Applicant's analysis, which is grossly underestimated due to Applicant's reliance on the model of thermal plume behavior put forward by Pritchard and Carter.
Pritchard's model is excessively simplistic and non-con-
servative. The model is overly sensitive to a few key
parameters such as the inverse-spreading rate, the measured ambient temperature, and the vertical entrainment.
It is a highly intuitive model that simply is unverified

by quality field data, and its applicability to surface
discharge situations such as Applicant's for a large range
of initial Froude numbers is quite questionable.

Pritchard's model does not handle the problem of differentiating the heat lost at the surface to the atmosphere and the heat retained in the deeper layers of the
river. While the assumption made by Pritchard may possibly be conservative with respect to the area within the
low temperature isotherms, it ignores the cumulative effects of the heat on benthic organisms and the lower layers of the river.

Pritchard's model is highly intuitive and only partially approximate with respect to the vertical spread of
the thermal plume. It does not include a three-dimension-
al model or include a term for diffusion or vertical entrainment that would give a solution for the vertical
thickness of the plume. Any accurate model of the vertical spread of a thermal plume must include the effects
of vertical shear in the velocity field and vertical density gradients that control vertical entrainment, such as
dependence on the Richardson number or some measure of
the vertical stability. Pritchard's model contains an
arbitrary choice of a constant mixed layer and an assumption that there is a critical depth of mixing. Pritchard
has no idea of how great a vertical region of the river
will be affected by the heat from Applicant's plant.

Pritchard's model also assumes that the river bottom
has no effect other than influencing the arbitrary choice
of a plume depth (i.e., one cannot assume a ten-foot
plume depth if the bottom is only eight feet down). Most
models of thermal plumes take this into account, because
the specific value of the bottom slope in inhibiting vertical mixing of the plume can be extremely important,
particularly in the sort of waters that lie off Applicant's plant.

Pritchard's model completely neglects buoyancy effects. There is no dependence in the model of the temperature distribution on the initial Froude number. The
model uses an integral technique in which the plume velocity and excess temperature above ambient are assumed to
have a "top-hat" distribution laterally and with depth at
each longitudinal position. In reality, the lateral temperature distribution at a given longitudinal position
will be a Gaussian bell shape. The vertical temperature
distribution will be J-shaped. In the case of Waterford
Unit 3, the additional lateral spreading due to buoyant
convective motions will distort the simple linear spread
assumed by Pritchard's model.

Pritchard's model is vastly oversimplified with respect to the transition zone between the region of domin-
ance of momentum jet entrainment and natural ambient mixing, which fails to handle the changeover from the plume
being controlled by its own velocity field to the plume
being controlled by natural mixing processes. Pritchard
arbitrarily assumes that the transition zone is fixed,

whereas in reality there is a transition from inertially
dominated flow to gravity dominated flow.

3.10 Petitioner contends that the plume from Waterford
Unit 3, taken together with the plume of Waterford Units
1 and 2 and Little Gypsy Steam Electric Station across
the Mississippi River from Waterford Unit 3, will cover
100% of the entire river to a depth of over 10 feet at
the 10°F. isotherm, and thus violate the zone of passage
criteria recently adopted by the U.S. Environmental Protection Agency.

3.11 Petitioner contends that Applicant's biological
preoperational monitoring program is inadequate and insufficient to provide a meaningful baseline for later
comparison in order to detect the magnitude of adverse
environmental effects from the operation of Applicant's
plant. It is critically important in any analysis of significant adverse effect to ascertain in the aquatic area
affected inventory of animals by genus and species.
Without such an inventory, it is impossible to conclude
whether there has been or will be a significant adverse
effect and any conclusions with respect to the absence of
significant adverse effect will be unsupported and therefore arbitrary. The inventory to be performed by the
Applicant in the area of this plant is cursory. Thus, no
meaningful baseline can be developed by the Applicant
which would serve to ascertain the magnitude of later adverse effects. Petitioners contend that Applicant's preoperational environmental monitoring program fails to include a comprehensive study of the fish present in the
area. Such an inventory and analysis of fish species
and their habits must precede any determination of significant adverse effects.

3.12 Petitioner contends that the Environmental Report
is inadequate to predict the effects of the Waterford
plant on the environment, particularly with respect to
aquatic ecology. For example, Appendix C prepared by
Ebasco Services indicates that 49 species of fish were
identified in the vicinity of the proposed Waterford site
(Luling) and that 17 species of fish were identified immediately at the Waterford site. These fish species are
summarized in Exhibit 11 and Exhibit 14 of Appendix C.
Appendix F of this report includes a very limited synopsis of various studies of thermal effects on fish. It
is significant to note that of the studies reported in
Appendix F only two species were identical to species reported at the Waterford site, namely the channel catfish
and hogchokers. Further, in the instances of these two
species both studies (Allen and Strawn, Heat Tolerance
of Channel Catfish, 1967, and Mihursky, Patuxent Thermal
Studies, 1969) indicated deleterious effects resulting
from heated effluents on these two species. The remaining data on fish in Appendix F are irrelevant to the
Waterford site. One would conclude from these data that
those species on which studies have been performed that

exist at the Waterford site will be endangered. It would
appear that the following quotation from paragraph 2,
page V-A-1 is either erroneous or not substantiated by
data:

> "However, studies of other power plants
> located on rivers and actual experience
> on the Mississippi River have shown no
> significant adverse environmental effects
> resulting from the discharge of condenser
> cooling water."

There is no substantiation for these conclusions,
and such statements, given the data presented, are con-
temptuous to both the Board and the public. Furthermore
the data reported in Appendix C indicate that inadequate
information is available on phytoplankton at the Waterford site (paragraph 3, page 22, Appendix C), therefore
rendering any conclusions on effects on phytoplankton invalid. Petitioner contends that, at a minimum, the Applicant's Environmental Report relative to aquatic ecology should:

(1) fully identify species of aquatic life in the
vicinity of the site and, the effects of thermal gradients on those specific species;

(2) give an exact prediction of the isotherms resulting from plant operation (Appendix E) for worst case conditions;

(3) relate these isotherms to <u>maximum</u> water temperatures over the season;

(4) predict the effect on the population of each
species for each thermal gradient as a function of the
river's seasonal temperature based on experimental data;

(5) propose a thermal monitoring program and an aquatic kill monitoring program after the plant is in operation;

(6) specify explicitly what steps will be taken, such
as reduced power output, plant shutdown, etc., in the
event that the deleterious effects exceed predictions.
For example, during the month of August when water temperature reaches 90° F, Applicant should state what steps,
if any, will be taken to reduce power output such that
thermal gradients will not exceed some specified amount.

Petitioner contends that steps (1) and (2) above
have only been partially completed and that steps (3),
(4), (5), and (6) have not even been discussed. Petitioner contends that with respect to aquatic ecology the Applicant's Environmental Report is totally inadequate.

3.13 Petitioner contends that the operation of Appli-

cant's plant with an open-cycle cooling system will have
a significant adverse effect on the quality of water in
the Mississippi River, and that no decision on a construction permit for this plant can fail to consider the present state of pollution of the river, its biological
characteristics, and the synergistic effects of the heat
proposed to be discharged from Applicant's plant together
with pollutants being discharged into the river by sources
other than Applicant's plant.

3.14 An indirect lethal effect of the thermal discharge
from Applicant's plant will be to increase the metabolic
rates of the aquatic biota, particularly fish, which increases the speed at which toxic substances affect the
organisms, and also can reduce the threshhold levels at
which the toxic substances can affect the organisms. Mercury and zinc are particularly influenced by temperature
increases, and many organic diseases also increase as a
result of elevated temperatures. This will represent a
significant adverse effect on the environment from the
operation of Applicant's plant with an open-cycle cooling
system.

3.15 An additional indirect lethal effect of the thermal
discharge from Applicant's plant will be the breakdown
of the social communications between species and intra-
species due to elevated temperatures. The more complex
the social behavior of a species, the earlier the effects
of the temperature on its predatory and reproductive behavior, with the subtle long-range result that the species
is eliminated, not directly but indirectly over a period
of several generations as its niche in the eco-system is
endangered and its reproduction reaches a state of collapse. While the research results along these lines are
meager, they tend to confirm that the game fish are the
first to suffer this fate. This will represent a significant adverse effect on the environment from the operation of Applicant's plant with an open-cycle cooling system.

3.16 During the summertime, the discharge from Applicant's proposed plant will significantly increase the population of blue-green algae in the Mississippi River.
Blue-green algae have distinctive and obnoxious odors,
and when a crop of such algae is driven by the wind onto
the river bank, it will severely limit the use of the
river bank for recreation. In addition, blue-green algae
contain chemicals that produce an obnoxious taste, and
these chemicals cannot be separated out of the drinking
water at any of the filtration plants downstream from Applicant's plant, such as the two St. Charles Parish Water
Work District plants 4.5 and 9.0 miles downstream, and
the two Jefferson Parish Water Works District plants 24.2
and 30.5 miles downstream, as well as the Carrollton Plant
of the New Orleans Sewage and Water Board 24.9 miles downstream. If Applicant's plant is permitted to be constructed and operated with an open-cycle cooling system util-

izing once-through cooling, the above drinking water systems will be rendered unfit for human consumption during
the summer months.

3.17 Petitioner contends that Applicant has used incorrect data to calculate zooplankton mortality for the proposed plant. Applicant relies on a Ginna plant study
which purportedly found a 2-3% plankton mortality through
the "pump condenser system" (Applicant's Supplement No. 3,
p. V-A-3). A more reliable study by the Grosse Isle Laboratory of the Environmental Protection Agency of the Big
Rock nuclear plant indicated that plankton mortality from
passage through the main circulating water pumps was 58%
and nearly 100% from passage through the service water
pumps.

3.18 Petitioner contends that the use of terms 'dilution'
and 'dispersion' are misleading. "...the lower Mississippi River rapidly dilutes and disperses the discharged
effluent by a factor of about 100 during most of the
year." (Draft Environmental Statement, V-24). It is
misleading in that 'dilution' and 'dispersion' do not
mean there are no biological consequences. ("...many
long-lived pollutants have ultimately biological effects
no matter how thoroughly diluted..." Julian McCaull,
Environment, September, 1972).

3.19 Petitioner contends that Applicant's analysis of
the environmental impact of the 23.5 mile 230 kv transmission line required by Waterford Unit 3 is erroneous:

> "It is estimated that only about 20% of
> the line will traverse timbered swamp, and
> the remainder will traverse uninhabited
> marsh." (Supplement 1, QE.6-1)

This statement perfectly reflects Applicant's state of
biological ignorance. This marsh is inhabited by many
biota and has been for centuries.

3.20 Petitioner contends that the radiological monitoring and surveillance programs planned by the Applicant
are inadequate to protect the health and safety of the
public, in that there are too few monitoring sites, the
monitoring at such insufficient sites is not frequent e-
nough to be meaningful and informative, and the monitoring proposed will not determine the concentrations and
biological magnification of major radionuclides in animal
and plant life and terrestrial and aquatic food chains in
the vicinity of the plant. There is no assurance in the
proposed monitoring and surveillance program that all of
the radionuclides of significance to terrestrial, aquatic
and human life will be regularly monitored in a manner
sufficient to detect hazards before they have already had
a significant deleterious effect on such life.

3.21 Petitioner contends that the radiological monitor-

ing program planned by the Applicant is inadequate in that
there is no connection between the various elements of the
aquatic food chain that will be sampled, and therefore
the data will be essentially meaningless. Petitioners
contend that any valid sampling would involve a determination of the actual elements of a particular food chain
(phytoplankton, benthos, zooplankton, larvae, juvenile
and adult fish) so that sampling at each of its stages
could determine the build-up of radioactivity in a meaningful way. Petitioner further contends that at least
half a dozen such aquatic food chains and half a dozen
comparative terrestrial food chains be sampled in order
to determine the radiological effects of the operation of
Applicant's plant. Unless such integral sampling is conducted, any conclusion as to the absence of adverse environmental effect would be arbitrary.

3.22 Petitioner contends that the implications of Applicant's environmental monitoring program are not adequately discussed. For example, Applicant states that levels
of I-131 will be monitored in milk, grass, and leafy garden vegetables for 2 years prior to the operation of the
plant as well as during plant operation (Environmental
Report, V-E and table V-E-1). Applicant does not state
the consequences of this data except to state that

> "The post operational environmental radio-
> activity monitoring program will be modi-
> fied if sample results indicate that the
> average quarterly plant discharge of radio-
> activity is in excess of the values speci-
> fied in the Atomic Energy Commission's
> proposed Appendix 1, Section IV, to 10 CFR
> 50." (Environmental Report, V-E-7).

Applicant further states

> "However, if any such effects [harmful or
> lasting environmental] were for some reason
> to become evident, as may be revealed by
> the monitoring programs mentioned in Sec-
> tion V-E of this report, steps will be taken
> to correct the situation." (Environmental
> Report, VII-1).

There is no indication at what level the plant would be
shut down, and Petitioner contends this is inadequate.

Dr. Ernest Sternglass, of the University of Pittsburgh and author of Low-Level Radiation cites measurements
of I-131 in milk in states and cities in the United States
as reported in Radiological Health Data and Reports,
August 1971. Measurements for 90% of the listings (for
every state and a number of cities) showed readings of 0
for both the monthly and yearly averages. A report prepared for Duquesne Light Co. prepared in August, 1972,
measured levels of I-131 in dairies near the U.S. Navy's

Shippingport nuclear reactor and found concentrations of
I-131 averaging 20 pCi/liter. (Pittsburgh Fair Witness,
December 15, 1972, page 8). Applicant's Table V-B-1
(Environmental Report V-B-5 Supplement No. 3) shows radiation doses to a child and adult's thyroid will increase
as a result of normal plant operation. Petitioner contends that any increase in I-131 is unacceptable. "It
can be stated unequivocally, and without fear of contra-
diction that no amount of radiation has ever been proved
to be safe." (Poisoned Power, Dr. John W. Gofman and
Dr. Arthur R. Tamplin, Rodale Press, 1971).

3.23 Petitioner contends that the environmental monitors
should be independent of management of Applicant's plant,
since to do otherwise is a conflict of interest. Applicant has made no provision for independent monitoring.
When the Monticello Nuclear Generating Plant of Northern
States Power released radioactivity into the Mississippi
River in July and November, 1971, management did not inform the Twin Cities Water Board until too late to stop
it from entering the city water supply (Petition for the
Intervenors in the Matter of Northern States Power Company, Docket No. 50-263), and Petitioner contends that
without independent monitoring this will happen to the
City of New Orleans, which gets its drinking water from
the Mississippi downstream of the proposed plant.

3.24 Petitioner contends that the employees at the Union
Carbide plant near Hahnville will receive dangerously
high doses in the event of a slug release of radioactive
liquid wastes from Applicant's plant, since the plant's
drinking water intake is only 1.6 miles from Applicant's
outfall. Applicant has no procedures planned to detect
such accidental releases or to warn Union Carbide of their
occurrence.

3.25 Petitioner contends that Applicant has done no studies of present rates of cancer, leukemia and genetic diseases among the population in a 100 miles radius of the
proposed plant. Thus it will be impossible to document
any increase in these diseases as a result of proposed
plant operation. Petitioner further contends that Applicant has given no consideration to the necessity of a
local control group involving a simultaneous and similar
monitoring in an area free from any nuclear power plant's
radiation.

3.26 Petitioner contends that the Staff has used totally
erroneous concentration factors in calculating the radiological effects of the plant's discharge on aquatic biota.
For example, the Staff uses a concentration factor of 30
for cesium-137 in fish; the literature is filled with instances of cesium bioaccumulation in fish on the order of
10,000 and the Public Health Service normally uses a concentration factor of 5800 in making its dose calculations.
Similarly, the Staff has used a concentration factor of
20 for strontium-90 in algae; Polikarpov has found that

algae concentrate strontium-90 at factors up to 500,000.

3.27 Petitioner contends that the Sewerage & Water Board
of New Orleans does not check for radioactive fission products in the water supply. Petitioner knows of no plans
by the Sewerage & Water Board to check for radioactive
fission products in the future, and Petitioner further
contends that if the Board's present incompetence in protecting the purity of our water supply is any indication
the Board could not do the job even if it wanted to.
(See Industrial Pollution of the Lower Mississippi River
in La., Environmental Protection Agency, April 1972).
Petitioner contends that granting a construction permit
to Applicant would endanger the health of the people whose
drinking water is taken from the Mississippi River (approximately 1,500,000 people take their drinking water
from the Lower Mississippi River below the proposed plant).

3.28 Petitioner contends that the proposed disposal and
storage of long-lived radioactive nuclear fission products
that will be generated by Waterford Steam Electric Station
3 represent a threat to the public health and safety:

> "What is really at issue is a moral ques-
> tion--the right of one generation of humans
> to take upon itself the arrogance of poss-
> ible compromising the earth as an habitable
> place for this and essentially all future
> generations. Nuclear power generation car-
> ries with it the prospect of visiting increas-
> ed cancer upon this and a thousand genera-
> tions to come. Additionally, nuclear power
> generation carries with it the prospect of
> genetic deterioration of humans that will
> insure an increase in most of the common
> causes of death in future generations.
>
> These seriously condemnatory statements
> are justified through elementary consid-
> erations concerning two classes of pro-
> found biological poisons which are inevi-
> table concomitants of nuclear power gen-
> eration: long-lived radioactive fission
> products and plutonium-239.
>
> LONG-LIVED RADIOACTIVE FISSION PRODUCTS.
> A 1000-megawatt (electrical) nuclear
> power station, breeder or non-breeder,
> gas-cooled, water-cooled, or sodium-cooled,
> will necessarily generate per year the
> long-lived radioactive fission products
> equivalent to those generated by 23 mega-
> tons of nuclear fission bombs. If the U.S.
> program of nuclear plant construction
> proceeds as now planned, we shall have at
> least 500 such plants by the turn of the
> century. The annual generation of long-

lived fission products will then be the
equivalent of at least 11,500 megatons
of nuclear fission bombs. The major long-
lived fission products, strontium-90 and
cesium-137, have half-lives on the order
of 30 years. Therefore, the inventory
will necessarily build up, until at a
steady state (several times 30 years) the
inventory will be 43 x 11,500, or approximately 500,000 megaton equivalents of long-
lived fission products.

The combined atmospheric weapons testing
of the U.S., the U.K., and the U.S.S.R. in
all time amounted to 250 megatons of nuclear fission. Distributed world-wide,
over land and sea, this 250 megatons led
to radiation doses that are not subject to
denial, and that provoked international
concern. Even neglecting the much smaller
area of the U.S. compared with that of the
whole globe (which will mean more concentrated dispersal of fission products), it
is clear that an annual dispersal of <u>one-
hundredth of one percent</u> of the long-lived
fission product inventory (meaning 99.99
percent annual containment of the inventory) would mean dispersing <u>50 megatons
annually</u> and will assuredly lead to high
radiation doses. And these doses will produce the cancers and genetic diseases discussed above. Is it assured that the nuclear power industry can guarantee 99.99
percent annual containment? And even this
is not good enough. Can such isolation of
fission product garbage with near perfec-
tion be achieved over centuries? Is this
a technical problem?

PLUTONIUM-239. Plutonium-239, the most
poisonous element ever handled in quantity
by man, is the very heart of the nuclear
power industry, breeder or non-breeder.
Dr. Donald Geesaman, an authority on plutonium hazard, has estimated that there
will be one human lung cancer for every
10,000 fine particles of plutonium inhaled.
Dispersed as fine insoluble particles (about
one micron in diameter), one pound of plu-
tonium-239 represents the potential for some
<u>nine billion</u> human lung cancer doses. Given
the 24,400-year half-life of plutonium-239,
any plutonium dispersed into the biosphere
presents a major carcinogenic hazard for
more than the next thousand human generations. The annual handling of plutonium-
239 in a fully developed nuclear power economy will be in the one-hundred-ton category, or some 200,000 pounds annually.
Comparing this with the one pound that can

> provide an intolerable potential lung can-
> cer burden, we estimate that better than
> 99.99 percent containment of plutonium-239
> is hardly good enough to avert disaster.
> And such a containment requirement is for
> a substance widely and authoritatively ex-
> pected to be of high desirability in il-
> licit commerce, since it is the simplest
> material to acquire for fabrication of nu-
> clear weapons. Who can guarantee the re-
> quisite containment of plutonium-239 will
> be achieved?" (Dr. John W. Gofman, The Case
> for a Nuclear Moratorium, pages 6 & 7.).

3.29 Petitioner contends that the following regulation
for implementation of the National Environmental Policy
Act of 1969, set forth in Appendix D to Part 50 of the
Commission's regulations, has not been met by the Applicant:

> "The Environmental Report required by
> paragraph 1 shall include a cost-benefit
> analysis which considers and balances the
> environmental effects of the facility and
> the alternatives available for reducing
> or avoiding adverse environmental effects
> of the facility and the alternatives avail-
> able for reducing or avoiding adverse en-
> vironmental effects, as well as the environ-
> mental, economic, technical and other bene-
> fits of the facility. The cost-benefit
> analysis shall, to the fullest extent prac-
> ticable, quantify the various factors con-
> sidered. To the extent that such factors
> cannot be quantified, they shall be dis-
> cussed in qualitative terms. The Environ-
> mental Report should contain sufficient
> data to aid the Commission in its develop-
> ment of an independent cost-benefit ana-
> lysis covering the factors specified in
> this paragraph.

> "The discussion of alternatives to the pro-
> posed action in the Environmental Report
> required by paragraph 1 shall be suffici-
> ently complete to aid the Commission in
> developing and exploring, pursuant to sec-
> tión 102 (2) (D) of the National Environ-
> mental Policy Act, 'appropriate alterna-
> tives * * * in any proposal which involves
> unresolved conflicts concerning alternative
> uses of available resources.'"

3.30 Petitioner contends that Applicant's consideration
of coal as the only alternative power source is inadequate.
(Environmental Report p. X-C). An alternative power
source is the geothermal energy stored in a geopressure

belt 750 miles long in the Northern Gulf of Mexico basin
which underlies the Coastal Plain inland for a distance
of 60 to 100 miles. (W.J. Hickel, Geothermal Energy,
page 16 (University of Alaska, 1972)). It has been estimated that this belt contains 10 tons of oil worth of geothermal power - in equivalent terms. (H.T. Meider and J.
Banwell, Geothermal Energy for the Future (United Nations,
1972); see comment to the AEC's draft environmental statement with regard to proposed Waterford Steam Electric
Station, Unit 3, submitted by Donald F. X. Finn, Executive
Director, Geothermal Energy Institute).

3.31 Petitioner contends that the environmental analyses
by the Applicant and Staff in their Environmental Report
and Draft Environmental Statement respectively have ignored other alternative sources of power, such as solar
energy. Petitioner contends that without such a consideration, both as a central station source for producing
electricity, or for individual buildings as a way of reducing electrical consumption, the environmental review
for Applicant's plant is inadequate.

3.32 Petitioner contends that Applicant has failed to
comply with §9.1 of the August 1972 AEC Guide to the Preparation of Environmental Reports for Nuclear Power Plants,
which requires a full discussion of alternatives not requiring the creation of new generating capacity, including energy conservation:

> §9.1 Alternatives not requiring the crea-
> tion of new generating capacity.
> Practicable means which meet the projected
> power demand with adequate system reliabil-
> ity and which do not require the creation
> of additional generating capacity should
> be identified and evaluated. Such alter-
> natives may include purchased energy, re-
> activation or upgrading an older plant,
> and/or base load operation of an existing
> peaking facility. Such alternatives should
> be analyzed in terms of cost, environmental
> impact, adequacy, reliability and other
> pertinent factors. The applicant is ad-
> vised that this analysis is of major import-
> ance because it provides the basis for
> justifying the creation of a new generating
> capability. [Emphasis added].

3.33 Petitioner contends that Applicant does not consider alternatives to increased use of electricity such as
(1) better construction and design of buildings:

> "Certain changes could be made in build-
> ing design and construction that will re-
> duce by at least 25 percent the energy re-
> quired to construct and maintain build-
> ings." ('A Matter of Design,' by Richard
> G. Stein and Associates, Architects,

Environment, October, 1972);

(2) replacing home electric heating by natural gas heating:

> "It is a fundamental principle of nature
> that heat energy can never be completely
> converted to electric energy. The prin-
> ciple is called the second law of thermo-
> dynamics. So some of the gas heat must
> be wasted. It never gets turned into
> electricity. Two-thirds of the gas ener-
> gy is wasted. Only one-third is convert-
> ed to electric energy." (Lewis Epstein,
> Instructor in Astronomy and Physics,
> Louisiana State University in New Orleans,
> published in NOLA Express #123);

(3) turning off lights at night in downtown office buildings where the lighting is not in use except for decora-
tion and advertising; (4) a balanced circulation of energy in city neighborhoods with plants and trees supplying cooling and fresh air rather than "air-conditioning":

> "The use of electricity to supply these
> sorts of heats [Direct space heating, water
> heating and air conditioning] involves a
> waste of natural resources that can only
> be described as capricious." (Wilson
> Clark, Energy Consultant for Environment-
> al Policy Center, 324 C St., SE Washington
> DC. The Case for a Nuclear Moratorium,
> page 27).

3.34 Petitioner contends that the Applicant and the
Staff have failed to comply with §8.5 of the August 1972
Guide to the Preparation of Environmental Reports for
Nuclear Power Plants, which requires that the adverse ef-
fects of generating electricity from the proposed plant
be considered:

> §8.5 Externalities.
> The Production of more, and perhaps lower
> cost electricity, could induce local in-
> dustry to increase the production of goods
> and services...[which] could lead to ad-
> verse environmental effects in themselves,
> such as increased air pollution. The ap-
> plicant should estimate both favorable and
> unfavorable effects.
> There could be other adverse effects on a
> region's economy. When the proposed fac-
> ility would increase a region's tax base,
> it would also add an additional burden
> to local services, such as water, sewage,
> education and transportation. The appli-
> cant should therefore estimate such ad-

verse effects as well as the benefits.

3.35 Petitioner further contends that Applicant does not document increased industrial and commercial need for electricity. Not only is there no documentation of this need, but there is also no analysis of the environmental impact of increased industry in the area or increased use of electricity by already existing industry.

3.36 Petitioner further contends that there is no discussion of the environmental consequences of the purpose of increased industrial use of electricity. For example, Petitioner contends that the electricity will be used for environmentally harmful purposes such as the production of non-returnable aluminum cans.

3.37 Petitioner contends that Applicant's analysis of projected load forecasts is unsound in that it overstates the future industrial needs of the State of Louisiana, the future population growth of the State of Louisiana, and fails to recognize that the demand for electricity will decrease on an absolute and percentage basis. Moreover, Petitioner contends that the Applicant has not considered all generating facilities that would be available, given certain interconnections, to consumers in its franchise area and, accordingly, Applicant has used a statistically erroneous geographic area in which to analyze a demand for electricity. Thus, Applicant's statement of electric reserves is misleading in that it does not cover all available reserves. Applicant's analysis assumes that the need for power is constant and firm and will remain so during at least the ten year period between 1970 and 1980. There is no basis for making this assumption or relying upon statistics during the period 1960 to 1970 because the factors governing each such period are not identical. For example, the rate of population increase during the ten year period, 1960 to 1970, was significantly greater than is or will be the rate of population increase during the period 1970 to 1980. Applicant has not taken this into account in its analysis.

3.38 Petitioner contends that Applicant's estimates of electrical load growth fail to consider the high cost and short supply of money and its effect on housing. Petitioner contends that the long time trend for the major part of housing in the future will no longer be single dwelling units but will be multiple dwelling units which will result in a lessening of electrical demand. Therefore Applicant's demand forecasts are not accurate. Furthermore, Petitioner contends that Applicant has failed to consider reduction in fertility rates in Applicant's service area and has failed to take into consideration the fact that the electrical load forecast is overstated by this amount of production not needed under the revised fertility assumptions.

3.39 In its estimates of load growth, Applicant has util-

ized an outmoded forecasting methodology. Applicant has
not broken down its load forecasting into components of
its system either by geographic area, by types of customer, or by class of service. Petitioner contends that certain parts, as enumerated above, may be growing much less
rapidly than the remainder. If this part is substantial
and its rate of growth differs significantly from that of
the total, failure to segregate it can result in misleading conelusions.

3.40 Applicant uses past growth rate as a basis for pre-
dicting the hypothetical future growth rate. "Electric
power requirements in this country have been doubling
every 10 years. For the Middle South Utility System of
which Louisiana Power & Light is a part, the doubling time
is every seven years. Further expansion is expected to
continue in much the same pattern." (Environmental Report, p. VIII-I). Applicant further states that this
growth is a result of increased consumption per person -
"While some of this growth is related to increases in
population, an ever greater proportion is related to increased power consumption per person." (Ibid.) Petitioner contends that this increased consumption per person is
not an irrevocable fact of nature, but is artificially
created by, for example, New Orleans Public Service Incorporated's (also a part of the Middle South System)
large scale advertising in the New Orleans Times-Picayune
promoting the increased use of all-electric homes and outdoor night electric lighting, and that if this advertising were stopped, electricity consumption per person
would not increase at such a rate as to double the need
for electricity every seven years.

3.41 Petitioner contends that LP&L's policy of giving
lower rates to large users of electricity further exacer-
bates the environmental situation and that if LP&L were
truly concerned about our environment, the price of electricity would be directly proportional to the usage.
Petitioner contends this would reduce the use of electricity, thus eliminating the alleged need for this nuclear power plant.

3.42 Petitioner contends that a decision as to whether
the consumption of more electricity should be a result of
this hearing should be a decision made on the basis of
conscious rational thought with full consequences known
and discussed in public, not be the arbitrary private decisions of the Applicant. Applicant has suppressed public
discussion of this so that Petitioner knows of many people in a 100 mile radius from the proposed plant who do
not even know of the proposed construction of plant and
are unaware of the consequences of this "incredible" increased usage of electricity that Applicant proposes.

3.43 Increased need for electricity is the fundamental
assumption on which Louisiana Power & Light postulates a
doubling of electricity need for the Middle South Utilit-

ies System every seven years (Environmental Report,
p. VIII-1). Applicant states "Further expansion is expected to continue in much the same pattern." (Ibid.)
Petitioner questions the validity of this assumption. If
it is true as Applicant alleges, that the need for electricity doubles every seven years, then Petitioner contends the result will be ecological disaster:

> "Consider for a moment one of the prime
> activities that results in environmental
> deterioration: the generation and use of
> electric power. Europeans live a pleasant,
> reasonable affluent life on somewhat less
> than one-half the per capita electric
> power consumption of Americans, and with
> careful planning their level of consump-
> tion could also be greatly reduced.
> Amazingly, though, the American power
> industry wants to increase our per capita
> consumption at a rate that will double our
> national use of power every decade. At
> this rate, every square inch of the United
> States would be covered with conventional
> power plants in two hundred years or so.
> This projected increase is the reason that
> the industry is vigorously promoting the
> construction of more heavily-subsidized
> nuclear power plants, perhaps the most
> dangerous single trend in the environment-
> technology area today." (Dr. Paul R.
> Ehrlich, How to Be a Survivor (Ballantine
> Books, 1971), page 71).

3.44 Petitioner notes that Middle South Utilities, the
parent company of LP&L, has an electricity exchange with
the publicly-owned TVA. Petitioner further notes that
the largest user of TVA electricity and, indeed, the
largest single consumer of electricity in the U.S. is the
U.S. Atomic Energy Commission (The Last Play, The Struggle
to Monopolize the World Energy Resources, James Ridgeway,
E.P. Dutton, 1973, page 20). The AEC consumed approximately 10 times more electric energy than has been produced in all U.S. atomic power plants (central stations).
(See the graph from 'Atomic Power: Fallacies and Fact,'
by Adolph J. Ackerman, IEEE Transactions on Aerospace and
Electronic Systems, September 1972.) Petitioner contends
that there should be an environmental report on this enormous use of electricity by the AEC with the purpose in
mind of reducing electricity consumption by the AEC, so
that TVA instead of supplying the electricity to the AEC
could transmit it to LP&L for the use of the people in
their service area. Petitioner further contends that
since the U.S. Atomic Energy Commission is the largest
single consumer of electricity in the country, the Commission is the primary cause of the alleged shortage of
electricity and thus should not be sitting in judgment
of this application.

3.45 Petitioner contends that there is at the present
time and will still be in 1977 sufficient reserve in the
Southwest Regional Group (SWRG) the Southwest Power Pool
(SPP) and the South Central Electric Companies (SCEC),
all of which Applicant is a member, to meet any power
needs offset by not building this plant. T. A. Phillips,
Chief of the Bureau of Power at the Federal Power Commission, admitted in a letter dated August 9, 1972 to R. C.
DeYoung of the AEC, that:

> "The Southwest Power Pool (SPP) of
> which the Applicant and MSU are mem-
> bers, reports reserve margins of 21.9
> percent of peak load for the 1977
> summer period." (p.4)

Petitioner contends that under the National Environmental
Policy Act Applicant's plant may not be constructed unless it is demonstrated that the electricity allegedly
needed from the plant is unavailable to the Applicant
from any other source.

3.46 Applicant's alleged need for uranium fuel is based
on alleged natural gas shortage of United Gas Pipeline
(Pennzoil) & others. Petitioner contends that there is
no documentation for this and that the alleged shortage
is possibly fraudulent insofar as there have not been independent studies of natural gas reserves. "There is
little way of knowing the extent of a gas shortage because the data on gas reserves is provided by the industry. The government itself does not make estimates of
reserves." (The Last Play, James Ridgeway, page 6.)

3.47 Petitioner contends that the calculation of radiological effects resulting from accidents in Section VI
of the Environmental Report is inadequate to the extent
that such accidents may endanger the lives and health of
millions of human beings living near the proposed plant.
In particular the Petitioner contends that any such calculations should be based on worst-case assumptions and
boundary conditions so that adequate evacuation procedures and safety measures can be formulated and implemented regardless of the low probabilities involved.
Petitioner finds these calculations inadequate for the
following reasons:

(1) Petitioner takes exception to the statement appearing on page VI-2 of the Environmental Report stating, "...the probability of occurrence is so small that
the environmental risk is extremely low and need not be
evaluated." Petitioner notes that the aforementioned
probability, however small, has not been quantified in
this report, although it must be in order for the above
statement to have merit. Furthermore, no matter how
small the resulting probability, Petitioner contends that,
at the minimum, in view of the potential seriousness of
the event, the Applicant should calculate the radiologi-

cal effects resulting from loss of containment and make
these data available to the public that must bear the
risk.

(2) Petitioner takes exception to the calculations
based on the formulas appearing on pages VI-2 and VI-3 of
this report. In particular the derivation of values for
the X/Q term in Table VI-1 are not presented.

3.48 Petitioner contends that using an annual 'average'
is not a worst-case assumption. Furthermore, the values
stipulated in Table VI-1 fall off roughly as the square
of the distance indicating that a spherical wavefront for
dispersion was assumed. This is not a worst-case assumption. Petitioner contends that the dispersion factor
should be derivated for a prevailing wind directly into
the New Orleans population for sudden ruptures such as a
LOCA and subsequent rupture of the containment. Dispersion calculations of toxic materials in the atmosphere
have been performed for over a decade for such toxic materials as liquid fluorine, hydrazine, etc., and Petitioner contends that the Applicant's Report and the Staff's
reports should be at least as definitive as these calculations, which they are not.

3.49 Petitioner contends that we human beings and this
Board in particular are trustees of evolution.

> "The ideologically most important fact
> about evolution is that the human species
> is now the spearhead of the evolutionary
> process on earth, the only portion of
> the stuff of which our planet is made
> which is capable of further progress.
> Men are the sole trustees, agents, re-
> presentatives, embodiments, or instru-
> ments -- each word has its merits and
> demerits -- of the only process of pro-
> gressive evolution with which we have
> any direct concern.

> "Man, in fact, is a microcosm -- but in
> a somewhat different sense from that of
> earlier centuries. He is, as it were,
> a distillation of the universe at large,
> the macrocosm. The picture that he con-
> structs of the universe, including of
> course himself, however distorted and
> full of gaps it may be, is the only re-
> presentation that exists on this earth
> of the macrocosm as a unit. And the
> novelties that he produces in history,
> however crude and misdirected some of
> them have been, involve the only large-
> scale advance of the evolutionary pro-
> cess still operating on our planet.
> There is thus a new categorical impera-

> tive that has taken form and voice
> from the facts of post-Darwinian
> science and humane studies -- that
> man's destiny, his duty and privi-
> lege in one, is to continue in his
> own person the advance of the cosmic
> process of evolution." (Sir Julian
> Huxley, Knowledge, Morality, &
> Destiny, 1957, page 94.)

Petitioner contends that the Environmental Report does
not discuss the genetic effects on evolution of the proposed nuclear power plant and therefore the report is inadequate and incomplete.

   Petitioner further contends that it would be an immoral act for this Board to grant a permit to this proposed nuclear power plant because of its deleterious effects on the evolution of life on earth and thus prays
that this Board deny the Applicant's permit.

> "For genetic effects there appears to be
> no possible threshhold dose below which
> some effect may not occur. Any amount of
> radiation, no matter how small, is bound
> to produce some mutations. Once completed,
> mutations are irreversible and almost
> all mutations are deleterious. Irradia-
> tion of a population from any source is
> bound to have some genetic consequences."
> (Water Quality Criteria, Jack Edward
> McKee and Harold W. Wold, editors. 2nd
> edition, State Water Quality Control
> Board, Sacramento, Ca., 1963, pages 345-
> 346.).

                    *   *   *

   In addition to the specific contentions made above,
Petitioner contends that Applicant will be shown to have
failed to comply with the National Environmental Policy
Act of 1969 for further reasons which will be set forth
later when information and documents not currently available in advance of the filing of this petition to intervene, such as the Final Environmental Statement, are
available, together with other documents to be produced
in accordance with pre-hearing discovery.

IV

FIRST PRELIMINARY
STATEMENT OF CONTENTIONS WITH RESPECT TO
APPLICANT'S LACK OF TECHNICAL
<u>AND FINANCIAL QUALIFICATIONS</u>

Petitioner contests a positive finding by the Atomic Safety and Licensing Board on the issues whether the Applicant is technically and financially qualified to design and construct the proposed facility, and whether such activities as would be authorized by the issuance of a construction permit would be conducted in compliance with the regulations of the Commission.

4.1 Applicant is not financially qualified to construct the plant because its present financial posture is seriously jeopardized by the rate at which net plant, capital and operating expenses are increasing in comparison to the substantially lower rate of increase in its sales. Applicant has over extended its construction program, and the resulting financial burden upon Applicant's financial resources by reason of the long-term and short-term indebtedness associated with these construction activities prevent it from being in the sound financial posture required to construct this plant and meet the requirements of the Act.

4.2 Petitioner contends that if the costs of the Waterford plant were to in any way approach the costs realistically calculated in Section III of this Petition, Applicant's financial stability would be undermined to the point that it would have to file for bankruptcy. As of December 31, 1971, Applicant's gross revenues for 1971 were only $153,642,743.36. The Staff's estimated total present worth of the proposed Waterford plant of $579,000,000 is itself 97.37% of Applicant's net utility plant after depreciation of $594,648,792.50 at the end of 1971. The proposed plant in effect represents an amount of money to be expended equivalent to Applicant's present net plant.

4.3 Petitioner states that to the best of his knowledge the Applicant's proposed plant is unable to obtain full liability coverage insurance from private companies because of high risk.

> "It is hardly reassuring to know that
> even the Price-Anderson act allows for
> only enough insurance to cover 8 percent
> of the damage that the government itself
> estimated would be caused <u>to property</u>
> <u>alone</u> by the most serious 'hypothetical
> accident' for a moderate-sized installa-
> tion. The estimated cost, $7 <u>billion</u>,
> is now thought to have been a very <u>low</u>
> estimate." (Drs. Paul R. & Anne H.

> Ehrlich, <u>Population, Resources,</u>
> <u>Environment</u>, W. H. Freeman and Co.,
> 1970.)

The above figures were based on the 500 MWt plant assumed
in WASH-740; Applicant's proposed design is <u>seven</u> times
larger (3560 MWt). Petitioner contends that since the
people of New Orleans and environs are not insured at all
against nuclear risks in their property policies, and Applicant is extremely under-insured with respect to nuclear liability, this is totally unacceptable and Applicant should not be granted a permit to construct the proposed plant.

4.4 Petitioner contends that Applicant has had no previous experience in constructing a nuclear power plant.
Waterford Unit 3 is the first nuclear plant to be built
by Louisiana Power and Light. Moreover, Applicant's
presently proposed engineering staff lacks the requisite
experience needed to supervise the design, construction,
and quality assurance plan implementation for a large
power reactor. Applicant's construction record and lack
of quality assurance on its other steam plants cause Petitioner to believe that Applicant's construction of this
plant would not meet the standards necessary to ensure
a safe plant.

4.5 Petitioner contends that Applicant has already
shown that it cannot comply with Commission regulations
during the limited amount of construction already done on
this plant. For example, the AEC Directorate of Regulatory Operations issued the Applicant a non-compliance
letter (RO:II:BJC 50-382/72-1) on June 28, 1972, citing
Applicant's failure to comply with 10 C.F.R. 50, Appendix
B, Criteria IV, XVII and XVIII:

> Contrary to the above, neither the archi-
> tect's specification, LOU-1564 Rev. 1,
> "Steel Containment Vessel," nor the pur-
> chase order, requires the designer, fabri-
> cator, or erector to have a quality as-
> surance program consistent with the pro-
> visions of the eighteen quality assurance
> criteria....
> LP&L has performed only two audits since
> June 1971. LP&L audited the nuclear steam
> system supplier and the architect's de-
> sign engineering utilizing a procedure
> designed for auditing a manufacturing fac-
> ility which appeared not be suitable for
> auditing an engineering organization;
> there was no indication that the audit re-
> sults were reviewed by LP&L management;
> there was no indication of planned follow-
> up action or reaudit.

Petitioner contends that this gross disregard for estab-

lished quality assurance requirements disqualifies Applicant for a construction permit.

4.6 Petitioner contends that the Board must take into
account, in reaching a determination with respect to the
qualification of this Applicant to design and construct
a nuclear power plant in accordance with the regulations
of the Commission, the moral integrity of Applicant's
management. Petitioner contends that the moral integrity
of a management that charges between 120% and 360% annual interest is open to question (See December 21, 1972
press release of the suit filed by Louisiana Attorney-
General William Guste).

                    *   *   *

     Petitioner reserves the right to amend the above
contentions regarding Applicant's technical and financial
qualifications upon completion of discovery and the production of Applicant's documents not available in advance of the filing of this Petition to Intervene.

V

FIRST PRELIMINARY
STATEMENT OF CONTENTIONS
WITH RESPECT TO
OTHER RELATED MATTERS

     Petitioner contends that for specific reasons set
forth below, until the legal and procedural defects already accumulated with respect to this application are
resolved, any hearing on this application for a construction permit would be contrary to law and prejudicial to
the public interest.

5.1 Petitioner contends that if Applicant's plant is
permitted to be constructed using an open-cycle cooling
water discharge, it will be in violation of the Federal
Water Pollution Control Act Amendments of 1972 (Public
Law 92-500, October 18, 1972), which states that "It is
the national goal that the discharge of pollutants into
the navigable waters be eliminated by 1985." Comity requires that this Board uphold this Act and not issue a
permit which would result in its violation.

5.2 Petitioner contends that the June 21, 1972 letter
from Robert A. Lafleur, Executive Secretary of the Stream
Control Commission of the State of Louisiana to Applicant
certifying that Applicant's proposed discharge complies
with Section 21(b) of the Federal Water Quality Improvement Act of 1970 is invalid, because the State of Louisiana has not adopted a mixing zone criterion, and therefore no determination with respect to the proposed discharge can be made.

5.3 Petitioner contends that the public notice procedures for this application have been inadequate and de-

fective. Based on a personal survey, Petitioner contends
that the vast majority of residents within a 100-mile
radius of the proposed plant have not seen the notices
in the Federal Register or the Times-Picayune. Petitioner contends that until a notice has been published in at
least one newspaper in every town within 100 miles of the
proposed plant, the public will have been deprived of
adequate notice of the proposed issuance of a construction permit and the holding of a hearing based on the
inadequate previous notice will be illegal.

5.4 Petitioner contends that the single most important
nuclear safety component of this proposed plant has already been completed without review of any Atomic Safety
and Licensing Board and without being under the jurisdiction of inspectors from the Directorate of Regulatory
Operations of the Commission. The reactor pressure vessel for the Waterford plant has already been fabricated
and is almost ready for shipment. It has not been built
in compliance with the most recent edition of the ASME
Boiler and Pressure Vessel Code, Section III, and therefore this Board has been deprived of the opportunity to
pass on its safety. Because the jurisdiction of the inspectors from the Directorate of Regulatory Operations
does not become official until the construction permit
has been issued, the reactor pressure vessel for this
plant has been completely fabricated without any effective regulatory inspection and review to ensure that the
vessel complies with all applicable codes and 10 C.F.R.
50.55a. Petitioner contends that for this Board to allow
this vessel to be installed at the Waterford plant,
should a construction permit be issued, would be contrary to law and due process.

5.5 Petitioner contends that the full Advisory Committee on Reactor Safeguards meeting on the Waterford reactor, held on January 12, 1973, was illegal and in violation of the Federal Advisory Committee Act of October
6, 1972 (Public Law 92-463, 92nd Congress, H.R. 4383).
Under the Act, all advisory committee meetings are to be
open to the public. Petitioner sent his consultant to
attend the meeting, but the consultant was barred from
attending the meeting by Mr. Ray Fraley of the ACRS staff,
pursuant to an illegal determination invalidly promulgated, purportedly on January 9, 1973 but in fact not
available to Petitioner's consultant until after the
meeting, by John V. Vinciguerra, whom the Commission has
improperly designated as its Advisory Committee Management Officer. Petitioner contends that the refusal to
admit his consultant to the meeting, although the two
other parties to this application were present at the
meeting, makes the meeting illegal, and therefore all
findings and reports resulting from matters considered at
that January 12, 1973 ACRS meeting will themselves be illegal, null and void.

5.6 Petitioner contends that Applicant has illegally at-

tempted to get favored treatment of its application at
the Commission by violating the Commissions' ex parte
rules. By Letter of June 20, 1972 Applicant's Vice-
President, J.M. Mooney, caused a number of Congressmen
and Senators in the United States Congress to write to
the Chairman of the Commission and ask that the Commission forego its orderly licensing procedures to alleviate
alleged blackouts and brownouts. Such letters involved
Congressmen John K. Rarick, Otto E. Passman, T. Edward
Hebert, Patrick T. Caffery, Speedy O. Long, and Senator
Russell B. Long. Petitioner contends that this political
pressure may have prejudiced the Staff's review of this
application.

5.7 Petitioner contends that Applicant's estimated expenditure of $13,300,00 by April 1, 1973 on site prepara-
tion for Waterford Unit 3 prior to the issuance of a construction permit for the nuclear plant cannot help but
prejudice this Board in favor of granting the permit.
Petitioner contends that the determinations made by the
Commission with respect to permitting such site preparation, embodied in the Commission's Determination of
July 28, 1972, were made without a hearing or participation of the public and therefore were made illegally.

5.8 Petitioner contends that whatever Board hears this
case should be wholly independent of the U.S. Atomic
Energy Commission. For reasons including the contention
above in Section III of this Petition regarding the Commission's role as the number one consumer of electricity
in the nation, and the Commission's deep involvement with
the promotion of nuclear power, a Board chosen by the AEC
rather than by Congress should not sit in judgment on
this case:

> Nothing has suited the promotional nuclear power
> interests better than keeping alive the mis-
> conception that a decision pro or con nuclear
> fission power rests upon esoteric technical
> arguments. The entire so-called 'public hear-
> ing' procedure is administered by the chief
> promotional interest, the U.S. Atomic Energy
> Commission. And concerned citizens have been
> led, like lambs to the slaughter, into the
> promoters' arena to contest a variety of valves,
> filters, cooling towers, and miscellaneous other
> items of hardware in specific nuclear power
> plants. A victory for citizens, in a specific
> encounter, comes in the form of an improved
> valve, an extra scrubber for radioactive ef-
> fluents or a brand new cooling tower. Such a
> 'victory' is a diversion from the really signi-
> ficant issues concerning the acceptability of
> nuclear power. Further, the illusion is created
> that safety has been substantially increased
> by the particular gadget addition or change.

(Dr. John W. Gofman, <u>The Case for a Nuclear
Moratorium</u>, p. 6).

5.9 Petitioner contends that there has been no showing
by the Commission that the technical members and alternative technical member of the Atomic Safety and Licensing Board in this proceeding are qualified and meet the
requirements of 10 C.F.R. Part 2, §2.721. Inasmuch as
the matters in controversy before this Board are complex
and cover a spectrum of disciplines, such a showing must
be made in order to assure that a valid determination
can be made by this Board. In addition, it is well-known
that members of the Atomic Safety and Licensing Panel at
large are drawn from the ranks of the nuclear industry
or have affiliations that may place them in positions of
conflict of interest. In order to verify that such is
not the case with respect to the technical members and
alternative technical members of this Board, Petitioner
respectfully requests that each such member produce for
the record a complete curriculum vitae, setting forth all
academic subjects and verified with transcripts from the
academic institutions attended, a determination by the
Commission of what areas of expertise for which the technical member is being tendered as competent and qualified, a complete list of all full time and part time occupational employment, including consultantships, fellow-
ships, etc., with a brief description of the nature of
the work and a list of actual direct as well as indirect
beneficiaries of the work performed. In addition, each
technical member and alternate should place into the record a complete bibliography of all his publications, and
include full copies of any having to do with the subjects
of nuclear safety, the environment, and other matters
related to the forthcoming construction permit hearing.

VI

CONCLUSION AND REQUEST
<u>FOR RELIEF</u>

Based on the foregoing, Petitioner respectfully requests that he be permitted to intervene as a party in this proceeding and the construction permit sought by the Applicant be denied for the reasons stated in this petition.

Respectfully submitted,

_____

Robert Head

_____

Luke Fontana
Attorney for Petitioner

(For Service)

Robert Head
P.O. Box 2342
New Orleans, LA 70116
(504) 524-5780

Luke Fontana, Esq.
824 Esplanade Avenue
New Orleans, LA 70116
(504) 524-0028

David Dinsmore Comey
109 North Dearborn Street, Suite 1001
Chicago, IL 60602
(312) 641-5570

Businessmen for the Public Interest
Settlement Agreement

BUSINESSMEN FOR THE PUBLIC INTEREST

109 N. Dearborn St., Suite 1001, Chicago, Ill. 60602
(312) 641 5570

PALISADES PLANT

SETTLEMENT AGREEMENT

Between

INTERVENORS

And

CONSUMERS POWER COMPANY

March 12, 1971

U.S. Atomic Energy Commission

Docket No. 50-255

TABLE OF CONTENTS

AGREEMENT

AGREEMENT, made this 12th day of March, 1971, by and between CONSUMERS POWER COMPANY, 212 West Michigan Avenue, Jackson, Michigan, hereinafter called "Consumers Power," and MICHIGAN STEEL HEAD AND SALMON FISHERMEN'S ASSOCIATION, 5619 Clato, Kalamazoo, Michigan, THERMAL ECOLOGY MUST BE PRESERVED (T.E.M.P.), 2312 Glenwood Drive, Kalamazoo, Michigan, CONCERNED PETITIONING CITIZENS, 2312 Glenwood Drive, Kalamazoo, Michigan, MICHIGAN LAKE AND STREAM ASSOCIATIONS, INC., 392 Fairbrook Court, Northville, Michigan, and SIERRA CLUB, 1050 Mills Tower, San Francisco, California (for itself and for each and all of its chapters), hereinafter called, jointly and severally, "Intervenors."

WHEREAS, pursuant to an application dated June 2, 1966 and assigned to AEC Docket No. 50-255, a permit to construct a pressurized-water-reactor nuclear power plant known as the Palisades Plant in Covert Township, Van Buren County, Michigan, was duly issued to Consumers Power by the U.S. Atomic Energy Commission (in this Agreement called by "AEC") on March 14, 1967 after a public hearing as required by law, without opposition by way of intervention, and pursuant to findings by the Atomic Safety and Licensing Board entered in favor of Consumers Power on all issues presented by the Notice of Hearing for construction permit; and

WHEREAS, by amendment to its application dated November 1, 1968, Consumers Power requested issuance of a license to operate the Palisades Plant at steady-state power levels up to and including 2200 thermal megawatts (in this Agreement called the "full-power license"); and

WHEREAS, on January 27, 1970, after review and proceedings required by law, the AEC's Advisory Committee on Reactor Safeguards issued its Report on the Palisades Plant which concluded that the Palisades Plant can be operated at power levels up to 2200 thermal megawatts without undue risk to the health and safety of the public, if due regard is given to the suggestions and comments contained in said ACRS Report, subject to the satisfactory completion of construction and preoperational testing; and

WHEREAS, On March 6, 1970, the AEC's Division of Reactor Licensing issued its Safety Evaluation with respect to the Palisades Plant which concluded, among other things, that there is reasonable assurance that the Palisades Plant can be operated as proposed without endangering the health and safety of the public; and

WHEREAS, on March 10, 1970, there was published in the Federal Register a notice that the AEC's Division of Reactor Licensing proposed to issue a provisional operating license to Consumers Power to operate the Palisades Plant as requested, which notice granted an opportunity for public hearing on the issuance of such license; and

WHEREAS, certain persons later to become Intervenors had meetings and discussions with representatives of Consumers Power to discuss such persons' concerns relating to environmental effects of the Palisades Plant, but such discussions did not alleviate the concerns of such persons, later to become Intervenors; and

WHEREAS, Intervenors requested a public hearing pursuant to said March 10, 1970 notice, upon the grounds, among others, that Intervenors were dissatisfied with the AEC's implementation of the National Environmental Policy Act and were dissatisfied with the design of the Palisades Plant insofar as radioactive and thermal effluents were concerned, and, accordingly, a public hearing (in this Agreement called "the proceeding") commenced before an AEC Atomic Safety and Licensing Board (in this Agreement called "ASLB") on June 23, 1970, which proceeding has not been concluded; and

WHEREAS, during the course of the proceeding Consumers Power filed a motion for issuance of a license authorizing fuel loading and low-power testing at power levels not to exceed one (1) thermal megawatt (in this Agreement called the "testing license") pending issuance of the full-power license; and

WHEREAS, the Intervenors have, since the proceeding began, vigorously contested the issuance of the requested operating licenses to Consumers Power because of Intervenors' contention, among other things, that the AEC, by such a hearing, is engaged in a continuing violation of the National Environmental Policy Act, the Federal Water Pollution Control Act, as amended, and the Atomic Energy Act of 1954, as amended; and

WHEREAS, during the course of said proceeding, Intervenors have questioned whether the Palisades Plant has been constructed in accordance with law and in accordance with Consumers Power's application, plans and specifications and if not so constructed, whether it may be operated safely; and

WHEREAS, the parties have made considerable expenditures of time and money in contesting the issuance of said operating licenses to date, and costly and time-consuming appeals from any decision of the ASLB in the proceeding are probable; and

WHEREAS, Intervenors are willing to forego in this proceeding final resolution of legal issues pursuant to the National Environmental Policy Act, the Federal Water Pollution Control Act, as amended, and the Atomic Energy Act of 1954, as amended, provided that certain steps are taken by Consumers Power, as provided in this Agreement, in order to resolve the contentions of Intervenors as regards radioactive and thermal effects and nuclear safety of the Palisades Plant; and

WHEREAS, the parties hereto desire to minimize further expenditures, to permit production of electrical energy from the Palisades Plant in accordance with the provisions of this Agreement, and to that end to resolve all controversies, differences and disputes between the parties hereto with respect to the design, construction, licensing and operation of the Palisades Plant, including but not limited to those which have heretofore arisen or might or could have arisen, or which may or could hereafter arise during the course of the proceeding or otherwise in AEC Docket No. 50-255 and in appeals therefrom and in actions in connection therewith before the ASLB, the AEC Atomic Safety and Licensing Appeal Board, the AEC and all other governmental agencies and all federal, state and local courts, except controversies, differences and disputes arising because of alleged breach of, or failure of performance pursuant to, this Agreement;

NOW, THEREFORE, in consideration of their mutual promises and undertakings herein, the parties hereto agree as follows:

SECTION 1 - CONDENSER COOLING SYSTEM MODIFICATION

§1.1 Consumers Power shall modify the condenser cooling system now installed in the Palisades Plant to a condenser cooling system substantially conforming to the conceptual design set forth in Appendix I hereto and in accordance with the principles set forth in this Section 1. The condenser cooling system as so modified (and in this Agreement called the "modified condenser cooling system") shall be so designed, constructed, operated and maintained as to form a closed cycle in which the condenser cooling water is continually recycled except for cooling system makeup water from and blowdown to Lake Michigan. The modified condenser cooling system shall include one or more wet-type cooling towers which may be of either the natural or the mechanical draft type, at Consumers Power's sole option, provided, that Consumers Power's obligation shall be to install either the natural or the mechanical draft type unless it is relieved from installing both types after exhausting all rights of hearing, appeal and requests for writs of certiorari to the highest state or federal court having jurisdiction, as provided in Section 10 of this Agreement. Design and construction of the cooling tower or towers shall conform to the latest applicable Cooling Tower Institute (CTI) codes and standards applicable at the time of detailed design, except to the extent the same may be contrary to any applicable law or rule, regulation or order of any governmental body having jurisdiction.

§1.2 Upon execution of this Agreement, Consumers Power will proceed immediately with all due diligence to arrange for the design, engineering, procurement of equipment and materials, and construction required to install the modified condenser cooling system as provided for herein and to make application to obtain all licenses, permits, consents or other authorizations of public bodies or officials which are required in connection with the design, construction, operation and maintenance of the modified condenser cooling system. In making and pursuing such application, Consumers Power shall pursue administrative remedies or court actions, or both, in the manner provided in Section 10 of this Agreement, and the rights and obligations of the parties in connection with such remedies or actions shall be governed and determined by Section 10 of this Agreement. The modified condenser cooling system shall be installed within forty-two (42) calendar months following the date of execution of this Agreement if Consumers Power installs a natural draft cooling tower or towers as part of the modified condenser cooling system, or within thirty-two (32) calendar months following the date of execution of this Agreement if Consumers Power installs a mechanical draft cooling tower or towers as part of the modified condenser cooling system. If, after Consumers Power has begun to arrange for the design, engineering, procurement of equipment and materials, and construction for a modified condenser cooling system utilizing either the mechanical draft or the natural draft type of cooling tower or towers, Consumers Power is relieved from installing or continuing to install the type of cooling tower or towers it first selects, and it is necessary to change to the alternative type of cooling tower or towers, the time for installation of a modified condenser cooling system utilizing the alternative type of cooling tower or towers shall commence from the date on which Consumers Power is relieved from installing or continuing to install the type of cooling tower or towers first selected. The modified condenser cooling system shall be placed in operation not later than the resumption of operation of the Palisades Plant after its first scheduled refueling following installation of said system, provided, that to the extent it can do so consistently with electrical system load requirements, Palisades Plant operating requirements and applicable license and other legal limitations, Consumers Power shall use its best efforts to schedule the first refueling following installation of the modified condenser cooling system so as to minimize the time between the completion of such installation and the initial operation of the modified condenser cooling system. The foregoing provisions of this §1.2 are subject to the condition that in the event the installation or the initial operation of such modified condenser cooling system is delayed (i) by reason of flood, strike, insurrection, riot, embargo, act of nature or the public enemy; or unavoidable delay in transportation or inability or unavoidable delay in procuring labor or materials; (ii) by reason of legal action by any third party; local, state or federal laws; or the rules, regulations, orders, actions or fail-

ure to act of any public body or official purporting to
exercise authority or control with respect to installation or operation of the modified condenser cooling system; or (iii) by reason of any cause beyond the reasonable control of Consumers Power, the time for performance
shall be extended (subject to the provisions of Section
10 of this Agreement as respects [ii] above) for a time
equal to the period of such delay. Moreover, until initial successful operation of the modified condenser cooling system, Consumers Power shall notify Intervenors
quarterly of all occurrences or conditions then known to
any officer of Consumers Power, or to an employee of Consumers Power who reports directly and regularly to any
such officer, which Consumers Power may claim forms a
basis for an extension of time for the installation and
operation of the modified condenser cooling system, and
shall notify Intervenors on a current basis of any occurrence or condition known to any officer of Consumers
Power, or to an employee of Consumers Power who reports
directly and regularly to any such officer, which Consumers Power then claims will form a basis for such an extension of time.

§1.3 Pending installation and operation of the modified condenser cooling system provided for in this Section 1, Consumers Power, insofar as Intervenors are concerned, may operate the Palisades Plant at any power
levels authorized by any AEC operating license issued to
Consumers Power, utilizing the existing once-through cooling system and releasing heated condenser cooling water
to Lake Michigan.

§1.4 As used in this Agreement the term "Palisades
Plant" means and refers to a single-unit nuclear electric
generating plant and shall not be deemed to include any
additional electric generating units that may hereafter
be installed at the Palisades Plant site.

SECTION 2 - LIQUID RADWASTE SYSTEM MODIFICATION

§2.1 Consumers Power shall modify the liquid radwaste system now installed in the Palisades Plant to a
liquid radwaste system substantially conforming to the
conceptual design set forth in Appendix II hereto and in
accordance with the principles set forth in this Section 2. The liquid radwaste system as so modified (and
in this Agreement called the "modified liquid radwaste
system") shall be so designed, constructed, operated and
maintained that at all times under normal operating conditions, radioactive materials in liquid discharges from
the Palisades Plant to Lake Michigan are reduced to essentially zero; provided, however, that radioactive materials in laundry waste system discharges which cannot be
treated in the dirty waste system of the modified liquid
radwaste system without the possibility of impairing the
function of dirty waste system equipment may be released
to Lake Michigan at levels which shall in no event exceed

25 picocuries per liter (2.5 X 10^{-8} microcuries/cc) on an
annual average basis; and provided further, that "essentially zero," as used herein, shall not be construed to
preclude liquid discharges to Lake Michigan containing
radioactive materials at levels, as sampled at the recycle
monitor tank before dilution, equivalent to or below then-current Lake Michigan background radioactivity levels, as
monitored offshore from the Palisades Plant prior to such
liquid discharges. As used in this Agreement "normal operating conditions" shall refer to operation of the
Palisades Plant during or in connection with which there
exist no abnormal events or circumstances such as (but
not limited to) steam generator tube leakages, fire, or
pipe breakage; and "abnormal operating conditions" shall
refer to operation of the Palisades Plant during or in
connection with which there exist any such abnormal
events or circumstances. All radioactive materials removed from liquid wastes by the modified liquid radwaste
system will be accumulated and prepared for shipment in
accordance with applicable rules, regulations and orders
of governmental authorities having jurisdiction and turned
over to a carrier or carriers licensed by governmental
authorities having jurisdiction for shipment to an authorized disposal area or areas. Consumers Power intends
to be alert to, and to utilize to the extent it is practical to do so, means of minimizing the amount of laundry
waste that cannot be treated in the dirty waste system.

§2.2 The parties recognize that under abnormal operating conditions it may be impossible or impractical to
achieve essentially zero release of radioactive materials
in liquid discharges from the Palisades Plant through operation of the modified liquid radwaste system. Consumers Power shall so operate the modified liquid radwaste
system as to ensure that radioactive materials in liquid
discharges to Lake Michigan resulting from abnormal operating conditions do not exceed, on a quarterly average
basis and on an individual isotopic analysis basis, ten
percent (10%) of applicable 10 CFR Part 20 limits in
effect as of December 1, 1970 and are reduced to essentially zero no later than sixty (60) consecutive days
after the commencement of such releases resulting from
abnormal operating conditions. Notwithstanding the foregoing, however, delay beyond said sixty (60) day period
in the reduction of radioactive materials in such liquid
discharges to essentially zero shall be excused (subject
to the provisions of Section 10 of this Agreement as
respects [ii] below) to the extent it is (i) due to inability to identify, locate or repair the abnormal operating condition; or due to flood; strike; insurrection;
riot; embargo, act of nature or the public enemy; or by
reason of unavoidable delay in transportation or inability or unavoidable delay in procuring labor or materials;
(ii) due to legal action by a third party; local, state
or federal laws; or the rules, regulations, orders,
actions or failure to act of any public body or official
purporting to exercise authority or control with respect

to such liquid discharges; or (iii) due to any cause beyond the reasonable control of Consumers Power; provided,
however, that radioactive materials in liquid discharges
to Lake Michigan from the modified liquid radwaste system during any such excused delay beyond said sixty (60)
day period shall not exceed, on a quarterly average basis
and on an individual isotopic analysis basis, one percent
(1%) of applicable 10 CFR Part 20 limits in effect as of
December 1, 1970; and provided further, however, that
Consumers Power shall undertake promptly to correct abnormal operating conditions which result in releases of
radioactive materials in liquid discharged to Lake Michigan from the modified liquid radwaste system at levels
greater than essentially zero.

§2.3 Upon execution of this Agreement, Consumers
Power will proceed immediately with all due diligence to
arrange for the design, engineering, procurement of equipment and materials, and construction required to install
the modified liquid radwaste system as provided for herein and to make application to obtain all licenses, permits, consents or other authorizations of public bodies
or officials which are required in connection with the
design, construction, operation and maintenance of the
modified liquid radwaste system. In making and pursuing
such applications Consumers Power shall pursue administrative remedies or court actions, or both, in the manner
provided in Section 10 of this Agreement, and the rights
and obligations of the parties in connection with such
remedies or actions shall be governed and determined by
Section 10 of this Agreement. The design of said system
shall be reviewed and approved by Combustion Engineering,
Inc. in the manner described in subsection B.1.c. and d.
of Article I of the February 8, 1966 Nuclear Equipment
Contract, as amended to December 1, 1970, between Consumers Power and Combustion Engineering, Inc. The modified liquid radwaste system shall be installed and placed
in operation no later than the resumption of operation of
the Palisades Plant after its first scheduled refueling
(which is expected to occur approximately seventeen [17]
calendar months following the date of commencement of escalation to full power following issuance of the full-
power license) or twenty-four (24) calendar months following the date of execution of this Agreement, whichever
occurs first. The foregoing provisions of this §2.3 are
subject to the condition that in the event the installation or the initial operation of such modified liquid radwaste system is delayed (i) by reason of flood; strike;
insurrection; riot; embargo; act of nature or the public
enemy; or unavoidable delay in transportation or inability
or unavoidable delay in procuring labor or materials;
(ii) by reason of legal action by a third party; local,
state or federal laws; or the rules, regulations, orders,
actions or failure to act of any public body or official
purporting to exercise authority or control with respect
to installation or operation of the modified liquid radwaste system; or (iii) by reason of any cause beyond the

reasonable control of Consumers Power, the time for performance shall be extended (subject to the provisions of
Section 10 of this Agreement as respects [ii] above) for
a time equal to the period of such delay. Moreover, until initial successful operation of the modified liquid
radwaste system, Consumers Power shall notify Intervenors
quarterly of all occurrences or conditions then known to
any officer of Consumers Power, or to an employee reporting directly and regularly to any such officer, which
Consumers Power may claim form a basis for an extension
of time for the installation and operation of the modified liquid radwaste system, and shall notify Intervenors
on a current basis of any occurrence or condition known
to any officer of Consumers Power, or to an employee reporting directly and regularly to any such officer, which
Consumers Power then claims will form a basis for such an
extension of time.

§2.4   Pending installation and operation of the
modified liquid radwaste system pursuant to the schedule
provided in §2.3 hereof, Consumers Power, insofar as
Intervenors are concerned, may operate the Palisades Plant
at any power levels authorized by any AEC license issued
to Consumers Power, utilizing the existing liquid radwaste
system; provided that radioactive materials in liquid discharges to Lake Michigan shall be at levels which are at
all times as low as practicable and which do not exceed,
on a quarterly average basis and on an individual isotopic analysis basis, and based on the assumptions used
in Section 11 of Consumers Power's Final Safety Analysis
Report to the AEC for the Palisades Plant as amended to
December 1, 1970, (i) under normal or abnormal operating
conditions as defined in §2.1 hereof and assuming no failed fuel, two percent (2%) of applicable 10 CFR Part 20
limits in effect as of December 1, 1970; and (ii) under
normal or abnormal operating conditions as defined in
§2.1 hereof and assuming some failed fuel, ten percent
(10%) of applicable 10 CFR Part 20 limits in effect as of
December 1, 1970.

SECTION 3 - GASEOUS RADWASTE SYSTEM

§3.1   No engineered feasible system is presently
available to reduce the gaseous radioactivity release from
a pressurized-water-reactor nuclear power plant to essentially zero. Work is presently in progress by reactor
vendors, national laboratories, and utility companies, including Consumers Power, on the development of systems or
components of systems to reduce gaseous waste releases to
essentially zero. Consumers Power will reasonably support the developmental progress of this type of system
and will retrofit such a system to the Palisades Plant
when it is available, provided that regulatory approvals
for such retrofitting can be secured and provided that,
in Consumers Power's reasonable judgment, (i) it is technically feasible to retrofit such a system to the Palisades
Plant at a reasonable cost, and (ii) the use of such a

system in the Palisades Plant would result in a whole-body radiation dose at the Palisades Plant site boundary (assuming a one percent [1%] failed fuel condition) significantly less than the whole-body radiation dose expected at the Palisades Plant site boundary (assuming a one percent [1%] failed fuel condition) utilizing the existing gaseous radwaste system. The latter whole-body radiation dose is described in Appendix III hereto.

SECTION 4 - HOT FUNCTIONAL TEST

§4.1 On or about February 5, 1971 Consumers Power commenced a hot functional test at the Palisades Plant covering the primary system and all nuclear auxiliary systems affected by the heatup of the primary system. The satisfactory performance and completion of such test shall be recorded in Palisades Plant records. At Consumers Power's request, the AEC furnished inspectors to review the test procedures, witness significant parts of the test and verify the test results as recorded in Palisades Plant records. Consumers Power agrees to permit a representative of Intervenors to inspect, at any reasonable time, the Palisades Plant records in which the testing contemplated by this §4.1 is recorded. Consumers Power will request the ASLB or the AEC to have copies of AEC inspection reports covering said test made available to Intervenors.

SECTION 5 - CONTROL ROD TESTS

§5.1 Consumers Power agrees to test in the Palisades Plant reactor, within thirty (30) days after initial fuel loading, all full-length control rods which are to be initially installed in the Palisades Plant reactor. The test shall be made in accordance with the Consumers Power procedure entitled "Control Rod Performance Test," dated January 8, 1971, a copy of which has been furnished to Intervenors, and shall subject said control rods to normal operating temperature, pressure, flow, and rod movements, including drops from the full-out and half-out positions. The reactor shall be held subcritical by boron concentration throughout the test. The data obtained from the test will be evaluated by Combustion Engineering, Inc. to assure that rod drop time requirements are met as provided in the "Control Rod Performance Test" procedure. If control rod drive motor current and drop time measurements made during the test demonstrate that any control rod exhibits any abnormality that would impair the ability of the rod to drop in an acceptable drop time, then Consumers Power shall either repair said rod or replace said rod with a control rod not exhibiting any such abnormality, prior to initial criticality.

§5.2 At the conclusion of zero power physics testing and prior to escalation to power, Consumers Power shall repeat the test contemplated by §5.1 hereof to verify drop times on all installed full-length control rods, and Combustion Engineering, Inc. shall evaluate the data obtained from such repeat test to assure that rod drop time requirements are met as provided in the "Control Rod Performance Test" procedure. If control rod drive motor current and drop time measurements made during the repeat test demonstrate that any control rod exhibits any abnormality which would impair the ability of the rod to drop in an acceptable drop time, then Consumers Power shall either repair said rod or replace said rod with a control rod not exhibiting any such abnormality, prior to escalation to power.

§5.3 Consumers Power shall require Combustion Engineering, Inc. to submit to Consumers Power a written report of its evaluations of the tests contemplated by this Section 5, and a copy of such report shall be filed as a part of the Palisades Plant records. Consumers Power agrees to permit a representative of Intervenors to inspect, at any reasonable time, the Palisades Plant records covering the procedures, measurements and evaluations of the tests contemplated by this Section 5.

SECTION 6 – MPSC APPROVAL; WITHDRAWAL OF INTERVENTION

§6.1 Upon execution of this Agreement, Intervenors shall cooperate with and take all appropriate action to assist and support Consumers Power in expeditiously obtaining the testing license, including but not limited to joining immediately with Consumers Power in presenting and filing in the proceeding the Stipulation (a copy of which is attached hereto as Appendix IV), which shall be executed by the parties' attorneys of record in the proceeding at the time of execution of this Agreement. Upon execution of this Agreement the parties' attorneys of record in the proceeding shall also execute, for later presentation and filing in the proceeding as provided in §6.6 hereof, the Stipulation (a copy of which is attached hereto as Appendix V) supporting issuance to Consumers Power of the full-power license containing the technical specifications in the form set forth in Exhibit A to said Appendix V (said form of technical specifications being called in the Agreement the "special technical specifications") as part of the Technical Specifications for the Palisades Plant. By execution of this Agreement, the parties authorize their respective attorneys of record in this proceeding to execute and file said Stipulations in the proceeding in accordance with this Agreement.

§6.2 Upon execution of this Agreement, Consumers Power shall, with all due diligence, make application to the Michigan Public Service Commission (in this Agreement called the "MPSC") for an order or other authorization (in this Agreement called the "MPSC order") approving Consumers Power's execution and performance of this Agreement and authorizing Consumers Power for rate-making purposes to include in its rate base its total investment in

the design, engineering, equipment and construction of
the modified condenser cooling system and the modified
liquid radwaste system, less depreciation, and to include
in its cost of service the expenses to be incurred in operating and maintaining the modified condenser cooling
system and the modified liquid radwaste system.

§6.3 Except as provided in (ii) of §6.4 hereof,
this Agreement (and all the rights and obligations of the
parties hereunder) shall terminate and the Stipulation
supporting the issuance to Consumers Power of the full-
power license containing the special technical specifications shall be of no further force or effect (i) if the
MPSC order is denied; or (ii) if the proceeding is reconvened to consider the issuance of the full-power license or any operating license other than the testing license prior to the granting or denial of the MPSC order;
or (iii) if, after the MPSC order has been granted, the
proceeding is reconvened to consider the issuance of the
full-power license or any operating license other than
the testing license prior to the expiration of all time
permitted by law for rehearing, appeal or review of the
MPSC order, or prior to the completion of any and all
rehearing, appeal or review of the MPSC order if rehearing, appeal or review thereof is sought by any person.

§6.4 No party hereto shall request that the proceeding be reconvened to consider the issuance of the
full-power license or any operating license other than
the testing license (i) prior to the granting or the
denial of the MPSC order, except that if the MPSC has
neither granted nor denied the MPSC order within sixty
(60) calendar days following the date of filing of the
application for the MPSC order, then Consumers Power
shall have the right to request the reconvening of the
proceeding to consider the issuance of the full-power license or any operating license other than the testing
license; or (ii) while there is pending any request for
rehearing, appeal or review of any granting of the MPSC
order, or during the time in which any such rehearing,
appeal or review of such granted MPSC order may be sought
under applicable law; provided, however, that, while
there is pending any such request for rehearing, appeal
or review of such granted MPSC order, or during the time
in which any such rehearing, appeal or review of such
granted MPSC order may be sought under applicable law,
Consumers Power shall have the right to request that the
proceeding be reconvened to consider the issuance of the
full-power license or any operating license containing
the special technical specifications, other than the
testing license, and if Consumers Power does so request
the proceeding to be reconvened, as provided in this (ii),
then Intervenors agree that they will join in such request, and the parties agree that this Agreement shall
not thereby terminate as provided in §6.3 hereof.

§6.5 Consumers Power shall promptly notify Inter-

venors of any request by any person for any rehearing,
appeal or review of the granting of the MPSC order. Intervenors shall have the right, insofar as Consumers
Power is concerned, to participate in any such rehearing,
appeal or review and Consumers Power shall pursue administrative remedies or court actions, or both, in connection with any such rehearing, appeal or review in the
manner provided for in Section 10 of this Agreement, in
order to assert the validity of the granting of the MPSC
order. If, after exhausting all such administrative
remedies or court actions or both, it is finally determined that the MPSC order, or any portion thereof, should
not have been granted:

      I.   and the MPSC order or portion thereof
is required for the performance by Consumers
Power of any provision or provisions of this
Agreement, then Consumers Power will be forever
relieved of any obligation to perform any provision or provisions of this Agreement (and
any and all other provisions of this Agreement
which require that said provision or provisions
be performed) as to which such invalidated MPSC
order or portion thereof is required;

      II.   and the MPSC order or portion thereof
is not required for the performance by Consumers
Power of any provision or provisions of this
Agreement, then notwithstanding such final determination, Consumers Power will not thereby
be relieved from performing any provision or
provisions of this Agreement.

§6.6   In the event Consumers Power is granted the
MPSC order prior to the time the proceeding is reconvened
to consider issuance of the full-power license or any
operating license other than the testing license, or if,
pursuant to (ii) of §6.4 hereof, Consumers Power requests
the reconvening of the proceeding while there is pending
any request for rehearing, appeal or review of such
granted MPSC order, or during the time in which any such
rehearing, appeal or review of such granted MPSC order
may be sought under applicable law, Consumers Power shall
promptly deliver to Intervenors a notice to that effect.
Intervenors shall thereupon cooperate with and take all
appropriate action not inconsistent with this Agreement
to assist and support Consumers Power in expeditiously
obtaining the full-power license containing the special
technical specifications, including but not limited to
joining with Consumers Power in presenting and filing
the Stipulation executed at the same time as this Agreement (a copy of which is attached hereto as Appendix V).
From the time of the execution of this Agreement Intervenors shall not, unless requested by Consumers Power in
order to support the issuance of the testing license and/
or the full-power license containing the special technical specifications, or unless directed or requested by

the ASLB, or unless permitted by this Agreement or the
Stipulations (copies of which are attached hereto as
Appendixes IV and V), take any further action in the proceeding or file any documents therein (other than the
aforesaid Stipulations) or initiate or participate in
any actions (including but not limited to administrative
remedies or court actions) dehors the proceeding with respect to or in connection with the testing license, or
the full-power license containing the special technical
specifications, or the issuance of said licenses.

§6.7   When (i) the full-power license has been issued to Consumers Power containing the special technical
specifications and (ii) the initial or final decision in
the proceeding has become the final action of the AEC
without amendment of the said full-power license so as to
remove or change the special technical specifications,
then Intervenors shall be deemed, without further action
on their part, to have withdrawn from the proceeding with
prejudice and without right thereafter (except as otherwise provided in §§6.9, 6.10 and 11.2 and Section 10 of
this Agreement) to take any further action in the proceeding or otherwise in AEC Docket No. 50-255; or to take
any action in any AEC proceeding to extend, renew or convert the full-power license from a provisional to a final
operating license or to amend the full-power license to
authorize operation of the Palisades Plant at any power
level higher than that authorized in the full-power license; or to appeal or to stay the effectiveness of any
or all decisions, findings, orders or rulings theretofore
or thereafter made or entered in the proceeding or otherwise in AEC Docket No. 50-255 or in any AEC proceeding to
so extend, renew, convert or amend the full-power license;
or to initiate or participate in any actions (including
but not limited to administrative remedies or court actions) dehors the proceeding with respect to or in connection with the testing license or the full-power license or the issuance of said licenses.   Moreover, upon
such issuance of the full-power license containing the
special technical specifications and the initial or final
decision in the proceeding having become the final action
of the AEC, as aforesaid in (i) and (ii) of this §6.7,
Intervenors shall also thereby be deemed to have waived
and forever relinquished any and all rights to take any
legal action with respect to any alleged noncompliance
of the Palisades Plant, the proceeding or any decision
in the proceeding, or the testing license or the full-
power license, with the National Environmental Policy Act,
the Federal Water Pollution Control Act as amended, the
Atomic Energy Act of 1954 as amended, the Federal Rivers
and Harbors Act of March 3, 1899 as amended, the Federal
Clean Air Act as amended, or with any other federal,
state or local statutes or ordinances and any rules, orders and regulations of the AEC or any other public official or agency under any of said Acts, statutes or ordinances.

§6.8 Consumers Power shall have the right to terminate this Agreement by notice to Intervenors if (i) the full-power license containing the special technical specifications has not been issued by the AEC Director of Regulation within one hundred fifty (150) calendar days after the date of execution of this Agreement (provided, that said 150-day period shall be extended by one day for each day that the completion of low-power testing under the testing license is delayed beyond thirty-five [35] calendar days from and after the date of issuance of the testing license), or (ii) there has been entered a court order or decree or an order of a public body or official having jurisdiction which, in the reasonable opinion of legal counsel for Consumers Power, renders improbable the issuance of such a full-power license within said 150-day period, as said 150-day period may be extended under (i) of this §6.8, or, if such court order or decree or order of a public body or official prevents the completion of the low-power testing, as said 150-day period may have been extended under (i) of this §6.8 prior to the entry of such court order or decree or order of a public body or official. Upon delivery of such notice this Agreement (and all the rights and obligations of the parties hereunder) shall terminate and the Stipulation (a copy of which is attached hereto as Appendix V) supporting the issuance to Consumers Power of such a full-power license, if theretofore filed in the proceeding, shall be withdrawn and shall be of no further force or effect.

§6.9 Nothing contained in this Section 6 shall preclude Intervenors from initiating any action or proceeding in AEC Docket No. 50-255 on account of Consumers Power's alleged breach of or failure of performance pursuant to this Agreement.

§6.10 Consumers Power shall give Intervenors advance notice of any change in the technical specifications of the full-power license respecting the construction, installation and operation of the modified radwaste and/or condenser cooling system proposed by Consumers Power after the issuance of said license. If Intervenors are of the opinion that any such proposed change is a breach of or failure of performance pursuant to this Agreement, they shall notify Consumers Power of such opinion within fifteen (15) business days following delivery of said notice by Consumers Power. If within ten (10) business days after delivery of such notice to Consumers Power, Intervenors request the AEC to hold a public hearing in connection with such proposed change, and if such request is reasonable, then Consumers Power will also request the AEC to hold a public hearing in connection with such proposed change. Nothing herein shall preclude Intervenors from initiating any action or proceeding, in addition to such an AEC hearing, to contest any such proposed change on the ground that it is a breach of or failure of performance pursuant to this Agreement.

SECTION 7 - RESERVATIONS

§7.1 Nothing in this Agreement shall prevent Consumers Power from taking any steps or measures in connection with the design, construction, modification or operation of the modified condenser cooling system and the
modified liquid radwaste system which contemplate modifications, procedures or modes of operation equal to or
better, considering the protection of the environment,
than the modifications, procedures or modes of operation
contemplated in this Agreement; provided, however, that
the foregoing provisions shall not authorize Consumers
Power to take any steps or measures to install and operate a modified condenser cooling system having an open-
cycle system utilizing Lake Michigan water for once-
through cooling or to install and operate a modified
liquid radwaste system which would release radioactivity
to the environment at levels above those contemplated in
Section 2 and Appendix II of this Agreement under the
conditions therein stated.

§7.2 The parties agree that Consumers Power's agreement to the modifications, procedures and modes of operation contemplated herein for the Palisades Plant and any
action taken by Consumers Power pursuant to this Agreement before or after the execution of this Agreement
shall not be deemed, construed, interpreted or claimed to
be an admission that the same or any similar modifications, procedures or modes of operation are necessary or
required at any other Consumers Power electric generating
plant.   The obligations of Consumers Power under this
Agreement are limited to the Palisades Plant.

SECTION 8 - OTHER PROCEEDINGS

§8.1 Intervenors shall not initiate, or take part
in directly or indirectly, or aid, advise or furnish information to any other person, corporation or association
in connection with, any suit, proceeding before any governmental agency, or other action, whether or not now
pending (including but not limited to the pending proceeding in AEC Docket Nos. 50-329 and 50-330 concerning
issuance of construction permits for Consumers Power's
midland Plant Units 1 and 2) to raise or contest issues
with respect to (i) the design, construction, licensing
or operation of the Palisades Plant, including but not
limited to the licensing or operation of the Palisades
Plant at power levels above 2200 thermal megawatts (except as otherwise permitted by §§6.9, 6.10 and 11.2 and
Section 10 of this Agreement); (ii) expenditures by Consumers Power to install and operate the modified liquid
radwaste system or the modified condenser cooling system
at the Palisades Plant; (iii) expenditures by Consumers
Power to obtain the testing and full-power licenses for
the Palisades Plant or expenditures in connection therewith or resulting therefrom.

SECTION 9 - INFORMATION AND REPORTS

§9.1 Not more frequently than quarterly, Consumers Power will answer reasonable requests for information respecting its performance under Sections 1, 2 and 3 of this Agreement when made in writing by one (1) of the representatives designated in or in accordance with Section 16 hereof on behalf of all of the Intervenors. Furthermore, Consumers Power shall, without request therefor, furnish to a representative of Intervenors, on behalf of all of the Intervenors, one (1) copy of all written reports Consumers Power is required to file with the AEC under the Plant Reporting Requirements of the Technical Specifications for the Palisades Plant.

§9.2 Upon execution of this Agreement, Consumers Power shall amend its proposed Technical Specifications for the Palisades Plant to add the following new item e. to subsection 6.6.1 of Section 6.6, "PLANT REPORTING REQUIREMENTS":

"e.   When a control rod or a part-length rod is misaligned as defined in 3.10.4.a of these Technical Specifications or when a control rod is inoperable as defined in 3.10.4.b of these Technical Specifications."

SECTION 10 - LEGAL VALIDITY

§10.1 If Consumers Power believes that the performance of any provision or provisions of this Agreement (including any corresponding special technical specifications included in the full-power license, whether or not specified in the notice) is contrary to or prevented by any local, state or federal law, or the rule, regulation, order, action or failure to act of any public body or official purporting to exercise authority with respect thereto, or the order or decree of any court, then Consumers Power shall promptly notify Intervenors thereof by telegram, telephone or other means and notify Intervenors thereof in writing within ten (10) business days thereafter, stating the basis for such belief. In the event Intervenors notify Consumers Power of their agreement with such belief within thirty (30) calendar days after delivery of the aforesaid written notice by Consumers Power (and from the time of the aforesaid telephonic, telegraphic, or other means of notice by Consumers Power and until the end of such thirty (30) day period whether or not such notification is given to Consumers Power by Intervenors) Consumers Power shall be relieved of any obligation to perform the provision or provisions in question and any and all other provisions of this Agreement which require that said provision or provisions be performed. However, notwithstanding its release from obligation as provided in this §10.1, Consumers Power shall have the right, in its sole discretion, to perform or

seek to perform said provision or provisions. In the
event Intervenors do not so notify Consumers Power within said thirty (30) day period, then Consumers Power
shall in good faith and with due diligence pursue administrative remedies or court actions (including appeals
or requests for writs of certiorari to the highest state
or federal court having jurisdiction), or both, to assert
the validity of the performance of said provision or provisions and/or the invalidity or unlawfulness of the law,
rule, regulation, order, decree, action or failure to act
that is the subject of the aforesaid written notice by
Consumers Power.

§10.2   In the event of an unfavorable ruling or the
inability to have the validity of the performance of such
provision or provisions (which are the subject of suit
and/or proceeding as contemplated in §10.1 hereof) upheld
after exhausting all rights of hearing, appeal and requests for writs of certiorari to the highest state or
federal court having jurisdiction, then Consumers Power
will forever be relieved of any obligation to perform the
provision or provisions in question and any and all other
provisions of this Agreement which require that said provision or provisions be performed.

§10.3   In the event Intervenors or one or more of
them seek to participate in any court action or administrative proceeding contemplated by §10.1 hereof, Consumers Power agrees not to oppose their participation and
to stipulate or take other appropriate action to induce
the court or agency to permit Intervenors or one or more
of them to participate in the proceeding.   Whether or not
Intervenors are permitted to participate, the parties
shall cooperate by exchanging all pertinent information,
documents, pleadings, or other papers filed or of record
in such court or agency proceeding.

§10.4   In the event Intervenors are not permitted
to participate as a party in any such court or administrative proceeding, Consumers Power agrees to consider
adopting and submitting evidence and arguments of Intervenors in support of Consumers Power's position before
the court or agency except and unless the same are, in
Consumers Power's judgment, defamatory, irrelevant, repetitious, inaccurate or otherwise improper.

§10.5   The parties agree that while Consumers Power
is pursuing the administrative remedies or court actions,
or both, contemplated in §10.1 hereof, Consumers Power
may operate the Palisades Plant in any manner permitted
by law; provided, however, Consumers Power agrees that
while it is pursuing said administrative remedies or
court actions, or both, it shall continue to perform all
of the provisions of this Agreement except any provision
or provisions (and any and all other provisions which require that said provision or provisions be performed) as

to which (i) it is prevented by a court order or decree
or is prevented by an order, notice or other action of
any public body or official having authority to enforce
such order, notice or other action without resort to a
court for enforcement; or (ii) it is prevented by the
lack of any permit, license, consent or other authorization of any public body or official which is required for
continued performance; or (iii) to do so would, in the
reasonable opinion of legal counsel for Consumers Power,
result in the violation of any criminal law or criminal
ordinance or the imposition of any criminal or civil
fine, criminal or civil penalty, or criminal or civil forfeiture; or (iv) there has been entered a court order or
decree or an order, notice or other action of a public
body or official which, while not preventing performance
of this Agreement by Consumers Power, would require shutdown of the Palisades Plant or a reduction in the electrical output of the Palisades Plant if Consumers Power
continued to perform.

§10.6 The special technical specifications to be
included in the full-power license shall provide that
Consumers Power shall be relieved of any obligation to
comply with said technical specifications to the extent
and during the time that Consumers Power is relieved from
performing any corresponding provision or provisions of
this Agreement pursuant to this Section 10.

SECTION 11 - DISPUTES

§11.1 If any dispute arises between Consumers
Power and Intervenors concerning the interpretation or
performance of this Agreement, they will first attempt
to resolve the same by good faith discussions directed
toward settlement by further agreement.

§11.2 Any party hereto shall have the right, if not
inconsistent with the terms of this Agreement, to enforce
any obligation of any other party hereto under this
Agreement in any action, including administrative actions
and actions in AEC Docket No. 50-255; provided, however,
the parties hereto agree that a breach of this Agreement
by any party cannot be adequately compensated or measured
by money damages and that the parties to this Agreement
with respect to enforcement thereof do not have an adequate remedy at law, except that a party hereto may enforce any obligation of any other party hereto and seek
money damages for breach of an obligation, if the breach
resulted from or was based upon conduct which is either
arbitrary, capricious or in bad faith.

§11.3 The parties agree that the obligations herein are not intended to create third party beneficiary
rights and are not enforceable at the instance of any
person who is not a party hereto except as, and to the
extent that, the provisions hereof may be enforceable

under applicable laws by any public body or official having authority to do so.

SECTION 12 - RATIFICATION AND APPROVAL

§12.1 Concurrently with the execution of this Agreement Consumers Power and each corporate Intervenor shall
deliver to each of the other parties verified evidence
of the authority of the person executing the same to do
so for and on behalf of the corporation represented by
such person. Within thirty (30) days after the execution
of this Agreement, each Intervenor which is a voluntary
association or other unincorporated organization shall
deliver to each of the other parties a verified certificate by the president or other authorized representative
thereof affirming that the members of the association or
organization have authorized or ratified and approved
this Agreement and the execution thereof on behalf of the
association or other unincorporated organization or that
such members are not required to specifically authorize
or ratify and approve this Agreement and the execution
thereof, and that such members will be jointly and severally bound by this Agreement without their specific
authorization or ratification and approval thereof.

SECTION 13 - BINDING EFFECT

§13.1 The promises and undertakings herein shall
be binding upon the parties signatory to this Agreement
and upon their heirs, representatives, seccessors and assigns; provided, however, that any transfer or assignment
by an Intervenor of this Agreement to another party
(whether or not the latter is a signatory hereof) or to
a successor, without the prior written consent of Consumers Power, shall be null and void; and provided further,
however, that Consumers Power shall consent to the transfer of this Agreement to a successor corporation of a
corporate Intervenor upon the merger or consolidation of
such corporate Intervenor with, or the transfer of substantially all of its assets to, another corporation having in general the same purposes and objectives as the
said corporate Intervenor and if said successor corporation is, by applicable law or otherwise, bound and obligated under this Agreement to the same extent and in
the same manner as said corporate Intervenor was so bound
and obligated prior to such merger, consolidation or
transfer of assets.

§13.2 Consumers Power agrees that any unincorporated Intervenor may transfer and assign this Agreement to
a nonprofit corporation hereafter organized under the
laws of the State of Michigan by all of the then members
(in this §13.2 called "incorporating members") of said
Intervenor and having in general the same purposes and
objectives as said unincorporated Intervenor, provided
(i) that said corporation agrees in writing with Consumers Power to assume and be bound by all of the obliga-

tions of Intervenors under this Agreement; (ii) that all
living incorporating members of said Intervenor, and all
living persons who were members in good standing of said
Intervenor on the date of its intervention in the proceeding or at any time during the proceeding (in this
§13.2 called "intervening members"), consent in writing
to said transfer and assignment; (iii) that all living
incorporating members and all living intervening members
of said Intervenor execute and deliver to Consumers Power
a written release, in a form satisfactory to Consumers
Power, forever releasing and discharging Consumers Power
from any and all obligations under this Agreement to each
said incorporating or intervening member; (iv) that said
Intervenor delivers to Consumers Power a complete list of
its incorporating and intervening members and the last-
known address of each said member, verified by the representative of said Intervenor who executes this Agreement; and (v) that compliance by said Intervenor and the
incorporating and intervening members thereof with the
conditions of this §13.2 shall be a condition precedent
to the effectiveness and validity of said transfer or
assignment.

SECTION 14 - PUBLICITY

§14.1   Intervenors and Consumers Power agree that
each party may disclose to others such of the terms of
this Agreement, as well as the reasons underlying such
party's having entered into the same, as such party may
determine or as may be required to effectuate the terms
hereof or as may be required by law or order of any governmental authority.

§14.2   The parties will issue a joint news release
announcing execution of this Agreement, as follows:

"Spokesmen for Consumers Power Company
and the groups which have intervened in AEC
licensing proceedings to contest the issuance of an operating license for the Company's Palisades Nuclear Power Plant on
Lake Michigan in Covert Township, Van Buren
County, Michigan, today announced that the
parties have entered into a settlement agreement.

"The Company announced that it will
proceed with a program to install and operate,
under AEC license limitations, cooling towers
and an essentially zero radioactive liquid
release system at the Palisades Plant.   The
modifications will be a major undertaking and
may take several years to complete.   It is
contemplated that the Plant will operate as presently constructed while the work is being done.

"Under the settlement agreement, install-

ation of the modifications is conditioned
upon receipt of an order of the Michigan
Public Service Commission approving the
Company's execution and performance of the
settlement agreement.

"The settlement agreement also provides
that the Intervenors will agree to the immediate issuance of a license to permit the
Company to load fuel and begin low-power
testing at the plant. When the Public Service Commission approval and a full-power
AEC license are obtained, the Intervenors
will also withdraw from the AEC proceeding
and waive all rights of appeal on the issues
they have been contesting.

"The proposed cooling towers will be
of the mechanical or natural draft type.
Except for the cleansing of lake water
residues from the towers, they will form a
closed circuit in which heated condenser
cooling water will be cooled and recirculated for use in the Plant.

"The modifications to the liquid radioactive waste system will essentially eliminate radioactive liquid discharges under normal
conditions. The existing system would release some radioactivity, although at levels
substantially below current AEC limits.

"A spokesman for the intervening groups
urged approval and installation of the modifications as soon as possible, describing the
Company's program as a major advance toward
protection of the environment through utilization of the latest and best technology.

"The intervenors' spokesman also said:
'We hope and trust that all state and federal
agencies whose approval is required for these
modifications will move quickly to permit the
parties to carry out their agreement, which we
believe will assure the environmental protection we have been seeking and is thus in the
public interest.'

"Spokesmen for both parties expect that
the AEC hearing can be concluded in the near
future and that issuance of a full-power operating license will soon follow."

The foregoing news release is not in any way intended,
and shall not be deemed, to add to or subtract from or
modify any of the rights and obligations of the parties
set forth in this Agreement, and shall not in any way be

used to interpret the provisions of this Agreement.

SECTION 15 - SERVICE OF PROCESS

§15.1 For the purpose of bringing suit in connection with this Agreement in any court in the State of
Michigan, any party may (in addition to any other procedures authorized by applicable law or rules) obtain service of process upon any other party by leaving a copy
of the Summons and Complaint with said other party's representative or representatives named in or pursuant to
Section 16 of this Agreement, and by sending by registered mail a Summons and a copy of the Complaint to said
other party at its address stated in the first paragraph
at page 1 of this Agreement (or, if such stated address
is changed and said other party has notified all parties
hereto of such change in writing, at said changed address
of said other party). Service of process made in accordance with the foregoing provisions shall constitute valid
service of process upon any party so served. This §15.1
shall not govern the method of service of process for any
suit brought elsewhere than in the State of Michigan.

SECTION 16 - NOTICES

§16.1 Except as otherwise specifically provided in
§10.1 hereof, any notice or other communication required
by this Agreement shall be in writing and delivered
either by messenger to the office of a representative of
a party during regular business hours or by registered
or certified mail, return receipt requested, postage prepaid to a representative of a party, as follows:

    (a) If to Consumers Power:

> P. A. Perry, Secretary
> Consumers Power Company
> 212 West Michigan Avenue
> Jackson, Michigan 49201

    (b) If to Intervenors:

> For all Intervenors except Sierra Club:

> Eric V. Brown, Sr., Esq.
> Brown, Colman & DeMent
> 125 W. Walnut Street
> Kalamazoo, Michigan 49007

> and

> Myron M. Cherry, Esq.
> McDermott, Will & Emery
> 111 West Monroe Street
> Chicago, Illinois 60603

For Sierra Club:

Lewis D. Drain, Esq.
Mika, Meyers, Beckett & Jones
311 Waters Building
Grand Rapids, Michigan 49502

Copies of all such notices and information
shall be delivered to:

David Dinsmore Comey
Businessmen For The Public Interest, Inc.
109 North Dearborn Street, Suite 1001
Chicago, Illinois 60602

Any party may change its representative or representatives at any time, provided, however, that (i) the
Sierra Club, and (ii) all Intervenors except Sierra Club,
shall each have one representative who shall have and
maintain a business address in the Lower Peninsula of the
State of Michigan, and all Intervenors except Sierra Club
may in addition have one representative who shall have
and maintain a business address in Cook County in the
State of Illinois; and provided further, that said party
shall notify the others in writing of any change in the
identity and/or address of its said representative or
representatives. Notices and other communications required to be made in writing pursuant to this Agreement
shall be deemed to be delivered on the day of actual delivery if by messenger or on the third calendar day after
the day of mailing, as the case may be.

SECTION 17 - TERMINATION

§17.1 If not previously terminated, this Agreement
and all rights and obligations of the parties hereunder
shall automatically terminate thirty-six (36) calendar
months after initial successful operation of the modified condenser cooling system or the modified liquid radwaste system, whichever is later, unless Consumers Power
is relieved of its obligation to install or operate one
or both of said systems pursuant to Section 10 of this
Agreement, in which event all rights and obligations of
the parties under this Agreement shall automatically terminate (i) thirty-six (36) calendar months after initial
successful operation of either the modified condenser
cooling system or the modified liquid radwaste system,
if Consumers Power is so relieved of its obligation to
install or operate the other system pursuant to said
Section 10; or (ii) twenty-four (24) calendar months after the date that Consumers Power is relieved of its obligation to install or operate the modified condenser
cooling system or the modified liquid radwaste system,
whichever date is later, if Consumers Power is relieved
of its obligations to install or operate both systems
pursuant to said Section 10. The foregoing provisions
are subject to the specific condition that any breach of,

or failure of performance pursuant to, this Agreement by
any Intervenor or Consumers Power, and the responsibility
or liability arising therefrom, which occurs prior to the
termination of this Agreement as aforesaid, shall survive
such termination. Consumers Power shall notify Intervenors of the date of initial successful operation of the
modified condenser cooling system or the modified liquid
radwaste system, or of the date that Consumers Power is
relieved of its obligations to install both of said systems, whichever is applicable under this §17.1. Consumers Power shall make available to a representative of
Intervenors such records as are necessary to support such
notification.

SECTION 18 - ENTIRE AGREEMENT

§18.1 This agreement supersedes all prior representations, negotiations and understandings of the parties
hereto, whether oral or written, and constitutes the entire Agreement of the parties with respect to the subject matter hereof. This Agreement shall not be changed,
supplemented or superseded, except in writing, duly executed on behalf of the parties hereto.

IN WITNESS WHEREOF, the parties have executed this
Agreement as of the day and year hereinabove first mentioned.

CONSUMERS POWER COMPANY   CONCERNED PETITIONING CITIZENS

By_____ By_____
     Senior Vice President

MICHIGAN STEELHEAD AND   MICHIGAN LAKE AND STREAM
    SALMON FISHERMEN'S   ASSOCIATIONS, INC.
    ASSOCIATION

By_____ By_____

THERMAL ECOLOGY MUST BE   SIERRA CLUB
    PRESERVED

By_____ By_____

Agreement dated in March, 1971   <u>APPENDIX I</u>
between Consumers Power Company
and Michigan Steelhead and Salmon
Fishermen's Association, et al.

MODIFIED CONDENSER COOLING SYSTEM

The modified condenser cooling system will be designed in accordance with the principles set forth in Section 1 of this Agreement and will substantially conform to the conceptual design described in this Appendix I. A sketch of the proposed modified condenser cooling system is shown in Exhibit A hereto. To accomodate this closed circuit system, modifications will have to be made to the plant. The existing cooling water intake structure will be modified so that the present lake inlet will go only to the service water pump bay. The existing service water pumps (not shown) will take suction from the cooling tower basin and from the lake, with the lake providing cooling tower makeup water. The existing circulating water pumps will be isolated from the lake inlet and instead will receive water from the cooling tower basin and discharge to the condenser. New circulating water pumps will be installed to carry the condenser discharge flow to the cooling tower inlet. The circulating water will pass through the tower into the basin below and then on to the modified intake structure where it will again be pumped through the condenser using the existing circulating water pumps, or will flow through the condenser by gravity.

Some water must be discharged from the cooling tower basin to the lake in order to control the concentration of salts or other impurities which are contained in the lake makeup water. This discharge is termed the tower "blowdown." Dilution pumps will be installed to add lake water to the blowdown prior to discharge into the lake. The dilution water flow will be such that the temperature of the mixed dilution water and blowdown will not exceed the ambient temperature of the receiving water at the shoreline by more than 5°F. The design heat rejection to the Lake as a result of this discharge will be as low as practicable consistent with available equipment, Palisades Plant and Consumers Power electrical system operating requirements, design optimization and other condenser cooling system design objectives, and will in no event exceed 500,000,000 BTU/hr.

Design and construction of the cooling tower or towers shall conform to the latest applicable Cooling Tower Institute (CTI) codes and standards applicable at the time of detailed design, except to the extent the same may be contrary to any applicable law or rule, regulation or order of any governmental body having jurisdiction.

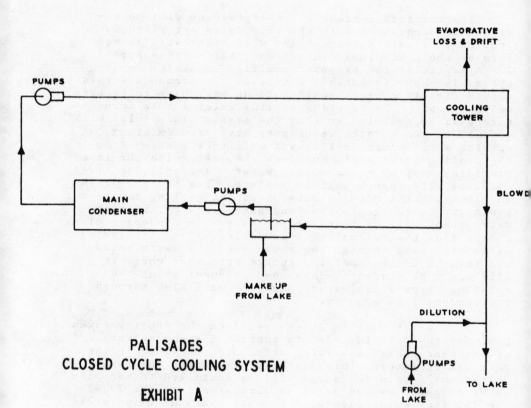

PALISADES
CLOSED CYCLE COOLING SYSTEM

EXHIBIT A

Agreement dated in March, 1971   APPENDIX II
between Consumers Power Company
and Michigan Steelhead and Salmon
Fishermen's Association, et al.

MODIFIED LIQUID RADWASTE SYSTEM

The modified liquid radwaste system will be designed
in accordance with the principles set forth in Section
2 of this Agreement and will substantially conform to the
conceptual design described in this Appendix II. The system will be designed to collect, store, process, monitor
and dispose of all liquid radioactive wastes from the
Palisades Plant. The integrated system will be basically
comprised of the following three subsystems: clean waste,
dirty waste and laundry. The subsystems are shown on
Exhibits A, B and C hereto, respectively.

The clean waste system processes high-activity, high-
purity (low solids) liquid wastes collected from four
basic sources: the letdown from the primary coolant system, the primary system drain tank, the radioactive-
chemical laboratory drain tank and the equipment drain
tank.

The letdown from the primary coolant system is the
largest source of both radioactivity and liquid to the
clean radwaste system. The main sources of this liquid
are thermal expansion of the primary coolant system and
dilution of the primary coolant for boron concentration
control.

The primary system drain tank serves as a collection
point in the containment building for seven sources of
liquid: chemical and volume control system heat exchanger drains, reactor shield cooling drains, safety injection tank drains, primary coolant pump seal leakage, primary loop drains, quench tank drains, and reactor flange
leakage drains.

The radioactive chemical-laboratory drain tank
serves as a collection point for the sample sink drains
and the clean radioactive chemical-laboratory drains.

The equipment drain tank serves as a collection
point for the spent resin shipping cask drains, radioactive steam generator blowdown, spent fuel pool heat
exchanger drains, spent fuel pool drain, spent resin storage tank drains, charging pumps relief line and drains,
chemical and volume control system ion exchangers and
filter drains, volume control tank drains, and waste gas
surge tank drain.

The liquids from the primary system drain tank and
the letdown pass through the vacuum degasifier where they
are joined by the liquids from the radioactive chemical

laboratory drain tank and the equipment drain tank. These
liquids are then collected and held up for natural decay
in the clean waste receiver tanks. After sufficient decay the liquids are pumped out of the clean waste receiver tanks, through the clean waste filter, the radwaste
ion exchangers and the treated waste monitoring tanks to
an evaporator. The evaporator will serve to further
clean the demineralized liquids and to separate out the
boric acid. The distillate from the evaporator will be
stored in the primary coolant system makeup tank from
which it will eventually be reused in the plant. The
concentrate from the evaporator will be essentially pure
boric acid and will be stored in the boric acid tank until further use or sent to the solid waste drumming station for packaging and eventual off-site disposal.

The dirty waste system collects low activity, high
solids liquid from the engineered safeguards rooms, the
volume control tank relief, access control area sink,
emergency shower, containment sump drains, vent stack
drains, pump leak-off, decontamination pit drains, spent
fuel cask washdown drains, contaminated lab drains, boric
acid area drains, component cooling loop drains, floor
drains, treated waste monitor tank drains and the component cooling water surge tank. These liquids are collected in the dirty waste drain tank from which they are
passed through the dirty waste filter to the filtered
waste monitor tank. The filtered liquids will then be
processed through an evaporator to further clean up the
liquids and to separate out any boric acid or other
solids. Like the clean waste distillate, the distillate
from the dirty waste evaporator will be recycled for reuse in the plant. The concentrate will be reused
as boric acid (if pure enough) or sent to the solid waste
drumming station for packaging and eventual off-site disposal.

The laundry wastes consist of the used wash water
from the plant laundry facility. This liquid may have
picked up some solids from clothing and is therefore filtered to remove contaminates. The liquid will be processed through the dirty waste system unless it contains
materials which cannot be so processed without the possibility of impairing the function of dirty waste system
equipment.

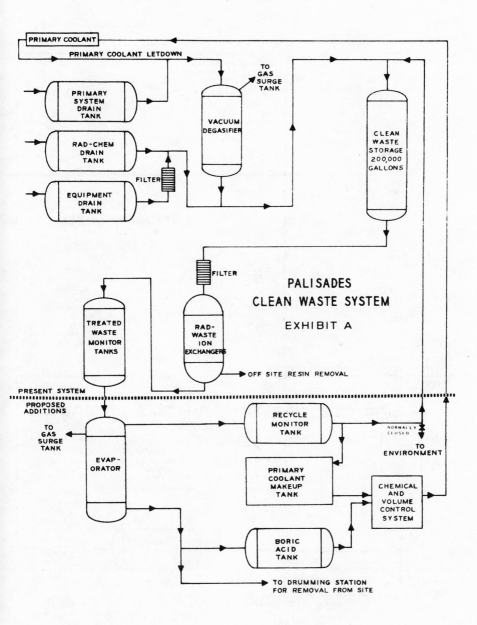

PALISADES
CLEAN WASTE SYSTEM

EXHIBIT A

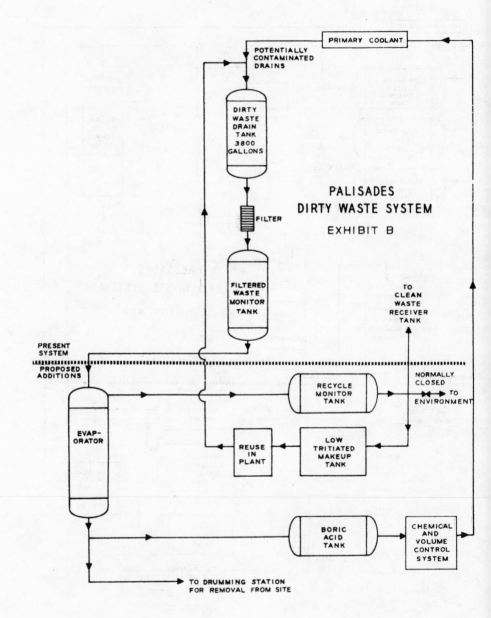

PALISADES
DIRTY WASTE SYSTEM
EXHIBIT B

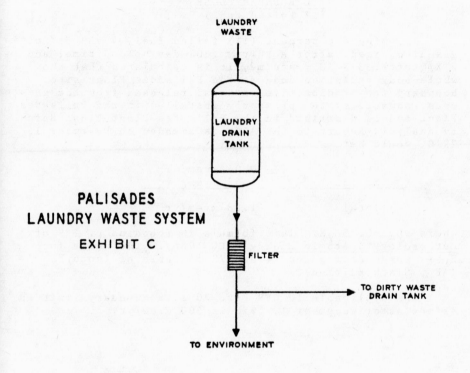

LAUNDRY
WASTE

LAUNDRY
DRAIN
TANK

PALISADES
LAUNDRY WASTE SYSTEM
EXHIBIT C

FILTER

TO DIRTY WASTE
DRAIN TANK

TO ENVIRONMENT

Agreement dated in March, 1971   APPENDIX III
between Consumers Power Company
and Michigan Steelhead and Salmon
Fishermen's Association, et al.

GASEOUS RADWASTE SYSTEM

SITE BOUNDARY DOSE
(1% Failed Fuel)

Assuming one percent (1%) failed fuel, 4,539 ft^3 of
gas discharged, after a thirty (30) day holdup time, and
a X/Q of 1.33 X 10^{-5} sec/m^3, it is calculated that the
whole-body radiation dose at the Palisades Plant site
boundary from radioactive material released from the gaseous radwaste system presently installed in the Palisades
Plant and as described in the Palisades Plant Final Safety Analysis Report to the AEC, as amended to December 1,
1970, would be:

$$
\begin{array}{lcl}
\text{Kr-85} & - & 0.06 \text{ mrem/yr} \\
\underline{\text{Xe-133}} & - & \underline{1.62 \text{ mrem/yr}} \\
\\
\text{Total} & - & 1.68 \text{ mrem/yr}
\end{array}
$$

where $_\gamma D_\infty = 0.25 \bar{E}_\gamma X$. This formula is found on p. 339 of
Meteorology & Atomic Energy (AEC 1968). The value for
$\bar{E}_\gamma$ is taken from pages 34 and 72 of Table of Isotopes
(AEC, Sixth Edition).

The applicable 10 CFR Part 20 site boundary limit in
effect as of December 1, 1970 is 500 mrem/yr.

Agreement dated in March, 1971   APPENDIX IV
between Consumers Power Company
and Michigan Steelhead and Salmon
Fishermen's Association, et al.

UNITED STATES OF AMERICA

ATOMIC ENERGY COMMISSION

In the Matter of   )
CONSUMERS POWER COMPANY)   Docket No. 50-255
(Palisades Plant)   )

STIPULATION BY AND BETWEEN ALL INTERVENORS
AND APPLICANT IN SUPPORT OF FUEL LOADING
AND LOW-POWER TESTING LICENSE

Applicant and Intervenors, by their respective
undersigned attorneys, and subject to the terms and provisions of an Agreement between Applicant and Intervenors
dated the 12th day of March, 1971 (hereinafter called
the "settlement agreement"), hereby stipulate and agree
as follows:

1. That in accordance with the Notice of Hearing
of May 18, 1970 in this proceeding, Applicant filed herein on July 21, 1970 a written motion for a license authorizing fuel loading and low-power testing of the
Palisades Plant at power levels not to exceed one thermal
megawatt (hereinafter called "the testing license");
that whereas Intervenors have heretofore contested the
granting of the testing license, Applicant and Intervenors entered into the settlement agreement and accordingly Intervenors no longer contest, but now support,
prompt issuance to Applicant of the testing license;
that, therefore, as regards fuel loading and low-power
testing of the Palisades Plant at Power levels not to exceed one thermal megawatt, there no longer is any "contested activity to be authorized" within the meaning of
the Notice of Hearing of May 18, 1970.

2. That, subject to paragraph 7 of this Stipulation, the Atomic Safety and Licensing Board (hereinafter
called "the ASLB") may, but solely for purposes of the
testing license, accept Applicant's evidence in this proceeding as uncontroverted within the meaning of §VI(b) of
Appendix A of the AEC's Rules of Practice and find that
there is good cause for the issuance to Applicant of the
testing license; and Applicant and Intervenors consent to
the entry of the proposed findings of fact, conclusions
of law and form of order contained in Exhibit A hereto,
or to findings of fact, conclusions of law and an order
by the ASLB not inconsistent with said Exhibit A.

3. That the testing license should be issued pursuant to Applicant's request; and that the initial de-

cision or order authorizing or directing the issuance of
the testing license, and the testing license as well,
should become effective at the earliest time permitted by
law and the rules and regulations of the AEC.

 4. That in support of the prompt issuance to Applicant of a testing license in accordance with this Stipulation, Intervenors:

> (i)   will not engage in any further
>   voir dire examination, cross-
>   examination, or direct examina-
>   tion herein;
>
> (ii)   will not make any further argu-
>   ment, objections, offers of proof,
>   motions or requests herein;
>
> (iii) will not submit or file or seek
>   leave to submit or file any plead-
>   ing, evidence, exhibit or other
>   document herein; and
>
> (iv)   will not take any other action here-
>   in or initiate or participate in
>   any actions (including but not
>   limited to administrative remedies
>   or court actions) dehors this pro-
>   ceeding with respect to or in con-
>   nection with the testing license,
>   or the issuance of said license,

unless requested by Applicant in order to support the issuance to Applicant of the testing license, or unless
directed or requested by ASLB, or unless permitted by
the settlement agreement or this Stipulation.

 5. That Intervenors will not file any exceptions to
any initial decision or order of the ASLB authorizing or
directing the issuance of the testing license issued in
accordance with this Stipulation.

 6. That, subject to paragraph 7 of this Stipulation, Intervenors consent to the filing in this proceeding and service upon the parties and persons required to
be served under the rules of practice of the AEC, of
written testimony, exhibits, pleadings and other documents by Applicant and the AEC Regulatory Staff with respect to Applicant's application for a license to operate
the Palisades Plant at power levels in excess of one
thermal megawatt prior to the reconvening of this proceeding to consider the issuance to Applicant of such an
operating license.

 7. That this Stipulation is entered into and submitted on condition that (unless Applicant and Intervenors shall otherwise stipulate), in any hearing or re-

convening of this proceeding to consider the issuance to
Applicant of a license to operate the Palisades Plant at
any power levels in excess of one thermal megawatt, Intervenors reserve the right to contest all issues, substantive and procedural, with respect to Applicant's
request for a license to operate the Palisades Plant at
such thermal power levels, including but not limited to
any right to file motions to strike any filings made pursuant to paragraph 6 of this Stipulation, and any right
of cross-examination, direct examination, argument, introduction of evidence or motions and demands for documents; and in any such hearing or reconvening of this
proceeding to consider the issuance to Applicant of a
license to operate the Palisades Plant at any power
levels in excess of one thermal megawatt, Intervenors
shall not be bound by and shall be free to challenge any
findings of fact or conclusions of law proposed in Exhibit A hereto or made by the ASLB in connection with or
for the issuance of the testing license, and that solely
for purposes of any such hearing or reconvening of this
proceeding, Applicant shall not object to Intervenors'
treating, and Intervenors may treat, such proposed findings of fact and conclusions of law as if never proposed,
made or entered.

8.   That Applicant and Intervenors will serve any
notice, request or motion that this proceeding be reconvened to consider the issuance to Applicant of a license
to operate the Palisades Plant at any thermal power
levels in excess of one megawatt at least five (5) days
before the requested date of reconvening, unless they
join in a notice, request or motion to reconvene this
proceeding for such purpose upon the expiration of a
shorter period of time.

9.   That concurrently with the filing of this Stipulation, the parties will file in this proceeding a true
copy of the settlement agreement.

10. That Intervenors shall not under any circumstances oppose the issuance to Applicant of the testing
license or challenge the validity of or seek to revoke or
suspend the testing license after it has been issued by
the Director of Regulation.

Judd L. Bacon, Esq.

Attorney for Applicant Consumers Power Company

Myron M. Cherry, Esq.

Attorney for all Intervenors except Sierra Club

Lewis D. Drain, Esq.

Attorney for Intervenor Sierra Club

Dated: March 12, 1971

EXHIBIT A
TO APPENDIX IV

UNITED STATES OF AMERICA
ATOMIC ENERGY COMMISSION

In the Matter of   )
CONSUMERS POWER COMPANY)   Docket No. 50-255
(Palisades Plant)   )

PROPOSED FINDINGS OF FACT, CONCLUSIONS OF LAW, AND FORM
   OF ORDER SUBMITTED JOINTLY BY APPLICANT AND
INTERVENORS RESPECTING AUTHORIZATION OF A FUEL
   LOADING AND LOW-POWER TESTING LICENSE

1. The findings and order of the Atomic Safety and Licensing Board hereinafter set forth are concerned with and limited to Applicant's request for the issuance of a provisional operating license authorizing fuel loading amd low-power testing of the Palisades Plant at power levels not to exceed one megawatt.

2. On May 18, 1970 the Commission entered a Notice of Hearing on the application of Consumers Power Company for a provisional operating license authorizing operation of the Palisades Plant at steady-state power levels up to and including 2200 megawatts thermal. The Notice of Hearing contained the following provisions authorizing the Board to consider and act upon any request by Applicant for a provisional operating license for fuel loading and low-power testing:

> "While the matter of the full power license is pending before the atomic safety and licensing board, the board may, upon motion in writing and upon good cause shown, consider and act upon such request as the applicant may make for a provisional operating license authorizing fuel loading and low power testing. Any such action by the atomic safety and licensing board shall be taken with due regard to the rights of all parties to the proceeding, including the right of any party to be heard to the extent that his contentions are relevant to the activity to be authorized. Prior to taking any such action, the atomic safety and licensing board shall with respect to any contested activity to be authorized, make appropriate findings in the form of an initial decision on the issues specified in this notice of hearing."

3. In accordance with the foregoing provisions of the Notice of Hearing, Applicant filed in this proceeding on July 21, 1970 a written motion requesting the Board to authorize the issuance to Applicant of a provisional op-

erating license authorizing fuel loading and low-power testing at power levels not to exceed one megawatt thermal (hereinafter referred to as the "interim provisional operating license"). Pending the disposition of Applicant's motion, evidence was received in the proceeding relating to matters relevant to the issuance of the interim provisional operating license.

4. Pursuant to a settlement agreement and stipulation between Applicant and all Intervenors in this proceeding dated March 12, 1971, which agreement and stipulation have been filed with the Board, Intervenors no longer contest, but now support, prompt issuance to Applicant of the requested interim provisional operating license. Therefore, the fuel loading and low-power testing to be authorized by such license is no longer a "contested activity" within the meaning of the above-quoted provisions of the Notice of Hearing.

5. Applicant has submitted evidence with respect to each of the numbered findings hereinafter made by the Board in respect to the issuance of the interim provisional operating license. Applicant's evidence includes, with respect to findings numbered (1), (3) and (7), those portions of the FSAR relevant to the activities to be conducted under the license [Applicant's Exhibits 51 through 58, received in evidence at Tr. 1639], together with supplementary testimony describing the testing program [Tr. 889-895; 992-994; 1853; Applicant's Exhibits 59 through 62, received in evidence at Tr. 1855], the control of radioactivity which might be generated during testing operations [Tr. 896-898; 994-1000], the upper limits of radiological effects associated with the most severe accidents which might occur during the testing period [Tr. 906-921; 1004-1022; 1031-1032], and the power history [Tr. 4642] and the fission product inventory [Tr. 4644-4645] during the testing period. With respect to finding numbered (2), the evidence includes the entire FSAR [Applicant's Exhibits 4 through 11, received in evidence at Tr. 1088], which describes both the design of the Palisades facility and the quality assurance and testing program designed to assure conformance of the license application, as well as supporting testimony by Applicant's project engineer [Tr. 2110; 2126-2127; 2558; 2600; 2634]. With respect to finding numbered (4), the evidence includes those portions of the Applicant's license application, including the FSAR, bearing on the technical and financial qualifications of the Applicant [Applicant's Exhibit 3, received in evidence at Tr. 1219; Applicant's Exhibit 50, received in evidence at Tr. 1842; Applicant's Exhibits 51, 55 and 57; Applicant's Exhibit 63, received in evidence at Tr. 1796; and Applicant's Exhibit 64, received in evidence at Tr. 1800]. Additional evidence as to Applicant's financial qualifications was supplied by Applicant's chief financial and accounting officers [Tr. 1386-1402; 1791-1802; 1812-1844]. With

respect to finding numbered (5), the evidence includes
the testimony of Applicant's Insurance Supervisor
[Tr. 1271-1279] and Vice President for Finance [Tr. 1845-
1848] and related documentary evidence [Applicant's Exhibits 3, 45, 46, 47, 48 and 66, received in evidence at
Tr. 1219, 1268, 1270, 1275, 1277 and 1848, respectively]
showing that Applicant has met the financial protection
requirements required by the Atomic Energy Act and AEC
regulations. With respect to finding numbered (6), Applicant's witnesses testified that the Plant was ready
for fuel loading and low-power testing prior to the end
of August, 1970 [Tr. 922-923; 1893-1894; 1910; 1927;
2539; 2555; 2870-2871].

   6.   Intervenors and Applicant have stipulated that
the Board may, but solely for purposes of the interim
provisional operating license, accept Applicant's evidence as uncontroverted within the meaning of §VI(b) of
Appendix A of the Commission's Rules of Practice and find
that there is good cause for the issuance to Applicant
of the interim provisional operating license, and the
Board so finds. The Board further finds that Intervenors'
and Applicant's stipulation is subject to the condition
that (unless Applicant and Intervenors shall otherwise
stipulate), in any hearing or reconvening of this proceeding to consider the issuance to Applicant of a license to operate the Palisades Plant at any power levels
in excess of one thermal megawatt, Intervenors reserve
the right to contest all issues, substantive and procedural,
with respect to Applicant's request for a license
to operate the Palisades Plant at such thermal power
levels, including but not limited to any right to file
motions to strike evidence hereafter filed in support of
such request and any right of cross-examination, direct
examination, argument, introduction of evidence or motions and demands for documents; and in any such hearing
or reconvening of this proceeding to consider the issuance to Applicant of a license to operate the Palisades
Plant at any power levels in excess of one thermal megawatt, Intervenors shall not be bound by and shall be
free to challenge any findings of fact or conclusions of
law made herein in connection with or for the issuance of
the testing license, and that solely for purposes of any
such hearing or reconvening of this proceeding, Applicant
shall not object to Intervenors' treating, and Intervenors may treat, such findings of fact and conclusions
of law as if never proposed, made or entered.

   7.   Based on the foregoing and the record of this
proceeding, this Board concludes, with respect to the
issuance of the interim provisional operating license,
that there is good cause for the issuance of said license
to Applicant, and that:

      (1)   Applicant has submitted to the Commission
   all technical information required by Provisional

Construction Permit No. CPPR-25, the Act, and the rules and regulations of the Commission to complete the application for the interim provisional operating license;

(2) Construction of the facility has proceeded, and there is reasonable assurance that it will be completed, in conformity with Provisional Construction Permit No. CPPR-25, the application, as amended, the provisions of the Act and the rules and regulations of the Commission;

(3) There is reasonable assurance that (i) the activities authorized by the interim provisional operating license can be conducted without endangering the health and safety of the public, and (ii) that such activities will be conducted in compliance with the rules and regulations of the Commission;

(4) Applicant is technically and financially qualified to engage in the activities authorized by the interim provisional operating license in accordance with the rules and regulations of the Commission;

(5) Applicant has satisfied the applicable provisions of 10 CFR Part 140, 'Financial Protection Requirements and Indemnity Agreements,' of the Commission's regulations;

(6) There is reasonable assurance that the facility will be ready for initial loading with nuclear fuel within 90 days from the issuance of the interim provisional operating license; and

(7) Issuance of the interim provisional operating license under the terms and conditions proposed will not be inimical to the common defense and security or to the health and safety of the public.

The Board further finds and concludes that there shall be reserved to Intervenors the rights, as hereinabove stated in paragraph 6, that Applicant and Intervenors have stipulated should be reserved to Intervenors.

8. WHEREFORE, pursuant to the Act and Commission's Regulations, IT IS ORDERED, that the Director of Regulation is authorized to issue to Consumers Power Company a provisional operating license authorizing fuel loading and low-power testing at a power level not to exceed one megawatt thermal, upon the following conditions:

(1) Such license shall be substantially in the form of the proposed provisional operating license filed herein by the AEC staff and distrib-

uted to the parties and consistent with this decision.

(2)   Such license shall be issued upon verification by the Commission's Division of Compliance
and a determination by the Director of Reactor Licensing that the Palisades Plant has been completed
in conformity with Provisional Construction Atomic
Energy Act of 1954, as amended, and the Rules and
Regulations of the Commission, and is ready for
fuel loading, and upon receipt by the Director of
Reactor Licensing of proof that Applicant has provided financial protection in the amount required
by the Commission's Regulations.

IT IS FURTHER ORDERED, in accordance with Section 2.764
of the Commission's Regulations, as amended effective
January 19, 1971, that this Order shall become effective
immediately upon its issuance subject to (i) the review
thereof and further decision by the Atomic Safety and
Licensing Appeal Board upon exceptions filed by any
party and (ii) such order as the Atomic Safety and Licensing Appeal Board may enter upon such exceptions or
upon its own motion within 45 days after the issuance of
this Order.

Agreement dated in March, 1971   <u>APPENDIX V</u>
between Consumers Power Company
and Michigan Steelhead and Salmon
Fishermen's Association, et al.

UNITED STATES OF AMERICA
ATOMIC ENERGY COMMISSION

In the Matter of   )
CONSUMERS POWER COMPANY)   Docket No. 50-255
(Palisades Plant)   )

STIPULATION BY AND BETWEEN ALL INTERVENORS AND
<u>APPLICANT IN SUPPORT OF FULL-POWER LICENSE</u>

Applicant and Intervenors, by their respective undersigned attorneys, and subject to the terms and provisions of an Agreement between Applicant and Intervenors
dated the 12th of March, 1971 (hereinafter called the
"settlement agreement"), hereby stipulate and agree as
follows:

1.   That this Stipulation shall be subject to withdrawal by the Applicant or the Intervenors in the event
the Regulatory Staff of the AEC fails, prior to the reconvening of this proceeding to consider the issuance to
Applicant of the full-power license or any operating license other than the testing license, to file in this
proceeding a form of full-power license, proposed to be
issued to Applicant, containing the special technical
specifications as part of the Technical Specifications
for the Palisades Plant. As used in this Stipulation:
the "full-power license" means a license to operate the
Palisades Plant at steady-state power levels up to and
including 2200 thermal megawatts; the "testing license"
means a license authorizing fuel loading and low-power
testing of the Palisades Plant at power levels not to exceed one thermal megawatt; and the "special technical
specifications" means the technical specifications in the
form set forth in Exhibit A hereto.

2.   That Intervenors have heretofore contested the
issuance to Applicant of the full-power license; that in
order to resolve their differences Applicant and Intervenors have entered into the settlement agreement, a true
copy of which has heretofore been filed in this proceeding; and that in accordance with the settlement agreement
and this Stipulation, Intervenors no longer oppose and
now support the prompt issuance to Applicant of the full-
power license containing the special technical specifications.

3.   That Applicant requests that the special technical specifications be included in the full-power license
as part of the Technical Specifications for the Palisades
Plant.

4. That in support of the prompt issuance to Applicant of the full-power license containing the special
technical specifications, Intervenors:

> (i) will not engage in any further voir
>   dire examination, cross-examination,
>   or direct examination herein;
>
> (ii) will not make any further argument,
>   objections, offers of proof, motions
>   or requests herein;
>
> (iii) will not submit or file or seek leave
>   to submit or file any pleading, evi-
>   dence, exhibit or other document
>   herein; and
>
> (iv) will not take any other action herein
>   or initiate or participate in any
>   actions (including but not limited to
>   administrative remedies or court
>   actions) dehors this proceeding with
>   respect to or in connection with the
>   testing license, or the full-power
>   license containing the special tech-
>   nical specifications, or the issu-
>   ance of said licenses,

unless requested by Applicant in order to support the issuance to Applicant of the full-power license containing
the special technical specifications, or unless directed
or requested by the Atomic Safety and Licensing Board
(hereinafter called the "ASLB"), or unless permitted by
the settlement agreement or this Stipulation.

5. That in support of the prompt issuance to Applicant of the full-power license containing the special
technical specifications, Intervenors:

> (i) withdraw all requests, demands and
>   motions heretofore made by them in
>   this proceeding;
>
> (ii) agree that the ASLB may accept the
>   evidence of the Applicant and of the
>   AEC Regulatory Staff and the conclu-
>   sions of the Advisory Committee on
>   Reactor Safeguards in this proceeding
>   as uncontroverted within the meaning
>   of §VI(b) of Appendix A of the AEC's
>   Rules of Practice; and
>
> (iii) consent to the entry of findings of
>   fact and conclusions of law not incon-
>   sistent with the settlement agreement
>   and this Stipulation, including but
>   not limited to findings of fact and

conclusions of law in favor of
Applicant on all issues specified
in the Notice of Hearing of
May 18, 1970 in this proceeding
on Applicant's application for a
provisional operating license for
the Palisades Plant as amended to
include the modifications contemplated by the special technical
specifications.

6. That Applicant shall file in this proceeding proposed findings of fact and conclusions of law and form of
an initial decision not inconsistent with the terms and
provisions of the settlement agreement and this Stipulation; and that the same shall contain, inter alia, findings of fact and conclusions of law to the effect that:

(i) Applicant has resolved to the satisfaction of the ASLB all evidentiary
issues regarding nuclear safety,
radiological protection, quality control, safe operation of the Palisades
Plant, and all other factors material
to Applicant's application for the
full-power license as amended to include the modifications contemplated
by the special technical specifications;

(ii) Intervenors shall be deemed to have
withdrawn from this proceeding when the
full-power license containing the special
technical specifications has been
issued to Applicant and the initial or
final decision in this proceeding has
become the final action of the AEC
without amendment of such license so as
to remove or change the special technical specifications; and

(iii) that the Intervenors will not lose or
waive any rights reserved in the Stipulation heretofore filed herein by Applicant and Intervenors in support of the
issuance of the testing license unless
and until Intervenors are deemed to have
withdrawn from this proceeding as provided in §6.7 of the settlement agreement and paragraph 8 of this Stipulation.

7. That the ASLB should authorize and order the issuance to Applicant of the full-power license containing
the special technical specifications in accordance with
the findings of fact and conclusions of law contemplated
by paragraph 6 of this Stipulation; and that the ASLB's
initial decision directing the issuance of said full-
power license, and said full-power license as well,

should become effective at the earliest time permitted by law and the rules and regulations of the AEC.

8.   That when (i) the full-power license has been issued to Applicant containing the special technical specifications and (ii) the initial or final decision in this proceeding has become the final action of the AEC without amendment of the full-power license so as to remove or change the special technical specifications, then Intervenors shall be deemed, without further action on their part, to have withdrawn from this proceeding with prejudice and without right thereafter (except as otherwise provided in the aforesaid settlement agreement) to take any further action in this proceeding or otherwise in this Docket No. 50-255; or to take any action in any AEC proceeding to extend, renew or convert the full-power license from a provisional to a final operating license or to amend the full-power license to authorize operation of the Palisades Plant at any power level higher than that authorized in the full-power license; or to appeal or to stay the effectiveness of any or all decisions, findings, orders or rulings theretofore or thereafter made or entered in this proceeding or otherwise in this Docket No. 50-255 or in any AEC proceeding to so extend, renew, convert or amend the full-power license; or to initiate or participate in any actions (including but not limited to administrative remedies or court actions) dehors this proceeding with respect to or in connection with the testing license or the full-power license or the issuance of ˷said licenses.   That, upon such issuance of the full-power license containing the special technical specifications and the initial or final decision having become the final action of the AEC, as aforesaid in (i) and (ii) of this paragraph 8, Intervenors shall also thereby be deemed to have waived and forever relinquished any and all rights to take any legal action with respect to any alleged noncompliance of the Palisades Plant, this proceeding or any decision in this proceeding, or the testing license or the full-power license, with the National Environmental Policy Act, the Federal Water Pollution Control Act as amended, the Atomic Energy Act of 1954 as amended, the Federal Rivers and Harbors Act of March 3, 1899 as amended, the Federal Clean Air Act as amended, or with any other federal, state or local statutes or ordinances and any rules, orders and regulations of the AEC or any other public official or agency under any of said Acts, statutes or ordinances.

9.   That if the aforesaid settlement agreement between Applicant and Intervenors shall be terminated prior to the issuance of the full-power license containing the special technical specifications, this Stipulation shall be withdrawn from this proceeding and shall thereafter be of no further force or effect.

10.   That when the Intervenors are deemed to have withdrawn from this proceeding, as provided in §6.7 in

the settlement agreement and paragraph 8 of this Stipulation, then Intervenors no longer shall claim, assert or have the rights reserved by them pursuant to the Stipulation heretofore filed herein by Applicant and Intervenors in support of the issuance of the testing license and this Stipulation.

_____
                                         Judd L. Bacon, Esq.
          Attorney for Applicant Consumers Power Company

_____
                                     Myron M. Cherry, Esq.
          Attorney for all Intervenors except Sierra Club

_____
                                     Lewis D. Drain, Esq.
          Attorney for Intervenor Sierra Club

Dated: March 12, 1971

SPECIAL TECHNICAL SPECIFICATIONS PURSUANT TO AGREEMENT

The licensee (in these special technical specifications sometimes called "Consumers Power") has entered into a settlement agreement dated in March, 1971, with the
parties who intervened in AEC Docket No. 50-255 prior to
December 1, 1970 to contest the issuance of an operating
license (in these special technical specifications sometimes called "Intervenors"), pursuant to which agreement
the licensee is to modify the condenser cooling system
and the liquid radwaste system now installed in the
Palisades Plant. The AEC is not a signatory to that
agreement or to the stipulations entered into and filed
in said Docket pursuant to that agreement, and is not
bound in any way by the provisions of such documents.

Pursuant to said settlement agreement, the licensee
has requested the inclusion of the following special
technical specifications respecting the modified condenser cooling system, the modified liquid radwaste system,
operation pending installation of modified systems, and
the licensee's reporting requirements. Consequently, the
following special technical specifications shall, like
other Palisades Plant technical specifications, be subject to enforcement by the AEC; provided, however, that
the inclusion of the following special technical specifications and their enforcement by the AEC shall be without prejudice to any position which the AEC may take,
in any forum or proceeding or otherwise, as to its jurisdiction with respect to the nonradiological effects of
production and utilization facilities or of source, by-
product and special nuclear materials.

The following special technical specifications are
additional requirements to any other requirements of the
Palisades Plant Technical Specifications. No such other
requirements of the Technical Specifications shall be effective to permit the licensee to fail to comply with any
requirement of the following special technical specifications. However, the licensee shall not be required to
comply with the following special technical specifications during the time and to the extent that the licensee
is relieved of obligation to comply therewith in accordance with their terms.

As used in these special technical specifications
the term "Palisades Plant" means and refers to a single-
unit nuclear electric generating plant and shall not be
deemed to include any additional electric generating
units that may hereafter be installed at the Palisades
Plant site.

SECTION S-1 – CONDENSER COOLING SYSTEM MODIFICATION

§S-1.1 Consumers Power shall modify the condenser
cooling system now installed in the Palisades Plant in
the manner provided in these special technical specifications. The condenser cooling system as so modified (and
in these special technical specifications called the
"modified condenser cooling system") shall be so designed,
constructed, operated and maintained as to form a
closed cycle in which the condenser cooling water is continually recycled except for cooling system makeup water
from and blowdown to Lake Michigan. The modified condenser cooling system shall include one or more wet-type
cooling towers which may be of either the natural or the
mechanical draft type, at Consumers Power's sole option,
provided, that Consumers Power's obligation shall be to
install either the natural or the mechanical draft type
unless it is relieved from installing both types after
exhausting all rights of hearing, appeal and requests for
writs of certiorari to the highest state or federal court
having jurisdiction, as provided in Section S-4 of these
special technical specifications. Design and construction of the cooling tower or towers shall conform to the
latest applicable Cooling Tower Institute (CTI) codes
and standards applicable at the time of detailed design,
except to the extent the same may be contrary to any applicable law or rule, regulation or order of any governmental body having jurisdiction. The blowdown shall be
diluted with Lake water prior to discharge into the Lake
so that the temperature of the mixed dilution water and
blowdown will not exceed the ambient temperature of the
receiving water at the shoreline by more than 5°F. The
design heat rejection to Lake Michigan as a result of
this discharge shall be as low as practicable consistent
with available equipment, operating requirements of the
Palisades Plant and Consumers Power's electrical system,
design optimization, and other condenser cooling system
design objectives, and will in no event exceed
500,000,000 BTU/hr.

§S-1.2 The modified condenser cooling system shall
be installed within forty-two (42) calendar months following the date of the aforesaid settlement agreement if
Consumers Power installs a natural draft cooling tower
or towers as part of the modified condenser cooling system, or within thirty-two (32) calendar months following
the date of the aforesaid settlement agreement if Consumers Power installs a mechanical draft cooling tower
or towers as part of the modified condenser cooling system. If, after Consumers Power has begun to arrange for
the design, engineering, procurement of equipment and
materials, and construction for a modified condenser
cooling system utilizing either the mechanical draft or
the natural draft type of cooling tower or towers, Consumers Power is relieved from installing or continuing to
install the type of cooling tower or towers it first se-

lects, and it is necessary to change to the alternative
type of cooling tower or towers, the time for installation of a modified condenser cooling system utilizing the
alternative type of cooling tower or towers shall commence from the date on which Consumers Power is relieved
from installing or continuing to install the type of
cooling tower or towers first selected. The modified
condenser cooling system shall be placed in operation not
later than the resumption of operation of the Palisades
Plant after its first scheduled refueling following installation of said system, provided, that to the extent
it can do so consistently with electrical system load
requirements, Palisades Plant operating requirements and
applicable license and other legal limitations, Consumers
Power shall use its best efforts to schedule the first
refueling following installation of the modified condenser cooling system so as to minimize the time between the
completion of such installation and the initial operation
of the modified condenser cooling system. The foregoing
provisions of this §S-1.2 are subject to the condition
that in the event the installation or the initial operation of such modified condenser cooling system is delayed
(i) by reason of flood, strike, insurrection, riot, embargo, act of nature or the public enemy; or unavoidable
delay in transportation or inability or unavoidable delay
in procuring labor or materials; (ii) by reason of legal
action by any party other than Consumers Power or Intervenors; local, state or federal laws; or the rules, regulations, orders, actions or failure to act of any public
body or official purporting to exercise authority or
control with respect to installation or operation of the
modified condenser cooling system; or (iii) by reason of
any cause beyond the reasonable control of Consumers
Power, the time for performance shall be extended (subject to the provisions of Section S-4 of these special
technical specifications as respects [ii] above) for a
time equal to the period of such delay.

§S-1.3   Pending installation and operation of the
modified condenser cooling system provided for in this
Section S-1, Consumers Power may operate the Palisades
Plant at any power levels authorized by any AEC operating
license issued to Consumers Power, utilizing the existing once-through cooling system and releasing heated
condenser cooling water to Lake Michigan.

SECTION S-2 - LIQUID RADWASTE SYSTEM MODIFICATION

§S-2.1   Consumers Power shall modify the liquid
radwaste system now installed in the Palisades Plant in
the manner provided in these special technical specifications. The liquid radwaste system as so modified (and in
these special technical specifications called the "modified liquid radwaste system") shall be so designed, constructed, operated and maintained that at all times under
normal operating conditions, radioactive materials in
liquid discharges from the Palisades Plant to Lake Michi-

gan are reduced to essentially zero; provided, however,
that radioactive materials in laundry waste system discharges which cannot be treated in the dirty waste system of the modified liquid radwaste system without the
possibility of impairing the function of dirty waste system equipment may be released to Lake Michigan at levels
which shall in no event exceed 25 picocuries per liter
$(2.5 \times 10^{-8}$ microcuries/cc) on an annual average basis;
and provided further, that "essentially zero," as used
herein, shall not be construed to preclude liquid discharges to Lake Michigan containing radioactive materials
at levels, as sampled at the recycle monitor tank before
dilution, equivalent to or below then-current Lake Michigan background radioactivity levels, as monitored offshore from the Palisades Plant prior to such liquid discharges. As used in these special technical specifications "normal operating conditions" shall refer to operation of the Palisades Plant during or in connection with
which there exist no abnormal events or circumstances
such as (but not limited to) steam generator tube leakages, fire, or pipe breakage; and "abnormal operating
conditions" shall refer to operation of the Palisades
Plant during or in connection with which there exist any
such abnormal events or circumstances. All radioactive
materials removed from liquid wastes by the modified
liquid radwaste system will be accumulated and prepared
for shipment in accordance with applicable rules, regulations and orders of governmental authorities having
jurisdiction and turned over to a carrier or carriers
licensed by governmental authorities having jurisdiction
for shipment to an authorized disposal area or areas.
Consumers Power intends to be alert to, and to utilize
to the extent it is practical to do so, means of minimizing the amount of laundry waste that cannot be treated in
the dirty waste system.

§S-2.2 It is recognized that under abnormal operating conditions it may be impossible or impractical to
achieve essentially zero release of radioactive materials
in liquid discharges from the Palisades Plant through
operation of the modified liquid radwaste system. Consumers Power shall so operate the modified liquid radwaste system as to ensure that radioactive materials in
liquid discharges to Lake Michigan resulting from abnormal operating conditions do not exceed, on a quarterly
average basis and on an individual isotopic analysis
basis, ten percent (10%) of applicable 10 CFR Part 20
limits in effect as of December 1, 1970, and are reduced
to essentially zero no later than sixty (60) consecutive
days after the commencement of such releases resulting
from abnormal operating conditions. Notwithstanding the
foregoing, however, delay beyond said sixty (60) day period in the reduction of radioactive materials in such
liquid discharges to essentially zero shall be excused
(subject to the provisions of Section S-4 of these special
technical specifications as respects [ii] below) to

the extent it is (i) due to inability to identify, locate
or repair the abnormal operating condition; or due to
flood; strike; insurrection; riot; embargo; act of nature
or the public enemy; or by reason of unavoidable delay
in transportation or inability or unavoidable delay in
procuring labor or materials; (ii) due to legal action by
a party other than Consumers Power or Intervenors; local,
state or federal laws; or the rules, regulations, orders,
actions or failure to act of any public body or official
purporting to exercise authority or control with respect
to such liquid discharges; or (iii) due to any cause beyond the reasonable control of Consumers Power; provided,
however, that radioactive materials in liquid discharges
to Lake Michigan from the modified liquid radwaste system during any such excused delay beyond said sixty (60)
day period shall not exceed, on a quarterly average
basis and on an individual isotopic analysis basis, one
percent (1%) of applicable 10 CFR Part 20 limits in effect as of December 1, 1970; and provided further, however, that Consumers Power shall undertake promptly to
correct abnormal operating conditions which result in
releases of radioactive materials in liquid discharges to
Lake Michigan from the modified liquid radwaste system at
levels greater than essentially zero.

§S-2.3   The modified liquid radwaste system shall be
installed and placed in operation no later than the resumption of operation of the Palisades Plant after its
first scheduled refueling (which is expected to occur
approximately seventeen [17] calendar months following
the date of commencement of escalation to full power following issuance of the provisional operating license authorizing Consumers Power to operate the Palisades Plant
at steady-state power levels up to and including 2200
thermal megawatts) or twenty-four (24) calendar months
following the date of the aforesaid settlement agreement,
whichever occurs first. The foregoing provisions of this
§S-2.3 are subject to the condition that in the event the
installation or the initial operation of such modified
liquid radwaste system is delayed (i) by reason of flood;
strike; insurrection; riot; embargo; act of nature or the
public enemy; or unavoidable delay in transportation or
inability or unavoidable delay in procuring labor or materials; (ii) by reason of legal action by a party other
than Consumers Power or Intervenors; local, state or federal laws; or the rules, regulations, orders, actions or
failure to act of any public body or official purporting
to exercise authority or control with respect to installation or operation of the modified liquid radwaste system; or (iii) by reason of any cause beyond the reasonable control of Consumers Power, the time for performance shall be extended (subject to the provisions of Section S-4 of these special technical specifications as
respects [ii] above) for a time equal to the period of
such delay.

§S-2.4   Pending installation and operation of the

modified liquid radwaste system pursuant to the schedule
provided in §S-2.3 hereof, Consumers Power may operate
the Palisades Plant at any power levels authorized by any
AEC license issued to Consumers Power, utilizing the existing liquid radwaste system; provided that radioactive
materials in liquid discharges to Lake Michigan shall be
at levels which are at all times as low as practicable
and which do not exceed, on a quarterly average basis and
on an individual isotopic analysis basis, and based on
the assumptions used in Section 11 of Consumers Power's
Safety Analysis Report to the AEC for the Palisades Plant
as amended to December 1, 1970, (i) under normal or abnormal operating conditions as defined in §S-2.1 hereof
and assuming no failed fuel, two percent (2%) of applicable 10 CFR Part 20 limits in effect as of December 1,
1970; and (ii) under normal or abnormal operating conditions as defined in §S-2.1 hereof and assuming some
failed fuel, ten percent (10%) of applicable 10 CFR Part
20 limits in effect as of December 1, 1970.

   §S-2.5 In line 8 of subsection 3.9.13 of Section
3.9, "EFFLUENT RELEASE" of the Technical Specifications,
add the following after "10 CFR 20":

      "for gaseous releases, and within the
      limits for liquid releases specified in
      the special technical specifications
      included herein at the request of the
      licensee pursuant to a settlement agree-
      ment dated in March, 1971."

SECTION S-3 - RESERVATIONS

   §S-3.1 Nothing in these special technical specifications shall prevent Consumers Power from taking any
steps or measures in connection with the design, construction, modification or operation of the modified condenser cooling system and the modified liquid radwaste
system which contemplate modifications, procedures or
modes of operation equal to or better, considering the
protection of the environment, than the modifications,
procedures or modes of operation contemplated in these
special technical specifications; provided, however, that
the foregoing provisions shall not authorize Consumers
Power to take any steps or measures to install and operate a modified condenser cooling system having an open
cycle system utilizing Lake Michigan water for once-
through cooling or to install and operate a modified
liquid radwaste system which would release radioactivity
to the environment at levels above those contemplated in
Section S-2 of these special technical specifications under the conditions therein stated.

   §S-3.2 The modifications, procedures and modes of
operation contemplated in these special technical specifications for the Palisades Plant and any action taken

by Consumers Power pursuant to said special technical
specifications or the aforesaid settlement agreement of
March, 1971 before or after the execution of said agreement shall not be deemed, construed, interpreted or
claimed to be an admission that the same or any similar
modifications, procedures or modes of operation are necessary or required at any other Consumers Power electric
generating plant. The obligations of Consumers Power
under these special technical specifications and said
agreement are limited to the Palisades Plant.

SECTION S-4 - LEGAL VALIDITY

§S-4.1 If Consumers Power believes that compliance
with any provision or provisions of these special technical specifications is contrary to or prevented by any
local, state or federal law, or the rule, regulation,
order, action or failure to act of any public body or official purporting to exercise authority with respect
thereto, or the order or decree of any court, then Consumers Power shall promptly notify Intervenors thereof by
telegram, telephone or other means and notify Intervenors
thereof in writing ten (10) business days thereafter,
stating the basis for such belief. In the event Intervenors notify Consumers Power of their agreement with
such belief within thirty (30) calendar days after delivery of the aforesaid written notice by Consumers Power
(and from the time of the aforesaid telephonic, telegraphic or other means of notice by Consumers Power and
until the end of such thirty (30) day period whether or
not such notification is given to Consumers Power by
Intervenors) Consumers Power shall be relieved of any obligation to comply with the provision or provisions in
question and any and all other provisions of these special
technical specifications which require compliance
with said provision or provisions. However, notwithstanding its release from obligation as provided in this
§S-4.1, Consumers Power shall have the right, in its
sole discretion, to comply with or seek to comply with
said provision or provisions. In the event Intervenors
do not so notify Consumers Power within said thirty (30)
day period, then Consumers Power shall in good faith and
with due diligence pursue administrative remedies or
court actions (including appeals or requests for writs
of certiorari to the highest state or federal court having jurisdiction), or both, to assert the validity of
compliance with said provision or provisions and/or the
invalidity or unlawfulness of the law, rule, regulation,
order, decree, action or failure to act that is the subject of the aforesaid written notice by Consumers Power.

§S-4.2 In the event of an unfavorable ruling or the
inability to have the validity of the compliance with
such provision or provisions (which are the subject of
suit and/or proceeding as contemplated in §S-4.1 hereof)
upheld after exhausting all rights of hearing, appeal

and requests for writs of certiorari to the highest state
or federal court having jurisdiction, then Consumers
Power will forever be relieved of any obligation to comply with the provision or provisions in question and any
and all other provisions of these special technical
specifications which require compliance with said provision or provisions.

§S-4.3   While Consumers Power is pursuing the administrative remedies or court actions, or both, contemplated in §S-4.1 hereof, Consumers Power may operate the
Palisades Plant in any manner permitted by law; provided,
however, that while Consumers Power is pursuing said administrative remedies or court actions, or both, it shall
continue to comply with all of the provisions of these
special technical specifications except any provision or
provisions (and any and all other provisions which require compliance with said provision or provisions) as
to which (i) it is prevented from complying by a court
order or decree or is prevented from complying by an
order, notice or other action of any public body or official having authority to enforce such order, notice
or other action without resort to a court for enforcement; or (ii) it is prevented from complying by the lack
of any permit, license, consent or other authorization of
any public body or official which is required for continued compliance; or (iii) continued compliance would,
in the reasonable opinion of legal counsel for Consumers
Power, result in the violation of any criminal law or
criminal ordinance or the imposition of any criminal or
civil fine, criminal or civil penalty, or criminal or
civil forfeiture; or (iv) there has been entered a court
order or decree or an order, notice or other action of
a public body or official which, while not preventing
compliance with these special technical specifications
by Consumers Power, would require shutdown of the Palisades Plant or a reduction in the electrical output of
the Palisades Plant if Consumers Power continued to comply therewith.

SECTION S-5 - REPORTING REQUIREMENTS

§S-5.1   Add the following new item e. to subsection
6.6.1 of Section 6.6, "PLANT REPORTING REQUIREMENTS" of
the Technical Specifications:

> "e.   When a control rod or a part-
> length rod is misaligned as
> defined in 3.10.4.a of these
> Technical Specifications or
> when a control rod is inoperable
> as defined in 3.10.4.b of these
> Technical Specifications."

CHAPTER 9

THE FEDERAL
POWER COMMISSION

> *The Federal Power Commission without question represents the outstanding example in the federal government of the breakdown of the administrative process.*
>
> —James J. Landis,
> *Report on Regulatory Agencies*
> *to President-elect Kennedy,*
> *December 1960*

Things haven't changed very much at the Federal Power Commission (FPC) in the decade since John F. Kennedy asked for a candid evaluation of the administrative agencies. There was a flurry of activity in the mid-1960s, but the basic patterns have persisted. However, some of the consequences have begun to intrude into the lives of ordinary people in noticeable ways.

In November 1965, millions of people in the northeastern part of the United States were given some cause to wonder just how well the process of regulating the power industry was working. Although the name of the FPC might not have occurred to many of them immediately, the total absence of electric power in an eight-state area certainly brought home to most inhabitants the distinct impression that something in the federal bureaucracy was not quite right. The FPC, after investigating the great blackout, made some much-needed recommendations on power plant siting and reliability. By way of self-defense, it pointed to all the days when there was enough electric power, and somewhat petulantly reported to the President: "The prime lesson of the blackout was that the electric utility industry must strive not merely for good but for virtually perfect service."

Most people assume that electricity and natural gas will always be there in the quantities they want, as close as the nearest wall outlet or the kitchen stove. The bills that come every month are small in comparison with many other expenses, and most people pay them uncomplainingly, assuming that they represent a reasonable charge. The generating plants which supply electricity are far removed from the people who use it, and few people have occasion to investigate the environmental costs of generating this power. Whatever it takes, the process is remote from their lives, and if they consider the process at all, most assume that the utility companies are doing their best to insure a safe and continuous supply of as much power as will be needed.

But power affects the lives of all people every day, and blackouts or brownouts have the effect of jolting them into realizing it. There are other effects of producing and using power which are no less serious for being less immediately obvious. The simplistic assertion that "all power pollutes" is often relied on by power companies to dismiss opposition to the environmental degradation induced by contemporary methods for producing electric power. Like Lord Acton's aphorism that "power corrupts," the assertion is a partial truth: as it is now being produced, power does pollute. And if the process is not changed, consumers will ultimately pay more than just a few dollars a year as the price of power.

The FPC, an independent regulatory commission, is the arm of the federal government charged with supervising the vast empire of the utility industry. Specifically, the Commission regulates electric power by licensing hydroelectric plants and approving rates for the wholesale interstate sale of electricity. The FPC also regulates the natural gas industry. The Commission approves interstate wholesale rates for interstate gas pipelines, determines rates charged by producers of natural gas in interstate commerce, authorizes construction of interstate pipelines, and has authority to allocate supplies of gas.

The utility business which the Commission regulates is the largest single industry in the United States, and it represents a coalition of *de facto* corporate states which cross state boundaries. This huge entity, with holdings in excess of $110 billion, dwarfs many of the fifty states by comparison. By the year 2000, the manifest destiny of this "Utility State" will result in its acquisition of 8 million acres of land just for transmission lines. Its power to tax the individual consumer through rates is subject only to the most cursory supervision by state regulatory commissions for retail rates, and to acquiescence by the FPC on wholesale interstate rates.

The Power Industry and the FPC

Starting at the end of the nineteenth century as an idea in Thomas Edison's mind, the electric power industry spread rapidly and raggedly throughout the country. Early companies often fought for customers by lacing towns with parallel and competing poles and wires. At one time Chicago was served by twenty separate electric power companies. Companies scrambled aggressively for hydroelectric power-generating sites. But cities soon began to reject the inefficiencies of overlapping power systems, and either granted exclusive franchises to furnish power or built their own municipal utility systems. The power industry quickly began to consolidate, and larger companies acquired domination over service areas.

By 1920 the random distribution of hydroelectric generating sites disturbed conservationists and others enough to result in enactment of the Federal Power Act [16 U.S.C. 792]. This statute was the origin of the FPC, creating a three-man Commission and establishing the power to grant fifty-year licenses for hydroelectric installations built on navigable rivers within federal jurisdiction. Under these licenses, the federal government retained the right to take over the projects when the license period ran out. But the Commission had little effect on the major development in the industry during the 1920s, which was the combination of small, private, local firms into large holding companies. The fraudulent financing involved in many of these elaborate holding company structures came to light during the Depression, and many of them were dismembered under the Public Utilities Holding Company Act of 1935 [15 U.S.C. 79].

In 1930 the Commission was expanded to five members. The expansion was part of its charter as an independent regulatory agency, with Commissioners nominated by the President and confirmed by the Senate. The Commission's jurisdiction was enlarged by the Public Utilities Holding Company Act, which authorized the Commission to set wholesale rates for electric power in interstate commerce and to regulate the interstate transmission of electric power. In addition, the Act gave the FPC authority to audit accounts of privately owned utility companies, to regulate securities and mergers of such companies, and to coordinate the generation, transmission, and sale of electricity.

The small municipally owned utilities (municipals) were able to resist the combinations of the 1920s, like the holding company empire of Samuel Insull, because of tax advantages which amounted to subsidies. They paid no federal or state income taxes and the cost of raising capital for investment was reduced, since those who purchased municipal utility bonds paid no income tax on the interest received. New Deal ventures into public power, such as the Tennessee Valley Authority (TVA) and the Bonneville Project, assisted the municipal power companies. These projects not only encouraged public power by their success, but also gave it assistance by selling low-cost hydroelectric power from the projects to municipals in preference to private companies and cooperatives. The New Deal public power projects also demonstrated that many private power companies were comparatively inefficient, dishonest, or both.

During the Depression, consumer-owned rural electric cooperatives were formed. As late as 1935, 90 percent of the farms in the United States had no electric service. Privately owned utilities had refused to extend their distribution to these unprofitable and isolated areas. The Rural Electrification Administration (REA) used low-interest loans to encourage the development of cooperatives, designed to provide electric power to rural areas which did not have sufficient revenue to attract power from private sources. (President Nixon recently proposed that the cheap 2 percent direct government loans to rural electric cooperatives be replaced by 5 percent federally insured loans.) The private utility industry was less hostile toward the rural electric cooperatives than they were toward municipal public-owned projects during this period, since the REA program applied only to areas which the private companies didn't want to serve anyway, and REA help was available to private companies if they wanted to enter these markets. But changes in population patterns since the 1930s have resulted in frequent conflicts between the rural electric cooperatives and privately owned utility companies. Now the cooperatives are as much the target of invective from private power company advertisements as are publicly owned power projects.

Despite the collapse of the original holding companies, tax advantages to municipals, and REA encouragement of cooperatives, privately owned electric power companies have continued to grow. This trend has continued even though privately owned utilities regularly charge their average residential customers significantly more for electricity than publicly owned companies and cooperatives [*Statistics of Privately Owned Electric Utilities* and *Statistics of Publicly Owned Electric Utilities*, Federal Power Commission, 1971, available from the Public Information Office, FPC, 825 N. Capitol St., N.E., Washington, D.C. 20426].

Among contending utilities, the victor is usually the largest company, rather than the company which can provide the best service. Municipally owned utilities are almost always at a disadvantage in these contests, since large private utility companies have vast resources upon which to rely. Among other tactics, private utilities conduct advertising campaigns which imply that public-owned utility companies are contrary to the "American way of life" and are either socialist or Communist in origin. They also have the power (subject to the FPC's not very watchful eye) to bring a small municipal company to its knees by refusing to allow it to interconnect or by charging confiscatory prices for connection. The significant economies of scale give larger private companies an advantage over smaller municipal companies, since their larger generating units are more efficient. Small systems can overcome this if they are able to "pool" by interconnecting with large sets of power systems or with each other. But if the large system refuses such interconnection, refuses to sell the power at a fair price, or refuses to "wheel" power from one small system to another, it can greatly handicap the small publicly owned utilities.

Use of these tactics by large privately owned power companies may well violate federal antitrust laws, but the FPC has been reluctant even to consider the possibility. However, the Justice Department recently filed a suit against the Otter Tail Electric Power Company for allegedly refusing to sell wholesale power or to "wheel" power to systems proposed for municipal takeover in an attempt to prevent municipal ownership from halting its expansion or cutting into its power empire. The case was decided by the Supreme Court against Otter Tail on 22 February 1973 (Sup. Ct. 71-991). A leading Washington antitrust lawyer, Worth Rowley, told public power officials that the suit represents a "prospective charter of freedom" against the monopoly power of privately owned companies.

The Federal Power Act specifically forbids "combinations, agreements, arrangements, or understandings, express or implied, to limit the output of electric energy, to restrain trade, or to fix, maintain, or increase prices for electrical energy or service" [16 U.S.C. 803(h)]. This provision, while in a section on conditions of licenses, appears to express a policy that applies to all public utilities and would be enforceable under 16 U.S.C. 825(a), which includes criminal penalties. Also, since the FPC is charged with enforcing national policy, enforcement of antitrust laws should be included as part of that policy. In practice, the Commission's record has been dismal. It took the Supreme Court, in the *El Paso* series of cases, to require the Commission to consider antitrust criteria as part of their broader "public interest" standard. The staff has rarely raised antitrust questions in processing cases, and a reporter familiar with the Commission commented that most of the commissioners had expressed opposition to the Justice Department's prosecution of the Otter Tail case.

The electric power industry is mostly owned by private companies, and that ownership is being increasingly consolidated. Private utility companies now control 76 percent of the electricity market; the federal government generates 13 percent; local publicly owned systems produce 10 percent; and cooperatives produce only 1 percent. The industry has been characterized by mergers and purchases, and several huge holding companies have again emerged. Although there are 3,000 utilities selling electricity, 90 percent of all sales come from only 150 systems, most of them privately owned. The monopoly power of a utility company is even more dramatic on a local scale. A utility is concentrated in a city, a state, or a region covering several states. Within its own area a utility company has a near-absolute monopoly over an essential service, subject only to minimal government supervision and a slight overlap at the edges with neighboring companies.

The major competition that electric utility companies face in most areas is gas. But because of apparent shortages of extracted gas at this time, gas companies are hard-pressed to meet their current obligations, much less to expand their limited markets. Some utility companies are beginning, however, to consolidate their monopoly positions by buying out the gas companies which represent potential competition. Their political and economic power permit these companies to be virtually above regulation by state utility commissions. The only other barrier to unlimited exercise of their monopoly power is the FPC's statutory duty to oversee wholesale rates and regulate the interstate power industry.

In 1938 the FPC went beyond electricity to natural gas regulation. The Natural Gas Act [15 U.S.C. 717] was passed in that year, and was expanded substantially in 1942. This statute gave the Commission jurisdiction over interstate transportation of natural gas and the sale of natural gas for resale. It also provided for regulation of interstate operations of natural gas companies, including jurisdiction over rates and accounts and certification of new sales or new construction. The Commission's jurisdiction was again expanded substantially by a 1954 U.S. Supreme Court decision holding that rates and sales of independent producers selling natural gas in interstate commerce are subject to FPC jurisdiction. But the Commission's rate making authority for gas is limited to wholesale rates, just as it is for electricity. The Commission has less power to require information and accounting from gas suppliers than it does from the electric power industry. The import and export of natural gas is also subject to FPC regulation [15 U.S.C. 717(b)].

Despite the implication of its name, the Federal Power Commission is not the only federal agency concerned with public power. Responsibility for energy policy on the federal level is fragmented among several agencies, ranging from the Atomic Energy Commission (AEC), which both promotes and regulates the nuclear power industry, through the TVA and Bonneville Power Administration, to the dam-building agencies, the Corps of Engineers and the Bureau of Reclamation. In addition, the FPC's jurisdiction is not only limited by statute, but also by its own deference to state regulatory agencies.

One of the greatest barriers to environmental protection by the FPC, if it should ever decide to exercise its authority, is the limitation on its licensing authority over electric generating projects under the Federal Power Act. The Commission has authority under the Act to license hydroelectric generating projects, but not to license fossil fuel projects, which are subject to state regulation. This limitation, currently being challenged in the federal courts, places a significant source of power and pollutants beyond the Commission's reach, since fossil fuel projects account for over 75 percent of all electricity generated. The hydro-electric generating plants licensed by the Commission account for only 15 percent, while nuclear plants produce the other 10 percent of all electric power. Also subject to state regulation is 50 percent of the sulfur dioxide and 25 percent of the particulate emissions in urban air pollution.

In addition to its limited licensing authority, the FPC only regulates the rates, securities, and services of hydroelectric power in interstate commerce when the states affected either have no regulatory agencies of their own, or when there is disagreement between state regulatory agencies. The statutory limitation on rate making authority to inter-state wholesale rates is strictly interpreted, and the Commission's exercise of rate making authority over such electricity is limited to 6 percent of national consumption. The Federal Power Act leaves to the state regulatory agencies supervision over retail rates and utility facilities which do not physically interfere with interstate commerce. But most state utility commissions must regulate not only electricity and gas, but also transportation, communications, and other basic utilities. In general, the state utility commissions are woefully understaffed, and dominated by the industries they regulate even more than their federal counterparts.

The failures of the FPC cannot be blamed entirely on statutory limitations of its power. It has licensed environmentally destructive electric generating projects; it has encouraged profligate use of electric power without regard for the environmental consequences of producing that power; and it has permitted private utilities to amass both economic and political power by its failure to promote fair interconnection between power systems and its abdication of antitrust responsibilities.

After receiving the Landis report which, as the introductory quotation for this chapter indicates, was critical of the FPC, President Kennedy took a step toward change. He appointed Joseph Swidler as chairman of the Commission. Swidler established a power rate bureau to exercise the Commission's jurisdiction over wholesale power rates. Under Swidler and his successor, Lee White, the Commission began to awaken from its lethargy. A number of power rate cases were developed, some antitrust questions were raised, and for the first time the Commission used its interconnection authority to require some power systems to interconnect with others on fair terms. A small step toward considering the effects of power generating projects was the institution of a requirement for license applicants to submit plans for the recreational development of hydroelectric projects. During this brief and mild period of activism, the Commission still did not encourage public participation in planning or in projects such as the National Power Survey. As one former staff member commented, "We had a feeling that *we* were representing the public, that it was *our* job." It was also during this period that the Commission proposed and supported legislation to increase its authority over the reliability of power sources, as well as a bill to establish a Utility Consumers Council. But the bills did not pass and this progressive period ended.

The end was marked by President Nixon's appointment in 1969 of Chairman John Nassikas, who was selected at the behest of Senator Norris Cotten of New Hampshire, the ranking Republican on the Senate Commerce Committee and a staunch ally of New England private power companies. In his public statements, the Chairman has repeatedly emphasized his belief that industry self-regulation, under supervision by state regulatory agencies, is sufficient to ensure that the power industry acts in the public interest:

> I have stated my belief a number of times that the primary
> responsibility for meeting the electric energy needs of the Nation

without undue impact upon the environment rests squarely upon the managements of the individual systems comprising the electric power industry. . . . I have also indicated that the principal regulatory responsibility for resolving environmental objectives consistent with federal standards rests with the state, regional, and local authorities. . . . Where action by one state cannot serve the common objectives of regional system planning and environmental considerations transcending state boundaries, regional organization by interstate compact should be established. [Speech to American Public Power Association, Memphis, Tennessee, 28 April 1970. Reprints are available from the Public Information Office of the FPC].

One example of this policy is Order 375-B of 15 April 1970. This order supposedly "clarifies" policies on recreational plans for hydroelectric projects to be submitted by applicants for licenses. An earlier commission announcement cited certain safety measures to be included in any submitted recreational plan. The "clarification" essentially repealed these measures, or, in the words of the press release, it was to "make clear that the examples of safety measures cited are not requirements but were intended merely as guidance." The "clarification" was sought by power companies which were concerned about the possibility of civil liability for failure to meet such standards, and the cost of buying equipment such as wastebaskets.

The FPC: Structure and Functions

At the top, the FPC is composed of five commissioners appointed for five-year terms by the President with the advice and consent of the Senate. The present commissioners are:

	Appointed	Current term expires
John Nassikas (Chairman) (Republican)	1969	1975
Albert B. Brook, Jr. (Republican)	1968	1974
Rush Moody (Democrat)	1971	1976
William Springer (Republican)	1973	1978
Don Smith (Democrat)	1973	1978

Most commissioners and many staff members come from the regulated industry and return to it after their term of government service is over.

For example, Pinkney Walker, while Dean of the Missouri Business School, was a frequent consultant for various utility companies, presenting arguments for higher rates. He replaced Commissioner Bagge, who quit the Commission before the expiration of his term to become president of the National Coal Association. Robert Morris was appointed in 1973 but rejected by the Senate because of his pro-industry associations.

The Commission is organized into Offices and Bureaus (see Appendix 9-A, p. 521), and, under the requirements of the Administrative Procedure Act (APA), there is a general separation between decision makers and the active staff. Decision makers include the commissioners and their personal staffs, hearing examiners, and the special assistants to the Commission. The special assistants serve as clerks to the commissioners, summarizing lengthy hearing records and preparing draft opinions. Because of the volume of decisions required of the Commission, the special assistants in effect make a great many decisions.

The active staff is divided into the Bureau of Natural Gas, the Bureau of Power, the Office of the General Counsel, the Office of Accounting and Finance, the Office of Economics, the Office of Public Information, and several internal housekeeping offices. The traffic cop of the entire bureaucratic system is the Secretary. His office receives all official documents, sets dates, routes documents to people, and issues routine clerical orders. When a filing such as a license application (Appendix 9-E, p. 556) comes to the Secretary, he sends copies to the engineers in the Bureau of Power and to lawyers in the Office of the General Counsel. The lawyers, working with the engineers, ultimately prepare a "blue order" which they circulate to the rest of the staff. Assuming that there are no hearings or adversary proceedings, this order then goes to the Commission for its decision. If formal proceedings are to be held, the Secretary makes sure that notice is given. The staff then prepares its position, the petitioners theirs, and the matter proceeds to a hearing examiner. The decision of the hearing examiner then goes to the Commissioners for review.

The Bureau of Power is organized in several divisions. The Division of River Basins prepares the Commission's plans of river basins, as required by the Federal Power Act, and calculates "head water benefits." Under the Act, hydroelectric licensees are required to pay the government for any benefits they receive at their facilities through upstream improvements to the river undertaken by the federal government.

The Division of Electric Resources and Requirements is responsible for gathering statistics about electric power, studying proposed interconnections, and preparing the various other studies of electric power plants and facilities which the Commission publishes.

The Division of Rates and Corporate Regulation is divided into a number of sections: Corporate Regulation, Electric Rate Investigations, Electric Rate Filings, Rate Reports, and Electric Systems Planning and Operations. The Rate Reports section publishes a useful compilation entitled *Typical Electric Bills*.

The Division of Licensed Projects handles hydroelectric licensing. This Division checks applications, investigates sites, and handles compliance actions. It includes a section on Recreation, Fish, and Wildlife.

Four Offices provide specialized services for the Bureau of Power and the Bureau of Natural Gas. These are the Office of the General Counsel, the Office of Accounting and Finance, the Office of Economics, and the Office of Public Information. The Commission's regional offices do little more than assist utilities with forms and make field inspections.

The production and transmission of electricity mars and destroys more of our wilderness than any other single activity of our industrial society, with the possible exception of highways. No landmark is really safe from being despoiled in order to generate electric power, as demonstrated by the plan to use part of the Grand Canyon as a hydroelectric generating site. Once a generating site is established, paths for transmission lines are ripped through the countryside. The sulfur dioxide emissions from power plants using fossil fuels are estimated to cause $10-15 billion a year in property damage alone. We are only beginning to recognize the impact of thermal pollution on marine life, and the residues of extracting and transporting fossil fuels for power generation, such as strip mine scars and oil slicks, are more and more in evidence. But the electric utility industry continues to promote greater consumption of electric power, and to predict that power output will quadruple in the next twenty years. This will require at least 150 new sites for major generating installations; transmission lines, which now cover 3 million acres, will be stretched across another million acres. One-sixth of the annual fresh water runoff will be required to cool the generators for these plants. This means that practically the entire fresh water flow of the United States during the dry season will pass through and be heated by electric generating units.

The FPC is the primary federal agency with the power, expertise, and the duty to formulate our national energy policy for the prevention of such an environmental catastrophe. The statutory charge to the FPC in 1935 to plan "for the purpose of assuring an abundant supply

of electric energy . . . with the greatest possible economy and with regard to the proper utilization and conservation of natural resources,"
along with its specific powers to collect information, prescribe accounting, and regulate interconnection, gave the Commission the power and
responsibility to see that electric energy is not generated at the expense
of our natural resources. The Commission's failure until now to carry
out its statutory mission, as demonstrated by continuing environmental
degradation and increasingly frequent power failures, is not encouraging.

The Commission does little national power planning of its own, relying mostly on industry estimates of what power will be needed and
where it will originate. The river basin surveys required by the Federal
Power Act are only catalogues of river basin demography, existing water
projects, and proposed water projects. The final report of the 1964
National Power Survey was written by the FPC staff, but the 1970 version was largely produced by industry representatives on the Task Force.
With the exception of a token Task Force on Environment appointed
in January 1970 for the 1970 Survey, there was no representation for
consumers or those concerned about the environment. Even this Task
Force was composed of government agencies' representatives, one representative of Commonwealth Edison, one engineering professor, and
one conservationist.

Just about anyone who lives in a metropolitan area is aware that the
reliability of electric power is less than perfect, particularly in the summer. In one way, it was fortunate for power companies that environmental protection groups began to oppose the wholesale destruction of
natural resources at about the time when the reliability of electric power
began to falter: It gave the companies a convenient place to focus the
blame. But it was unfortunate for purposes of intelligent decision making on power and natural resources, because it led to a false dilemma of
choosing between having power and protecting the environment.

The Storm King project, in New York's Hudson River Valley, was
not built as planned by the summer of 1969 because of the resistance
of environmental protection groups. But even if it had been completed
on schedule it would not have prevented the brownouts of that summer. It was not the environmentalists who caused a completed project—
the Queens plant—to break down; had it been operating there would
have been no brownouts. Nor was it environmentalists who delayed the
Indian Point No. 2 plant, a delay which admittedly "resulted from other
factors such as design problems, strikes, and shortages of skilled labor"
[1 *Environmental Law Reporter* 20292 (1971)]. The generating facilities coming on the line this year and next were ordered five or more

years ago, before the general opposition to power plants became so
intense.

A major shortcoming has been the industry's failure to anticipate the
growth in demand generated by its own promotion. As a result, according to A. H. Aymond, president of the Edison Electric Institute, the
equipment manufacturers are "having difficulty in the shops in meeting
specifications to reach the standards that the industry needs for these
high temperatures and pressures." Research and development for pollution control and reliability have been minimal—about one-quarter of 1
percent of gross revenues.

Aggravating the problem has been a shortage of sufficient supplies of
fuel to run those plants which are operating. Fuel shortages present a
problem even if there were no immediate shortage of coal or oil reserves in the United States, and these sources of electrical energy, as
well as the other two sources—natural gas and uranium—are to some
extent interchangeable.

Coal is responsible for 57 percent of the electric power produced in
the nation. Fortunately there is a bountiful supply of coal in the U.S.—
enough to last for at least 600 years at the present rate of consumption.
But coal companies have been reluctant to develop new mines, believing
that uranium fuel would satisfy future needs. Railroads, operating under
the same faulty assumption, have cut back on purchases of coal cars.
The U.S. has increased enormously the amount of coal it exports—from
34 million tons in 1961 to 66 million tons—and these increased exports
have intensified the shortage of railroad cars for domestic deliveries.
Many cities and states have wisely limited the permissible sulfur content
of coal in order to reduce air pollution. Thus, demand for low-sulfur
coal has greatly increased, but sufficient supplies have yet to be developed. Serious questions about the adequacy of nuclear safety standards
and radioactive waste disposal have delayed the "clean" nuclear generating plants which many utilities had expected to take the place of
fossil fuel plants.

Natural gas burns much cleaner than coal or crude oil, and for that
reason is a more desirable fuel from an environmental point of view.
It is attractive to the consumer because it is usually a cheaper source
of power. But companies have been less than diligent in gas exploration,
claiming that they are not allowed enough profit to justify developing
new reserves. The industry's sincerity in claiming that there are not
sufficient reserves for immediate use has been brought into question by
its failure to disclose information concerning the extent of known reserves. Lee White, former chairman of the FPC, remarked in a May 1969

address: "The industry cannot have it both ways—it cannot reasonably claim a gas shortage exists and at the same time continue to refuse to make the basic data available."

In order to study the gas resources of the United States and to determine the extent of the shortage, if any, the FPC has formed a National Gas Survey Executive Advisory Committee. But the Committee is composed almost entirely of industry representatives. Of the thirty-nine original members, only three could possibly be considered consumer representatives as of Oct. 73: Virginia Knauer, President Nixon's Consumer Advisor; Russell Train, of the Environmental Protection Agency; and L. E. Fouraker, Harvard Graduate School of Business. The Chairman of the Committee is W. M. Elmer, Chairman of the Board of Texas Gas Transmission Corporation. Under subsequent pressure from environmental and consumer groups, the number of nonindustry members was increased.

Residual oil which would normally be used to replace coal and gas is not available either. The United States tends to produce more specialized petroleum products and less residual oil. Various international complications such as higher Venezuelan prices, the closing of the Suez Canal, and import quotas have limited the amount of low sulfur oil available in the United States. To compound the problem further (and reduce interfuel competition), ownership of the various energy sources is interrelated. For example, oil companies control natural gas production and 45 percent or more of the known U.S. uranium reserves. Since 1965, eight of the ten largest coal-mining companies, which produce half the coal in the U.S., have been purchased either by oil companies or mineral companies, or other large "energy corporations."

The reason for blackouts is not that we don't have enough power, but that we don't have enough power in the right places. There is 25 percent more power generated in the United States than can be used at peak demand periods. The problem is that most of this power is generated in the West and Midwest and cannot find its way to the power-hungry East. This inability to use available power is caused by poor interconnection resulting from industry unwillingness to tie in with other systems, and poorly constructed interconnections. An example of a grid both critical and inadequate for interconnection is the PJM intersection, handling power for Pennsylvania, New Jersey, and Maryland. If the PJM intersection were larger, New York might have avoided some brownouts. During the 1969 power failure a cooperative in the Dakotas named Basin Electric offered to supply power, but it had to be turned down because the PJM wasn't big enough to handle the Basin Electric power block. The industry is reluctant to interconnect even when the equipment is adequate, but it is willing to build unnecessary plants in order to remain autonomous. In comparison, the European Power Pool is fully interconnected from Portugal to Austria and from Denmark to Italy. But the FPC has only made some recommendations for better interconnection to insure reliability, and has not given serious consideration to the possible solution of a "national grid" for transmitting power to the areas which need it. Sweden, the Soviet Union, and Great Britain have done far more research than the United States in extra high voltage direct current, by far the most economical method for transmitting large blocs of power long distances. We have failed also to promote multiple use utility and transportation corridors to accommodate, with a minimum of land, the corridors which a national grid would require.

There is a danger that a national grid could come under the domination of a few very large, inadequately regulated, private utility companies. Utility companies are becoming larger and fewer already. There were 1,060 private utility companies in 1945, and today there are only 267. The control wielded by these few companies is intensified by their interlocking directorates with the largest banks and by the benign regulation of the FPC.

But intensive development of alternate energy sources, such as fuel cells, would make such a system as a national grid unnecessary. Fuel cells for the production of electricity already exist, but their cost is still much higher than conventional means. There are several other undeveloped technological possibilities for solving our energy problems: "super conductivity" would reduce the energy waste involved in the transportation of electricity by lowering the temperature of transmission lines to almost absolute zero; nuclear fusion is virtually self-generating, and, unlike nuclear fission, is radioactively "clean"; subterranean steam, solar energy, and magnetohydrodynamics are other possible solutions. But at present these alternatives are barely being considered by the FPC or the regulated utilities.

So far, the FPC's answer to power shortages has been to promote *voluntary* coordination among the over 3,000 separately owned utility systems. The utilities have responded by creating the National Electric Reliability Council (NERC), made up of twelve electric utility organizations. NERC is a consultative body, with no governmental status, which is supposed to develop national reliability criteria. However, smaller utilities and representatives of state and federal regulatory agencies are generally excluded from NERC proceedings.

There are many problems related to insufficient power supply, poor management, poor quality control, poor interconnection, poor planning, and limited fuel supply—but central to all of them is our rapidly increasing demand for power. The population of the United States increases 1 percent annually, while the demand for electricity increases 7 percent. At the present rate, demand will double every ten years. Most spokesmen for the FPC and the utility industry assume that this geometrical increase in demand will continue. But the rate of demand increase does not just happen. To understand why demand increases seven times faster than the population grows, and what the FPC has to do with it, requires knowledge about two of the utility industry's promotional practices—advertising and promotional rate structures.

It is an annual irony when utility companies, which have advertised all year long to encourage the purchase and use of electrical appliances such as air conditioners, take to the air each summer to urge people not to use them—just when they are most needed. The utility industry spends millions of dollars annually encouraging people to use electricity which will not be there to use. In 1969, industry expenditures on sales and advertising were eight times their expenditures on research and development. The FPC has not seriously questioned this practice, let alone taken steps to limit the utilities from passing on to consumers the costs of artificially stimulating demand for electricity.

One reason for the increased use of electricity is that those who use more pay at a lower rate. A person who uses only 250 kilowatt-hours (kwh) per month pays about 3 cents per kwh, while a person using 750 kwh per month pays less than 2 cents per kwh, and so on. These are appropriately called "promotional rates," and they serve to encourage large users to use more. It amounts to a subsidy paid by small residential users of electric power to support large industrial users.

If the rate structure were revised to charge those who use excessive amounts of electricity more per kwh, or the same rate paid by small users, it would be an undeniable incentive to conserve energy. Such a revision might also encourage other methods of conserving energy, such as increasing insulation in homes and buildings to reduce the energy needed for heating and cooling (*The Potential for Energy Conservation,* Office of Emergency Preparedness, October 1972). While it is the states, not the FPC, which set the retail promotional rates, the FPC could have considerable influence in changing them. If the Commission restructured interstate wholesale rate schedules, it would be a powerful inducement for the states to follow suit. (More dramatically, utilities could be prohibited from promoting the increased use of scarce energy —as the Oklahoma Corporation Commission has in fact done.)

But there is little hope for such action if the attitude of former Commissioner Pinkney Walker is shared by present Commissioners. During his confirmation hearing before the Senate Commerce Committee, he was reminded by Senator Hartke that the country is short on energy, and was then asked how he would feel about the idea of increasing the cost of electricity with volume increases for the purpose of reducing excess consumption. He stated three times: "I should not want to increase costs with that basic purpose. . . . I should not favor that with that sole purpose" [Hearing before the Committee on Commerce, U.S. Senate, Nomination of Pinkney C. Walker of Missouri to be Member of the Federal Power Commission, 6 May 1971, p. 29].

> Three men were having lunch not far from the Capitol building in Washington. One was a wealthy businessman, the second a cost-plus defense contractor, the third an electric utility official. It was a good lunch and a big check. The first man reached for the check and said, "I'll take it. I'm in the seventy percent bracket, and it will only cost me thirty percent of the total."
>
> "Don't be silly," said the cost-plus contractor, "I can cover it in my expenses and it won't cost me anything."
>
> But the utility official took the check and said, "Boys, it's my pleasure. I'll slip it in the rate base and earn six percent on it forever." [Anecdote told by Senator Lee Metcalf]

Since competition does not determine what prices utilities will charge their customers, they must be arbitrarily determined. The FPC determines the extent of profit in interstate wholesale of electricity, and the states regulate the allowable return for retail power sales. Although a return of 6 percent on the total invested capital has historically been considered equitable, most utility companies receive more. This rate of return should not be confused with the usual method of computing profit by sales ratio. The utility industry makes among the highest percentages of after-tax profit on total sales of any industry. In 1964 leading manufacturing corporations averaged 6.1 percent in after-tax profit out of each sales dollar; the utilities took home 14 percent.

Utility rates are usually computed in the following manner by federal and state regulatory agencies. The company is allowed a certain percentage return on its net invested capital, called the rate base. The projected operating expenses are then added to arrive at the net operating income—what they will charge their customers. An example from *Overcharge*, by Senator Lee Metcalf and Vic Reinemer (New York: David McKay, 1967), illustrates the calculations:

rate base ($300 million) X rate of return (6%) = net operating income ($60 million revenue minus $42 million operating expenses, or $18 million)

If the utility companies are able to increase either the rate base or the rate of return, their profit margin increases. If any of the three factors is increased, the customers will have to pay more for electricity. The more utility consumers pay for power, the more profit the companies make; the more profit the companies make, the greater their rate base; and the greater the rate base, the more the consumers ultimately will pay. When the utilities overcharge their customers because of lower operating expenses than anticipated, tax benefits, or miscalculations, they retain the excess profits. This increases the rate base, and ultimately increases the charges to consumers.

Consumers also ultimately pay for miscellaneous expenditures of the utility companies, including legal fees to assure the companies of vigilant representation at the FPC and state utility commissions, and the cost of promotional advertising to increase demand. The business expenses of utilities also include the cost of institutional advertising by investor-owned utilities (known as IOUs) attacking government-owned utilities.

The FPC's authority over wholesale electricity rates comes from the declaration in the 1935 Federal Power Act that "federal regulation of matters relating to. . .that part of [the electricity] business which consists of the transmission of electric energy in interstate commerce and the sale of such energy at wholesale in interstate commerce is necessary in the public interest" [16 U.S.C. 824]. The Act requires that rates and charges within the FPC's jurisdiction be "just and reasonable," and not give any "undue preference or advantage." Every utility must file its wholesale interstate rates with the Commission, and may not change them without permission; the utility has the burden of proof to show that a change is proper [16 U.S.C. 824(d)]. The Commission itself may set the rate if it finds any charges to be improper.

But this apparently sweeping jurisdiction is, in practice, rather limited. In 1969 Commissioner White testified that FPC jurisdiction actually is exerted over rates affecting only about 10 percent of all electric power. The Federal Power Act excludes from FPC jurisdiction "facilities for the transmission of electric energy consumed wholly by the transmitter" [16 U.S.C. 824(b)]. This exclusion refers to facilities, not to rates, and applies to powers other than rate regulation, such as those involving interconnection and disposition of property. Commissioner White explained that FPC rate regulation only covers 10 percent of the power generated because "for the most part electric utilities are vertically integrated—the same company generates electricity and transmits it throughout its system and distributes it to the ultimate consumer" [Hearings on Utility Consumers' Counsel Act of 1969, p. 301]. In other words, most interstate "sales" are actually transactions within one company, and therefore are considered beyond the FPC's reach. But that section of the statute does not refer to the Commission's *rate making* jurisdiction, and the Act, in giving jurisdiction over transmissions in interstate commerce and wholesale sales, defines these terms in ways strongly suggesting that transactions between units of the same firm are included. A wholesale sale "means a sale of electric energy to *any* person for resale" (emphasis added). Electricity is transmitted in interstate commerce "if transmitted from a State and consumed at any point outside thereof," with no specification that the transmitter and purchaser be independent corporate entities. The 1935 Act, coming during an era of vast interstate holding companies, could hardly have overlooked the interstate character of many utility companies. But the Commission not only has disclaimed jurisdiction over such transactions, it also has limited its jurisdiction further by authorizing mergers and combinations among utilities, permitting the creation of more interstate combines which the FPC claims to be immune from its rate regulation.

The Commission's rate regulation staff has been inadequate even for those areas in which it concedes jurisdiction. When Chairman Swidler arrived at the Commission in 1961, no power rate bureau even existed, and the Commission's entire rate supervision responsibility rested with two or three people in the Natural Gas division. The Landis Report said that in September 1960, "the Commission announced that it would take 13 years with its present staff to clear up its pending 2,313 producer rate cases."

The Commission's rate authority over natural gas has been more vigorously used than the authority over electric power, partly because gas distributors have an economic interest in opposing rate increases sought by gas producers and pipelines, and therefore contest them. This contrasts with the power side, however, in which utilities are vertically integrated—producing, transmitting, and distributing the power themselves—with the result that there is no countervailing force to challenge rate increases.

The FPC's influence over utility rates extends beyond its direct rate making responsibilities. "Operating costs" are fundamental in calculating the return allowed and rates to be paid, and operating costs are determined by what the regulatory agency allows to be included "above the lines"—an accounting term which means a legitimate business expense included in the rates. If the expense is below the line, it must be borne by the shareholders. In calculating operating costs, regulatory agencies naturally use the utilities' accounts. Although they are not bound to use them, as a practical matter understaffed agencies (especially state regulatory commissions) usually follow whatever accounting system is presented to them.

The significance of the Federal Power Act's accounting provisions is thus more than just procedural. The Act "plainly confers power to regulate and to establish a system of accounts—a power which is as broad and all inclusive as words can make it" [*Southwestern Electric Power Co.* v. *FPC*, 304 F.2d. 29 (5th Cir. 1962)]. Under this authority, the Commission has promulgated a uniform system of accounts which utilities must use when filing their required statements with the FPC, and most state commissions also require the same system. The FPC also makes rulings from time to time on the allowability of particular types of expenditures. While the FPC's accounting does not necessarily bind the states and the utilities, as a practical matter, "when a particular item of operating expense is forced 'below the line' it stays there" [*Southwestern Power, supra,* 39-40]. Only a few state agencies have anything approaching the FPC's ability to audit utility books and ensure conformity with the accounting requirements, so the FPC's accounting authority gives it considerable *de facto* influence over state-set electric power rates.

One problem is that the FPC gets around to auditing a utility's books only once every five years on a regular schedule. When it comes upon violations it does little more than meekly ask the utility to correct them. As a result, the FPC must share some responsibility for what Senator Lee Metcalf estimates is about a $60 per person annual overcharge in electricity bills [*Overcharge*, p. 228]. These overcharges do not just result from excessive rates of return allowed by states, but from excessive operating expenses included in the rate base.

One practical accounting shortcoming concerns the FPC requirement that utilities itemize "expenditures for the purpose of influencing public opinion with respect to the election or appointment of public officials, referenda, legislation, or ordinances. . . or for the purpose of influencing the decisions of public officials," in order to deduct them from operating expenses [*Accounts*, 426.4]. In a recent case a Commission accountant discovered a virtual cornucopia of expenditures by Otter Tail Power Co. in local elections, apparently in an effort to keep the towns from leaving the Otter Tail system and starting their own municipal systems. None of these expenditures had been listed in the proper account; the company's disingenuous explanation was that it believed the account to apply only to expenditures on national politics. Utilities which deduct these expenditures obtain enormous political leverage, as well as directly increasing rates.

Citizen access to the Commission's accounting work could generally take two forms. First, accounting rules and policy are set by rule making, which outsiders may initiate or comment upon. Second, the public can try to force the Commission to investigate accounts or classify certain expenditures. A requirement by the FPC for complete utility reporting would be a useful source of information for the public, and might serve as a restraint of utility expenditures.

In addition to all the other industry shortcomings which the FPC has managed to overlook, the utility industry has the dubious distinction of being among the most discriminatory employers in the United States. In June 1968 the Equal Employment Opportunity Commission (EEOC) reported that the utility industry—particularly the electric power companies—was, according to 1966 and 1967 data, the worst employer of minorities of any industry grouping. In 1969 the Chairman of the EEOC, Mr. William H. Brown III, addressed the Edison Electric Institute, and, noting that virtually no progress had been made in their discriminatory hiring practices, said: "I cannot accept the excuse, from any of these companies which are such painfully good examples of exclusion, that qualified minorities and women just could not be found."

In 1970 Brown remarked: "Our patience with the inaction of the utilities industry is running short," and cited an EEOC survey of over 100 major utilities, which indicated that the industry employs blacks at only about half the rate of other major businesses. Of the industry's 80,000 officials and managers, there are fewer than 300 black and 200 Spanish-surnamed Americans. Blacks held 4.8 percent of all jobs, and Spanish-surnamed Americans held 1.2 percent of all jobs. After reminding the utility industry that it was the third time in as many years that a Chairman of the EEOC had to bring this to the industry's attention, he concluded: "The utilities industry, however, has succeeded in staying peculiarly remote from many of the intense demands for equal opportunity. This industry, by its unique position, has been shielded by its legalized status as a monopoly. . ." [Remarks by William H. Brown III, Chairman EEOC, Washington, D.C., National Energy Policy Conference, Washington, D.C., 18 February 1970]. Having gone to industry three times with no success, Brown then threatened to take the case to the Federal Power Commission. "I think FPC would seriously question whether a utility company with employment figures such as those cited today. . .is truly operating in the public interest."

He thought wrong, as he learned in 1970. That year the California Rural Legal Assistance Fund (CRLA) challenged a license application by Pacific Gas and Electric on the grounds that their discriminatory employment practices were not in the public interest. The FPC acknowledged that discrimination by industry was a real problem, but refused to consider any action. "We cannot lawfully resolve the issue of whether an electric utility's employment practices are discriminatory because this would require [the Commission] to act in an area in which it has no statutory basis for jurisdiction." CRLA chose not to appeal the FPC ruling to the Court of Appeals, so the Commission has not yet had its responsibilities authoritatively pointed out.

The FPC reiterated its position in 1972, after a coalition of civil rights and public interest organizations filed a petition for rule making asking the agency to assert its jurisdiction and issue rules requiring equal employment opportunity and nondiscrimination in the employment practices of regulated companies. The Commission swiftly rejected this petition, claiming that it "lacks the legal authority" to deal with the issues. Although claiming to be "fully supportive of the National policies of this Nation directed at the elimination of discriminatory treatment of persons," the Commission ignored entirely an authoritative opinion it had received a few months earlier from the Justice Department demonstrating clearly that it has ample authority to issue nondiscrimination regulations. Instead, the agency sought to pass the buck by explicitly inviting "judicial review and final resolution of the findings and conclusions set forth in this Opinion" [FPC Opinion No. 623, Declaratory Opinion and Order on Petition for Issuance of a Rule Relative to Employment Practices, Docket No. R-447, issued 11 July 1972].

Although the FPC says it cannot take into account discriminatory hiring practices when issuing licenses, the Commission requires licensees maintaining recreation facilities for public use to permit all persons, regardless of race, color, religious creed, or national origin, unobstructed use of such facilities. The Federal Power Act authorizes the Commission to license projects which are "desirable and justified in the public interest" [Section 797(e) 4], and it gives the Commission authority to include in a license "Such other conditions not inconsistent with the provisions of this chapter as the Commission may require" [Section 10(g)]. It would be well within the Commission's statutory mandate to consider employment discrimination by licensees, particularly in view of Congressional declarations of the public's interest in equal employment opportunity [see Title VII, Civil Rights Act of 1964, 42 U.S.C. 2000; Civil Rights Act of 1870, 42 U.S.C. 1981].

Federal courts have held that Congress intended "to give the Commission wide latitude in the performance of its license and regulatory functions" [*Metropolitan Edison Co.* v. *FPC*, 169 F.2d 719 (3d Cir. 1948)], and that the Commission must itself examine all issues relevant to the public interest, including antitrust laws which the Commission has no authority to enforce. Other federal regulatory agencies have been ordered to take into account the very issues that the FPC has ignored. In *Office of Communications of United Church of Christ* v. *FCC* [359 F.2d 994 (D.C. Cir. 1965)], the Federal Communications Commission (FCC) was ordered to hold evidentiary hearings on racial discrimination by licensees. In the opinion, (then) Judge Warren Burger noted that although a broadcaster was not exactly a utility company, it was enough like one to merit similar regulation. It would not appear to stretch the argument to suggest that a company such as Pacific Gas and Electric, which indisputably is a utility, would also be subject to regulation.

If the FPC has trouble finding statutory authority to act against employment discrimination, it could try the Equal Protection Clause of the Fourteenth Amendment, which prohibits a state or individual acting under cover of state authority to discriminate against racial, religious, or ethnic groups, or the Fifth Amendment's similar direction to the federal government and its agencies [*Bolling* v. *Sharpe*, 347 U.S. 497 (1954)]. If the Fourteenth Amendment was violated when a state parking authority leased premises to a restaurant which discriminated, the Fifth Amendment would seem to be violated when a federal agency grants a license to a company which discriminates in its hiring practices.

It will take some sort of affirmative action through the FPC before utilities change their employment practices. As a protected monopoly, the utility industry is not threatened by minority business enterprise programs, and it cannot be affected by informal consumer pressure such as boycotts. Unlike many other industries, utilities are scarcely affected by government contract compliance action. Raising the issue through rule making petition or by intervening in a rate increase proceeding or hydroelectric license case have so far proved ineffective in pressing the Commission to take affirmative action. As these efforts have demonstrated, it will require appeal to the federal courts before the FPC is forced to act, an action which the Commission itself has explicitly invited. At this time, an appeal is in fact planned by the public interest groups which unsuccessfully petitioned the FPC for such regulatory action in 1972.

Access at the FPC

Citizen access at the FPC has been largely focused on hydroelectric licensing proceedings, rule making proceedings, and, to a limited extent, rate making. But before jumping into a formal proceeding, one must know about the informal avenues of information and communication.

Commissioners and staff members frequently attend and give speeches at industry conventions, seminars, and other events. Although the FPC has rules prohibiting private (*ex parte*) contacts with parties who are involved in current formal proceedings, the rules are applied in only a small fraction of FPC cases. Get copies of speeches made by more FPC officicals to industry groups, and attend the conventions when you can. Don't be reluctant to ask for interviews with FPC officials when you have questions to ask.

Even if the FPC were vigorous in attempting to get information from industry on environmental side effects, it would still have problems with the Office of Management and Budget (OMB), which screens all government requests to industry for information (see p. 72). Under the Federal Reports Act, the OMB (formerly the Budget Bureau) must approve all government requests for information to ten or more businesses. The original purpose of this requirement was to avoid duplication of effort, but the clearance procedures have created an industry board of censors, with effective power to bar any questions which they don't want asked. An Advisory Council on Federal Reports, composed of various industry groups, meets regularly with the OMB to review any proposed questionnaire to be sent to the industry. In effect, the Advisory Council can exercise veto power over the questions, and clearance by the OMB will be withheld until the questionnaire is revised to satisfy industry representatives. The Edison Electric Institute, the trade association for the private electric utilities, seems to be one of the most active industry representatives in using this device.

The FPC has recently established an Office of the Advisor on Environmental Quality, to serve as the Commission's environmental advocate and as the Commission's contact for persons concerned about environmental consequences of FPC decisions. It is important for those concerned about the environment to be aware of this office, but not to be overly optimistic about its function. An "environmental advisor" or "consumer advisor" may serve as a spokesman for environmentalists and consumers in a government agency, but may also be used as a bureaucratic lightning rod—an exposed position to attract attention and divert efforts from affecting the decision making structure. The first appointee to the FPC's Office of the Advisor on Environmental Quality, Mr. Frederick Warren, is an engineer, a former officer in the Army Corps of Engineers, advisor to the AEC, and private consulting engineer. In describing his attitude toward environmental protection, Mr. Warren sounds much like utility industry representatives. The environment must be put to "optimum use," which is determined by considering all factors—economics and production of power as well as environmental protection. In an interview he maintained that his role is not to preserve the environment in a natural state. "The National Park Service or Wilderness people might want to adopt that policy, but we have to consider a broad range of potential benefits to be derived from a project." He argues that he is opposed to an exclusive (natural state) use of our resources because he believes that may not be the best possible use. He is far from sympathetic to environmental protection intervenors in FPC cases. When asked if he felt the brownouts of the past might be the result of poor interconnections rather than environmental intervenors, he replied:

> Oh no, I disagree entirely. There may be some slight transmission problem in the Northeast where they may at times have trouble getting electricity through but the environmentalists are becoming a major factor in this. Because of their intervention industry is losing their flexibility to plan ahead in determining the best sites. Something must be done about this. [Interview with J. Shelby Bryan, Center for Study of Responsive Law, May 1971]

As with all the agencies, Congress can be an important source of information and assistance. Requests for information forwarded by your Senator or Representative will be treated better than if they come directly from you. The Senate and House Commerce Committees "oversee" the FPC, and their hearings can be much more informative than FPC sources. A well-publicized hearing can subject the Commission to close scrutiny by a staff which has information not available to ordinary citizens. An important congressional ally to remember is Senator Lee Metcalf of Montana, and his knowledgeable executive secretary, Vic Reinemer.

The Office of Public Information at the FPC is the brightest spot in the FPC for consumers. Although it is somewhat technical, the free weekly publication *FPC News* is essential. Free copies of recent Commission opinions are also available from the Office of Public Information (Office of Public Information, FPC, 825 N. Capitol St., N.E., Washington, D.C. 20426). The coin-operated photocopying machines at the FPC take only quarters—the same excessive price at which most machines at federal agencies are set. But the charge for photocopying done by the agency is a surprisingly reasonable (for a federal agency) 9 cents per page. However, it takes a few days, and there is a minimum $2 charge.

Daily press releases are sent to newspapers, and can be picked up at the FPC Washington office (see address above). Notices of hydroelectric permit proceedings are published in newspapers in the area of the project, and such notices are sent to government agencies and officials—such as Fish and Game Commission, city officials, and Congressmen—concerned with the area. Industry representatives often rely on expensive "watching services" which monitor the FPC for actions of interest to their clients.

The collected opinions of the Commission are available from the Government Printing Office (G.P.O.) as *FPC Reports*, but the cost for a set is $200. The FPC Rules of Practice and Procedure are available from the G.P.O. for $1.50. A complete list of FPC publications can be found in Appendix 9-B (p. 522).

Like most federal agencies, the FPC has the power to acquire, analyze, and retain voluminous amounts of useful information that would be either impossible or prohibitively expensive for a private organization to acquire. But, also like most federal agencies, the FPC is often reluctant to share its information with members of the public. The Commission's rules implementing the Freedom of Information Act (FOIA) are in Section 1.36 of the Commission's Rules of Practice and Procedure. [18 C.F.R.] They allow the public to inspect all "public records," which includes financial, statistical, and other reports to the Commission, power system statements, statements of claimed cost of licensed projects, original cost and reclassification studies, proposed accounting entries, and rates or rate schedules. The Commission also allows public access to correspondence relating to any of these categories. The list of what members of the public may see is specific and detailed. You should study it carefully before asking the Commission for information. The exemptions for "confidential" information are almost identical to those in the FOIA itself. The exemption which is most heavily relied on is Section 1.36(c)(14)(v) of the Commission's Rules, which reads as follows:

> (14) All other records of the Commission [are to be made public] except for those that are: ....(v) Interagency or intra-agency memoranda or letters which would not be available by law to a party other than an agency in litigation with the agency. . . .

One of the most significant information cases is *International Paper Co. v. FPC* [438 F.2d 1349 (2nd Cir. 1971), *cert. den.*, 404 U.S. 827]. The Commission had denied a request for memoranda of a policy or legal nature to the Commission from staff attorneys and policy advisors in the Commission's consideration of four cases. None of the four cases was set for contested hearing and the relief sought was granted by the Commission with no hearing. International Paper asked for the memoranda sent to the Commission by its staff advisors, and argued "that since the position of agency staff members participating in a hearing will become a matter of public record, in the absence of a hearing, all staff memoranda lose their privileged status" [38 FPC 825 at 826]. The Commission refused on the basis of Section 1.36(c)(14)(v), and went on to hold that the documents were not subject to disclosure under the "good cause shown" argument of Section 1.36(d) of the Commission's Rules.

The most basic form of citizen access to any government agency is a complaint. A complaint is usually an appeal to the agency to correct some practice under its jurisdiction which offends a fundamental sense of fairness. The way an agency handles such complaints frequently is an accurate index of its general responsiveness. Basically, you have a right to complain to the FPC about anything a regulated company is doing that it is not supposed to do, or is not doing that it is supposed to do. The regulations specifically provide that:

> Any person, including any State or local commission, complaining of anything done or omitted to be done by any licensee, public utility or natural gas company in contravention of an act, rule,

regulation, or order administered or issued by this Commission, may file a complaint with the Commission. If the complaint relates to a provision in a tariff or a contract on file with the Commission it should be identified. A copy of the complaint will be forwarded by the Commission to such licensee, public utility or natural gas company who shall be called upon to satisfy the complaint or to answer the same in writing within 30 days after the date of service of the complaint unless the Commission with or without motion shall prescribe a different time. A copy of the response or answer shall, at the time it is forwarded to the Commission, be served upon the complainant. If, in the judgment of the Commission, a violation of an act, rule, regulation, or order, administered or issued by this Commission, has been alleged and has not adequately been satisfied it will either invite the parties to an informal conference, set the matter for a formal hearing, or take any other action which in the judgment of the Commission would be appropriate. In the event that a hearing is held the complainant automatically will be a party thereto and need not file a petition for leave to intervene. [18 C.F.R. 1.6]

A complaint can be made by letter, and the formal requirements are not elaborate. It should contain the name and address of the complainant, the name and address of the party against whom the complaint is made, and a statement of the facts to show some violation of a statute administered by the Commission, or of a rule, regulation, or order issued by the Commission. Supporting material can also be submitted. It is not required, but the Commission prefers to have ten copies of everything. Those are the formal requirements for submitting a complaint. The reality of how complaints are handled is not quite so simple.

The citizens of Snohomish, Washington, had moved to Echo Lake in order to avoid the noise and pollution of Seattle. As one of the area residents said, they went there to avoid "noisy city, noisy airports, railroads, and highways, and heavy industry." But El Paso Natural Gas (EPNG) was right behind them, and in 1958 the company decided to build a 4,000-5,000 hp. compressor station in the area for transporting natural gas, assuring residents that they would hardly know it was there. But, as an FPC report later put it, El Paso failed to give "adequate consideration to the impact of noise levels on existing residents in the choice of the compressor station site. The property is uniquely located in a basin where even minimal sound levels tend to be magnified." In other words, Echo Lake had a good reason for its name.

It finally got to the people around Echo Lake, and on 14 January 1967, eighty-three of them signed a complaint to the FPC that said, in part:

> An intolerable situation [has been] created in our community by the presence of EPNG's compressor. Excessive vibration causes damage to buildings in the surrounding area, Echo Lake's former mirror like surface is a thing of the past, and the noise is excessively loud due to the beat of the engine 24 hours a day, 7 days a week with a sound like a freight train.

They also stated that they were landowners in the area. The Commission sent a copy of the complaint to EPNG, asking for an explanation. The company replied that there was a "minimum of background noises with which urban dwellers and many rural dwellers have become familiar," and that they wouldn't be able to get around to taking any remedial action on the noise problem until there was less demand for gas—when the winter season was over. The FPC was satisfied with this explanation and a few minor modifications by the company.

But one resident persisted and wrote another letter to the FPC in November 1968, alleging that the noise was still so bad that the plaster on his walls was cracking, that there were gas leaks, and that he was about to put his house up for sale. The Commission forwarded the letter to EPNG. A Congressman from Washington then wrote the FPC demanding an explanation, a complaint from another resident was received, and the Commission requested a complete report from EPNG on the problem and what they had done to abate it. The company then asked for an extension, which was granted by the Commission. But the FPC also sent two staff engineers on a field trip to observe the problem. After reviewing the reports, the FPC decided that the complaints might have been valid at one time, but that time had passed; although it would be possible to remove the compressor, the Commission felt that it would not be economically practical or in the public interest.

The Echo Lake case is a discouraging example of what to expect from the FPC in response to informal complaints. It also illustrates a few guidelines to follow to get any response at all from the Commission. Put your complaints in writing and be as specific as possible. Get as many people as possible to join in the complaint, and emphasize the substantiality of their interests, such as owning property. Enlist Congressional support if you can, and be persistent.

A protest is somewhat more formal than a complaint. It is limited to a matter which the Commission has under consideration, such as a rate increase proposal or licensing of a hydroelectric project. "Any person" may file a protest to any matter under consideration by the Commission. Although no particular form is required, it should contain the name and address of the protestant, the proceeding or matter to which the protest is addressed, and a concise statement of the protest. Also, "If possible 10 copies of the protest should be forwarded to the Commission." But filing a protest doesn't make you a party with any right to participate in the proceeding; for that, you have to file a separate petition to intervene. A protest will not be considered by the Commission as establishing the truth of its assertions, and is not even considered to be part of the official record in the case.

> If a hearing has been ordered, the protest will be placed into a public file associated with, but not part of the record upon which the Commission's decision is made, and will be available for such further exploration of the substantive matters raised therein by the Commission staff and the other parties as may be appropriate. [18 C.F.R. 1.10]

For example, assume that for twenty-five years residents near a hydroelectric project have been complaining that the water level has been kept too low and has been killing the fish. Assume further that there have been 200 such letters over the period. When a citizen group intervenes in a licensing proceeding on the project, the letters would be excluded from the record on which the decision is made.

One form of citizen participation more elaborate than a complaint or protest, but not requiring investment of time and money for intervention, is a petition for rule making. It can be as narrow or broad as you want to make it. The major problem with such a petition, as with rule making petitions to any agency, is that the FPC is not required to take any action. But if the Commission does adopt the rule you propose, it will have the force of law under the Federal Power Act or the National Gas Act. A successful intervention, on the other hand, may be limited in its effect to the facts of that particular case, especially if it does not involve an appeal to the courts.

A petition for rule making must include the text of the proposed rule and a memorandum of the legal arguments and facts to support the rule. The petition, like all documents filed with the Commission, must include your name, and the name and address of a person to whom correspondence should be sent—either you or your attorney. It must "state clearly and concisely the petitioner's grounds of interest in the subject matter, the facts relied upon, and the relief sought and shall cite by appropriate reference the statutory provision or other authority relied upon for relief and shall conform to the requirements of § § 1.15 and 1.16" [18 C.F.R. 1.7(a)]. For example, a petition for the Commission to require regulated companies to report on minority employment and to take measures to abolish discrimination in hiring might be in a form similar to a petition filed with the Interstate Commerce Commission (see Chapter 6). The legal authorities would include those discussed in Chapter 4. If the petition alleges facts, they must be "verified," that is, the person signing the petition must also sign a notarized oath that the facts are true to the best of his knowledge and belief. Although there are no "parties" to your rule making petition who must be served with copies, as there are if you intervene in other proceedings, you still are required to send an original and fourteen copies of your petition to the Secretary of the Commission [18 C.F.R. 1.15(b)].

The most effective form of citizen participation in FPC proceedings, and the most expensive in terms of time, effort, and money, is intervention. A petition to intervene (see Appendix 9-F, p. 558) can be filed in just about any Commission proceeding, ranging from licensing of a hydroelectric project to setting wholesale rates for electricity or gas. It is somewhat similar to a protest, but a protest, as mentioned before, is more of a method to allow people to let off steam, and is not a part of the record in a formal proceeding or considered in making a decision after a hearing [18 C.F.R. 1.10(a)]. Intervention is authorized both by statute and by the Commission's regulations. The Federal Power Act and the Natural Gas Act have identical provisions:

> In any proceeding before it, the Commission in accordance with such rules and regulations as it may prescribe, may admit as a party any interested State, State commission, municipality, or *any representative of interested consumers* or security holders, or any competitor of a party to such proceedings, or *any other person whose participation in the proceeding may be in the public interest.* [15 U.S.C. 717n(a), 16 U.S.C. 825g(a) (emphasis added)]

The Commission has issued regulations that spell out in a little more detail, and with more limitations, who is allowed to intervene as a party:

> A petition to intervene may be filed by any person claiming a right to intervene or an interest of such nature that intervention is

necessary or appropriate to the administration of the statute under which the proceeding is brought. Such right or interest may be: (1) A right conferred by statute of the United States; (2) An interest which may be directly affected and which is not adequately represented by existing parties and as to which petitioners may be bound by the Commission's action in the proceeding (the following may have such an interest: *consumers served by the applicant*, defendant or respondent; holders of securities of the applicant, defendant or respondent; and competitors of the applicant, defendant or respondent; (3) Any other interest of such nature that *petitioner's participation may be in the public interest*. [18 C.F.R. 1.8(b) (emphasis added)]

An example of the sort of interest which has been upheld by the courts as having a right to be represented was in the "Storm King" hydroelectric case, which will be described in a little more detail later. In that case, the federal court of appeals said that those with a special interest in aesthetic, conservational, and recreational consequences of a power project would be "aggrieved," under Section 313(b) of the Federal Power Act, and would have a right to intervene [*Scenic Hudson Preservation Conference* v. *FPC*, 354 F.2d 608 at 616 (2d Cir. 1965)].

Two other possible FPC proceedings for consumer intervention are those to set wholesale gas and electric rates, but the right of individual consumers and consumer groups to participate in such cases has not been clearly established.

The Rules of Practice and Procedure do not describe the procedures for electric rate proceedings in the same detail in which they describe gas rate proceedings. The Rules simply provide, "Proceedings to determine just and reasonable rates, charges, etc., under section 206(a) of the act are initiated by complaint or by Commission order served on the parties and interested State agencies and published in the *Federal Register*." Staff studies and recommendations are submitted and a hearing is held after publication in the *Register*. The best place to start is by scanning the *FPC News* regularly for notices of proposed rate increases.

For gas rate proceedings the procedures are described in more detail in Section 2.59 of the Rules of Practice and Procedure. After a pipeline company files for a gas rate increase:

(a) The Commission will give prompt public notice of the application and fix a date for the filing of any petitions for or notices of intervention. (b) Any suspension order issued by the Commission will designate the presiding examiner, who thereafter will control the proceeding until the completed record is certified to the Commission. (c) Any Commission order granting intervention will direct the natural gas company proposing the rate change to serve copies of its filings upon all interveners promptly thereafter unless such service has already been effected pursuant to Part 157 of this chapter. (d) The suspension order will also fix the date by which the Commission staff and all interveners proposing to present evidence shall serve their testimony and exhibits upon the presiding examiner and all parties. This date may be deferred in exceptional cases. (e) The suspension order will ordinarily fix the date for a prehearing conference. (f) The conference set by the Commission's suspension order shall be an integral part of the proceeding. All parties will be expected to give adequate study, in advance of such conference, to all material distributed in the case. A primary purpose of the conference will be to exclude immaterial and irrelevant evidence, stipulate non-controverted facts, and define the issues. (g) At the conclusion of the prehearing conference the presiding examiner will set the date for service by the applicant of its rebuttal case, if any, and will at the same time fix a date as early as possible after such service date for hearing on the issues remaining to be tried. [18 C.F.R. 2.59]

After the hearing is over a settlement conference is held between the same parties who participated in the pretrial conference. If the parties agree on a price rate in the settlement conference, the agreement is sent by the trial examiner to the commissioners, who usually accept it. If no agreement is reached, the trial examiner writes up what he believes the rate should be, based on the accounts and the hearings, and sends the entire record to the commissioners, who then decide the rate issue.

A major cost of intervention is the requirement that copies of all documents filed must be served on all other parties, either by mail or in person [18 C.F.R. 1.17]. For example, in one area rate proceeding, the Permian Basin Area Rate case, there were 384 parties. The photocopying and postage fees for every page submitted are a powerful incentive for brevity.

As a practical matter, most consumer or environmental protection groups cannot hope to match the financial resources of the pipeline companies in presenting a case. What they can do is to raise issues at the prehearing conference and at the hearing which would not otherwise be considered. At the hearing their major function is to cross-examine industry expert witnesses, since expert witnesses of their own would be expensive.

To give you an idea of what the regulated companies spend in coping with the FPC, one interstate gas transmission company paid $231,942 for outside legal counsel in 1969. Remember that most companies have internal legal departments of their own, and that such an expenditure is merely for *extra* legal expenses. The same company indicated that it spent $255,314 in one year for rate filing and certificate proceedings before the FPC. The annual reports which regulated companies file with the Commission list such expenditures, and are available for public inspection.

One reason why participation in FPC hearings is so expensive, aside from legal fees and expert witnesses, is the cost of a transcript. If you intend to participate effectively, especially if you rely on cross-examination, it is necessary to have a daily copy of the transcript from the previous day. That will cost you 84 cents per page for "immediate" delivery, by 9:00 P.M. the day of the hearing, or nine hours after close of the day's proceedings, whichever is later. For "daily" delivery, 8:00 A.M. the next morning, the charge is 64 cents per page. For "ordinary" delivery within five days, the charge is 28 cents per page. As with all the other administrative agencies, these charges are paid to a private reporting company, currently the Columbia Reporting Company, which provides the FPC with free copies and also provides any other federal agency with one free copy on request. But no provision of the FPC contract with Columbia prohibits photocopying, as some other contracts do, and the Commission's copy should be available as a public document for inspection and copying at the same 9 cents per page as for other documents. But so far this has not been tried. The Commission usually holds four hours of hearings per day, and daily transcript will be about 125 pages. The daily cost will be from $80 to $105, depending on the speed of delivery.

One attempt at intervention in an FPC gas case is particularly worth noting, because the intervenor raised a whole spectrum of consumer issues, including a request for relief from the overwhelming expenses of participating in an FPC proceeding. Although the FPC turned him down on almost all the issues, including the request for financial relief, the Commission now points to its refusal as establishing the criteria for *in forma pauperis* status at the FPC [FPC reply to questionnaire of Subcommittee on Administrative Practice and Procedure, Senate Judiciary Committee; proceedings of the Administrative Conference of the United States, 7 December 1971].

The proceeding, R-389A, was a rule making proceeding to establish national interim rates for independent producers of natural gas pending completion of area rate proceedings. An essential issue was whether existing rates were high enough to insure adequate supplies. The comprehensive petition was filed by Anthony Martin-Trigona, on behalf of People Organized to Win Effective Regulation (POWER), on 30 July 1970. The petition was filed pursuant to Section 1.7 of the Rules of Practice and Procedure.

The group asked that:

1. The Commission immediately suspend any and all rate increases until a comprehensive plan for future energy source development and consumption be promulgated for public analysis.
2. POWER be allowed to intervene as a party, and be allowed an initial $10,000 in costs and fees payable by the Commission on proper proof of expenditure for POWER to secure counsel and act as a public interest and consumer surrogate in lieu of the Commission.
3. Hearings on any and all rate increases be held in major consumer cities.
4. The public be invited and indeed encouraged to intervene and participate in the rate increase proceedings in opposition to such rate increases.
5. Members of Congress and other political candidates be prohibited from participation in the proceeding, either directly or indirectly.
6. Any and all commissioners who had been publicly identified with increased rates disqualify themselves from consideration and participation in the proceedings, with special reference to the Chairman of the Commission, who must disqualify himself.
7. The Commission revert to normal unexpedited procedures for the consideration of these issues, with customary retroactive safeguards for rebates and other consumer protection.

The Commission concluded that POWER's points 1, on suspending rate increases, and 7, on procedures, would be given consideration as part of the response to the notice of rule making. In reply to point 3, concerning hearings on rate increases being held in major consumer cities, the Commission noted that hearings had already been held in Midland, New Orleans, Denver, Pittsburgh, and Chicago. But the Commission granted the request to the extent that further oral hearings were held in Los Angeles, New York City, and Boston.

As to point 4, the Commission blandly said that they invited and encouraged the participation of any and all interested persons in the proceeding, and agreed that anyone would be able to file late for good cause shown. On point 5 of POWER's motion, the Commission noted that *ex parte* communications in any proceeding pending before the Commission are prohibited by the Commission's Rules of Practice. Insofar as direct participation is concerned, the Commission maintained that public officials have the right to express their views and the views of their constituents in the proceeding when their statements are made on the record and are subject to rebuttal by any party.

POWER asked the Chairman to disqualify himself, asserting that the test for disqualification—whether "a disinterested observer may conclude that [the agency] has in some measure adjudged the facts as well as the law of a particular case in advance of hearing it"—meant that the chairman's identification with increased gas rates should preclude him from being able to represent the public interest. The Chairman declined to disqualify himself, and a judicial appeal was dismissed as premature.

POWER's request for the Commission to defray its expenses as a public interest intervenor was also denied, but in the process the FPC at least admitted the existence of some conditions under which it might pay some costs. Despite the Commission's denial in this case, it does have statutory authority to pay such expenses, since both the Federal Power Act and the Natural Gas Act provide that:

> *The Commission may employ such attorneys* as it finds necessary for proper legal aid and service of the Commission or its members in the conduct of their work, or *for proper representation of the public interest* in investigations made by it, or cases or proceedings pending before it, whether at the Commission's own instance or upon complaint, or to appear for or represent the Commission in any case in court; and the expenses of such employment shall be paid out of the appropriation for the Commission. [15 U.S.C. 717s(c) relating to natural gas proceedings, with almost exact wording in 16 U.S.C. 825m(c) relating to electric or hydroelectric proceedings (emphasis added)]

As the POWER petition phrased its argument:

> Normally, an administrative agency need not pay legal fees and costs for an outside group to represent the public interest. There is a strong presumption that the agency itself is representing the

public interest. But where, as in the pending case, the agency is actively working against the public interest by seeking and indeed encouraging rate increases for natural gas suppliers, then the agency has a clear legal responsibility to see that the public interest is represented by someone. POWER (the intervenor) hereby demands designation as that surrogate, and further demands that the Commission pay all costs and fees associated with POWER's intervention in these proceedings on behalf of the consumer interest.

Although this is an issue of first impression at the Commission, other federal administrative agencies have already established that where public interest surrogates intervene in a proceeding—in a case where the Commission is a neutral party—a financial beneficiary party may pay the costs of the public group. Thus, for example, the Federal Communications Commission has upheld the payment of legal expenses to a public group opposing a broadcast station license renewal, where a final settlement is arrived at and the public opposition is dismissed with payment of legal fees by the incumbent licensee. In a case such as the pending one, where the Commission itself has become an advocate of increased rates through the open statements of its chairman, the Commission itself has a mandatory duty to pay the fees and costs of groups opposing this action and seeking to vindicate the public interest. [*Request for Disqualification of Chairman; Notice of Intervention as a Matter of Right; Request for Appointment of Consumer Counsel; Opposition to Any and All Pending and Prospective Rate Increases; Statements in Support of Relief Sought,* by Anthony R. Martin-Trigona, filed in Docket No. R-389A (30 July 1970)].

But the Commission refused, not on the ground that it lacked authority, but because "the Commission has not and will not abdicate its mandate to represent the public interest. Therefore, a volunteer surrogate will not be appointed in lieu of the Commission" [*Order Extending Time for Filing Responses, and Setting Further Oral Hearings, and Responding to Motions,* Docket No. R-389A (28 August 1970)].

The FPC did admit to a limited *in forma pauperis* procedure by stating that parties who could not obtain a transcript because of financial hardship should file a statement under oath that they could not pay such costs, and that a transcript and service of process might be provided for parties without funds [Order of 25 September 1970].

In terms of getting what it requested, the POWER petition failed. But since the FPC committed itself to the idea of *in forma pauperis* status in the course of denying the petition, it appeared to succeed in laying the basis for future successes. Although the FPC seemed reluctantly to be inviting another group to make the idea reality, its handling of a more recent case shows that *in forma pauperis* status will still not be easy to attain. In that case, SOUP (Students Opposing Unfair Practices) and the Washington Urban League sought to intervene in an action brought by Gulf Oil to amend an FPC order issuing a certificate of public convenience and necessity for sale to Texas Eastern Transmission Corporation of 4.4 trillion cubic feet of natural gas. Intervention was allowed, and the parties then moved to proceed *in forma pauperis*. They asked that they be allowed to:

1. Borrow from the FPC one copy of the transcript, rather than purchase it.
2. Serve only Gulf, rather than all of the parties involved (about 65).
3. File only one copy rather than multiple copies.

The Urban League's motion was denied on the ground that it had funds in its treasury, even though these were earmarked for expenses other than litigation. The Commission held that SOUP's motion must show not only that its corporate treasury was without funds, but also that its members could not individually or collectively bear the costs. It said, "The opportunity to adopt the corporate form simply as a subterfuge masking the wealth of its members is too apparent." SOUP refused to supply an accounting of the financial status of its members and its motion was denied. A motion for emergency relief made to the U.S. Court of Appeals (D.C. Circuit)(No. 72-1103) was denied.

The FPC was born as a quasi-conservation agency; at least it was directed to give great consideration to the conservation of natural resources in its licensing of hydroelectric projects. That power still represents the most accessible FPC proceeding for environmental protection groups, and it has been the focus of most citizen access at the Commission until now.

Part I of the Federal Power Act requires that nonfederal entities must obtain a license from the FPC to construct or operate a hydroelectric project across or along navigable waters of the United States, or to construct a hydroelectric project connected to electric transmission lines crossing between states (see J. G. Kerwin, *Federal Water Power Legislation* [New York: AMS Press, 1926] for a detailed history). A hydroelectric "project" includes not only the dam, reservoir, and power house, but also the associated land and facilities. The license for a "project" sets forth requirements regarding the land area, recreation facilities, and "primary" transmission lines. But the definition of "primary" transmission lines can be varied almost at will by the licensee. If a project involves several dams and reservoirs, each dam and reservoir, together with the land and other facilities, is called a "development." Licensing also includes nonfederal power facilities which use a head of water created by federal dams.

Projects in national parks or national monuments cannot be licensed without express authorization from Congress [16 U.S.C. 797(a)], and a project within a government reservation can be licensed only if it will "not interfere or be inconsistent with" the purposes of the reservation, and subject to condition imposed on the reservation [16 U.S.C. 797(e)]. License applications made by states or municipalities are theoretically given preference over private applications, and preference among license applications is also supposed to be given to those projects which are best adapted to conserve and use the water resources of the region in the public interest [16 U.S.C. 800]. To be licensed, a project must be "necessary or convenient" for navigation, power, or using surplus water or energy from government dams, but no project will be licensed if the Commission thinks the federal government itself should undertake it [16 U.S.C. 807].

The procedures for licensing hydroelectric projects are established under Sections 797(f), 802, and 808 of Title 16 in the U.S.C. If an application for a preliminary permit is filed (see Appendix 9-E, p. 556), the Commission gives notice in writing to the state or municipality which will be affected, and publishes a notice for four weeks in a local newspaper. A preliminary permit allows the applicant to secure data and perform acts required in preparation for a license.

16 U.S.C. 799 specifies that licenses can only last for fifty years (see Appendix 9-C, p. 529), and cannot be transferred without Commission approval [16 U.S.C. 801]. Projects must be adapted to a comprehensive plan for improving and developing waterways for commerce, water power, recreational purposes, and other beneficial public uses [16 U.S.C. 803(a)]. They must be maintained, but Commission approval is required for substantial alterations to projects which do not conform to the original plans.

Licensees must pay, under Commission orders, for benefits accruing to them because of storage reservoirs or other headwater improvements which belong to other licensees or government projects. Licensees are forbidden to join with other licensees to limit electricity or increase prices. They must construct navigation structures at their own expense, or convey land to the federal government if it is needed to construct navigation facilities.

The Commission fixes depreciation rates for licenses, public utilities, and natural gas companies, as well as approving the expenses to be charged to depreciation [16 U.S.C. 825(a), 15 U.S.C. 717(h)]. Water power project licensees and natural gas companies are given the power of eminent domain to acquire property for facilities under 16 U.S.C. 814 and 15 U.S.C. 717f(h).

Unfortunately, the Commission's exercise of jurisdiction over licensing has been limited. It has failed to enforce license conditions and formal licensing procedures. Denial or substantial modification by the Commission on a major project is resisted as being disruptive of power reliability. The Storm King case is illustrative, not only of the Commission's refusal to allow citizen intervention, but also of its deference to industry arguments.

In 1963 Consolidated Edison (Con Ed) sought to license a huge hydroelectric facility at Storm King Mountain, on a scenic portion of the Hudson River. Since it planned the facility to be operational by 1968, its own planning procedures required it to know the site, design, and major engineering details of the project by 1958 at the latest. Yet, by delaying the application until 1963, Con Ed virtually assured a favorable FPC decision. At that late date, alternative power sources to meet the 1968 demand could not readily be found. Thus, the FPC was offered a choice between granting the license or risking power blackouts.

A conservation group, the Scenic Hudson Preservation Conference, attempted to intervene in the license hearing, but the FPC refused to allow them to participate. Scenic Hudson objected to the project primarily on the grounds that it would deface the natural beauty of the area and would endanger the fish resources of the Hudson River. Con Ed asserted that the plant was essential to meet the power needs of New York City, that there was no alternative source of power, and that fish life would not be adversely affected. All of the planning and assessments for the project were done in absolute secrecy. No outsiders were consulted to offer alternative suggestions. Oblivious to strong citizen opposition, the FPC summarily licensed the plant. The Commission accepted Con Ed's contentions without question, and failed to consider the questions which are supposed to be raised when granting a license. As the U.S. Court of Appeals for the Second Circuit subsequently found, the Commission failed to assess the impact of the plant upon fish, wildlife, and scenic assets. It also held that the Commission's

assessment was incomplete on a variety of other issues, including
". . .among other things, cost, public convenience and necessity and the
absence of reasonable alternatives."

It was suggested at the original hearings that Con Ed install gas turbines as an alternative to the project, but Con Ed's experts scoffed at
the suggestion as mere gadgetry. They asserted that turbines were inefficient for large-scale power production, and were too noisy. But the
company apparently changed experts, for in 1967 Con Ed installed
gas turbines on barges in the Hudson River, as Kitzmiller/Scenic
Hudson had suggested, to provide reserve capacity and quick starting
capability for main units. By 1970 the company had installed gas turbines with 1.4 million kilowatt capacity, and they are adding units
capable of generating 636 thousand kilowatts to meet peaking and reserve needs. This power is equal to the planned capacity of Storm King,
and there are indications that these units generate power less expen-
sively than the Storm King plant would have [Statement of William
Michael Kitzmiller, The Role of Citizen Action in the Implementation
of Technology Assessment, conducted by George Washington University's Program of Policy Studies in Science and Technology. Seminar
Series, Spring 1971].

Con Ed's assertions concerning potential harm to fish life were even
less reliable, and the FPC heard only one witness on the subject before
issuing the license. Marine biologists who opposed the project were not
even allowed to testify. Instead the Commission accepted completely
the opinion of Con Ed's witness, Dr. Alfred Perlmutter, who testified
that he could almost guarantee that the proposed plant would have
little effect on fish life. He dismissed the contention that striped bass
spawning would be affected by the project because most spawning
grounds for striped bass were "much farther up the river" (FPC Hearings on Project 2338, p. 132). In any case, he continued, where they
spawned was immaterial because striped bass eggs "sink to the bottom of
the river and probably stick there until they hatch" (*Ibid.*, p. 155).

But the FPC should not have been so ready to rely on the single
witness. In subsequent hearings ordered by the Court of Appeals, three
Interior Department witnesses testified that 90 percent of the striped
bass spawning takes place right at the point where the plant would be
operating. They testified further that striped bass eggs do not sink to
the bottom, but remain suspended in the water. If, in fact, they did
sink to the bottom, the witnesses said they would probably smother
(*Ibid.*, pp. 2334-2351).

Refused a hearing by the FPC, Scenic Hudson appealed to the U.S.

Court of Appeals for the Second Circuit, which ordered a hearing and chastised the FPC:

> In this case, as in many others, the Commission has claimed to be the representative of the public interest. This role does not permit it to act as an umpire blandly calling balls and strikes for adversaries appearing before it; the right of the public must receive active and affirmative protection at the hands of the Commission [*Scenic Hudson Preservation Conference* v. *FPC*, 354 F.2d 608 (2d Cir. 1965)].

The conservationists who intervened to seek denial of the license were able to win substantial modifications in the project design. But this was after an expenditure of nearly a million dollars, and donated services worth several million more, during a battle which is still not over.

Although the FPC has a statutory responsibility to "plan. . .with regard to the proper utilization and conservation of natural resources," the courts have had to remind the Commission of its environmental responsibilities in other cases. In *Udall* v. *Federal Power Commission*, which reversed an FPC decision to grant a license, Justice Douglas said:

> The test is whether the project will be in the public interest. And that determination can be made only after an exploration of all issues relevant to the public interest including future power demand and supply, alternate sources of power, and public interest in the reaches of wild rivers and wilderness areas, the preservation of anadromous fish for commercial and recreational purposes and the protection of wildlife [387 U.S. 428, 450 (1967)].

The National Environmental Policy Act of 1969 (NEPA) [42 U.S.C. 4331] declared "The Congress recognizes that each person should enjoy a healthful environment and that each person has a responsibility to contribute to the preservation and enhancement of the environment." Title I, Section 102 of the Act orders all agencies of the federal government to make reports on all "actions significantly affecting the quality of the human environment." Specifically, the FPC will be required in all future licensing proceedings to make a study of the environmental impact of a proposed project [Section 102(C)]. The adverse environmental effects of the proposed projects, which cannot be avoided by reasonable alternatives, must be justified by other stated considerations of national policy [Sec. 102(C) (ii)]. Where short-term uses of resources are proposed, the Commission must now show them to be consistent with the maintenance and enhancement of the long-term productivity of the environment [Sec. 102(C) (iv)].

The studies which must be made on all proposed projects which will affect the environment, called "102 Statements," offer a rare opportunity for those concerned with the environmental consequences of decisions made by the FPC, as well as those made by other agencies. One example of such FPC decisions is the licensing of new hydroelectric projects, such as the Storm King plant. Another opportunity is in the licensing of existing projects now operating without FPC licenses.

There are a large number of hydroelectric projects currently operating which, contrary to the requirements of the Federal Power Act, have failed to obtain licenses from the FPC. Some of them are shown in Appendix 9-D (p. 542). The number of such delinquent projects was increased in 1965 with the Taum Sauk decision, in which the U.S. Supreme Court held that many projects which were in operation and unlicensed should be licensed by the FPC. The Court affirmed the Commission's licensing authority over the Union Electric Company's Taum Sauk pumped-storage hydroelectric project. Although it was located on a small stream entirely within the State of Missouri, the project affected the interests of interstate commerce by reason of the interstate transmission of electric energy generated by the project [*FPC* v. *Union Electric Co.*, 381 U.S. 90 (1965)]. Before that ruling, the Commission had tried to impose licenses only on those projects constructed on navigable waters.

There currently are 191 projects which have already obtained licenses and another 203 applications pending. In the licensing of these 394 projects, there have been no interventions. Seventy other projects have agreed to submit to FPC licensing. Another 147 projects maintain that they will contest FPC jurisdiction. This represents a rare opportunity for citizen intervenors. Since they are operating in violation of the Act, delinquent project owners are vulnerable. The FPC can impose conditions for further operation, and municipalities have an opportunity to take over such projects, since they are given preference in initial licensing. The Commission has the authority to backdate the license to the time of the original trespass, and to collect the annual charges which should have been paid for the entire period [*Niagara Mohawk Power Corp.* v. *FPC*, 379 F.2d 153 (1967)].

At the very least, intervenors should be able to require imposition of conditions for future operations. But it will take such intervention if the licenses are to be more than rubber stamps. The FPC Advisor on

Environmental Quality, Frederick H. Warren, has admitted that 102 statements were now being prepared on projects which did not originally obtain licenses but are now applying for them. When asked if he would impose environmental conditions on these late-license applicants, he replied: "We aren't going to impose a bunch of conditions on these people at the same time that we are asking them to obtain licenses." But he later modified this statement by noting that he felt some conditions were being imposed during licensing. When asked if he thought that the FPC would close down such a project solely on the basis of adverse environmental effects, he said: "I don't think that we are just going to go in there and shut down some project which is generating electricity and. . .providing economic benefits."

If you intend to intervene in an FPC proceeding to license a hydroelectric project, you should become acquainted with Commission staff personnel. They are of varying temperaments and can sometimes be of assistance regarding Commission procedures. They may occasionally even provide information about unpublicized plans and proposals. Members of Congress can also help, if only by forwarding correspondence to the Commission and asking questions. In the Blue Ridge Project (Number 2317) a Congressional hearing was arranged, in addition to Congressional inquiries being sent to the FPC. In another proceeding involving the Arizona Power Company, Congress enacted a moratorium on licensing along one stretch of the Colorado River.

The range of *issues* which can be raised by interventions is broad. There are all the environmental issues, from downstream water flow to the adequacy of the environmental impact statement; there are, as well, antitrust considerations, such as whether small, competing utilities can participate on equal terms in any pooling arrangements or in ownership of the facility itself.

The *procedures* for intervening in a hydroelectric license proceeding are similar to those for intervening in a rate case. When public notice is given by the Commission of a proposed project, a deadline for filing petitions to intervene will be included in the notice. The formal requirements for a petition to intervene are found at Section 1.8 of the Commission's Rules of Practice and Procedure. Appendix 9-F (p. 558) provides an outline of these requirements. If a petition to intervene is not filed by the deadline given in the notice, Subsection 1.8(d) requires the petitioner to show some "good cause" why intervention should be allowed. Late interventions have been allowed in cases where timely petitions of intervenors with similar positions have been filed, or in which no substantial delay would result from participation by the late-filing intervenors. If the intervention petition is very late and raises new issues, it is better if you can persuade a governmental body to intervene. Tactically, it is usually advisable whenever possible to submit interventions allied with governmental bodies. These can range from municipalities to federal agencies such as the Department of Interior or the Environmental Protection Agency (EPA).

When an application for a license is filed, representatives of the applicant usually make contact with the staff engineers on the case who are assigned to the Bureau of Power's Division of Licensed Projects. After the Bureau has reviewed the application, a very brief description of the proposed project is published in the *Federal Register* and in local newspapers near the project site.

The position of the Bureau of Power on a particular project is in part developed during the early stages of a license proceeding, before an order setting the case for hearing is issued. During this period there is normally considerable contact between staff personnel and representatives of the applicant regarding questions about the project. Access to the supplemental information provided to the staff before the hearing order can be of tremendous assistance in understanding the project and its alternatives. A hearing will be required if any intervenor or member of the staff raises an issue of fact concerning the project.

A speeded-up procedure used in the Bear Swamp Project (Number 2669) may be used in future license proceedings. This procedure at least presents the appearance of a public-spirited applicant working with a diligent Commission staff. Under the Bear Swamp procedure, a prehearing conference and hearing are to be held within a year after the application's filing, which limits the time for opposition to build. At the prehearing conference, a schedule for filing direct testimony and hearing dates are set. Both the prehearing conference and the hearing are presided over by an Examiner, who will often push for a settlement, frequently to the disadvantage of any intervenors. Direct testimony is presented in writing before the actual hearing. At the hearing itself, witnesses are sworn and adopt the direct testimony (with any correction); then they are subject to cross-examination. Additional statements may also be filed, but they do not have the weight of sworn testimony. With the Examiner's permission, depositions may be taken for out-of-town witnesses. Discovery of information in the hands of other parties is conducted through letters. Because of the detailed technical nature of the problems and the data being in widely separate locales, extensive use of discovery is necessary to obtain adequate information for intervention.

After the applicant's witnesses are sworn at the first session of the hearing and are subject to questions on their written testimony, the Commission's staff and the intervenors give their direct testimony. A second session of the hearing is then held, at which the applicant's witnesses are again available for cross-examination, followed by the intervenor's witnesses, representatives of other government bodies, and Commission staff representatives. Answering testimony may follow immediately, or a third hearing session may be held, with answering testimony served in writing before the hearing. Intervenors might find it useful to have government witnesses available for clarifying questions before they are cross-examined at the second hearing. This helps in understanding the government position, and in preventing the hearing from conforming to the applicant's terms.

Direct testimony by intervenors or allied government bodies is the most effective method of participating in these proceedings. Testimony by expert witnesses is more effective than simply relying on cross-examination to point up omissions and distortions in testimony by witnesses of the applicant and government. Nonetheless, cross-examination of such witnesses can be useful, and cross-examiners should ask to see the witnesses' work papers.

The most important action for an intervenor in a license proceeding is to raise issues which otherwise would not even be considered. These are some of the issues you should consider raising in a license application proceeding:

1. Inundation of land, tax losses, displacement from homes and jobs, ecological effects, road displacements, and community disruption.
2. Transmission lines—routes, tower design and width, provisions for undergrounding, pole design, and electrical interference in the surrounding area.
3. Anticompetitive power company activity.
4. Flood control and navigation plans.
5. Changes in downstream flows.
6. Changes in water quality in and below the reservoir, such as temperature, chemical composition (especially dissolved oxygen), and outlet design.
7. Evaporation losses in reservoirs over those in streams.
8. Provisions for safe and adequate recreation, such as parks, boat facilities, beaches, camping, hiking, wilderness, and wildlife preserves.

9. Provisions for fish and wildlife—displacement of animals and provisions for fisheries.
10. Federal development.
11. Coordination of projects with other power needs and plants.
12. Air pollution.
13. Practices used by the licensee in acquisition of land.
14. Structural adequacy and stability.
15. Surplus profits and amortization.

Expert witnesses add to the cost of intervention. Sometimes the witnesses may be obtained at a lower cost from public power bodies, universities, or by contacting retired government employees. Some sources to check for possible expert witnesses are the American Public Power Association and interested Congressmen. Members of the Commission staff may refer you to experts in the field.

After the hearing, briefs are filed with the Presiding Examiner, who renders an Initial Decision. Briefs on exceptions to this decision are then filed with the Commission, and the Commission may schedule oral argument. After a Commission decision, a petition for rehearing may be filed. If such a petition is denied, the Commission decision may be appealed to a U.S. Court of Appeals.

Some techniques to use in limiting costs of intervention, such as casting issues as questions of law rather than fact, or shifting the burden, or adducing facts to other parties or the staff, are described in "Some Thoughts of an Environmental Lawyer in the Wilderness of Administrative Law" (Sive, 70 *Columbia Law Review* 612, 1970). Another useful text is edited by M. Baldwin and J. Page, *Law and the Environment* (New York: Walker, 1970). One possible intervenor technique would be to subpoena personnel in the upper administrative reaches of the Bureau of Power, or the FPC's Environmental Advisor. Another technique involves subpoenaing personnel from other government agencies concerned with consequences of the proposed project, such as the EPA or the Department of the Interior.

Usually you should beware of open-ended license conditions, under which a decision on some point is deferred while a license is granted. Such provisions are frequently not enforced, or enforced only after protracted proceedings to require enforcement. A licensee who already has a project is obviously in a different position than a mere applicant. Even if conditions are included in the license, they may be amended or overlooked after the heat of a license application proceeding. An example is the history of the recreation plan in Duke Power Company (Project Number 2503).

But under some conditions, an open-ended license can be useful. Normally when a license is granted it will be neither revoked nor amended for its duration—usually fifty years. But the Commission has the power to condition licenses to provide for periodic evaluation of projects during their license terms, with the possible imposition of additional requirements directed at maintaining comprehensive development.

But an intervenor should agree to an open-ended license only if there is an uncertain condition which, either because of potential advances in technology or a possible change of circumstances, would make it desirable to hold the licensee to a different or stricter requirement than those presently imposed. Some typical open-ended conditions now used relate to water releases, joint use of project reservoirs and properties by the licensee and others, installation of additional capacity, coordination of project operation both electrically and hydraulically with other projects and power systems, and construction, maintenance, and operation of facilities to conserve and develop fish and wildlife resources. The right of the Commission to impose such conditions was upheld in *California* v. *FPC*, 345 F.2d 917 (9th Cir. 1965).

A related action would be to initiate proceedings to enforce conditions of licenses already granted. These are now rare. They may be begun by the Commission, at the request of another agency, or upon a formal complaint, under Section 1.6 of the Commission's Rules of Practice and Procedure. But since the Commission has complete discretion in deciding whether to act on such a complaint, intervenors might argue for provisions in a license article to govern how proceedings to enforce the license may be initiated. In the case of open-ended license conditions, intervenors should at least argue that adequate provisions for notice, clear standards and plans, and specific provisions for the initiation of enforcement proceedings be contained in such a license article.

Although it is much better for conditions to be imposed as a part of licenses, the FPC has authority to modify a license even though there are no open conditions imposed on it. Section 10(g)(803c) of the Federal Power Act states that a licensed project "shall conform to such rules and regulations as the Commission may from time to time prescribe for the protection of life, health, and property." The Act also provides, in Section 10(c), that "Each licensee hereunder shall be liable for all damages occasioned to the property of others by the construction, maintenance, or operation of the project works appurtenant or accessory thereto, constructed under the license. . . ." These sections represent opportunities for both Commission action to cure activity by licensees which threatens the environment, and legal action by citizens to secure compensation for past damage.

Licenses may also be revoked for violations of their conditions, under 16 U.S.C. 820, if the Commission requests the Attorney General to institute proceedings for such revocation. Similarly, any violation of the Federal Power Act or of regulations can be remedied by the Attorney General seeking an injunction or mandamus in District Court. Under 16 U.S.C. 825m, the FPC itself may sue to enjoin violations or enforce compliance. Willful failure to comply with a Commission *order* can result in a $1,000 forfeiture, and those who willfully and knowingly violate the Act may be punished by a fine of $5,000 and two years imprisonment. Violation of an FPC *rule* is punishable by a fine of $500 a day.

The relicensing of hydroelectric projects represents a valuable opportunity to judge the performance of the licensees with the possibility of improving their future performance. Many of these opportunities will come in the next ten years, since hydroelectric licenses can only be granted for a maximum of fifty years, and most of the major projects were licensed in the 1920s. When the licenses expire, the projects can be taken over by the government or relicensed (see Appendix 9-C, p. 529). According to Section 808 of the Federal Power Act:

> If the United States does not, at the expiration of the original license, exercise its right to take over, maintain, and operate any project or projects of the licensee, as provided in Section 807 of this title (giving Congress ten years to decide on takeover at the expiration of each license), the Commission is authorized to issue a new license. . . . *Upon such terms and conditions as may be authorized or required* . . . to a new licensee (or the original licensee) . . . . (emphasis added)

In plain language, this means that the relicensing proceeding is a day of judgment for the original licensee: The project can be taken over by the federal government, a license to operate it can be granted to another applicant (with compensation to the licensee), or the license may be renewed under strict conditions.

This condition was included in the Act because Congress has required its permission to construct dams on navigable waters, under the concept of "superior servitude"—i.e., the public has a right to navigation over private dams. Because of early technology, hydroelectric energy was considerably cheaper than steam thermal. Conservationists considered it unfair that private hydroelectric project owners should be able to charge market (steam) prices, and pocket the considerable difference. They argued that the rights should be rented to private owners by the government in order to protect the public interest. Others, arguing that it was important to encourage maximum development of cheap hydroelectric power, proposed that the utilities sell power at cost with a reasonably regulated return added on. The compromise reached in the Federal Water Power Act of 1920 [16 U.S.C. 791-823] allowed for fifty-year licenses, after which the federal government could recapture the project's "economic rent" accumulated over the years. The law allows for collection of excess profits for the first twenty years, and the creation of an amortization fund for the next thirty. At the end of the fifty-year license period, the cost of the project would be calculated by subtracting depreciation and excess profits from the original cost. Specifically, Section 14 of the Act [16 U.S.C. 807] provides that the federal government may acquire, upon payment of net investment and any severance damages, nonpublic hydroelectric power plants upon expiration of their FPC licenses or upon "mutual agreement." Alternatively, the Commission may issue a new license to the original licensee or to a new applicant.

But the Act didn't provide any procedures—an oversight corrected by an amendment in 1968 (Pub. L. 90-451). Basically, the amendment permits the Commission to combine for consideration in one proceeding the questions of whether a project should be recaptured or relicensed, and it authorizes the Commission to issue a nonpower license whenever the Commission finds that all or part of a project should no longer be used for power purposes. Under the procedure, the Secretary of the FPC gives notice of the expiration date of a license five years in advance, and the Commission includes in its annual report a list of all project licenses which will expire in the next six years (see Appendix 9-C, p. 529). This notice includes the expiration date of the license, the licensee's name, the project number, the principal project works included under the license, the geographical location of the project by state, county, city, and stream, and the project's installed capacity.

No earlier than five years before the expiration of the license, and not later than three years before expiration, a licensee may file an application for a new license, a nonpower license, or a statement renouncing the right to file. Any other person, including a municipality, may also apply for a power or nonpower license, no earlier than five years prior to the expiration date, and not later than two and one-half years prior to that date (or six months after notice of the filing by the original licensee, whichever is earlier). Extensions of time may be granted for good cause.

There are several nonindustry groups with interests which could be served by intervening in hydroelectric relicensing proceedings, and a number of tactical options are open to them. A group of citizens generally dissatisfied with the manner in which a project has been run could intervene to urge at least three possible alternatives: They could argue that the government should recapture the project, that the license should be granted to someone else, or, if the license is reissued to the present holder, that it include certain conditions. Another party which might intervene is the municipality served by the project. A municipality could take over the project to obtain revenue, a cheaper supply of power, and better service for residents. Although it is clear that municipalities must be given preference in licensing a new project [16 U.S.C. 800], the FPC insists that this preference does not extend to relicensing proceedings. But the American Public Power Association disagrees [see Hearings of Senate Committee on Commerce on S.2445, No. 90-62, 26 and 27 February 1968; Hearings of Subcommittee on Communications and Power, House Interstate and Foreign Commerce Committee on H.R. 12698 and 12699, No. 90-40, 11-13 June 1968].

Another possible intervenor could be a publicly owned utility in the area, which might also want to obtain a license to operate the project, particularly if it had been denied power or had been charged confiscatory rates by the present license holder.

Regardless of the specific group or the alternative proposed (recapture, a new licensee, or relicensing with conditions), there are several possible issues for intervenors to raise, including:

1. Whether the project has been run economically.
2. Whether the project has unnecessarily damaged the environment.
3. Whether the project has violated federal laws (such as equal employment or antitrust).
4. Whether the project has complied with FPC regulations.

Just about any issue which can be raised by intervenors in an initial license proceeding (see p. 510) can be raised in a relicensing proceeding, but the situation is quite different. The applicant is not just presenting promises of what he will do; there is a fifty-year record of what he has already done. It might be useful to compare the promises the licensee made about such things as preserving natural resources and providing recreational facilities with what has actually been done.

The relicensing of a hydroelectric project is in some ways like the FCC license renewal proceedings for radio and television stations, except that hydro projects only come up after fifty years, while broadcast licenses must be renewed every three years. But the similarity suggests yet another tactic—the negotiated settlement. In several instances intervenors in broadcast license proceedings have withdrawn in exchange for promises of improvements in employment and programming (see Chapter 7 for details). Similarly, intervenors in license proceedings before the AEC for nuclear power plants have negotiated settlements for measures to conserve wildlife and reduce the hazards of radioactivity (see Chapter 8). Hydroelectric licensees would, in all probability, be equally capable of reaching such agreements.

But nothing is as simple as it looks, and either recapture of a project by the government or transfer to a new licensee requires grappling with the byzantine computation of net worth—the compensation to be paid to the previous licensee. The Act [16 U.S.C. 807] provides that if, at the expiration of a license, the government takes over or recaptures a project, it must pay the licensee its net investment in the project, not in excess of fair value, and any reasonable severance damage incurred (damage resulting to the former licensee's remaining property as a consequence of the taking). If a party other than the government takes over a project, the new licensee receiving authorization to operate all or part of the project must then pay the old licensee at the same rate.

"Net investment" in a project is the actual original cost of the project plus "additions and betterments," after subtracting depreciation and accumulated "excess earnings." Among other problems, the Act didn't define the "excess" in "excess earnings." Section 10(d) of the Act does make it clear that, after the first twenty years of operation, a percentage of a project's earnings in excess of a reasonable rate of return are to be held in a reserve account until termination of the license. The Commission has determined that a fair return on "net investment" for any year shall be one and one-half times the "weighted average annual embedded cost" rate of long-term debt, or 6 percent, whichever is higher. The purpose of 10(d) was to reduce the competitive advantage of hydro projects by making certain that at least some portion of their surplus earnings would be retained, rather than being distributed in the form of dividends, to be applied in reducing the recapture or relicensing price.

Unfortunately, the Commission reversed an earlier ruling [Docket No. R-297, Order No. 370, 27 September 1968] which would have required the licensee to set up an amortization fund for any excess profits derived from the first twenty years of operations. So the price of a project that is recaptured by the government or licensed to another applicant will be higher than might appear from reading Section 10(d) of the Act.

When the present licensee applies for renewal, it must furnish estimates which would be critical if the Commission decided to order relicensing to another applicant or recapture: the project's fair value, the net investment, and the severance damages if the license is not renewed. The applicant is also required to furnish other information, such as an explanation of why additional capacity is not being proposed, and the effect the relicensing to another applicant would have on the supply of electrical energy and rates charged [Order No. 384, Docket No. R-335, issued 17 July 1969, amending Part 16 and portions of Parts 2 and 4.34, F.R. 12269].

The greatest opportunity for citizen participation in FPC proceedings is probably in the relicensing of hydroelectric projects. The opportunity is limited, both in potential impact and in time. Hydroelectric projects are not as significant in terms of national environmental degradation as the fossil-fueled plants and the processes, such as strip mining, that supply them. But they are legally vulnerable when they are up for renewal. That period of vulnerability, as already described, will expire for most of these projects at the end of the 1970s. If they are then renewed for fifty-year terms, they will disappear from public access for another half-century—the demi-Brigadoons of administrative law.

Those are not the only points of access at the FPC, but they are the ones least difficult to use. Participating in rate making is expensive and complex, but it could have considerable effect. Petitions for rule making can be as simple or complex as you want to make them, and could conceivably cover concerns from equal employment by regulated companies to the use of advertising to increase consumption of power. The problem is that there is no way to force the agency to take any action on them.

Although there may be some precedent [*Mills* v. *Electric Auto-Lite Co.*, 396 U.S. 375 (1970), Award of Counsel Fees in Action under Sec. Exch. Act] for reimbursing intervenors in agency proceedings, this procedure has not yet been practiced by the FPC. In a recent hydroelectric plant licensing case, intervenors were denied an order requiring either the power company or the FPC to pay their expenses and fees incurred, if their participation in the hearing was found to have been in the public interest. Their request included experts' fees and attorney's fees. The court held that in the absence of a clear Congressional mandate in the Federal Power Act for awarding counsel fees and of "a showing of compelling need, it would be premature for us to inject the federal courts into this area of administrative discretion" [*Green County Planning Board* v. *FPC*, 2d Cir., 17 January 1972, 2 ELR 20018, No. 71-1991].

In addition, a recommendation adopted in December 1971 by the Administrative Conference of the United States on public participation in Administrative Hearings excluded a proposal that agencies experiment with means for assisting citizen groups in meeting the expenses of such participation. It merely recommended that agencies minimize certain expenses, not that they reimburse the litigation costs of public intervention (see Chapter 18).

The Commission has frequently pointed to its response in the Martin-Tregona POWER case as an example of its provisions for participation *in forma pauperis* by citizen groups. Since it has expressed its standards, in the course of rejecting a petition, there is an express opportunity for citizen groups to apply under conditions which would meet those standards. If such an effort succeeded, it would be a major advance toward reducing the immense financial expense that is the greatest single barrier to citizen access at the FPC.

Organization Chart of the Federal Power Commission

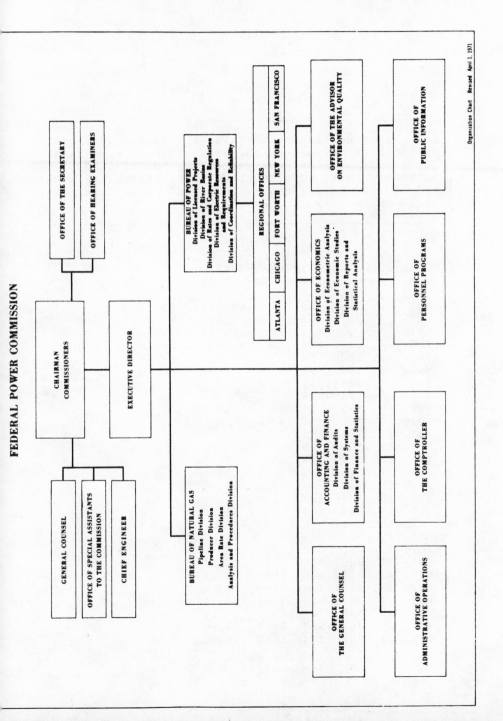

FEDERAL POWER COMMISSION

Organization Chart Revised April 1, 1971

OFFICE OF THE SECRETARY

OFFICE OF HEARING EXAMINERS

CHAIRMAN COMMISSIONERS

EXECUTIVE DIRECTOR

GENERAL COUNSEL

OFFICE OF SPECIAL ASSISTANTS TO THE COMMISSION

CHIEF ENGINEER

BUREAU OF POWER
Division of Licensed Projects
Division of River Basins
Division of Rates and Corporate Regulation
Division of Electric Resources and Requirements
Division of Coordination and Reliability

REGIONAL OFFICES
ATLANTA   CHICAGO   FORT WORTH   NEW YORK   SAN FRANCISCO

OFFICE OF ECONOMICS
Division of Econometric Analysis
Division of Economic Studies
Division of Reports and Statistical Analysis

OFFICE OF THE ADVISOR ON ENVIRONMENTAL QUALITY

OFFICE OF PUBLIC INFORMATION

OFFICE OF PERSONNEL PROGRAMS

BUREAU OF NATURAL GAS
Pipeline Division
Producer Division
Area Rate Division
Analysis and Procedures Division

OFFICE OF ACCOUNTING AND FINANCE
Division of Audits
Division of Systems
Division of Finance and Statistics

OFFICE OF THE COMPTROLLER

OFFICE OF THE GENERAL COUNSEL

OFFICE OF ADMINISTRATIVE OPERATIONS

FPC Publications List

February 12, 1973

The following listing contains the latest editions of
publications issued by the Federal Power Commission.
Copies are available only from the SUPERINTENDENT OF
DOCUMENTS, U.S. GOVERNMENT PRINTING OFFICE, Washington
D.C. 20402, unless otherwise noted. Remittance must
accompany order.

ADMINISTRATIVE

FEDERAL POWER COMMISSION REPORTS
    (Opinions, Decisions and Orders)

        Vol. 1, Jan. 1931 to June 1939, $3.50
        Vol. 2, July 1939 to Dec. 1941, $4.25
        Vol. 3, Jan. 1942 to Sept. 1943, $4.25
        Vol. 4, Oct. 1943 to Dec. 1945, $4.25
        Vol. 5, 1946, $2.75
        Vol. 6, 1947, $4.50
        Vol. 7, 1948, $4.25
        Vol. 8, 1949, $4.00
        Vol. 9, 1950, $4.00
        Vol. 10, 1951, $5.75
        Vol. 11, 1952, $5.50
        Vol. 12, 1953, $5.25
        Vol. 13, 1954, $5.25
        Vol. 14, 1955, $4.50
        Vol. 15, Jan.-June 1956, $5.75
        Vol. 16, July-Dec. 1956, $5.00
        Vol. 17, Jan.-June 1957, $3.50
        Vol. 18, July-Dec. 1957, $3.25
        Vol. 19, Jan.-June 1958, $4.00
        Vol. 20, July-Dec. 1958, $3.50
        Vol. 21, Jan.-June 1959, $3.50
        Vol. 22, July-Dec. 1959, $4.25
        Vol. 23, Jan.-June 1960, $3.50
        Vol. 24, July-Dec. 1960, $4.25
        Vol. 25, Jan.-June 1961, $5.50
        Vol. 26, July-Dec. 1961, $3.50
        Vol. 27, Jan.-June 1962, $5.00

```
Vol. 28, July-Dec. 1962, $4.50
Vol. 29, Jan.-June 1963, $4.50
Vol. 30, July-Dec. 1963, $5.50
Vol. 31, Jan.-June 1964, $5.75
Vol. 32, July-Dec. 1964, $5.50
Vol. 33, Jan.-June 1965, $5.00
Vol. 34, July-Dec. 1965, $8.25
Vol. 35, Jan.-June 1966, $6.25
Vol. 36, July-Dec. 1966, $7.00
```

PRELIMINARY PRINTS of Federal Power Commission
   Reports. Monthly (Opinions, Decisions, and Orders)
   Subscription - $26.50 per year
                  $ 6.75 Foreign postage
      (Prices of single copies varies according to size.)

FEDERAL POWER ACT - Indexed -- March 1, 1971.
   (A-110 - $1.00)

NATURAL GAS ACT - Indexed -- April 1, 1965.
   (A-11 - 25 cents)

LIST OF UNITS OF PROPERTY for Use in Connection with the
   Uniform System of Accounts for Natural Gas Companies,
   effective January 1, 1961.
   **(A-73 - 15 cents - Available only from the FPC.)

REGULATIONS UNDER THE FEDERAL POWER ACT, January 1, 1970.
   Also includes forms under Federal Power Act. Loose-
   leaf edition. Subscription includes the basic book and
   all supplements for indefinite period.
   *(A-105 - $2.50)
   OUT OF PRINT

REGULATIONS UNDER THE NATURAL GAS ACT, August 1, 1967.
   Also includes approved forms under the Natural Gas Act.
   Loose-leaf edition. Subscription includes the basic
   book and all supplements for indefinite period.
   **(A-96 - $3.50)

RULES OF PRACTICE AND PROCEDURE, January 1, 1966. Also
   includes General Policy and Interpretations, Organization and the Administrative Procedure Act. Indexed.
   Loose-leaf edition. Subscription includes the basic
   book and all supplements for indefinite period.
   *(A-92 - $1.50)
   OUT OF PRINT

NOTE: The latest revisions of these publications appear
in the Code of Federal Regulations-Title 18-Conservation
of Power and Water Resources, which may be purchased from
the Superintendent of Documents, U.S. Government Printing Office, Washington, D.C. 20402 for $2.00 a part.
(*Parts 1 to 149, **Parts 150 to end of code.)

UNIFORM SYSTEM OF ACCOUNTS PRESCRIBED FOR PUBLIC UTILITIES
AND LICENSEES, January 1, 1970. Loose-leaf edition.
Subscription includes basic book and all supplements
for an indefinite period.
*(A-106 - $6.00)

UNIFORM SYSTEM OF ACCOUNTS PRESCRIBED FOR NATURAL GAS
COMPANIES, September 1, 1968. Loose-leaf edition.
Subscription includes basic book and all supplements
for an indefinite period.
**(A-102 - $3.50)

REGULATIONS TO GOVERN THE PRESERVATION OF RECORDS OF
PUBLIC UTILITIES AND LICENSEES, December 12, 1962.
*(A-77 - .15 cents - Available only from the FPC.)

REGULATIONS TO GOVERN THE PRESERVATION OF RECORDS OF
NATURAL GAS COMPANIES, December 12, 1962.
**(A-78 - 15 cents - Available only from the FPC.)

ELECTRIC POWER

ALL-ELECTRIC HOMES, ANNUAL BILLS, 1971. Includes compilation of annual bills for electric power consumption in all-electric homes; data for individual utilities on the number of homes served with estimates of
the average annual kwh consumption; and amounts used,
with estimated normal figures, for heating and cooling.
(R-79 - 35 cents)

DEPRECIATION PRACTICES OF ELECTRIC UTILITIES, 1966.
Report on depreciation practices of electric utilities
under FPC jurisdiction having annual operating revenues of $1 million or more.
(S-201 - $1.00)

ELECTRIC POWER STATISTICS. Consists of monthly pamphlets
summarizing the production and sale of electric energy,
capacity of generating plants, consumption of fuel for
production of energy, and electric utility system loads
for all utilities of all types of ownership; also sales,
revenues, and income of privately owned electric utilities; by states and geographic divisions. Subscription
price does not include any back issues.
(S-17 - $5.50 per year. Single issue - 50 cents)

HYDROELECTRIC PLANT CONSTRUCTION COST AND ANNUAL PRODUC-
TION EXPENSES, 1970. Shows cost of plant, production
expenses, statistics on plant capacity, plant output
and characteristics for plants in U.S. and Puerto Rico.
Plant data based on annual reports and statements
filed with FPC.
*(S-220 - $2.00)

---

*Indicates new edition

HYDROELECTRIC POWER EVALUATION, 1968. A guide for evaluation of the hydroelectric power aspects of water resource developments. Also includes guidelines for planning hydroelectric developments as parts of comprehensive river basin plants.
    (P-35 - 65 cents)

HYDROELECTRIC POWER EVALUATION, Supplement No. 1, July
1969.
    (P-38 - 25 cents)

HYDROELECTRIC POWER RESOURCES OF THE UNITED STATES, DEVEL-
OPED AND UNDEVELOPED, 1968. Shows developed potential
hydroelectric power capacity available for possible
development in U.S. as of January 1, 1968. Contains 13
tables, with data arranged by major drainages and river
basins, and by geographic divisions and states. Also
includes maps showing locations of both federal and
FPC-licensed plants.
    (P-36 - $1.75)

NATIONAL ELECTRIC RATE BOOK. Consists of individual State
rate books covering rates charged by publicly and privately owned electric utilities in communities of 2,500
or more population (each state revised at least once
annually). Subscription price does not include any back
issues.
    (R-16 - $22.50 per year.
    Individual State Book - 45 cents)

RECREATION OPPORTUNITIES AT HYDROELECTRIC PROJECTS LI-
CENSED BY THE FPC - 1970. Lists over 5,200 recreational
areas available to the general public at FPC-licensed
hydroelectric projects in 42 states, including play-
grounds, picnic and camping areas, boating facilities,
fishing and hunting areas, hiking or riding trails,
trailer parks, and other lodging facilities. Contains
24 four-color map pages showing the location of recreational facilities in relation to major cities and
highway routes.
    ($2.00)

SALES OF FIRM ELECTRIC POWER FOR RESALE, 1966-70. Contains data on the sales of electric power for resale
under firm power rate schedules by privately owned
electric utilities and federal projects to associated
utilities, non-associated utilities, municipalities,
and cooperatives.
    (S-221 - $1.00)

STATISTICS OF PRIVATELY OWNED ELECTRIC UTILITIES IN THE
UNITED STATES, 1970. Presents data on stocks, bonds,
revenues, expenses, sales, utility plants income earned
surplus, balance sheets and physical quantities for
Class A and Class B companies. Also includes information on rates of return, investment tax credits, and
research and development expenditures.
    (S-214 - $3.25)

STATISTICS OF PUBLICLY OWNED ELECTRIC UTILITIES IN THE
UNITED STATES, 1970. Contains financial and operating
data for publicly owned electric utilities (municipal
and federal projects) taken from annual reports filed
with FPC.
   (S-219 - $1.50)

STEAM-ELECTRIC PLANT CONSTRUCTION COST AND ANNUAL PRO-
DUCTION EXPENSES, 1970. Reports operating results
for steam-electric plants in the U.S. and Puerto Rico.
Based on data from annual reports and statements filed
with FPC by electric utilities. Gives information on
capacity, demand, capability, costs and construction.
   •(S-222 - $1.75)

TYPICAL ELECTRIC BILLS, 1971. Gives residential bills in
cities of 2,500 population and more; commercial and
industrial bills in cities of 50,000 population or more.
   (R-78 - $1.50)

WORLD POWER DATA, 1969. Presents statistics on electric
generating capacity and electric energy production for
almost all countries of the world and a number of their
dependencies.
   (P-41 - 30 cents)

NATURAL GAS

DEPRECIATION PRACTICES OF NATURAL GAS COMPANIES, 1969.
First FPC report on depreciation practices of the large
interstate natural gas pipeline companies under its
jurisdiction. Studies 79 companies with annual gas
operating revenues exceeding $1 million.
   (S-225 - $2.25)

NATIONAL GAS SUPPLY AND DEMAND, 1971 - 1990. Staff Report No. 2
   (S-218 - $1.75)

SALES BY PRODUCERS OF NATURAL GAS TO INTERSTATE PIPELINE
COMPANIES, 1970. Tables in the report include sales
by states, and by pricing areas, sales to individual
purchasers; and interstate pipeline companies' purchases from producers and their own production.
   (S-217 - $3.75)

STATISTICS FOR INTERSTATE NATURAL GAS PIPELINE COMPANIES,
1971. Presents detailed statements of the balance
sheet, income and earned surplus accounts, operating expenses, operating revenues, customers and sales, gas
utility plant investment, gas account and certain physical property data of interstate natural gas pipeline
companies.
   •(S-223 - $2.25)

SPECIAL REPORTS

FIFTY-FIRST ANNUAL REPORT OF FPC, 1971
    (A-111 - $1.25)

GLOSSARY OF IMPORTANT POWER AND RATE TERMS, ABBREVIA-
    TIONS, AND UNITS OF MEASUREMENT, 1965.
    (A-91 - 20 cents)

FEDERAL AND STATE COMMISSION JURISDICTION AND REGULATION
    OF ELECTRIC, GAS AND TELEPHONE UTILITIES, 1967. Out-
    lines powers of state commissions to regulate electric,
    gas and telephone utility industries. Results are from
    a survey of state jurisdiction and regulation of elec-
    tric, gas and telephone utilities in 50 states, District
    of Columbia, Puerto Rico, and the Virgin Islands.
    (S-184 - 60 cents)

1970 NATIONAL POWER SURVEY
    Part I - $4.25 - Commission's own report laying out
    a long-range guide for efficient development of the
    nation's electric power industry through 1990.

    Part II - $6.00 - Reports by the Northeast, East
    Central and Southeast Regional Advisory Committees and
    a report covering these three areas by the Fossil Fuel
    Resources Committee.

    Part III - $5.25 - Reports by the South Central, West
    Central and West Regional Advisory Committees.

    Part IV - $4.00 - Reports by four technical advisory
    committees -- Generation, Transmission, Distribution,
    and Load Forecasting Methodology.

MAPS

PRINCIPAL ELECTRIC FACILITIES, 1971. Set of 8 regional
    maps showing high voltage lines of 69 kv and above, and
    generating stations exceeding 5,000 kw. Lists plant
    and ownership. Each generating station is numbered and
    each operating utility has a letter code for identifi-
    cation. Congested areas shown as enlarged inserts.
    Scale 1 inch = 32 miles for all regions except Region 8
    where scale varies from area to area.

    Region 1 - Me., N.H., Vt., Mass., Conn., R.I., N.Y.,
               Pa., N.J., Md., D.C., Del., Va. and W. Va.
    Region 2 - Wis., Mich., Ill., Ind., Ohio and Ky.
    Region 3 - N. & S. Dak., Minn., Nebr., Iowa, Kans. and
               Mo.
    Region 4 - Wash., Oreg., Idaho, Mont. and Wyo.
    Region 5 - Calif., Nev., Utah, Ariz., Colo. and N.Mex.
    Region 6 - Texas, Okla., Ark. and La.

Region 7 - Tenn., N. & S.C., Ga., Ala., Miss. and Fla.
Region 8 - Alaska, Hawaii, Puerto Rico and the Virgin
            Islands
   (M-92 - 50 cents for each regional map)

PRINCIPAL ELECTRIC FACILITIES IN THE UNITED STATES, 1966.
   Displays high voltage lines of 69 kv or more and electric utility generating stations of 10,000 kw or more.
   Lists power plants by states, with generating capacity
   in thousands of kw. Eight colors. Scale 1 inch = 55
   miles. Size 44 x 64 inches.
   (M-78 - $1.25)

MAJOR NATURAL GAS PIPELINES, June 30, 1972. Shows major
   existing pipelines, those under construction or authorized but not yet started, and proposed pipelines.
   Also shows location of major natural gas fields, and
   imports and exports of Canadian and Mexican gas, with
   the names of the companies keyed to numbers placed at
   points of sale. Directional arrows indicate whether
   each sale is an import or export. All pipelines are
   numbered with corresponding index at bottom. Does not
   include Alaska or Hawaii. Five colors. Scale 1 inch =
   170 miles. Size 13 x 18 inches.
   °(M-96 - 15 cents)

PRINCIPAL NATURAL GAS PIPELINES IN THE UNITED STATES,
   June 30, 1968. Presents major sources and generalized
   areas of gas supply as well as storage areas. Covers
   350 companies, with reference number keyed to index
   at bottom of map. Also index of 19 principal systems
   included. Scale 1 inch = 55 miles. Size 44 x 64
   inches.
   (M-83 - $1.75)

FREE MAILING SERVICES MAINTAINED BY
THE FEDERAL POWER COMMISSION
441 G street, N.W., Washington, D.C. 20406

_____   RU - All orders in rulemaking dockets.

_____   RO - All opinions.

_____   FPC News - includes all news releases, daily
        lists of formal documents issued, announcements
        of new publications and reports, notices of
        pipeline and electric rate revisions, list of
        independent producer rate change filings and
        list of independent producer rate schedule
        quality statements. MAILED WEEKLY.

Expiration of Hydroelectric Licenses

FEDERAL POWER COMMISSION

NEWS RELEASE   WASHINGTON, D.C. 20426

IMMEDIATE RELEASE
NOVEMBER 28, 1972   No. 18762

FPC LISTS 39 HYDROELECTRIC PROJECTS SUBJECT

TO TAKEOVER DURING FISCAL 1973-78 PERIOD

      The Federal Power Commission today published in the Federal Register a list of the 39 hydroelectric power projects for which FPC licenses will expire during the six-year period ending June 30, 1978.

      The Commission said the public notice was being given so the Congress would have adequate opportunity to decide whether, upon expiration of the licenses, to take over the projects as provided under Section 14 of the Federal Power Act. The FPC said its notice also would give the licensees and others adequate notice and opportunity to file timely applications for new licenses.

      Under Section 14 of the Federal Power Act, the United States may acquire, upon payment of net investment and any severance damages, non-public hydroelectric power projects upon expiration of their FPC licenses, which are issued for maximum periods of 50 years. FPC licenses include private companies, states, municipalities, and individuals. However, state and municipal projects are exempt from the takeover provisions of the Federal Power Act.

      The accompanying table lists all of the project licenses which will expire between July 1, 1972 and June 30, 1978. The Commission publishes each year in its annual report and in the Federal Register a similar table showing Federal licenses for projects subject to takeover or relicensing within the next six years.

-FPC-

For further information
386-6102 (Area Code 202)

PROJECTS FOR WHICH LICENSES WILL EXPIRE BETWEEN
JULY 1, 1972 AND JUNE 30, 1978, WHICH ARE
SUBJECT TO TAKEOVER OR RELICENSING

License Expiration Date	License
July 27, 1972	Pacific Gas & Electric Co.
Sept. 26, 1972	Portland General Electric Co.
Oct. 12, 1972	Pennsylvania Electric Co.
Oct. 31, 1972	Jesse I. Smith
Dec. 1, 1972	Pacific Gas & Electric Co.
Feb. 6, 1973	Arkansas Power & Light Co.
Apr. 26, 1973	Southern California Edison Co.
June 6, 1973	Ford Motor Co.
June 8, 1973	Alabama Power Co.
June 30, 1973	Owens-Illinois, Inc.
July 4, 1973	Utah Power & Light Co.
Aug. 24, 1973	Minnesota Power & Light Co.
Sept. 18, 1973	Michigan Gas & Electric Co.
Oct. 23, 1973	Pacific Gas & Electric Co.
Oct. 26, 1973	Minnesota Power & Light Co.
Apr. 10, 1974	North Counties Hydro-Electric Co.

PROJECTS FOR WHICH LICENSES WILL EXPIRE BETWEEN JULY 1, 1972 AND JUNE 30, 1978, WHICH ARE SUBJECT TO TAKEOVER OR RELICENSING

Project No.	State	County or Town
175	California	Fresno
135	Oregon	Clackamas
309	Pennsylvania	Clarion
719	Washington	Chelan
96	California	Madera and Fresno
271	Arkansas	Montgomery, Garland and Hot Springs
344	California	Riverside and San Bernardino
362	Minnesota	Hennepin and Ramsey
349	Alabama	Elmore, Tallapoosa and Coosa
2180	Wisconsin	Lincoln
20	Idaho	Bannock and Caribou
346	Minnesota	Morrison
401	Michigan	St. Joseph
233	California	Shasta
469	Minnesota	St. Louis and Lake
287	Illinois	La Salle

PROJECTS FOR WHICH LICENSES WILL EXPIRE BETWEEN JULY 1, 1972 AND JUNE 30, 1978, WHICH ARE SUBJECT TO TAKEOVER OR RELICENSING

Stream	Installation (kw.)
North Fork, Kings River	128,200
Clackamas River and Oak Grove River	51,000
Clarion River	28,800
James and Phelps Creeks	318
San Joaquin River	34,100
Ouachita River	65,300
San Gorgonio River	2,300
Mississippi River	14,400
Tallapoosa River	154,200
Wisconsin River	3,000
Bear River	14,000
Mississippi River	12,000
St. Joseph River	1,700
Pit River	292,250
Kawishiwi River	4,000
Fox	3,689

PROJECTS FOR WHICH LICENSES WILL EXPIRE BETWEEN
JULY 1, 1972 AND JUNE 30, 1978, WHICH ARE
SUBJECT TO TAKEOVER OR RELICENSING

Facilities under license	Period of license (years)
Diversion dam, afterbay dam, conduit, powerhouse, transmission line	50
Storage reservoir, diversion dam, forebay reservoir, conduit, powerhouse and transmission line	50
Dam and powerhouse	50
2 diversion dams, 2 conduits and powerhouse	20
Dam, conduit, powerhouse, transmission lines	50
2 dams, 2 reservoirs, 2 powerhouses	50
2 diversion dams, 2 canals, 2 forebay tanks, 2 penstocks, 2 powerhouses, and transmission lines	50
Powerhouse	50
Dam, reservoir, powerhouse	50
Dam, integral powerhouse, transmission line	35-1/2
Dam and integral powerhouse, reservoir	50
Dam and integral powerhouse	50
...do...	50
3 dams, 3 powerhouses, 3 reservoirs, penstocks, pressure tunnels, surge tanks, transmission lines	50
Dam, reservoir, penstocks, powerhouse, and transmission line	49-1/8
Dam, reservoir, headrace and powerhouse	50

June 24, 1974   Escondido Mutual Water Co.

June 26, 1974   Pacific Power & Light Co.

June 30, 1974   Wisconsin Public Service Corp.

June 30, 1974   Wisconsin Michigan Power Co.

Sept. 28, 1974   Pennsylvania Power & Light Co.

Dec. 14, 1974   Georgia Power Co.

Dec. 31, 1974   Mosinee Paper Mills Co.

Feb. 27, 1975   Southern California Edison Co.

Apr. 29, 1975   Pacific Gas & Electric Co.

Nov. 6, 1975   Alabama Power Co.

Nov. 10, 1975   Louisville Gas & Electric Co.

Nov. 23, 1975   Pacific Gas & Electric Co.

Dec. 31, 1975   The Montana Power Co.

Dec. 31, 1975   Public Service Co. of New Hampshire

Feb. 19, 1976   The Susquehanna Power Co. and
                       Philadelphia Electric Power Co.

Feb. 24, 1976   Union Electric Co.   -

June 3, 1976   Crown Zellerbach Corp.

June 7, 1976   The Washington Water Power Co.

Aug. 18, 1976   Kentucky Utilities Co.

Nov. 22, 1976   Carolina Power & Light Co.

Aug. 4, 1977   South Carolina Electric & Gas Co.

July 19, 1977   Wisconsin Power & Light Co.

176	California	San Diego
308	Oregon	Wallowa
1979	Wisconsin	Lincoln
2131	Wisconsin and Michigan	Florence, Wis. and Dickinson, Mich.
487	Pennsylvania	Wayne and Pike
485	Alabama and Georgia	Chambers and Lee, Ala., Harris, Ga.
2207	Wisconsin	Mosinee
382	California	Kern
178	...do...	...do...
618	Alabama	Elmore, Chilton, and Coos
289	Kentucky	Jefferson
137	California	Amador and Calaveras
1869	Montana	Sanders
2140	New Hampshire	Merrimack
405	Maryland and Pennslyvania	Cecil, Harford, Md., York, Lancaster, Pa.
459	Missouri	Miller, Morgan, and Candor
588	Washington	Clallam
621	Idaho	Nez Perce
539	Kentucky	Mercer
432	North Carolina	Haywood
516	South Carolina	Lexington, Richland, New-berry & Saluda Counties
710	Wisconsin	Shawno County

San Luis Rey	700
East Fork Wallowa River and Royal Purple Creek	4,200
Wisconsin	4,200
Menominee	7,200
Wallenpaupack	40,000
Chattahoochee	65,000
Wisconsin	3,050
Kern	9,200
...do...	8,500
Coosa	100,000
Ohio	80,320
North Fork Mokelumne	192,800
Clark Fork	30,000
Merrimack	7,200
Susquehanna	474,500
Osage	172,000
Elwha	12,000
Clearwater	10,000
Kentucky	2,040
Big Pigeon	108,600
Saluda River	200,000
Wolf River	700

Diversion dam, conduit dam, reservoir,   50
2 powerplants and transmission lines

2 diversion dams, 2 pipe conduits and   50
powerhouse

Dam, reservoir and powerhouse   36-1/2

Dam, reservoir, powerhouse and   36-1/2
transmission line

Dam, dike, reservoir, conduits and powerhouse   50

Dam, reservoir, powerhouse and   50
transmission line

Dam, reservoir, 2 powerhouses and   37
2 transmission lines

Diversion dam, conduit, powerhouse, and   50
transmission line

Diversion dam, conduit, powerhouse, and   50
transmission line

Dam, powerhouse, storage reservoir, and   50
transmission line

Powerhouse and appurtenant facilities   50

6 dams and storage reservoirs, forebays,   50
diversion facilities, water conduits, 5
powerhouses, transmission lines

Dam, powerhouse. reservoir, and trans. line   38

Dam, reservoir, and powerhouse   38

Dam, reservoir, powerhouse, and trans. line   50

Dams, reservoir, powerhouse, and trans. line   50

Dam, reservoir, powerhouse, and trans. line   50

Dam, reservoir, powerhouse, and 2 trans. lines   50

Powerhouse and transmission line   50

Dam, reservoir, and powerhouse   50

Dam, reservoir, powerhouse   50

Dam, reservoir, powerhouse & transmission line   50

Oct. 7, 1977   New England Fish Company

Sec. 14 of the Federal Power Act (16 U.S.C. 807), re-
serving the right to the United States to take over the
project works upon expiration of the license at a price
to be determined under that Section, but may be waived
pursuant to Sec. 10(i) to the Act (16 U.S.C. 803(i)).
Sec. 14 is not applicable to any project owned by a
State or municipality, pursuant to Act of Aug. 15, 1953
(67 Stat. 587).

2251   Alaska   Evans Island

San Juan Lake & stream   100

3 dams, reservoir 20

Unlicensed Hydroelectric Projects

PWR-LP

Mr. Shelby Bryan
c/o Center for Study of Responsive Law
1156 - 19th Street, N.W.
Washington, DC. 20036

July 21, 1971

Dear Mr. Bryan:

In response to your letter request of June 18, 1971, there are enclosed a number of tables listing unlicensed hydroelectric projects for which the owners have either agreed or have not agreed, for various reasons described by the table headings, to file applications for Commission license.

Your attention is invited to the fact that this information on unlicensed projects is as of June 30, 1970, which coincides with the date of the information on licensed projects contained in the Commission's annual report for fiscal year 1970 previously furnished you.

By handwritten notations on the enclosed tables we have indicated the projects whose status changed during fiscal year 1971; i.e., those for which applications for license were received and those which were removed from service due to the fact that they were, in the judgment of their owners, at the end of their economic life and it was impractical to rehabilitate and continue them in operation.

Very truly yours,

Secretary

Enclosure:
    Tables

cc: Senator Metcalf w/encl.

<u>TABLE V</u>   6/30/70

Hydroelectric Projects Constructed Without a Valid Federal
Permit or FPC License for which Owners have stated Their
Intention to File License Application

Owner Plant	Installed Capacity KW	River	State
Bangor Hydro-Electric Co.			
* Orono	2,325	Stillwater	Maine
* Stillwater	1,950	Stillwater	Maine
Howland	1,875	Piscataquis	Maine
Ellsworth	8,900	Union	Maine
Central Maine Power Co.			
Kezar Falls	350	Ossippe	Maine
Headwater Storage Reservoirs			Maine
Central Vermont Public Serv. Corp.			
Middlebury, Lower	2,250	Otter Creek	Vermont
Weybridge	3,000	Otter Creek	Vermont
Hydeville	270	Castleton Creek	Vermont
Pittsford	3,600	East Creek	Vermont
Glen	2,000	East Creek	Vermont
Patch	400	East Creek	Vermont
Silver Lake	2,200	Silver Lake	Vermont
Salisburg	1,300	Leicester	Vermont
Carver's Falls	1,560	Poultney	N.Y.
The Connecticut Light & Power Co.			
Bantam	320	Bantam	Conn.
Combined Paper Mills, Inc.			
* Combined Locks	2,375	Fox	Wisc.
Duke Power Co.			
Lake Tohoma	240	Buck Cr.	N.C.
Great Northern Paper Co.			
Thirteen Headwater Reservoirs	--	W. Br. Penobscot	Maine
Idaho Falls, City of			
Lower Hydro No. 4	3,000	Snake	Idaho
City Project	2,000	Snake	Idaho
Upper Hydro No. 3	2,400	Snake	Idaho

---

*Application for license received as of 6/30/71

TABLE V (Continued)   6/30/70
                                                          p. 2

Owner Plant	Installed Capacity KW	River	State
International Paper Co.			
** Ticonderoga No. 38	1,750	Ticonderoga	N.Y.
Newton Falls Paper Mill, Inc.			
Newton Falls	2,200	Oswegatchie	N.Y.
New York State Electric & **Gas Corp.**			
High Fall	14,100	Saranac	N.Y.
Cadyville	2,400	Saranac	N.Y.
Mill "C"	2,250	Saranac	N.Y.
Kent Falls	6,400	Saranac	N.Y.
Niagara Mohawk Power Corp.			
Oak Orchard	350	Oak Orchard Creek	N.Y.
* Brown Falls	15,000	Oswegatchie	N.Y.
* Eel Weir	2,700	Oswegatchie	N.Y.
* Flat Rock	6,000	Oswegatchie	N.Y.
Heuvelton	1,040	Oswegatchie	N.Y.
Oswegatchie	800	Oswegatchie	N.Y.
Allens Falls	4,400	St. Regis	N.Y.
Parishville	2,400	St. Regis	N.Y.
Hogansburg	700	St. Regis	N.Y.
Chasm	3,325	Salmon	N.Y.
Macomb	1,000	Salmon	N.Y.
Bennetts Bridge	26,750	Salmon	N.Y.
Lighthouse Hill	7,500	Salmon	N.Y.
Theresa	1,615	Indian Cr.	N.Y.
Baldwinsville	640	Seneca	N.Y.
Middle Falls	1,040	Battenkill	N.Y.
Schuylerville	1,200	Fish Cr.	N.Y.
Victory Mills	1,280	Fish Cr.	N.Y.
Piercefield	2,400	Raquette	N.Y.
Yaleville	725	Raquette	N.Y.
Diamond Island	1,200	Black	N.Y.
* South Edwards No. 2	2,680	Oswegatchie	N.Y.
Franklin Falls	2,265	Saranac	N.Y.
Union Falls	2,400	Saranac	N.Y.
Northern States Power Co.			
* Trego	1,200	Namekagon	Wisc.
Hatfield	4,800	Black	Wisc.
** Colfax	1,200	Red Cedar	Wisc.

        **Removed from service (too costly to operate) as of
6/30/71

TABLE V (Continued)   6/30/70
                                                      p. 3

Owner Plant	Installed Capacity KW	River	State
Norway, City of			
Sturgon Falls	3,500	Menominee	Mich.
Oswego, N.Y., City of			
High Dam No. 6	7,600	Oswego	N.Y.
Pacific Power & Light Co.			
Cline Falls	1,000	Deschutes	Oregon
Eagle Point	2,813	S.F. Big Butte Creek	Oregon
Albany	800	So. Santiam	Oregon
Stayton	600	No. Santiam	Oregon
Sealright-Oswego Falls Corp.			
Oswego Falls	9,000	Oswego	N.Y.
Riverside	800	Oswego	N.Y.
Spartan Mills			
Berry Shoals	1,200	South Tyger	S.C.
Startex Mills	1,200	Middle Tyger	S.C.
James White Estate			
Barnett Shoals	2,800	Oconee	Georgia
Springfield, City of			
Cobble Mountain	33,000	Little	Mass.
Wolverine Power Co.			
Edenville	4,800	Tittabawassee	Mich.
Sanford	3,300	Tittabawassee	Mich.
Smallwood	1,200	Tittabawassee	Mich.
Secord	1,200	Tittabawassee	Mich.
Total	242,838		

VI - A   6/30/70

Hydroelectric Plants for which Owners, Claiming
Special Acts of Congress, Have Not Agreed to
File Application for License in Response to
Commission Letters of May 4, 1962, Oct. 30, 1962
and July 13, 1965

Owner Plant	Existing Capacity KW	River	State
East Bay Municipal Utility Dist			
Pardee	15,000	Mokelumne	Cal.
Indiana & Michigan Elec. Co.			
Berrien Springs	7,200	St. Joseph	Mich.
Los Angeles, City of & its Dept.			
of Water & Power			
S. Francisquito No. 1	58,125	Acqueduct	Cal.
Cottonwood	1,545	Cottonwood Cr.	Cal.
Franklin Canyon	2,000	Acqueduct	Cal.
San Fernando	5,600	Acqueduct	Cal.
S. Francisquito No. 2	42,000	Acqueduct	Cal.
Haiwee	5,600	Acqueduct	Cal.
Big Pine	3,200	B. Pine Cr.	Cal.
Control Gorge	37,500	Owens	Cal.
Middle Gorge	37,500	Owens	Cal.
** Adams Main	5,000	Owens	Cal.
** Adams Aux.	2,400	Owens	Cal.
Upper Gorge	37,500	Owens	Cal.
Pleasant Valley	3,200	Owens	Cal.
Moline Water Power Co.			
Moline	3,600	Miss.	Ill.
Northern States Pwr. Co.			
(Wisconsin)			
St. Croix Falls	23,200	St. Croix	Wisc.
San Francisco, Public Util. Comm.			
of the City and County of			
Moccasin Creek	70,000	Toulumne Div.	Cal.
Early Intake	3,600	Cherry Cr.	Cal.
Cherry Creek	135,000	Cherry Cr.	Cal.
Canyon	67,500	Toulumne	Cal.
St. Croix Paper Co.			
Grand Falls	9,000	St. Croix	Maine
Woodland	8,980	St. Croix	Maine

	VI - A		6/30/70
			p. 2
Owner	Existing		
	Capacity		
Plant	KW	River	State

Owner / Plant	Existing Capacity KW	River	State
St. Regis Paper Co.			
Sartell	2,340	Miss.	Minn.
Union Electric Co.			
Keokuk	124,800	Miss.	Iowa
The Washington Water Pwr. Co.			
Little Falls	32,000	Spokane	Wash.
Post Falls	11,250	Spokane	Idaho
	─────────		
Total	754,640		

VI - B   6/30/70

Hydroelectric Plants for which Owners, Claiming
Valid Federal Permits, Have Not Agreed to File
Application for License in Response to Commission
Letters of May 4, 1962, Oct. 30, 1962 & July 13, 1965

Owner Plant	Existing Capacity KW	River	State
Boise Cascade Corp. (Successor to Minnesota & Ontario Paper Co.)			
International Falls	5,600	Rainy	Minn.
Public Serv. Co. of Colo.			
Shoshone	14,400	Colorado	Colo.
Salt River Project Agricultural Improvement Dist.			
Cross Cut	3,000	Cross Cut	Ariz.
Stewart Mountain	10,400	Salt	Ariz.
Mormon Flat	7,000	Salt	Ariz.
Horse Mesa	30,000	Salt	Ariz.
Roosevelt	19,696	Salt	Ariz.
Wisconsin Michigan Pwr. Co.			
Appleton	1,440	Fox	Wisc.
Wisconsin Pwr. & Lt. Co.			
Kilbourn	8,200	Wisconsin	Wisc.
Prairie du Sac	28,500	Wisconsin	Wisc.

Total   128,236

VI - C   6/30/70

Hydroelectric Plants for which Owners, Citing Dis-
claimer of Jurisdiction by the Commission on
Declaration of Intention Filings, Have Not Agreed
to File Application for License in Response to
Commission Letters of May 4, 1962, Oct. 30, 1962,
and July 13, 1965

Owner Plant	Existing Capacity KW	River	State
Central Hudson Gas and Electric Co.			
Neversink	25,000	Neversink	N.Y.
Centralia, Wash., City of			
Centralia	9,000	Nisqually	Wash.
Consumers Power Co.			
** Ada	2,000	Thornapple	Mich.
Cascade	2,560	Thornapple	Mich.
Danville, City of, Gas and Elec. Dept.			
Pinnacles	10,125	Dan	Va.
Kentucky Utilities Co.			
Dix	28,500	Dix	Ky.
Lower Colo. River. Auth.			
Marshall Ford (Mansfield Ord.)	67,600	Lower Colo.	Texas
Marble Falls	30,000	Lower Colo.	Texas
Granite Shoals	45,000	Lower Colo.	Texas
Inks	12,500	Lower Colo.	Texas
Buchanan	33,750	Lower Colo.	Texas
Austin	13,500	Colorado	Texas
Northern Indiana Public Service Co.			
Oakdale	11,000	Tippecanoe	Ind.
Norway	6,720	Tippecanoe	Ind.
Orange & Rockland Utilities, Inc.			
Grahamsville	18,000	Rondout Cr.	N.Y.

Total   315,255

VI - D   6/30/70

Municipal Hydroelectric Plants for which Owners,
Claiming Lack of Jurisdiction by Commission and
Citing other Reasons, Have Not Agreed to File
Application for License in Response to Commission
letters of May 4, 1962, October 30, 1962, and
July 13, 1965

Owner 　Plant	Existing Capacity KW	River	State
Abbeville, City of			
Rocky River	2,800	Rocky	S.C.
Consumers Public Pwr. Dist.			
Boelus	2,000	Middle Loup	Neb.
Spencer	2,640	Niobrara	Neb.
Guadalupe-Blanco River Auth.			
H5	2,400	Guadalupe	Texas
H4	2,400	Guadalupe	Texas
TP4	2,400	Guadalupe	Texas
Nolte TP5	2,480	Guadalupe	Texas
Abbott TP3	2,800	Guadalupe	Texas
Dunlap TP1	3,600	Guadalupe	Texas
Hamilton, City of, Dept. of			
Public Utilities			
Hamilton	2,250	Miami R.C.	Ohio
Hudson River-Black River			
Regulating Dist., Board of			
Conklingville Dam &			
Sacandaga Reservoir	Storage	Sacandaga	N.Y.
Imperial Irrigation Dist.			
Drop No. 4	19,600	All American Canal	Cal.
Drop No. 3	4,800	All American Canal	Cal.
Drop No. 2	10,000	All American Canal	Cal.
Pilot Knob	33,000	All American Canal	Cal.
Metropolitan Dist. Comm.			
Commonwealth of Mass.			
Wachusett	6,400	S.B. Nashua	Mass.
Oakdale	3,500	Quabbin Aq.	Mass.
Winsor	1,200	Swift	Mass.

VI - D   6/30/70
                                              p. 2

Municipal Hydroelectric Plants for which Owners,
Claiming Lack of Jurisdiction by Commission and
Citing other Reasons, Have Not Agreed to File
Application for License

Owner Plant	Existing Capacity KW	River	State
The Metropolitan Sanitary Dist. of Greater Chicago Lockport	19,900	Illinois	Ill.
Nebraska Public Pwr. System Kearney	1,500	Platte	Neb.

N.Y. State Dept. of Public Works
  Crescent
  Vischer Ferry
	5,600
	5,600
		Mohawk
		Mohawk
			N.Y.
			N.Y.

Passaic Valley Water Comm. Little Falls	2,400	Passaic	N.J.
Paterson, City of SUM	3,680	Passaic	N.J.
Providence, City of Water Supply Board Gainer	1,500	Pawtuxet	R.I.

Richmond, City of, Dept.
of Public Works
  Hollywood
  Bird Park
	2,024
	1,125
		James
		James
			Va.
			Va.

Rochester, City of Rochester	1,840	Zumbro	Minn.
Seattle, City of, Dept. of Lighting Cedar Falls	22,856	Cedar	Wash.
Spokane, City of Up River	3,900	Spokane	Wash.
Truckee-Carson Irrigation Dist. Lahontan	2,400	Carson	Nevada
Turlock Irrigation Dist. LaGrange	3,900	Tuolumne	Cal.
Total	182,495		

VI - E   6/30/70

Hydroelectric Plants for which Owners Have Not
Agreed to File Application for License for Reasons
Cited and on which Additional Navigational
Research May be Required

Owner Plant	Existing Capacity KW	River	State
Brown Company, American Writing Paper Div.			
Holyoke Mills	3,510	Conn. Canal	Mass.
Boot Mills			
Lowell	4,975	Merrimack Canal	Mass.
Lowell	2,400	Merrimack Canal	Mass.
Lowell	1,300	Merrimack Canal	Mass.
Dole-Suncook, Inc.			
Allentown	1,800	Suncook	N.H.
Graniteville Co.			
Sibley	2,100	Savannah Canal	Ga.
Enterprise	1,200	Savannah Canal	Ga.
Kimberly-Clark Corp.			
Kimberly	2,700	Fox	Wisc.
John P. King Mfg. Co.			
King	2,250	Savannah Canal	Ga.
Marseilles Land & Water Co.			
Marseilles	2,024	Illinois	Ill.
Owens-Illinois Glass Co.			
Holcombs Rock	1,875	James	Va.
Rowland Industries, Inc.			
Canal Street	1,920	Merrimack Canal	Mass.
S.D. Warren Co.			
Dundee	2,400	Presumpscot	Maine
Eel Weir	1,800	Presumpscot	Maine
Total	32,254		

VI - F   6/30/70

Hydroelectric Plants for which Owners, for
Reasons Given, Have Not Agreed to File
Application for License in Response to
Commission Letters of May 4, 1962, Oct. 30,
1962, and July 13, 1965

Owner Plant	Existing Capacity KW	River	State
Burlington Industries			
** High Shoals No. 3	1,700	South Fork	N.C.
** Cherokee Falls	1,750	Broad	S.C.
Calif. Elec. Pwr. Co.			
Bishop Creek No. 6	1,800	Bishop Creek	Cal.
Central Hudson Gas & **Electric Co.**			
Sturgeon Pool	14,400	Wallkill	N.Y.
Dashville	4,800	Wallkill	N.Y.
High Falls	2,120	Rondout	N.Y.
Central Maine Pwr. Co.			
Lewiston	4,800	Androscoggin Canal	Maine
Hill	2,160	Androscoggin Canal	Maine
Androscoggin	2,782	Androscoggin Canal	Maine
Central Pwr. & Lt. Co.			
Eagle Pass	9,600	Rio Grande Canal	Texas
Cone Mills Corp.			
Cliffside	1,625	Second Broad	N.C.
Fall River Rural Elec. **Coop.**			
Teton River	1,870	Teton	Idaho
Georgia-Pacific Corp.			
Plant No. 1	2,400	Saranac	N.Y.
Plant No. 2	1,080	Saranac	N.Y.
Habersham Mills			
Habersham	1,640	Soque	Ga.

| | VI - F | | 6/30/70 |
| | | | p. 2 |
Owner Plant	Existing Capacity KW	River	State
Home Stake Mining Co.			
Spearfish	4,000	Spearfish Cr.	S.D.
Maurice	4,000	Spearfish Cr.	S.D.
Idaho Pwr. Co.	13,500	Malad	Idaho
Lower Malad	7,200	Malad	Idaho
Upper Malad	8,000	Spring	Idaho
Thousands Springs	2,500	Spring	Idaho
Clear Lake			
N.Y. State Elec. & Gas Corp.			
Rainbow Falls	2,640	Ausable	N.Y.
Keuka	2,000	Keuka Lake	N.Y.
Northern States Pwr. Co. (Wisc.)			
Apple River	3,000	Apple	Wisc.
Pelzer Mills			
Pelzer	5,300	Saluda	S.C.
Public Serv. Co. of N.H.			
** Salmon Falls	2,000	Salmon Falls	N.H.
Jackman	3,200	Contoocook	N.H.
Rocky Mount Mills			
Rocky Mount	1,600	Tar	N.C.
Sellers Mf. Co.			
Saxapahaw	1,500	Haw	N.C.
Sierra Pacific Pwr. Co.			
Washoe	1,500	Truckee	Nev.
Verdi	2,400	Truckee	Nev.
Fleish	2,000	Truckee	Nev.
Farad	2,800	Truckee	Cal.
Southern Calif. Edison Co.			
Mill Creek No. 1	800	Mill Creek	Cal.
Fontana	1,920	Lytle Creek	Cal.
Sierra	480	San Antonio Cr.	Cal.
Ontario No. 1	600	San Antonio Cr.	Cal.
Ontario No. 2	320	San Antonio Cr.	Cal.

| | VI - F | | 6/30/70 |
| | | | p. 3 |

Owner Plant	Existing Capacity KW	River	State
Standard Packaging Corp.			
Sheldon Springs	1,750	Missisquoi	Vermont
Utah Pwr. & Lt. Co.			
Pioneer	5,000	Ogden	Utah
Riverdale	3,750	Weber	Utah
** Snake Creek	1,180	Snake Creek	Utah
Swan Creek	300	Swan Creek	Utah
Granite	1,500	Big Cotton- wood Creek	Utah Utah
Fountain Green	320	Big Springs	Utah
Western Mass. Elec. Co.			
* Indian Orchard	4,900	Little Chicopee	Mass
Dwight	2,080	Little Chicopee	Mass.
* Ludlow	3,200	Little Chicopee	Mass.
* Red Bridge	3,600	Little Chicopee	Mass.

| | Total | 156,087 |

Total Table VI-A thru
F (all projects)   1,568,967

What Licensees Must Tell the FPC

The FPC requires hydroelectric licensees to file several forms which may contain valuable information. If these are closely examined you may discover that the licensee has not always been entirely honest with the Commission. Misleading information may be grounds for denying renewal of a license or perhaps, if serious enough, grounds for revocation before expiration of a license. This is some of the information which licensees are required to file.

Applicants for licenses for proposed major projects must submit these exhibits:

A--certified copy of articles of incorporation.

B--certified copy of resolution of shareholders.

C--copies or citations of relevant State hydroelectric, water power and irrigation laws.

D--evidence of compliance with relevant State laws concerning each step of project construction.

E--evidence of the nature of and State authorization for water rights.

F--full details as to the acquisition of and ownership rights in all land.

G--financial ability and feasibility studies.

H--statement of proposed operations plans under various physical conditions.

I--estimates of capacity and electrical output.

J--general map showing necessary structural and other locations.

K--detail maps of Exhibit J showing additional information.

L--design drawings of various structures.

M--descriptions of various equipment.

N--cost estimates for development of project and annual cost of operation.

O--detailed time statements.

P--statement as to authority to build.

Q--brief history of constructed works.

R--maps, locations and descriptions of proposed recreational uses of the licensed facilities, such as camping, picnicking, bathing, fishing, etc. (Racial and religious discrimination is barred in the operation of recreational facilities.)

S--a report on the effect the project will have upon the fish and wildlife resources in the project area. This report shall be made after consultation with the U.S. Fish and Wildlife Service, Department of the Interior. It shall state proposed facilities necessary for the protection and enhancement of wildlife resources.

The Commission has provided for two other exhibits, T and U, which will have to be filed with every license application. These exhibits are probably a response to the Supreme Court's directive that the Commission employ the "comprehensive development" standard of Section 10(a) of the Federal Power Act, established in the High Mountain Sheep case. (Udall v. FPC, 387 U.S. 428)

In Exhibit T applicants (other than state or municipal applicants seeking relicensing) will be required to establish that federal development or federal recapture is not necessary to realize comprehensive development.

In Exhibit U, which must be filed for all projects that have a capacity of more than 25,000 kilowatts, applicants will have to describe all the undertakings of the applicant to interconnect and coordinate its generation and transmission facilities with those of others for purposes of sales, purchases or exchanges of various types of capacity, energy, transmission, or other servicing, including all requirements service, partial requirements service, economy energy transactions, reserve sharing and point to point or displacement deliveries of electric power and energy. Moreover, the exhibit must disclose the

(1) nature and extent of the applicant's consultation with other electric systems, power pools, or power planning groups in formulating its plan for development and utilization of the optimum output of the project, including the disposition of excess power and energy from the project to others than the applicant and the terms of any such disposition; (2) the nature and extent of applicant's activities in correlating the generating and transmission capability of the project with the needs and resources of its system and of other interconnected systems.

The Commission's purpose for instituting Exhibit U was to provide that "an applicant seeking to utilize the nation's waterways for the development of power has an obligation to look beyond its own needs to those of the region in which it operates." In other words, if a municipality has got less than favorable treatment when trying to purchase electricity from the licensee, that municipality may find Exhibit U useful for intervention or negotiation.

Intervention Petition Guide

Petitioning the FPC

The first problem in filing a petition to intervene in an FPC proceeding is to establish your "standing," or right to participate. The same basic rules apply whether you are petitioning for denial of a license, imposing conditions on a license, federal recapture, or other matters.

"Standing" to participate is recognized if there is a right conferred by a statute of the United States, or an interest which may be directly affected and which is not adequately represented by existing parties, and as to which the petitioners may be bound by the Commission's action. Some parties who may have such standing are consumers served by the applicant, defendant, or respondent in a proceeding; holders of securities of the applicant, defendant, or respondent; and competitors of the applicant, defendant, or respondent. You may also have standing if the Commission thinks that your interest is of such nature that participation would be in the public interest.

Form and Contents of Petition (Rule 183(c))

Petitions to intervene must set out clearly and concisely the facts from which the nature of the petitioner's alleged right or interest can be determined, the grounds of the proposed intervention, and the position of the petitioner in the proceeding, so as fully and completely to advise the parties and the Commission as to the specific issue of fact or law to be raised or controverted, by admitting, denying or otherwise answering, specifically and in detail, each material allegation of fact or law asserted in the proceeding, and citing by appropriate reference the statutory provisions or other authority relied on. Other requirements are in Sections 1.15 to 1.17 of the Rules.

Filing and Service of Petition (Rule 1.8(d))

"Petitions to intervene and notices of intervention may be filed at any time following the filing of a notice of rate or tariff change, or of an application, petition, complaint, or other document seeking Commission action, but in no event later than the date fixed for the filing of petitions to intervene in any order or notice with respect to the proceedings issued by the Commission or its Secretary, unless, in extraordinary circumstances for good cause shown, the Commission authorizes a late filing."

Action on Petitions (Rule 1.8(f))

"As soon as practicable after the expiration of the
time for filing answers to such petitions or default thereof, as provided in paragraph (e) of this section, the
Commission will grant or deny such petition in whole or in
part or may, if found to be appropriate, authorize limited
participation. No petitions to intervene may be filed or
will be acted upon during a hearing unless permitted by the
Commission after opportunity for all parties to object
thereto."

Limitation in Hearings (Rule 1.8(g))

"Where there are two or more intervenors having substantially like interests and positions, the Commission
or presiding officer may, in order to expedite the hearing,
arrange appropriate limitations on the number of attorneys
who will be permitted to cross-examine and make and argue
motions and objections on behalf of such intervenors."

All papers filed with the Commission--except pro-
tests--must follow a standard form, and be filed with the
Secretary of the Commission in Washington, D.C. The formal
requirements are in Sections 1.15-1.17 of the Rules.

Title. Pleadings, documents, or other papers filed
with the Commission in any proceeding shall clearly show
the docket designation and title of the proceeding before
the Commission. They shall also show, in the title of the
particular pleading or other document filed, the name of
the person in whose behalf the filing is made. If more
than one person is involved, a single name only need be
included in the title.

Copies. The FPC, like other federal agencies, requires multiple copies of all filings. The rules provide
that "except as may be otherwise required by the rules
or regulations of the Commission, at the time pleadings,
documents, or other papers other than correspondence, are
filed with the Commission, there shall be furnished to the
Commission an original and nineteen copies of such papers
and exhibits, if any." Thus for rule making petitions or
petitions to intervene in licensing, relicensing, or rate
cases you will have to submit an original and nineteen
copies. But for a protest letter the Commission only asks
for ten copies, and only the original is necessary. For
complaints, ten copies must be submitted.

Form. Pleadings, documents, or other papers filed in
proceedings, if not printed, shall be typewritten on paper
cut or folded to letter size, 8 to 8 1/2 inches wide by 10

1/2 to 11 inches long, with left-hand margin not less than
11 1/2 inches wide and other margins not less than 1 inch.
The impression shall be on only one side of the paper,
unless there are more than four pages, and shall be double
spaced, except that quotations in excess of a few lines
shall be single spaced and indented. Mimeographed, multi-
graphed, hectographed, or planographed copies will be
accepted as typewritten, provided all copies are clearly
legible. If documents are printed, they shall not be less
than 10-point type on unglazed paper, cut or folded so as
not to exceed 8 1/2 inches wide by 11 inches long, with
inside margin not less than 1 inch wide, and with double-
leaded text and single-leaded, indented quotations. Pleadings, documents, and papers other than correspondence shall
be bound at the left side only. All applications to the
Commission shall be signed in ink by the party in interest,
or by his or its attorney, as required by the rules, and
shall show the office and post office address of the same.
Any paper containing defamatory, scurrilous, or unethical
matter will be rejected by the Commission.

Subscription and Verification

Documents must be "subscribed" (signed) (i) by the
person filing the same, and severally if there be more than
one person so filing; (ii) by an officer thereof if it be a
corporation, trust, association, or other organized group,
who may be required to be supplemented by appropriate evidence of the authority of the officer or attorney subscribing such pleadings. The signature of the person,
officer or attorney subscribing any pleading or matter
filed with the Commission constitutes a certificate by such
individual that he had read the pleading or matter being
subscribed and filed and knows the contents thereof, and
believes them to be true. Any facts alleged in the matter
filed shall be verified under oath by the person filing
before a notary public.

Services (Rule 1.17)

After you have completed drawing up a petition it must
be notarized and all parties must be served with a copy of
it.   Service is usually accomplished by mailing copies of
the petition to the parties. After serving one copy by
delivery or by mailing to each participant, you must send
the Commission the original petition with a sworn certificate of service and nineteen copies of the petition. This
is a sample certificate of service. For more detailed explanation of service, along with alternative methods, see
Sec. 1.17 of the Rules of Practice.

I hereby certify that I have this day served the foregoing document upon all parties of record in this proceeding in accordance with the requirements of Sec. 1.17 of
the Rules of Practice and Procedure Dated as ....
................this .... day of ....,
1972.

                              ....
                              (signature)

Of counsel for

....

According to the Rules, all "Applications and petitions for amendment or modification of orders, answers,
protests, intervening petitions, supplements or amendments
thereto or to applications, complaints or petitions, motions, briefs, notices, and all other papers, except depositions, filed in proceedings pending before the Commission
upon its docket, when filed or tendered to the Commission
for filing, shall show service thereof upon all participants to the proceeding." The Secretary of the FPC
suggests that you include in the copy of the petition you
send to the adverse party a transmittal letter. This
would merely be an explanation of what the petition is, and
would bring the petition to their attention.

If you find the requirement of filing nineteen copies
oppressively expensive, you may submit a request for waiver
to the Commission. However, your petition won't be acted
on until the Commission rules on your waiver request, and
by then the time for filing the petition may have run out.
The Commission also has a little surprise for you, if your
petition is accepted. The Commission will send you, from
time to time, a "service list." The list contains the
names of all interested parties, and you are required to
send them all a copy of your petition. Depending on the
case, this list can be quite lengthy and quite expensive
for you. For example, in the Martin-Tregona Rate Intervention there were 200 industry parties who intervened.

CHAPTER 10

THE CIVIL
AERONAUTICS BOARD

*If I were to charge you several hundred
dollars for the privilege of standing in line
in a humid, crowded terminal, clutching two
or three small but exquisitely heavy and
awkward bags, in order to spend six or seven
hours in the cramped steerage of a rumbling,
lurching conveyance to the accompaniment of
rattling dishes, screaming infants, flushing
toilets, and the squeaking, booming sound-
track of a mindless GP movie, you would
probably punch me in the mouth. With
reason. Yet this sort of humiliating slaveship
treatment is what practically every long-
distance traveler pays plenty for—in the name
of pleasure, escape, and relaxation today.*
—L. E. Sissman, "The Bus Line in the
Sky and other Expensive Indignities,"
Atlantic, September 1971

Aviation and the CAB: 1938 and Now

When the Civil Aeronautics Board (CAB) was born in 1938, air transportation was a small, struggling industry, with only 311 aircraft
(mostly DC-3s), slightly over a million passengers, and total passenger
revenues of under $30 million [1968 CAB Annual Report, p. 103].

But leaders of the industry, aware of the inherent advantages of
aviation and the advances that developing technology would bring,
were anxious to protect their companies from the rigors of competition,
and lobbied for establishment of a comprehensive federal regulatory
scheme similar to the ones already established for railroads, trucking,
and telecommunications. This objective was achieved with the enactment of the Civil Aeronautics Act of 1938, subsequently renamed the
Federal Aviation Act [Federal Aviation Act of 1958, 49 U.S.C. 1301].

The CAB is now well over thirty years old, and is entrusted by statute with regulating one of the most important industries in our economy. In 1970, with a fleet of more than 2,000 jet aircraft, U.S. scheduled airlines transported almost 170 million passengers a total of 130 billion miles and received more than $7.6 billion in passenger fares [Air Transport Association of America, *1971 Air Transport Facts and Figures*, annual report, pp. 3, 23]. Although there has been some revision of the law, the basic pattern of protective regulation of airlines that was established in 1938 still exists today.

Under the Federal Aviation Act of 1958, the major aviation regulatory responsibilities are divided between the CAB and the Federal Aviation Administration (FAA), which is now part of the U.S. Department of Transportation (DOT). There is often considerable confusion about which agency has jurisdiction over a particular area of aviation, even among the agencies themselves. But a basic rule of thumb is that the CAB regulates the economic and service aspects of commercial airlines, while the FAA is responsible for the physical, safety, and developmental aspects of all nonmilitary aviation. A third agency concerned with aviation was created by the Department of Transportation Act of 1966 and given the duty of investigating aviation accidents and determining their probable causes, as well as making recommendations to improve air transportation safety. This agency, theoretically independent of the others, is the National Transportation Safety Board.

Air travel has become the backbone of our national transportation system, and determinations in such basic matters as air fares, routes, airport location and design, and noise and exhaust standards touch on vital consumer and environmental interests. Even when the immediate issues seem insignificant, they can have enormous ramifications. For example, when the CAB recently permitted the airlines to round off all fares upward to the next highest dollar (rather than rounding off to the nearest dollar), the result was a direct loss to consumers of $50 million [CAB Press Release 70-79 (19 June 1970)]; only after consumer advocates publicly embarrassed the agency by pointing out this unfair and illegal move did the CAB rule that in the future fares could not be rounded upward but had to be rounded to the *nearest* dollar [*Washington Star*, 8 September 1970; see also Remarks of Sen. Steven Young, Congressional Record, 1 July 1970, S-10393].

Industry Groups Within CAB Jurisdiction

There are several segments of the airlines and related industries that fall within the CAB's jurisdiction to some degree. They can be conveniently lumped into such categories as domestic trunk carriers, foreign air carriers, local service air carriers, supplemental air carriers, all-cargo air carriers, and air taxis. Tour operators and travel agents may also, from time to time, become involved with the CAB.

The trunk carriers are the major airlines authorized by the CAB to operate scheduled services over specified routes within the United States and on international routes. These are, basically, the airlines which were in existence in 1938 and sought enactment of the Civil Aeronautics Act to guarantee their survival and growth. These companies still detest the idea of competition in their industry. Included in this group are American, Braniff, Continental, Delta, Eastern, National, Northwest, Trans World, United, and Western. While Pan American has no domestic routes, it is also generally included in this group. Two trunk carriers, Northeast and Trans Caribbean, disappeared by merger with other airlines during 1972.

The foreign air carriers are the airlines based in other countries which fly to the United States under license from the CAB. Some of the best known of these are Air France, SAS, Air Canada, Lufthansa, BOAC, Japan Air Lines, KLM, and Alitalia.

Local service carriers are authorized to operate scheduled services over specified regional and local routes. The local service carriers are also the beneficiaries of millions of dollars of public subsidies administered by the CAB. For example, in 1971 the CAB made subsidy payouts of approximately $63 million to these companies [Civil Aeronautics Board, Bureau of Economics, Subsidy for United States Certificated Air Carriers, May 1971]. They include Alaska, Allegheny, Aloha, Frontier, Hawaiian, Hughes Air West, North Central, Ozark, Piedmont, Southern, and Texas International. Mohawk Airlines recently disappeared as a result of a merger with Allegheny.

Supplemental carriers are a small group of airlines which are not authorized to operate any regular or scheduled services, but are permitted by the CAB to operate charter flights within the U.S., and between the U.S. and specified international areas. Historically, the supplemental or charter airlines (sometimes called "nonskeds") have provided a most important competitive factor which has restrained scheduled carriers to some extent from raising fares beyond their exist-ing high levels [See, e.g., Hearings Before the Antitrust Subcommittee of the House Committee on the Judiciary, "Monopoly Problems in Regulated Industries," Part I, Volume 2, Airlines, 84th Cong., 2d Sess. (1957)]. In this category are Capitol International, Modern Air Trans-port, Overseas National Airways, Saturn, Southern Air Transport, Trans International, and World Airways. An eighth supplemental, Universal, was recently forced into bankruptcy when the Board delayed in renew-ing its basic operating authority.

All-cargo carriers are authorized by the CAB to operate flights carry-ing freight, express, and mail over specified domestic and international routes, and include Airlift International, Flying Tiger, and Seaboard World.

Air taxis, often called commuter airlines, operate relatively small planes on specific routes under exemptions from regulation by the CAB. These companies are under the safety jurisdiction of the FAA, although they have been permitted by that agency to operate under considerably less stringent safety requirements than the certificated air carriers. Only the larger air taxis are required to file information reports with the CAB as to the extent of their operations. There are approximately 3,500 air taxi operators in the U.S., of which about 250 provide regularly sched-uled flights [*Washington Post*, 30 August 1970, Potomac Supplement, p. 11; see also CAB, Commuter Air Carrier Traffic, Twelve Months Ending 30 June 1970 (February 1971)]. Much of the growth of this segment of the air transport industry has resulted from agreements by commuter airlines to take over routes which local service carriers no longer wished to service ["Emerging Patterns in the Regulation of Local Air Carriers," Remarks by Hon. Whitney Gillilland, Vice Chairman, Civil Aeronautics Board, before the 81st Annual Convention, National Asso-ciation of Regulatory Utility Commissions, 9 October 1969]. Approx-imately 180 commuter airlines perform either air mail service or sched-uled passenger services, and 13 of these are permitted to operate with larger aircraft.

In addition, there are a few airlines which operate entirely within the boundaries of a single state, and thus are not legally subject to regula-tion by the CAB. While few in number (at present, intrastate carriers operate only in California and Texas), these airlines have been of great significance in demonstrating how CAB economic regulation has abused the public by keeping air fares too high and generally preventing any meaningful competition in the airline industry [William Jordan, *Airline Regulation in America: Effects and Imperfections* (Baltimore: Johns

Hopkins, 1970)]. The most prominent of the intrastate carriers, Pacific Southwest Airlines (PSA), has been a continuing embarrassment to the certificated carriers and the CAB by operating between major California cities at competitive fares roughly half of what the other carriers charge for interstate passengers.

Instead of regulating travel agents, the CAB has largely handed that job over to the trade associations of the airlines themselves, the Air Transport Association of America (ATA) and the International Air Transport Association (IATA). These organizations determine such matters as who is entitled to become a travel agent and how much they are to be paid for their services, subject to the Board's ultimate blessing [CAB Order 70-12-165, Docket Nos. 21305 and 21121, 31 December 1970; see also statement of K. G. J. Pillai, Executive Director of Aviation Consumer Action Project, Before Subcommittee on Tourism of Senate Commerce Committee, 18 November 1971]. There are approximately 6,000 travel agents operating in the U.S. subject to this private regulation.

Tour operators are individuals and companies which sell tour packages to travelers, including air transportation and certain land accommodations. Often these arrangements are made by the tour operator in conjunction with an airline. In recent years this segment of the industry has been the subject of great concern, and many unsuspecting travelers have been swindled or stranded far from home by unscrupulous tour operators. Nevertheless, the CAB has done little or nothing to provide effective protection for the public or regulation of the rates charged. [Petition of Aviation Consumer Action Project for rule making for certification and regulation of indirect air carriers, including tour operators, 4 February 1972, CAB Docket No. 24204; see also Transcript of Meeting of CAB Consumer Advisory Committee, 22 October 1971, p. 51].

Participating in CAB regulatory proceedings is not easy, and is particularly difficult to do alone. Simple enforcement proceedings may easily take as long as six or seven years, and one favorite technique of the Board in dealing with troublesome cases is to lock them away in a filing cabinet and simply forget them. Route and fare cases are incredibly complex, entailing thousands of pages of hearing transcripts and paperwork that is most appropriately measured by weight. Pressure groups, including trade associations, lobbyists, and a highly specialized segment of the bar, are extremely well organized in the aviation field and can be expected to exert powerful and subtle influences to advance the special interests of their clients. For example, when American

Airlines sought CAB approval for a proposed merger with Western Air Lines, its top executives and Washington lawyers quietly pushed the case through private meetings with the Board members and heavy pressure applied by high White House officials.

It is important to understand that industry groups do not necessarily work under the same ethical or procedural constraints that are normally observed in legal proceedings. One interesting example was recently brought to light by the Aviation Consumer Action Project (ACAP) in a proceeding set up by the CAB to determine what should be done to regulate smoking on passenger flights. Lorillard, a tobacco company which produces such brands as Kent, True, Old Gold, and Spring cigarettes, directed its advertising agencies to inundate the Board with letters opposing the proposed regulation. The company's lawyer instructed that the letters, which he had drafted, should purport to be from individual citizens and conceal any connection with the company. ACAP pointed out that such letters should be stricken from the record unless identification of their true source is given [Motion of Aviation Consumer Action Project for Rectification of Record, 18 January 1973, CAB Docket No. 21708].

Outside Influences

One of the most powerful of the private pressure groups involved in aviation is the ATA, a Washington-based lobby composed of major U.S. scheduled airlines. Virtually no legislation or regulation concerning commercial aviation can be passed, and no appointment to the CAB or FAA can be made, without the approval of the ATA, which calls itself the principal spokesman for the scheduled airline industry.

Some of the methods used by the ATA in dealing with the CAB were exposed several years ago in an extraordinary affidavit filed with the Board by one of its top staff officials, who had become frustrated with the Association's tactics to stifle a CAB investigation [*The Wall Street Journal*, 2 August 1963, p. 2; see Affidavit of J.W. Rosenthal, CAB Docket No. 10281]. The ATA was accused of "activities designed to bring pressure on the Board to obtain favorable decisions based on pressures rather than the merit of the cases." The outraged CAB staff also produced internal ATA documents showing that the association's education program was actually nothing more than a propaganda effort geared "to thoroughly indoctrinate the Board and its staff." One ATA memo was quoted as saying there should be "an organized campaign to find out who has influence on the individual members, and a follow-up to educate those people."

There is no evidence to indicate that there have been significant changes in ATA's methods in recent years. The Association admits to spending at least $50,000 in 1971 "to defray the cost of industry entertainment and participation in a variety of meetings of organizations involving local and state political leaders." Total ATA expenditures in 1970 were in excess of $7.5 million, according to ATA's own records [Air Transport Association of America, minutes on file at CAB]. This may be compared with the CAB's operating budget for all of its regulatory activities, which was $11.3 million for 1970 and less than $10 million in 1969 [1970 CAB Annual Report, p. 69].

The ATA prints volumes of propaganda which can usually be obtained at no charge, such as *The Supersonic Transport—Fantasy and Fact, How the Airlines are Reducing Jet Pollution, Airlines and the Military—How the Scheduled Airlines Meet Defense Transport Needs,* and including an annual publication entitled *Facts and Figures about Air Transportation.* The Association recently initiated what it has called a "new communications offensive," a million-dollar propaganda program designed to stifle growing criticism of the airlines by consumers and environmentalists ["The Airlines' New Flight Plan: A Communications Offensive," remarks of Daniel B. Priest, ATA Vice President—Public Relations, before the Advertising and Sales Executives' Club, Kansas City, Missouri, 2 June 1971].

The chief figures at ATA are its long-time president, Stuart G. Tipton; executive vice president Paul R. Ignatius, former Secretary of the Navy; and senior vice president Clifton P. von Kann, retired U.S. Air Force General. It should be realized that all of ATA's funds, including expenditures for influence-peddling and propaganda, are provided by the airlines through their dues and assessments; ultimately, by virtue of the CAB's regulatory policy, it is all paid for by the consumers themselves.

The IATA, headquartered in Montreal, is the trade association of virtually all U.S. and foreign scheduled airlines which operate on international routes. The power of this organization is awesome indeed, for it in fact fixes the prices (and other conditions of service) for air travel around the world [see K. G. J. Pillai, *The Air Net* (New York: Grossman, 1970)]. This huge cartel, which excludes the public, the press, and even governmental agencies from its price-fixing conferences, operates under a blanket immunity from the antitrust laws granted complacently by the CAB in 1955 [CAB Order E-9305, 15 June 1955]. Like its domestic counterpart, the ATA, IATA also licenses and controls travel agents, determining who may engage in that business and on what terms.

The American Society of Travel Agents (ASTA) has approximately 3,500 members in the U.S. and Canada. Although this organization participates frequently in CAB cases, it almost invariably takes the side of the scheduled airlines and their trade associations, ATA and IATA.

The Air Line Pilots Association, (ALPA), is the most powerful labor organization in the airline industry. Representing nearly 4,000 airline employees, including both pilots and stewardesses, ALPA's main emphasis has been on its negotiations with management concerning wages, but it has participated in CAB proceedings by which its members may be affected, and in safety matters at the FAA. ALPA has criticized the CAB for holding closed-door meetings with top airline executives, urging that any such future conferences be open to the public [ALPA Press Release 71.51, 16 August 1971]. Other airline unions also participate on occasion in CAB proceedings.

The Association of Local Transport Airlines (ALTA) represents the local service airlines before Congress and the CAB on matters relating to such issues as subsidies, air fares, and routes that affect the special interests of those companies.

National Air Carrier Association (NACA) is the trade association and publicity arm of the supplemental airlines. It has been active and effective in promoting their interests before Congress and the CAB, particularly in making a case for the merits of low-cost charter services. At the same time, NACA has in effect been a supporter of the IATA price-fixing mechanism which has helped to keep the fares of the scheduled airlines artificially high, so that the lower-priced charter services of the NACA carriers appear more attractive. NACA has also been engaged in establishing its own international organization of supplemental carriers, a junior version of IATA, which the CAB has approved in principle [CAB Order 71-10-14, 4 October 1971]. NACA maintains a mailing list and will provide information concerning the operations of the charter airline industry upon request (NACA, 1730 M Street, N. W., Washington, D.C. 20036).

The Aero Club of Washington is an industry social club with about 500 members, including lobbyists and airlines executives, aircraft manufacturers, the aviation trade press, and high-ranking government and military officials. The Aero Club has monthly luncheon meetings at the Army-Navy Club in Washington. Membership dues are $20 a year. Although the Club does not formally participate in hearings or regulatory proceedings, its influence in aviation matters is substantial. For example, featured guests at Aero Club luncheons have included the Chairman of the Senate Aviation Subcommittee, the Chairman of the CAB, the Administrator of the FAA, and heads of major airlines and aerospace firms. Frequently these occasions are used to pass along valuable bits of information and predictions about existing and future regulatory policy.

Until very recently, the only participants in the process of regulating airlines who were not representing the industry itself were municipalities and chambers of commerce seeking expanded air services to their areas. By and large, their involvement has been at the request and behest of the airlines. However, some public interest organizations have begun to provide representation for other consumer and environmental interest affected by CAB decisions. You may want to coordinate your efforts with these groups, some of which are described below.

ACAP (Aviation Consumer Action Project, P.O. Box 19029, Washington, D.C. 20036) is a nonprofit consumer organization founded in 1971 by Ralph Nader and other consumer advocates. ACAP's purpose is to promote and advocate the interests of consumers and the general public before the CAB and other decision making bodies in the field of aviation. It has participated extensively in CAB proceedings and monitors that agency's performance on a continuing basis, in addition to pressing for improved safety and environmental standards in aviation. This group, which has become the most vigorous spokesman for consumer interests in the airline industry, provides a clear demonstration of the importance of establishing and working through effective consumer organizations to bring about improvements in industry and greater responsibility in government agencies. ACAP is funded entirely by voluntary donations from consumers and citizens who support its objectives of improving the air transportation system. A printed report of ACAP's activities will be mailed upon request, and copies of special reports issued by the group, covering such topics as discrimination in employment at the CAB and air pollution from jet aircraft, as well as briefs, complaints, and petitions in various cases, are available at a copying cost of usually 10 cents a page.

Consumers Union (CU), the largest consumer organization in the country, tests products and services, disseminates consumer information, and publishes *Consumer Reports*. CU has recently established a legal staff in Washington (Consumers Union, 1714 Massachusetts Avenue, N.W., Washington, D.C., 20036) to represent its members in administrative and judicial proceedings and, upon invitation, in Congressional hearings. CU has become an active participant in several CAB proceedings.

The Sierra Club (1050 Mills Tower, San Francisco, California 94104) is a well-known conservation organization which has participated actively in a number of cases involving airport planning and environmental effects. Friends of the Earth (620 C Street, S.E., Washington, D.C. 20003) is an environmental protection group which was very active in the Congressional debates over federal funding of the SST. The Center for Study of Responsive Law (P.O. Box 19367, Washington, D.C. 20036) is a nonprofit research organization which, among other studies, conducts continuing research on various transportation and aviation matters, including air safety, airline economics, and the role of trade associations.

Natural Resources Defense Council (NRDC) (1710 N Street, N.W., Washington, D.C. 20036) is another environmental protection organization of lawyers, scientists, and private citizens which works primarily through court actions and participation in the administrative process.

Several other groups claiming to speak for consumer interests have been established in the aviation field, but some of these have historical ties with the industry that may affect the positions they take.

Americans for Charter Travel (ACT) (1125 19th Street, N.W., Suite 602, Washington, D.C. 20036) is primarily involved in advocating the availability of low-cost charter travel before the CAB and in Congressional hearings. ACT has received financial support in the past from NACA.

The Airline Passengers Association (Box 2758, Dallas, Texas 75221) is principally a commercial organization selling insurance and other special services to its members, with very close affiliations with major airlines. Some of its claims appear questionable, such as its promise to provide a "luggage protection" service to assure the "quick and safe return" of your luggage if it is lost. It publishes a quarterly magazine, at $1 per copy, which generally contains a series of laudatory articles on various airlines and aircraft, and profiles of government and industry officials. Membership, without insurance, is $7.50 per year; with insurance coverage, membership costs up to $75 a year. This association also claims to represent its members before Congressional committees and regulatory agencies, but it has not made its presence felt in these arenas as an effective proponent of consumer interests.

There are many other agencies of the federal, state, and local governments that become involved in federal regulatory proceedings concerning aviation. For example, the DOT participates in many hearings and proceedings before the CAB. Mergers and other economic regulatory matters before the CAB often elicit the interest and activity of the Antitrust Division of the Department of Justice. Frequently the White House has become involved in matters pending before the CAB, although this is generally not made known to the public or other participants [see, e.g., *Aviation Daily* 195 (11 June 1971: 225)]. Route and service cases before the CAB almost invariably include local governmental or development agencies as well as local chambers of commerce and booster clubs.

Public interest advocates should understand the great importance that participation of such other government agencies may have in CAB proceedings, and should actively seek the support of other agencies. For example, the active opposition of the Justice Department's Antitrust Division to a proposed airline merger can mean its defeat. This is well understood by the airline industry and its advocates, who have developed sophisticated strategies for eliciting support or silencing opposition from these agencies. A clear example came to light during CAB hearings on a proposed merger between American and Western Airlines. The companies retained special Washington counsel experienced in lobbying the officials of various executive departments as well as influential members of Congress. Well before the merger hearings began, the airlines' representatives quietly visited with at least fifty municipal governments and chambers of commerce in areas that might be affected, and also with the Undersecretary of Transportation, the Assistant Attorney General of the Antitrust Division, the Secretary of Transportation, and a Special Assistant to the President. At these private meetings the airlines urged that the proposed merger was a good idea and should not be opposed. No one was present, of course, to present facts or arguments on the other side of the case, but the airlines were still only partially successful. The DOT supported the merger when the CAB hearing was held, but the Department of Justice submitted a strongly worded brief arguing that the merger would increase the domination of the industry by a few companies [*Washington Post*, 1 September 1971, p. A.2.]. The Board rejected the merger on grounds that it would upset the "competitive balance" of the industry.

In addition to the executive agencies and departments of government, key members of both houses of Congress can also be extremely influential in the aviation agencies. Letters or inquiries from any

Senator or Congressman, for example, get special attention at the CAB, as they do in other agencies.

The potential impact of Congressional involvement was illustrated in a 1970 case in which a group of thirty-two Congressmen, led by Rep. John Moss (D.-Calif.), challenged the CAB's practice of holding secret, closed meetings with top airline officials to work out the details of passenger fare increases. The Congressmen claimed that these *ex parte* meetings violated the procedural requirements for rate regulation proceedings, and that the large fare increases approved by the Board as a result of such meetings were illegal. When the CAB rejected these contentions, the Moss group filed an appeal in federal court. The court handed down a ruling which sustained the views of the Congressmen [*Moss* v. *CAB*, 430 F. 2d 891 (D.C. Cir. 1970)] and was highly critical of the CAB:

> In any case, ignoring the general public's interests in order to better serve the carriers is not the proper response to the difficulties supposedly created by an outdated or unwieldy statutory procedure. After all, there is more to rate making than providing carriers with sufficient revenue to meet their obligations to their creditors and to their stockholders. [*Ibid.*, p. 901]

The Moss decision had a deep impact on the CAB, which had expected to win the case, rather than receive an extensive dressing-down by the court. Internally, the CAB staff was forced to re-evaluate some of the agency's attitudes and procedures in rate making. The Moss decision was, in effect, a new charter for consumer participation in CAB proceedings. It is improper, the court ruled, for the agency to fence out the public from rate making procedures:

> Congress requires public participation in making rates because it is the public who pays them. And under this Act . . . there is no statutory provision for reparations to the public if the rates charged are unreasonable. Hence observance of safeguards to protect the public *before* the rates are imposed is imperative. [*Ibid.*, p. 902]

The "clubby" attitude of agency personnel and industry representatives presents a formidable practical barrier to citizen access throughout the federal government. At the CAB (and also at the FAA) it is intensified by the mystique of aviation. It is common for people in these agencies to retain an almost adolescent enthusiasm for flying, with wing emblems or other aeronautical symbols worn as lapel buttons or tie tacks, and models or photos of planes (generally donated by the regulated companies) in their offices. They resent the intrusion of any countervailing interests into their tight world. Of course there are many employees who do not conform to these mental or emotional stereotypes, particularly among the younger professional staff members. Many within the agency are sensitive to and sympathetic with consumer and environmental interests, in contrast with the industry orientation among their supervisors. Yet public dissent is generally restricted and frowned upon, and the more zealous public interest proponents within the agency are frustrated and forced to wait quietly for changes which may be slow in coming. But you should be aware of possibly substantial but quiet support or assistance from friendly staff members, even when the official agency stance toward you is hostile.

In addition to repeated interpersonal contacts between agency officials and representatives of the regulated industries, there is a constant flow of people moving from the agency into lucrative industry jobs. A few recent examples of this are:

1. Monte Lazarus, who moved from the influential job of Administrative Assistant to the CAB Chairman into United Air Lines as a top Washington lobbyist in 1973.
2. Irving Roth, who left a top CAB staff position as director of the Bureau of Economics to become a vice president at United Air Lines.
3. J. W. Rosenthal, former director of the CAB's Bureau of Operating Rights, now a lawyer and officer of Flying Tiger Lines.
4. Robert Burstein retired as director of the Bureau of Enforcement at the CAB and then became an officer at NACA in 1970.
5. Edward Driscoll served as Executive Director of the CAB before becoming president of the NACA.
6. Russell Adams, Donald W. Nyrop, and Robert P. Murphy, former CAB board members, were given positions in the airlines as vice president of Pan American, president of Northwest Airlines, and Executive Director of ALTA, respectively.

The pattern by which government officials are "promoted" to higher-paying jobs in the regulated industry is illustrated by Najeeb Halaby, former head of the FAA. While he was at the FAA, Halaby was approached several times by the president of Pan American World Airways and offered a job on an "if you ever leave the government" basis. He went directly to Pan Am when he left the FAA, with a $40,000 raise to start, and subsequently served for several years as president of the company [*The Wall Street Journal*, 5 October 1971, p. 37].

Although relatively few high regulatory officials in the CAB enter the government directly from positions in the regulated industry, many of the public servants employed by these agencies have developed long-standing friendships with those they are supposed to be regulating. Chan Gurney, a former CAB member and more recently a "consultant" for American Airlines, lunched with the present Board members to discuss old times and other matters while he was in Washington during the hearings in the American-Western merger case. A recent CAB chairman, Secor Browne, was taken to task by columnist Jack Anderson for vacationing at the private villas of high Pan Am officials in the Caribbean and Hawaii, but denied any impropriety. They are just friends, the Chairman explained, and he paid for his own lodgings. The current chairman, Robert Timm, has spent a vast amount of his time visiting with airline officials around the country.

The CAB: Structure and Functions

The CAB is one of the "independent" agencies, like the Federal Trade Commission (FTC) and the Interstate Commerce Commission (ICC), meaning that it is structured as a multimember commission, theoretically independent from the direct policy or political control of the current administration, with the exception of decisions on international routes and foreign air carrier permits, which can be reversed by the President.

The agency is responsible for regulating economic aspects of commercial air transportation, with a mandate under the Federal Aviation Act of 1958 [49 U.S.C. 1301 *et seq.*] to decide:

- Who may operate airline services.
- Which cities receive airline services, and by which carriers.
- Whether or not published airline fares, rates, and regulations are reasonable and in the public interest.

It is also charged with:

- Preventing favoritism and discrimination in airline services.
- Preventing monopolies and regulating airline mergers and agreements.
- Establishing and enforcing rules for airline treatment of passengers.
- Prevention of unfair or deceptive practices in air transportation.
- Investigation of the competence and efficiency of those managing or controlling the airlines.
- Deciding the level of operating subsidies to be given to local service airlines.

The CAB itself is composed of five members appointed by the President, with the "advice and consent" of the Senate, for six-year terms. No more than three of the five members may be from the same political party. The President also designates one of the members as chairman and another as vice chairman. As a practical matter, the chairman tends to have special influence on the CAB's operations and activities, due to his control of administrative matters and his power to appoint key agency personnel. Generally the chairman is recognized as the Board's chief spokesman in Congressional hearings, and in dealings with industry, the public, and the press.

Historically, as with other regulatory agencies, the background and qualifications of appointees to the CAB have been spotty, at best. While there have been some exceptionally able members, the Board has often served as a resting place for defeated Congressmen and cronies of political figures.

The current members of the CAB are:

1. Robert D. Timm, chairman. A Republican Party adherent from the state of Washington, Timm has a reputation as the most consistently anticonsumer member of the Board. A former state legislator with close ties to banking and insurance interests, he was head of the Washington Utilities and Transportation Commission when appointed by President Nixon to the Board in early 1971, for a term expiring at the end of 1976.

2. Whitney Gillilland, vice-chairman. A Republican originally appointed by President Eisenhower, he is generally considered one of the more conservative members of the Board and seldom takes exception to industry positions. Often referred to as

"Judge" because of his background as a state judge in Iowa, the pleasant, courtly Gillilland also served as chairman of the Foreign Claims Settlement Commission. Term expires December 31, 1977.

3. G. Joseph Minetti, a Democrat, was appointed to the Board in 1956. Of the present members, he is regarded as the most sympathetic to consumer interests—which isn't saying much. Recently renominated, his current term expires December 31, 1979.

4. Lee R. West, a Nixon Democratic appointee, is a former state court judge from Oklahoma. While he has no known experience or background in aviation, transportation, or utility regulation, *The Wall Street Journal* reported at the time of his nomination that he had strong but quiet backing for the CAB job from American Airlines. His term will expire December 31, 1978.

5. Richard J. O'Melia, a Republican, was appointed to the Board by President Nixon in 1973 after several years as the CAB's director of enforcement. In that job he won high marks from the big airlines by harassing and terrorizing charter groups, supplemental airlines and anyone else who threatened the industry's inflated price structure. Consumer problems were largely ignored, unrecognized or rebuffed under his command. O'Melia's present term will expire December 31, 1974.

The Board itself actually deals with only a small part of the agency's regulatory business. Most of the work is done by the CAB's relatively small staff of approximately 640 persons. The CAB staff is organized into bureaus and offices with specialized functions. Some of particular concern or interest to consumers are:

Office of the Managing Director/Secretary. This is one of the key positions in the agency. The Managing Director's principal function is to assist the chairman in controlling the executive, administrative, and personnel aspects of the agency, but he is often deeply involved in policy matters. Other functions of this office are *Congressional relations, public information,* and *internal management,* including agency budgeting and accounting. Under the present setup, this job includes the functions of the Office of the Secretary, described below.

Office of Consumer Affairs. This is a relatively new office which reports to the Office of the Chairman. It has a very small staff, consisting of the Director, an assistant, four analysts, and clerical personnel.

It is primarily responsible for handling consumer complaints directed to the Board, although its official mandate calls for it to bridge any "communication gaps" in helping the public "to understand what the commercial aviation industry offers and the role of the Civil Aeronautics Board in promoting and regulating air transportation."

Office of the General Counsel. This office advises the Board and other parts of the staff on a wide variety of legal and policy issues. It also assists in the preparation of Board orders, opinions, rules, and other legal documents. The position of General Counsel is generally regarded as one of the most sensitive and important staff jobs at the CAB. From time to time this office will provide opinions, upon request by consumers and public interest groups (as well as others), as to the legal application or interpretation of CAB rules, regulations, or procedures.

Bureau of Economics. This office is responsible for conducting research and advising the Board on economic policies and programs. It often participates actively in proceedings before the Board on economic questions such as fares, and has generally been a proponent of fare reductions. While this bureau has a good reputation for the professionalism of its work product, its recommendations are often disregarded by the Board.

Bureau of Operating Rights. The responsibilities of this important staff office are primarily related to licensing matters. The Bureau participates in formal Board hearings through submission of economic exhibits and analyses, and through the furnishing of expert witnesses. It is also responsible for antitrust matters that may affect air transportation, such as interlocking relationships among airlines and other transportation companies, and mergers of airlines. This Bureau also has the "delegated authority" to approve agreements between air carriers by "staff action," without hearings or other formalities.

Bureau of Enforcement. This bureau is responsible for instituting and prosecuting actions against companies under CAB jurisdiction which have violated economic provisions of the Federal Aviation Act, or orders or regulations of the Board. It has wide investigative powers to look into alleged or suspected violations. In practice it has proved extremely reluctant to prosecute the major airlines for violations of the law, although smaller companies which fall within its regulatory grasp (such as tour agents, freight forwarders, and low-cost charter airlines) often have the book thrown at them. While officials of this bureau are at times outwardly cordial to consumer representatives, a number of attorneys and researchers have reported bizarre encounters with them involving direct hostility and harassment. Enforcement actions against major carriers, even where clear abuses are apparent, usually require the application of continuing intense pressure by public interest and consumer groups. The Bureau of Enforcement has been a major source of delay at the agency, especially in consumer protection cases. But its real priorities were illustrated during the summer of 1972 when several officials of the bureau, together with IATA officials, interrogated passengers arriving to board transatlantic flights at Kennedy Airport in New York about whether their tickets had been properly paid for, and in a number of cases made the passengers pay more money to the airlines before being permitted to board their flights. Meanwhile, the bureau was doing nothing about widespread and well-documented patterns of fraud and illegal overcharges by airlines, brought to light by *Consumer Reports* editor John Galloway, which resulted in passengers' being cheated by many millions of dollars a year.

Bureau of Administrative Law Judges. Formerly designated as hearing examiners, members of this Bureau act as trial judges for the Board, presiding at formal hearings and rulings on motions. They receive evidence, issue subpoenas, render initial decisions and recommended decisions based on the evidence, and generally perform the quasi-judicial functions of hearing examiners described in Chapter 4. Their decisions may be reversed by the Board.

Office of the Secretary. This office is generally concerned with the formalities of CAB proceedings, including the examination of formal applications, petitions, and complaints for compliance with the Board's procedural regulation. Its *Docket Section* maintains the official docket file of formal proceedings, and makes official service on all parties of notices, decisions, and other documents filed by the CAB in each proceeding. The *Minutes Section* records Board Actions and maintains the official minutes of Board meetings.

Each of the bureaus and major offices has a variety of functions. With respect to some matters that come before it, a bureau has authority "delegated" to it by the Board to make a determination on behalf of the Board. In other cases the staff will function in a purely advisory capacity. The complexity which the varying degrees of delegation to staff can entail is illustrated by the following description given by the head of the Bureau of Operating Rights of that Bureau's functions:

> Our basic and primary function as I say is to license air service of a variety of sorts. . . .
> The procedures are three-fold. We have an extensive delegation of authority from the Board to process markets of routine impor-

tance and we utilize that very extensively. In markets of more complexity, such as those affecting exemptions or major suspensions, we are agents of the Board. We recommend courses of action to the Board internally and the Board issues a green order effectuating either our recommendation or their own decision.

Finally in the area of the major proceedings, the more important cases, the process involves a public hearing and we have a staff who act as bureau counsel, as trial attorneys, and we also have expert witnesses who are either economists or accountants or statisticians. We participate in these proceedings in a fashion similar to any other party, and our recommendations are made publicly, and there is no private communication with the Board. [CAB Transcript of Conference on Consumer Committee and the Airlines, 20 April 1971, p. 30]

During the winter of 1969 Chairman Secor Browne announced that he was establishing the Consumer Advisory Committee, which was intended to help bridge the obvious and growing gap between the Board's activities and the interests of airline passengers and other consumers. To this unpaid council he appointed eight individuals having some knowledge of or involvement in consumer issues related to airline services.

By its charter, the consumer committee was prohibited from discussing "any matter then pending before the Board" or actually participating in any cases before the Board. Nevertheless, the committee held open public meetings about once a month and discussed a wide range of issues and problems relating to consumer and environmental concerns in airline regulation. On a number of occasions representatives of environmental and consumer organizations, as well as individual consumers, came to committee meetings to discuss particular problems and issues of concern to them. Problems raised at these meetings were relayed by the committee to the CAB's Office of Consumer Affairs or other offices for appropriate investigation or action. In addition, the committee made numerous recommendations to the chairman of the CAB for specific procedural revisions or innovations designed to facilitate consumer communication and participation in Board proceedings. Few of these recommendations were acted on by the Board.

Unfortunately, this laudable experiment in improving consumer input into CAB operations was short-lived. Its activities were brought to an abrupt and untimely end by Chairman Secor Browne in May 1972. Monte Lazarus, Browne's executive assistant who was in charge of committee functions, told reporters that the premature termination was necessary because the Consumer Advisory Committee had "strayed into policy issues" such as passenger fares and the effect of CAB policies on airport noise and pollution. He did not explain how the Committee was supposed to function without considering the critical substantive problems which affect consumers on a day-to-day basis [*Washington Post,* 31 May 1972]. The real reason for abolition of the Committee was that Browne was embarrassed by the members' unexpected militancy in stressing consumer issues, and their constant exposure of the Board's lack of interest in consumer problems.

CAB Information

The regulations of the CAB are contained in the third volume (Part 200 to End) of Title 14, Code of Federal Regulations (C.F.R.), which may be purchased for $3 from the Government Printing Office (G.P.O.) The regulations are also available in loose-leaf form on a subscription basis from the Board for $12 per year. This includes the basic volume plus subsequent revisions and amendments.

The Federal Aviation Act is contained in Title 49 of the U.S. Code, Sections 1301 to 1542. It may be purchased in a pamphlet from the CAB for 30 cents, and also is contained in a useful paperback volume entitled *Aeronautical Statutes and Related Material* (containing applicable provisions of the Department of Transportation Act, the Administrative Procedure Act, and pertinent Executive Orders, antitrust laws, treaties, and other materials), available from the G.P.O. or the CAB for $2.50.

The CAB also issues regular press releases describing Board activities and operations, and the Office of Information is normally willing to put interested citizens or groups on the list free of charge. Press release list number 11 was recently set up to include matters of special interest to consumer organizations, omitting most of the highly technical or routine matters. Many other publications are available free or on a paid subscription basis from the CAB Office of Information. These include: speeches of CAB members (free); all CAB economic orders and opinions ($85 a year); calendar of prehearing conferences, hearings, and oral arguments ($7 a year); examiners' prehearing conference reports ($15 a year); examiners' initial and recommended decisions ($48 a year); notices of proposed rule making proceedings ($9 a year); periodic statistical reports on airline traffic and air carrier finances; and various reports and studies by the Bureau of Economics (free as long as available). The Office of Information will provide a free list of all publications available from the CAB.

In most cases, single copies of all Board publications are available to any interested person upon request in person or in writing. In addition, charges for subscription services may be waived for public libraries, governmental agencies at any level, colleges and universities, and nonprofit organizations. Any request for such free subscriptions should be made in writing to the Office of Information, with a brief explanation of your need or interest in receiving the material and verification of your nonprofit status.

One of the CAB's most important functions is the collection and compilation of crucial information about the industry it is supposed to regulate. The CAB economics staff, for example, conducts continuing research into various aspects of air carrier economics on such subjects as "Characteristics of Air Travelers," "Development of the International Cargo Markets, " and an "Economic Study of Air Freight Forwarding." Other bureaus also conduct studies on matters within their particular jurisdictions. Less formal studies and surveys are made on such matters as the diversion of air carrier assets into nonaviation conglomerate enterprises.

The Bureau of Accounts and Statistics is responsible for prescription and administration of standard methods of accounting for certificated air carriers, and the collection and maintenance of regular financial and commercial reports from the airlines. The most important set of reports is filed on the CAB's "Form 41," which requires a wide variety of detailed balance sheets and other information, including the substantial legal fees paid by airlines to the firms retained by them. These reports are available for inspection in the CAB Public Reference Room.

One very useful source of information about CAB actions is the *Aviation Law Reporter,* published by the Commerce Clearing House, 4025 W. Peterson Avenue, Chicago, Ill. 60646, which compiles some regulatory decisions of the CAB and other aviation agencies. Published in four loose-leaf volumes, it is available on a subscription basis for $285 a year, and is also available for inspection at the CAB and in some other libraries. A handy industry reference source is the *World Aviation Directory*, published twice yearly by Ziff-Davis Publications Co., 1156 15 St., N.W., Washington, D.C. 20005 ($25 per copy), which contains names and addresses for aviation companies, officials, and government agencies throughout the world.

Consumer Reports, published monthly by the Consumers Union (Orangeburg, N.Y. 10962), contains occasional articles about airline practices and CAB regulatory actions. A one-year subscription costs $8.

In addition, there are a number of specialized magazines and trade journals that follow closely the activities of the CAB and the operations of the airline industry. Even more than in many other industries, some of the trade publications see their primary function as pleasing the airline and aerospace executives who buy subscriptions. The most notorious of these is the *Aviation Daily,* available for $325 a year, which is the staunchest defender of anything done by the big airlines or their trade associations, IATA and ATA, and which is vitriolic in attacking those who would question the airlines' wisdom. Another publication, slightly more evenhanded and objective in reporting on consumer and environmental developments affecting the airlines, is *Aviation Week and Space Technology,* published by McGraw-Hill. But it has an unfortunately strong prejudice when it comes to military appropriations or subsidies for aerospace development, and it is still fuming about the opposition to the SST by Senator Proxmire and others. *Travel Management Daily*, a relative newcomer to the field, is a newsletter primarily oriented toward the interests and concerns of travel agencies and airline sales departments. *Travel Weekly,* published twice a week in tabloid format, also covers some consumer news of interest to the travel industry, but it refuses to sell or give copies to members of the public, consumer organizations, or anyone outside the travel fraternity.

A subscription to one of these publications might be useful, and they are also available in the CAB library and in some public libraries.

Under the Board's public information regulations (contained in Part 310 of the regulations), records and information not routinely available from the Office of Information may be available for inspection and copying at the CAB Public Reference Room or other CAB offices. These regulations contain an index of the type and location of information generally available, as well as a list of the records and information that the Board claims can be withheld from public inspection. But that list is not necessarily the final word. For example, the regulations purport to prohibit public inspection of "consumer complaint files which would disclose the identity of private complainants," but these files were opened to the public after investigators from the Center for Study of Responsive Law filed suit under the Freedom of Information Act (FOIA) [CAB Press Release 70-14, 2 February 1970]. Previously secret minutes and agenda material concerning the operations of IATA, which fixes air fares for international travel, were finally opened up on demand by ACAP [Letter from Harry J. Zink, Acting Executive Director, CAB, to K. G. J. Pillai, 14 June 1971].

A request to inspect a copy of (or have copied) any of the Board's records may be made to the appropriate office in person, by telephone, or in writing, according to the regulations. The request should be as specific as possible and should identify the materials, as far as possible, by name, date, number, or other data sufficient for the Board's staff to locate and prepare it for inspection. An exorbitant fee of 35 cents per page is charged for copying services by the CAB staff, with a minimum charge of $1; coin-operated copying machines are available in the Public Reference Room, but be forewarned that the charge for using these machines is still 15 cents per page—reduced in 1972 from a quarter at the urging of the Consumer Advisory Committee.

If access to any requested record is denied by the office which has it (or should have it), or by the Public Reference Room, the denial may be appealed to the managing director, who has authority delegated by the chairman to handle such appeals. The regulations provide that the appeal shall be by letter, and shall identify the material requested and denied in the same manner as it was identified to the first office which denied the request. An appeal letter is also required by the regulations to be filed within ten days after denial, and to indicate the dates of request and denial as well as "the expressed basis for the denial." In addition, the regulations say that "the letter of appeal shall state briefly and succinctly the reasons why the record should be made available" [14 C.F.R. 310.9].

The requirement that reasons for disclosure be given is clearly inconsistent with the FOIA. The CAB is off base, for example, in trying to shift the burden of proof onto the applicant, demanding that he explain why public records should be made available, rather than having the agency justify its suppression. Nevertheless, the CAB has a history of stretching any technicalities and loopholes built into the regulations to incredible lengths in attempting to deny public access to agency documents that citizens have a right to examine.

One example of the CAB's reluctance to disclose information to the public occurred in the fall of 1969. Investigators from the Center for Study of Responsive Law wrote to the Board and the managing director (then known as executive director), requesting access to a CAB survey on the adequacy of airline handling of consumer complaints, as well as the CAB's lists, based on that study, of carriers considered to be deficient or effective in complaint handling. This request was denied by the assistant director of the Bureau of Enforcement. The CAB later took the position that the proper procedures had not been followed because the Center investigators did not appeal to the managing director a *second time* for access to the requested records, and did not also seek another "review" of the staff's denial by the Board itself, which would mean still another round of delay [Affidavit of Charles F. Kiefer, Executive Director of CAB, filed in Civil Action No. 3349-69, *Robertson* v. *Kiefer,* U.S. District Court for the District of Columbia, February 1970; see also CAB Press Release 70-14, *supra*].

It was until recently the policy of the CAB that decisions of the managing director are not "administratively final" so as to provide a basis for judicial review. This outrageous tool for administrative delay was quietly abandoned by the Board under growing criticism by consumer spokesmen and administrative law experts. The amended—and much improved—regulation now makes it clear that the managing director must decide on FOIA appeals within seven business days, and, in the case of a negative decision, must state the basis for denial. In certain cases the matter may be referred to the Board within the seven-day period, and the Board is ordinarily required to act on the matter within twenty days of the date of the request. In either case, the requirement for duplicate appeal has been removed, and CAB regulations now make clear that a decision by either the managing director or the Board is administratively final for purposes of judicial review, and not subject to any further petitions for reconsideration.

It is important to pursue demands for CAB information which you wish to examine, despite initial denials and the likelihood of delay. For one thing, information is usually withheld only when agency bureaucrats fear it would prove embarrassing to them or the airlines. Second, there is a good probability of prevailing in most suits against the CAB under the FOIA, and merely filing suit can be enough to jar the information loose. Finally, experience demonstrates that the information can be of great utility to the public—such as the files of consumer complaint letters, the Board's studies of airline complaint handling, the long secret records of IATA price-fixing conferences, and records of informal negotiations between airlines and the Bureau of Enforcement to compromise violations of the Federal Aviation Act.

Access at the CAB

In 1967 the CAB's enforcement staff conducted a massive nine-month study to evaluate the airline industry's handling of consumer complaints. The purposes of this research were to give the Board "a clear insight into the basis for consumer dissatisfaction," which was growing rapidly, and to form a basis for recommendations to improve the industry's public image. Unfortunately, as discussed briefly above, the CAB chose to suppress the results of this project, rather than to release the information to the public, until a suit was filed under the FOIA in 1969 [CAB Press Release 70-14, 2 February 1970].

When the agency's report was finally made available, it proved to be clear evidence of the value that honestly objective and critical evaluation by an agency might have for consumers [*Washington Star,* 3 February 1970]. Because its authors assumed no one would ever see the report except those in the industry's inside circles, it contained information and analysis virtually unprecedented among CAB studies, including the identification and comparative rating of individual airlines on complaint-handling abilities and attitudes toward consumers [Memorandum to the Board on Phase 3—Consumer Survey from Robert Burstein, Director, Bureau of Enforcement, dated 13 December 1967].

Seven of the airlines, including Pan American, Northwest, and National, were identified as doing a "poor" job in dealing with passenger grievances. Seven other carriers, however, were rated "very good" in the report. These included American, Eastern, Trans World, and United. Other carriers were given ratings of "good" or "fair."

The secret CAB memorandum noted that some of the airlines "displayed a complete lack of interest in the problems of consumers and our survey as well." Another criticism expressed was that, "too often, when a complaint deserves a substantive answer, the complainant receives a brush-off or a defensive letter." On the other hand, the survey also pointed out that some carriers were concerned enough about consumer complaints to hold daily "briefing sessions" among supervisory personnel to discuss the previous day's performance. It noted that:

> These carriers place particular emphasis on the quality of service they have rendered to their passengers on the previous day, and responsible department heads are required to provide detailed information on delays and irregularities which occurred and to

report what has been done to accommodate inconvenienced passengers or correct the deficiencies. [*Ibid.*]

Why this kind of information should be kept from members of the public by their government officials is hard to understand. Nevertheless, the instincts of the CAB seem to be those of a trade association which abhors the thought of any outside criticism of its members, regardless of how well deserved.

In response to Congressional and public criticism about the suppression of this survey, the CAB in late 1970 issued a new "consumer complaint survey" report, purportedly to revise and update the first [Civil Aeronautics Board, 1969 Consumer Complaint Survey Report (1970)]. This time, however, there was to be no embarrassment for the industry. There was no criticism or rating of individual carriers. The laudatory reports on the various airlines were essentially written by the companies themselves. Nevertheless, even this tame survey could not hide the growing consumer problems throughout the airline industry. For example, it revealed that in 1969 over 200,000 passengers had their personal baggage lost, damaged, or seriously delayed. At least 45,000 people were bumped from planes, without justification or warning. Other frequent complaints included misinformation about fares and flight, inadequate service, and rudeness or indifference on the part of airline employees.

If you have a grievance about the way you are treated by an airline, the first step is usually to file a claim (in the case of lost baggage or tickets) or to write a letter to the company, setting forth your complaint and requesting whatever relief you feel is appropriate.* However, do not be surprised if you are treated like a petty criminal in response, particularly if the company thinks you are young. Many airlines are convinced that most complaints from passengers are fraudulent attempts to cheat the company. Pan American's widely publicized vice president for consumer relations, for example, recently suggested that new personnel be assigned in the CAB's office of consumer affairs to

---

*You should be aware that an airline may later argue that failure to give written notice of a claim within a very short time, in some cases as little as seven days, extinguishes all of your rights to obtain relief in court. General Tariff Rule 40, incorporated in the tariffs of most airlines, sets a forty-five-day limit for giving the carrier written notice of loss, damage, or delay of baggage on domestic flights or "any other claim" (excepting only personal injury or death). While such tariff provisions are of questionable validity, they are routinely accepted by the CAB and frequently asserted by the carriers to prevent consumer redress. Thus, even if you are not sure you are going to press the matter, for your own protection it is a good idea always to give some written notice as soon as possible.

investigate passenger complaints, in order to help the carriers ascertain the existence of fraudulent claims. One carrier, Aspen Airways, is reported to have gone to the extent of arranging for employees to get into the hotel rooms of persons who have filed lost baggage claims to look for the luggage there [CAB Transcript of Conference on Consumer Committee and the Airlines, 20 April 1971, pp. 84-85].

In sending a complaint letter to an airline, it is advisable to write to the president of the company, who just may happen to read it. In any case, it is certain to get more attention even if it is relayed down to a subordinate within the company. Even when corresponding with some other employee of the company, it is a good idea to send a carbon copy to the president. It is also useful to send copies to public interest groups, such as ACAP and CU.

Your letter should be as detailed and specific as possible, including such pertinent information as dates, times, flight numbers, and as many names as you can remember of airline employees with whom you dealt. Photocopies (but not originals) of ticket stubs, baggage claim checks, and other relevant evidence should also be enclosed. It may be useful in many cases to have your letter or supporting statement notarized in order to emphasize that you are telling the truth. Be sure to keep copies of any correspondence with the company.

It is not particularly useful, in writing an airline, to threaten never to patronize that company again. While this is a natural and common impulse, such threats are not taken seriously by the airlines, since they know that the industry's structure and limited number of companies makes it a virtual impossibility to avoid particular carriers if you are a frequent traveler.

Writing the company will occasionally help resolve your problem. Often, however, the airline will be unresponsive; even the CAB itself often has difficulty getting a straight answer. Some typical examples were given by Jack Yohe, director of the Board's consumer office, in a recent meeting with airline officials:

> Here is one carrier who failed to answer the question put to it by the CAB Office of Consumer Affairs on whether part 250 was being complied with. We asked the carrier. They never responded. They came back with an answer that was absolutely unresponsive.

> Here is another one we sent out, after a complaint from the public; it questions the legality of selling seats in the lounge area of a plane. The carrier came back with a nice answer but never answered the question.

Here is one complaint about a certain flight. Just for the sake of numbers I will say Flight 123. The carrier reply dealt with Flight 456. It never said anything about the flight referred to in the complaint from the traveler. Then when we went back, we still never got an answer. . . .

We had one complaint that came in on baggage damage. The answer came back from the carrier to the complainant, about service deficiencies, which the complainant never discussed in his letter. No mention was made of his baggage damage. And so it goes. [*Ibid.*, pp. 74-75]

Another frequent airline ploy in dealing with consumer complaints is to claim the reason the company will not provide redress is that it is prohibited from doing so by the CAB. But in the great majority of cases in which the airline replies that the CAB requires or prohibits something, the airline itself has established the regulation or rule, filed it with the CAB, and received rubber stamp approval. The director of customer relations of one airline has admitted that many more people who deal with the carriers are becoming wise to this device. "Apparently," he says, "these are knowledgeable people. . . . I find this becoming more prevalent. At least more passengers are writing to me and saying you filed this regulation. Why don't you be honest and say this is what your company has decided to do" [*Ibid.*, pp. 99-100].

Each airline is required to keep an up-to-date copy of its tariffs and all conditions, rules, and regulations at each ticket office or agency, and they must be made available for you to inspect upon request (see p. 606). You might take a look at them the next time you find yourself spending a few extra hours at the airport between flights—or after being "bumped" off your flight. You are not required to give a "reason" for wanting to inspect the tariffs or the associated rules and regulations, and the airline employees are required "to lend assistance to seekers of information" [*An Introduction to Airfreight Rates*, p. 7, CAB Office of Consumer Affairs, Washington, D.C. 20428, 40 cents]. Tarrifs are also on file in the Tariffs Section at the CAB and may be examined there by any interested person.

There is virtually no other way to find out exactly what your rights as an airline passenger are, and in what ways the carrier is limiting its responsibility to you. The ticket forms used by most airlines contain, in tiny print, only brief allusions to the mysterious documents noted above. You are strongly advised, at some point, to try reading the small print "conditions of contract" printed on back of the ticket, and the carriers' tariff rules.

If you read the fine print you may learn what many travelers, such as the one who wrote the following letter to *The New York Times*, learn only from bitter experience:

To the Editor:

My suitcase, which I had given to the clerk at an airline counter at Kennedy Airport, failed to appear when I arrived in Copenhagen last summer, and to this day it is still missing. Since I travel with only one, large suitcase, everything was lost; and when all of one's traveling valuables are in one container, the total value is obviously quite high. The items in my bag included a camera, strobe light, binoculars, fly-casting equipment and electric razor, as well as much clothing. I calculated the value at over $1,200. After having to waste time shopping for basic articles of clothing while on vacation, I soon learned that no one is legally responsible for the major part of the loss incurred. The airline representative merely pointed to the fine print on the plane ticket and offered the maximum settlement of approximately $330. One only becomes aware of this sort of discrepancy when one's suitcase is lost; otherwise the fine print is there to be ignored. If the airlines were obliged to clearly bring the figure of $330 to the eyes of travelers, everyone would take proper precautions to avoid such treatment and costly losses.

> —Robert Unger, Westbury, L.I.
> [Letter to *Travel* editor, 15 August 1971, section 10, p. 4]

It is unknown to most passengers that if their baggage is lost, stolen, rifled, damaged, or seriously delayed, they may not obtain full or fair settlement from the airline which is responsible. This is because of an obscure tariff provision on file at the CAB, by which most airlines have unilaterally declared that they will not accept responsibility beyond a current level of $500 per passenger (or $360 for international flights). With a couple of suits, a good camera, some jewelry, or important business papers in a suitcase, the limit is easily exceeded, as it was in Mr. Unger's case. The worst part is that the limitation on liability is effectively kept secret until the loss has been suffered. Timely knowledge would at least give passengers the opportunity to obtain insurance or excess coverage, or warn them not to put valuable items in their luggage.

It is common practice within the airline industry to "oversell" flights whenever possible—that is, to sell more tickets than the number of seats available in the plane—on the assumption that some passengers will not show up. This obviously can and does result in a great deal of confusion and inconvenience to passengers who are "bumped off" the flight even though they had "confirmed reservations." This is one area in which the CAB has taken some action, although it is inadequate.

A CAB regulation known as Part 250 (found in the C.F.R., Title 14) sets forth rules which the carriers are required to observe when a flight is oversold. If the carrier is not able to find alternate accommodations which will get the passenger to his destination within two hours of his scheduled arrival time (or four hours, in the case of a foreign flight), then the airline must promptly refund his ticket and tender a penalty payment to the passenger in the amount of the ticket value for the flight from which he was bumped. This is known as "denied boarding compensation." The penalty is limited to a maximum of $200, however, with a minimum of $25. The airline is required by this regulation to tell affected passengers of their rights under Part 250 as soon as they are denied boarding for an oversold flight, but this rule is often violated. Violations of these requirements may result in penalties being assessed against the airline involved, so it is very important to let the Office of Consumer Affairs know if your rights under Part 250 have been neglected [see CAB Order 72-7-42, Enforcement Action Against TWA].

There are obvious deficiencies in this regulation of which airline passengers should be aware. First, it may be entirely unacceptable to many passengers to be delivered several hours late; by that time the trip may have lost its purpose (such as in the case of an important meeting or appointment). Second, the CAB has ruled that the penalty payment is considered "liquidated damages," which means that the bumped passenger who accepts the money thereby forfeits all rights to obtain a more reasonable compensation for his loss and inconvenience. Victimized passengers should be aware that this is one area of consumer abuse for which the courts have held the airlines may be liable, and for which punitive damages may be recovered [460 F. 2d 14 (9th Cir. 1972); *Nader v. Allegheny Airlines,* U.S. District Court, Washington, D.C. (October 18, 1973) reprinted in *Congressional Record,* November 15, 1973, [7371].

What had been another serious defect in the denied boarding compensation rule has recently been changed—to the passenger's benefit. Only those holding "confirmed reservations" may qualify for compensation under the rule if they are bumped. Most people think that they hold a "confirmed reservation" for a flight if they call the airline and are told their reservation is "confirmed." This has not been the case. Typical airline tariffs had defined a "confirmed reservation" as one for which the passenger has actually purchased his ticket. Thus, "confirmed" telephone reservations were often dishonored by the airlines, leaving passengers completely without recourse. The CAB's Consumer Advisory Committee suggested to the Board that it should be considered a deceptive practice for an airline to represent to consumers that they have "confirmed reservations" when in fact they do not under the carrier's own tariff. In June 1973 the Board ruled that the airlines had the option of declaring whether or not they would honor telephone reservations. If they do so file, the passenger now is entitled to "denied boarding compensation."

Schedule irregularities, especially flight delays, have consistently been one of the top subjects of complaint for airline consumers, and for good reason. Airlines have persisted for years in publishing completely unrealistic schedules that they know cannot be met. The result of this deceptive scheduling is massive inconvenience for people who have relied on the schedules to arrange business meetings, connecting flights, or personal matters.

The CAB has repeatedly proclaimed that it is a violation of the law for an airline to publish a schedule that does not reasonably reflect the actual times of arrival and departure of its flights [14 C.F.R. 234.3; see also Notice of Proposed Rule Making dated 11 April 1956, *Federal Register,* 18 April 1956, p. 2533]. Yet the Board refuses to enforce its edict or protect the public from misleading and unreasonable published schedules. A third-party complaint filed in early 1972 by ACAP against eleven major airlines detailed massive violations of the Board's regulations, with some of the offenders operating 50 or even 60 percent of their flights on major routes more than fifteen minutes late. ACAP also asked the Board, in addition to enforcement action, to issue new regulations to provide some level of compensation to passengers inconvenienced by deceptive scheduling practices. True to its first loyalty to the airlines, rather than to the public, the Bureau of Enforcement refused to institute an enforcement proceeding as requested by the complaint [Letter from Richard O'Melia to Aviation Consumer Action Project, 13 July 1972, CAB Docket No. 24362], completely ignoring its own communications to airlines a few years earlier threatening enforcement action unless the noncompliance with schedules was corrected [Letter from Robert Burstein to Northwest Airlines, 9 February

1968; Letter from William Lundin to Delta Airlines, 17 January 1968].

Any provision of the tariffs of an airline is subject to change without any notice to passengers. This means that even if you have paid in full for your ticket and made your plans for a trip, the airline retains the right to refuse to transport you unless you pay additional amounts of money which may be demanded when you arrive at the airport. Similarly, basic changes in rules may be made without notice regarding such matters as reservations, confirmation, or routing, necessitating abrupt changes or cancellation of your trip.

Unknown to most passengers, airlines maintain tariff regulations which give them absolute liberty to refuse transportation on the ground of body odor, bad breath, extreme ugliness (in the airlines' opinion) [Air Traffic Conference of America, Trade Practice Manual Resolution No. 10.6, paragraph 2A, Approved by CAB 31 December 1962, Agreement No. 16614; this rule states that "Persons who have malodorous conditions, gross disfigurement, or other unpleasant characteristics so unusual as to offend fellow passengers should not be transported by any Member], or disability by virtue of "conduct, status, age, or mental or physical condition" unless the person is accompanied by an "attendant." The airlines have this power even over a person who has a confirmed ticket and a doctor's certificate as to his ability to make the trip. This rule, established by mutual airline agreement, is written in such vague and imprecise terms that it creates continuing possibilities for abuse and arbitrary rejections of unattractive, disabled, or crippled persons. As a result, disabled persons have found it impossible to tell whether their plane reservations will be honored, or if they will be rudely stranded by airline personnel who do not want to be bothered. The rule, developed from a 1962 agreement among the airlines, has made airline travel a virtual nightmare for thousands of disabled veterans and others who only need assistance in boarding and deboarding the plane, except for the few who can afford to take along an "attendant" when they travel. ACAP has filed a rule making petition with the CAB to change this. ACAP petition (Appendix 10-B, p. 625) asks the Board to declare that airlines have an absolute duty to serve all persons without discrimination, regardless of appearance or disabilities, and that each carrier should make provisions for providing reasonable assistance to those persons. The petition also asks the Board to issue uniform rules which would be binding on all airlines to define these responsibilities. As a result, the CAB has initiated an investigation to determine what problems exist in this area, and what might be done about them [CAB Docket No. 23904, Transportation of Physically

Disabled Persons, Advance Notice of Proposed Rule Making, 14 October 1971, 36 F.R. 20309].

Each year thousands of frustrated consumers write to the CAB seeking assistance in resolution of problems that have arisen in their dealings with airlines. The number of complaints addressed to the Board has risen dramatically in recent years, an increase that industry spokesmen claim is almost entirely attributable to increased public awareness of the Board's existence and functions. In 1965 the Board was receiving about 1,500 complaints a year [Letter from CAB Chairman Charles S. Murphy to Attorney General Nicholas Katzenbach, 15 November 1965], but by mid-1972 the rate had risen to over 10,000 a year [CAB Press Release 72-143, 17 July 1972].

Still, relatively few consumers are aware of the CAB's functions or of how to file a complaint with the CAB about airline service. One particularly meritorious recommendation, made by the CAB's Consumer Advisory Committee, was to require the airlines, by way of signs or printed cards, to inform their customers about the CAB and its complaint procedures. The Board has never followed up on this recommendation, although it would improve substantially the flow of information to it about problems in the industry.

Complaints sent to the Board in the form of letters are dealt with by the staff as "informal" complaints, as opposed to a "formal" complaint, which must comply with a number of requirements as to form and content and to which is assigned an official docket number. For most consumers, the "informal" procedure is less burdensome and a useful way to communicate a problem, although it lacks the legal impact of a formal complaint. Informal complaints and communications should be sent to: Office of Consumer Affairs, Civil Aeronautics Board, Washington, D.C. 20428.

But the degree of responsiveness to an informal complaint may not be very high. A frustrated consumer from Boston wrote to the Board members: "You august gentlemen are derelict in your duty and you should all resign without delay" [Remarks of Whitney Gillilland, Vice Chairman, Civil Aeronautics Board, before the Association of Local Transport Airlines, 30 September 1971]. A citizen from Pittsburgh, angry at the CAB's inaction on discriminatory fares, opined: "The CAB seems to me a parasite on the body of mankind" [*Ibid*]. A lawyer wrote to ACAP:

Since I speak from experience involving several of my clients, I am conscious of the need for a militant consumer group to repre-

sent the interests of the public in air travel. . . . The correspondence which I have received from [the Consumer Affairs Office of
the CAB] leads to the almost inescapable conclusion that it is an
arm or branch office of the airlines.

A small businessman whose baggage was lost by an airline was informed by the company that he was "not going to get a cent." When he
was unable to obtain any assistance from the CAB, he angrily wrote to
Changing Times magazine, which had recommended sending complaints
to the Board:

> As you can see by the enclosed letters, I wrote to and received a
> letter from the CAB as you people suggested in your April, 71
> issue.
> From personal experience I have found the CAB to be overpaid
> double talkers who are known for being able to send mail free of
> charge. Letters that contain one hundred words or more say
> *NOTHING.*
> If the "Office of Consumer Affairs" is to help people with miss-
> ing luggage, (my case), and get a letter like the one they sent me,
> GOD help the people.

Nevertheless, there is some possibility that your complaint to the
CAB may result in greater success than these people achieved, or in the
initiation of formal action by the CAB. One example worth noting
occurred in the spring of 1969 when Mr. Stanley Cohen of Washington,
D.C., editor of *Advertising Age,* wrote to the CAB to complain about
the lack of adequate and comprehensible notice by airlines of their
tariff provisions which limit liability for lost baggage in international
travel. His letter made several specific suggestions for amendment of
existing CAB regulations, including a requirement for notice of baggage
liability limitations, and a requirement that all notices of liability limitations be stated in terms of dollars. But it was not until after Senator
Warren Magnuson, chairman of the powerful Senate Commerce Committee, wrote to the Board several months later expressing his concern
for the problems described in Mr. Cohen's letter, that the CAB staff
determined to treat the letter as a "petition for rule making." During
the next several months, staff members of the Office of General Counsel, Bureau of Economics, and Bureau of Enforcement conferred and
agreed on the need for Board action. Among other things, the staff
reviewed the number and subject matter of complaints that had been

received during the preceding years relating to baggage liability limitations and inadequacy of notice. A formal rule making proceeding was initiated in May 1970 and published in the *Federal Register* [35 F.R. 7513]. Over the strenuous objection of the ATA and IATA, the CAB finally issued a regulation requiring the airlines to give passengers more adequate notice of their limitations of liability for the loss, delay, or damage of baggage. This new rule became effective early in 1972 [14 C.F.R. 221.176].

Another example of action based on consumer complaints was a fine of $87,000 imposed on TWA in July 1972 for violating the denied boarding compensation regulations. This was one of the few pro-consumer enforcement actions ever taken by the Bureau of Enforcement and was initiated under the prodding of the Office of Consumer Affairs [CAB Order 72-7-42, 13 July 1972].

Even if no action results, it is still worth something to complain to the CAB if you have been wronged, since there is a growing tendency in the industry and the Board to point to numbers of complaints as indicative of the quality of air service. Complaint statistics, by airline and by subject matter, are now issued monthly by the CAB and watched closely by the carriers. As mentioned before, when rule making is proposed, the CAB is likely to review its consumer complaint files to see how many complaints have been received dealing with a particular problem. Thus, filing a complaint is the one way available for individual consumers to "cast a vote" about the quality of service from a particular airline. Rising complaints also catch the ear of members of Congress who monitor the CAB.

As with consumer letters to carriers, an informal complaint to the CAB should contain as much specific detail as possible, including names, dates, flight numbers, and any documentation, such as copies of ticket stubs, that may be available. It can be helpful to include sworn affidavits setting forth the facts in considerable detail, to emphasize to the Board's staff that you are telling the truth.

Another method which greatly increases the likelihood of agency responsiveness is to send your complaint to a Congressman or Senator (as Mr. Cohen did), who will generally forward it to the Board with a request for a follow-up report. Congressional complaints or inquiries are indicated by special red tabs in the CAB's files and get special treatment from the CAB staff. It is important to send copies of every complaint or petition to your Congressional representatives, to consumer organizations such as ACAP, and to Virginia Knauer's Office of

Consumer Affairs in the Department of Health, Education, and Welfare (Room 3300, HEW N. Bldg., 330 Independence Avenue, S.W., Washington, D.C. 20201), so they are continually made aware of current problems.

The CAB's time-honored method for dealing with consumer complaints has been to send a copy of the complaint to the airline involved, with a request that the company please work out the problem with the complainant, and to send a form letter or postcard to the complainant indicating that his or her letter has been received. Months or even years might pass before the complainant hears anything more—if he ever does. However, with the establishment of the CAB's Office of Consumer Affairs, the Board indicated its desire to improve communications and service to consumers who have grievances. "I envision this as an ombudsman type function that will provide the public a single and readily accessible contact point," ex-chairman Secor Browne said in setting up the new office. "It will ensure better handling of the thousands of communications the Board receives from air transportation users, and should contribute materially to improved service to the public." Whether it is successful in this task, of course, remains to be seen.

The Director of the Office of Consumer Affairs, Jack Yohe, outlined for the Consumer Advisory Committee how the Complaints Section handles consumer complaints:

> Complaints from customers are received generally in one of three ways. They are written and addressed directly to the Board, they come to the Board as a carbon copy of a letter written and addressed to the carrier(s) involved, or they come to us through an inquiry of a Senator, Congressman or the President's Committee on Consumer Affairs. If the carrier involved is mentioned in the complaint, we get in touch with the carrier regardless of how we receive the complaint.
>
> All complaints addressed to the Board are answered by acknowledgement or substantive reply depending on the content of the complaint. Our acknowledgement may consist of a brief letter or a preprinted post card. Congressmen's and Senators' inquiries are answered over the signature of either the Chairman or the Director, Office of Community and Congressional Relations. We do not acknowledge receipt of carbon copies of letters addressed to air carriers.
>
> The Section's inquiry of the air carrier includes a request that it write directly to the complainant explaining its actions in the

particular situation causing the complaint and that it send the Section a copy of the letter. The replies from the carriers are reviewed to make certain that the points raised by the complainant are covered and that the carrier has complied with the Federal Aviation Act, the Board Regulations, and the carrier's own tariff.

If a violation is evident, the case is referred to either the Investigation Division of the Bureau for further investigation or to the Legal Division for further action. The case is not closed until we have reasonably established that the carrier's response has satisfied the complainant within reason and within the limits of the law, that no violation is evident, that the carrier has taken or will take corrective action where necessary, and that further correspondence or communication will be of no benefit. If there is any question about the carrier's response, further inquiry is made of the carrier posing specific questions about the questionable aspects of the complaint and/or the answer.

At the time the complaint is received, it is recorded by case number, by complainant's name (including name of Congressman when applicable), by subject of complaint, and by air carrier involved. Data is compiled on consumer complaints on a monthly basis.

The Office of Consumer Affairs reports that it has been modifying its methods of processing complaints to improve its effectiveness and eliminate unnecessary paperwork where possible. Mr. Yohe, for example, advocates greater use of the telephone to assist in obtaining relief for airline consumers where possible, and has been known to look over a complaint letter, immediately call up the president or top consumer relations official of the airline involved, and ask why they can't work the matter out satisfactorily. The Office has been successful on several occasions in actually helping citizen complainants, a rare occurrence in the CAB's history. The Board claims that, as of 30 June 1972, over $250,000 in reimbursements has been paid by air carriers and indirect air carriers (freight forwarders and tour operators) to consumers who wrote the Office of Consumer Affairs for assistance [CAB Press Release 72-143, 17 July 1972]. Thus it may be extremely helpful to call the director of the Office of Consumer Affairs personally about your complaint, and ask him to help resolve the problem. (Allow five to seven days after writing for your letter to be received and sorted before you call.) The number is: 202-382-6376.

Consumers also may file "formal" complaints, which are often

referred to as "third-party complaints," seeking enforcement action by
the Board with respect to specific violations of the Federal Aviation
Act or the Board's rules and regulations, or petitions for rule making
seeking the issuance or amendment of a regulation by the CAB to deal
with specific or general abuses. Any such "formal" documents should
be addressed to the Docket Section, Civil Aeronautics Board, Washington, D.C. 20428, and should comply with the CAB's Rules of Practice,
set forth in Part 302 of the regulations and briefly summarized below.
Such documents should generally be typed (or printed) on standard
letter or legal size bond. The text should be double-spaced (except for
footnotes or long quotations, which may be single-spaced), with margins
of at least one inch (one and one-half inches for left margin). The initial
document filed by any party in a particular proceeding must state, on
the first page, the name and mailing address of the person who may be
served with any subsequent documents that may be filed in the proceeding. Generally a signed original and nineteen copies of any formal
document must be filed [14 C.F.R. 302.3, 302.8]. The document
should also contain a caption indicating the substance of the matter
involved, as well as a title (such as "Complaint," "Petition," or "Request
for Investigation") indicating the nature of the document itself. If the
document is filed in compliance with these formal requirements, it is
then assigned a "docket" or case number. The CAB may strike any
document filed which is not in "substantial conformity" with the rules
[14 C.F.R. 302.5].

In addition to the copies which must be furnished to the Board, the
Rules also require service of formal complaints upon any other party to
the proceeding, such as any specific airline or company against which
the complaint is being lodged. Service may be made by regular or registered mail, or by personal delivery. Generally it is adequate to address
the president or any other officer of a company for this purpose,
except that once a proceeding is under way, documents should be
addressed to the person or persons designated by the parties to receive
service. Any such complaint or other document seeking action against
specific parties should be concluded with an appropriate certificate of
service.

The substantive content of a complaint or petition depends upon the
subject matter and the applicable legal and factual circumstances. As
general guidelines, the document should identify the statutory section
or regulatory provision under which relief is sought, describe the facts
as clearly and concisely as possible, and set forth the legal and policy
arguments that support the claim for CAB action. Examples are

provided in Appendices 10-A (p. 618) and 10-B (p. 625 for general guidance in the format and contents of formal pleadings, including a complaint charging deceptive advertising and sales practices by an airline and a tour operator, and a petition for rule making to prohibit discrimination against physically disabled persons in air transportation.

Once a formal complaint is filed, it is supposed to be reviewed promptly by the CAB staff. Upon conclusion of this review, the Director of the Bureau of Enforcement is required by the CAB's own regulations [14 C.F.R. 302.205] either to dismiss the complaint, giving his reasons for this action, or to file a "petition for enforcement," initiating a formal investigation or enforcement proceeding concerning the alleged violations. In practice, this process may take months or years. Complainants should not give up in despair when delay tactics are encountered, however, for there are legal means available to force the agency to do its duty. For example, a citizen's complaint against several airlines, banks, and financial firms, alleging widespread violations of requirements of the Federal Aviation Act for disclosure of airline ownership details, was filed in August 1970. Answers were then filed by the respondents named in the complaint, and by November 1970 the case was ready for disposition [CAB Docket No. 22468]. When more than two and one-half years passed with no response from the Bureau of Enforcement, the complainant filed suit in U.S. District Court. The District Judge, expressing shock at the Board's conduct, ordered the Director of Enforcement to dispose of the matter within thirty days [*Nader* v. *Browne*, C.A. 1240-72, U.S. District Court, District of Columbia, Order of Judge Green dated 10 November 1972], which the Director did on the last day by dismissing the complaint and ignoring the established violations of the law.

The purported aim of a formal enforcement proceeding is to impose some form of punishment if the respondent is found to have violated the law, or to eliminate the practices involved. However, the CAB staff is usually willing to settle for a nonpenalizing order prohibiting the offender from committing further violations of the same nature. Actual fines or other penalties against air carriers have been rare, despite the severity of violation. For example, in the five-year period ending in the summer of 1969, only one major U.S. airline was subject to a civil penalty by the CAB. That was a $1,000 fine against Pan American in 1965.

Even the initiation of formal enforcement proceedings does not necessarily mean that action will be taken in the near future. The experience of Herbert A. Goldberger of Cranston, Rhode Island, bears witness to the unbelievable delays that are common in CAB enforcement proceedings.

Mr. Goldberger first complained to the Board in January 1966 that American Airlines had violated the Federal Aviation Act in arbitrarily excluding him from its plush "Admirals Club" facilities at major airports, which are restricted to persons listed in *Who's Who*, top corporate officials, and other favored passengers of American [CAB Docket No. 16895]. Six months later, the Bureau of Enforcement filed a formal complaint and petition for enforcement against American (and at the same time initiated proceedings against other airlines maintaining similar restricted waiting rooms and facilities). The Bureau asserted, in no uncertain terms, that the airline "clubs" and lounges illegally discriminate against excluded passengers, and constitute unfair practices and unfair methods of competition which are prohibited by the law.

In 1971, after numerous private negotiations between the Board and American's lawyers had apparently stalled the proceedings, Mr. Goldberger's lawyer wrote to the enforcement director: "Our client is considerably upset, and for very good reason. Your Board's failure to act during these several years is supportive of the charges made from time to time that your agency is catering to the airlines and not to the consumer public. There is no justification whatever for this undue delay." It was a cry in the wilderness, unheeded by the Board. In December 1972 Mr. Goldberger's lawyer again wrote to the Board. "As it is now some seven years since action was commenced in this matter," he wrote, "we would appreciate receiving a report from you by return mail as to when our client may expect that this matter will be resolved." The response from the CAB's managing director was a classic of bureaucratic noncommitment: "Your concern over the delay in the disposition of this matter is easily understood. It is presently before the Board for decision and I am certain will be handled at the earliest possible time." Finally, Mr. Goldberger was forced to petition the U.S. Court of Appeals to review the Board's inability or unwillingness to act, even after seven years.

To be sure, all formal complaints to the Board do not yield such frustrating inaction. A complaint filed by ACAP against alleged fraud by Trans World Airlines and a tour operator, Flying Mercury, Inc., in the sale of tours to Europe, finally resulted in an enforcement proceeding being initiated by the Bureau of Enforcement after a year of inaction. ACAP protested strenuously the Bureau's delay, its failure to pursue other clear law violations that were discovered in the investigation, and its practice of conducting private discussions with the respondents in the case; the Bureau's response was to try to prevent ACAP from participating in subsequent stages of the case [CAB Docket Nos. 23628 and 24697].

If the Bureau of Enforcement dismisses the charges, the complainant may file a motion with the Board to review this action, setting forth the grounds for appeal. Such a motion must be filed within twenty days after the letter of dismissal has been served, and must conform to the formal requirements of Rule 18 of the Rules of Practice [14 C.F.R. 302.18]. The Board may then sustain or reverse the action of the enforcement director in dismissing the complaint. At that point, if the Board refuses to pursue the complaint, an appeal may be taken to the U.S. Court of Appeals, to review the Board's action.

Rule making proceedings at the CAB are not nearly as formal as adjudicatory cases, and rarely involve hearings. The procedures for filing a petition for rule making have been discussed. Section 302.38 provides that, if the Board determines "that the petition discloses sufficient reasons in support of the relief requested to justify the institution of public rule making procedures," it will then issue an appropriate public notice, which is published in the *Federal Register*. Otherwise, the Board is required to notify the petitioner and other interested parties that the rule making is not being initiated, together with the grounds for the denial. In addition, of course, the Board may initiate rule making proceedings or investigations on its own initiative. This is done by issuing and publishing in the *Federal Register* a Notice of Proposed Rule Making (NPRM) or Advance Notice of Proposed Rule Making (ANPRM), if the proposal is at a very preliminary and tentative stage.

Once a rule making proceeding or investigation has been instituted, any person may file comments, evidence, or arguments within a specified period (usually from thirty to ninety days). Such comments should be typed, and nineteen extra copies are generally required. The Board, however, is usually more lenient with respect to citizen participation in rule making than it is in formal hearing cases, and will often accept informal or handwritten comments for consideration in the rule making proceeding. Indeed, in a recent rule making proceeding dealing with the question of smoking on airliners, the Board expressly invited "individual members of the public" to participate by submitting a letter without the necessity of multiple copies. The result was an unprecedented volume of consumer participation as thousands of citizens took the opportunity to present their views.

The Board has been substantially more responsive to consumer petitions and comments in rule making proceedings than it has been to formal complaints. In response to a 1970 rule making petition filed by a group of law students asking the agency to assure that airlines were complying with federal laws against employment discrimination, the Board did, over nineteen months later, institute a half-hearted rule making inquiry as to its powers to take such action [CAB Docket No. 24636; see CAB Press Release 72-154 (1 August 1972)]. In another case, the CAB in 1972 opened a major rule making proceeding into the problem of cigar, pipe, and cigarette smoking on passenger flights in response to a petition by Ralph Nader—but only after a delay of two years, nine months, and two days, and a lawsuit filed by Nader to compel Board action. The steps leading to this proceeding are described more fully below.

Filing comments in CAB rule making proceedings is relatively easy and often useful. The airlines and other industry groups rarely miss an opportunity to express their views in a rule making proceeding, often through their trade association. Comments may be brief or extensive and may make whatever arguments or produce whatever evidence you deem pertinent to the inquiry. Generally comments should be typed and presented in the format required for pleadings before the CAB, with the required number of copies (usually an original and nineteen unless the CAB order indicates a smaller number), although comments from individual members of the public and civic organizations are often acceptable in the form of a letter, telegram, or other informal communication. Nonindustry comments can make a difference. For example, suggestions made by ACAP to tighten up proposed regulations governing reporting of airline stock ownership were incorporated into the final rule [Docket No. 23962; see 14 C.F.R. 245]. In addition, the number of comments received in support or opposition of a proposal are often taken by the Board and its staff as an indication of the public's interest in the matter.

One of the most formidable obstacles facing any citizen or group dealing with the CAB is neglect, usually intentional. While the Board's own rules generally call for complaints or petitions to be dealt with in a reasonable time, in practice this requirement is frequently ignored, with the result that the petitioner is unable to press his or her case. Many important cases filed at the Board have never been dealt with at all—the CAB simply assigns them a number, puts them in a file drawer, and does nothing more. Usually the petitioner, after months or years of inaction, loses interest or gives up in disgust. This is just what the bureaucrats want, of course.

Citizens are not powerless to compel government officials to do their duties, however, and it is important to develop effective methods of dealing with such inaction. One possible approach was suggested in a lawsuit filed by Ralph Nader and an associate in June 1972. This step was taken after years of inaction on a 1969 petition filed by Nader asking the Board to establish rules to deal with the problem of smoking on airliners, as it affects the health, comfort, and safety of passengers— a long-time source of complaint by airline passengers—and a 1970 third-party complaint asking the Bureau of Enforcement to require airlines and financial institutions to comply with the ownership reporting requirements of the Federal Aviation Act. The plaintiffs sought a court order requiring the Board members and the enforcement director to act on the cases, as the CAB's own regulations require. The suit also asked the Court to assess on the defendants a penalty of 5 percent of their salary for the period of time during which they neglected to act on the complaint and petition. The plaintiffs argued that the penalty should be paid to the Treasurer of the United States to compensate the government for the officials' failure to perform their duties while accepting their salaries from the government. Although the suit was successful in getting action from the CAB on both the petition and the third-party complaint, the U.S. District Judge declined to assess the proposed penalty [*Nader* v. *Browne*, U.S. District Court, District of Columbia, Civil Action No. 1240-72, Order dated 10 November 1972]. An appeal from this decision has been taken to the U.S. Court of Appeals.

Learning about either formal hearing cases or rule making proceedings before the CAB in time to participate is a serious problem, and operates as an effective barrier for many individuals and organizations that may wish to be heard. Few have the resources to be able to read the notices published in the *Federal Register* each day, although asking to be put on the CAB list for press releases may help to some degree. The agency's underlying disinterest in effective citizen participation was demonstrated in its cavalier approach to the problem of informing members of the public about what is going on. In a response to the Senate Administrative Practice Subcommittee's inquiry, the Board members asserted laconically: "It is believed that those persons that are affected by the Board's activities know enough about them" [Letter from John H. Crooker, Jr., Chairman, Civil Aeronautics Board, to Sen. Edward M. Kennedy, 7 April 1969, reprinted in Committee Print of Senate Judiciary Committee, Subcommittee on Administrative Practice and Procedure, Responses to Questionnaire on Citizen Involvement and Responsive Agency Decision-Making, 9 September 1969]. The CAB's Consumer Advisory Committee urged the Board, through its Office of Consumer Affairs, to establish a consumer bulletin containing information about proceedings of interest to consumers, but no action has yet been taken.

Airline fares are under the regulatory jurisdiction of the CAB. This does not mean, however, that the CAB "sets" the fares, as is commonly believed; rather, the law contemplates that each airline will determine its own fares and charges, which it publishes in loose-leaf books known as tariffs. New or revised fares as well as the airlines' rules and regulations are submitted to the CAB prior to their becoming effective, and the agency may either permit them to go into effect or disapprove them. Airlines are barred from charging more or less than is set forth in the tariffs.

Thousands of new tariff filings containing prices, conditions, and rules for fares are filed with the CAB each year. They are deposited in the Board's Tariff Section in Room 814, where they are required to be available for public inspection. However, at least one knowledgeable reporter complained to the Consumer Advisory Committee that these important filings often disappear as soon as they are filed, either by accidental loss or by theft [Statement of Donald Knoles, editor of *Travel Management Daily*, to CAB Consumer Advisory Committee meeting, 24 March 1971]. But the Tariff Section at the CAB is a model of bureaucratic chaos, and it is not at all unlikely that new tariff filings could be misplaced for days.

Actually, most airlines use the services of a tariff agent who prints, files, and publishes these tariff documents for them. Mr. C. C. Squires, the tariff agent for most domestic airlines, has offered to provide copies of every passenger and air freight tariff filed by his company to any interested party for reimbursement of postage alone, which is estimated to run between $300 and $400 a year. His address is: C. C. Squires, Airline Tariff Publishers, Inc., 1825 K Street, N.W., Washington, D.C. 20006.

Carriers are also required to have their applicable tariffs on file and freely available for inspection by any person at their offices [14 C.F.R. 221, IV]. But don't be surprised if you can't understand them when you inspect them. Tariffs are unbelievably complicated publications, and can be almost impossible to decipher. The CAB itself has only a few employees who are really qualified to read and understand all aspects of airline tariffs, and such specialists are relatively rare even within the airlines.

Tariff filings that contain significant changes in an airline's rates, fares, rules, or conditions of service (as opposed to technical amendments) are required to be accompanied by the carrier's detailed "justification," which includes a full explanation of the changes and the reasons for them, and the economic data to support the need for the new tariff. This should include such items as estimates of the costs of service and of the effects of the changes upon passengers and revenues, and examples of how the new fares will compare with existing fares [14 C.F.R. 221.165]. In reality, this important requirement for justification data in support of new or increased fares is largely ignored. The Board has permitted fare increases to take effect even in cases where the carrier has submitted no information at all to support the changes. The effect of this is to greatly increase the burden of consumers who would challenge such fare increases, since there is no evidence of what rationale the carrier or the Board is using for the increases.

When a new or revised tariff is filed, a number of possible courses are open to the Board. It may simply permit the tariff to become effective, which is what happens with the great majority of filings each year. It may reject the tariff if it is not filed in accordance with the Board's procedural regulations and orders. It may suspend the new tariff for up to ninety days for an investigation, and this suspension period may be extended for an additional ninety days if the investigation is not completed in that time. Or the Board may permit the tariff to become effective while it undertakes an investigation. If at the end of its investigation the Board determines that the proposed tariff "is or will be unjust or unreasonable, or unjustly discriminatory, or unduly preferential, or unduly prejudicial," it can set the rate which the carrier must use. Actually the quoted words have little meaning in practice, serving primarily as incantation used by the CAB whenever it decides, for one reason or another, to disapprove of a carrier's tariff.

Any citizen has the right to file a petition for suspension, a complaint, comments, or opinions concerning new tariff filings. Citizen participation in tariff matters, however, has been a rarity at the CAB, largely because of the great complexity, obscurity, and technicality of the issues and procedures involved. Robert Sherer, director of the Bureau of Economics at the CAB, recently acknowledged: "In the past, all too often these complaints have been limited to competing carriers. The public has not entered into this process of complaining very often against fare filings" [CAB Transcript of Conference on Consumer Committee and The Airlines, 20 April 1971, p. 14]. In fact, it is virtually impossible for an ordinary citizen to learn of a fare filing in time to register a complaint, since carriers are not required to make any public announcement or otherwise alert their customers to what is going on—

particularly where a substantial fare increase is proposed. The CAB Consumer Advisory Committee made several recommendations for improvements in this area, such as establishment of a daily register of important tariff filings, notification to wire services and local media of proposed changes, and a requirement that carriers notify passengers of planned fare increases, but the Board has largely neglected to pursue these suggestions.

The time for filing complaints against a tariff is very short. Generally tariffs are not permitted to become effective less than thirty days from the date of their publication. A complaint requesting suspension of a tariff must be received by the Board at least eighteen days prior to its effective date, which means that generally the complaint must be lodged within twelve days of the tariff filing [14 C.F.R. 302.505]. The carrier must file its answer within six days of the complaint [*Ibid*]. Any such complaint must identify the carrier, the tariff (with specific reference to its "CAB number"), and the specific items or provisions being complained against. The petition or complaint should also state the reasons why the contents of the tariff are believed to be unlawful, and set forth whatever facts or analysis may be available to support that assertion [14 C.F.R. 302.502]. Like other documents filed at the Board, a petition or complaint against a tariff should be typewritten on durable paper not larger than eight and one-half by fourteen inches.

Regulations governing the filing of tariffs are set forth in Part 221 of the Board's regulations, Title 14 C.F.R., while the procedural rules governing the filing of complaints are in Part 302, discussed earlier in this chapter. A sample complaint against carrier tariffs is contained in Appendix 10-A (p. 618).

The CAB has done almost nothing to educate ordinary consumers about its tariff procedures by which passenger fares are set, or about the public's right to participate in these important matters. By contrast, the Board has been highly solicitous of and helpful to business organizations, such as commercial shippers, which might have an interest in airline freight tariffs. For example, the CAB has issued a pamphlet for the benefit of commercial shippers, entitled *An Introduction to Airfreight Rates*. This useful booklet's expressed aim is to meet the need "for clarification of the rate-making process in air transportation, and particularly the role of the shipper in this process." Indeed, it was noted, "the Board, the staff, and facilities of the CAB are available to lend all reasonable assistance to any person on any matter within our authority and responsibility."

The shippers' booklet, prepared by the Bureau of Economics staff, contains brief, clear summaries of various aspects of domestic and international airfreight rates, the processes by which they are determined, factors affecting the rates, tariff procedures, specific information on how to obtain CAB orders, tariffs, rate agreements, and other information, and how to participate in the process. Unfortunately, the CAB has not issued a comparable guide to assist airline passengers in access to CAB proceedings, despite recommendations to that effect by the Consumer Advisory Committee. The Board did, however, heed the Committee's recommendation to the extent of publishing a brief booklet on some of the problems that airline passengers frequently encounter. While this booklet, entitled *Consumer Guide for Air Travelers,* falls short of assisting consumer participation at the agency, it does include a number of useful tips for travelers. Both *An Introduction to Airfreight Rates* and the *Consumer Guide* are available free upon request from the CAB Office of Consumer Affairs.

Once a complaint and answer have been filed, the Board's Bureau of Economics reviews all the available material, including the carrier's justification statement. "And then the burden falls upon my staff to try to find out where the truth lies," Bureau Director Sherer has noted, "and all too often there is a lot of argument, and not much fact, and it is very difficult." The economics staff makes a recommendation to the Board regarding the proposed tariff, and the Board then must either dismiss the complaint or initiate a formal proceeding to investigate the fare, either with or without suspending it pending the proceeding.

Public hearings may be held at the CAB, normally before one of the agency's administrative law judges, in various kinds of regulatory matters:

- Rate making involving the legality of airline rates, fares, or conditions.
- Mergers and agreements involving airline companies.
- Route cases, in which one or more carriers are seeking to begin or terminate service between particular points.
- Enforcement proceedings, in which a carrier is charged with some violation of law or regulations.

Theoretically, any interested party can participate in a CAB hearing. There is no register of authorized practitioners, as required by some agencies. As a practical matter, however, the Board and its administrative law judges have created barriers to participation by citizens, so that members of the regulated industry, governmental agencies, and commercial groups have far easier access to these proceedings than members of the public or representatives of consumer or environmental organizations. Two levels of participation are contemplated in Part 302 of the CAB regulations. Rule 15 provides for formal intervention as a party in hearing cases which may be "permitted" for any person "whose intervention will be conducive to the ends of justice and will not unduly delay the conduct of such proceeding" [14 C.F.R. 302.15]. Rule 14 [14 C.F.R. 302.14], on the other hand, provides for limited participation in hearings by interested persons. Under Rule 14 status, the participant has the right "to present any evidence which is relevant to the issues," to present a written statement on the issues involved in the case, and, with the consent of the official conducting the hearing, to cross-examine witnesses. But Rule 14 intervenors have no rights to file an appeal to the Board or to present oral arguments to the Board. In practice, Rule 14 participants are not taken very seriously at the Board, either by the agency or by industry representatives.

One of the most critical stages in a proceeding at the CAB is the prehearing conference, at which the issues to be decided in the hearing are established and defined. Attendance at this conference is very important, because the administrative law judge will generally refuse to inquire into any matter not brought up at the conference and contained in its report. In addition, this is the time when information requests are made by and upon the various parties, and passed upon by the judge. The schedule for the hearing and for presentation of evidence is also established in the prehearing conference report.

Generally, requests for intervention should be made prior to or at the prehearing conference, although such petitions can be filed up to the day before the hearing begins if "good cause" can be shown for the person's lateness in application, or if the applicant is a city, a "public body," or a chamber of commerce. Do not expect a sympathetic response to your late-filed intervention petitions, since the Board is usually glad to have some technical reason for rejecting consumer participants. For example, a petition filed by the NRDC to intervene in a general fare investigation hearing was rejected because of lateness, although NRDC was not even in existence at the time of the prehearing conference. The Board ruled that NRDC was not a "public body," which would permit it to file late intervention in the same manner as chambers of commerce, although it was incorporated for the exclusive purpose of environmental protection and public interest advocacy [CAB Order 71-4-176, Docket No. 21866-9, Domestic Passenger Fare Investigation].

Petitions for intervention under Rule 15 should comply with the formal requirements for filing documents set forth in Part 302 of the Board's regulations, and should be served on every party to the proceeding. The parties then have seven days to answer or oppose such a petition. The petition should refer to the factors set forth in Rule 15 as relevant considerations in determination of a petition to intervene, specifically:

1. The nature of the petitioner's right under the statute to be made a party to the proceeding.
2. The nature and extent of the property, financial, or other interest of the petitioner.
3. The effect of the order which may be entered in the proceeding on petitioner's interest.
4. The availability of other means whereby the petitioner's interest may be protected.
5. The extent to which petitioner's interest will be represented by existing parties.
6. The extent to which petitioner's participation may reasonably be expected to assist in the development of a sound record.
7. The extent to which participation of the petitioner will broaden the issue or delay the proceeding.

In addition, the CAB has issued further requirements that apply to public interest organizations seeking to intervene under Rule 15 in cases pending before the Board. Following a ruling that ACAP and similar public interest and consumer organizations are not "public bodies" entitled to any of the privileges extended to chambers of commerce and municipal agencies, the Board stated as follows in a footnote:

The Board welcomes the views of any person, and has provided in Rule 14 a procedure by which such views can be placed in the record of a proceeding. On the other hand, neither the Federal Aviation Act nor the courts have placed on the Board the requirement of permitting formal intervention (with all the potential for added delays and increased costs which such intervention implies) to groups which have no direct and substantial economic interest in the proceeding at hand and which may in reality turn out to consist of no more than one or a few individuals. . . . Thus it is incumbent on applicants for intervention to disclose sufficient facts to enable the Board to ascertain that they are "responsible spokesmen for representative groups" having a significant interest in the subject matter of the proceeding. . . . [CAB Order 71-11-43, Docket No. 22916, American-Western Merger Case, adopted 11 November 1971, footnote 6]

Among the factors that the Board demanded be included by ACAP were the names of its founders, the members of its board of advisors and their role in determining the policy of the organization, and the number and geographic distribution of members of the public who have lent it their support. In short, the agency unilaterally, and without the normal procedures of rule making, established a requirement that any prospective intervenor such as ACAP must demonstrate that it "is in fact a broadly based organization representing a significant segment of the public" [*Ibid*]. The Board, by restricting citizens, consumers, and environmental organizations from participation in public proceedings, while facilitating representation of financial and commercial interests, has made clear where its true loyalties lie. Although ACAP has successfully intervened and participated in numerous subsequent cases, the CAB has continually demonstrated its antipathy to such groups and reinforced the procedural barriers that are likely to be encountered.

In the hearing the judge usually allows oral argument, statements, and proposed findings and conclusions to follow the presentation of direct and rebuttal evidence and cross-examination of witnesses. After considering the evidence in the record, he reaches an initial or recommended decision which becomes final thirty days after it has been served upon all parties, unless a petition for discretionary review by the Board is filed by one of the parties. If you are participating under Rule 14, you do not have the right to file such a petition. But the Board may decide on its own initiative to review the decision. Another procedure which is sometimes followed under CAB regulations is for the judge to pass the buck by certifying the record in a proceeding directly to the Board, without issuing an initial or recommended decision, and for the Board itself to prepare a "tentative decision."

Parties have ten days after service of a judge's initial decision or a tentative decision of the Board to file objections to conclusions which they consider wrong. These must be clearly and separately stated, and served on the Board and all other parties. After that, parties are entitled to file briefs, reply briefs rebutting the arguments of other parties, and requests for oral argument. After all of these procedural steps, the Board disposes of the case by entering a final decision (subject to petitions for reconsideration, which may be filed within twenty days).

A case involving important environmental challenges by citizen groups demonstrates clearly the difficulties that may be experienced in seeking full participatory rights before the agency. Organizations comprised of Washington, D.C., area residents sought to intervene, under Rule 15, in a case involving possible certification of regular helicopter operations in the area. The groups included the Palisades Citizens' Association, a nonprofit District of Columbia corporation, and the Committee Against National, an unincorporated association of persons residing in the District of Columbia and adjacent areas of Maryland and Virginia, concerned with "the nature, composition, and operating characteristics of all aviation in the Washington, D.C.–Baltimore, Md. service areas." The groups and their members (many of whom lived directly in the flight path of the proposed helicopter operations) claimed a specific concern about the environmental effects, including noise, fumes and particulate emissions, safety hazards, visual intrusions, and radio and television interference, which would result from the proposed services. Although the proposed route would take the helicopters over the homes and businesses of the would-be intervenors, the CAB administrative law judge denied their petition to intervene as full parties, restricting them to limited participation under Rule 14.

The ruling was upheld by the Board, although the petitioners were finally permitted to participate before the Board in oral argument, and to file a brief. In its opinion upholding the ruling, the Board demonstrated its attitude toward the raising of questions about the environmental impact of proposed actions by citizen intervenors:

> The applicants' assertions of "environmental impact" upon them are highly generalized, and the effect upon their individual interests of any certification herein is both remote and speculative. The applicants do not allege any unique injury which will not be shared equally by all similarly situated property owners. Furthermore, there is no showing that the environmental impact of helicopter operations may be expected to differ from that inflicted by any other aircraft which may pass at low altitudes over residential areas, or that this proceeding is essentially different in this respect from any other new route case. [CAB Order No. E-25,704]

The Board ruled that "the Federal Aviation Act does not in terms confer any right of intervention upon members of the public who may be interested in or affected by new air operations. . . ." The groups then challenged the CAB's action before the U.S. Court of Appeals. The court reasoned that, since the groups had in fact been permitted to participate in oral argument and to submit written briefs to the Board, they had not been substantially injured by the agency's ruling [*Palisades Citizen Association* v. *CAB,* 420 F.2d 188 (D.C. Cir. 1969)]. But the court also took the occasion to chastise the CAB for its indifference to environmental concerns:

> In affirming the Board's order in this case let us first caution the Board that questions relating to environmental impact of proposed services upon persons and property lying below the routes are substantial and clearly relevant to the Board's certification inquiry. . . . No agency entrusted with determinations of public convenience and necessity is an island. It fits within a national system of regulatory control of industry. Its decisions affect not only its primary interest groups but also the general public at large. . . . To say that the environmental impact of that service is not a proper consideration of the Board in its certification hearing is folly. [*Ibid.*]

Although the proposed helicopter service was approved by the Board, it was never initiated.

Other federal agencies, such as the Department of Defense, the Department of Transportation, and the General Services Administration, sometimes intervene in CAB proceedings, and they may be potential allies for citizen intervenors. Frequently they intervene in rate or service cases to protect the interests of the agency as a shipper, but agencies such as the Justice Department, Health, Education, and Welfare's Office of Consumer Affairs, or the Environmental Protection Agency also could represent consumer or environmental interests.

The token gesture made by the CAB toward consumers— the Office of Consumer Affairs—offers the initial point of citizen access within the CAB for most complaints. Your complaints will usually be directed at a specific airline, so as a rule they should be copied and sent to several places: the airline involved, the CAB Office of Consumer Affairs, your Congressman, ACAP, and other outside groups that may be interested. Even if your complaint is not resolved to your satisfaction, adding to other similar complaints may contribute to saving others from the same kind of abuse. There is strength in numbers.

Petitions for rule making take more time and effort, but they can have much greater impact for the future, since many consumer complaints about the airlines are directed at specific continuing practices which the CAB has ample authority to prohibit. Intervening in formal proceedings is much more difficult, as the Palisades Citizens discovered. For that kind of participation, you either have to be in Washington, or have a legal representative there. ACAP is the first public interest project of this kind. With sufficient support it can continue to serve as an effective consumer voice at the CAB.

Conclusion

This chapter has made no attempt to minimize the hurdles and frustrations that are frequently encountered in seeking meaningful citizen access to the CAB. Nevertheless, some groups and individuals have been able to survive these obstacles and have had an important impact in moving the agency's orientation toward the interests of citizens and consumers. The highest level of success has been achieved by those who are aware of the realities of the game and who, just as industry does, bring to bear a variety of strategies designed to reinforce the desired objectives. Some of the strategies that should be considered are described below.

Members of the CAB have frequent informal meetings with airline and industry proponents to discuss their problems and desires, and they are frequently asked to address meetings or conventions of such people. Yet it is almost unheard of for consumers to call upon these officials to discuss consumer or public interest points of view. Indeed, the Board members live in virtual isolation in Washington, far from most of the people and communities affected by their actions, with personal contacts largely restricted to the inbred aviation fraternity. A visit to one or more of the Board members in Washington, or an invitation to address a community organization where you live, should be considered as strategies to help sensitize these public officials to the public's interests, and to heighten their responsiveness to consumers.

Experience has shown that there is no substitute for effective organization in attempting to get an agency to respond to citizen needs. There is definitely power in numbers, and the CAB, like other agencies, can be impressed when masses of people band together in a consumer demand. Thus it is very important for citizens to join with and support groups which have established expertise and effectiveness in dealing with the CAB, such as ACAP and CU. Similarly, getting hundreds or thousands of other people to sign a petition to the Board to write individual letters, as occured in the rule making proceeding on smoking in airplanes, is another important tactic.

One important problem deserves mention here. Groups seeking to distribute information to passengers about airline consumer issues, or to obtain their signatures on petitions, have been thrown out of airports and threatened with arrest, although such activities are entirely lawful under the U.S. Constitution. Thus the airlines have been able to prevent consumer groups from establishing effective communications with fellow passengers victimized by their unjust practices. Before you attempt such endeavors, it is a good idea to contact the airport authorities and find out what reasonable rules and regulations (e.g., obtaining a permit, agreeing to clean up litter, not obstructing traffic) may apply. If you are denied the right to engage in these activities, you may have to get a lawyer to bring suit for you.

One of the most effective strategies in dealing with the airlines and the CAB is publicity. If you have been defrauded, overcharged or otherwise abused, and the airline refuses to do anything about it, take the story to a newspaper or television reporter. A story chastising or criticizing either the company or the agency not only makes other citizens aware of the situation, but may even bring about swift remedial action to avoid any further exposure.

Direct action, such as peaceful picketing in front of an airline's office or headquarters, can do wonders in drawing public focus to a particular issue and the company's involvement. For example, in 1971 ACAP protested exclusion of the press and consumer groups from IATA's price fixing conferences by picketing in front of their convention in downtown Montreal. The result was to focus attention on these secret activities and to force the conference participants and officials into greater recognition of how their activities affect the public. Another form of direct action that could be used in some circumstances is a consumer boycott, in which public dissatisfaction with particularly recalcitrant conduct by an airline can be translated into a debit on its profit and loss statement.

It is important to send copies of complaints to your representatives in Congress, and it is also important in some cases to draw more deeply upon Congressional resources. For example, some Congressmen have become so outraged at CAB anticonsumer actions that they have brought suit—and won—in federal court [*Moss* v. *CAB*, 430 F.2d 891 (D.C. Cir. 1970)]. The possibility of a Congressional hearing at which he will be called upon to defend the agency's failure to protect the public can generate concern in any bureaucrat, and even a strong statement against the agency's inaction, reprinted in the Congressional

Record, can be helpful. Finally, some problems call for legislative reforms which will clarify the agency's duties and powers. A good illustration was provided in a bill sponsored by Senator Lee Metcalf (D-Mont.) which was enacted in 1972 as the Federal Advisory Committee Act [Public Law 92-463]. This law grew in part out of hearings chaired by Senator Metcalf in which abuses by the CAB, in setting up a "financial advisory committee" consisting of bankers and airline financial interests, and using it to provide secret high-level access to CAB officials, were disclosed. As a result of the Congressional pressure the committee was disbanded, and the 1972 law prohibits repetition of this pattern of special influence [see *Advisory Committees,* Hearings Before the Subcommittee on Intergovernmental Relations, Senate Government Operations Committee, Part 1 (1971)].

Citizen action advances with practice and persistence. Better and more effective ideas come forth from involvement and continual probing for the strategies to change conditions that restrain the just interests of the consumer. More citizens with these attitudes mean greater momentum for more responsive government at the CAB as well as other agencies.

Sample Complaint (Deceptive Practices)

CIVIL AERONAUTICS BOARD
WASHINGTON, D. C. 20428

AVIATION CONSUMER ACTION PROJECT,
 	
 and
 	
 CONSUMERS UNION OF UNITED STATES, INC.,
 	
                   Complainants,
 	
    v.
 	
 EASTERN AIR LINES, INC.,
 	
                   Petitioners.
	))))))))) Docket_____)))))))

VERIFIED COMPLAINT

Communications with respect
to this matter should be
addressed to:

Reuben B. Robertson, III
   1156 19th Street, N.W.
   Washington, DC 20036
   (202) 833 3400
Attorney for Aviation
   Consumer Action Project

Peter Schuck
   1714 Massachusetts Avenue,
   N.W.
   Washington, DC 20036
   (202) 785 1906
Attorney for Consumers Union
   of United States, Inc.

January 24, 1973

CIVIL AERONAUTICS BOARD
WASHINGTON, D. C. 20428

AVIATION CONSUMER ACTION PROJECT	)
and	)
CONSUMERS UNION OF UNITED STATES, INC.,	)
Complainants,	) Docket_____
v.	)
EASTERN AIR LINES, INC.,	)
Petitioners.	)

VERIFIED COMPLAINT

1. This complaint is filed pursuant to Section 1002
of the Federal Aviation Act and 14 CFR 302.201.

2. Complainant Aviation Consumer Action Project (ACAP)
is a non-profit corporation, existing under the laws of the
District of Columbia. ACAP is engaged in the advocacy of
consumer issues before the Civil Aeronautics Board and
other agencies and courts on behalf of its supporters.

3. Complainant Consumers Union of United States, Inc.
is a non-profit corporation, existing under the laws of
the State of New York. Consumers Union tests products and
services, disseminates consumer information, and represents its 350,000 members in administrative, judicial and,

upon invitation, legislative proceedings. It is the publisher of Consumer Reports, which has a paid circulation
of approximately 2.2 million.

4. Respondent Eastern Air Lines, Inc. is an air
carrier within the meaning of the Federal Aviation Act
and is subject to the jurisdiction of the Board.

5. Pursuant to Section 403(a) of the Federal Aviation Act, Eastern has filed with the Board tariffs setting
forth the rates, fares, and charges for certain passenger
service provided by it between Washington, New York/
Newark, and Boston known as air shuttle service. Among
other things, such tariffs include "family plan" fares,
applicable at all times except from 2:00 p.m. through
midnight each Friday and Sunday. Under the family plan,
a discount of 25 to 33 percent applies to the fare of
immediate family members accompanying a passenger who is
paying the full fare for such transportation.

6. Eastern does not in fact apply the family plan
fares to eligible members of families travelling together
on the air shuttle. Specific evidence of this is shown
in the attached copies of passenger tickets issued by
Eastern to supporters of ACAP for its air shuttle service
on November 20, 1972 (Attachment A). Although the family
plan fare was applicable, the full fare of $26.00 was
charged to both husband and wife, who were travelling
together and seated together on the aircraft. Eastern was
on notice that the passengers were eligible for the family

plan fare, in that both tickets were paid for with a credit card issued to the husband and the voucher in each case was signed by the wife. Eastern failed to notify these passengers of the existence or applicability of the family plan fares and failed to charge the correct amount for the transportation provided.

7. Eastern, either intentionally or negligently, overcharges many passengers on its air shuttle service in this manner. A survey made by Consumers Union, a summary of which is appended hereto (Attachment B), shows that Eastern has not adequately trained its employees with respect to the applicability of family plan fares, and that several married couples, interviewed at Eastern's terminal upon disembarkation from the air shuttle, indicated they had been charged the full fare rather than the family plan fares to which they were entitled.

8. Such acts and practices are in violation of Sections 403(b) and 404(a) of the Federal Aviation Act.

9. Supporters and members of ACAP and Consumers Union are adversely affected by the aforesaid acts and practices.

WHEREFORE, ACAP files this complaint and urges the Board to initiate an investigation and enforcement proceeding with respect to the alleged violations; to include within such proceeding the issues of whether Eastern systematically fails to apply applicable family plan fares for air shuttle and other services, and whether other

carriers are also engaged in such practices; to impose
appropriate sanctions, provided in the Federal Aviation
Act, with respect to such violations, including an order
requiring past overcharges to be refunded by the carrier.

                              Respectfully submitted,

                              Reuben B. Robertson, III
                              Attorney for Aviation
                              Consumer Action Project

                              Peter Schuck
                              Attorney for Consumers
                              Union of United States, Inc.

CIVIL AERONAUTICS BOARD
WASHINGTON, D. C. 20428

AVIATION CONSUMER ACTION PROJECT,   )
)
    and   )
)
CONSUMERS UNION OF UNITED STATES, INC.,   )
)
                Complainants,   ) Docket_____
)
    v.   )
)
EASTERN AIR LINES, INC.,   )
)
                Petitioners.   )

VERIFICATION

I, Reuben B. Robertson, III hereby depose and state
that I am an attorney for the complainant Aviation Consumer Action Project; that such organization is incorporated pursuant to the laws of the District of Columbia;
that I have read the foregoing complaint and know the
contents thereof; and that the matters therein stated are
true upon information and belief, and as to such matters
I believe them to be true.

_____

Subscribed and sworn to before
me, a Notary Public in and for
the District of Columbia, this
24th day of January, 1973.

_____

My Commission Expires:
January 14, 1977

CIVIL AERONAUTICS BOARD
WASHINGTON, D. C. 20428

AVIATION CONSUMER ACTION PROJECT,   )
)
    and   )
)
CONSUMERS UNION OF UNITED STATES, INC.,   )
)
                     Complainants,   ) Docket_____
)
    v.   )
)
EASTERN AIR LINES, INC.,   )
)
                     Petitioners.   )
)

VERIFICATION

I, Peter Schuck, hereby depose and state that I am attorney for the complainant Consumers Union of United States, Inc.; that such organization is incorporated pursuant to the laws of the State of New York; that I have read the foregoing complaint and know the contents thereof; and that the matters therein stated are true upon information and belief, and as to such matters I believe them to be true.

Subscribed and sworn to before
me, a Notary Public in and for
the District of Columbia, this
24th day of January, 1973.

My Commission Expires:
January 14, 1977

Sample Rule Making Petition
(On Handicapped Passengers)

BEFORE THE
CIVIL AERONAUTICS BOARD
WASHINGTON, D. C. 20428

In the Matter of Petition of   :
                                                :
AVIATION CONSUMER ACTION PROJECT   : Docket_____
                                                :
For Rulemaking to Prohibit Discrimination   :
In Air Transportation Against Physically   :
Disabled and Crippled Persons   :
                                                :

Communications with respect to this proceeding should be
addressed to:

> K.G.J. Pillai
> Aviation Consumer Action Project
> Post Office Box 19029
> Washington, D.C. 20036

PETITION

Aviation Consumer Action Project (ACAP) hereby
respectfully petitions the Civil Aeronautics Board, pursuant to Rule 38 of the Board's Rules of Practice in Economic Proceedings, 49 CFR 302.38, to institute a rulemaking proceeding addressed to the increasingly serious
and shocking problems of crippled and disabled persons
who are the victims of brutal, arbitrary and patently
discriminatory practices by certificated air carriers
under the CAB's jurisdiction. The existing pattern of
abuse is condoned and protected by the CAB through its
rubber stamp approval of carrier devised tariff rules,
regardless of how cruel or senseless they may be. The
CAB has a statutory duty to protect all citizens, including those of us who are crippled or physically disabled, from unjust discrimination in air transportation.
We respectfully urge the Board, by prompt investigation
and rulemaking, to fulfill this mandate and responsibility

to the public. Proposed rules to deal with carriers' obligations with respect to crippled and physically disabled persons are set forth in Appendix A to this Petition. Further facts and reasons demonstrating the urgent need for the enactment of such rules are contained below.

Aviation Consumer Action Project, petitioner herein, is a non-profit public interest organization founded for the purpose of advocating the interests of consumers and other members of the public in aviation matters, including regulatory proceedings before the C.A.B. It is financed exclusively by the voluntary donations of its supporters.

I. ARBITRARY REFUSALS TO TRANSPORT AND MISTREATMENT OF CRIPPLED AND PHYSICALLY DISABLED PERSONS ARE SERIOUS AND GROWING PROBLEMS IN THE AIRLINE INDUSTRY

ACAP has recently received several complaints from its supporters and others disclosing shocking and unconscionable instances of insulting, discriminatory and unjust treatment of crippled and disabled passengers by airlines. Often these unfortunate people are simply refused transportation, while sometimes they are carried only after being subjected to penalizing conditions. In large part the fate of such persons depends upon the idiosyncratic will or mood of the airline personnel with whom they come in contact.

The following bitter experience of one of ACAP's supporters is set forth to illustrate the kind of treatment that disabled persons frequently encounter.

During April, 1971 Mr. Ralf Hotchkiss, who is an engineer and writer, was engaged to be interviewed on a nationwide radio program of Canadian Broadcasting Company in Montreal. Mr. Hotchkiss is physically disabled and uses a wheelchair for personal conveyance. He made a reservation on Northeast Airlines flight 304 from Washington National Airport to Montreal.

Upon reaching the airport, however, Mr. Hotchkiss was informed by a Northeast ticket agent, Miss Latorri, that people in wheelchairs were never permitted to travel alone. He thought at first that she must have been joking and told her that what she said was ridiculous, since for years he personally had travelled by air throughout the United States without difficulty. When it appeared that the agent was serious, however, Mr. Hotchkiss then spoke to the Northeast station manager, Mr. Schaeffer, who was then serving as the boarding agent for flight 304.

Mr. Schaeffer stated to Mr. Hotchkiss that no one in a wheelchair was permitted to travel without an attendant. He was told that this "rule" had been forced on the airlines by the CAB; and that while the rule had been on the books for a long time, the airline had only recently (within the previous three or four weeks) sent orders for its enforcement, in fear of some crackdown (by the CAB, presumably).

Mr. Hotchkiss immediately recruited two young men also booked on flight 304 to serve in the embarrassing capacity of "attendants" to him for the flight. Mr. Schaeffer, the Northeast manager, spoke to them, however, to discourage them from accompanying Mr. Hotchkiss, and successfully convinced them that it would be wiser for them not to accept the grave responsibilities which would be involved.

Mr. Hotchkiss then left the Northeast gate, insulted and outraged by this incident. However, he was soon stopped by a small boy who had run after him and said that "lots of people" on the flight wanted to accompany him. He returned to find that at least one couple were in fact willing to volunteer for this duty.

Mr. Hotchkiss was then accepted for the flight, since the Northeast personnel apparently felt they had no alternative under their applicable "rule." The baggage personnel then took Mr. Hotchkiss' wheelchair to load it in the baggage compartment, while he proceeded to strap himself into one of the airlines' standard loading chairs. However, as he was being moved up the stairs onto the plane, someone apparently realized that the volunteer couple was getting off at Boston, while Mr. Hotchkiss had reservations to Montreal. He was then summarily removed from the plane, given back his wheelchair, and informed that there was no chance of his going to Montreal.

However, the airline personnel offered to telephone CBC in Montreal to cancel his appearance. They also called the other airlines serving Montreal, American and Eastern, and informed him that they were subject to the same rule and would not be allowed to take him, either.

When Mr. Hotchkiss demanded denied boarding compensation, he was informed by Mr. Schaeffer that it did not apply to him and would not be paid.

Mr. Hotchkiss asked Mr. Schaeffer to put in writing the reason he had been refused transportation by the carrier, but Mr. Schaeffer stated that he would not sign anything, and that the fact that Mr. Hotchkiss was still there at Washington would be "physical witness" to the facts. When Mr. Hotchkiss asked for an explanation of why new instructions had been issued not to admit wheel-chair riders, Mr. Schaeffer stated that it had been decided that "it had gone far enough." At this point, Mr. Schaeffer stated that if Mr. Hotchkiss had any more questions he should have his lawyer get in touch with Northeast Airlines' lawyer, but failed to state the name, address or other information regarding the company's lawyers. Mr. Schaeffer closed the conversation by stating that, "as of right now, no one here will answer any more questions whatsoever."

ACAP respectfully submits that incidents of this nature are absolutely unacceptable on the part of regulated common carriers. This incident speaks for itself with respect to the competence and responsibility of the management of the airline involved; but it is a parody of public law and an insult to the CAB that it could be attributed to the lawful mandate of a federal agency which is supposed to protect citizens. Unfortunately, this is not an isolated incident.

What is especially chilling is the fact that this kind of abuse appears to be growing more serious at precisely the time when the number of injured persons relying on airlines for public transportation is growing rapidly. Thousands of young American men are now returning home from military service in which they were permanently crippled or disabled. The sacrifices these men have already made in the service of their country must not now be compounded by the crude, arrogant behavior of airlines which care more for personal gain than public service. Additionally, the recent discontinuance of rail passenger service in many parts of the country leaves air travel as the only viable means of conveyance for many.

We urge the Board to take prompt action which will protect these people from such arbitrary and discriminatory treatment and will reaffirm the obligation of airlines to provide service for all persons.

ACAP will be willing to present the testimony of Mr. Hotchkiss and others who have had similar experiences before the Board, if necessary.

II. EXISTING TARIFF RULES OF AIRLINES CONCERNING THE TRANSPORTATION OF CRIPPLED AND DISABLED PERSONS ARE ARBITRARY AND UNREASONABLE

The right of physically disabled or crippled persons to travel by air is arbitrarily curtailed and circumscribed by a tariff rule formulated by the airlines and approved by the CAB. This rule (Rule 15, CAB No. 142; CTC (A) 53) purports to guarantee the right of airlines to "refuse" transportation on the ground of physical fitness of passengers. The relevant parts of Rule 15 read as follows:

"Rule 15. Refusal to Transport.

(A) Carrier will refuse to transport or will remove at any point, any passenger...

* * *

(2) Passenger's Conduct or Condition

whose conduct, status, age, or mental or physical condition is such as to...

(a) Render him incapable of caring for himself without assistance, unless...

(i) he is accompanied by an attendant who will be responsible for caring for him enroute, and

(ii) with the care of such attendant, he will not require unreasonable attention or assistance from employees of the carrier;

(b) Make such refusal or removal necessary for the reasonable safety or comfort of other passengers; or

(c) Involve any unusual hazard or risk to himself or to other persons...or to property.

(C) Liability

Carrier is not liable for its refusal to transport any passenger or for its removal of any passenger in accordance with the preceding paragraphs of this rule, but such carrier will, at the request of the passenger, refund in accordance with Rule 390 (Refund-Involuntary).

This unconscionable rule, insofar as it permits the airlines to refuse transportation to physically disabled passengers, should be removed from the files of the CAB. The rule requires such passengers not only to pay additional fares for "attendant(s)" but also to give assurance that they will not ask for "unreasonable attention or assistance" from carrier employees. One pertinent issue here is whether the employees of carriers, whose salaries are ultimately paid by passengers, are responsible for helping passengers in need of reasonable assistance for their transportation, or whether they should be principally employed for profit-making purposes such as the sale of sex appeal, alcohol, tobacco and duty-free goods. We believe that the employees have the primary responsibility to help physically disabled passengers. Again, crippled people, whose source of income is naturally limited, should not be asked to pay double fare--fares for passenger plus fare for attendant--for air transportation. The assessment of a double fare is discriminatory and probably illegal because a crippled passenger alone does not occupy more space in an airplane than any other passenger. Further, airlines have no right to require a crippled person to hire paid attendants when fellow passengers express willingness to help him or if he believes that someone will help him during the flight. At any rate, the airlines should not have the right to deny transportation to a crippled person by insisting that the same "attendant" should help such passenger both at the point of origin and at the point of destination.

Another obnoxious aspect of Rule 15 is the stipulation that carriers could refuse transportation to crippled persons on the ground of the "comfort" of other passengers. It is amazing that carriers can refuse transportation of disabled persons for the sake of comfort of other passengers while the same airlines habitually disregard the comfort of passengers who sit near chain-smokers. Another infirmity of Rule 15 is the provision which disqualifies crippled persons from the benefits of denied boarding compensation assured by Part 250 of the Board's Economic Regulations.

The conditions for international travel by physically handicapped persons are prohibitive, and the airlines discretion to refuse air transportation to such persons is absolute. For instance, one tariff rule reads as follows: "Pan American and Braniff will, upon advance arrangement and subject to the availability of space and appropriate equipment on interchange flights, accept an incapacitated passenger accompanied by an able bodied attendant who shall care for such passenger during the trip. The charge for the carriage of incapacitated passengers, including the attendant, will be as follows: On stretchers in Jet Aircraft: 4 normal all year adult first class fares." Tariff rule applicable for TWA flights will charge the stretcher passenger and attendant a total of "four one-way adult first class fares from origin to destination." These carriers' own tariff rules indicate that the stretcher passengers and disabled persons are charged arbitrary fares without giving due regard to the space occupied by those persons.

By contrast, "TWA will permit, on its international flights, the use of two seats for the single applicable adult fare, when a passenger, due to his size, requires the use of two seats exclusively for himself." Further, there are carriers operating on the same routes which carry disabled persons without surcharges. Thus BOAC will charge "the invalid passenger and each attendant... the normal fare for the journey to be undertaken according to the class of travel." TWA also stipulates that "stretcher passengers will not be accepted for trip of less than 700 miles" and that "only one stretcher passenger per flight [will be] accepted." It seems that in the case of international transportation these rules concerning stretcher passengers are also applicable to physically disabled, crippled or infirm persons who use wheelchairs or other supporting instruments. It is just incredible that the CAB approved these whimsically stupid rules formulated by ruthless profiteers in air transportation.

III.   CARRIERS' TARIFF RULES CONCERNING TRANS- PORTATION OF PHYSICALLY DISABLED PERSONS ARE ILLEGAL UNDER THE FEDERAL AVIATION ACT

The tariff rules of airlines governing transportation of physically disabled persons which purport to grant the carriers broad rights to deny transportation, totally without standards or recourse, are illegal under the Federal Aviation Act of 1958. Section 404(a) (49 U.S.C. 1374) of the Act provides that "it shall be the duty of every air carrier to provide and furnish interstate and overseas air transportation, as authorized by its certificate, upon reasonable request therefor, ...and to establish...just and reasonable classification, rules, regulations and practices relating to such air transportation...." Rule 15 of CAB No. 142 not only disregards the admonition contained in section 404(a) but also violates the various provisions of the Act which prohibit unjust discrimination (e.g., Sections 404(b); 102(c)).

The Act never authorized the carriers to refuse transportation on the grounds of passengers' body shape or physical condition. The only ground on which an air carrier
is authorized to refuse transportation is safety as
specified in section 1111 (49 U.S.C. 1511). Further, we
submit that a government action permitting the exclusion
of persons from the use of a common carrier facility on
the grounds of physical infirmity amounts to the denial of
equal protection of the law prohibited by the United States
Constitution.

WHEREFORE, for all the foregoing reasons the Aviation
Consumer Action Project requests that the Board institute
a rulemaking proceeding to guarantee the right of disabled persons to travel by air, without being subject to
arbitrary discretion or conditions imposed by air carriers,
and grant such other and further relief as may be appropriate. ACAP or one or more of its supporters may, at a
future date, supplement the recommendations presented
herewith.

Respectfully submitted,

AVIATION CONSUMER ACTION PROJECT

By: /s/ K.G.J. Pillai
K.G.J. Pillai

/s/ Reuben B. Robertson
Reuben B. Robertson, III

June 4, 1971

APPENDIX A

PROPOSED RULE REGARDING TRANSPORTATION
OF DISABLED PERSONS BY AIR

(1) DEFINITIONS. For purpose of this part, a
"DISABLED PERSON" means a person who is physically disabled, retarded, infirm, invalid, crippled or otherwise
incapacitated to travel without the aid and help of airline employees or attendants, whether or not such person
is in a wheelchair or stretcher during or prior to flight.

(2) CONDITIONS FOR CARRIAGE

(a) It shall be the duty of every air carrier
to provide and furnish, upon reasonable request, interstate and overseas air transportation for disabled persons.

(b) The fares, rates and charges to be received
as compensation by the air carrier for transportation
furnished in accordance with paragraph (a) of this section
shall not exceed the fares, rates and charges normally
received by such carrier from able bodied persons for the
same or identical transportation.

(c) In case an attendant accompanies the disabled person to take care of the latter aboard the plane,
the carrier shall provide transportation for such attendant after receiving one-half of the fare paid by the
disabled passenger, as compensation for such transportation.

(d) It shall be the primary responsibility of
every employee of the air carrier to render all reasonable
and required help to a disabled passenger at the origin,
stopover and destination points and aboard the aircraft
at no additional cost to such disabled passenger.

(3) The provisions of this rule shall be equally
applicable to each domestic carrier and any carrier which
provides and furnishes foreign transportation and which is
authorized to serve any point in the United States by
virtue of a foreign air carrier permit issued by the Board.

(4) In addition to the penalties otherwise provided
for by the Federal Aviation Act, any carrier employee involved in the violation of any provision of this part
shall be subject to a fine of not exceeding $1000 for
each such violation.

CHAPTER 11

THE FOOD AND
DRUG ADMINISTRATION

> *The thing that bugs me is that the people*
> *think the FDA is protecting them—it isn't.*
> *What the FDA is doing and what the public*
> *thinks it's doing are as different as night and*
> *day.*
> —Dr. Herbert L. Ley, Jr., former Commissioner
> of the Department of Health, Education
> and Welfare's Food and Drug Administration,
> *The New York Times*, 31 December 1969

People may not have a clear idea of exactly what the Food and Drug Administration (FDA) does, but they are now probably less inclined to assume that the FDA is watching over the safety and quality of everything they eat or take to make themselves feel better. The FDA is part of the Department of Health, Education, and Welfare. The reported slips, such as contaminated intravenous fluids, and the agency's tendency to delay action against such chronic hazards as PCBs, DES, and hexachlorophene, should be enough to disabuse anyone of that comforting notion. And many of the hazards which have come to FDA's attention would have gone unnoticed if outsiders had not determinedly brought them to the fore. It is this sort of citizen participation that can multiply the effectiveness of the Administration's small work force, as well as countering the pressure which industry lobbyists can bring to bear. But it must be knowledgeable to be effective, and the purpose of this chapter is to provide you with the basis for such knowledge.

To begin with, the FDA regulates the safety and quality of much more than just foodstuffs and pharmaceuticals. A complete list of the products under its jurisdiction would look like an inventory of a one-stop shopping center, since it also includes cosmetics and medical devices. But not all federal regulation of food quality is carried out by the FDA; meat inspection, meat quality grading, and standards for meat products are regulated by the Department of Agriculture (see Chapter

12). The FDA's varied jurisdiction has resulted from the grafting of a whole series of statutes on the Food, Drug and Cosmetic Act of 1938. These include the Food Additives Amendment of 1958, the Color Additive Amendments of 1960, the Kefauver Drug Amendments of 1962, and the Animal Drug Amendments of 1968. Other statutes administered in whole or in part by FDA are the Import Milk Act, the Filled Milk Act, the Import Tea Act, the Federal Caustic Poison Act, Sections of the Public Health Service Act, and the Fair Packaging and Labeling Act of 1965. The newest statute to be administered by FDA is the Drug Listing Act of 1972, Public Law 92-387. The FDA is a part of the Department of Health, Education, and Welfare (HEW), and is thus a "line" agency of the Executive Branch, rather than being an independent regulatory commission.

FDA resources do not begin to match its statutory responsibilities. For fiscal year 1973, FDA sought $144 million to administer the statutes enumerated above, plus the three statutes (the Poison Prevention Packaging Act of 1970, 15 U.S.C. 1471; the Federal Hazardous Substances Act, 15 U.S.C. 1261; and the Flammable Fabrics Act, 15 U.S.C. 1191) whose administration has been transferred to the new Consumer Product Safety Commission (CPSC) by the Consumer Product Safety Act of 1972, PL 92-573 (see Chapter 17). To administer these programs FDA requested 6,216 positions. President Nixon has vetoed the HEW appropriations bill twice. (Note: FDA sought $18 million and 1,127 positions to administer "consumer product safety programs," i.e., those now transferred to the new Commission. In the past few years the FDA has spent much of its time in reorganizing and re-reorganizing itself, with considerable energy and money going for transfers of people and offices from Washington to field offices and back again.)

The FDA allocates its resources like a fireman, racing from one crisis to another, often leaving fundamental problems smoldering to present new crises. The list of crisis efforts includes pesticides in cranberries, panalba (drug), cyclamates, vichyssoisse, hexachlorophene, mercury levels in fish, and hazardous toys. In addition to preventing a rational and well-planned program, this crisis orientation has become so embedded in the FDA that very little is done about a problem unless a public alarm is raised. There is considerable internal rivalry between competing regulatory programs, such as food regulation and drug regulation, for the use of limited money, personnel, and laboratories. In one way this crisis orientation and internal rivalry presents an opportunity for citizen access. At least it indicates some willingness to respond to public initiative, instead of the massive bureaucratic indifference which characterizes some other agencies.

FDA Activities

Although the FDA's legal authority and responsibility is a mass of legislative accretion, its activities can be divided into seven general areas. These are:

1. Establishing mandatory standards of identity, quality, and quantity for foods.
2. Regulating the safety of food additives.
3. Safety regulation of artificial colors added to foods, drugs, and cosmetics.
4. Enforcing the Fair Packaging and Labeling Act provisions which apply to food, drugs, devices, and cosmetics.
5. Regulating cosmetics, drugs, and devices, which includes insuring that drugs, cosmetics, and devices are not adulterated or misbranded, and that new drugs be shown to be safe and effective prior to marketing.
6. Regulating vaccines, blood and other biological products (a function transferred in July 1972 from the National Institutes of Health to FDA).
7. Regulating animal drug safety.

The tools for consumers to use in influencing FDA action in these areas are limited, but they have been effective in the past, and can be made more effective in the future. The most important opportunities are presented by the procedures which the FDA must follow in promulgating regulations. These procedures provide for the right of any interested party to initiate, comment, and participate in hearings on any proposed regulation.

In addition to working through the formal procedures for establishing regulations, consumer groups should make contact with FDA district offices to assist them in, and prod them into, eliminating violations of existing food and drug laws. The Administration maintains nineteen district offices, ninety-seven resident inspector posts, and a staff of consumer specialists, at least one of whom is stationed in each district office. Appendix 11-B (p. 660) contains a list of the FDA district offices. Informal contact is a necessary prerequisite for formal participation, and the best place for you to start with the FDA is to get in touch with the nearest local office. In its responses to questions from Senator Kennedy's Subcommittee on Administrative Practice and Procedure, the FDA said that it encourages members of the public to contact its local offices about unsatisfactory food, drugs, cosmetics, or devices in the marketplace. Collecting and presenting such complaints to the FDA local offices is a first step for you to get to know about FDA, and also a way of establishing your status with the FDA as a concerned citizen. In addition to correcting some marketplace deficiencies, such activity can provide you with the background and familiarity with administrative procedures which can be useful in participating at a higher level.

The basic information which you need to participate in FDA proceedings is in Title 21 of the Code of Federal Regulations (C.F.R.). The C.F.R. can be found in most law school libraries, but if you are going to be dealing with the FDA on a regular basis it is probably better to buy the paperbound volumes from the Government Printing Office (G.P.O.). The total cost of the five parts of 21 C.F.R. is $8.10. To keep up with the FDA's activities, start with *FDA Consumer,* a magazine which FDA publishes monthly, with news about its current activities. Among other things it contains the monthly lists of food products and drugs which have been recalled. This can also be ordered from the G.P.O. for $3.50 per year. *The Chemical Feast,* by James S. Turner (New York: Grossman Publishers, 1970, 95 cents), the Ralph Nader Study Group Report on Food Protection and the FDA, is an essential source of information up to 1970. The Health Research Group, 2000 P Street, N.W., Washington, D.C., should be contacted for materials on FDA since 1970.

The FDA Public Information Office is another source of information. Ask to be put on the FDA mailing list for all news releases, "fact sheets," speeches by FDA officials, and the current directory of state food and drug officials. Sooner or later it will probably be necessary for you to get information from the FDA by phone, and a current telephone directory for the agency will speed up the process. The FDA directory is part of the Department of Health, Education, and Welfare Telephone Directory, which costs $2.75 (Fall 1972 edition) from the G.P.O. (Catalog number HE-1.28:972). Commerce Clearing House, a private publisher of topical law reports (4025 W. Peterson Avenue, Chicago, Ill. 60646) has two specialized services for attorneys: the *Food, Drug, and Cosmetic Law Journal* and the *Food, Drug, and Cosmetic Law Reports.* These are relatively expensive ($20 and $335 per year) but are useful if you can find them in a law library. Two good trade journals in the field are *Food Chemical News,* and FDC Reports ("The Pink Sheet"), although both are expensive ($175 and $180 per year). Of course, the *Federal Register* is the daily official notice to the world of what the FDA and the other federal administrative agencies are doing. A subscription costs only $25 per year and is a necessity for any consumer groups attempting to monitor Federal administrative agencies. The *Federal Register* traditionally has maintained a rather dry and foreboding appearance and has been written in technical language. Recent changes, however, should help make it comprehensible to consumers. The most important change is that effective 3 January 1973 a preamble is required in each proposed rule making and final rule making document "that describes the contents of the document in a manner sufficient to apprise a reader who is not an expert on the subject area of the general subject matter of the document."

The FDA has been less than enthusiastic about following the policy of the Freedom of Information Act (FOIA), despite the official statement that HEW policy "is one of the fullest responsible disclosure limited only by the obligations of confidentiality and the Administration necessities recognized by the Act" [45 C.F.R. 5.12]. For example, in one instance records which had been freely available for public inspection and copying when in the custody of the National Commission on Product Safety were restricted after this temporary Commission completed its term and the files were turned over to FDA. The FDA proposed new FOIA regulations on 4 May 1972, and they are claimed to indicate a less restrictive attitude toward release of information. Requests for information should be made under these new regulations and perhaps some information will be now available (5600 Fishers Lane, Rockville, Md. 20852). FDA channels requests for significant information through the Associate Commissioner for Compliance.

Complaining to the FDA

The simplest thing to do with a government agency is to complain, and the FDA has indicated that it wants to hear complaints. In responding to questions from the Kennedy Subcommittee on Administrative Practice and Procedure, the FDA said: "Consumer complaints are one of the principal sources of FDA intelligence. The subject matter of these complaints runs the gamut from drug reactions and food 'poisonings' to filth in foods and economic problems." Since the FDA claims to rely on this type of information, a basic form of citizen participation is for you and any consumer group to which you belong to provide consumer complaints on a regular and extensive basis. Appendix 11-A (p. 658) offers some guidelines for reporting to the FDA.

Since the FDA primarily regulates foods and drugs, you and all members of your group should make it a routine practice to examine every food or drug product purchased. This habit will add only a few minutes to each trip, but it could provide the information for an effective consumer complaint to the FDA. The Administration says that it urges consumers to evaluate product information and to write or call FDA district offices if they find FDA-regulated products that are "deficient or unsatisfactory in any way." Take them up on it!

But don't limit your information to the complaints that you and other members have. Devise some way to collect and process the complaints of other people in your community. One way is to establish a telephone number to which dissatisfied consumers can report their experiences. Make copies of a simple form to record information uniformly and make it more useful, and set up a schedule of people to answer the phone. Concentrating on such complaints can lead to more popular support and greater effectiveness for your efforts.

The FDA has a well-established routine for dealing with consumer complaints. As it was described in response to questions of the Administrative Practices and Procedure Subcommittee, there are six steps in its complaint-processing procedure:

1. A call or letter is received by headquarters or one of our field offices.

It is important to establish liaison with the field office through routine inquiries before making the "call or letter" with the information you have collected. Phone calls of importance should be followed up by letters recording their contents.

2. A preliminary evaluation of the complaint is made to expedite those which may involve serious health hazards.

In complaining to the FDA, you should include an opinion about the hazardous nature or deceptiveness of the product and, if possible, get some expert opinion to support it. Insist on a prompt response explaining how serious the FDA feels the complaint is and why. Complaints are rarely dismissed openly as being worthless. Instead, they are ignored or referred or studied to death. If the agency refuses to explain the action it has taken—or refuses to take any action—that refusal itself can become an issue on which your group can take action. If the complaint is ignored or rejected, take it to the Commissioner of FDA, the Assistant Secretary for Health of HEW, the Secretary of HEW, *and above all, write to your own Congressman and Senators.*

If the complaint is serious and the supporting information well-prepared, these other routes may force the FDA to act. The press and consumer organizations should also be notified.

3. Complaints of a general nature are answered by the headquarters staff or field offices. Those relating to specific products are referred to the field office nearest the consumer's residence.

Include in the complaint an evaluation as to whether it is of "a general nature" or one "relating to specific products," and present whatever evidence there is for the classification. Then follow the complaint through the various administrative channels which precede the FDA's decision on whether to act on the complaint nationally or locally. If the FDA decides to act nationally, insist on being informed at every stage on all details in order to evaluate the effectiveness of the FDA action. The FDA may have good reasons for an action such as referring the matter to a field office. But explaining such reasons is a part of FDA's job, and you should insist on such an explanation.

4. The field office evaluates the complaint and responds to the consumer. In many cases, an FDA inspector may contact the consumer directly for additional information. If in the course of the investigation, a sample is collected from the consumer, a report of analysis will be furnished on request.

In collecting the information to present a complaint, get as many samples as possible of food, drugs, labeling, advertising, and other supporting information. If photocopies can be made, include them with the complaint. Descriptions of items which cannot be included with the complaint should be attached to the complaint. If the complaint is about the purity or safety of a product, ask for an analysis. But when you ask for an FDA analysis, try to get another analysis from an independent source. Often university scientists will be willing to help in such cases, and in some communities there are independent laboratories that charge for basic analysis. Sometimes these charges are modest enough to be acceptable for a small consumer group (see Appendices 18-B, p. 904, and 18-C, p. 910 for other possible sources of technical assistance). Ask to meet with the FDA inspector handling the complaint.

5. When all the facts are collected and the investigation is complete, the Agency, through the field office, decides on the appropriate response.

The FDA has a wide range of possible sanctions from which to choose. It can send a warning letter to a firm or individual; the products involved can be seized or recalled; the product can be banned from shipment in interstate commerce; in serious cases the individuals responsible can be fined or jailed; or the FDA may do nothing at all.

6. The complaint and the answer are filed for further reference.

Such files can be important sources of future action by the FDA. They are also important to a complaining group, which should maintain its own file of complaints and answers. In the FDA's own words: "The analysis of consumer complaints can provide trends which may indicate a need for a change in Agency policy or perhaps introduction of new legislation relating to a particular problem." Getting access to FDA complaint files under the FOIA might be useful in discovering areas in which action should be taken, but has not.

In summary, gather as much information as you can to present a well-documented complaint to the FDA. The complaint should include:

1. A specific statement of the abuse in the marketplace.
2. Detailed evidence, including samples of advertising, labels, and other documentary support for the complaint, and descriptions of product samples supporting the complaint (always indicating when and where supporting evidence was obtained).
3. An assessment of the seriousness of the complaint, and whether it involves a health or economic issue.
4. Whether the issue is general in nature or about a specific product in a local area.
5. A request to meet with an FDA inspector for analysis of the product involved.
6. A request to be kept informed about the progress of the complaint through the FDA decision making process.

Using the complaint mechanism this way, backed up by solid evidence and followed up by periodic inquiry, may begin to move the FDA to more vigorous consumer protection. It will also reveal in detail exactly where internal agency weaknesses lie and where major restructuring of the food and drug laws is needed. In this way the complaint process offers an opportunity not only for correcting individual abuses, but also for showing where energies for regulatory and legislative change can best be spent.

Public Information

When the Kennedy Subcommittee asked the FDA: "What attempts are made to solicit views of affected groups that otherwise might not become involved in the administrative process on their own initiative?" the response was, "Considerable publicity (press releases and 'items' in the trade press) have offered the opportunity for organizations, other than these [advisory] committees, and the general public to become involved in the work of FDA by expressing their views where applicable." So don't be shy about expressing your opinion to the FDA about one of their news releases—it is an invitation to comment. The FDA also uses fact sheets, radio and television spots, films, slide shows, exhibits, and workshops in an effort to "promote citizen and industry awareness of its activities." A tremendous amount of information, and sometimes misinformation, comes from the FDA's Public Information Office. It is important to collect, review, and criticize this material, because it can be either an important method of consumer protection or a public relations scheme for disguising inaction. Let the FDA know if it has prepared good information which answers important questions accurately. When the information is biased, inaccurate, or incomplete, be persistent until you find out what you want to know.

The FDA also claims that "one of the methods now being used to improve communications with the public is through a continuous review of consumer questions—whether these are presented at consumer conferences around the country or through consumer mail. This provides a guide to the information gaps that may exist, and we are able to tailor educational materials to meet the need." Just as with consumer complaints, the questions presented to the FDA and the answers given by the agency should be made public. A review of this material might be useful in locating specific consumer concerns and FDA responses to them.

During the last three years the FDA also "has developed a program of industry workshops" designed to explain and discuss, in depth, problems and possible solutions with various industry groups. Find out when these are being held and go to them. While such conferences often have huge fees, you can frequently get in free or for a nominal sum if you contact the sponsoring organization and explain your financial position. There is no reason why federal tax money should be used to run exclusive workshops designed to smooth the way for industry. Press the FDA to hold consumer workshops and joint consumer-industry workshops. Such workshops could bring consumers into direct confrontation with industry spokesmen, and representatives of the two groups sitting in the same room might work out some new solutions to problems.

Information Policies of the FDA

When the FOIA was signed into law, President Johnson said: "No one should be able to pull curtains of secrecy around decisions which can be revealed without injury to the public interest." The Food, Drug, and Cosmetic Act, 21 U.S.C. 331(j), from which the FDA gets its primary operating authority, prohibits "[t]he. . .revealing, other than to the Secretary or officers or employees of the Department, or to the courts when relevant in any judicial proceeding under 'this chapter,' any information. . .concerning any method or process which as a trade secret is entitled to protection," and Section 303(a) [21 U.S.C. 333(a)] provides that anyone violating this prohibition can be fined $1,000, or sentenced to prison for one year, or both.

On 5 May 1972 the FDA published in the *Federal Register* proposed regulations to amend its present regulations on public disclosure of information. Supposedly most of what has previously been withheld would now be opened to the public; in fact, huge areas of secrecy remain. The regulations would:

1. Make public safety and effectiveness data for food additives, color additives, and antibiotic drugs, but not make them available for new drugs.
2. Require manufacturers to identify and justify all claims of confidentiality for data previously submitted to FDA in support of the marketing of a new drug. Such identification and justification would be required with each new application.
3. Make public all adverse reaction and complaint data which has been submitted to the Agency as required by law. Data not required by law and voluntarily submitted will also be available

(*HEW News,* U.S. Department of Health, Education, and Welfare, Public Health Service, Food and Drug Administration, Thursday, 4 May 1972).

Confronted with a statutory mandate for disclosure of government information and criminal penalties for disclosing vaguely defined "trade secrets," most FDA personnel are cautious about what is released. The information policies of the FDA have been restrictive and they should be a primary target for your efforts. The FOIA, and tactics to use in applying it, are described in Chapter 3. Regulations issued under the Act by HEW which apply to the FDA are located at 45 C.F.R. 5.1 *et seq.* The requirements for withholding information by the FDA are located at 21 C.F.R. 4.1. These have been amended as of March 1973.

Acting under these regulations, the FDA keeps secret an enormous amount of information about potential threats to the public health. All information contained in New Drug Applications, Food Additive Petitions, investigative files on food and drug firms, and the results of studies conducted by FDA scientists or under FDA contracts currently is routinely withheld. In trying to get information from the FDA, it is important to remember that at least three categories may be involved:

1. Information which FDA officials are prohibited from releasing.
2. Information which they are required to release.
3. Some information which may or may not be released, as the FDA decides.

It is essential that these distinctions be kept clearly in mind when seeking information. Different kinds of arguments must be used depending on the class into which the information falls, or which the FDA claims it falls.

If the FDA claims that it is prohibited from releasing the information you want, the counterargument is that it does not fall into the prohibited class. If the FDA claims that the information sought is exempt from disclosure on the basis of the FOIA, there are two possible responses. One is to argue that the information is not within the class of material exempt from disclosure pursuant to the FOIA. Even if the material is exempt, the other response is to argue that the FOIA does not compel the use of a relevant exemption, and an argument may be made that release is in the public interest.

Unfortunately, HEW regulations implementing the FOIA blur the distinctions between information prohibited from release and information which may be exempt at the FDA's discretion:

> . . .kinds of material which are exempt from mandatory disclosure. . .[r]especting Food and Drug Administration regulatory activities: Trade secrets or commercial or confidential information [This is a subtle but important change from the Food and Drug Act prohibition on the release of "any method or process which as a trade secret is entitled to protection"], voluntarily revealed in requests for opinions and related records indicating that a person, firm or product is or is not in compliance with the law; records relating to factory inspections, sample collections, seafood inspection, and other examinations and investigations by the Food and Drug Administration; Investigational New Drug files; New Drug Applications and master files other than final printed labeling; report and records relating to individual adverse drug reaction(s) data in support of petitions relating to pesticide chemicals, food standards, food additives, and color additives, and master files relating thereto; files relating to certification of insulin, antibiotics, and color additives, and master files relating thereto; notices of hearings issued to individuals and firms under 21 U.S.C. 335 and records related thereto; records relating to. . .regulatory activities of the Food and Drug Administration. Note: Certain documents in some of the above files may be available upon request identifying the particular documents. [45 C.F.R. 5 Appendix A(11)]

This regulation is relied on to justify the withholding of nearly all information obtained by the FDA while conducting its regulatory mission. The note assumes that in all but a very few cases information will be withheld. This situation presents two important tactical considerations.

The first is that requests for information must be properly prepared, presented, and followed up administratively in order to lay a foundation for possible court appeals. The procedure to be followed in making a request for information is set forth in detail in Sections 5.51 to 5.53 and 5.80 to 5.85 of the regulations [45 C.F.R.]. Briefly, the steps to be followed are:

1. Oral requests for information which are denied must be put in writing immediately and sent to the official making the oral denial.
2. The written request should identify the requested records by

brief descriptions including the name, number or date, and any other information sufficient to identify and locate them.

3. Ask what the fee for searching and copying in providing the documents (in accordance with Subpart E of Appendix F) will be.

4. If the denial of the request is made in writing instead of orally, it should be received within thirty days.

5. A request for review of a denial must be in writing, and a decision reviewing the denial is supposed to be "promptly communicated" to the person requesting it.

At this point the stage has been properly set for appeal to the courts.

The second consideration presented by the FDA's intransigence is that obtaining information often becomes a major campaign in itself. Such a campaign may be costly in time, energy, and money. The potential cost should be estimated before getting deeply involved in the battle, and that cost should be weighed against other alternatives. Sometimes a choice must be made as to whether the information is essential to the effort; sometimes the choice is between getting the information (while conceding the FDA's authority to withhold it) and waging a costly battle to establish your right to it.

The Personal Touch:
Liaison with the FDA Staff

An informal but fundamental method of dealing with the FDA is to maintain regular personal contact with the local, regional, and (whenever necessary and possible) national staffs. You or a member of your group should begin by making an appointment with the regional director or resident inspector closest to you. The purpose of the meeting should be to explain to the official what you intend to do and what you expect the FDA to do, and to assess the FDA's response to you.

Each FDA district office has a district director in overall charge of activities in the district. Although he has some autonomy in making decisions for his district, in the final analysis he is responsible to the Washington headquarters. He does have the opportunity to make quarterly and annual reports in which he can comment critically about the support he and his district activities have been receiving. For example, the district directors have been very critical of the Washington staff for placing food supply sanitation low on the list of food protection goals. If a citizens group can raise and document a serious complaint and convince the district director of its importance, it gives him more of an opportunity to influence the FDA headquarters staff. Once a vigorous, well-organized, and effective citizen action group is established, reporting on it is likely to become a regular feature of the district director's reports to Washington.

The district staffs also include inspectors and chemists, who are the front line of the FDA, but who are likely to be restricted by the orders of their superiors. The inspectors do both food and drug inspections, looking for violations of the law in the marketplace, insuring that recalls are carried out as required, and generally acting as the policemen of retail sales. The chemists work in district laboratories, testing samples brought in by the inspectors for trace elements or other adulterants, evaluating contents of products against the claims on the label, and conducting other routine chemical analyses to insure that the products regulated by the FDA meet legal requirements. Arrange with the district director to visit the laboratories and accompany an inspector on routine rounds to learn how these key people do their jobs. Find out what equipment or other support the chemists and inspectors need to carry out their jobs, and try to help them obtain this equipment. District offices often can improve their activity just by getting the necessary equipment.

Two other FDA officials in each district office should also be contacted. One is the consumer consultant and the other is the science adviser. The consumer consultant or specialist has the job of explaining FDA activities to consumer and community groups and coordinating joint efforts with them. The science adviser is a part-time consultant to the FDA who usually works one day a week in the FDA district laboratory, with the objective of improving the quality of the scientific work done there. Among other things, he reviews the working methods of the chemists, evaluates the equipment needs of the laboratories, and reviews any proposed scientific writings by FDA district scientists. He is usually a laboratory scientist from a local university, and as such has a commitment to both the FDA and the community. He often has important information about the way in which the district laboratory carries out its mission and what needs to be done to improve it. If either of these posts is vacant in a district, find out why and demand that it be filled. The consumer specialist and the science adviser are two of the most important people in maintaining communications between the FDA and the community which it serves.

There are only nineteen district offices of the FDA, but there are ninety-seven resident inspector posts. A resident post usually has one or two inspectors who serve in a subdistrict office, located in a city other than the one containing the district office. The inspectors in these posts have much the same relationship with the district office that the district office has with the Washington headquarters. Such inspectors should be approached in much the same way that district directors are approached, except that more routine liaison with these offices is sometimes required to insure that their work is not lost in the longer bureaucratic channels through which they must go. A report for a resident inspector must go to the district for action. If it is to be acted upon at that level, it often must go to Washington before action is taken. This leads to great delay, lost reports, or even complete disregard of recommendations originating outside the district office.

The ease with which the resident inspector's work can be sidetracked is a major obstacle. Close liaison—calling on a weekly or daily basis to discover what action is being taken—can help speed up communication.

Although it can be useful, you should not be content with quiet behind-the-scenes action. When a meeting is arranged with FDA officials about an important subject, a press release should be prepared about the meeting and its significance. See Appendix 11-C, p. 662. If, after some effort, it is discovered that officials are dragging their feet or ignoring important issues, that should be called to the attention of the press.

Advisory Committees

According to the FDA, "The members of the various advisory committees are primarily citizen scientists, mostly from universities and non-profit research institutions. . . .[T]hey are advisory committees, not executive committees. . . .[F]actors other than purely their scientific findings may have to be considered by him [the Commissioner] in making judgments." As of 1 February 1973 the FDA had established thirty-eight permanent advisory committees, and was authorized by the Secretary of HEW to establish three more. These committees provide massive amounts of information for the Commissioner of FDA to use in making his decisions, and the information is given special weight as an expression of disinterested scientific expertise. Because of this, it is essential to monitor their activities to insure that they include representation of all sides in the many controversial scientific issues which they consider.

Such monitoring should be somewhat easier with passage of the Federal Advisory Committee Act, P.L. 92-463. Section 10 of this Act sets forth the requirements for advisory committee procedures, including a requirement that "each advisory committee meeting shall be open to the public," unless the meeting is determined in writing by the President or agency head to be "concerned with matters listed in Section 552(b) of Title 5, United States Code" (the FOIA). Another important provision of this Act is the requirement in Section 11 that "except where prohibited by contractual agreements entered into prior to the effective date of this Act, agencies and advisory committees shall make available to any person, *at actual cost,* copies of transcripts of agency proceedings or advisory committee meetings." This provision, if complied with, should end the practices of agencies making transcripts available only through private contractors at prohibitive costs of from 75 cents a page.

The advisory committees cover many different topics. In the medical field these have included a Medical Advisory Board, a Cardiovascular and Renal Disorder Advisory Committee, and a Drug Experience Advisory Committee. Others have been the Food Standards Advisory Committee, the Protocols for Safety Evaluation Advisory Committee, the Research in the Biological and Physical Sciences Advisory Committee, the Safety of Pesticide Residues in Food Advisory Committee, and the Advisory Committee on Veterinary Medicine. As their titles indicate, these committees play a vital role in the FDA regulatory process; unfortunately, that role is almost invisible. It is essential to learn when, where, and why an advisory committee of concern to you is meeting. The *Federal Register's* "Highlights" section lists the meetings about a week in advance. Since most of these are held in the Washington area, you may want to encourage a Washington consumer group to attend a particularly important meeting. For example, when a group of women concerned about the effects of birth control pills located the meeting of the FDA advisory committee considering the question, they arranged to attend the meeting and raised some important questions. The experience of seeing the advisory committee at work enabled them to sharpen their arguments about the pill and to raise the credibility of their attack on inadequate warnings. The result was much stronger action by the FDA in informing pill users of dangerous side effects than would have been taken if the FDA had followed the usual process of arriving at its decision in bureaucratic silence.

The most important advisory committee for consumers is the National Advisory Food and Drug Council. The FDA decided that the members of this group "should represent collectively the areas of science, industry, consumer groups, law, medicine, pharmacy, veterinary medicine, education, agriculture, communications, labor, government, voluntary health organizations, and women's organizations." Its seventeen members are invited to present prepared statements on what their colleagues expect from the FDA. At their meetings they have considered such issues as the FDA's international role, its role in the poverty program, food standards, new drug applications, and enforcement of the Fair Packaging and Labeling Act. The Council officially alerts the FDA to the views of organized groups concerned with FDA activities. Unfortunately, meetings of the Council have often been one-sided attempts by the FDA to get endorsements for programs already decided upon.

Ask your district office for information about this Council—how it functions, when it meets, how its members are chosen, and how to obtain copies of its minutes. Then convey any information you have to the Council, particularly to the consumer representative, if there is one at the time, and try to participate in naming the members. Since the FDA professes to learn consumer opinion through the Council, it should be willing to listen to consumers' opinions about how it is composed and how it works.

Other advisory committees should be approached in the same manner. Many of them deal with topics on which lay consumers are perfectly qualified to comment, such as food standards. Even the committees dealing with purely technical and scientific data should not be totally isolated from consumer opinion. The consumer role in relation to these committees should be to insure that scientists with proper credentials and the confidence of the consuming public are appointed to them. One or two seats on each committee should be reserved for representatives chosen by members of the consuming public. The number of scientists raising serious questions of safety and quality about foods and drugs today is large enough for there to be scientists qualified to present all sides of each scientific debate for each committee.

There is also now an informal FDA ad hoc Consumer Representative Committee which meets monthly in Washington, D.C., to discuss current regulatory issues. Among the issues discussed have been nitrates and nitrites and the GRAS (Generally Recognized As Safe Recognized) list review, etc. In February 1973 this group won the right to nominate six qualified scientists to six scientific panels reviewing the safety of food additives. The review is being conducted by the Federation of American Societies of Experimental Biology, under FDA contract.

Rule Making

An important procedure for influencing the FDA, and one which offers a wide range of possible participation, is the process by which FDA establishes a regulation.

Rule making under the Food, Drug, and Cosmetic Act is of two types—formal (rule making on a record after opportunity for a trial-type agency hearing) and informal (rule making after notice and opportunity for interested persons to participate through "submission of written data, views or arguments, with or without opportunity for oral presentation").

21 U.S.C. 371 specifies which rules require formal rule making procedure: food definitions and standards of identity, special dietary regulations, emergency permit control, tolerances for poisonous ingredients in food, drug assay methods, habit-forming drugs, and drugs liable to deterioration. The Secretary of HEW (or the Commissioner of FDA), on his own initiative or by petition from interested persons, is required to publish the proposed regulation and give all interested persons an opportunity to present their views thereon, orally or in writing. The Secretary is required to act upon each such proposal as soon as practicable thereafter. Adversely affected parties are given thirty days to file objections "specifying with particularity the provisions of the order deemed objectionable, stating the grounds therefor, and requesting a public hearing upon such objections." The Secretary is required to stay the effectiveness of the order to which objection is made, and after due notice to hold a formal public hearing "for the purpose of receiving evidence relevant and material to the issue raised by such objection." At the hearing, any interested person may be heard in person or through a representative. After completion of the hearing, the Secretary is required by order to act on the proposed regulation, "based only on substantial evidence of record at such hearing." Persons adversely affected by such order, in a case of actual controversy, are given ninety days to petition the federal courts of appeal for judicial review.

While the above procedure opens up a possibility for consumer advocates and consumer organizations to participate as "interested persons" in such a formal hearing, the time and expense required makes such participation unlikely. Thousands of dollars and months or years of effort may be required. Participation before the hearing stage, by filing written comments on the original petition, for example, is more feasible.

With regard to rule making under other sections of the Act, the practical possibilities for meaningful participation are much greater. Most of the recent FDA rule making that has been of broad interest to consumers—the proposals for "over-the-counter" drugs review, voluntary cosmetic registration of ingredients, nutritional labeling—has been informal rule making. The procedure has involved publication of a general notice of proposed rule making in the *Federal Register,* with at least thirty (usually sixty) days allowed for public participation through submission of written data, views, or arguments "with or without opportunity for oral presentation." After consideration of the relevant matter presented, the agency is required to "incorporate in the rules adopted a concise general statement of their basis and purpose."

Under informal rule making, consumers and consumer organizations can attempt to influence the FDA simply by writing their views on the proposed rule to the FDA. (The *Federal Register* notice includes both the deadline for comments and the address to which comments should be sent.) Such a comment can be as simple as a letter saying you think the proposal is inadequate, or as complex as a trial brief with technical appendices. Recent statements by the FDA in the *Federal Register*, however, indicate that the Agency is really looking for hard data on a particular proposal, so be as specific and detailed as you can, given the limitations on your time and resources.

FDA Legislative Development Program

An important factor in determining what the FDA will and will not do is what it asks Congress for authority and money to do. It maintains an Office of Legislative and Governmental Services for the purpose of proposing such legislative changes. It is important to find out how the office runs—the information it publishes (for example, it publishes a directory of all state and local food and drug officials with periodic supplements which every consumer group should have), who its contacts are in each state and local community (it maintains a wide range of communication with officials outside Washington), and what legislative plans it has.

At the same time that you are gathering this information and learning who are the decision makers in the office, you should be preparing information for inclusion in the FDA legislative package. According to the FDA, "in submitting recommendations for new legislation, the

Districts take into consideration suggestions brought to their attention by consumers, consumer groups and industry associations." This notation should be viewed by any organized consumer group as a call to prepare and present to the FDA district office nearest them proposals for legislative reform.

The Office of Legislative and Governmental Services prepares a legislative package each year. To begin the process it asks the bureaus, independent offices, and districts of the FDA to submit recommendations regarding legislation needed to improve its ability to carry out its "functions and responsibilities." In addition, the Agency claims to compile throughout the year "suggestions for new legislation" through long-range planning activities or "when received from consumers and other sources." The FDA's averred willingness to receive and consider the legislative suggestions of consumers represents an opportunity for consumer groups to provide creative suggestions.

Once the list of recommendations is prepared, it is circulated back to the bureaus, districts, independent offices, and staff of the Commissioner's office for comment. When the legislative program returns to the nearest district office, you should demand the opportunity to present comments on the entire program, including the disposition of any suggestions that your consumer organization had originated. Comments prepared by the district offices, along with other comments from the FDA hierarchy, are reviewed and, where possible, necessary, or desirable in the opinion of the legislative office, the proposals are modified and forwarded to the Commissioner for review and endorsement.

Those proposals endorsed by the Commissioner are forwarded to the HEW Assistant Secretary for Health and Science for coordination with the rest of the Department's legislative program. The whole program is then passed to the economic review section of the Office of Management and Budget (OMB, formerly the Bureau of the Budget) for review before inclusion in the President's overall legislative program and budget. The opportunities for a consumer group to influence the FDA's proposals are limited once the first suggestions are made. However, you should see that, once the district office has received your comments on the legislative office's proposals, these comments are communicated to all levels at which the program is considered. A letter outlining the proposal in detail and presenting arguments for it should be sent first to the Commissioner. Following this, the same information should be sent to the Office of the Secretary of HEW, to OMB, and to your Congressman and Senators.

Legislative efforts should be only supplemental to your work. All of this involved activity is done to get a proposal, whatever it may be, before Congress with the endorsement of the FDA. The purpose of your suggestions is to give the FDA an opportunity to consider and respond to new legislative proposals. Offering this opportunity builds your record of responsibility and might even convince the FDA to adopt a proposal.

Issues and Actions

There are many important questions about the regulation of foods and drugs which are not now within the FDA's legislative authority. For example, whether or not there should be a list of chemicals generally recognized as safe for use in food, whether or not food additives should be established as necessary and effective in expanding the food supply, and whether or not the FDA should be required to test all chemicals under its jurisdiction for safety and effectiveness, are all questions currently being debated which can only be solved by Congressional action. Organized consumer activity designed to influence the answers to these questions should be directed toward Congress and not the FDA. The Nader Congress Project Report, *Who Runs Congress,* by Mark Green, James Fallows, and David Zwick (New York: Grossman Publishers, 1972) should be read for general background, particularly Chapter 9.

On the other hand, many important questions of national concern are primarily, if not exclusively, up to the FDA. Whether the FDA should require all chemicals under its control to be tested for long-range mutagenic, teratogenic, and carcinogenic hazard potential, and whether the FDA should require drug companies to inform users of drugs directly about any or all possible hazards related to taking the drugs, are questions which the FDA routinely answers by its daily actions. It is on these questions that organized consumer action should be focused.

The general tools which have been described for approaching the FDA on such issues are limited, but they can be effective. Whether you decide to focus your efforts on filing complaints, getting and evaluating FDA public information, getting information from the FDA under the FOIA, informal liaison, the advisory committees, or the rule making process, you should concentrate your work on important issues with continuing impact. Here are nine such issues for you to consider:

1. How should the FDA review the list of food additives generally recognized as safe?
2. How much information about the dangers of drugs should be presented directly to the consumer by drug companies?
3. How much of the information on food and drug safety and quality now contained in the massive FDA files and withheld from the public should be made available?
4. What should be the regulation for nutritional quality of foods formulated from substitute products such as soy beans?
5. Should the FDA require all foods and drugs to be tested for mutagenic (pertaining to hereditary change), teratogenic (birth defects), and carcinogenic (pertaining to cancer) potential before allowing them to be marketed? (Currently there is a vigorous debate among FDA officials about this question, with one side arguing that public health requires the testing and the other side arguing that such testing is too expensive.)
6. Should the FDA provide stricter control over the use of drugs in food-producing animals? Currently there are two controversies about animal drugs within FDA. One concerns the use of hormones; the second concerns antibiotic drugs used on food animals. British authorities have raised serious questions about these drugs.
7. Is the FDA properly conducting routine monitoring devices to discover whether or not food and drug contaminants such as PCBs, heavy metals (mercury and others), and excessive food additives are getting into the food supply?
8. Are FDA personnel properly distributed to insure maximum protection of public health? Currently more than half of the FDA's employees are located in the Washington headquarters.
9. Does the FDA have a sufficient scientific capacity? From the problems which develop to crises before being noticed, criticism of science advisers, and discovery of important scientific data in old unused files, it appears that the FDA might not be effectively using or requesting adequate scientific research.

Because the products which the FDA is supposed to regulate for safety are known and used by most consumers, citizen participation and complaints can have a stronger impact on this agency than on other agencies which regulate complex economic practices further removed from people's daily experiences. This is being shown by a few consumer groups, but much more progress can be forthcoming with broader knowledge about how to go about creating a more responsive agency.

FDA Fact Sheet: How the Consumer Can Report to FDA

	U.S. DEPARTMENT OF HEALTH, EDU-CATION, AND WELFARE
FACT	Public Health Service
FDA SHEET	FOOD AND DRUG ADMINISTRATION
	5600 Fishers Lane
	Rockville, Maryland 20852

HOW THE CONSUMER CAN REPORT TO FDA

Consumers sometimes come across a food, drug, or cosmetic they think is mislabeled, unsanitary, or otherwise harm-ful.

If you report a legitimate grievance to the Food and Drug Administration, you are doing a public service. Such a report can, and often does, lead to the detection of a violation of the Federal Food, Drug, and Cosmetic Act, to the seizure of products that break the law, and to the punishment of law-breakers. Of course, the FDA will not take action solely on your complaint, but it will investi-gate your report promptly and act if necessary.

Here are some guidelines to follow in reporting suspected violations of the Federal Food, Drug, and Cosmetic Act.

Where to Report. You may refer your complaint in writing or by phone to the nearest FDA Field office or resident inspection station. FDA has 10 Regional offices, 19 District offices, and 97 resident inspection stations throughout the United States. In other major cities not listed, you can find the address and phone number of the nearest FDA office in the telephone directory under U.S. Government, Department of Health, Education, and Welfare, Food and Drug Adminis-tration. If you wish, you may write about your complaint directly to FDA headquarters. The address is Food and Drug Administration, 5600 Fishers Lane, Rockville, Maryland 20852. The complaint will reach the correct person.

How to Report

1. Report your grievance promptly.
2. State clearly what appeared to be wrong.
3. Describe the label of the product and give any code marks that appear on the

container. (In the case of a canned
food, these are usually embossed into
or stamped on the lid of the can.)

4. Give the name and address of the store
where the article was bought.

5. Save whatever remains of the suspect
product or the empty container for
your doctor's guidance or for use in
case of an investigation.

6. Hold any unopened container of the
product bought at the same time.

7. If an injury is involved, see a doctor
at once.

8. Also report the suspect product to the
manufacturer, packer, or distributor
shown on the label of the product and
to the store where you bought it.

With a medicine, you may suspect the product is harmful
because you experience an unusual reaction. You should
report this to your doctor immediately. The reaction may
be a "side effect" rather than an indication of any defect in the medicine. Therefore, it may not be necessary
to complain to FDA. However, your physician will want to
know of such a reaction for his own information and for
reporting to the FDA or the American Medical Association.
The FDA, the AMA, and reputable drug manufacturers are
concerned about unusual reactions to specific drugs.

Other complaints on foods, drugs, and cosmetics should be
referred to the following:

1. Suspected false advertising -- the Federal Trade
Commission.

2. Meat and poultry products -- the U.S. Department
of Agriculture.

3. Sanitation of restaurants -- local health authorities.

4. Products made and sold exclusively within a
state -- local or state Health Department or
similar law enforcement agency.

5. Suspected illegal sale of narcotics or dangerous
drugs ("Dangerous" drugs include stimulants, de-
pressants and hallucinogens) -- the Bureau of
Narcotics and Dangerous Drugs, U.S. Department
of Justice.

FDA Districts

ATLANTA DISTRICT

BALTIMORE DISTRICT

BOSTON DISTRICT

BUFFALO DISTRICT

CHICAGO DISTRICT

CINCINNATI DISTRICT

DALLAS DISTRICT

DENVER DISTRICT

DETROIT DISTRICT

KANSAS CITY DISTRICT

60 Eighth Street, N.E.
Atlanta, GA 30309
404 526 5265

900 Madison Avenue
Baltimore, MD 21201
301 962 3396

585 Commercial Street
Boston, MA 02109
617 223 3174

599 Delaware Avenue
Buffalo, NY 14202
716 842 6906

Main Post Office Bldg.
Room 1222
433 W. Van Buren Street
Chicago, IL 60607
312 353 5863

1141 Central Parkway
Cincinnati, OH 45202
513 684 3503

3032 Bryan Street
Dallas, TX 75204
214 749 2735

5604 New Customhouse
   Building
20th and California
   Streets
Denver, CO 80202
303 297 4335

1560 E. Jefferson Ave.
Detroit, MI 48207
313 226 6262

1009 Cherry Street
Kansas City, MO
816 374 5521

LOS ANGELES DISTRICT   1521 W. Pico Blvd.
                                            Los Angeles, CA 90015
                                            213 688 3771

MINNEAPOLIS DISTRICT   240 Hennepin Avenue
                                            Minneapolis, MN 55401
                                            612 725 2121

NEW ORLEANS DISTRICT   U.S. Customhouse Bldg.
                                            423 Canal Street
                                            Room 222
                                            New Orleans, LA 70130
                                            504 527 2420

NEW YORK DISTRICT   850 3rd Avenue
                                            Room 700
                                            Brooklyn, NY 11232
                                            212 788 5000, ex. 1300

NEWARK DISTRICT   970 Broad Street
                                            Room 831
                                            Newark, NJ 07102
                                            201 645 3265

PHILADELPHIA DISTRICT   U.S. Customhouse
                                            Room 1204
                                            2nd & Chestnut Streets
                                            Philadelphia, PA 19106
                                            215 597 4390

SAN FRANCISCO DISTRICT   Federal Office Bldg.
                                            50 Fulton Street
                                            Room 518
                                            San Francisco, CA 94102
                                            415 556 2062

SAN JUAN DISTRICT   P.O.Box 4427
                                            San Juan Station
                                            Puerto Rico 00905
                                            809 622 0443

SEATTLE DISTRICT   Federal Office Bldg.
                                            909 First Avenue
                                            Room 501
                                            Seattle, WA 98104
                                            206 583 5304

LABEL, Inc., News Release:
Labeling of Product Ingredients

LABEL, Inc.
Law Students Association for Buyers' Education and Labeling
Room 226
2020 F Street, N.W.
Washington, D.C. 20006
Telephone: 293-6478

FOR RELEASE: 12 Noon, Thursday, February 25, 1971

News Conference:
12 Noon, Thursday, February 25, 1971
Room 22, The George Washington University Law School
720 - 20th Street, N.W.
Washington, D.C.

LABEL announced it will file a petition this afternoon before the Food and Drug Administration charging that FDA regulations have resulted in inconsistent, ineffective, and misleading food labeling regulations, and among charges made are that:

(1)   Many products list no ingredients whatsoever on their labels.

(2)   Some products list several of their ingredients, but neglect to inform the consumer that this is only a partial disclosure.

(3)   Retailers and distributors often receive a more informatively labeled product than the consumer.

Because of weak FDA regulations, LABEL said the presence of many potentially harmful ingredients, such as caffeine and monosodium glutamate are hidden from the public.

The petitioners demanded that the FDA issue a new regulation to require complete declaration of all ingredients contained in food products.   LABEL contends that the FDA is not complying with the Congressional statute which calls for action by the FDA that will "promote honesty and fair dealing in the interest of consumers."

LABEL, a nonprofit corporation, is an acronym for Law Students Association for Buyers' Education and Labeling. The members of LABEL, all second year law students at the George Washington University Law School, are: Arthur Koch, Chairman; Louis Kaufman, Gary Laden, Joan Levy, and Ellis

Saul. The group was conceived in an Unfair Trade Practices Course taught by Professor John Banzhaf. It has been working closely with Jim Turner of the Center for Study of Responsive Law. Additionally, Giant Food, Inc., in cooperation with LABEL, has voluntarily undertaken a more complete labeling program.

Note:

Speakers at the News Conference include:

(1) Arthur Koch, Chairman, LABEL, Inc.

(2) Mrs. Esther Petersen, Consumer Consultant to Giant Food, Inc.

(3) Professor John Banzhaf, The George Washington University Law School.

(4) Mr. James Turner, Author of The Chemical Feast, and an attorney for the Center for Study of Responsive Law.

(5) A representative from The Virginia Citizens Consumer Council.

NEWS CONFERENCE STATEMENT
Arthur Koch, LABEL Chairman

My name is Arthur Koch, and I am Chairman of LABEL,
Inc., an acronym for Law Students Association for Buyers'
Education and Labeling. We are a group of five George
Washington University Law Students who, under the direction
of Professor John Banzhaf, are working together to seek a
more complete ingredient labeling on all food products.

We are here today to announce that as soon as this
press conference concludes, we will file a formal petition
with the Food and Drug Administration requesting enactment
of a rule to require that all food manufacturers and distributors list on the label all ingredients contained in
the food products they put forth for consumption.

We file this petition hoping that the Food and Drug
Administration will rise to the occasion and take notice
of nationwide inadequacies in the labeling of almost all
food products. The petition is filed on our own behalf as
a consumer group concerned about the existing inability of
all consumers to learn what composes the foods they buy
and eat. Our petition illustrates how present FDA regulations provide privileged sanctuaries for literally hundreds of potentially harmful hidden ingredients.

It is our privilege to be working closely with Giant
Food, Inc., which, under its Consumers' Bill of Rights,
has voluntarily undertaken a more complete labeling program in response to our efforts. We have also been working with Mr. James Turner of the Center for Study of
Responsive Law who has been laboring tirelessly for the
consumer in the area of Food and Drug Law.

We sincerely hope the FDA will respond to our call.

CHAPTER 12

THE DEPARTMENT
OF AGRICULTURE

The U.S. Department of Agriculture (USDA) is involved in just about everything that is concerned with the growing and processing of food, including rural housing loans, electrification, food standards, and food inspection. Here we will focus on some of the things that the USDA does about some of the food you eat, and the price you pay for one particular basic food product—milk. These programs have been chosen because they involve basic consumer interests, and because they offer some potential for you to have some say in them. To give you an idea of the range of other USDA activities, the functions selected for discussion here are all directed by the Assistant Secretary for Marketing and Consumer Services, which is only one of six major departments within USDA. (For perspective, see the organization chart in Appendix 12-A, p. 688.)

Most of the functions to be discussed involve animal products in one way or another—the composition of processed foods, the labeling of meat products, and the price of milk. The function that goes beyond this rough categorization—grading standards—involves both meat and agricultural products. If you have been through the chapter on the Food and Drug Administration (FDA), you may have a sense of déjà vu in reading some of this material. The functions of the FDA and the USDA parallel and occasionally overlap. A graphic example was in the fall of 1971, when incidents of botulism in canned soup made people uneasy over their dinners. The initial case involved poisoning from a can of vichyssoise, and the agency involved was the FDA. Subsequent instances of suspected botulin contamination of other soups brought the USDA into the matter, however. The reason? The later cases involved chicken vegetable soup, and where meat is (a "meat product" with over 3 percent meat), the Department is, so long as it involves interstate commerce. The same rule of thumb—if a product has meat, it's a USDA problem—applies to pork, poultry, and other meat products.

Shortly after World War II, we started eating more and more canned and otherwise processed foods. Perhaps it was because of the ubiquitous spam and ham-and-lima beans in military rations. In any case, we began to get increasing amounts of meat protein from processed foods, and we now receive 36 percent of our meat protein from meat pies, pizza, hot dogs, hamburgers, and other processed sources. One problem with this is that meat is an expensive ingredient, and it is easy for processors of these foods to stretch or adulterate them with fat, water, and fillers such as cereal. When people buy foods such as chile con carne, beef stew, or spaghetti with meatballs in a supermarket, they are likely to assume that the food has about the same ingredients it would have if it were prepared at home. They are likely to be wrong. Because the USDA refuses to require percentage labeling of ingredients in processed meat products, there is no way for you to know how much fat is in a hot dog and hamburger, how much beef is actually in beef stew, or how many meatballs are in a can of spaghetti and meatballs.

Standards of Identity

Although USDA won't require food producers to tell you the percentages of real food and extenders in products, it has set some limits on the imagination of food processors by setting standards of quality [*Federal Register*, Vol. 35, No. 193, 3 October 1970]. There are two kinds of standards, *standards of composition* and *standards of identity*. *Standards of composition*, which are more common, state the minimum meat, minimum water, and maximum fat content of particular foods. "Breakfast sausage," for example, can't be more than 50 percent fat, and stews must be at least 25 percent meat. *Standards of identity* include the standards of composition, but also specify ingredients other than meat, water, and fat, with prescribed flavor, texture, and color. Standards of identity have been set for only a few products, such as corned beef hash and the hot dog. As an example, corned beef hash is limited to a maximum of 15 percent fat and 72 percent moisture; of the total ingredients, at least 35 percent must be beef; the list of optional ingredients includes garlic, onions, potatoes, and spices [9 C.F.R. 319.303]. The hot dog cannot contain more than 30 percent fat or 10 percent moisture [9 C.F.R. 319.180].

The standards are prepared by the Product Standards Staff of USDA's Animal and Plant Health Inspection Service. A food manufacturer with a new processed meat product must send the formula or recipe to this branch. USDA then checks the proposed recipe against a microfilm file of labels and formulations already approved. If the recipe is simply a new formulation of a common product such as chile con carne or beef stew, it must comply with the standards of composition or identity which have already been set. If the product belongs to a food category for which no standards have been set, USDA makes a series of investigations based on the reference to the "common or usual name of the food" in the Federal Meat Inspection Act [21 U.S.C. 601, Subchapter I(n)(9)] to determine what the standard should be. The investigations usually consist of determining the standards generally used by manufacturers of the product. Information is also sought from restaurants and other professional food preparers, and from cookbooks and nutrition manuals, to get some indication of what the consumer expects to receive when he purchases the food.

After a new standard is developed, it is usually published in the *Federal Register* with a request for comments if the product is fairly widely used, or if industry or consumer groups have expressed an interest. The latest list of meat standards can be found in the 3 October 1970 *Federal Register*, Volume 35, No. 194, Part 319: *Definition and Standards of Identity in Composition*, p. 15597, which you can get for 25 cents from the G.P.O. (See p. 25 on how to order from G.P.O., and see Appendix 12-E, p. 693, for Consumer Reference List Standards for Meat and Poultry Products.)

Commenting on standards published in the *Federal Register* is the major method of consumer participation in the standards-setting process. The somewhat unusual example of the fatty hot dog serves as an illustration. For over thirty years the nutritional value of the hot dog has been constantly shrinking, while the frankfurter got fatter. In the early 1930s the average fat present in cooked frankfurters was 18.6 percent, and protein was 19.6 percent, which was about the same ratio as the meat that went into them. But by 1969 average fat content had increased to 34 percent (up to 51 percent in some brands), while protein had declined to 11.8 percent. When you buy steaks, roasts, chops, and other cuts, you can control the intake of animal fats by trimming. But with products prepared from emulsified meat mixtures, such as frankfurters, it is impossible to estimate or separate the fat level. The advice of the American Heart Association and the American Medical Association to avoid excessive intake of saturated fats made the prospect of an ever-fatter hot dog a public health issue as well as an issue of economic deception. (Harrison Wellford, *Sowing the Wind*, New York: Grossman Publishers, 1972, Chap. IV).

In 1969 USDA proposed setting the limit on fat in frankfurters at 33 percent. Not coincidentally, that level was the industry norm. The USDA initially had set the limit at 30 percent, instead of the 25 percent maximum advocated by nutritionists and public health officials in the Secretary of Agriculture's Ad Hoc Committee Report. The Department had taken an unprecedented step in scheduling hearings on the new standard in four cities, but after a change of political parties in power and industry pressure, the hearings were reduced to one, in Washington, and the proposed limit was raised to 33 percent. In the hearing, industry representatives argued that consumers preferred a fatty hot dog. But the manufacturers were reluctant to disclose the fat content on labels.

The hearing received an unusual amount of publicity, partly because the Consumer Federation of America was represented by their general counsel, Ed Berlin, and partly because the White House Consumer Advisor, Virginia Knauer, participated. As Ed Berlin put it in arguing for a 25 percent maximum:

> We begin with the premise that when the consumer purchases sausage products, she assumes that she is purchasing meat, not fat. Therefore, fat should be a permissible ingredient only to the extent that its presence is established as necessary. This should be the thrust of the Department's investigation, not an inquiry to establish prevailing industry practices and then merely ratify them.

But the latter nearly was the thrust of the inquiry. Virginia Knauer appeared and argued for a 30 percent limit. The conflict between her office and the USDA was settled when a weight-watching President Nixon called her to give his support to the 30 percent limit. With that word from the top, the decision was made: fat would be limited to 30 percent. But a proposal to require hot dog labels to disclose percentages of ingredients was rejected.

USDA now supervises the 30 percent standard with quarterly checks of retail sausage products, and the results of these analyses were made available to the public after associates of the Center for Study of Responsive Law successfully sued the Department under the Freedom of Information Act (FOIA). Appendix 12-D (p. 691) provides a list of current meat and poultry inspection programs. You can get current test results from the Field Operations branch of the Animal and Plant Health Inspection Service, and older tests are available from the Scientific

Services branch of the same division. The results give the percent of fat in samples of cooked sausage products by manufacturer.

Having Your Say

The frankfurter controversy was newsworthy not just because of the importance of frankfurters and the role played by a cholesterol conscious President: It was and is the only occasion when the USDA permitted a public hearing on a proposed standard. Consumer participation in setting food standards is rare enough, and you should not wait until another public hearing to have your say. You can be sure that if industry feels its self-interest is being violated, it will be very vocal about it, as this hot dog case so aptly shows. Anything affecting gross profits is fair game, whether it be at the state or local level.

In Michigan, for instance, the state legislature usurped the federal statute by providing for a minimum 12 percent protein level in sausage products and limiting this content to "skeletal fresh meat." Three large meat-packing companies protested this upgrading of quality in a lawsuit filed in the Michigan U.S. District Court on the ground that the costs involved would cause them "irreparable injury." In a late 1971 decision the court ruled that the stiffer state law took precedence. The U.S. Court of Appeals held in a subsequent decision that the "supremacy clause" allowed federal law to take precedence over the state standards.

Having your say at the USDA isn't much different from participating in rule making at other agencies: You can complain whenever you feel like writing a letter; you can watch the *Federal Register* and submit comments on proposed standards; you can file petitions for new rules or standards; and you can appear at a hearing, if any more are ever held.

Individual letters of complaint may not prompt much action, but a bulging file may spur someone to move, and is useful to counter the industry argument that everybody is happy with our food supply. Remember that the USDA is concerned with the quality and labeling of meat and poultry products. Document your complaint with examples, and make specific suggestions (such as labels giving percentages of ingredients). Send your letters to Animal and Plant Health Inspection Service, U.S. Department of Agriculture, Washington, D.C., 20250.

Since states and cities also have some control over local products,

send copies to your state and local agencies, too. Be liberal with your
carbon (or photo-) copies. Send them to others who may be interested,
such as your Congressman, and to consumer groups such as Consumers
Union, the Consumer Federation, or others listed in Appendix 12-C
(p. 690).

Proposed standards published in the *Federal Register* include this
paragraph:

> Consideration will be given to any written data, views or arguments
> pertaining to the proposal which are received by the Hearing Clerk,
> U.S. Department of Agriculture, Room 112, Administration Build-
> ing, Washington, D.C. 20250.

Almost all of the comments received are industry arguments against any
restrictions on their products. (See Appendix 12-B, p. 689, for names
and addresses of some industry trade journals.) However, there have
been two recent cases of strong consumer feedback. One occurred in
mid-1969, when USDA received 1,066 letters from consumers denouncing a proposal which would allow 15 percent poultry meat in hot dogs
without special labeling. According to one newspaper account, this was
"the largest number ever received on proposed changes in meat and
poultry inspection regulations." In response to this expression of consumer concern the Department first proposed and then canceled a
public hearing on the proposal. A similar incident in late 1971 provoked
some 447 comments, 90 percent of which were from consumers in-
censed over a proposal which allowed manufacturers to add the chemical SAPP (sodium acid pyrophosphate) to fix color in hot dogs. Since
they obviously did not have their own testing facilities, the consumers
provided no specific evidence that SAPP was harmful; SAPP was opposed as just one more additive in an already chemicalized product.

Neither of these proposals was settled in favor of the consumer,
partly because consumers failed to involve their Congressmen directly
in their petitions. In the SAPP case, however, several USDA staff members endorsed the consumer position. You should read the *Federal
Register* regularly and submit your own comments. The *Consumer
Register* supplement to *Consumer News* (see p. 26) may be of some
help in translating the *Federal Register*'s opaque prose. In addition, the
Center for Study of Responsive Law publishes a newsletter (the *Consumer Protection Report*) which comments on and interprets some of
the current proposals in the *Federal Register* pertaining to food questions. By opening lines of communication between the meat and poultry

inspector and the consumer, it also acts as a voice for the interests of both in the regulatory system.

When drafting your letter, send out two copies. One will be kept in the Hearing Clerk's office, and the other will go to the Animal and Plant Health Inspection Service. Get the comments in by the deadline listed in the announcement. If that is impossible, send a letter to the Hearing Clerk requesting an extension of time for comment. Comments based on medical opinion or nutritional values will carry more weight than personal preferences. But individual comments can be influential if there are enough of them. If you are in Washington, you can look at all of the comments submitted on specific subjects in the Hearing Clerk's office (Room 112, USDA Building, 12th and Independence Avenues, S.W., Washington, D.C. 20250) as required by 7 C.F.R. 1.27. Most of the comments you see will be from the industry groups.

If you want to change a regulation, rather than simply respond to changes proposed by USDA, the petition is the only tool available. USDA regulations simply authorize an interested party to petition for "the issuance, amendment or repeal of a rule" [7 C.F.R. 1.28]. But to have a chance of being effective, your petition should be carefully drafted and supported by evidence. The petition in Appendix 12-F (p. 699) serves as an example, although it deals with meat additives rather than standards of identity.

In 1972 two Washington, D.C., consumers and the Center for Science in the Public Interest filed a petition with USDA demanding that it severely restrict the uses of sodium nitrite and nitrate, chemical additives used in most processed meat products, including luncheon meat, bacon, ham, hot dogs, and corned beef. The twenty-one page petition cited extensive scientific evidence that nitrites, when combined with other chemicals called amines commonly found in food, drugs, tobacco, and beer, may form nitrosamines. Nitrosamines, according to Professor William Lijinsky, are "among the most potent carcinogens [cancer-producing substances] we know. . . ." The petition asked the Secretary of Agriculture to stop the cosmetic use of nitrite to make meat red and to permit other uses only upon a showing by the meat industry that nitrite is necessary, in carefully approved amounts, to prevent botulism and other bacteriological disease.

The Secretary denied the petition, and the issue is now before the courts. The petition has already stirred wide discussion in the press and in scientific circles about the need to find substitutes for potentially hazardous substances like nitrite. It is as important to get wide support for your petition as it is to make it legally and factually persuasive.

Get legal assistance in drafting a petition, and send preliminary drafts and proposals to organizations such as those in Appendix 12-C (p. 690) before you submit the proposal to the Department. Try to get those organizations to join in the petition. You should also enlist the support of your Congressman or other members of Congress. Remember that the USDA, like other agencies, is not required to do anything at all with a petition. If the petition is docketed as a proposal for rule making, that is only the first step. Trade associations (such as the National Broiler Council, the National Independent Meat Packers Association, and the American Meat Institute) will flood the agency with volumes of arguments. You can and should inspect these carefully and submit counter-arguments of your own.

For example, you should not hesitate to write to meat companies or trade associations to request the sources of their statements. Most universities, particularly land grant institutions, have departments of food technology and nutrition which may analyze technical arguments for you and help prepare your comment. In some cases the comment or petition need not be technical at all. In the SAPP case, numerous consumer statements disapproving any additional chemicals for hot dogs were received, although no health risks from SAPP itself were documented.

The hot dog hearings were probably such a discomfiting experience for the Department that similar opportunities in the future are likely, without a consumer resurgence, to be rare. Unfortunately, calling a public hearing is entirely up to the Secretary of Agriculture; there is no formal method to request such hearings. If you think that an issue, such as a proposed regulation in the *Federal Register*, deserves a public hearing, write to the Secretary of Agriculture and say so. You might compare the significance of the proposal with that of the fat limits in hot dogs, for which hearings were held. Enlist all of the popular and Congressional support available for your request. Ask for hearings to be held in several locations, since Washington hearings alone are easily dominated by the trade associations with offices in Washington. If the USDA refuses to hold hearings, Congressional committees may decide to hold their own. If a request for a hearing is refused, send copies of the correspondence to Senator Ribicoff, Chairman of the Government Operations Subcommittee on Executive Reorganization.

Labeling of Food Products

From the information on labels, you know more about the food you buy for your pets than the food you eat and feed to your children. The label of a dog food has not only a list of ingredients, but also an analysis of those ingredients, giving percentages of nutritional components. The purchaser of human food, however, finds the label devoid of information which would help him maximize the nutritional reach of his food dollar. As presently used, the primary function of the label is to sell the product. It identifies the contents only to the extent that the description will promote sales, or to meet the minimal legal requirements. Rarely, if ever, does the label communicate any nutritional information to consumers. The FDA has recently made some changes aimed at offsetting this void through voluntary compliance in nutritional labeling.

In cases in which a manufacturer makes a nutritional claim in its advertising or on its label, full nutrition labeling becomes mandatory. This includes information relating to size, calories, carbohydrates, proteins, fats, and vitamin percentages. When a product contains more than 50 percent of the recommended daily intake for proteins, vitamins, and minerals, it must be classified as a "dietary supplement." Although most of the new reforms are voluntary in nature, the FDA hopes that pressure within the industry will force broad compliance. USDA has not yet adopted similar regulations for the processed food which it inspects. However, if acceptance spreads industry-wide, as FDA hopes it will, the meat processors may be forced to take similar action. Consumers should give USDA their views on this subject.

Food labeling has a direct impact on a consumer's health as well as his buying power. When brands of food cannot be compared on the basis of their nutritional value or fat content, food manufacturers lack incentives to develop products with, for example, high protein or low cholesterol. The need for adequate labeling is especially urgent for poor people whose food dollar must be directed to foods of the greatest nutritional value, particularly since processed foods constitute a higher proportion of the diet of poorer consumers than those with higher incomes. But a poor consumer who buys a macaroni and cheese dinner must guess the percentage of cheese in that dinner; when he buys corned beef hash, he has no idea how much of the hash is potatoes and how much is meat.

The mounting evidence which points to a relationship between diet, especially consumption of saturated fats, and coronary disease indicates another risk of inadequate labeling. A recent report by the Inter-Society Commission for Heart Disease Resources asked the food industry to make major revisions in food processing to moderate fat and cholesterol content. Citing studies which showed that a 25 percent decrease in serum cholesterol yields a 53.5 percent reduction in coronary heart disease, it urged a new approach to labeling which would allow the consumer easily to identify nutrient content in all foods, including commercially prepared mixed dishes, and encouraged the manufacture of nutritious products low in saturated fats and cholesterol [*Feedstuffs* (2501 Wayzata Blvd., P.O. Box 67, Minneapolis, Minnesota 55404), 26 December 1970, p. 34]. Similar demands have been made by the New Foods and Food Safety Panels of the White House Conference on Food, Nutrition, and Health, and by a large number of consumer groups.

The consumer relies upon labels attached to packaged foods as the prime source of information about their contents, nutritional value, and safety. It does him little good to know that there is a connection between diet and heart disease if he can't get information about the foods he eats by reading the labels.

The Department of Agriculture's Labels and Packaging staff has authority to regulate the labeling on all processed foods. Part 317 of the Meat Inspection Regulations, published in the *Federal Register*, 3 October 1970, sets the guidelines for labeling, marking devices, and containers of all meat products. The regulations prohibit misleading labeling in any form. Section 317.2(3) prohibits the use of the terms meat, meat by-products, and meat food products in a context which is not common to consumers—unless accompanied by terms descriptive of the product. Section 317.8 generally prohibits any false or misleading marking, label, or other labeling, as well as any statement, word, picture, design, or device which conveys any false impression or gives any false indication of origin or quality, or is otherwise false or misleading.

The Department examines over 100,000 labels a year to see if they meet these standards. In order to be approved, every label must provide information meeting these requirements:

1. The common or usual name, if any, or a descriptive name of the product's contents.
2. The official market inspection.
3. The official number of the establishment inspected.
4. A net weight statement.
5. A name and address of the firm responsible for the product.

6. An ingredient statement if composed of two or more ingredients (Section 317.2(f) requires the list of ingredients to show the common or usual names of the ingredients arranged in descending order of prominence).
7. A warning statement such as "Keep Refrigerated," if applicable.

If the label specifies the number of servings in the package, the size of each serving must be stated, and if a photograph or drawing of the product appears on the label, it must be an accurate representation of the contents. For example, if a macaroni and cheese dinner is pictured on the label with peas and tomatoes, the legend "Serving Suggestion" or "Suggested Serving" must be marked on the label.

USDA has exercised its authority over labels primarily to see that they do not purposely mislead the consumer. The Department is far less concerned with labels which fail to tell the consumer anything of value for his nutrition or health. Concern for nutritional labeling as outlined in the new FDA regulations is not considered a part of the overall program. Yet in 1968 over 103,000 labels were approved, and 3,000 were rejected for false or misleading statements. Compared to the effect on the consumer's health from inadequate listing of contents, these rejections often seem trivial. A label marked "California style spiced beef" was rejected because there is no recognized "California style," and the label lacked the clear statement that the product was actually made in Pennsylvania ["Labels that Flunk the Test," by H. E. Steinhoff, *Agricultural Marketing* Vol. 14, No. 5 (May 1969), p. 16. Washington, D.C.: Consumer and Marketing Service, USDA. Magazine discontinued in 1971]. A proposed bacon package was rejected because the photograph on the label had been tinted red to give the bacon a leaner look.

There is little precedent for consumer involvement in government decisions about food labels, and the few cases on record offer little encouragement, except for one. As already mentioned, a proposal for percentage labeling of fat content for frankfurters was rejected during the hearings on fat in hot dogs.

Another case, however, looks more hopeful. The USDA interpretation of Section 317.8 of the Department's regulations, which states that "meat and the names of particular kinds of meat. . . shall not be used in such a manner as to be false or misleading," was challenged in a petition submitted to the Secretary of Agriculture in October 1969 by the Federation of Homemakers, a consumers' organization. That section, together with 319.180, sets the standards for "all meat" hot dogs. Under

the Department's interpretation of this section, a producer may manufacture a hot dog which is 30 percent fat, 58 percent water, 3.5 percent
curing additives, and 2 percent corn syrup solids, and still prominently
label and advertise his product as being "all meat" or "all beef" or "all
pork." An "all meat" hot dog can even have 15 percent chicken in it.
But if the sausage includes nonfat dry milk or any other milk product,
the label must include that information, i.e., "nonfat dry milk added,"
"calcium reduced dried skim milk added" [Section 317.8 (16)]. The
"all meat" hot dog now captures 70 percent of the market and is considered by most consumers to be a higher quality product, since the
term "all meat" suggests erroneously that the sausages are of higher
nutritional value.

The USDA ignored the petition. The attorney for the organization,
Ed Berlin, then went to court. On 5 May 1971 the U.S. District Court
for the District of Columbia ruled that the "all meat" labels were illegal.
A subsequent U.S. Court of Appeals decision on 18 August 1972 upheld this judgment and further required that the USDA come up with
labels that would more accurately describe types of frankfurters. Since
then USDA has published a proposal in the 23 December 1972 edition
of the Federal Register (pp. 28430-31) that withdraws the "all meat"
classification and limits "cooked sausage" to the use of "skeletal muscle
meat" only. In the past, almost any part of the animal could be used,
including eyes, ears, lungs, and bladders. The new proposed regulation
also requires that hot dogs made with dried milk or other such binders
include the name of this ingredient in the title of the product. Although
poultry is still allowed in quantities up to 15 percent without a separate
label, the new proposal represents a step forward for the consumer.
Three years of letters, petitions, and court cases were required to move
USDA in this direction.

A similar labeling case involving salmonella bacteria has not been as
successful. The case began as a petition by the New Jersey Public Health
Association asking USDA to place a warning on all raw meat and poultry
products as to their possible contamination with disease-producing
bacteria such as salmonella. The petition grew into a five-plaintiff lawsuit charging that it was USDA's responsibility to inform the public on
the proper storage, cooking, and handling precautions necessary to
minimize the risk of salmonella and other bacterial food poisoning. The
enormity of the problem is reflected in estimates of 2 million Americans being afflicted with this type of poisoning each year. Meat and
poultry are major sources of salmonella food poisoning. Although this
suit was recently lost in the U.S. District Court, it is now on appeal.

As the fate of the "all meat" and salmonella labeling petitions indicates, the USDA is not always receptive to consumer participation, although their attitude may have changed somewhat since the Court of Appeal's ruling. Check the *Federal Register's* table of contents for label proposals as well as ingredient standards, and send your comments. You can also request that USDA put you on its mailing list for notices of labeling proposals. When a particularly significant label change is proposed, submit a petition to the Secretary of Agriculture asking for a hearing, with copies to your Congressman. If you find a label that you think is misleading or inaccurate, report it to the Regional Consumer Protection Office of the U.S. Department of Agriculture for your area.

The recommendations of the New Foods Panel of the White House Conference on Food, Nutrition, and Health offer several possible proposals for use in a petition for rule making (conference held in December 1969 and the proposals were published in 1970). The panel urged that a complete statement of ingredients should be required on every new food label, regardless of whether there is a government standard for the product. It also urged that the amount of the characterizing ingredient be listed on a percentage basis, and that technical designation of ingredients be simplified to make it more understandable by consumers. As protection for allergenics, commonly used generic names of foods should be declared in terms of their sources, such as wheat protein hydrolysate, rather than just protein hydrolysate, potato starch rather than just starch, and peanut oil rather than just vegetable oil. Another possibility for a rule making petition would be to urge that the protein, saturated fat, and water level of all meat products be listed on the label, as is now required by the FDA for all products with nutritional claims.

Grading Standards: Jumbo and Up

At the USDA, food inspection is supposed to make sure that food is safe for you to eat, standards of identity are supposed to insure that food is what it says it is, and labeling requirements make the producers give you some idea of just what is inside the container. Grading is supposed to tell you how far the food you buy is above the minimum quality required to be sold. Unfortunately, grades are often impossible to determine, or, if determinable, incomprehensible. For example, a No. 1 avocado is a better avocado than a No. 1 apple is as an apple.

Some "better" grades, such as those for beef, are actually worse for you. In practice, the U.S. grademark is primarily designed to lend sales appeal to a food product. As the 1966 Yearbook of Agriculture put it, "Commercial firms use the U.S. grade standards and employ the grading service only if it helps them in marketing their products."

Industry orientation is inevitable in the grade-setting process because the program is voluntary, and industry pays for it. Over $50 million in fees is paid annually for the services of approximately 6,000 federal and state graders. The reassurance that some consumers derive from knowing that the official USDA shield and grademark is used only on products packed in USDA-approved plants operating under continuous inspection would be shaken if they had a better idea of how such inspection actually works. (See Wellford, *Sowing the Wind,* New York: Grossman Publishers, 1972, $7.95.)

An explanation of grade standards for specific foods is given in Title 7 of the Code of Federal Regulations (C.F.R.). Grade standards for fresh fruits and vegetables may be found in 7 C.F.R. 51; for processed fruits and vegetables, 7 C.F.R. 52; meat and meat products, 7 C.F.R. 53; rabbits, 7 C.F.R. 54; egg products, 7 C.F.R. 55; eggs, 7 C.F.R. 56; dairy products, 7 C.F.R. 58; rice, dry peas, and lentils, 7 C.F.R. 68; and poultry, 7 C.F.R. 70.

Grading terms are often designed to impart a specious aura of quality to second and third choice commodities rather than to inform the consumer of the product's quality. Not only are the names for grades misleading, but the same name often has a different meaning for different products. For example, apples, cantaloupes, and avocados which are wholesale graded U.S. No. 1 are actually not equivalent grades. Avocados graded U.S. No. 1 rank first, followed by U.S. Combination avocados, and then U.S. No. 2 (which are thus number three in quality) [7 C.F.R. 51.3050]. U.S. No. 1 cantaloupes rank second in quality behind U.S. Fancy [7 C.F.R. 51.475]. U.S. No. 1 apples rank third on the scale behind U.S. Fancy [7 C.F.R. 51.301] and U.S. Extra Fancy [7 C.F.R. 51.300]. If you are looking for large olives and you innocently choose a can marked "large," you have selected nearly the smallest olive on the market (seventh on a scale of nine). There are nine sizes of olives, and the largest is called "Super Colossal," followed by "Colossal," "Jumbo," "Giant," and "Mammoth"—to name only the top five [7 C.F.R. 52.5445].

These misleading distinctions are well known to food processors and wholesalers, but ordinary consumers are barely aware of them. An elementary improvement, and a good proposal for a rule making petition, would be to establish a uniform grading system for all products so that consumers would be able to determine the relative quality of what they buy.

Grading has much more significance than just as a sorting process. The qualities in food products that are rewarded by higher grades influence producers in what they produce and consumers in what they consume. The best example of this is in beef grading. Because higher grades are awarded for greater fat "marbling" in beef, cattle are fed in feedlots for long periods of time in order to increase fat, and are bred to produce high fat levels. Although cattle can be bred to reach market weight without much fat and still be extremely palatable, the grading system provides incentives to increase the level of saturated fat in the American diet. The previously mentioned Inter-Society Commission for Heart Disease Resources also called for changes in grade standards to achieve a low saturated fat, low cholesterol diet "because so much evidence already points to the diet's implication in the large number of heart attacks in the U.S." But the changes have not been made. Until grades are changed, beef cattle will continue to be kept in stalls and fed heavily to produce meat with a high fat content. Pork has no consumer grades because it does not have the characteristic fat marbling that largely determines beef, lamb, and veal grades. Fat also rates a high grade for poultry. The White House Conference on Food, Nutrition, and Health (Panel III-4, Recommendation 4–Grading Standards) recommended that higher grades be given to meat with less fat. That proposal might also be a good subject for a rule making petition.

It would also be an improvement if grades were clearly communicated to consumers. Only about a dozen products, including potatoes, tomatoes, corn, carrots, brussel sprouts, and cranberries, are graded specifically for consumer use. Wholesale grades are extensively used for marketing and processing information, but they provide little knowledge in the retail store. Such grades are extremely difficult to locate, since they are usually marked on crates, barrels, and packaging materials which are discarded when products are unpacked for convenient and attractive display in the store. Canned and frozen fruits and vegetables infrequently or never bear grade symbols. These products should be clearly graded, particularly in view of the growth of cheaper private brand canned or frozen fruits and vegetables which producers choose to label as supreme or top quality, rather than grade C government grade.

Beef, lamb, chicken, turkey, butter, and eggs usually carry the USDA grade shield. Meat is almost always sold with the wholesale grade prominently displayed, since there is no other brand name to use for advertising purposes. Eggs use a consumer grade [7 C.F.R. 56.217], and are

tising purposes. Eggs use a consumer grade [7 C.F.R. 56.217], and are
so clearly marked that the USDA's Economic Research Service [USDA-
Economic Service Research Marketing Research Report No. 876, Consumer's Knowledge and Use of Government Grades for Selected Food
Items] found a higher degree of consumer awareness of egg grades than
of the grading of any other product. Eggs are clearly marked with both
the grade and the size. The top two consumer grades, AA and A, have
firm yolks and thicker whites than grade B eggs [USDA C&MS PA-708,
7 C.R.F. 58.200], while egg sizes vary from Jumbo (thirty ounces per
dozen), decreasing by three ounces per size to Peewee (fifteen ounces
per dozen). It would be an improvement if other products had a clearly
communicated system of consumer grades.

Unfortunately, consumers in general are likely to assume that the
government is grading foods that are not graded. When asked by the
USDA's Economic Research Service whether government grades existed
for the food items they purchased, 89.7 percent of the consumers said
grades existed for beefsteak, 82.16 percent for turkey, 71.3 percent for
eggs, 70.12 percent for bacon, and 70 percent for fresh milk. White
bread was the only food item queried that many did not believe was
government graded. But neither milk nor bacon is graded at all [USDA-
Economic Research Service Marketing Research Report No. 876, Consumer's Knowledge and Use of Government Grades for Selected Food
Items]. A simple system of charts explaining the grading system and
displayed in supermarkets would make the system much more useful.

If products are being sold in your area which you think are below
the grade with which they are marked, you should take your complaint
to the local USDA graders. Most complaints now are made by wholesalers and packers challenging grades awarded to competing products.
Before complaining, you should get copies of the grading standards for
the particular product. These are issued in pamphlet form and are free
on request to the Fresh Products Standardization and Inspection
Branch, Fruit and Vegetable Division, Consumer and Marketing Service,
USDA, Washington, D.C. 20250. Then document your case as carefully
as possible with examples. To register your complaint, look under U.S.
Government in the local phone book for the Department of Agriculture,
or Animal and Plant Health Inspection Service, if listed. Explain that you
are calling about food grading and give the details of your complaint.

You can also submit your comments when grading standards are
being considered. These are published in the *Federal Register* for new
products which have never been graded before, or for old products with
standards the industry or USDA decides are outmoded or inadequate.

Comments should be sent to Hearing Clerk, Room 112, Administration Building, USDA, Washington, D.C. 20250.

Although letters indicating individual preferences may have a cumulative effect, it is better if you can present documented arguments with the support of some organization. If you propose a change in the grading standards, say exactly what is wrong with the old standards, what should be substituted, and why.

The not-so-great potato case was the first time the Standardization and Inspection Branch of the Fruits and Vegetables Division ever received more than one letter from a consumer on a grade standards question. The proposals for changes in potato standards were apparently generated by consumers who were "interested in being able to buy better quality and more uniformly sized potatoes in the retail stores" [35 *Federal Register* 18258]. Six hundred and sixty-two letters were received on the proposed potato standards, and about 45 percent of them came from consumers. Unfortunately, most of the proposed changes (such as proposals that No. 1 potatoes have less sprout damage, a larger diameter, a weight minimum, and be fairly well matured) were dropped from the final standard after industry opposition, some of which was channeled through Congress. As one official in the Standardization Section put it: "It was pressure, pure and simple, that we had to back off on the size. We would have liked to have done a lot more." Because of this, potatoes which meet standards for U.S. No. 1 are not always best.

Milked Prices

Although most people know that the USDA pays people for not growing things, and provides subsidized prices for crops that are grown, few realize that the price that they pay for milk is also determined under USDA procedures. Under this system, milk is priced beyond the means of many people who need it most. During the first six months of life, the average child gets over half of his total nutrients from cows' milk. However, in many cities milk is a luxury food beyond the reach of a poverty budget. According to the *Household Food Consumption Survey 1965-1966*, Report #1: Food Consumption of Households in the U.S. (Washington, D.C.: USDA Consumer and Food Economics Institute, Spring 1965) per capita consumption of milk averages 1.2 pints a day, while the recommended amount of milk per capita consumption is 1.3

pints per day. And accordng to an estimate in 2 *Antitrust Law and Economic Review*, Foreword, pp. 7 and 8 (Summer 1969), consumers are paying at least 30 percent more (over $3.7 billion annually) for milk than they should be.

This important source of basic nutrition is not getting to the people who need it, and one reason is an artificially inflated price. According to the editor of *Antitrust Law and Economic Review*, the competitive price of a half gallon of milk in 1969 in a free market should have been 40 cents. But the national average was around 60 cents, and the major reason for the disparity was the fact that the price of milk is determined not by the free market, but by federal and state agencies that use artificial supports and a system of marketing orders. The USDA contributes to the rising cost of milk in two ways. The Agricultural Act of 1949 (as amended) requires the Secretary of Agriculture to support prices for milk and butterfat between 75 and 90 percent of parity [7 U.S.C. 1446(c)]. Every April the Secretary announces a support price for manufactured milk products—butter, cheese, and nonfat dry milk. The government purchases these products through the Commodity Credit Corporation at the prices it pledges to pay. Continuance of the costly agricultural support program for manufactured milk artifically inflates the prices of fluid milk by putting a floor under the price the farmer receives. The support price for butter further inflates the price of milk, because butter is a milk extract. If the consumer seeks to escape the influence of butter on the price of milk by buying filled milk— milk from which the butterfat has been extracted and vegetable fat substituted—the USDA, in some areas, has insisted on classifying this product as Class 1 milk, carrying the same price as fluid milk.

A more significant role played by the USDA—and one which offers some opportunity for consumer participation—is the system of federal milk marketing orders established by the Agricultural Marketing Agreement Act. This Act sets the terms under which handlers who distribute milk in specified marketing areas buy the milk from dairy farmers. Marketing orders are supposed to promote orderly marketing conditions through a uniform system of classified prices throughout the market. The orders require milk dealers to pay specified minimum prices to farmers for milk, and the prices vary according to the value of the end product. Through the marketing order system, dairy farmers, in effect, have the power to vote themselves a monopoly over fluid milk supplies. A complete compilation of all federal milk marketing orders, as of 1 January of each year, is available from the Superintendent of Documents, and is republished each year in about April in Title 7 of the C.F.R. in five volumes arranged by geographical areas.

The problem with the marketing order system for milk is that the original basis for the price fixing no longer exists. It was designed to strengthen the bargaining position of milk producers at a time when milk could only be shipped relatively short distances and had to be sold quickly regardless of price. There was a need thirty years ago for some procedure which every metropolitan area could use for encouraging the production of an adequate supply of milk. But new methods of transporting milk now make any market accessible to any other within the continental United States. If it were not for the barriers of milk orders, surplus milk could be shipped to areas where it is in demand.

Thirty years ago, milk producers were not well organized, and were often at the mercy of large dairy companies which had a market for fluid milk. If a dairy farmer wanted to be on the company's list of accepted producers, he had to do as the company said. The marketing order program gave producers time to organize and gain enough power to bargain at the same level with the company. But now the milk producers' cooperatives are enormously powerful. They control at least 90 percent of the fluid milk supply in the country, and exercise considerable political pressure through their donations to campaign funds. The chief result of the present program is increased prices for milk.

The marketing order system works this way. Marketing orders must first be proposed, either by the Secretary of Agriculture or any other person. Any person other than the Secretary who proposes a marketing order must file a written application with the administrator of the Agricultural Marketing Service (AMS), together with at least four copies of the proposal requesting the Secretary to hold a hearing [7 C.F.R. 900.3]. The Dairy Division of the AMS is responsible for investigating each hearing proposal and recommending whether a hearing on the proposal be held. Normally proposals for hearings on a new order are made by dairy farmer cooperatives representing producers who supply milk to the marketing area for which an order is sought. The inquiry prior to the recommendation of hearing on a proposed new order must establish that:

1. Marketing conditions in the area are susceptible to improvement by the issuance of a milk order.
2. Evidence pertinent to the consideration of a milk order will be forthcoming at the hearing.
3. The proponents of the order appear to have the support of a substantial number of producers in the market.
4. Marketing of milk in the area affects interstate commerce.

There is a tradition that hearings are not called unless the USDA is willing to increase prices. Producers rarely object to higher prices, and the Department only recommends lower prices if they are requested by producers. If the Director of the Dairy Division recommends that a hearing notice be issued, the notice is published in the *Federal Register* [7 C.F.R. 900.4(b)(1)(i)].

Dairy economists and statisticians who analyze economic conditions in dairying can rarely predict the future of the milk market with confidence, and the Secretary of Agriculture thus is eventually faced with deciding whether a milk marketing order is justified largely as a matter of personal judgment. After the hearings, the Secretary may recommend an increase, no change, or a decrease in the minimum price of milk. An order is issued after analysis of the evidence introduced at the public hearing in order to give dairy farmers, milk dealers, and the general public an opportunity to comment on the effect of a proposed milk order. Interested persons can file written exceptions to the findings, conclusions, and provisions of the recommended order. A vote must be taken of all the producers who supplied milk to the defined marketing area during a designated period [7 U.S.C. 608 c(19)], and the order must be approved (by two-thirds if the order establishes a market-wide pool, by three-fourths if it is an individual pool) before it is issued.

The public hearings present a limited opportunity to be heard for those who ultimately pay the prices set there. At present, they are almost entirely industry proceedings. Few, if any, consumer spokesmen ever appear at these hearings. They are rarely publicized in advance except through the *Federal Register*, and if there is any newspaper coverage of proposed hearings, it is relegated to the commodity section of the financial pages of local newspapers. In addition to lack of effective notice, any consumer participation would be hampered by the nature of evidence considered relevant by hearing examiners. The hearings are characterized by volumes of dairy statistics which can be manipulated to prove any argument [Testimony of Rodney Leonard, former Administrator of Consumer and Marketing Service, in Organizing Federal Consumer Activities, Hearings, Subcommittee of the Committee on Government Operations, House of Representatives, 91st Cong. 1st Sess., 1969, p. 136].

Nevertheless, these hearings offer an unused opportunity for participation by consumer representatives, particularly metropolitan area consumer groups. Although asking for a hearing might be a major undertaking, many groups would probably be able to present testimony at hearings called at producers' requests, and after such hearings there are still opportunities to submit comments. The voting by producers, who must approve such orders, presents an unusual opportunity for consumer participation. Producers do not usually object to fixed higher prices but they might reconsider if they were presented with the possibility that people would refuse to buy at those prices. Although milk is a basic food, most of its nutrients are available from other sources. A carefully planned program for people to get those nutrients from other sources, with accompanying publicity, might be effective in persuading producers to reconsider their guaranteed price increases.

Meat Inspection: Opportunities for Consumer Action

All raw meat and poultry products, and other foods containing at least 2 percent chicken and 5 percent meat, are subject to inspection by either the USDA or a state meat inspection service. Appendix 12-D (p. 691) gives the addresses of federal inspection programs. While meat shipped across state lines has been inspected by USDA since the passage of the Federal Meat Inspection Act (21 U.S.C. 601) in 1906, intrastate meat for many years was left to the discretion of the states, many of which failed to provide any inspection at all. This situation was changed in 1967 when, after shocking disclosure of filth in meat plants, Congress passed the Wholesome Meat Act (81 Stat 584), which amended the 1906 law to require that states develop inspection programs "at least equal to" federal standards. Comparable legislation for poultry inspection (82 Stat 791) was enacted in 1968.

Forty-two states now have meat inspection systems "certified" by the federal government as equal to USDA's standards (33 states have "certified" poultry inspection systems). Plants under state inspection produce about 10 percent of the meat and poultry consumed annually in the United States. The adequacy of state inspection continues to be a matter of controversy. At hearings on amendments to the Wholesome Meat Act by the House Committee on Agriculture in 1972, the American Meat Institute (lobby for the interstate packers), labor unions, and consumer groups all questioned whether state inspection really did measure up to federal standards. The federal government pays one-half the cost of the state inspection programs.

Federal and state inspection affects meat and poultry products only at the point of slaughtering and processing. Municipal health and inspection services are responsible for inspecting meat products at points of retail sale, such as restaurants and supermarkets.

If the consumer has a complaint about a meat product—if, for example, he thinks there is too much water in his ham or too much fat in his hamburger, or he finds a worm in his chili con carne or a rodent's foot in his chicken soup (all actual cases)—there are several things he can do. First he should examine the product and see whether it is state or federally inspected (federally inspected products bear a "U.S. Inspected" mark).

If the product has a USDA mark, check the telephone directory to see if there is a local USDA Meat and Poultry Inspection Office in your area. There is usually one in any large city and sometimes even in smaller towns where there are a number of packing plants in the area. Although this local office cannot act directly on your complaint or give you specific information about a product, it can refer your request to a Compliance Staff located in one of USDA's five regional offices.

This regional office is your second and more direct source for getting information or filing a complaint. There are offices in Philadelphia, Atlanta, Des Moines, Dallas, and San Francisco. Each office is comprised of a Compliance Staff and a Meat and Poultry Inspection Staff. They are not always located in the same building, so you must first call the USDA Regional Office of Meat and Poultry Inspection and ask for the Compliance Staff. Copies of your complaint should be sent to the House and Senate Committees on Agriculture, your local Congressman and Senators, and to the Center for Study of Responsive Law's *Consumer Protection Report* (P.O. Box 19367, Washington, D.C., 20036).

The citizen also has the right to contact a local U.S. meat inspector and request a visit to a federally inspected plant (the same can be requested of state inspectors as well).

For the consumer who wishes to learn about local products and companies which have fallen afoul of the meat laws, USDA's detention records and letters of warning are now available for public review. The detention records list products which have been detained by USDA because they were contaminated or adulterated, or for other reasons. Unfortunately they do not give the name of the company producing the product, but tell only where it was sold and why it was detained or eventually condemned. The letters of warning are notices by USDA to meat and poultry processors suspected of violating federal meat laws. Here the name of the company is given.

These records were made available as a result of a lawsuit under the FOIA by Harrison Wellford of the Center for Study of Responsive Law. As of 15 January 1973, USDA is making its detention records and letters of warning available in its five regional offices as well as in its Compliance Office in Washington, D.C.

This information can be useful in several ways. When the consumer prepares a complaint, he can check the records to see if meat from the same store has been detained in the past, a fact that will lend substance to his complaint. If a consumer suspects that a ham he purchased has been adulterated with water, he can check to see if the company producing the ham has been cited for such violations in the past. Such disclosure encourages obedience to the meat laws. Packers will be much more likely to clean up their own operations if they know their letters of warning will be made public. Armed with this information, the consumer can avoid chronic violators of federal inspection laws, making the marketplace a more effective regulator of meat and poultry quality.

Ralph Westcott, a Compliance Staff official at USDA's headquarters in Washington, has said that, "within reason," the regional staffs would be able to check on individual cases for you, but that they would encourage you to go to their offices and look through the files yourself. Written requests will also be answered.

If you are interested in checking on the quality of any products produced under state rather than federal inspection, you may request to see USDA's State Program Evaluation Reports. These are individual plant surveys taken periodically by USDA personnel in state-inspected establishments. The reports were released recently after an FOIA suit was brought by Peter Schuck, now with Consumers Union, in order to gain access to surveys taken in six specific states. The suit had been motivated by concerns about the quality of the state programs and whether they were in fact "equal to" federal standards. Copies of these can be reviewed at USDA's Compliance Office for Meat and Poultry Inspection in Washington. When they are available, Mr. Westcott will reproduce copies of USDA's survey of individual plants, if the consumer has a particular state plant about which he is concerned.

If a consumer has information which indicates that either a state or federal plant is producing unsanitary or adulterated meat, he should also contact the General Accounting Office (GAO), Washington, D.C., 20548. The GAO is an investigative arm of Congress which has released a series of highly critical reports on federal meat and poultry inspection. These reports, which are public and can be ordered from the GAO, spotlight plant inspection failures such as poor rodent and insect control, inadequate sanitation, contamination from peeling paint, and rusty or corroded processing equipment. The consumer should also write to his Congressman asking specifically that he request a GAO investigation of the plant in question.

Organization Chart of the U. S. Department of Agriculture

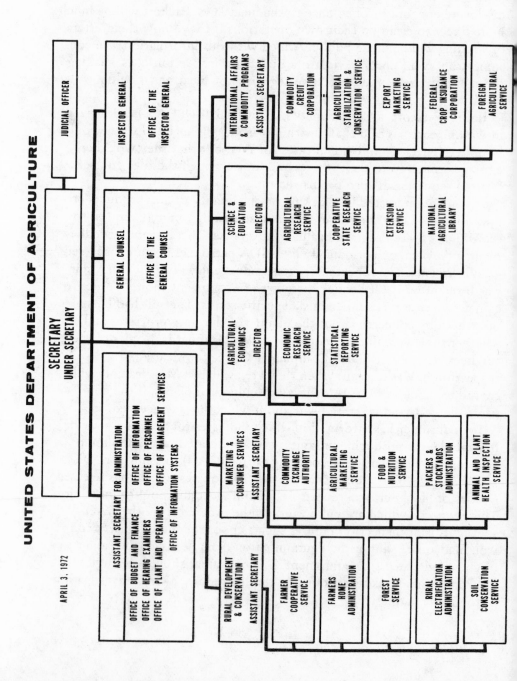

UNITED STATES DEPARTMENT OF AGRICULTURE

APRIL 3, 1972

JUDICIAL OFFICER

SECRETARY
UNDER SECRETARY

INSPECTOR GENERAL
OFFICE OF THE INSPECTOR GENERAL

GENERAL COUNSEL
OFFICE OF THE GENERAL COUNSEL

ASSISTANT SECRETARY FOR ADMINISTRATION

OFFICE OF BUDGET AND FINANCE
OFFICE OF HEARING EXAMINERS
OFFICE OF PLANT AND OPERATIONS
OFFICE OF INFORMATION
OFFICE OF PERSONNEL
OFFICE OF MANAGEMENT SERVICES
OFFICE OF INFORMATION SYSTEMS

INTERNATIONAL AFFAIRS & COMMODITY PROGRAMS
ASSISTANT SECRETARY

COMMODITY CREDIT CORPORATION
AGRICULTURAL STABILIZATION & CONSERVATION SERVICE
EXPORT MARKETING SERVICE
FEDERAL CROP INSURANCE CORPORATION
FOREIGN AGRICULTURAL SERVICE

SCIENCE & EDUCATION
DIRECTOR

AGRICULTURAL RESEARCH SERVICE
COOPERATIVE STATE RESEARCH SERVICE
EXTENSION SERVICE
NATIONAL AGRICULTURAL LIBRARY

AGRICULTURAL ECONOMICS
DIRECTOR

ECONOMIC RESEARCH SERVICE
STATISTICAL REPORTING SERVICE

MARKETING & CONSUMER SERVICES
ASSISTANT SECRETARY

COMMODITY EXCHANGE AUTHORITY
AGRICULTURAL MARKETING SERVICE
FOOD & NUTRITION SERVICE
PACKERS & STOCKYARDS ADMINISTRATION
ANIMAL AND PLANT HEALTH INSPECTION SERVICE

RURAL DEVELOPMENT & CONSERVATION
ASSISTANT SECRETARY

FARMER COOPERATIVE SERVICE
FARMERS HOME ADMINISTRATION
FOREST SERVICE
RURAL ELECTRIFICATION ADMINISTRATION
SOIL CONSERVATION SERVICE

Meat and Poultry Trade Journals

Feedstuffs
2501 Wayzata Blvd.
P.O.Box 67
Minneapolis, MN 55404

Broiler Industry
Garden State Publishers
4411 Landis
Sea Isle City, NJ 08243

The National Provisioners
15 W. Huron Avenue
Chicago, IL 60610

Meat Magazine
Harbrace Publishers, Inc.
Harbrace Building
Duluth, MN 55802

Meat Processing
Davies Publishers
645 N. Michigan Avenue
Chicago, IL 60611

Poultry Meat
Watt Publishing
Mount Morris, IL 61504

Public Interest and Consumer Groups Concerned with the Department of Agriculture

Edward Berlin
Berlin, Roisman and Kessler
1712 N Street, N.W.
Washington, DC 20036

Center for Study of
    Responsive Law
1156 19th Street, N.W.
Washington, DC 20036

Consumer Federation of
    America
1012 14th Street, N.W.
Washington, DC 20005

Consumers Union
Washington Office
1714 Massachusetts Ave., N.W.
Washington, DC 20036

Amalgamated Meat Cutters
    and Butchers Workmen
Washington Office
100 Indiana Avenue, N.W.
Washington, DC 20001

Meat and Poultry Inspection Programs

Western Region

Meat and Poultry Inspection Program
Consumer and Marketing Service
U.S. Department of Agriculture
Room 102, Building 2-C
620 Central Avenue
Alameda, CA 94501
415/273 7402

Alaska
Arizona
California
Colorado
Hawaii
Idaho
Montana
Nevada
Oregon
Utah
Washington
Wyoming
Samoa, Guam

Southwestern Region

Meat and Poultry Inspection Program
Consumer and Marketing Service
U.S. Department of Agriculture
Room 5-F41, 1100 Commerce Street
Dallas, TX 75202
214/749 3747

Arkansas
Kansas
Louisiana
Missouri
New Mexico
Oklahoma
Texas

North Central Region

Meat and Poultry Inspection Program
Consumer and Marketing Service
U.S. Department of Agriculture
Room 419, U.S. Courthouse Building
East First and Walnut Streets
Des Moines, IA 50309
515/284 4043

Illinois
Indiana
Iowa
Michigan
Minnesota
Nebraska
North Dakota
Ohio
South Dakota
Wisconsin

Southeastern Region

Meat and Poultry Inspection Program
Consumer and Marketing Service
U.S. Department of Agriculture
Room 216, 1718 Peachtree Street, N.W.
Atlanta, GA 30309
404/526 3911

Alabama
Florida
Georgia
Kentucky
Mississippi
North Carolina
Puerto Rico
South Carolina
Tennessee
Virgin Islands

Northeastern Region

Meat and Poultry Inspection Program
Consumer and Marketing Service
U.S. Department of Agriculture
7th Floor, 1421 Cherry Street
Philadelphia, PA 19102
215/597 4219

Connecticut
Delaware
District of Columbia
Maine
Maryland
Massachusetts
New Hampshire
New Jersey
New York
Pennsylvania
Rhode Island
Virginia
Vermont
West Virginia

Standards for Meat and Poultry Products

UNITED STATES DEPARTMENT OF AGRICULTURE
Consumer and Marketing Service

STANDARDS FOR MEAT AND POULTRY PRODUCTS

A Consumer Reference List

To be labeled with a particular name--such as "All Beef Franks" or "Chicken Soup"--a Federally inspected meat or poultry product must be approved by the U.S. Department of Agriculture as meeting specific product requirements. Following are products for which percentages of meat, poultry, or other ingredients have been established. (This list does not include all products for which requirements have been set, nor does it necessarily include all requirements for those products that are listed.)

Red Meat Products (all percentages of meat are on the basis of fresh uncooked weight unless otherwise indicated)

* BARBECUED MEATS - Weight of meat when barbecued can't exceed 70% of the weight of the fresh uncooked meat. Must have barbecued (crusted) appearance and be prepared over burning or smoldering hardwood or its sawdust.
* BARBECUE SAUCE WITH MEAT - At least 35% meat (cooked basis).
* BEANS WITH BACON IN SAUCE - At least 12% bacon.
* BEANS WITH FRANKFURTERS IN SAUCE - At least 20% franks.
* BEANS WITH HAM IN SAUCE - At least 12% ham (cooked basis).
* BEEF WITH BARBECUE SAUCE - At least 50% beef (cooked basis).
* BEEF WITH GRAVY - At least 50% beef (cooked basis). GRAVY WITH BEEF - At least 35% beef (cooked basis).
* BEEF SAUSAGE (raw) - No more than 30% fat.
* BEEF STROGANOFF - At least 45% fresh uncooked beef or 30% cooked beef, and at least 10% sour cream or a "gourmet" combination of at least 7.5% sour cream and 5% wine.
* BREADED STEAKS, CHOPS, etc. - Breading can't exceed 30% of the finished product weight.
* BREAKFAST SAUSAGE - No more than 50% fat.

August 1970

* BURRITOS - At least 15% meat.
* CHILI CON CARNE - At least 40% meat.
* CHILI CON CARNE WITH BEANS - At least 25% meat.
* CHILI SAUCE WITH MEAT - At least 6% meat.
* CHOP SUEY (AMERICAN STYLE) WITH MACARONI AND MEAT -
    At least 25% meat.
* CHOP SUEY VEGETABLES WITH MEAT - At least 12% meat.
* CHOW MEIN VEGETABLES WITH MEAT - At least 12% meat.
* CONDENSED, CREAMED DRIED BEEF OR CHIPPED BEEF - At
    least 18% dried or chipped beef (figured on
    reconstituted total content).
* CORN DOG - Must meet standards for frankfurters and
    batter cannot exceed the weight of the frank.
* CORNED BEEF AND CABBAGE - At least 25% corned beef.
* DEVILED HAM - No more than 35% fat.
* EGG FOO YUNG WITH MEAT - At least 12% meat.
* ENCHILADA WITH MEAT - At least 15% meat.
* EGG ROLLS WITH MEAT - At least 10% meat.
* FRANKFURTERS, BOLOGNA, OTHER COOKED SAUSAGE - May
    contain meat and meat by-products; no more than
    30% fat, 10% added water, and 2% corn syrup;
    no more than 15% poultry unless its presence is
    reflected in product name; no more than 3.5%
    cereals and nonfat dry milk, with product name
    showing that they're added. / "ALL MEAT" - Only
    muscle tissue with natural amounts of fat; no
    by-products, cereal, or binders. / "ALL BEEF" -
    Only meat of beef animals.
* FRITTERS - At least 35% meat.
* FROZEN BREAKFASTS - At least 15% meat (cooked basis).
* FROZEN DINNERS - At least 25% meat or meat food
    product (cooked basis, figured on total meal
    minus appetizer, bread and dessert).
* HAM - Not permitted to weigh more after processing
    than the fresh ham weighs before curing and
    smoking. Hams containing up to 10% added water
    must be labeled as "HAM - WATER ADDED." If
    added water exceeds 10%, must be labeled
    "IMITATION HAM."
* HAMBURGER OR GROUND BEEF - No more than 30% fat.
* HAM AND CHEESE SPREAD - At least 25% ham (cooked
    basis).
* HAM CHOWDER - At least 10% ham (cooked basis).
* HAM CROQUETTES - At least 35% ham (cooked basis).
* HAM SPREAD - At least 50% ham.
* HASH - At least 35% meat (cooked basis).
* LASAGNA WITH MEAT AND SAUCE - At least 12% meat.
* LIMA BEANS WITH HAM OR BACON IN SAUCE - At least 12%
    ham or cooked bacon.

* LIVER SAUSAGE, LIVER LOAF, LIVER PASTE, LIVER
    CHEESE, LIVER PUDDING, LIVER SPREAD, and
    similar liver products - At least 30% liver.
* MACARONI AND CHEESE WITH HAM - At least 12% ham
    (cooked basis).
* MACARONI AND BEEF IN TOMATO SAUCE - At least 12%
    beef.
* MEAT CASSEROLES - At least 25% fresh uncooked meat
    or 18% cooked meat.
* MEAT PIES - At least 25% meat.
* MEAT RAVIOLI - At least 10% meat in ravioli, minus
    the sauce.
* MEAT SALADS - At least 35% meat (cooked basis).
* MEAT TACOS - At least 15% meat.
* MEAT TURNOVERS - At least 25% meat.
* OMELET WITH BACON - At least 12% bacon (cooked
    basis).
* OMELET WITH HAM - At least 18% ham (cooked basis).
* PEPPER STEAKS - At least 30% beef (cooked basis).
* PIZZA WITH MEAT - At least 15% meat.
* PIZZA WITH SAUSAGE - At least 12% sausage (cooked
    basis) or 10% dry sausage, such as pepperoni.
* PORK SAUSAGE - Not more than 50% fat.
* PORK WITH BARBECUE SAUCE - At least 50% pork
    (cooked basis).
* SAUERKRAUT WITH WIENERS AND JUICE - At least 20%
    weiners.
* SCALLOPED POTATOES AND HAM - At least 20% ham
    (cooked basis).
* SCALLOPINE - At least 35% meat (cooked basis).
* SCRAPPLE - At least 40% meat and/or meat by-
    products.
* SPAGHETTI SAUCE WITH MEAT - At least 6% meat.
* SPAGHETTI SAUCE AND MEAT BALLS - At least 35% meat
    balls (cooked basis).
* SPAGHETTI WITH MEAT AND SAUCE - At least 12% meat.
* SPAGHETTI WITH MEAT BALLS AND SAUCE - At least 12%
    meat.
* SPANISH RICE WITH BEEF OR HAM - At least 20% beef
    or ham (cooked basis).
* STEWS (BEEF, LAMB, and the like) - At least 25%
    meat.
* SUKIYAKI - At least 30% meat.
* SWEET AND SOUR PORK OR BEEF - At least 25% fresh
    uncooked meat or 16% cooked meat, and at least
    16% fruit.
* SWISS STEAK WITH GRAVY - At least 50% meat (cooked
    basis). /GRAVY AND SWISS STEAK - At least 35%
    meat (cooked basis).

* TAMALES - At least 25% meat.
* TAMALES WITH SAUCE ¬ (or WITH GRAVY) - At least
    20% meat.
* TONGUE SPREAD - At least 50% tongue.
* VEAL BIRDS - At least 60% meat and not more than
    40% stuffing.
* VEAL CORDON BLEU - At least 60% veal, 5% ham, and
    containing Swiss, Gruyere or Mozzarella cheese.
* VEAL FRICASSEE - At least 40% meat.
* VEAL PARMAGIANA - At least 40% breaded meat product
    in sauce. Breaded meat portion - At least
    28% meat (cooked basis).
* VEAL STEAKS - Can be chopped, shaped, cubed, frozen.
    Beef can be added with product name shown as
    "VEAL STEAKS, BEEF ADDED, CHOPPED, SHAPED, AND
    CUBED." No more than 20% beef or must be
    labeled "VEAL AND BEEF STEAK, CHOPPED, SHAPED
    AND CUBED." No more than 30% fat.

Poultry Products (all percentages of poultry--chicken,
turkey, or other kinds of poultry--are on cooked deboned
basis unless otherwise indicated)

* BREADED POULTRY - No more than 30% breading.
* CANNED BONED POULTRY:
    -- BONED (kind), SOLID PACK - At least 95%
       poultry meat, skin and fat.
    -- BONED (kind) - At least 90% poultry meat,
       skin and fat.
    -- BONED (kind), WITH BROTH - At least 80%
       poultry meat, skin and fat.
    -- BONED (kind), WITH SPECIFIED PERCENTAGE OF
       BROTH - At least 50% poultry meat, skin and
       fat.
* CHICKEN CACCIATORE - At least 20% chicken meat, or
    40% with bone.
* CHICKEN CROQUETTES - At least 25% chicken meat.
* CHOPPED POULTRY WITH BROTH (BABY FOOD) - At least
    43% poultry meat, with skin, fat, and seasoning.
* CREAMED POULTRY - At least 20% poultry meat.
* POULTRY A LA KING - At least 20% poultry meat.
* POULTRY BARBECUE - At least 40% poultry meat.
* POULTRY BURGERS - 100% poultry meat, with skin and
    fat.
* POULTRY CHOP SUEY - At least 4% poultry meat. / CHOP
    SUEY WITH POULTRY - At least 2% poultry meat.
* POULTRY CHOW MEIN, WITHOUT NOODLES - At least 4%
    poultry meat.

* POULTRY DINNERS - At least 18% poultry meat.
* POULTRY FRICASSEE - At least 20% poultry meat.
* POULTRY FRICASSEE OF WINGS - At least 40% poultry
    meat (cooked basis, with bone).
* POULTRY HASH - At least 30% poultry meat.
* POULTRY NOODLES OR DUMPLINGS - At least 15% poultry
    meat, or 30% with bone. / NOODLES OR DUMPLINGS
    WITH POULTRY - At least 6% poultry meat.
* POULTRY PIES - At least 14% poultry meat.
* POULTRY RAVIOLI - At least 2% poultry meat.
* POULTRY ROLLS - Binding agents limited to 3% in
    cooked roll.
* POULTRY SALAD - At least 25% poultry meat.
* POULTRY SOUP - At least 2% poultry meat.
* POULTRY STEW - At least 12% poultry meat.
* POULTRY STROGANOFF - At least 30% poultry meat.
* POULTRY TAMALES - At least 6% poultry meat.
* POULTRY TETRAZZINI - At least 15% poultry meat.
* POULTRY WITH GRAVY - At least 35% poultry meat. /
    GRAVY WITH POULTRY - At least 15% poultry meat.
* SLICED POULTRY WITH GRAVY - At least 35% poultry.

Complete standards of identity currently exist for
three meat products. These standards require specific
ingredients to be present as follows:

* CORNED BEEF HASH - Must contain at least 35% beef
  (cooked basis). Also must contain potatoes (either
  fresh, dehydrated, cooked dehydrated, or a mixture
  of these types), curing agents, and seasonings. May
  be made with certain optional ingredients such as
  onions, garlic, beef broth, or beef fat. May not
  contain more than 15% fat nor more than 72% moisture.

* CHOPPED HAM - Must contain fresh, cured, or smoked
  ham, along with certain specified kinds of curing
  agents and seasonings. May also contain certain
  optional ingredients in specified amounts, including
  finely chopped ham shank meat, dehydrated onions,
  dehydrated garlic, corn syrup, other chemical substances as permitted in the Federal standard, and not
  more than 3% water to dissolve the curing agents.

* OLEOMARGARINE OR MARGARINE - Must contain either the
  rendered fat, oil, or stearin derived from cattle,
  sheep, swine, or goats; or a vegetable food fat, oil,

or stearin; or a combination of these two classes of
ingredients in a specified proportion. Must contain
--individually or in combination--pasteurized cream,
cow's milk, skim milk, a combination of nonfat dry
milk and water or finely ground soybeans and water.
May contain optional ingredients specified in the
standard, including butter, salt, artificial coloring, vitamins A and D, and permitted chemical substances. Fat in finished product may not exceed
80%. Label must indicate whether product is from
animal or vegetable origin or both.

Sample Petition: Restriction of the Addition of Sodium Nitrate or Sodium Nitrite to Meat or Meat Food Products

BEFORE THE
UNITED STATES DEPARTMENT OF AGRICULTURE

Harrison Wellford, Marcy Schuck, on
behalf of herself and her infant child,
Christopher, and Center for Science in
the Public Interest,

Petitioners

TO: Honorable Earl Butz
       Secretary of Agriculture

   PETITION REQUESTING THE AMENDMENT OF SECTION
   318.7(c) OF THE DEPARTMENT'S MEAT INSPECTION
   REGULATIONS TO RESTRICT THE ADDITION OF
        SODIUM NITRATE OR SODIUM NITRITE TO
   MEAT OR MEAT FOOD PRODUCTS, AND OTHER RELIEF

     Petitioners request the Secretary of Agriculture to
exercise his authority under Section 5, Section 21, and
other sections of the Wholesome Meat Act, 81 Stat. 584 et
seq., as amended, 21 U.S.C. Sections 601 et seq. (hereinafter "the Act"), to take the following actions:

     1.   Immediately prohibit (a) the use of sodium
nitrite (hereinafter "nitrite") in meat or meat food
products (hereinafter "meat products") for the uses now
approved under Section 318.7(c) of the Meat Inspection
Regulations, as amended June 15, 1971 (hereinafter "the
Regulations"), i.e., "to fix color," and (b) the use of
sodium nitrate (hereinafter "nitrate") as a source of
nitrite to the extent that such nitrite is used "to fix
color."

     2.   Immediately prohibit the use of nitrate and
nitrite in bacon products, and in meat products intended
for babies. Because baby foods have a slow turnover and
may remain on supermarket shelves for months, USDA should
initiate seizure or recall actions for baby food products
to which nitrite or nitrate has been added.

     3.   With respect to meat products not mentioned in
(2), immediately convene a scientific panel of dis-
tinguished scientists to determine (a) the efficacy of
nitrites in the prevention of botulism under ordinary

meat processing conditions; (b) if efficacious, whether the use of nitrite as an anti-botulism agent in meat products is necessary, taking into account the availability of equally efficacious, less hazardous substitute additives or processes; and (c) if no such substitute exists, the smallest quantity of nitrate and nitrite that must be added to meat products in order to achieve the necessary anti-botulism effect in each such product.

4. With respect to meat products not mentioned in (2), require that all uses of nitrate and nitrite in meat products terminate as of September 1, 1972, unless such scientific panel determines that nitrite is efficacious in the prevention of botulism under ordinary meat processing conditions, and that no equally efficacious, less hazardous substitute additive or process is, or within a reasonable length of time can be made, available. In the event of such a determination, the Secretary shall immediately require that meat products not mentioned in (2) thereafter contain no more than the smallest quantity of nitrate and nitrite found by such panel to be necessary to prevent botulism in each such product.

5. To the extent that nitrate and nitrite are permitted for use in meat products, require (under Section 7 and other sections of the Act, and under Part 317 of the Regulations) that all meat products containing nitrate or nitrite bear an appropriate label designating the presence in the meat product of nitrate or nitrite.

A steadily accumulating body of scientific and other evidence establishes a number of propositions, which together constitute reasonable grounds for granting this petition. These propositions include the following:

(1) Nitrite, and nitrate, after reduction to nitrite, may combine with hemoglobin in the blood of children and certain susceptible adults to form methemoglobin, destroying the oxygen-carrying capacity of the blood.

(2) Nitrite, and nitrate, after reduction to nitrite, may cause the formation of nitrosamines through interaction with secondary and tertiary amines.

(3) Nitrosamines cause cancer in a wide variety of test animals, and there is a strong presumption that they are carcinogenic for man.

(4) Nitrosamines have been detected in hot dogs (up to 80 ppb), bacon (up to 106 ppb), dried beef, smoked fish, cured pork, and other meat products.

(5) Nitrosamine formation has been observed in vivo in some mammalian species, and there is a strong presumption that such formation can occur in man.

(6) The addition of nitrite and nitrate to meat products is responsible for the presence of nitrosamines in such products.

(7) No safe level of carcinogenic nitrosamines in meat products has been determined.

(8) Nitrites and nitrates in bacon and baby food meat products are used for cosmetic purposes only, i.e., to fix a red color in the product. There is no botulism danger from ingestion of these products and thus no justification for permitting the use therein of such dangerous substances.

(9) The United States Department of Agriculture (hereinafter "USDA") has failed to determine whether the levels of nitrite and nitrate added to meat products other than bacon and baby food meat products are in excess of amounts necessary to protect against botulism.

(10) Any benefits from the cosmetic uses of nitrite are greatly outweighed by the potential hazards of nitrosamine formation caused by nitrite.

(11) USDA's failure to identify nitrate and nitrite as ingredients of meat products on the product label violates both the Act and USDA's own Regulations thereunder.

Taken altogether, the evidence summarized herein in support of these propositions requires that USDA act promptly to grant the relief requested above.

I. PETITIONERS

Petitioner Harrison Wellford is a resident of Washington, D.C. and is a consumer of meat products. As a consultant to the Center for Study of Responsive Law, a non-profit, tax-exempt organization engaged in public interest research, petitioner Wellford directed a task force studying USDA and has authored a book and several articles concerned with the activities and policies of USDA. Pursuant to these concerns, petitioner Wellford has also initiated several actions and proceedings within and against USDA.

Petitioner Marcy Schuck is a resident of Washington,
D.C. and is a consumer of meat products. She is the
mother of an infant son, Christopher Schuck, who is also
a resident of Washington, D.C. and is a consumer of baby
food meat products.

Petitioner Center for Science in the Public Interest
is a non-profit, tax-exempt organization in Washington,
D.C. engaged in public interest research on consumer and
environmental problems.

II. AUTHORITY FOR PETITION

Petitioners are authorized to submit this petition
and obtain a final order with respect thereto by Section
4(d) of the Administrative Procedures Act (5 U.S.C. Section
553(e)), and 7 C.F.R. Section 1.28, which authorize an
interested party to petition the Department for "the
issuance, amendment or repeal of a rule."

III. OTHER RELEVANT PROCEEDINGS

A. The Petition to the Secretary of Health,
Education and Welfare Concerning the Use of
Nitrate and Nitrite in Foods and Drugs

Soon after the filing of this petition, petitioners
expect to file a petition (hereinafter "the HEW petition")
with the Secretary of Health, Education and Welfare pursuant to Section 409(h) of the Food, Drug, and Cosmetic
Act (21 U.S.C. Section 348(h) and 21 C.F.R. Section 121.74),
which authorize petitions for the amendment or repeal of
food additive regulations issued pursuant to Section 409
of that Act.

The HEW petition will request that the Secretary of
HEW restrict the use of nitrate and nitrite in food and
drugs. The HEW petition will request that the use of
nitrate or nitrite in food products be permitted only if
and to the extent that (a) such substances are demonstrated to be actually necessary to prevent botulism
contamination of such products and (b) no equally efficacious, less hazardous substitute additive or process
is, or within a reasonable time can be made available.

B. Request for Information from USDA Relating to
    the Use of Nitrate and Nitrite in Meat Products

On January 21, 1972, petitioner Wellford wrote to Dr.
William J. Minor, Chief of the Products Standards Branch,
Consumer and Marketing Science, USDA, requesting various
information pertaining to the issues raised by this petition. No response has yet been received from USDA.

C. Recent Action Against Nitrate and Nitrite in
    Norway

In November, 1971, the National Health Department of
Norway banned the use of nitrate and nitrite as coloring
agents in meat after experiments showed that small doses,
when combined with other ingredients, can cause cancer in
animal organs. The ban will not take effect until January
1, 1973, unless the meat industry by that time can
establish that nitrite is necessary to prevent botulism.
Norway, therefore, places the burden of proof as to the
safety of nitrites on the meat industry.

IV. APPLICABLE LAWS

Section 1(m) (1) of the Act defines an "adulterated"
meat product as one which, inter alia, "bears or contains
any poisonous or deleterious substance which may render it
injurious to health; . . . ." Under the Act, a product
that is "adulterated" is, by reason of that fact, "misbranded" as well. (Section 1(n)(1)) Various other provisions of the Act (e.g., Sections 3, 5, 21) prohibit the
introduction into interstate commerce of adulterated meat
products, and require the Secretary of Agriculture to
issue rules and regulations to prevent such introduction.

Section 318.7 of the Regulations authorizes the addition to cured meat products of 500 parts per million (ppm)
of nitrate as a source of nitrite, and 200 ppm of nitrite
in the finished product, to fix color. These are the
only direct food additive uses of nitrate and nitrite
authorized under the Act.

The Food, Drug and Cosmetic Act, 21 U.S.C. Section
301 et seq., is administered by HEW and regulates exclusively the use of all food additives, including nitrate
and nitrite, the only relevant exception being "any substance used in accordance with a sanction or approval
granted prior to September 6, 1958 pursuant to . . . the

Meat Inspection Act of March 4, 1907, as amended and
extended." (Section 201(s)(4) of the Food, Drug and
Cosmetic Act) Thus, any direct food additive use in
meat products (a) of nitrate other than as a source of
nitrite, and (b) of nitrite other than to fix color,
cannot be authorized by USDA; such uses were not and are
not sanctioned under the Meat Inspection Act, as amended
and extended.

Section 1(n)(11) of the Act provides that a meat
food product is "misbranded . . . if it bears or contains
any artificial flavoring, artificial coloring, or chemical
preservative, unless it bears labeling stating that fact:
Provided, That, to the extent that compliance with the
requirements of this subparagraph (11) is impracticable,
exemptions shall be established by regulations promulgated by the Secretary." Various other provisions of
the Act prohibit the introduction into interstate commerce
of misbranded meat products, and require the Secretary
to issue rules and regulations to prevent such introduction.

Section 301.2(ii)(11) of the Regulations similarly
requires the labeling of artificial flavoring, artificial
coloring, or chemical preservatives. And Section 317.2(j)
(12) provides that "containers of other products packed
in, bearing, or containing any chemical preservative
shall bear a label stating that fact."

V. THE DANGERS TO MAN OF NITRATE AND NITRITE

The scientific evidence concerning the human health
hazards associated with the use of nitrate and nitrite in
the food supply is abundant and, for the most part, not
controversial. This evidence clearly demonstrates that
nitrate and nitrite have no place in the human food supply
unless and only to the extent that they can be shown to be
indispensable for the prevention of botulism.

A. Acute Effects

Nitrates are relatively non-toxic to living systems
(Regulation of Food Additives and Medicated Animal Feeds:
Hearings Before Intergovernmental Relations Subcommittee
of the House Committee on Government Operations, 92nd
Congress, 1st Session, March 1971 (hereinafter "Fountain
Subcommittee Hearings"), p. 12). They are of concern
chiefly because they are a source of nitrites through

conversion by means of bacteriological action in foods and in the human body. The following discussion, then, will be confined almost wholly to nitrites.

In the human body, nitrites react with hemoglobin to produce methemoglobin, a pigment suppressing the ability of red blood cells to carry oxygen. Theoretically, one gram of nitrite can convert up to approximately 1855 grams of hemoglobin to methemoglobin (Fountain Subcommittee Hearings, p. 212). Infants seem to be especially prone to this type of poisoning, and several deaths have been reported over the years from this source (Fountain Subcommittee Hearings, p. 12). In addition, there are many cases on record of death and serious acute effects from the misuse of nitrite in food. Dr. A.J. Lehman, former Director of FDA's Division of Pharmacology and Toxicology, has warned that "only a small margin of safety exists between the amount of nitrite that is safe and that which may be dangerous. The margin of safety is even more reduced when the smaller blood volume and the corresponding small quantity of hemoglobin in children is taken into account." (Dr. A.J. Lehman, "Nitrates and Nitrites in Meat Products," Association of Food and Drug Officials of the United States, Vol. XXII, No. 3, July, 1958) Dr. Lehman's statement was prompted by over a dozen cases of nitrite poisoning of children in 1955 and 1956.

The danger of methemoglobin formation from nitrite, while principally a health hazard to children, may also constitute a hazard to persons suffering from anemia and to fetuses during the latter stages of pregnancy when the fetal blood system has been established. (Fountain Subcommittee Hearings, pp. 145-146)

Baby food manufacturers insist that these chemicals are added to infant foods only to impart a red color to infant meat products. In a letter of January 11, 1971 to petitioner Center for Science in the Public Interest, for example, Dr. Robert A. Stewart, Director of Research of Gerber's Baby Foods, stated:

> To reiterate, nitrite and nitrate are not
> food preservatives. They are not used for
> the purpose of destroying or controlling
> bacteria. They do cure meat by producing
> chemical changes resulting in the charac-
> teristic color and flavor of cured ham,
> bacon, etc.

In a letter of January 13, 1971 to petitioner Center for Science in the Public Interest, Dr. I.J. Hutchings,

General Manager of Research and Development for the Heinz Company, stated that Heinz does not add <u>any</u> nitrate or nitrite to baby foods:

> The Heinz Company does not add either sodium nitrate or nitrite to infant foods; and to the best of my knowledge, it is added to only limited items by other baby food manufacturers.
>
> When sodium nitrate and nitrite are added to infant foods, they are not used in the true sense of preservatives (i.e. to prevent bacteriological growth), but are present to preserve the color of certain meat varieties.

And in a letter of February 3, 1971 to petitioner Center for Science in the Public Interest, Beech-Nut, Inc. indicated that it adds to its baby foods amounts of nitrate and nitrite too small to serve any purpose other than as a color fixative.

Under the circumstances, then, it is irresponsible for USDA to permit <u>any</u> nitrate or nitrite in baby foods. According to the Joint FAO/WHO Expert Committee on Food Additives, "Nitrate should on no account be added to baby foods" and "Food for babies should not contain added nitrite." (WHO Technical Report, Series No. 228, pp. 72, 75) Given the danger to fetuses, children, and others from methemoglobin formation, and given the danger from nitrosamine formation discussed below, the addition of nitrate or nitrite to such foods is clearly an "adulteration" within the meaning of the Act. Cosmetic considerations cannot be permitted to outweigh the human health hazards associated with the use of these substances in such foods.

B.   Chronic Effects

The danger of methemoglobin formation from nitrite ingestion is a hazard peculiar to infants and others with oxygen-carrying deficiencies in their blood. In addition, however, nitrites present serious chronic health hazards to <u>all</u> humans who eat meat products cured with nitrites or nitrates.

The scientific community is in universal agreement that nitrites under certain conditions, interact with secondary amines to form nitrosamines. (FDA, Review on the Chemistry and Toxicology of Nitrates, and Nitroso

Compounds (Nitrosamines) as óf August 28, 1970, reprinted
in Fountain Subcommittee Hearings, p. 604) And it is
equally undisputed that most nitrosamines tested are
carcinogenic, and some highly so, to a wide variety of
mammalian and non-mammalian species. According to Dr.
William Lijinsky, a leading cancer researcher, nitrosamines are among the most potent carcinogens we know and
are certainly the most widely acting group of carcinogens.
(Fountain Subcommittee Hearings, p. 132)

Nitrosamines cause cancer in a wide variety of
species, including the rat, hamster, mouse, guinea pig,
dog, and monkey. (P.N. Magee, "Toxicity of Nitrosamines:
Their Possible Human Health Hazards," Fd. Cosmet. Toxi-
col., vol. 9 (1971))

There appears to be no published report of any
animal species that is resistant to carcinogenisis by
these agents. (Magee, p. 215) Experiments with rats
show that nitrosamines attack many different organs of
the animals, including the lungs, liver, esophagus, and
other sites. (Lijinsky and Epstein, "Nitrosamines as
Environmental Carcinogens," Nature, vol. 225, No. 5227
(1970)) Recent studies on the toxicity of nitrosamines
have concluded that they are a threat to human beings.
Dr. P.N. Magee of England's Courtault Institute of Bio-
chemistry warns that the nitroso compounds have "many of
the properties that might be predicted for an environmental carcinogen to which man would be susceptible."
(Magee, p. 215) A cancer researcher at Oak Ridge National
Laboratory, Dr. William Lijinsky, and Dr. Samuel Epstein,
Swetland Professor of Environmental Health and Human
Ecology at Case Western Reserve Medical School, conclude
that "nitrosamines seem to be a major candidate class of
carcinogens that are likely to be causally related to
human cancer in industrialized society." (Lijinsky and
Epstein, p. 223) An FDA Status Report on the toxicology
of nitrites and nitrosamines states that since nitrosamines "can induce tumors in a wide spectrum of experimental animals, including the non-human primate, these
compounds may have a high potential for induction of neo-
plasia in man" (Reprinted at Fountain Subcommittee
Hearings, p. 608).

Danger from human exposure to nitrosamines derives
from two sources--their presence in human food and their
formation in the body.

Nitrosamines have recently been found in many food
products, including frankfurters in amounts up to 80 ppb,

in bacon (after frying) up to 106 ppb, in dried beef and
cured pork products up to 48 ppb, in ham up to 5 ppb, and
in fish up to 26 ppb.   (Memo to file of September 13,
1971 by Dr. Harry Mussman, Director of Laboratory Services,
USDA; Joint USDA-HEW press release of February 5, 1972;
Fountain Subcommittee Hearings, p. 619)   Since a limited
sampling program for nitrosamines has only recently been
inaugurated by USDA, these findings are suggestive of
significant contamination of the food supply with highly
carcinogenic nitrosamines.

In addition to exposure from the formation of nitrosamines in food, there is also the distinct possibility
of human exposure from the formation of nitrosamines in
the human stomach.   Nitrosamine formation from the interaction of nitrites and secondary amines is favored by the
acid conditions of the mammalian stomach.   (Magee, p. 214)
This reaction has been established in vitro in cats,
rabbits, dogs, and man, and it has been established in
vivo in cats and rabbits, species whose gastric juices are
similar in pH to man.   (Magee, p. 214)   The presence of
nitrosodiphenylamine was found in the stomachs of 31
human subjects given a combination of nitrate and a secondary amine.   (Magee, p. 215)

The pervasiveness of secondary amines in foods,
alcohol, tobacco smoke and other common substances, and
the possibility of their interaction with nitrite added
to food under pH conditions prevailing in the human
stomach, have caused Drs. Lijinsky and Epstein to conclude: "In vivo formation of nitrosamines from ingested
nitrite and certain secondary amines is potentially a
serious problem, especially because nitrosamines are
possibly more significant in human cancer in industrialized society than are polynuclear compounds, azo dyes or
aflatoxins."   (Lijinsky and Epstein, p. 23)

The great weight of scientific opinion holds that
chronic exposure to carcinogens such as nitrosamines,
even in the amounts to which humans are likely to be
exposed, constitutes a grave risk to human health.
(Report to the Surgeon General, USPHS, April 22, 1970 by
Ad Hoc Committee on the Evaluation of Low Levels of Environmental Chemical Carcinogens, National Cancer
Institute); (Lijinsky and Epstein)

According to Dr. Lijinsky, "Nitrosamines...seem to
be most effective in eliciting tumors when they are
applied as small doses over a long period, rather than
as large single doses.   These are precisely the conditions

under which we would be exposed to nitrosamines if they
are, indeed, formed by interaction of amines with nitrites
in our diet." (Fountain Subcommittee Hearings, p. 132)

Nitrosamines produce cancer of the liver in rats at
dietary levels as low as 2 parts per million, the lowest
levels tested. The FDA Status Report noted that "because
of these multiple observations on carcinogenicity in
experimental animals and since low levels (2 ppm) of
dimethylnitrosamine produced malignant tumors in the rat,
a 'no effect' level for this formed compound has not been
established." (Fountain Subcommittee Hearings, p. 608)

The Food, Drug and Cosmetic Act, including the Food
Additive Amendment of 1958, 21 U.S.C. Section 348, not
only places the burden of proof of food additive safety
on the food manufacturers, but provides in the Delaney
Clause that no additive shall be deemed to be safe if it
is found to induce cancer in man or animal. (Section
348(c)(3)(A))

It is only because of a quirk in the law--namely,
that USDA approved nitrate and nitrite as curing agents
under the Meat Inspection Act prior to the passage of the
1958 Amendments--that their use in meat is not subject to
the Food, Drug and Cosmetic Act, including the Delaney
Clause. The same standard of safety, however, should
apply.

Under the standard imposed by the Delaney Clause, the
use of nitrate and nitrite in meat or meat food products
would clearly be prohibited. Dr. Virgil Wodicka, Director
of FDA's Bureau of Foods, recognized this fact in testimony
before the Fountain Subcommittee at a time when nitrosamines had not yet been found in foods:

> If it were demonstrated that the nitrites
> added to meat or fish produced nitrosamines
> in the meat or fish and those nitrosamines
> were then consumed, this could not be per-
> mitted under the Delaney amendment. (p. 540)

> We could not permit the use of nitrites
> if it led to the formation of nitrosamines
> in food. (p. 541)

And another FDA official, Dr. Ramsey, stated in 1971
that in view of the suspected hazards from nitrosamine
formation, it would be "impossible" for FDA to approve the

present level of nitrite if the compound had just been
discovered (cited in Chemicals and the Future of Man:
Hearings Before the Subcommittee on Executive Reorganization and Government Research of the Senate Committee on
Government Operations, 92nd Congress, 1st Session. April
1971 (hereinafter "Ribicoff Subcommittee Hearings,"
p. 54).

While no cases of human cancer have definitely been
traced to exposure to nitrosamines, cancer researchers
stress that this is not a basis for assuming that there
is no such danger, particularly in view of the crudity and
lack of specificity of epidemiological data. Indeed,
there is wide agreement among such scientists that any
unnecessary exposure to a carcinogen constitutes a health
risk for man. A National Cancer Institute Committee
recently reported to the Surgeon General that "any substance which is shown conclusively to cause tumors in
animals should be considered carcinogenic and therefore a
potential cancer hazard for man.... It is essential to
recognize that no level of exposure to a carcinogenic substance, however low it may be, can be considered to be a
'safe' level for man." For these reasons, some scientists
predict that "reduction of human exposure to nitrites and
certain secondary amines, particularly in foods, may
result in a decrease in the incidence of human cancer."
(Lijinsky and Epstein, p. 23)

It is clear, then, that the human health dangers from
nitrate and nitrite use in meat products, while not quan-
tifiable, are significant and perhaps irreversible. Apart
from the cosmetic efficacy of nitrate and nitrite, however,
only one benefit from such use has even been suggested--the
prevention of botulism--and the anti-botulism effects of
these chemicals with respect to most cured meat products
are either non-existent or highly questionable.

The Botulism Hazard

There is evidence that in meat products the botulism
danger is limited to hermetically-sealed, shelf-stable,
cured meat products which do not require further cooking
before eating. The spores of Clostridium botulinum are
extremely rare in meat. (R. Greenberg et al., Appl.
Microbiol., 14:789, 1966; Fountain Subcommittee Hearings,
p. 236) In the rare event that they are present, the
following conditions help determine whether they produce
the toxins which cause human illness:

(1)   there must be an anerobic (oxygen-free) environment
       in or around the meat product for the spores to
       exist and multiply.

(2)   cooking meat at temperatures above 250 degrees F.
       for 2.7 minutes kills the spores, and cooking at
       temperatures above 176 degrees F. for 15 minutes or
       less kills the toxins produced by the spores. (G.M.
       Dack, Food Poisoning, 3rd ed., Univ. of Chicago
       Press, 1956, pp. 102-03) At boiling temperature (212
       degrees F.), the toxins would be killed even sooner.

(3)   Types A and B botulism, the types commonly found in
       meat, will not multiply and produce toxins when meat
       is   refrigerated at temperature below 40 degrees F.

       The following meat products carry no botulism hazard
and therefore can be immediately cleansed of nitrite without increasing the risks of food poisoning:

(1)   bacon: USDA officials have stated publicly that
       bacon poses no botulism hazard whatsoever. According
       to Mr. R. Paul Elliott, Chief of USDA's Chemistry and
       Microbiology Branch, "Bacon...which is always heated
       thoroughly, could not, under any circumstances become
       a hazard from botulism." (Fountain Subcommittee
       Hearings, p. 262) Nevertheless, nitrite is added to
       bacon to fix its red color and enhance flavor without
       any identification on the product label. Highly
       carcinogenic nitrosamines have recently been found
       in bacon in amounts up to 106 ppb after it had been
       fried. Since botulism poses no hazard in bacon, the
       use of nitrate and nitrite in bacon should be sus-
       pended immediately.

(2)   baby foods containing cured meat products: Baby
       foods are sterilized by heat processing above 250
       in hermetically sealed containers. This process
       kills any botulinum spores and toxins which may be
       present. According to statements from Gerber, Swift,
       Beech-Nut and Heinz officials, nitrites are used in
       baby foods to fix their color and enhance their
       taste, not to destroy or control bacteria. Because
       there is no botulism danger, the Heinz Company felt
       no need to add any nitrite or nitrate to its infant
       foods. Gerber, Beech-Nut, and Swift, on the other
       hand, added nitrites to some of their baby food meat
       products, but for cosmetic purposes only. Since
       botulism does not exist as a hazard in these products

and since any added nitrite or nitrate increase
the risks of carcinogenic nitrosamine formation,
the use of nitrite and nitrate in these products
should be suspended immediately.

The extent, if any, of the botulism hazard in frankfurters has not been definitely determined, but the available evidence strongly suggests that no such hazard exists.
There is some doubt whether the permeable skinned frankfurter possesses the anerobic environment necessary for
the survival of <u>Clostridium botulinum</u>. Second, since
frankfurters are refrigerated, any spores of botulism
present would be unlikely to multiply and produce toxins.
Third, since frankfurters are cooked before eating, any
toxins present would almost certainly be killed before
consumption. USDA officials have publicly stated that
"any food that must be cooked [before eating] will not be
a hazard from botulism from any toxin formed before
cooking, because the toxin is easily destroyed by heat."
(<u>Fountain Subcommittee Hearings</u>, p. 262)

Fourth, at least one company already markets a frankfurter devoid of nitrate, nitrite, or any other chemical
preservative. The Maple Crest Sausage Company of Rochester, New York has sold a frozen nitrite-free, preservative-
free frankfurter for several years. Consumers Cooperative
is planning to market a similar product soon in the Washington, D.C. area. And Giant Foods, a large retail chain,
plans to market a non-frozen frankfurter free of chemical
preservatives.

It is noteworthy that USDA imposes no <u>minimum</u> nitrate
or nitrite level requirement on frankfurters or other meat
products. If nitrate or nitrite were necessary to prevent
botulism, USDA would have to insure that sufficient levels
of these substances were present. In testimony before the
Fountain Subcommittee in 1971, the following exchange
occurred between Dr. Goldhammer of the Subcommittee staff
and Mr. Elliott of USDA (<u>Fountain Subcommittee Hearings</u>,
p. 237):

     Mr. Goldhammer: The question I asked was, do you not
                         have a minimum nitrite content de-
                         clared in your regulation, because
                         below that minimum you may not have
                         preservation? Just as the FDA had
                         to do in connection with the chubs.

     Mr. Elliott: You are quite right. It is a very
                         good point.

The absence of such minima, the absence of even a single reported outbreak of botulism since at least 1950 attributable to meat or poultry to which nitrites were not added (Fountain Subcommittee Hearings, pp. 383-88), together with the nitrite-related human health hazards documented above, require that a heavy burden of proving the existence of an anti-botulism effect from nitrite rests on those seeking to justify its use.

It therefore appears that the botulism risk in frankfurters, if it exists at all, is exceedingly remote, and that alternative processing methods to prevent botulism are available. The frankfurter is the nation's most popular processed meat product; billions are consumed each year. It is a special favorite of children. Any addition of nitrate or nitrite which is not necessary to protect against botulism creates particularly high risks in these products. Therefore, the use of nitrites in frankfurters should be suspended, unless scientific data is produced within six months (a reasonable period for the development of such data) demonstrating that there is a botulism hazard in frankfurters and that nitrite, in strictly specified amounts, is necessary to protect against it.

VI. PRAYER FOR RELIEF

For the reasons set forth above, petitioners request that the Secretary grant the relief set forth on pages 1 and 2 of this Petition.

Respectfully submitted,

Peter H. Schuck
400 - 7th Street, S.E.
Washington, DC. 20003

Attorney for Petitioners

February 9, 1972

CHAPTER 13

THE NATIONAL HIGHWAY TRAFFIC SAFETY ADMINISTRATION

> *In 1970, some 55,330 persons died in traffic accidents, 2 percent less than in 1969, a difference of 1,100 lives. The Federal Highway Administration estimates that the number of miles traveled . . . went up by about 5 percent in both 1970 and 1971.*
>
> *The reduction of 1,100 deaths in 1970 was the first substantial drop in motor vehicle fatalities since 1958. It was largely attributed by safety experts to increased use of seat belts, improved highways and driver education, and certain safety features in the new automobiles mandated by the National Traffic and Motor Vehicle Safety Act of 1966.*
>
> —The New York Times,
> 12 December 1971, p. 82

Actions of the National Highway Traffic Safety Administration (NHTSA) may affect your life and limb. NHTSA is part of the Department of Transportation. Had the NHTSA never come into existence, and had the auto companies continued to ignore safety in their products as they had before 1966, the number of fatalities in 1972 due to auto accidents could have been increased by as many as 8,000 over the actual number of 57,000. However, for the first time since the passage of both the National Traffic and Motor Vehicle Safety Act and the Highway Safety Act of 1966, the rate of motor vehicle fatalities (as a function of vehicle-miles traveled) did not drop in 1972. Many of the easily achieved safety standards have now been effected, and until most occupants are properly protected in crashes, either by passive restraints (air bags) or mandatory safety belt-use laws with improved belt designs, it is unlikely that any dramatic drop in the rates of motor vehicle deaths and injuries will be experienced. These future gains in auto safety are going to be achieved only against concerted efforts to water down and postpone rule making by both industry and the government itself. Saving lives on the country's roads will require constant and well-informed oversight of the NHTSA by motorist-consumers to counteract the constant and skillful stalling tactics of auto industry lobbyists.

Until a few years ago it was commonly assumed that people who were killed or injured in automobile crashes had only themselves or other drivers to blame. The message presented by most safety organizations and the automobile industry was that accidents were primarily caused by "the nut behind the wheel," and that they could be prevented if people would only drive more carefully. But about seven years ago the public and Congress began to realize that it would be easier to build safer cars than to change human behavior. One tangible result of this change in attitude is the NHTSA, a small agency in the Department of Transportation (DOT) which is responsible for carrying out two acts of Congress, the National Traffic and Motor Vehicle Safety Act [15 U.S.C. 1391 *et seq.*] and the Highway Safety Act [23 U.S.C. 401 *et seq.*].

Before getting into descriptions of what you can do with the NHTSA, you should know what the agency is, and something about the laws it administers. The National Traffic and Motor Vehicle Safety Act authorizes the NHTSA (formerly called the National Highway Safety Bureau) to set federal motor vehicle safety standards, requires manufacturers to notify owners of safety defects, and provides penalties for manufacturing cars which violate the federal safety standards or for failure to notify owners about safety defects.

Violators of the Act are subject to fines of $1,000 per vehicle or piece of equipment in violation, with a maximum of $400,000 per violation. The Act also authorizes the agency to develop used car standards (to be met in vehicle inspections) and tire quality grading standards, to support research, including an experimental safety vehicle program to demonstrate just how safe a car can be made, and to investigate possible violations of standards and possible motor vehicle safety defects.

The Highway Safety Act requires all states to adopt comprehensive highway safety programs. The NHTSA is delegated responsibility for setting uniform standards for highway safety which will have the effect of improving driver and pedestrian performance. The standards are also required to cover the state's record system for accident reporting and investigation; vehicle registration and inspection; traffic laws and codes and their enforcement; highway designs, markings, and hazards; and emergency services. States which do not comply with the Highway Safety Act may have 10 percent of their federal aid highway funds withheld. Despite considerable noncompliance by the states, highway funds have never been withheld for this reason.

In 1972 the Congress passed the Motor Vehicle Information and Cost Savings Act. This Act has four titles which are designed to protect the motorist as consumer. The Secretary of Transportation designated the NHTSA to carry out the requirements of the Act. The first title requires that the NHTSA set standards for the damageability of automobile bumpers, but gives no deadlines for the issuance of these standards. The second title requires that damageability, crashworthiness, and ease of diagnosis and repair of automobiles be studied, and that the results be communicated to the public in usable form. The final date for compliance with this title is 1 February 1975. The third title authorizes diagnostic inspection demonstration projects to determine the feasibility of such inspections. Vehicle inspections under this title must commence by 1 January 1974. The fourth title concerns odometers and makes it unlawful to defraud by disconnecting or changing an odometer. It also requires disclosure of the mileage of vehicles when sold or transferred.

In dealing with the NHTSA, it helps to know where it has been in its short life. The Administration is actually a composite of two agencies, originally established within the Department of Commerce under the National Traffic and Motor Vehicle Safety Act and the Highway Safety Act, but which have always acted as a single unit. In April 1967 these two agencies were transferred to the new cabinet department created by the Department of Transportation Act. Two months later they were merged officially into one organization, the National Highway Safety Bureau [Exec. Order No. 11,357, 3 C.F.R. 656, 15 U.S.C. 1392]. From June 1967 to March 1970 the agency was part of the Federal Highway Administration along with the Bureau of Public Roads, an older organization concerned almost exclusively with road-building. For the first year after President Nixon took office in January 1969, the Bureau didn't have a director. In March 1970 the Secretary of Transportation reorganized the agency, removed it from its subsidiary position in the Federal Highway Administration, and established it as an operating administration reporting directly to him. The Federal-Aid Highway Act of 1970 changed the name to the National Highway Traffic Safety Administration.

Structure of the NHTSA

As federal agencies go, the NHTSA is small, with only 750 employees. It has a headquarters organization in Washington, D.C. and ten regional offices. The regional offices (addresses in Appendix 13-A, p. 742) are responsible for field administration of grants to assist states in developing highway safety programs. The agency is divided into three major branches, with Associate Administrators in charge of each: Motor Vehicle Programs, Traffic Safety Programs, and the Research Institute. The Motor Vehicle Programs office develops and enforces motor vehicle safety standards and investigates safety defects, carrying out the provisions of the National Traffic and Motor Vehicle Safety Act. The Traffic Safety Programs office is responsible for funding comprehensive state highway safety programs under the Highway Safety Act. The Research Institute contracts for and provides research information to the other branches.

An organization chart of the agency (in Appendix 13-B, p. 744) will give you a rough idea of who answers to whom, and some of the titles will give you an idea of what they answer for. The headquarters in Washington include, in the Offices of the Administrator, Civil Rights, the Executive Secretariat, the Office of Consumer Affairs and Public Information (formerly just Public Information), the Chief Counsel, and the Chief Scientist. Also in Washington are the Office of Planning and Programming and the Office of Administration.

The Administrator, currently Dr. James Gregory, is the head of the agency, and he has an assistant—the Deputy Administrator. The Director of Civil Rights is responsible not only for seeing that the Administration is an equal opportunity employer, but also for checking on all contractors and states receiving federal assistance under the Highway Safety Act.

The Director of Consumer Affairs and Public Information is responsible for keeping you and other members of the public informed about what the agency is doing. The office, however, is one of the less informative government information offices, partly because of its small staff, and partly because of its primary interest in press communications and its failure to do much more than issue press releases. The Executive Secretariat provides general housekeeping support for the Administrator and other organizations such as the National Highway Safety Advisory Committee, the National Motor Vehicle Safety Advisory Council, and Youth Organizations United Toward Highway Safety (YOUTHS), an advisory group of people under twenty-five. Anything you send directly to the Administrator will go first to this office. The Chief Counsel is the Administrator's lawyer. He (and his assistants) review all of the materials which form the basis for rule making on standards issued under the Act, prepare legal materials for enforcement, and handle litigation. If you ask the NHTSA for information it does not wish to disclose, the Chief Counsel will provide the Administrator with the applicable exemption under the Freedom of Information Act (FOIA).

The Associate Administrator for Motor Vehicle Programs is in charge of the job of making cars safer. There are four offices under him: Crashworthiness, Operating Systems, Standards Enforcement, and Defects Investigation.

An office responsible for setting standards for vehicles in use, which was set up in 1967, was eliminated in 1972. "Vehicles in use" means used cars, and the National Traffic Motor Vehicle Safety Act gave the NHTSA the job of establishing federal safety standards for used cars "no later than one year" after it had finished studying the area. The study report was submitted to Congress in June 1968. On 31 January 1973 Dr. Carl Nash of Ralph Nader's Public Interest Research Group sued the NHTSA Administrator and the Secretary of Transportation in the District of Columbia Federal District Court to force issuance of vehicle-in-use standards. The Judge ordered that the standards be issued no later than 5 September 1973.

The Office of Crashworthiness is responsible for developing motor vehicle standards which will make it possible for people to survive automobile crashes. One development of this office is a requirement for use of a "passive" restraint system, such as an airbag that inflates upon collision, which demands no action on the part of a vehicle occupant. The NHTSA estimates that passive restraints would save between 7,000 and 21,000 lives every year if they were used in all cars. A partial passive restraint system will be mandatory for 1976 model cars. As currently written, the passive occupant restraint standard would protect all passengers in frontal barrier crashes up to thirty miles per hour (mph), in side impacts up to twenty mph, and would prevent passenger ejection in a rollover at thirty mph. These requirements were to have been mandatory for 1976 model cars and 1978 model light trucks and multipurpose passenger vehicles, but a recent court decision in *Chrysler* v. *DOT* required that the deadline be delayed until an adequately objective test dummy could be developed and specified. Although the delay will probably not exceed one year, there is an expectation that some auto manufacturers may move for further delay.

The Office of Operating Systems develops standards for systems in cars such as lighting, fuel, brakes, and tires, the crucial elements in the prevention of crashes.

The Office of Standards Enforcement relies heavily on a testing program contracted to about twenty-five testing laboratories, analyzing data obtained from manufacturers, field investigations, automotive journals, and to a lesser extent, consumer complaints. Every year the NHTSA establishes priorities among standards to determine which will be emphasized in compliance testing. For instance, in 1969 the standards with high priority were those for brakes, tires, headlights, and steering. Low on the priority list are those standards which are difficult to enforce because of ambiguities or other inadequacies in their definition. Although aware of the problem, the agency has been slow to attend to this issue. The Office of Standards Enforcement selects vehicles for testing, and requires manufacturers to submit information on measures taken to comply with safety standards. If enough information suggesting a violation accumulates, the office may initiate a formal investigation. The manufacturer is notified and is allowed to present views and evidence. During the course of the investigation neither the government's nor the manufacturer's evidence is available to the public. After the investigation is completed, information other than trade secrets can be obtained from the Office of Standards Enforcement. A citizen's lawsuit now pending asks that all information known to both the manufacturer and the government be available to the public whether the matter is under investigation or not.

The Office of Defects Investigation is concerned with safety defects in motor vehicles, whether or not the vehicle system is covered by safety standards. Since the standards themselves cover only a narrow range of the possible safety problems with any car, the role of Defects Investigation is crucial. This is the office which determines the need for defect notification campaigns, popularly called "recall campaigns," because many manufacturers also agree to correct safety defects in their cars. Consumer letters complaining about safety defect problems in cars (whether written to DOT or to other government agencies) are forwarded to NHTSA, analyzed, and fed into a computer. The computer is used to detect defect trends and spot the need for potential recall efforts. Computer printouts summarizing the contents of letters received by NHTSA are available at the agency for public inspection.

The office is staffed with engineers and technicians who investigate defects. After the office completes its work and determines that a defect notification campaign is needed, the case goes to the Office of the Chief Counsel for clearance. If no safety defect is found, the investigation is closed and the file is open for public inspection. Although the files of investigations in progess are closed, the agency from time to time issues releases listing the makes, models, years, and components suspected of being defective or in violation of a standard.

The agency's Traffic Safety Programs are directed at supervising programs at the state and local level which are funded under the Highway Safety Act. The supervision is carried out by three offices: State and Community Comprehensive Programs, Standards Development and Implementation, and Alcohol Countermeasures. The State and Community Comprehensive Programs are devoted to assisting states and regional offices in developing the comprehensive highway safety programs required by the Highway Safety Act. These programs are based on sixteen highway safety program standards (see Appendix 13-C, p. 745) established by the NHTSA. Each state submits a "work program" annually, outlining what the state and its participating subdivisions have planned to improve highway safety in the coming year. These state programs often begin at the local level, and present opportunities for involvement in developing your state's highway safety program. Local communities decide what they need to make traffic safer in their area, and then apply to the governor's highway safety representative to participate in the state program. The state allocates federal and state funding requests to various parts of its program and submits the entire program to the NHTSA for approval. These programs are negotiated and subsequently evaluated through the regional offices under guidelines promulgated by the Office of State and Community Comprehensive Programs. A scorecard which rates each state's progress in establishing highway safety programs is in Appendix 13-D (p. 749).

The actual development of the highway safety program standards is done by the Office of Standards Development and Implementation. This office endorses the Uniform Vehicle Code published by the National Committee on Uniform Traffic Laws and Ordinances (955 North L'Enfant Plaza, S.W., Washington, D.C. 20024). All states have now adopted the Uniform Vehicle Code as the basis for their traffic codes. The Office of Alcohol Countermeasures sponsors traffic safety programs directed at problems created by the combination of using alcohol, or other drugs, and driving. This program was heavily funded beginning in 1971 in a major attack via state and pilot programs on drinking and driving.

It is important to remember that all of these offices are primarily concerned with the traditional approach to highway safety—laws and educational programs aimed at changing the behavior of drivers. While there is relatively little opportunity for citizens individually to affect the development of these programs, there are frequent opportunities for participation in overseeing and improving the comprehensive state highway safety programs.

The Research and Development Programs are concerned with both drivers and automobiles. There are five operating offices: Accident Investigation and Data Analysis, Vehicle Structures Research, Experimental Safety Vehicle Programs, Driver Performance Research, and Operating Systems Research. You should know how research is carried out in order to understand how the agency arrives at motor vehicle safety and state program standards. Motor vehicle standards must be supported by adequate test data, especially since the automobile manufacturers are quick to furnish data showing that proposed standards are not needed, or are not objective or feasible. First the NHTSA decides what is going to be studied. This is done by "cabinet-level" meetings between the Administrator and the Associate Administrators for Motor Vehicle Programs, Traffic Safety Programs, and Research and Development. After deciding on a general subject to be studied, such as crash survivability, the next step is to establish data requirements, such as determining the ability of doors to stay shut in collisions and the capacity of the human body to absorb energy in crashes. Data are then obtained from accident investigations and experiments, trends projected, and safety standards developed. Once the standards are established, the research process continues to evaluate their effectiveness.

The Office of Accident Investigation and Data Analysis investigates a small number of actual highway collisions, somewhat like investigations of airplane crashes. This is done primarily by fifteen multidisciplinary accident investigation teams, composed of doctors, engineers, lawyers, and police officers, under contract to the agency. These teams are based at universities and research centers across the country. This office also maintains the National Driver Register, and if you have had a driver's license denied, revoked, or suspended for more than six months by any state, your name is on the Register. The National Accident Summary is another computerized collection of information, this one on automobile accidents from all over the country measured according to eleven variables. The office also maintains on computer tape annotations of most highway safety literature, results of research contracts, and reports of the accident investigation teams.

The Office of Vehicle Structures Research uses controlled laboratory experiments to find out what happens to vehicles in accidents. Since the agency has no test facilities (an old facility in Ohio is being renovated for use beginning in 1974), all of this work is done through contracts awarded to outside research facilities. The National Traffic and Motor Vehicle Safety Act also gave the NHTSA the job of developing an experimental safe car, and the Office of Experimental Safety Vehicle Programs is in charge. Contracts have been awarded to AMF, Inc., Fairchild Hiller, General Motors, and Ford. The prototypes were delivered and tested in 1972. A follow-up contract has been awarded to AMF. The ESV program also involves extensive cooperation with foreign governments and auto makers.

The Research Institute Programs have a close relationship with the automobile manufacturing industry. For example, the General Motors "long form" for accident investigations is used by the agency, and there is considerable cooperation in exchanging data bank information. But the NHTSA has been reluctant to press the automobile industry for information. It has never asked General Motors for results of its 3,000 investigations carried out every year on late model cars, and automobile manufacturers have never been asked to forward results of their tests on vehicle crashworthiness.

The Associate Director for Administration takes care of the financial and administrative details for the agency. One office under him, Contracts and Procurement, might interest you if you're an inventor with an idea for an automobile safety device. All unsolicited proposals to the agency are cleared through this office [National Highway Safety Bureau Order 4.0500, 12 August 1970]. An unsolicited proposal is "a formal written offer to perform work under contract or grant, submitted by an organization or individual on its or his own initiative not in response to a request for a proposal." Such proposals are then sent to the Associate Director in charge of the area with which the proposal is concerned. "If the submission has even the slightest probability of either current or future use," the proposal will be sent to an appropriate reviewing office, which will recommend whether or not the project should get financial support. It is then returned to Contract and Procurement for a final decision. All of the unsolicited proposals which the NHTSA has received are maintained in computer storage by subject in the Office of Research and Development. Few have been granted funding, however, since the agency has always had limited funds available, and there has been considerable competition among the programs for adequate money to research key issues.

The Associate Director for Planning and Programming is in charge of evaluating programs now under way, planning future programs, and preparing basic legislative materials.

National Traffic and Motor Vehicle Safety Act:
Making Safer Cars

The National Traffic and Motor Vehicle Safety Act gives the NHTSA the power to establish motor vehicle safety standards which must be practicable, meet the need for motor vehicle safety, and provide objective criteria [15 U.S.C. 1391(2)]. Forty-five standards have been promulgated as of January 1973, ranging from the requirement for seatbelts (Standard No. 208) to a standard specifying burn resistance for materials used in automobile interiors (No. 302). All proposed and issued standards are published in the *Federal Register,* and at least thirty days generally is provided for comment on proposals by any interested party. The agency must, under the Administrative Procedure Act (APA), invite all interested parties to comment on proposed standards. Under agency rules petitions for reconsideration of final standards may be filed for thirty to sixty days after issuance. Summary descriptions of all standards which have been issued are in Appendix 13-E (p. 757), along with descriptions of some NHTSA regulations (such as Part 575, which requires manufacturers to tell consumers about vehicle passing, acceleration ability, and stopping distances [49 C.F.R. 575]).

The statute also required the Secretary of Transportation to establish a National Motor Vehicle Safety Advisory Council [15 U.S.C. 1393(a)]. The Council has twenty-two members (listed in Appendix 13-F, p. 768). The NHTSA is required by law to consult the Council in developing motor vehicle safety standards [15 U.S.C. 1393(b)], but the Council's contributions often have been too late and too meager to have any appreciable effect on the agency's decision making. It has, however, taken initiatives in the past, such as urging the Secretary of Transportation in 1969 to develop and issue passive restraint standards. Recent appointments have unfortunately shown a heavy emphasis on political loyalty and little concern for safety expertise. The Council meets monthly, and most of its meetings are open to the public. To learn the exact locations and dates of Council meetings, follow the *Federal Register* or write the Executive Secretary, National Highway

Traffic Safety Administration, Department of Transportation, Washington, D.C. 20590. Transcripts of Council meetings are available for inspection in the Washington office of the NHTSA. The Council is only an advisory body, but it could have much more effect by taking strong and timely stands on issues before the Administration. Letters to the Advisory Council or to individual members might encourage a more active role. The Council published annual reports in 1967 and 1968, but these have been discontinued. A first step in monitoring the Council's recent activities would be to ask for a copy of the report made by the Chairman of the Council to the Secretary of Transportation on the past year's activities.

The Act prohibits [15 U.S.C. 1397(a)]:

1. Manufacturing or offering for sale any new vehicle or equipment not in conformity with the applicable federal safety standards.
2. Failure to produce records or refusing entry to a facility to carry out the purposes of the Act.
3. Failure to issue a certificate notifying first purchasers that vehicles meet the applicable standards.
4. Failure to furnish notification of safety-related defects to first purchasers or subsequent warranty holders.

The Act also gives federal district courts the power to restrain or stop the sale of any vehicle found violating a standard [15 U.S.C. 1399(a)]. The Act authorizes any inspections or investigations necessary to enforce safety standards, including the power to enter and inspect factories and warehouses.

The NHTSA also has broad powers under the Act to require manufacturers to furnish information so that the NHTSA can determine whether they are complying with standards. The Act also gives the agency authority to make manufacturers furnish performance information to new car buyers [15 U.S.C. 1401(d)]. Currently, manufacturers are required to tell new car buyers about passing and acceleration performance, stopping ability, and tire-load capacity. These requirements were issued in 1969. Neither the Administrator nor the engineers are interested in improving these performance data for consumers, even though no such information which is comparable for all cars is otherwise available.

Also discontinued by former Administrator Douglas Toms was a program for comparative crash testing of vehicles and the development of an index rating cars by their crash survivability qualities. As a consequence, most car buyers are just as uninformed today about the safety qualities of individual vehicles as they were before the safety laws were passed in 1966.

Wholesale recalls of automobiles by their manufacturers are not made because the companies cannot rest until every car is perfect. The law requires each manufacturer to notify first purchasers and warranty holders when it is determined that a safety defect exists, or when vehicles do not comply with applicable safety standards [15 U.S.C. 1402(c)]. This notification must be made by certified mail to both dealers and owners. It must "contain a clear description of such defect, an evaluation of the risk to traffic safety reasonably related to such defect, and a statement of the measures to be taken to repair such defect." But, according to a letter sent by the NHTSA to automobile manufacturers in May 1971, there has been "a serious failure to comply" with the statute in these letters. Many of the notices described the defects in technical terms, but neglected to say how or whether such defects would be dangerous. Without warning of the possible consequences, owners would have little incentive to have the defects repaired. A prime example is the General Motors letter which denied the existence of the safety defect, found by the agency in the 1961-1969 Corvair heater, which passes carbon monoxide fumes from the engine area into the passenger compartment. There are now regulations on how the defect notifications must be written.

Often in response to complaints, the agency will investigate potential safety defects. After affording the manufacturer the opportunity to present his views and evidence, the Secretary has the discretion to find that a defect exists and to order the manufacturer to send notification to owners in accordance with the law. The law does not, however, give the agency authority to order manufacturers to recall and remedy vehicles. Although many have done so voluntarily, the absence of this authority frequently allows manufacturers to bargain with the agency as to the scope of its finding.

The agency also has authority over automobile tires. The Act and standards require that all auto tires meet minimal federal safety standards and be labeled with the maximum permissible load the tire can bear, an indication that the tire meets federal standards, and identification of the manufacturer. However, most tire manufacturers are identified on their products only by a code rarely understood by consumers (see Appendix 13-G, p. 770). The Act also directed issuance by 1968 of a tire quality grading system "in order to assist the consumer to make an informed choice in the purchase of motor vehicle tires" [15 U.S.C. 1423]. It is now estimated by the agency that this grading system will become effective in 1974. A 1970 amendment authorized the NHTSA to require auto and tire manufacturers to develop a record keeping system for identification of first purchasers to facilitate immediate notification upon discovery of defects. The names and addresses of all purchasers of new cars and tires are now recorded on forms supplied by manufacturers. The 1970 amendments also required the NHTSA to set "limits on the age of tire carcasses which can be retreaded" [15 U.S.C. 1426]. The limitation on tires which can be retreaded and standards for retread tires have been delayed by lawsuits brought by the retreading industry which were decided in favor of the industry.

Despite its broad responsibilities in the field of auto safety, the NHTSA has had no testing facilities of its own, although the previously mentioned site in Ohio is in the process of renovation. In 1968 a report was submitted, as authorized by the original legislation, estimating that $10 million would be required to construct minimal compliance testing facilities, and more than $100 million would be needed for proper research facilities. In the authorization amendments for fiscal years 1970-1972 Congress granted authority to proceed with construction, with the significant limitation that if expenditures were to exceed $100,000, additional Congressional approval from the four authorizing committees would be required.

The Congressional committees which watch over the NHTSA's motor vehicle programs are the Senate Commerce Committee and the House Committee on Interstate and Foreign Commerce, while the House and Senate Public Works Committees oversee the Highway Safety Act. These committees play an important role in influencing the agency's policies. For example, after a father-son team of inventors demonstrated their impact-absorbing bumper system to members of the Senate Commerce Committee in 1971, the NHTSA disclosed that it was re-evaluating its own proposed exterior vehicle damage standard, which it had issued six weeks earlier [*Washington Post*, 29 May 1971, p. 1]. After the re-evaluation, the standard was beefed up. Four members of the Senate Commerce Committee are usually identified as auto safety advocates: Magnuson of Washington, Hart of Michigan, Moss of Utah, and Hartke of Indiana. Representative John Moss of California plays a similar role in the House.

The Highway Safety Act:
The Older Way

The traditional approach to highway safety, making drivers and highways safer, is also the responsibility of the NHTSA, although with the removal of the NHTSA from the Federal Highway Administration in early 1970, primary authority and responsibility for safety in highway design remained with the Highway Administration. The Highway Safety Act of 1966 provides for federal matching funds to develop comprehensive highway safety programs at the state and local level. These programs are supposed to be established under NHTSA standards to improve driver performance, driver licensing examinations, pedestrian performance, accident reporting and investigation, highway design and maintenance, vehicle codes and laws, and emergency services. So far sixteen standards have been established (see Appendix 13-C, p. 745) on subjects such as driver education programs and licensing of commercial driving schools and instructors, traffic control devices, police traffic services, drivers' license requirements, and emergency medical services. The programs must include participation by county and municipal governments. No state has adopted all sixteen of the standards. Although the NHTSA has authority to reduce federal highway funds (which average $5 to $6 billion a year) by 10 percent to states which do not meet the standards [Highway Act of 1966, 23 U.S.C. 402(c)], and is not supposed to fund highway safety programs in states which have not adopted the standards, as of January 1973 no state has been denied federal funds because of its failure to adopt the standards. Former Administrator Toms has said that individual Senators and Representatives have objected to such sanctions against their own states.

On 18 July 1972 the NHTSA proposed a complete revision of the Highway Safety Program Standards into eight categories. One of the new proposals would require that states pass mandatory safety belt usage laws, and another would legalize in all states right turns against red lights after a full stop. The comment period closed on 1 February 1973.

In order to adopt new highway safety program standards, the NHTSA must submit them to Congress at least ninety days prior to the effective date [23 U.S.C. 402(h)]. The agency also has the power to waive any of the standards on a temporary basis for the purpose of evaluating new or experimental programs to see if they would be in the public interest [23 U.S.C. 402(a)]. One such waiver, in California, was made to evaluate a spot-check system of vehicle inspection instead of mandatory inspection for all motor vehicles.

The Highway Safety Act also established the National Highway Safety Advisory Committee, composed of the Undersecretary of Transportation, the Federal Highway Administrator, and thirty-five presidential appointees [23 U.S.C. 404]; members are listed in Appendix 13-H (p. 776). The Committee is supposed to advise the NHTSA on safety standards and make recommendations. It is required to meet once a year, and rarely meets more often than that. The Committee cooperates with a private organization called Safety Through Action to Enlist Support (STATES). STATES is made up of representatives of national organizations such as insurance companies and automobile trade associations. Its primary function, according to its representatives, is to encourage state and local highway safety programs. Each state has an assigned STATES field representative and a resource coordinator who work closely with the NHTSA regional office and the governor's representative to encourage adoption of highway safety programs.

The STATES field representatives and resource coordinators are useful sources of information if you are concerned about state and local highway safety programs. They have brochures on each of the sixteen highway safety standards, and can furnish worksheets describing each state's program. The worksheets detail which standards have not been adopted in the state, set priorities for adoption of standards, and give progress reports. There are also "conformity charts" available from STATES which compare progress in each state in terms of selected safety standards. Information on the STATES program is available from either of these two addresses: National Coordinator, Mr. Vince Gallalee, Field Service Department, National Safety Council, 425 N. Michigan Avenue, Chicago, Illinois 60611; National Chairman, Mr. Roy D. Chapin, Jr., Highway Users Federation for Safety and Mobility, 1776 Massachusetts Avenue, N.W., Washington, D.C. 20026.

NHTSA Information

The first step in keeping up with the NHTSA is to get on the mailing list for free materials. Write to the Office of Consumer Affairs and Public Information, National Highway Traffic Safety Administration, Department of Transportation, Washington, D.C. 20590, and ask to receive any (or all) of the following free materials: the annual report, news releases, consumer protection bulletins, monthly compliance reports, *Highway Safety Literature,* multidisciplinary accident investigation summaries, recall booklets, and the list of current safety defect investigations.

The annual report is the agency's summary of activity for the preceding year. It is required to be submitted to the Congress on 1 March of each year. The news releases are summaries of recent agency actions which are given to the press. Although they are designed to present the NHTSA's point of view and need to be read with a skeptical eye, a current file of news releases is a good way of keeping up with NHTSA activities. Consumer protection bulletins are issued to alert consumers about potential motor vehicle hazards, and to solicit consumer comments. These are frequently unpublicized by the regular news media because they are written in bland language and the agency has invested little effort in broadcasting them. Thus they have been of negligible value except for use in consumer newsletters. Monthly compliance reports, usually issued as press releases, list, by make and model, the motor vehicles or parts that have been tested for compliance with safety standards, and state whether each passed or failed safety tests. These reports also contain tabular summaries of investigations to see if individual test failures indicate violations of safety standards. *Highway Safety Literature,* published by the agency, is a very useful periodical for research on auto safety. It contains annotations of all publications received by the agency's documentation library, all NHTSA publications, all of the agency's accident investigation reports and compliance test reports, summaries of completed agency research, and staff speeches and papers. Each issue also contains instructions on how to get complete copies of the annotated material. A complete bibliography of all the material annotated in *Highway Safety Literature* is stored on computer tape by the NHTSA, and if you are doing research and have a relatively narrow topic, this bibliography can provide you with a list of all applicable published information.

The multidisciplinary accident investigation summaries are brief reports of investigations carried out by the multidisciplinary investigation teams. The summaries, which are available at no cost on a regular basis, also contain instructions on how to obtain detailed reports on each accident investigated. Recall booklets describe each recall campaign conducted by manufacturers. Issued quarterly, they describe all such campaigns carried out during the previous three months. The description includes dates of notification, make, model, and year of vehicles, descriptions of the defects involved, and number of vehicles to be recalled. The summaries of recall campaigns conducted during the year are also published annually. Both the annual and quarterly summaries contain instructions on how to obtain detailed information on each campaign, including information exchanged among the manufacturer, owner, dealer, and the agency. The monthly list of safety defect investigations indicates vehicles which might be recalled in the future.

Another useful research tool is a bibliography of research reports. This describes all research completed by or under contract with the NHTSA, along with identification numbers for ordering specific reports. Other NHTSA publications available from the agency and the Government Printing Office (G.P.O.) are listed in Appendix 13-I (p. 778).

To find out if your car model has been subject to a recall campaign, or is under investigation for possible safety defects, write directly to the NHTSA, with the vehicle make, model, and year (or the particular piece of equipment), the manufacturer, the vehicle identification number (located on the top left side of the dash panel or the left front door jamb), and the suspected defect. Or you can ask for copies of recall booklets for previous years and go through them yourself. By sending the same information to the NHTSA with an inquiry, you can request information on how many other cars with similar defects have been reported. But if you want the names and addresses of other owners, you will have to dig it out for yourself at the agency in Washington, D.C. By ordering copies of past monthly compliance summaries, you can tell whether a particular model or piece of equipment has been tested and whether it meets a particular motor vehicle safety standard.

Much of the agency's information is available for inspection in the documentation facilities. These are in the Technical Reference Division, Room 5108, National Highway Traffic Safety Administration, Department of Transportation, 400 7th Street, S.W., Washington, D.C. 20590. The division has an excellent auto safety library, open to the public, which contains files on completed defect and compliance investigations (either of which can be obtained, in many cases, on microfiche from the division at 50 cents per card, each card containing upward of forty pages from the file), and computer printouts of consumer letters complaining of defects.

In the legal docket, Room 5217, is the "Red Book." This is a digest of interpretations and informal views expressed by the NHTSA on provisions of the Acts which the agency enforces, and interpretations of

standards issued by the agency. The NHTSA warns that these interpretations, which are issued in response to individual questions, are not to
be relied on by people other than the original questioners. But they do
serve as a useful tool to determine agency attitudes. The docket room
also contains all comments on rule making actions both from within
the agency and from interested persons (usually auto and equipment
makers) outside the agency. Because of its technical nature, consumers
rarely comment on rule making, leaving the agency without pressure
and views from *all* interested parties. Much other information, such as
maps, photographs, drawings, and research reports, can also be inspected
at the Washington headquarters. Copies of such material can be obtained
by mail, although there are bureaucratic and financial barriers to such
access. Requests for such items must be in writing, and must be in sufficient detail so that the item can be identified and located with a
"reasonable" amount of effort.

The standard charge for photocopying documents is 25 cents per
page. The DOT issued new regulations on public information (49
C.F.R., Part 7) in the 28 March 1972 *Federal Register* (p. 6315) which
say in part [7.87]:

> (c) Documents may be furnished without charge or at a reduced
> charge, if the Director of Public Affairs, or the head of the oper-
> ating administration concerned, as the case may be, determines
> that waiver or reduction of the fee is in the public interest, be-
> cause furnishing the information can be considered as primarily
> benefiting the general public.

Cited as being eligible for such a reduction are nonprofit activities for
public safety, health, or welfare; schools; and students studying in the
field of transportation. If you wish to use these rules to obtain such
documents, you should read the complete notice from the C.F.R.
(1973) or from the *Federal Register* (see Appendix 13-J, p. 780).

Like other federal agencies, the NHTSA publishes material in the
Federal Register, and checking the *Federal Register* regularly for proposed and issued standards and regulations is a necessary part of keeping up with the agency. (See p. 26 on how to get the *Federal Register*.)

The DOT FOIA regulations include an affirmative policy statement
that records are to be made available to the public to the fullest extent
possible. The rules are fairly specific in spelling out what materials will
be withheld from the public under the statutory exemptions from dis-

closure, in marked contrast to the regulations of some other agencies, which merely restate the general terms of the Act.

Even if information falls into one of the categories which are made exempt from the general rule of disclosure by the statute, the agency nevertheless has the discretion to release the material. In promulgating regulations under the FOIA, the Secretary of the DOT said:

> The policy of the Department will be to make all information available to the public except that which must not be disclosed in the national interest, to protect the right of an individual to personal privacy, or to ensure the effective conduct of public business. To this end, the [regulation] provides that information will be made available to the public *even if it falls within one of the exemptions set forth in section 552(b)*, unless the release of that information would be inconsistent with the purpose of the exemption (emphasis added). [32 *Fed. Reg.* 9284 (1967)]

Agency refusals of requests for information must be accompanied by written explanations. If you receive such a refusal, the next step is to make a written application for reconsideration. If the application for reconsideration is refused, that refusal is a final administrative decision which can then be appealed to the courts. (See *Ditlow* v. *Volpe,* No. 2370-72, District Court for the District of Columbia, filed 30 November 1972.)

How to Be Heard in NHTSA Proceedings:
What You Can Do

There are three general ways for you to be heard in the NHTSA proceedings:

1. By writing complaint letters about safety defects and safety standard noncompliance.
2. By submitting your comments on proposed safety standards.
3. By submitting petitions for reconsideration of safety standards already in force, or petitions for new standards.

Don't underestimate the potential impact of a complaint letter. One letter about a sticking accelerator in a 1970 Buick Skylark eventually resulted in a recall of 12,000 vehicles. Several cogent letters to the agency and to Ralph Nader started an investigation of Chevrolet engine mounts which led to the largest recall ever—6.7 million cars. Consumer letters provide important information to the agency as well as serving to remind them that there are others besides industry who are affected by their decisions. Letters are frequently useful to alert the Office of Defects Investigation to safety-related defects which may warrant notification and recall, or to noncompliance with safety standards.

About 14,000 letters are received every year, and the Executive Correspondence Unit handles most of them, forwarding them to the appropriate divisions. As is the case with most agencies, letters forwarded from the President's Consumer Advisor or from members of Congress are usually handled first, so you should try to get your letter forwarded by your Congressman, with a request for response. Letters concerning automobiles which do not indicate safety problems are usually forwarded to other agencies. For example, a letter about air pollution from automobile exhaust would be forwarded to the Environmental Protection Agency (EPA).

It is most important that your letter include enough information to identify your car. At a minimum, this should include the make, model, year, vehicle identification number, and details of your complaint. If the defect caused a collision, tell whether there were any warning signs beforehand, and describe the collision as completely as possible. Each letter is reviewed by an engineer in the Office of Defects Investigation, and saved for future reference. Usually you will receive an answer from either the Executive Correspondence Unit or the reviewing engineer. The information which is extracted from your letter is tabulated and recorded along with information from other letters. Each month this information is analyzed by cumulative computer printouts to spot possible defect trends. This trend-spotting is also available to you. By writing the agency and requesting a copy of the printout for a particular make, model, and year, you can find out how many other cars of the same make, model, and year have had similar reported problems. Copies of vehicle or equipment consumer complaint letters are automatically forwarded by the agency to the manufacturer for consideration. In the past manufacturers treated consumer complaints with considerable disdain. Now that the agency reviews complaint letters, the manufacturers also give them consideration.

If the Office of Defects Investigation believes that a safety-related problem is serious enough to warrant further investigation, it sends a formal Information Request to the manufacturer asking for technical information, and sometimes has tests run by an independent laboratory under contract. If the agency decides that there is a safety-related defect, it begins negotiations with the manufacturer, requesting that notification of the defect be sent to motor vehicle owners. It is important to remember that the NHTSA has authority only to make the manufacturer notify owners of such defects; it does not have power to force the manufacturer to recall the defective automobiles or to pay for corrections. Recognizing the difficulties the agency has experienced in trying to pursuade manufacturers to recall and remedy whenever notification is sent, several bills have been introduced in the 93rd Congress (on which Senate hearings were held in January 1973) to give the agency authority to mandate recall.

One method of participating in the agency's rule making procedures is by submitting comments on proposed safety standards. Another way is by submitting petitions for reconsideration of a safety standard which has been issued, while a third is by attempting to initiate safety standards by submitting petitions for rule making. There are several stages to NHTSA rule making which you need to understand in order to make effective use of any of these methods.

The first possible step in rule making is the Advance Notice of Proposed Rule Making (ANPRM), which is optional and not used often. It is published in the *Federal Register,* stating the agency's intention to develop a safety standard in a particular area and inviting comments from industry and the public (all interested parties). In effect, it is an administrative way of making the agency aware of anticipated concepts, disadvantages, or impacts of the rule making before it is issued in proposal form. The ANPRM is most likely to be used in proposing a standard expected to be controversial, and consumer groups should be aware of this function. As a result of a request from Ralph Nader, for example, an ANPRM was issued in 1972 for a collision avoidance standard. Such a standard might require a radar or sonar device to detect objects in the path of a vehicle with which the vehicle might collide. The device might also apply the brakes or steer the vehicle to avoid the collision.

The Notice of Proposed Rule Making (NPRM) is the first formal step in creating a safety standard. Also published in the *Federal Register,* it describes a proposed safety standard and the test requirements which it will incorporate, and invites comments. Each NPRM gives the address to which comments should be sent and a deadline for submission of the comments. Submitting such comments is the most important way of affecting rule making. If there isn't enough time for you to prepare comments for submission before the deadline, send a letter asking for an extension of the deadline. While such extensions are not automatically granted, if they are supported by reasonable grounds they will often be honored.

Technical meetings following issuance of the NPRM are usually held for more controversial proposed standards. These are public meetings to discuss the provisions of a proposed standard, and are usually held in Washington. The so-called "air bag rule," motor vehicle safety standard 208, was preceded by a technical meeting to discuss the feasibility of passive restraints such as air bags. If the agency believes that a technical meeting is necessary, it may announce it in the NPRM, or by other notice in the *Federal Register*. The announcement will include the place and the name of the person in charge. If you want to participate in a technical meeting, you should write the person in charge, describing your interest and what you would like to discuss. If you think that a technical meeting on a proposed standard would be useful, but none has been announced, you may petition for one to be held. Such a petition is more likely to be granted if it is submitted with a statement explaining the need, and is from a group rather than an individual, especially if several groups join in the petition. The format of a technical meeting is that of presentations by interested parties, followed by a relatively informal discussion in which agency officials answer questions about the proposed rule. The questions raised are usually industry objections to the cost of the standard and the amount of technological change required. Transcripts of meetings are made and placed in the public docket. They may be inspected there and copies of them may be obtained from NHTSA for 25 cents or less per page or from the reporter company at the commercial rate.

Sometimes a second NPRM is issued. This is not required and is usually done when there is substantial disagreement within the agency about the rule, or when the agency believes that significant revisions in the proposed rule are needed. The period for comments on a second NPRM is usually shorter than that for a first NPRM.

The next step is publication in the *Federal Register* of the rule itself. But this is not the final stage in the rule making process. After a rule is published there follows a thirty-day period for submission of petitions for reconsideration. At this stage any industry efforts to block a rule will be intensified. During this thirty-day period, industry representatives often increase the volume and heat of their objections to proposed standards, insisting that they are useless and/or dangerous, unreasonable, and expensive. While technical comments during this period are helpful, expressions of approval for standards are also useful, as are refutations of industry objections. Under the impact of a blitz of petitions for reconsideration, the NHTSA is likely to reissue the rule in substantially weaker form. The manufacturer or any party "adversely affected" by a rule may petition for review in federal court within sixty days after a rule is issued. It is important to recognize that any person who comes into contact with motor vehicles is "adversely affected" by the rule making if it results in a reduction of the actual, proposed, or practicable levels of safety in vehicles on the road. This is especially true in view of recent court trends toward broadening traditional doctrines of standing to challenge agency action.

To participate in the rule making process, it is very useful to know what other comments have been received by the agency in response to the public notices. All of the comments received are placed in the Central Docket, Room 5217, 400 7th Street, S.W., at NHTSA headquarters in Washington [49 C.F.R. 553.35]. The docket file will include copies of all public notices, comments received, petitions and requests for extensions of period for comment, and records of all meetings relating to a proposed rule. Photocopies of docket files are available at the agency rate, but sometimes they will lend copies of the docket overnight or over a weekend so that photocopies can be made on other machines at more reasonable prices. Summaries of material in the docket are also made by engineers and attorneys working on the proposed rule. If you cannot examine the docket file in person, requesting a copy of the summary is a less expensive way of getting a general idea of what has been said about a proposed rule.

To find out in which areas the agency plans to issue rules and when the rules are planned to go into effect, get a copy of the Program Plan for Motor Vehicle Safety Standards, which is updated every year or two. This explains the general plans of the NHTSA for future rule making and the areas to be emphasized. You should also check the *Federal Register* regularly. This does not mean that you have to read it from cover to cover every day; it is enough to scan the table of contents to see if any notices from the NHTSA are in that issue. Another way of finding out which safety standards are being proposed is to get on the mailing list for press releases. Both the *Federal Register* notice and the press release will describe the proposed rule and give the deadline for comments.

To find out if there has been an NPRM, check the index to the *Federal Register* in your local library. If you cannot obtain it there, the Center for Auto Safety (P.O. Box 7250, Washington, D.C. 20044) will send you a copy on request of any proposed or issued rule if you will enclose a stamped, self-addressed envelope. If the Center has done relevant research in an area, the staff will also provide copies of their work for the cost of copying and mailing. The Center is interested in hearing about other organized citizen efforts to become involved in the activities of the NHTSA or in more general automotive safety questions.

Usually the agency wants you to submit ten copies of comments on proposed standards, but this is not a requirement. If you have any technical or professional expertise, such as engineering or medical training, phrase your comments in technical terms and indicate your background and experience. Although such expertise makes comments more useful, ordinary expressions of opinion are also helpful. Also send a copy of your comments to the National Motor Vehicle Safety Advisory Council. The Council is supposed to represent the "public" point of view on proposed standards, and if you express your opinions to them they may take a more vigorous stand on proposed standards. Comments should be sent to the Chairman of the Council at the NHTSA.

There are two general types of standards set by the NHTSA: "performance standards" and "design standards." A design standard requires that a particular design or device be used for all vehicles, while a performance standard only requires the vehicle to function in a certain way under specified conditions, allowing the manufacturer to use whatever design he thinks will meet the required performance level. For example, an occupant restraint standard could be set in terms of either performance or design. A performance standard would require that, in a collision at a certain speed, the crash forces exceeding a specified level should not be permitted to reach the occupants. A design standard, on the other hand, would require a certain type of restraint device (such as seatbelts or air bags) to be used on vehicles to accomplish this result. The law permits the agency to set both types of standards, but exhibits a preference for performance standards.

It is also possible to participate in the rule making process by starting it. This can be accomplished by a simple letter describing what kind of safety features you think are needed on motor vehicles, or a detailed technical proposal for a rule, with engineering specifications for the suggested rule spelled out in the petition. Such petitions are submitted to "establish, amend, or repeal a rule" under the provisions of 49 C.F.R. 553. Petitions should be sent in duplicate to the Central Docket Room at the NHTSA, which will forward them to appropriate divisions within the agency. Remember that the law stipulates that a safety standard must be practicable, must meet a need for vehicle safety, and must be stated in objective terms.

An informal petition might be in the form of a letter asking the agency to consider a rule, such as one to protect pedestrians from autos and trucks or to require better rear view mirrors. No particular format is necessary for such an informal petition. An ordinary letter setting forth your views as clearly as possible is enough. If you can get other interested people to sign the letter, so much the better. The letter in Appendix 13-K (p. 786) is an example of an informal petition for standardized and impact resistant bumpers. As the NHTSA reply indicates, a standard was proposed by the agency, and the letter was placed in the docket on the proposed rule.

A technical petition, on the other hand, would describe the engineering specifications in detail. Appendix 13-L (p. 788) is an example of a petition presented in technical form, with a supporting brief. Instead of merely asking the NHTSA to "(1) standardize bumper heights and (2) construct bumpers that will withstand low speed impacts without sustaining damage," as the informal letter did, the petition proposes a standard which

> establishes requirements for the impact resistance and the configuration of front and rear vehicle surfaces, to prevent low-speed collisions from impairing the mobility and the safe operation of specified vehicle systems, to reduce G-loading on passengers, and to reduce the frequency of override or underride in higher speed collisions.

The petition goes on to describe the specific Society of Automotive Engineers (SAE) test to be used under the rule. It helps if you can submit your petition in the more formal form, since the final standard will be phrased in just such technical terms, and the technical specifications incorporated into the standard can make a great deal of difference which may not be apparent on the surface. Thus, it is preferable for the petitioner to draft exactly what he wants so that the agency, in exercising its interpretive discretion, does not misconstrue the petitioner's request. For example, the NHTSA had proposed that bumpers be tested by striking the bumper of a car which was standing still. The Students Mobilizing on Auto Safety Hazards (SMASH) petition argues in some detail that the SAE test of driving a test car into a barrier is a better way of telling how well bumpers bump.

All petitions for rule making are reviewed by engineers and attorneys.

If the agency is already considering an NPRM in this area, the petition may be treated as a docket submission. If such a standard is not under consideration, the agency may "grant" the petition. This does not mean that the proposed rule will be issued in the words of the petition. It can mean that the NHTSA will incorporate the general proposal of the petition in its own NPRM, or that the ideas in the petition will be used as a point of departure for a proposed rule.

Because the agency has not always been prompt or responsive in answering petitions for rule making, legislative proposals are now under consideration in the 93rd Congress to give individuals the right to petition and to require the agency to respond. Also under consideration are legislative proposals giving individuals the right to intervene in agency enforcement activities, a key to adequate preservation of legal rights in judicial review.

Although it is possible to have some impact on NHTSA decision making by using just the material in this book and working by yourself, your efforts will be more effective if you also read other materials and cooperate with other people engaged in similar efforts. One book which you will need is R. Nader, L. Dodge, and R. Hotchkiss, *What To Do With Your Bad Car: An Action Manual For Lemon Owners* (New York: Bantam Books, 1971, $1.50). In addition to providing guidelines for self-help in dealing with the automobile industry, this book has an extensive bibliography of materials for further research, and describes several consumer organizations active in auto safety. One of these organizations in particular concentrates on monitoring the activities of the NHTSA: The Center for Auto Safety, P.O. Box 7250, Washington, D.C. 20044.

Other consumer groups which deal with the NHTSA are listed in Appendix 13-M (p. 799). Unfortunately, the influence of these groups is relatively minor compared to the well-financed and continuing influence presented by industry groups, which also monitor the NHTSA. Several of these groups are listed in Appendix 13-N (p. 800).

Three general methods of dealing with the agency have been described in this chapter: writing complaint letters, submitting comments on proposed standards, and submitting petitions. If you try one of these approaches, let others know what you are doing by sending copies to consumer groups and to members of Congress (both your own Congressman and members of the Senate and House Commerce Committees). While the NHTSA advisory councils have not played a particularly significant role in the past, they might be incited to more vigor if their members began to hear from the public. One way for you to do this is to select a member of one of the groups (see Appendices 13-F, p. 768 and 13-G, p. 770) who has some geographic or organizational link to you, and write him a letter. Although efforts for better highway safety programs are inherently less efficient than making safe cars, they need and can benefit from vigorous consumer support. See how your state measures up according to Appendix 13-D (p. 749), then get in touch with your governor's highway safety representative and find out what is being done to improve the state safety program.

If you have some professional or technical expertise, you can make a particularly valuable contribution. One of the fundamental problems with the NHTSA, which it shares with other agencies, is that most of the experts it sees are either from industry or on their way there. Groups such as the Center for Auto Safety, the Insurance Institute for Highway Safety, and Physicians for Auto Safety (see Appendix 13-M, p. 799) have been established to make the most efficient use of expertise outside the auto industry, and they need the assistance of interested physicians and professionals in all fields.

Citizen action does not depend on Washington leadership, and you can have a significant impact by organizing in your own community (see Chapter 18). Such a local group can have considerable influence on the state and local level by working for adoption of a comprehensive highway safety program. It can also participate in NHTSA activities, from writing letters all the way to drawing up and submitting a technical rule making petition. You should also let your Senators and Representatives know your concern about traffic and highway safety. The Congress can affect traffic safety both by overseeing the NHTSA and by passing new legislation. The level of your activity can be as little or as great as your energy and concern. But remember that although superficially you are dealing with legal minutiae and technical engineering details, fundamentally you are saving human lives.

NHTSA Regional Offices

Address

Region I   James F. Williamson, Regional Adminis-
7:45 am--4:15 pm   trator, NHTSA, Transportation Systems
                    Center, 55 Broadway, Cambridge, Massa-
                    chusetts 02142, Tel: (617) 494-2681.
                    (Connecticut, Maine, Massachusetts, New
                    Hampshire, Rhode Island, and Vermont)

Region II   Dean Van Gorden, Regional Administrator,
7:45 am--4:15 pm   NHTSA, Room 400, 200 Mamaroneck Avenue,
                    White Plains, New York 10601, Tel: (914)
                    761-4250, Ext. 312, 313, 314. (After
                    FTS hrs. and Saturday 761-8761) (New
                    Jersey, New York, and Puerto Rico)

Region III   Vincent D. Walsh, Regional Administra-
8:00 am--4:30 pm   tor, NHTSA, Room 817-B, Federal Build-
                    ing, 31 Hopkins Plaza, Baltimore, Mary-
                    land 21201, Tel: (301) 962-3877. (Dela-
                    ware, District of Columbia, Maryland,
                    Pennsylvania, Virginia, and West Virginia)

Region IV   Lawrence E. Thompson, Regional Adminis-
7:45 am--4:15 pm   trator, NHTSA, Suite 400, 1720 Peachtree
                    Road, N.W., Atlanta, Georgia 30309, Tel:
                    (404) 526-5537. (Alabama, Florida,
                    Georgia, Kentucky, Mississippi, North
                    Carolina, and Tennessee)

Region V   Gordon Lindquist, Regional Administra-
8:00 am--4:40 pm   tor, NHTSA, Suite 214 Executive Plaza,
                    1010 Dixie Highway, Chicago Heights,
                    Illinois 60411, Tel: (312) 756-1950.
                    (Illinois, Indiana, Michigan, Minnesota,
                    Ohio, and Wisconsin)

Region VI   E. Robert Anderson, Regional Administra-
8:00 am--4:30 pm   tor, NHTSA, 819 Taylor Street, Room
                    11A26, Fort Worth, Texas 76102, Tel:
                    (817) 334-2021. (Arkansas, Louisiana,
                    New Mexico, Oklahoma, and Texas)

Region VII   C. Robert Wright, Regional Administra-
7:45 am--4:15 pm   tor, NHTSA, P.O. Box 7085, Country Club
                    Station, Kansas City, Missouri 64113,
                    Tel: (816) 361-7887. (Iowa, Kansas,
                    Missouri, and Nebraska)

Region VIII   R.C. O'Connell, Regional Administrator,
7:45 am--4:15 pm   NHTSA, 9393 W. Alameda Avenue, Lakewood,
                     Colorado 80226, Tel: (303) 234-3253.
                     (Colorado, Montana, North Dakota, South
                     Dakota, Utah, and Wyoming).

Region IX   Bradford Crittenden, Regional Adminis-
7:45 am--4:15 pm   trator, NHTSA, 450 Golden Gate Avenue,
                     Box 36112, San Francisco, California
                     94102, Tel: (415) 556-6415. (Arizona,
                     California, Hawaii, and Nevada).

Region X   William L. Hall, Regional Administrator,
7:45 am--4:15 pm   NHTSA, 5140 Federal Office Building,
                     Seattle, Washington 98104, Tel: (206)
                     442-5934. (Alaska, Idaho, Oregon, and
                     Washington).

Organization Chart of the National Highway Traffic Safety Administration

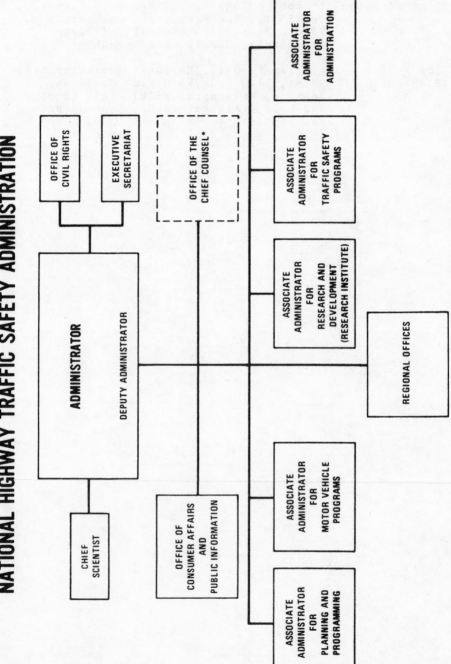

NATIONAL HIGHWAY TRAFFIC SAFETY ADMINISTRATION

- OFFICE OF CIVIL RIGHTS
- EXECUTIVE SECRETARIAT
- ADMINISTRATOR
- DEPUTY ADMINISTRATOR
- CHIEF SCIENTIST
- OFFICE OF THE CHIEF COUNSEL*
- OFFICE OF CONSUMER AFFAIRS AND PUBLIC INFORMATION
- ASSOCIATE ADMINISTRATOR FOR PLANNING AND PROGRAMMING
- ASSOCIATE ADMINISTRATOR FOR MOTOR VEHICLE PROGRAMS
- ASSOCIATE ADMINISTRATOR FOR RESEARCH AND DEVELOPMENT (RESEARCH INSTITUTE)
- ASSOCIATE ADMINISTRATOR FOR TRAFFIC SAFETY PROGRAMS
- ASSOCIATE ADMINISTRATOR FOR ADMINISTRATION
- REGIONAL OFFICES

*Provides legal services to the Administrator, performing these services under the professional supervision and direction of the General Counsel, DOT, who is finally responsible for providing opinions and other legal services to the Administrator; the Administrator; the General Counsel

Purposes of 16 Highway Safety Program Standards

Copies of the 32-page booklet, <u>Highway Safety Program Standards</u>, describing in full detail the 16 Standards and providing pertinent background information on each of them, may be obtained from the Superintendent of Documents, Washington, DC 20402. Price 45¢

Each of the Standards (number 1 through 16) is also available printed individually, and verbatim, on separate pocket size cards (8 1/2" x 3 1/2"). One copy of each may be obtained free from the National Highway Safety Bureau--Documentation Center, Washington, DC 20591.

1.   PERIODIC MOTOR VEHICLE INSPECTION

To increase, through periodic motor vehicle inspection, the likelihood that every vehicle operated on the public highway is properly equipped and is being maintained in reasonably safe working order.

2.   MOTOR VEHICLE REGISTRATION

To provide a means of identifying the owner and type, weight, size and carrying capacities of every vehicle licensed to operate in the State, and to make such data available for traffic safety studies and research, accident investigation, enforcement, and other operational uses.

To provide a means for aggregating ownership and vehicle information for: (a) accident research; (b) planning and development of streets, highway and related facilities; and (c) other operational uses.

3.   MOTORCYCLE SAFETY

To assure that motorcycles, motorcycle operators and their passengers meet standards which contribute to safe operation and protection from injuries.

4.   DRIVER EDUCATION

To insure that every eligible high school student has the opportunity to enroll in a course of instruction designed to train him to drive skillfully and as safely as possible under all traffic and roadway conditions.

To insure that commercial driver training schools achieve and maintain a corresponding level of instruction for beginning drivers with recognition of differences between the needs of adults and adolescents.

To provide education courses offering driving instruction to adults.

5.   DRIVER LICENSING

To improve the quality of driving by implementing more effective and uniform licensing procedures, and thereby to reduce the number of accidents while also increasing the efficiency of traffic flow.

6.   CODES AND LAWS

To eliminate all the major variations in traffic codes, laws and ordinances on given aspects of highway safety among political subdivisions in a State, to increase the compatibility of these ordinances with a unified overall State policy on traffic safety codes and laws, and to further the adoption of appropriate aspects of the Rules of the Road section of the Uniform Vehicle Code.

7.   TRAFFIC COURTS

To provide prompt impartial adjudication of proceedings involving motor vehicle laws.

8.   ALCOHOL IN RELATION TO HIGHWAY SAFETY

To broaden the scope and number of activities directed toward reducing traffic accident loss experience arising in whole or part from persons driving under the influence of alcohol.

9.   IDENTIFICATION & SURVEILLANCE OF ACCIDENT LOCATIONS

To identify specific locations or sections of streets and highways which have high or potentially high accident experience, as a basis for improvement, selective enforcement, or other operational practices that will eliminate or reduce the hazards at the location so identified.

10.   TRAFFIC RECORDS

To assure that appropriate data on traffic accidents, drivers, motor vehicles and roadways are available to provide:

1. A reliable indication of the magnitude and nature of the highway traffic accident problem on a national, State and local scale;

2. A reliable means for identifying short-term changes and long-term trends in the magnitude and nature of traffic accidents;

3. A valid basis for

   a. The detection of high or potentially high accident locations and causes

   b. The detection of health, behavioral and related factors contributing to accident causation

   c. The design of accident, fatality and injury countermeasures

   d. Developing means for evaluating the cost and effectiveness of these measures

   e. The planning and implementation of selected enforcement and other operational programs.

11. EMERGENCY MEDICAL SERVICES

To provide an emergency care system that will:

I.   Provide quick identification and response to accidents;

II. Sustain and prolong life through proper first aid measures, both at the scene and in transit;

III. Provide the coordination, transportation, and communications necessary to bring the injured and definitive medical care together in the shortest practicable time, without simultaneously creating additional hazards.

12. HIGHWAY DESIGN, CONSTRUCTION & MAINTENANCE

To assure (a) that existing streets and highways are maintained in a condition that promotes safety, (b) that capital improvements either to modernize existing roads or to provide new facilities meet approved safety standards, and (c) that appropriate precautions are taken to protect passing motorists as well as highway workers from accident involvement at highway construction sites.

13. TRAFFIC CONTROL DEVICES

To assure the full and proper application of modern traffic engineering practice and uniform standards for traffic control devices in reducing the likelihood and severity of traffic accidents.

14. PEDESTRIAN SAFETY

To emphasize the need to recognize pedestrian safety as an integral, constant and important element in community planning and all aspects of highway transportation and to insure a continuing program to improve such safety by each State and its political subdivisions.

15. POLICE TRAFFIC SERVICES

To reduce the deaths and injuries by improving police traffic services in all aspects of accident prevention programs and police traffic supervision, post accident procedures to aid crash victims and to bring those responsible for the accidents to justice.

16. DEBRIS HAZARD CONTROL AND CLEANUP

To provide for the assignment of official responsibilities and for the planning, training, coordination and communications necessary to assure the recognition, reporting, and prompt correction of conditions or incidents that constitute potential dangers; that incident sites are restored to a safe condition; and that traffic movement is expeditiously resumed.

Highway Safety Program Standards

ABOVE AVERAGE

STANDARD	Va.	N.H.	Del.	S.D.	Me.	Colo.	D.C.	Mass.	Utah	N.Y.	Mich.	Calif.	Penn.
Periodic Motor Vehicle Inspection (301)	100	100	88	100	88	88	100	85	88	100	50	50	88
Motor Vehicle Registration (302)	100	100	82	100	100	96	82	100	100	100	100	96	100
Motorcycle Safety (303)	100	100	100	100	95	100	100	100	50	100	90	45	95
Driver Education (304)	85	100	90	90	90	70	90	100	100	85	90	100	100
Driver Licensing (305)	94	89	82	68	83	72	72	79	98	89	84	99	52
Codes and Laws (306)	100	100	100	100	100	100	80	0	100	100	100	0	80
Traffic Courts (307)	80	90	100	70	100	90	100	100	80	90	70	90	70

Alcohol Safety (308)	95	95	95	95	95	75	50	95	80	80	100	95	80
Identification & Surveillance of Accident Locations (309)	68	77	61	36	66	83	90	75	49	67	91	61	87
Traffic Records (310)	100	99	100	81	81	81	81	80	100	73	74	81	99
Emergency Medical Services (311)	35	55	25	25	50	75	45	60	85	100	75	75	100
Highway Design, Construction & Maintenance (312)	78	82	68	64	70	63	77	73	53	65	66	61	83
Traffic Control Devices (313)	58	90	66	65	34	63	78	74	62	63	86	90	92
Pedestrian Safety (314)	57	85	84	74	71	86	91	57	66	77	81	84	90
Police Traffic Services (315)	78	92	95	76	79	91	52	92	74	83	72	79	95
Debris Hazard Control & Cleanup (316)	100	100	80	80	100	100	100	100	100	100	100	100	100
TOTALS	1254	1255	1258	1260	1262	1281	1288	1322	1325	1336	1387	1405	1485

AVERAGE

STANDARD	Idaho	Md.	Ohio	N.J.	Ariz.	Minn.	Ore.	Wash.	S.C.	Wisc.	N.C.	Conn.	Ill.	Mont.
Periodic Motor Vehicle Inspection (301)	88	0	41	93	0	0	44	0	98	0	88	0	0	0
Motor Vehicle Registration (302)	87	100	100	100	96	96	100	100	69	100	100	96	73	69
Motorcycle Safety (303)	65	90	90	100	90	85	75	90	100	90	70	90	40	60
Driver Education (304)	100	100	90	75	73	97	75	100	100	100	100	86	100	90
Driver Licensing (305)	77	69	51	53	92	90	53	88	73	73	85	59	60	80
Codes and Laws (306)	100	100	20	100	100	100	100	100	100	100	20	100	100	100
Traffic Courts (307)	100	100	90	90	100	60	70	55	70	60	90	100	100	70
Alcohol Safety (308)	75	75	95	75	95	100	100	95	80	75	95	95	90	100

Identification & Surveillance of Accident Locations (309)	59	55	65	36	54	57	78	89	50	58	76	60	64	56
Traffic Records (310)	65	100	100	81	66	81	81	86	69	81	100	81	81	57
Emergency Medical Services (311)	25	65	100	30	90	65	35	45	40	50	45	25	90	100
Highway Design, Construction & Maintenance (312)	68	53	62	60	58	78	75	75	67	67	67	53	65	63
Traffic Control Devices (313)	54	68	62	74	62	75	77	62	49	82	70	71	67	67
Pedestrian Safety (314)	77	79	77	64	68	85	69	57	69	57	45	71	81	73
Police Traffic Services (315)	95	79	76	84	90	97	97	72	82	73	72	75	89	92
Debris Hazard Control & Cleanup (316)	100	100	100	95	72	40	75	55	50	100	40	100	60	80
TOTALS	1235	1233	1219	1210	1206	1206	1204	1169	1166	1166	1163	1162	1160	1157

AVERAGE

STANDARD	Vt.	Tex.	Mo.	Tenn.	R.I.	Hawaii	N.M.	Okla.	Fla.	La.	Ark.	Neb.	Ky.
Periodic Motor Vehicle Inspection (301)	100	87	100	0	88	88	84	88	100	88	88	88	88
Motor Vehicle Registration (302)	100	96	100	100	100	82	96	73	50	100	96	69	69
Motorcycle Safety (303)	100	85	85	90	100	100	65	55	75	100	75	40	100
Driver Education (304)	90	75	80	90	53	75	100	90	75	75	60	75	100
Driver Licensing (305)	46	75	67	55	81	87	65	50	65	100	54	66	54
Codes and Laws (306)	0	100	80	100	100	100	100	100	100	100	100	100	80
Traffic Courts (307)	80	60	75	60	90	80	80	60	80	40	80	40	25
Alcohol Safety (308)	100	80	60	95	80	100	80	60	80	95	100	80	100

Identification & Surveillance of Accident Locations (309)	55	54	54	48	49	21	49	66	64	39	34	41	33
Traffic Records (310)	81	81	81	86	73	71	67	67	57	81	74	62	84
Emergency Medical Services (311)	60	60	25	10	60	10	55	40	25	25	0	35	70
Highway Design, Construction & Maintenance (312)	61	63	52	62	56	38	35	49	66	41	41	53	53
Traffic Control Devices (313)	62	58	43	74	50	57	39	68	63	50	20	40	53
Pedestrian Safety (314)	80	49	78	61	29	56	68	52	80	35	60	73	53
Police Traffic Services (315)	60	75	81	62	24	44	24	97	68	82	84	71	60
Debris Hazard Control & Cleanup (316)	80	50	80	100	58	80	80	59	10	0	70	100	10
TOTALS	1155	1148	1141	1093	1091	1089	1087	1074	1058	1051	1036	1033	1032

BELOW AVERAGE

STANDARD	Ala.	Alaska	Kans.	Miss.	Iowa	W.Va.	Ind.	N.D.	P.R.	Ga.	Wyo.	Nev.
Periodic Motor Vehicle Inspection (301)	0	0	0	78	0	88	88	0	80	100	88	0
Motor Vehicle Registration (302)	82	61	50	49	50	60	100	87	96	100	50	96
Motorcycle Safety (303)	90	65	0	15	40	75	70	85	75	75	10	90
Driver Education (304)	44	43	90	70	90	85	46	65	11	80	86	100
Driver Licensing (305)	43	46	49	48	63	37	83	63	42	42	59	80
Codes and Laws (306)	0	80	100	100	100	100	100	100	100	100	100	100
Traffic Courts (307)	25	80	70	0	35	50	50	60	100	25	70	45
Alcohol Safety (308)	80	75	55	65	70	80	80	100	75	95	75	100

Identification & Surveillance of Accident Locations (309)	36	47	50	54	40	22	30	33	50	22	46	51
Traffic Records (310)	80	53	69	63	71	81	68	53	68	57	56	76
Emergency Medical Services (311)	45	35	25	0	65	0	0	20	35	15	15	50
Highway Design, Construction & Maintenance (312)	43	71	60	43	43	71	46	59	45	49	46	43
Traffic Control Devices (313)	26	70	59	73	55	71	45	62	50	50	42	45
Pedestrian Safety (314)	75	78	61	59	31	52	41	66	69	58	33	40
Police Traffic Services (315)	64	45	44	75	80	24	30	92	19	97	26	70
Debris Hazard Control & Cleanup (316)	30	70	10	40	8	0	40	50	100	64	45	0
TOTALS	1010	1007	995	986	953	938	884	883	861	826	759	739

Summary Description of
Safety Standards

STANDARD NO. 101 - Control Location, Identification and
Illumination - Passenger Cars (Effective 1-1-68), Multipurpose Passenger Vehicles, Trucks and Buses (Effective
9-1-72)

Requires that essential controls be within the reach
of the driver restrained by a lap belt and upper torso
restraint, and that certain of these controls be identified when mounted on the instrument panel. Illumination
requirements will become effective September 1, 1972.
The purpose of the standard is to facilitate control selection and ensure accessibility.

STANDARD NO. 102 - Transmission Shift Lever Sequence,
Starter Interlock, and Transmission Braking Effect - Pas-
senger Cars, Multipurpose Passenger Vehicles, Trucks, and
Buses (Effective 1-1-68)

Requires that transmission shift lever sequences have
the neutral position placed between forward and reverse
drive positions. Its purpose is to reduce the likelihood
of driver error in shifting. Also required is an interlock to prevent starting the car in the reverse and forward drive positions, and an engine-braking effect in one
of the lower gears at vehicle speeds below 25 miles per
hour.

STANDARD NO. 103 - Windshield Defrosting and Defogging
Systems - Passenger Cars, Multipurpose Passenger Vehicles,
Trucks, and Buses (Effective 1-1-68)

Requires that all vehicles manufactured for sale in
the continental United States be equipped with windshield
defrosters and defogging systems, and (Effective January
1, 1969) meet certain performance requirements.

STANDARD NO. 104 - Windshield Wiping and Washing Systems -
Passenger Cars, Multipurpose Passenger Vehicles, Trucks
and Buses (Effective 1-1-68)

Specifies the windshield area to be wiped and requires
washer and high performance, two-speed wipers on all passenger cars. The wipers must be able to sweep the wind-

shield at least 45 times a minute regardless of engine
load. An amendment, effective January 1, 1969, broadens
the application of the initial standard to cover smaller
passenger cars, multipurpose passenger vehicles, trucks
and buses. Tables prescribing the minimum size of wiped
areas have been added for the smaller passenger cars.

STANDARD NO. 105 - Hydraulic Brake Systems - Passenger
Cars (Effective 1-1-68)

     In order to ensure adequate braking performance under
normal and emergency conditions, this standard requires
each passenger car to have: a foot brake capable of stopping under certain specified conditions, a parking brake
capable of holding on a 30-percent grade, a warning light
that indicates failure of the hydraulic brakes, and a system designed to provide residual braking in case of failure of the service brake.

STANDARD NO. 106 - Hydraulic Brake Hoses - Passenger Cars
and Multipurpose Passenger Vehicles (Effective 1-1-68)

     Vehicles must be equipped with hoses meeting require-
ments of this standard.

STANDARD NO. 107 - Reflecting Surfaces - Passenger Cars,
Multipurpose Passenger Vehicles, Trucks, and Buses
(Effective 1-1-68)

     The reflection of the sun and bright lights into the
driver's eyes from shiny surfaces in his line of sight
has long been a safety hazard. This standard requires
that windshield wiper arms, inside windshield moldings,
horn rings, and the frames and brackets of inside rearview mirrors have dull surfaces which will greatly reduce
the likelihood of hazardous reflection into the driver's
eyes.

STANDARD NO. 108 - Lamps, Reflective Devices, and Associ-
ated Equipment - Passenger Cars, Multipurpose Passenger
Vehicles, Trucks, Trailers, Buses, and Motorcycles
(Effective 1-1-68)

     This standard specifies requirements for lamps, re-
flective devices, and associated equipment for signaling
and to enable safe operation in darkness and other conditions of reduced visibility. It was originally applicable
to multipurpose passenger vehicles, trucks, trailers, and
buses 80 inches or more in overall width.

     Effective January 1, 1969, the requirements of the
standard were applicable to all passenger cars, motorcycles, multipurpose passenger vehicles, trucks, buses,
and trailers, irrespective of overall width.

     Several revisions were made in the standard, effec-
tive January 1, 1972, including the extension of require-

ments to cover all applicable replacement equipment. Another amendment, effective January 1, 1973, affects turn
signal and hazard warning signal flashers.

STANDARD NO. 109 - New Pneumatic Tires - Passenger Cars
(Effective 1-1-68)

Specifies tire dimensions and laboratory test requirements for bead unseating resistance; strength, endurance, and high-speed performance; defines tire load
rating; and specifies labeling requirements.

STANDARD NO. 110 - Tire Selection and Rims - Passenger
Cars (Effective 4-1-68)

Specifies requirements for original equipment tire
and rim selection on new cars to prevent tire overloading.
These include placard requirements relating to load distribution as well as rim performance requirements under
conditions of tire deflation.

STANDARD NO. 111 - Rearview Mirrors - Passenger Cars and
Multipurpose Passenger Vehicles (Effective 1-1-68)

Specifies requirements for rearview mirrors to provide the driver with a clear and reasonably unobstructed
view to the rear. It requires an outside rearview mirror
on the driver's side, and when the inside mirror does not
provide a sufficient field of view because of the size or
location of the rear window, an additional outside mirror
on the passenger side is required. Also, the inside
mirror must be designed to reduce the likelihood of injury
on impact.

The mirror may protrude further than the widest part
of the vehicle body to the extent necessary to produce a
field-of-view meeting or exceeding the field-of-view requirements of the standard.

STANDARD NO. 112 - Headlamp Concealment Devices -
Passenger Cars, Multipurpose Passenger Vehicles, Trucks,
Buses, and Motorcycles (Effective 1-1-69)

Specifies that any fully opened headlamp concealment
device shall remain fully opened whether either or both
of the following occur: (a) any loss of power to or
within the device or (b) any malfunction of wiring or
electrical supply for controlling the concealment device
occurs.

STANDARD NO. 113 - Hood Latch Systems - Passenger
Cars, Multipurpose Passenger Vehicles, Trucks and Buses
(Effective 1-1-69)

Specifies requirements for a hood latch system for
each hood. A front opening hood, which in any open position partially or completely obstructs a driver's forward

view through the windshield, must be provided with a
second latch position on the hood latch system or with a
second hood latch system.

STANDARD NO. 114 - Theft Protection - Passenger Cars
(Effective 1-1-70)

This standard requires that each passenger car have
a key-locking system that, whenever the key is removed,
prevents normal activation of the car's engine and also
prevents either steering or self-mobility of the car, or
both.

STANDARD NO. 115 - Vehicle Identification Number -
Passenger Cars (Effective 1-1-69)

Specifies requirements for an identification number
for all passenger cars to facilitate recognition of unauthorized vehicle use resulting in crashes. The number
will be sunk or embossed upon either a part of the vehicle (other than the glazing), which is not designed to
be removed except for repair, or on a separate plate
which is permanently affixed to such a part. The number
must be visible from outside the vehicle.

STANDARD NO. 116 - Hydraulic Brake Fluids (Effective
3-1-72)

Specifies minimum physical characteristics for two
grades of brake fluids, DOT 3 and DOT 4, for use in hydraulic brake systems in all motor vehicles. Also establishes labeling requirements for brake fluid containers.

STANDARD NO. 117 - Retreaded Pneumatic Tires - Passenger
Cars (Effective 1-1-72)

Requires retreaded tires to meet performance requirements similar to those for new passenger car tires;
and prohibits certain practices in the manufacture of retreaded tires which might weaken the completed tire. Certain labeling requirements also are specified.

STANDARD NO. 118 - Power-Operated Window Systems -
Passenger Cars and Multipurpose Passenger Vehicles
(Effective 2-1-71)

Requires that power-operated window systems be inoperative when ignition is in an off position or when key
is removed.

STANDARD NO. 119 - Tires for Vehicles Other Than Passenger Cars (Proposed Effective 9-1-73)

Specifies tire dimensions and laboratory test requirements for strength, endurance, and high-speed performance; defines tire load rating; and specifies labeling requirements.

STANDARD NO. 120 - Tire and Rim Selection and Rim Performance for Vehicles Other Than Passenger Cars (Proposed Effective 1-1-73)

Specifies requirements for original equipment tire and rim selection on new multipurpose passenger vehicles, trucks, and buses to prevent tire overloading. These include placard requirements relating to load distribution as well as rim performance under conditions of tire deflation.

STANDARD NO. 121 - Air Brake Systems - Trucks, Buses, and Trailers (Effective 9-1-74)

Establishes performance and equipment requirements on vehicles equipped with air brake systems.

STANDARD NO. 122 - Motorcycle Brake Systems - Motorcycles (Effective 9-1-73)

Establishes equipment and performance requirements on brake systems appropriate for two-wheeled and three-wheeled motorcycles. Each motorcycle is required to have either a split hydraulic service brake system or two independently actuated service brake systems.

STANDARD NO. 123 - Motorcycle Controls and Displays (Effective 9-1-74)

Specifies requirements for the location, operation, identification and illumination of motorcycle controls and displays and for stands and footrests.

STANDARD NO. 124 - Accelerator Control Systems - Passenger Cars, Multipurpose Passenger Vehicles, Trucks and Buses (Effective 9-1-73)

Establishes requirements for the return of a vehicle's throttle to the idle position when the driver removes the actuating force from the accelerator control, or in the event of a breakage or disconnection in the accelerator control system.

STANDARD NO. 125 - Warning Devices (Effective 1-1-74)

Establishes shape, size and performance requirements for reuseable day and night warning devices that can be erected on or near the roadway to warn approaching motorists of the presence of a stopped vehicle. It applies only to devices that do not have self-contained energy sources.

STANDARD NO. 126 - Truck-Camper Loading - Slide-in Campers (Effective 1-1-73 and 9-1-73)

Specifies requirements for labeling truck-campers including a vehicle identification number, weight, center of gravity, and loading instructions.

STANDARD NO. 201 - Occupant Protection in Interior Impact - Passenger Cars (Effective 1-1-68)

Over a wide range of impact speeds, the injuries
suffered by drivers and passengers are largely determined
by the extent to which the structures on the inside of
the vehicle have been designed to cushion the heads and
other parts of the bodies hitting them. This standard
specifies requirements to afford impact protection for
occupants; it contains requirements for padded instrument
panels, seat backs, sun visors, and armrests.

An amendment effective January 1, 1970, requires
that interior compartment doors (glove compartment doors)
remain closed during a crash.

STANDARD NO. 202 - Head Restraints - Passenger Cars
(Effective 1-1-69)

Specifies requirements for head restraints to reduce
the frequency and severity of "whiplash" type and other
neck injuries in rear-end and other collisions.

STANDARD NO. 203 - Impact Protection for the Driver From
the Steering Control System - Passenger Cars (Effective
1-1-68)

Specifies requirements for minimizing chest, neck,
and facial injuries by providing steering systems that
yield forward, cushioning the impact of the driver's
chest and absorbing much of his impact energy in front-
end crashes. Such systems are already proving highly
effective in reducing the likelihood of serious and fatal
injuries.

STANDARD NO. 204 - Steering Control Rearward Displacement - Passenger Cars (Effective 1-1-68)

Specifies requirements limiting the rearward displacement of the steering control into the passenger
compartment to reduce the likelihood of chest, neck, or
head injuries.

STANDARD NO. 205 - Glazing Materials - Passenger Cars,
Multipurpose Passenger Vehicles, Motorcycles, Trucks, and
Buses (Effective 1-1-68)

Specifies requirements for all glazing materials
used in windshields, windows, and interior partitions of
motor vehicles. Its purpose is to reduce the likelihood
of lacerations to the face, scalp, and neck, and to minimize the possibility of occupants penetrating the windshield in collisions.

STANDARD NO. 206 - Door Locks and Door Retention Components - Passenger Cars (Effective 1-1-68), Multipurpose
Passenger Vehicles (Effective 1-1-70) and Trucks (Effective 1-1-72)

Specifies load requirements for door latches and
door hinge systems to minimize the probability of failure
as a result of forces encountered in vehicle impacts.

STANDARD NO. 207 - Anchorage of Seats - Passenger Cars
(Effective 1-1-68), Multipurpose Passenger Vehicles,
Trucks and Buses (Effective 1-1-72)

Establishes requirements for seats, their attachment
assemblies, and their installation, to minimize the possibility of failure as a result of forces acting on the
seat on vehicle impact.

STANDARD NO. 208 - Occupant Crash Protection

This standard amends Standard No. 208, Seat Belt
Installations, by specifying requirements for both active
and passive occupant crash protection systems for passenger vehicles, trucks, and driver's seats in buses. The
following optional solutions are permitted:

Passenger Cars (Effective 1-1-72)
  1) Passive protection at all seats
  2) Lap belts at all positions, plus meeting
     injury criteria at front outboard positions
  3) Lap and shoulder belts at all outboard
     positions

Bus Driver Seat (Effective 1-1-72)
  1) Complete passive protection
  2) Belts conforming to Standard No. 209

Passenger Cars (Effective 8-15-73)
  1) Passive protection at all positions
  2) System providing passive protection for
     front seating positions
  3) Belt ignition interlock system

Passenger Cars (Effective 8-15-75)
  1) Passive protection in all seating positions

Multipurpose Passenger Vehicles and Trucks (Effective 8-15-75)
  1) Required to meet one of three options required
     for passenger cars, effective August 15, 1973,
     noted above

Multipurpose Passenger Vehicles and Trucks (Effective 8-15-77)
  1) Full passive protection

STANDARD NO. 209 - Seat Belt Assemblies - Passenger Cars,
Multipurpose Passenger Vehicles, Trucks, and Buses
(Effective 3-1-67)

Specifies requirements pertaining to the manufacture
of seat belt assemblies. The requirements apply to
straps, webbing or similar material, as well as to all
necessary buckles and other fasteners, and all hardware
designed for installing the assembly in a motor vehicle
and to the installation, usage and maintenance instructions for the assembly.

STANDARD NO. 210 - Seat Belt Assembly Anchorages - Passenger Cars (Effective 1-1-68), Multipurpose Passenger
Vehicles, Trucks and Buses (Effective 7-1-71)

Specifies the requirements for seat belt assembly
anchorages to ensure effective occupant restraint and to
reduce the likelihood of failure in collisions. Included
is a requirement for anchorages for lap and upper torso
restraint belts in all forward facing outboard seats
(four in standard sedans).

STANDARD NO. 211 - Wheel Nuts, Wheel Discs, and Hub Caps -
Passenger Cars and Multipurpose Passenger Vehicles (Effective 1-1-68)

Requires that "spinner" hub caps and other winged
projections (both functional and non-functional) be deleted from wheel nuts, wheel discs, and hub caps. Its
purpose is to eliminate a potential hazard to pedestrians
and cyclists.

STANDARD NO. 212 - Windshield Mounting - Passenger Cars
(Effective 1-1-70)

This standard requires that, when tested as described, each windshield mounting must retain either:
(1) not less than 75 percent of the windshield periphery;
or (2) not less than 50 percent of that portion of the
windshield periphery on each side of the vehicle longitudinal centerline, if an unrestrained 95th percentile
adult male manikin is seated in each outboard front seating position. The purpose of the standard is to keep the
vehicle occupants within the confines of the passenger
compartment during a crash.

STANDARD NO. 213 - Child Seating Systems (Effective
4-1-71)

Specifies requirements for child seating systems to
minimize the likelihood of injury and/or death to children in vehicle crashes or sudden stops. Includes requirements for providing information for proper installation and use.

STANDARD NO. 214 - Side Door Strength - Passenger Cars
(Effective 1-1-73)

This standard specifies requirements for side doors
of passenger cars to minimize the safety hazard caused by
intrusion into the passenger compartment in a side impact
accident.

STANDARD NO. 215 - Exterior Protection - Passenger Cars
(Effective 9-1-72)

Requires passenger cars to withstand barrier impacts
of 5 m.p.h. front, and 2-1/2 m.p.h. rear, without damage
to lighting, fuel, exhaust, cooling and latching systems.
An amendment, effective September 1, 1973, was issued to
upgrade the barrier impact speed to 5 m.p.h. front, and 5
m.p.h. rear, and to correct the mismatch that exists between passenger car bumpers by requiring impacts by a
weighted pendulum at 5 m.p.h. front and rear.

STANDARD NO. 216 - Roof Crush Resistance - Passenger Cars
(Effective 8-15-73)

Sets minimum strength requirements for passenger car
roofs to reduce the likelihood of roof collapse in a
rollover accident. The standard provides an alternative
to conformity with the rollover tests of Standard No. 208.

STANDARD NO. 217 - Bus Window Retention and Release -
Buses (Effective 9-1-73)

Specifies requirements for retention of bus windows
to prevent occupant ejection in a crash, and specifies
requirements for emergency exits for escape.

STANDARD NO. 301 - Fuel Tanks, Fuel Tank Filler Pipes,
and Fuel Tank Connections - Passenger Cars (Effective
1-1-68)

Specifies requirements for the integrity and security of fuel tanks, fuel tank filler pipes, and fuel tank
connections to minimize fire hazard as a result of
collision.

STANDARD NO. 302 - Flammability of Interior Materials -
Passenger Cars, Multipurpose Passenger Vehicles, Trucks,
and Buses (Effective 9-1-72)

This standard specifies burn resistance requirements
for materials used in the occupant compartment of motor
vehicles in order to reduce deaths and injuries caused by
vehicle fires.

SUMMARY DESCRIPTION OF
OTHER REGULATIONS

PART 566 - Manufacturer Identification (Effective 2-1-72)

Requires manufacturers of motor vehicles and motor
vehicle equipment (except tires) to which a motor vehicle
safety standard applies, to submit identifying information and a description of the items they produce to the
Department of Transportation. Revised information also
is required when necessary to keep the entry current.

PART 567 - Certification Regulations (Effective 8-31-69)

This part specifies the content and location of, and
other requirements for, the label or tag to be affixed to
motor vehicles and motor vehicle equipment manufactured
after August 31, 1969. This certificate will provide the
consumer with information to assist him in determining
which of the Federal Motor Vehicle Safety Standards are
applicable to the vehicle or equipment, and its date of
manufacture.

PART 568 - Vehicles Manufactured in Two or More Stages
(Effective 1-1-72)

This part requires the furnishing of information
relative to a vehicle's conformity to motor vehicle safety standards. It requires that the incomplete vehicle
manufacturer to list each standard applicable to the
types of vehicles into which the incomplete vehicle may
be manufactured that is in effect at the time of manufacture of the incomplete vehicle.

PART 569 - Regrooved Tires - Applies to all motor vehicle
regrooved or regroovable tires manufactured or regrooved
after March 1, 1969

The regulation allows only tires designed for the
regrooving process to be regrooved; specifies dimensional
and conditional requirements for the tire after the regrooving process; and sets forth labeling requirements
for the tire which is to be regrooved.

PART 573 - Defect Reports (Effective 10-1-71)

This part specifies manufacturer requirements for
reporting safety-related defects to the National Highway
Traffic Safety Administration; for providing quarterly
reports on defect notification campaigns and vehicle
production; for providing copies of communications with
dealers and purchasers concerning defects; and for maintaining owner lists.

PART 574 - Tire Identification and Record Keeping

Applies to manufacturers, brand name owners, re-
treaders, and distributors and dealers of new and retread

tires for use on motor vehicles, and to manufacturers and
dealers of motor vehicles. Requires tire identification,
recording and reporting of names of tire purchasers. It
became effective May 22, 1971.

PART 575 - Consumer Information Regulations

This part requires every manufacturer of motor vehicles manufactured after January 1, 1970, to provide the
following information to first purchasers of motor vehicles:

Vehicle stopping distance. Manufacturers of passenger cars and motorcycles must provide information
on stopping distance at specified speeds and under
various conditions.

Tire reserve load. Manufacturers of passenger cars
must provide information as to the difference between the load imposed on a tire by the vehicle and
the maximum load rating for the tire at recommended
inflation pressures.

Acceleration and passing ability. Manufacturers of
passenger cars and motorcycles must provide information on acceleration and passing ability under low
and high-speed conditions.

National Motor Vehicle Safety Advisory Council

Mr. Leslie N. Bland
Leslie N. Bland and Co.
2235 S. Michigan Avenue
Chicago, IL 60616

Mr. Judson B. Branch
Chrmn., Executive Committee
Allstate Insurance Company
Allstate Plaza
Northbrook, IL 60062

Mrs. Katherine K. Burgum
Dean, College of Home
   Economics
North Dakota State Univ.
Fargo, ND 58102

Mr. Francis G. Dwyer
Chrmn., Rhode Island Bridge
   & Turnpike Authority
37 Bellevue Street
Newport, RI 02840

Mr. Earl Hathaway
482 St. Andrews Drive
Akron, OH 44303

Col. James J. Hegarty
Director, Department of
   Public Safety
Phoenix, AZ 85009

Dr. Henry Hill, President
Riverside Research Laboratory
300 Neck Road
Haverhill, MA 91830

Mr. Dale C. Hogue
Attorney at Law
P.O. Box 1024
Middleburg, VA 22117

Dr. Donald F. Huelke
University of Michigan
   Medical School
Medical Science II Bldg.
Ann Arbor, MI 48102

Mr. Ralph T. Millet
66 Otter Cove Drive
Old Saybrook, CT 06475

Mr. John N. Noettl
Director, Membership
   Services
Automobile Club of Missouri
3917 Lindell Boulevard
St. Louis, MI 63108

Mr. Lawrence M. Patrick
Professor, Bio-Mechanics
   Research Center
Wayne State University
Detroit, MI 48202

Mr. William A. Raftery
Executive Vice President &
   General Manager
Motor & Equipment Manu-
   facturers Association
MEMA Headquarters
222 Cedar Lane
Teaneck, NJ 07666

Mr. William B. Robertson
Special Assistant to the
   Governor of Minority
   Groups & Consumer Affairs
State Capitol
Richmond, VA 23219

Mr. Frank Sawyer
Chairman and President
General Rental Corporation
209 Columbus Avenue
Boston, MA 02117

Mr. Herbert D. Smith
Vice President -
   Public Affairs
Uniroyal, Inc.
1230 Avenue of the Americas
New York, NY 10020

Mr. Trevor O. Jones
Director, Advanced
  Product Engineering
General Motors Corporation
Warren, MI 48090

Dr. John D. States
Associate Clinical Prof.
University of Rochester
15 Prince Street
Rochester, NY 14607

Dr. George S. Sutherland
President, Rocket Research
  Corporation
York Center
Redmond, WA 90852

Ms. Marcy Taylor
1800 Broadway, Apt. 603
San Francisco, CA 94109

Mr. Vincent L. Tofany
Commissioner, New York
  Dept. of Motor Vehicles
Swan Street Building
South Mall
Albany, NY 12226

Mr. Ivan J. Wagar
Editor, Cycle World
3512 Graysby Avenue
San Pedro, CA 90732

Dr. Arthur H. Keeney
Wills Eye Hospital
1061 Spring Garden Street
Philadelphia, PA 19130

Tire Information Charts

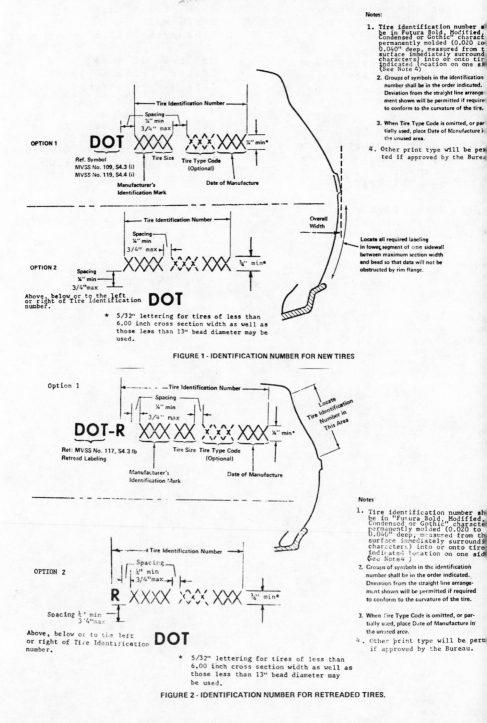

Notes:

1. Tire identification number s be in Futura Bold, Modified Condensed or Gothic characte permanently molded (0.020 to 0.040" deep, measured from t surface immediately surround characters) into or onto tir indicated location on one s (See Note 4)

2. Groups of symbols in the identification number shall be in the order indicated. Deviation from the straight line arrangement shown will be permitted if require to conform to the curvature of the tire.

3. When Tire Type Code is omitted, or par tially used, place Date of Manufacture i the unused area.

4. Other print type will be per ted if approved by the Burea

Locate all required labeling in lower segment of one sidewall between maximum section width and bead so that data will not be obstructed by rim flange.

* 5/32" lettering for tires of less than 6.00 inch cross section width as well as those less than 13" bead diameter may be used.

FIGURE 1 - IDENTIFICATION NUMBER FOR NEW TIRES

Notes:

1. Tire identification number sh be in "Futura Bold, Modified, Condensed or Gothic" characte permanently molded (0.020 to 0.040" deep, measured from th surface immediately surround characters) into or onto tire indicated location on one sid (See Note 4)

2. Groups of symbols in the identification number shall be in the order indicated. Deviation from the straight line arrangement shown will be permitted if required to conform to the curvature of the tire.

3. When Tire Type Code is omitted, or partially used, place Date of Manufacture in the unused area.

4. Other print type will be perm if approved by the Bureau.

* 5/32" lettering for tires of less than 6.00 inch cross section width as well as those less than 13" bead diameter may be used.

FIGURE 2 - IDENTIFICATION NUMBER FOR RETREADED TIRES.

LIST OF NEW TIRE MANUFACTURERS AND CORRESPONDING
IDENTIFICATION CODE MARKS
(Based on the following Alpha-numeric code with letters:
ABCDEFHJKLMNPTZVWXY and Nos. 123456789)

Manufacturer	Identification code
ance Tire & Rubber Co., td.	CD.
Armstrong Rubber Co	CE, CF, CH, CV.
n Rubber Co	AT.
igestone Tire Co., Ltd	EH, EJ, EK, EL, EM, EN, EP.
lisle Tire & Rubber Division f Carlisle Corp.	UU.
t	HT, HU, HV.
tinental A.G	CM, CN, CP, CT, CU.
per Tire & Rubber Co	UP, UT.
Dayton Tire & Rubber Co	HX, HY.
man Rubber Manufacturing o.	DY.
Dunlap Tire & Rubber Co	DA, DB, DC, DD, DE, DF, DH, DJ, DK, DL, DM, DN, DP, DU.
Firestone Tire & Rubber Co	VA, VB, VC, VD, VE, VF, VH, VJ, VK, VL, VM, VN, VP, VT, VV, VW, VX, VY, WA, WB, WC, WD, WF, WH, WJ.
Gates Rubber Co	BW, BX, BY.
General Tire & Rubber Co	AA, AB, AC, AD, AE AF, AH.
B. F. Goodrich Co	BA, BB, BC, BD, BE, BF, BH, BJ, BK, BL, BM, BN, BP.
Goodyear Tire & Rubber o.	MA, MB, MC, MD, ME, MF, MH, MJ, MK, ML, MM, MN, MP, MT, MU, MV, MW, MX, MY, NA, NB, NC, ND, NE, NF, NH, NJ, NK, NL, NM, NN, NP, NT, NU, NV, NW, NX, NY, PA, PB, PC, PD, PE, PF.
ng Ah Tire Co., Ltd	EF
International BV. Rubber o.	BV
ue Rubber Co., CJ. Ltd	CJ
Kelly-Springfield Tire Co	PH, PJ, PK, PL, PM, PN, PP, PT, PU, PV, PW, PX, PY, TA, TB, TC, TD, TE, TF, TH, TJ, TK, TL, TM, TN, TP, TT, TU, TV, TW, TX, TY, UA, UB, UC, UD, UE, UF, UH, UJ, UK, UL, UM, UN.
ber-Colombes Co	EV, EW, EX, EY.
owa Rubber Ind. Co., Ltd	

Manufacturer	Identification code
The Lee Tire & Rubber Co	JA, JB, JC, JD, JE, JF, JH, JJ, JK, JL, JM, JN, JP, JT, JU, JV, JW, JX, JY, KA, KB, KC, KD, KE, KF, KH, KJ, KK, KL, KM, KN, KP, KT, KU, KV, KW, KX, KY, LA, LB, LC, LD, LE, LF.
Madras Rubber Factory, Ltd.	WT.
The Mansfield Tire & Rubber Co.	WL.
Mansfield-Denman-General Co., Ltd.	LV.
McCreary Tire & Rubber Co	CY.
Metzeler A.G	EA, EB, EC.
Michelin Tire Corp	FF, FH, FJ, FK, FL, FM, FN, FP, FT, FU, FV, FW, FX, FY, HA, HB, HC, HD, HE, HF, HH, HJ, HK, HL, HM, HN, HP.
Mitsuboshi Belting, Ltd	LX, LY.
The Mohawk Rubber Co	CA, CB., CC
Nitto Tire Co., Ltd	EE.
Okamoto Riken Gumo Co., Ltd.	ED.
Olympic Tire & Rubber Co. Pty., Ltd.	WM, WN.
Pennsylvania Tire & Rubber Company of Mississippi.	WK.
Phoenix Gummiwerke A.G	AX AY.
Pirelli Tire Corp	XA, XB, XC, XD, XE XF, XH, XJ, XK, XL, XM, XN, XP.
Samson Tire & Rubber Co., Ltd.	AW.
Schenuit Industries, Inc	WP.
The Seiberling Tire & Rubber Co.	AV.
Semperit Gummiwerke A.G	BT, BU.
Sumitomo Rubber Industries	ET. EU.
The Toyo Rubber Industry Co., Ltd.	CW, CX.
Trelleborg Rubber Co	LW.
Uniroyal Inc	AJ, AK, AL, AM, AN, AP, AU, LH, LJ, LK, LL, LM, LN, LP, LT, LU.
Veith-Pirelli A.G	XT.
Vredestein	DV, DW.
Vredestein-Radium	DX.
The Yokohama Rubber Co., Ltd.	FA, FB, FC, FD, FE.

TABLE I—SIZE CODE FOR MOTOR VEHICLE TIRES

Tire size code:	*Tire size designation[1]*	*Tire size code:*	*Tire size designation*	*Tire size code:*	*Tire size designation*
AA	4.00–4	CP	6.2–12	E7	160 R 13
AB	3.50–4	CT	6.20–12	E8	165–13
AC	3.00–5	CU	6.90–12	E9	165 R 13
AD	4.00–5	CV	23.5 x 8.50–12 ST[2]	FA	165–13/6.45–13
AE	3.50–5	CW	125–12	FB	165/70 R 13
AF	6.90–6	CX	125 R 12	FC	170 R 13
AH	3.00–8	CY	125–12/5.35–12	FD	175–13
AJ	3.50–6	C1	135–12	FE	175 R 13
AK	4.10–6	C2	135 R 12	FF	175–13/6.95–13
AL	4.50–6	C3	135–12/5.65–12	FH	175/70 R 13
AM	5.30–6	C4	145–12	FJ	185–13
AN	6.00–6	C5	145 R 12	FK	185 R 13
AP	3.25–8	C6	145–12/5.95–12	FL	185–13/7.35–13
AT	3.50–8	C7	155–12	FM	185/70 R 13
AU	3.00–7	C8	155 R 12	FN	195–13
AV	4.00–7	C9	155–12/6.15–12	FP	195 R 13
AW	4.80–7	DA	4.80–10	FT	195/70 R 13
AX	5.30–7	DB	3.25–12	FU	D70–13
AY	5.00–8	DC	3.50–12	FV	B78–13
A1	H60–14	DD	4.50–12 LT	FW	BR78–13
A2	4.00–8	DE	5.00–12 LT	FX	C78–13
A3	4.80–8	DF	7.00–12	FY	7.50–12
A4	5.70–8	DH	5.00–13	F1	140 R 12
A5	16.5 x 6.5–8	DJ	5.00–13 LT	F2	6.5–13
A6	18.5 x 8.5–8	DK	5.00 R 13	F3	185/60 R 13
A7	CR70–14	DL	5.20–13	F4	A70–13
A8	2.75–9	DM	5.20 R 13	F5	A78–13
A9	4.80–9	DN	5.50–13	F6	CR78–13
BA	6.00–9	DP	5.50–13 LT	F7	2.25–14
BB	6.90–9	DT	5.50 R 13	F8	2.75–14
BC	3.50–9	DU	5.60–13	F9	3.00–14
BD	4.00–10	DV	5.60–13 LT	HA	6.70–14 LT
BE	3.00–10	DW	5.60 R 13	HB	165–14 LT
BF	3.50–10	DX	5.90–13	HC	2.50–14
BH	5.20–10	DY	5.90–13 LT	HD	5.00–14 LT
BJ	5.20 R 10	D1	5.90 R 13	HE	5.20–14
BK	5.9–10	D2	6.00–13	HF	5.20 R 14
BL	5.90–10	D3	6.00–13 LT	HH	5.50–14 LT
BM	6.50–10	D4	6.00 R 13	HJ	5.60–14
BN	7.00–10	D5	6.2–13	HK	5.90–14
BP	7.50–10	D6	6.20–13	HL	5.90–14 LT
BT	9.00–10	D7	6.40–13	HM	5.90 R 14
BU	20.5 x 8.0–10	D8	6.40–13 LT	HN	6.00–14
BV	145–10	D9	6.40 R 13	HP	6.00–14 LT
BW	145 R 10	EA	6.50–13	HT	6.40–14
BX	145–10/5.95–10	EB	6.50–13 LT	HU	6.40–14 LT
BY	4.50–10 LT[2]	EC	6.50–13 ST	HV	6.45–14
B1	5.00–10 LT	ED	6.50 R 13	HW	6.50–14
B2	3.00–12	EE	6.70–13	HX	6.50–14 LT
B3	4.00–12	EF	6.70–13 LT	HY	6.70–14
B4	4.50–12	EH	6.70 R 13	H1	6.95–14
B5	4.80–12	EJ	6.9–13	H2	7.00–14
B6	5.00–12	EK	6.90–13	H3	7.00–14 LT
B7	5.00 R 12	EL	7.00–13	H4	7.00 R 14
B8	5.20–12	EM	7.00–13 LT	H5	7.35–14
B9	5.20–12 LT	EN	7.00 R 13	H6	7.50–14
CA	5.20 R 12	EP	7.25–13	H7	7.50–14 LT
CB	5.30–12	ET	7.25 R 13	H8	7.50 R 14
CC	5.50–12	EU	7.50–13	H9	7.75–14
CD	5.50–12 LT	EV	135–13	JA	7.75–14 ST
CE	5.50 R 12	EW	135 R 13	JB	8.00–14
CF	5.60–12	EX	135–13/5.65–13	JC	8.25–14
CH	5.60–12 LT	EY	145–13	JD	8.50–14
CJ	5.60 R 12	E1	145 R 13	JE	8.55–14
CK	5.9–12	E2	145–13/5.95–13	JF	8.85–14
CL	5.90–12	E3	150 R 13	JH	9.00–14
CM	6.00–12	E4	155–13	JJ	9.50–14
CN	6.00–12 LT	E5	155 R 13	JK	135–14
		E6	155–13/6.15–13	JL	135 R 14

[1][2] See footnotes at end of Tables.

size code : Tire size designation	Tire size code : Tire size designation	Tire size code : Tire size designation
.... 10.00-20 ML	6T........ 27 x 8.50-15	8K........ 2-19R
.... 10.00-22 ML	6U........ 27 x 9.50-15	8L........ 2-19¾
.... 10.00-24 ML	6V........ 29 x 12.00-15	8M........ 2-22
.... 11.00-20 ML	6W........ 31 x 13.50-15	8N........ 2-22½
.... 11.00-22 ML	6X........ 31 x 15.50-15	8P........ 2¼-15
.... 11.00-24 ML	6Y........ 38 x 20.00-16.1	8T........ 2¼-16
.... 11.00-25 ML	61........ 44 x 41.00-16.1	8U........ 2¼-17
.... 12.00-20 ML	62........ 44 x 41.00-20	8V........ 2¼-18
.... 12.00-21 ML	63........ 48 x 20.00-20	8W........ 2¼-19
.... 12.00-24 ML	64........ 48 x 25.00-20	8X........ 2¼-19
.... 12.00-25 ML	65........ 48 x 31.00-20	8Y........ 2¼-20
.... 13.00-20 ML	66........ 3.40-5	81........ 2½-8
.... 13.00-24 ML	67........ 4.10-4	82........ 2½-9
.... 13.00-25 ML	68........ 4.10-5	83........ 2½-16
.... 14.00-20 ML	69........ 175-14 LT	84........ 2½-17
.... 14.00-21 ML	7A........ 11-14	85........ 2½-18
.... 14.00-24 ML	7B........ E78-14 LT	86........ 2½-19
.... 14.00-25 ML	7C........ G78-15 LT	87........ 2½-19R
.... 10.3-20 ML	7D........ H78-15 LT	88........ 2¾-19
.... 11.1-20 ML	7E........ 180 R15	89........ 2¾-16
.... 12.5-20 ML	7F........ 185-16 LT	9A........ 2¾-17
.... 9-22.5 ML	7H........ 205-16 LT	9B........ 2¾-17R
.... 9.4-22.5 ML	7J........ 215-16 LT	9C........ 3-10
.... 10-22.5 ML	7K........ F78-16 LT	9D........ 3-12
.... 10.3-22.5 ML	7L........ H78-16 LT	9E........ Not Assigned
.... 11-22.5 ML	7M........ L78-16 LT	9F........ Not Assigned
.... 11-24.5 ML	7N........ 135 R10	9H........ 15.50-20
.... 14-17.5 ML	7P........ 6.95-14 LT	9J........ 18.50-20
.... 15-19.5 ML	7T........ 7-14.5 MH [2]	9K........ 19.50-20
.... 15-22.5 ML	7U........ 8-14.5 MH	9L........ 2¼-14
.... 16.5-19.5 ML	7V........ 9-14.5 MH	9M........ 2½-20
.... 16.5-22.5 ML	7W........ 4.25/85-18	9N........ 2¾-16R
.... 18-19.5 ML	7X........ A78-14	9P........ 2¾-18
.... 18-22.5 ML	7Y........ 7.50-18MPT	9T........ 10-20
.... 19.5-19.5 ML	71........ 10.5-18 MPT	9U........ 11-24
.... 23-23.5 ML	72........ 12.5-18 MPT	9V........ 11.25-24
.... 18-21 ML	73........ 12.5-20 MPT	9W........ 15 x 4½ x 8
.... 19.5-21 ML	74........ 14.5-20 MPT	9X........ 14.75/80-20
.... 23-21 ML	75........ 10.5-20 MPT	9Y........ Not Assigned
.... 6.00-13 ST	76........ 10.5-20	91........ Not Assigned
.... 7.35-14 ST	77........ Not Assigned	92........ Not Assigned
.... 8.25-14 ST	78........ 150 R12	93........ Not Assigned
.... 7.35-15 ST	79........ 150 R14	94........ Not Assigned
.... 8.25-15 ST	8A........ 1¾-19	95........ Not Assigned
.... 12.00-22 ML	8B........ 1¾-19¾	96........ Not Assigned
.... 4.30-18	8C........ 2-12	97........ Not Assigned
.... 3.60-19	8D........ 2-16	98........ Not Assigned
.... 3.00-20	8E........ 2-17	99........ Not Assigned
.... 4.25-18	8F........ 2-17R	
.... MP90-18	8H........ 2-18	
.... 3.75-19	8J........ 2-19	
.... MM90-19		
.... 3.25-7		
.... 2.75-16		
.... 4.00-16		
.... Not Assigned		
.... 25 x 7.50-15		

e letters "H," "S," and "V" may be included in the tire size designation adjacent to
n place of a dash without affecting the size code for the designation.

used in this table the letters at the end of the tire size indicate the following: LT—
ht Truck, ML—Mining & Logging, MH—Mobile Home, ST—Special Trailer, TR—
ck (comparable size in passenger car size).

Tire size code:	Tire size designation	Tire size code:	Tire size designation	Tire size code:	Tire size designation
U6	H70–15	XN	12–16.5	18	19.5–19.5
U7	HR70–15	XP	185 R16	19	6.00–20
U8	J70–15	XT	4.50–17	2A	6.50–20
U9	JR70–15	XU	2.00–17	2B	7.00–20
VA	K70–15	XV	2.25–17	2C	7.50–20
VB	KR70–15	XW	2.50–17	2D	8.25–20
VC	L70–15	XX	2.75–17	2E	8.5–20
VD	LR70–15	XY	3.00–17	2F	9.00–20
VE	17–400TR	X1	3.25–17	2H	9.4–20
VF	185–300TR	X2	3.50–17	2J	10.00–20
VH	185–300LT	X3	6.50–17	2K	10.3–20
VJ	AR78–15	X4	6.50–17 LT	2L	11.00–20
VK	BR78–15	X5	7.00–17	2M	11.1–20
VL	C78–15	X6	7.50–17	2N	11.50–20
VM	D78–15	X7	8.25–17	2P	11.9–20
VN	E78–15	X8	7.50–17 LT	2T	12.00–20
VP	ER78–15	X9	225/70 R14	2U	12.5–20
VT	F78–15	YA	G50C–17	2V	13.00–20
VU	FR78–15	YB	H50C–17	2W	14.00–20
VV	G78–15	YC	195/70 R15	2X	6.50–20 LT
VW	GR78–15	YD	4.20–18	2Y	7.00–20 LT
VX	H78–15	YE	8–17.5 LT	21	13/80–20
VY	HR78–15	YF	11–17.5	22	14/80–20
V1	J78–15	YH	7–17.5	23	2.75–21
V2	JR78–15	YJ	8–17.5	24	3.00–21
V3	L78–15	YK	8.5–17.5	25	2.50–21
V4	LR78–15	YL	9.5–17.5	26	2.75–20
V5	N78–15	YM	10–17.5	27	10.00–22
V6	17–15(17–380 LT)	YN	14–17.5	28	11.00–22
V7	17–400 LT	YP	9–17.5	29	11.1–22
V8	11–15	YT	205/70 R15	3A	11.9–22
V9	11–16	YU	2.25–18	3B	12.00–22
WA	L84–15	YV	2.50–18	3C	14.00–22
WB	11.00–15	YW	2.75–18	3D	11.50–22
WC	2.25–16	YX	3.00–18	3E	4.10–18
WD	2.50–16	YY	3.25–18	3F	4.10–19
WE	3.00–16	Y1	3.50–18	3H	7–22.5
WF	3.25–16	Y2	4.00–18	3J	8–22.5
WH	3.50–16	Y3	4.50–18	3K	8.5–22.5
WJ	5.00–16	Y4	6.00–18	3L	9–22.5
WK	5.10–16	Y5	7.00–18	3M	9.4–22.5
WL	5.50–16 LT	Y6	7.50–18	3N	10–22.5
WM	6.00–16	Y7	8.25–18	3P	10.3–22.5
WN	6.00–16 LT	Y8	9.00–18	3T	11–22.5
WP	6.50–16	Y9	10.00–18	3U	11.1–22.5
WT	6.50–16 LT	1A	11.00–18	3V	11.5–22.5
WU	6.70–16	1B	6.00–18 LT	3W	11.9–22.5
WV	7.00–16	1C	6.00–20 LT	3X	12–22.5
WW	7.00–16 LT	1D	L50C–18	3Y	12.5–22.5
WX	7.50–16	1E	7.00–18 LT	31	15–22.5
WY	7.50–16 LT	1F	12–19.5	32	16.5–22.5
W1	8.25–16	1H	2.00–19	33	18–22.5
W2	9.00–16	1J	2.25–19	34	215/70 R15
W3	10–16	1K	2.50–19	35	225/70 R15
W4	8.25–16 LT	1L	2.75–19	36	L70–18
W5	9.00–16 LT	1M	3.00–19	37	9.00–24
W6	11.00–16	1N	3.25–19	38	10.00–24
W7	19–400 C	1P	3.50–19	39	11.00–24
W8	165–400	1T	4.00–19	4A	12.00–24
W9	235–16	1U	11.00–19	4B	14.00–24
XA	185–16	1V	9.5–19.5	4C	3.50–7
XB	19–400 LT	1W	10–19.5	4D	Not Assigned
XC	G45C–16	1X	11–19.5	4E	12.5–24.5
XD	E50C–16	1Y	7–19.5	4F	11–24.5
XE	F50C–16	11	7.5–19.5	4H	12–24.5
XF	7.00–16 TR	12	8–19.5	4J	13.5–24.5
XH	7.50–16 TR	13	9–19.5	4K	7.00–20 ML [2]
XJ	8.00–16.5	14	14–19.5	4L	7.50–20 ML
XK	8.75–16.5	15	15–19.5	4M	8.25–20 ML
XL	9.50–16.5	16	16.5–19.5	4N	9.00–20 ML
XM	10–16.5	17	18–19.5		

[1][2] See footnotes at end of Tables.

Tire size code	Tire size designation
	135-14/5.65-14
	145-14
	145 R 14
	145-14/5.95-14
	155-14
	155 R 14
	155-14/6.15-14
	155/70 R 14
	165-14
	165 R 14
	175-14
	175 R 14
	185-14
	185 R 14
	185/70 R 14
	195-14
	195 R 14
	195/70 R 14
	205-14
	205 R 14
	215-14
	215 R 14
	225-14
	225 R 14
	620 R 14
	690 R 14
	A R78-13
	195-14 LT
	185-14 LT
	A80-22.5
	B80-22.5
	C80-22.5
	D80-22.5
	E80-22.5
	F60-14
	G60-14
	J60-14
	L60-14
	F80-22.5
	G80-22.5
	H80-22.5
	J80-22.5
	A80-24.5
	B80-24.5
	B R 78-14
	D70-14
	D R70-14
	E70-14
	E R70-14
	F70-14
	F R70-14
	G70-14
	G R70-14
	H70-14
	H R70-14
	J70-14
	J R70-14
	L70-14
	L R70-14
	C80-24.5
	D80-24.5
	E80-24.5
	F80-24.5
	G77-14
	B78-14
	C78-14
	C R78-14
	D78-14
	D R78-14
	E78-14
	E R78-14

Tire size code	Tire size designation
L7	F78-14
L8	F R78-14
L9	G78-14
M A	G R78-14
M B	H78-14
M C	H R78-14
M D	J78-14
M E	J R78-14
M F	205-14 LT
M H	G80-24.5
M J	H80-24.5
M K	7-14.5
M L	8-14.5
M M	9-14.5
M N	6.60 R 15
M P	2.00-15
M T	2.25-15
M U	2.50-15
M V	3.00-15
M W	3.25-15
M X	5.0-15
M Y	5.20-15
M1	5.0-15
M2	5.50-15L
M3	5.50-15 LT
M4	5.60-15
M5	5.60 R 15
M6	5.90-15
M7	5.90-15 LT
M8	6.00-15
M9	6.00-15 L
N A	6.00-15 LT
N B	6.2-15
N C	6.40-15
N D	6.40-15 LT
N E	6.40 R 15
N F	6.50-15
N H	6.50-15L
N J	6.50-15 LT
N K	6.70-15
N L	6.70-15 LT
N M	6.70 R 15
N N	6.85-15
N P	6.9-15
N T	7.00-15
N U	7.00-15 L
N V	7.00-15 LT
N W	7.10-15
N X	7.10-15 LT
N Y	7.35-15
N1	7.50-15
N2	7.60-15
N3	7.60 R 15
N4	7.75-15
N5	7.75-15 ST
N6	8.00-15
N7	8.15-15
N8	8.20-15
N9	8.25-15
P A	8.25-15 LT
P B	8.45-15
P C	8.55-15
P D	8.85-15
P E	8.90-15
P F	9.00-15
P H	9.00-15 LT
P J	9.15-15
P K	10-15
P L	10.00-15
P M	7.50-15 LT
P N	7.00-15 TR [a]

Tire size code	Tire size designation
PP	8.25-15 TR
PT	9.00-15 TR
PU	7.50-15 TR
PV	125-15
PW	125 R 15
PX	125-15/5.35-15
PY	135-15
P1	135 R 15
P2	135-15/5.65-15
P3	145-15
P4	145 R 15
P5	145-15/5.95-15
P6	155-15
P7	155 R 15
P8	155-15/6.35-15
P9	165-15
TA	165-15 LT
TB	165 R 15
TC	175-15
TD	175 R 15
TE	175-15/7.15-15
TF	175/70 R 15
TH	180-15
TJ	185-15
TK	185 R 15
TL	185/70 R 15
TM	195-15
TN	195 R 15
TP	205-15
TT	205 R 15
TU	215-15
TV	215 R 15
TW	225-15
TX	225 R 15
TY	235-15
T1	235 R 15
T2	J80-24.5
T3	ER60-15
T4	D78-13
T5	A78-15
T6	D R70-13
T7	H R60-15
T8	E60-14
T9	205/70 R14
UA	215/70 R14
UB	H60-15
UC	E60-15
UD	F60-15
UE	F R60-15
UF	G60-15
UH	G R60-15
UJ	J60-15
UK	L60-15
UL	4.60-15
UM	2.75-15
UN	2.50-9
UP	2.50-10
UT	5.00-9
UU	6.7-10
UV	C70-15
UW	D70-15
UX	D R70-15
UY	E70-15
U1	ER70-15
U2	F70-15
U3	F R70-15
U4	G70-15
U5	GR70-15

[a] See footnotes at end of Tables.

National Highway Safety Advisory Committee

Dr. James E. Aaron
Coordinator, Safety Center
Southern Illinois University
Carbondale, IL 62901

Mr. John Almeida, Jr.
Chairman of the Board and
  President
Almeida Bus Lines, Inc.
1091 Kempton Street
New Bedford, MA 02740

Mr. Forest C. Braden
President, Braden Machinery
Box 1631
Yuma, AZ 85364

Mr. Vincent Paul Brevetti
Attorney at Law
118-21 Queens Boulevard
Forest Hills, NY 11375

Mr. J.B. Creal
Executive Vice President
American Automobile Assoc.
1712 G Street, N.W.
Washington, DC 20006

Mr. Mark Donohue
Penske Racing Enter., Inc.
3628 Winding Way Road
Newtown Square, PA 19073

Mrs. Mary Emrick
Public Relations Dept.
Standard Oil of California
Room 1125
225 Bush Street
San Francisco, CA 94104

Mr. John Everroad, Pres.
Cummins Medwest Co., Inc.
5515 Center Street
Omaha, NE 68106

Hon. Sherman G. Finesilver
Judge, U.S. District Court
Denver, CO 80202

Mrs. Mildred Gnau, Pres.
National Assoc. of Women
  Highway Safety Leaders
3112 Monticello Boulevard
Cleveland Heights, OH 44118

Dr. Walter W. Gray
Director, Driver and Traf-
  fic Safety Instructional
  Demonstration Center
Indiana State University
Terre Haute, IN 46609

Mr. Joel K. Gustafson
Florida House of Repre-
  sentatives
2455 E. Sunrise Boulevard
Fort Lauderdale, FL 33304

Mr. Daumants Hazners
Chairman, Division of En-
  gineering & Architecture
Mercer County Community
  College
Trenton, NJ 08608

Mr. Clarence Hoffman
4424 Arthur Place, N.E.
Columbia Heights, MN 55421

Mr. Cooper T. Holt
Executive Director
Veterans of Foreign Wars of
  the U.S.
200 Maryland Avenue, N.E.
Washington, DC 20002

Mr. Elmer Huntley
Washington State Senate
Thornton, WA 99176

Hon. Henry F. McQuade
Chief Justice, State
  Supreme Court
Supreme Court Building
Boise, ID 83702

Mr. Murray W. Miller
General Secy. & Treasurer
International Brotherhood
  of Teamsters
25 Louisiana Avenue, N.W.
Washington, DC 20001

Mr. Thomas C. Morrill
Vice President, State Farm
  Mutual Automobile In-
  surance Company
112 E. Washington St.
Bloomington, IL 61701

Hon. Ruth Peck
Arizona House of Repre-
  sentatives
510 E. Medlock Drive
Phoenix, AZ 85012

Mr. Manuel Quevedo, Jr.
Community Relations Con-
  sultant
1454 Wall Avenue
San Bernardino, CA 92404

Mr. Wayne E. Rapp
Vice President, Walker
  Manufacturing Company
1201 Michigan Boulevard
Racine, WI 51402

Mr. Gordon M. Scherer
Ohio State Representative
1717 Carew Tower
Cincinnati, OH 45202

Mr. Joe R. Seacrest
Executive Editor
The Lincoln Journal
P.O. Box 81689
Lincoln, NE 68505

Mr. Thomas J. Skutt
Special Tax Counsel & Secy.
33d & Dodge Streets
Omaha, NE 68131

Mr. Cordell Smith
Coordinator of Highway
  Safety
729 State Services Bldg.
Denver, CO 80203

Mr. J.W. "Bill" Stevens
Board of County Commission-
  ers of Broward County
201 S.E. Sixth Street
Room 248
Fort Lauderdale, FL 33301

Mr. Harold W. Sullivan
Vice Chairman, Air
  Resources Board
State of California
17235 Otsego Street
Encino, CA 91316

Mr. Paul J. Sullivan
Asst. District Attorney
130 Spruce Street, Apt.19A
Philadelphia, PA 19106

Mr. John K. Tabor
Law Offices - Kirkpatrick,
  Lockhart, Johnson &
  Hutchinson
1500 Oliver Building
Pittsburgh, PA 15522

Mr. Thomas Miller Thompson
Chairman of the Board
General American Trans-
  portation Corporation
120 Riverside Plaza
Chicago, IL 60680

Mrs. Leota M. Westfall
Highway Traffic Safety
  Center
Room 68 Kellogg Center for
  Continuing Education
Michigan State University
East Lansing, MI 48823

Mr. Joseph S. Wilcox, Jr.
President, Wilcox Land and
  Development Corporation
One E. Putnam Avenue
Greenwich, CT 06830

Dr. Ruth E. Winkler
Optometrist
1872 E. 15th Street
Tulsa, OK 74104

Mr. Louis Petitto
Byron Construction Co.,Inc.
P.O. Box 1589
Clarksburg, WV 26301

Dr. Robert L. Hess
Director, Highway Safety
  Research Institute
University of Michigan
Ann Arbor, MI 48105

Publications of the NHTSA

Alcohol Countermeasures, Report on 1971 Forum. June 30,
    1971. Available from Superintendent of Documents -
    60¢.

Annual Report. Highway Safety Act of 1966 and National
    Traffic and Motor Vehicle Safety Act of 1966. The
    Fifth Annual Report of the Department of Transporta-
    tion on activities under the Highway Safety Act of
    1966 and the National Traffic and Motor Vehicle
    Safety Act of 1966 for the period January 1 through
    December 31, 1970. Available from Superintendent of
    Docments.

Annual Report to the Secretary on Accident Investigation
    and Reporting Activities - 1971, February 1972.
    Available from the National Technical Information
    Service - $3.00.

Audiovisual Catalog of the National Highway Traffic
    Safety Administration. December 1970 - October 1971.
    Available from the Technical Reference Division,
    NHTSA.

Compliance Test Reports KWIC Index. May 1971. Available
    from the National Technical Information Service -
    $6.00.

Drug Use and Highway Safety: A Review of the Literature.
    (by James L. Nichols) July 1971. Available from
    Superintendent of Documents - $1.25.

An Evaluation of a Safety Belt Interlock System. February
    1971. Available from National Technical Information
    Service - $3.00.

Motor Vehicle Safety Defect Recall Campaigns. Annual and
    quarterly reports available from January 1968 to the
    present from Superintendent of Documents.

Multidisciplinary Accident Investigation Summaries. From
    Vol. 1, No. 1 (May 1970), some available from
    National Technical Information Service, remainder
    can be viewed at Technical Reference Division,
    NHTSA, along with complete accident reports.

Tri-Level Accident Investigation Summaries, Level 3A
    Injury Causation. From Vol. 1, No. 1 (November
    1971), available from National Technical Information
    Service - $3.00 each.

Performance Data for New 1973 Passenger Cars and Motor-
    cycles. Compiled from data furnished by vehicle
    manufacturers (also available for 1970-72 vehicles).
    For sale by Superintendent of Documents.

Executive Summaries - National Highway Traffic Safety
    Administration Contractors Reports. From January
    1968, available from Superintendent of Documents.

Federal Motor Vehicle Safety Standards. September 25,
    1969, looseleaf with supplements. For sale as a
    subscription from Superintendent of Documents.

Highway Safety Literature: An Announcement of Recent
    Acquisitions. Available from General Services
    Division, NHTSA, on request.

International Conferences on Passive Restraints. Avail-
    able from National Technical Information Service.

Report on the International Technical Conferences on Ex-
    perimental Safety Vehicles. Available from the
    Superintendent of Documents.

Manual on Uniform Traffic Control Devices for Streets and
    Highways, 1971. Available from Superintendent of
    Documents - $3.50.

Highway Safety Program Manuals. January 1969 (17 vol-
    umes). For sale from the General Services Division,
    NHTSA.

Program Plan for the Motor Vehicle Safety Standards.
    October 1971. Available from the National Tech-
    nical Information Service - $4.75.

R&D, Highway and Safety Transportation System Studies
    1971. In progress during fiscal year 1971. Avail-
    able from Superintendent of Documents - $2.75.

Reports and other publications on the Alcohol Safety
    Programs of the NHTSA are available from the Office
    of Alcohol Countermeasures, NHTSA.

School Bus Safety Problems. November 1971. Available
    from Superintendent of Documents - 70¢.

Technical Reports of the National Highway Traffic Safety
    Administration; a Bibliography, 1967-1971. Avail-
    able from National Technical Information Service.

Department of Transportation:
Public Availability of Information

DEPARTMENT OF TRANSPORTATION:
Public Availability of Information
[49 C.F.R. Part 7]

The following are excerpts from the rules and regulations of the Department of Transportation which govern the application of the Freedom of Information Act. For the complete regulations, consult the Code of Federal Regulations

§7.3 Policy.

In implementing section 552 of Title 5, United States Code, it is the policy of the Department of Transportation to make information within the Department available to the public to the greatest extent possible in keeping with the spirit of that section. Therefore, all records of the Department, except those that the Department specifically determines must not be disclosed in the national interest, for the protection of private rights, or for the efficient conduct of public business, are declared to be available for public inspection and copying as provided in this part. Each officer and employee of the Department is directed to cooperate to this end and to make records available to the public promptly and to the fullest extent consistent with this policy. A record may not be withheld from the public solely because its release might suggest administrative error or embarrass an officer or employee of the Department.

Subpart C--Publication in
Federal Register

§7.21 Applicability.

This subpart implements section 552(a)(1) of Title 5, United States Code, and prescribes rules governing the publication in the FEDERAL REGISTER of the following: following:

(a) Descriptions of the organization of the Department, including its operating administrations and the established places at which, the officers from whom, and the methods by which, the public (1) may secure information; and (2) make submittals or requests or obtain decisions.

(b) Statements of the general course and methods by which the Department's functions are channeled and determined, including the nature and requirements of all formal and informal procedures available.

(c) Rules of procedure, descriptions of forms available or the places at which forms may be obtained, and instructions as to the scope and contents of all papers, reports or examinations.

(d) Substantive rules of general applicability adopted as authorized by law, and statements of general policy or interpretations of general applicability adopted by the Department.

(e) Each amendment, revision, or repeal of any material listed in paragraphs (a) through (d) of this section.

Subpart D--Availability of Opinions,
Orders, Staff Manuals, Statements
of Policy, and Interpretations: Indexes

§7.31 Applicability.

(a) This subpart implements section 552(a)(2) of Title 5, United States Code. It prescribes the rules governing the availability, for public inspection and copying, of the following:

(1) Any final opinion (including a concurring or dissenting opinion) or order made in the adjudication of a case.
(2) Any policy or interpretation that has been adopted under the authority of the Department, including any policy or interpretation concerning a particular factual situation, if that policy or interpretation can reasonably be expected to have precedential value in any case involving a member of the public in a similar situation.
(3) Any administrative staff manual or instruction to staff that affects any member of the public, including the prescribing of any standard, procedure, or policy that, when implemented, requires or limits any action of any member of the public or prescribes the manner of performance of any activity by any member of the public. However this does not include staff manuals or instructions to staff concerning internal operating rules, practices, guidelines and procedures for Departmental inspectors, investigators, examiners, auditors and negotiators, the release of which would substantially impair the effective performance of their duties.

§7.33 Access to materials and index.

(a) Except as provided in paragraph (b) of this section, material listed in §7.31(a) is available for inspection

and copying by any member of the public at document inspection facilities of the Department. The index of
material available at each facility is also located at the
facility. Information as to the kinds of materials available at each facility may be obtained from that facility
or the headquarters of the operating administration of
which it is a part.

(b) The material listed in §7.31(a) that is published
and offered for sale is indexed but is not required to be
kept available for public inspection. However, whenever
practicable, it will be made available for public inspection at any document inspection facility maintained by the
Office of the Secretary or an operating administration,
whichever is concerned.

Subpart G--Procedures for Reconsidering
Decisions Not To Disclose Records

§7.71 General.

(a) Each officer or employee of the Department who,
upon a request by a member of the public for a record
under this part, makes a determination that the record is
not to be disclosed, will give a written statement of his
reasons for that determination to the person making the
request.

(b) Any person to whom a record is not made available
within a reasonable time after his request, and any person
who has been given a determination pursuant to paragraph
(a) of this section, that a record he has requested will
not be disclosed, may apply to the head of the operating
administration concerned, or in the case of the Office of
the Secretary, to the General Counsel of the Department,
for reconsideration of the request. No determination that
a record will not be disclosed is administratively final
for the purposes of judicial review unless it was made by
the head of the operating administration concerned (or his
designee), or the General Counsel, as the case may be.

(c) Each application for reconsideration must be in
writing and must include all information and arguments
relied upon by the person making the request.

(d) Whenever the head of the operating administration
concerned, or the General Counsel, as the case may be, determines it to be necessary, he may require the person
making the request to furnish additional information, or
proof of factual allegations, and may order other proceedings appropriate in the circumstances. The decision
of the head of the operating administration concerned, or
the General Counsel, as the case may be, as to the availability of the record is administratively final.

(e) The decision by the head of the operating administration concerned, or the General Counsel, as the case may

be, not to disclose a record under this part is considered
to be a withholding by the Secretary for the purposes of
section 552(a)(3) of Title 5, United States Code.

Subpart H--Fees

§7.81   General.

(a) This subpart prescribes fees for services performed
for the public under Subparts D and E of this part by the
Department of Transportation.

(b) This subpart does not apply to any special study,
special statistical compilation, table or other record
requested under section 9(n) of the Department of Transportation Act.   The fee for the performance of such a service is the actual cost of the work involved in compiling
the record.   All moneys received by the Department in payment of the cost of the work are deposited in a separate
account administered under the direction of the Secretary,
and may be used for the ordinary expenses incidental to
the work.

§7.83   Payment of fees.

The fees prescribed in this subpart may be paid by
check, draft, or postal money order, payable to the
Treasurer of the United States.   Except as provided in
§7.43(f), the fees are payable in advance.

§7.85   Fee schedule.

(a) Except as provided in paragraph (j) of this sec-
    tion, search for a record under Subpart E of
    this part, when required, including making it
    available for inspection-$3.00

(b) Copies of documents by photocopy or similar method:
    Each page not larger than 11x17 inches-$.25

(c) Copies of documents by typewriter, each page-$2.50

(d) Certified copies of documents:
    (1) With Department of Transportation seal-$2.00
    (2) True copy, without seal-$1.00

(e) Photographs: black and white glossy print, 8x10
    inches or smaller, each-$1.00
(f) Duplicate data tapes - each reel of tape or frac-
    tion thereof-$40.00
    The applicant must furnish the necessary number
    of blank magnetic tapes. The tapes must be
    compatible for use in the supplier's computer
    system, 1/2 inch wide and 2,400 feet long, and
    must be capable of recording data at a density
    of 556 or 800 characters per inch. Unless
    otherwise designated, the tapes will be recorded

at 556 CPI density. The Department of Transportation is not responsible for damaged tape.
However, if the applicant furnishes a replacement for a damaged tape, the duplication process is completed at no additional charge.

(g) Microreproduction fees are as follows:
(1) Microfilm copies, each 100-foot roll or
less-$8.00
(2) Microfiche copies, each standard size sheet
4x6 inches, 60 copies-$.50

(h) Data processed records, each 1,000 lines or fraction thereof-$5.00

(i) Preprinted materials, shelf stock, one color,
standard sizes:
(1) Each page (excluding blanks)-$.05
(2) Minimum charge-$1.00

(j) Other records: The fee for a copy of a record not
described in paragraphs (b) through (i) of this
section will be supplied on request. The amount
of that fee will be the cost of producing and
handling. The fee for a search and copy of any
record where the cost will obviously be more
than $3.00 will be determined in accordance
with the policy on user charges set forth in
section 483(a) of title 31, United States Code.
In addition, fees covering items that are
peculiar to the records of any operating administration may be prescribed in the appendix to
this part that applies to that administration.

§7.87 Services performed without charge or at a reduced
charge.

(a) No fee is charged for time spent in preparing
correspondence related to a request and in
making determinations pursuant to §7.71

(b) No fee is charged for documents furnished in response to:
(1) A request from an employee or former employee of the Department for copies of personnel
records of the employee;
(2) A request from a member of Congress for his
official use;
(3) A request from a State, territory, U.S.
possession, county or municipal government, or
an agency thereof;
(4) A request from a court that will serve as a
substitute for the personal court appearance of
an officer or employee of the Department;
(5) A request from a foreign government or an
agency thereof, or an international organization.

(c) Documents may be furnished without charge or at a
    reduced charge, if the Director of Public
    Affairs, or the head of the operating adminis-
    tration concerned, as the case may be, deter-
    mines that waiver or reduction of the fee is in
    the public interest, because furnishing the
    information can be considered as primarily bene-
    fiting the general public. Examples of requests
    that may fall within this paragraph are reason-
    able requests from groups engaged in a nonprofit
    activity designed for the public safety, health,
    or welfare; schools; and students engaged in
    study in the field of transportation.

§7.89 Transcripts.

Transcripts of hearings and oral argument are available for inspection. Where transcripts are prepared by a
nongovernment contractor, and the contract permits the
Department to handle the reproduction of further copies,
the provisions of Subpart H apply. Where the contract for
transcription services reserves the sales privilege to the
reporting service, any duplicate copies should be purchased directly from the reporting service.

§7.91 Alternate sources of information.

In the interest of making documents of general interest publicly available at as reasonable a cost as possible,
alternate sources are arranged whenever practicable. In
appropriate instances, material that is published and
offered for sale may be obtained from the Superintendent
of Documents, U.S. Government Printing Office, Washington,
D.C. 20402; the Commerce Department's National Technical
Information Service (NTIS), Springfield, Va. 22151; the
National Audio-visual Center, National Archives and
Records Service, General Services Administration, Washington, D.C. 20405; or the Consumer Product Information Coordinating Center, General Services Administration, Washington, D.C. 20407.

Informal Petition on Bumpers

February 3, 1971

The Honorable John Volpe
Secretary of Transportation
Department of Transportation
Washington, D.C.

Dear Sir:

As a concerned citizen I have attached petitions signed
by 643 people at my place of employment, asking you to use
your powers to encourage the auto makers to (1) standardize
bumper heights and (2) construct bumpers that will withstand low speed impacts without sustaining damage.

The persons who have signed these petitions are a
cross-section of people commonly referred to as the "silent
majority." At my company we employ 900 persons, from
janitors to skilled assemblers, to a variety of professional management.

While we complain about the high cost of auto insurance
we understand that insurance companies are in business
to show a profit. But, to reduce auto collision insurance
rates 20% by getting rid of cosmetic bumpers on today's
automobiles and replacing them with bumpers that will
withstand "bumps" we are certainly in favor of that.

Therefore, we ask you to help establish regulations
to encourage auto makers to make the necessary changes
to produce a safer, more economical automobile. I stand
willing to aid further in the accomplishment of this goal
if need be.

Very truly yours,

/s/
Thomas Choinski
Director of Safety
Thermo King Corporation

cc: Mr. Robert Anderson, Minnesota Safety Council
     Mr. Bud Malone, Commissioner, Minnesota Dept. of
          Labor and Industry
     Mr. Robert P. Miskelly, Public Affairs, Allstate
          Insurance Company

U.S. DEPARTMENT OF TRANSPORTATION
NATIONAL HIGHWAY TRAFFIC SAFETY ADMINISTRATION
Washington, D.C. 20591

In Reply Refer to: 40-30

March 12, 1971

Mr. Thomas Choinski
Director of Safety
Thermo King Corporation
314 West 90th Street
Minneapolis, Minnesota 55420

Dear Mr. Choinski:

The Secretary has requested that we reply to your letter
of February 3, 1971 and the accompanying petition from
the employees of the Thermo King Corporation. The
Department of Transportation has for some time been
interested in the development of better and safer bumpers.
To this end our agency, the National Highway Traffic
Safety Administration, has proposed a motor vehicle safety
standard to regulate bumper height and effectiveness.

A copy of the proposed standard is enclosed for your information. Your letter has been entered in the appropriate rulemaking docket.

Sincerely,

/s/
Lawrence R. Schneider
Acting Chief Counsel

Enclosure

SMASH Formal Petition on Bumpers and Supporting Brief

SMASH--STUDENTS MOBILIZING ON AUTO SAFETY HAZARDS

SMASH submits the following substitute exterior protection rule and supporting brief pursuant to 49 C.F.R. 553.17 and 49 C.F.R. 553.31.

Exterior Protection - Passenger Cars

S1.   Purpose and scope. This standard establishes requirements for the impact resistance and the configuration of front and rear vehicle surfaces, to prevent low-speed collisions from impairing the mobility and the safe operation of specified vehicle systems, to reduce G-loading on passengers, and to reduce the frequency of override or underride in higher speed collisions.

S2.   Application. This standard applies to passenger cars.

S3.   Definition. "Vehicle corner" means the part of a vehicle contacted by a vertical plane that is tangent to the vehicle and at an angle of 45° to the vehicle's longitudinal centerline.

S4.   Test device. The test specified in S6 shall be conducted with a SAE J850 rigid barrier. An add-on contoured impact face shall be used for angular impacts.

S5.   Requirements. The vehicle shall meet the following requirements before, during, and after all phases of testing.

S5.1   The engine of the vehicle shall be running.

S5.2   Upon impact, the vehicle shall not touch the barrier except for the face of the bumper, which shall be flush with the barrier on 90° angular impacts.

S5.2.1   The barrier shall be impacted by the bumper at a standard height between 14 and 20 inches, that standard height to be determined by the Bureau.

S5.3   Each lamp or reflective device shall be free of cracks and shall comply with the applicable visibility requirements of section S4.3.1.1 of Motor Vehicle Safety Standard number 108.

S5.4   The aim of the headlamp shall be adjustable in accordance with the applicable requirements of Standard number 108.

S5.5   The latching systems of the vehicle's hood, truck, and doors shall be operable in the normal manner.

S5.6   The vehicle's fuel and cooling systems (including air conditioner cooling systems) shall have no leaks or constricted fluid passages and all sealing devices and caps shall be operable in the normal manner.

S5.7   The vehicle's exhaust system shall have no constrictions or open joints.

S5.8   The following parts shall be fully operable in the normal manner: brakes, internal engine parts, steeering mechanism, transmission, drive train, tires, and bumper systems.

S5.9   The turning radius of the tires shall be unimpaired by any sheet metal or other vehicle surfaces.

S5.10   At speeds between 1-20 m-p-h, the relationship between the frame force in G's and the impact velocity in m-p-h shall be no greater than that shown in Figure I.

S5.11   The vehicle frame shall be free of any structural defects.

S5.12   There shall be no debris on the roadway resulting from any of the test impacts. This includes, but is not limited to, lights, windshields, side and rear windows, chrome, grill, door handles, sheet metal, and other trim.

S5.13   Following impact the vehicle shall be driven away under its own power.

S5.14   General. Front wheels shall be parallel to the vehicle's longitudinal centerline.

S5.14.1   The vehicle is at empty weight plus maximum capacity of all fluids necessary for operation of the vehicle.

S5.14.2   The tires shall be inflated to the vehicle
manufacturer's recommended pressure for the specified
loading condition.

S5.14.3   The brakes shall be disengaged, the transmission
in neutral.

S6.   Test procedure. The test vehicle shall impact
the barrier at a speed of 11 (eleven) feet-per-second
three times on its front, three times on its rear, and
three times on each of its 4 (four) corners.

SMASH--STUDENTS MOBILIZING ON AUTO SAFETY HAZARDS

Memorandum In Support Of Proposed Rule

Today's bumpers no longer serve to protect the integrity of the vehicle and its passengers. The bumpers on
cars of 40 to 50 years ago served this purpose, but due to
Detroit's emphasis on style over function this purpose has
all but been forgotten.

Although the National Highway Safety Bureau has
recognized part of this problem in their statement of
purpose (Federal Register volume 35, number 228), there
are other essential safety factors which have yet to be
considered. Furthermore, we feel the Bureau's proposal
would fail to accomplish its stated purpose. In fact,
the potential danger to passengers at speeds above the
test speed may be greater as a result of the proposed rule.

In developing its proposal, the Bureau has failed to
give adequate consideration to existing technology, bypassing such advances as the hydraulic and water bumpers.
At the hearings,conducted by the Bureau on April 2, 1970,
a spokesman for hydraulic bumpers stated, "Our 4 1/2 inch
bumper stroke system is designed to absorb energy at 7 1/2
miles-per-hour in barrier crashes, or 15 miles-per-hour
vehicle to vehicle crashes." (Docket file 19, 110 page
36.) This statement and others are evidence of the
Bureau's neglect, prompting us to make this proposal.

After carefully examining the Bureau's proposal, we
have reached several conclusions as to the value of the
test procedure. We are recommending that the pendulum
test be scrapped in favor of a barrier test, that additional car parts be added to the list of those which must
be unimpaired following the crash test, that the 5 m-p-h
test impact be upgraded up 7 1/2 m-p-h, and that the
standards for bumper implacement be more exacting.

It is our contention that such modifications to the
proposed rule are technically feasible and will result in
much greater passenger safety, with only a small rise in
cost.

I. PENDULUM TEST v. BARRIER TEST. The Bureau proposes
that the device used to test the bumper's effectiveness be
a pendulum (S5.2). This pendulum would strike the stationary test vehicle several times at the prescribed speed
(S6.1 and S6.2). This testing device is not a realistic

simulation of actual collisions. Instead the testing should be done with the well-known barrier test (SAE J850 Standard Rigid Barrier). Here the test vehicle is driven into a rigid, flat vertical barrier at the prescribed speed.

A. The impact force of the barrier test is greater than that of the pendulum test due to the fact that the pendulum bounces back after impact, thus diffusing kinetic energy. With the barrier test, this crash energy is transmitted through the bumper to the vehicle; further there is a much greater transfer of momentum from the pendulum to the car further minimizing the test effectiveness.

B. The specified pendulum, which has a front striking surface 16 inches wide with a vertical width which tapers to a point (see NHSB Figures 1 & 2), would not strike the entire front or rear of the car at once as would the barrier, further reducing the test's effectiveness.

C. Unlike the barrier test, in the pendulum test the engine of the test vehicle is not running, eliminating several essential safety tests:

1. The possibility of the transmission gear shifting because of the impact is not tested.

2. Any test for fluid leakage (S4.4) cannot be dependable since the fluids are not circulating.

3. Moving parts are not operating, thereby precluding the discovery of greater damage caused by their movement or dislocation. An example of this would be the non-operation of the fan, which eliminates the possibility that the spinning fan will be pushed into the radiator causing a leak or other damage.

4. The possibility of fire or explosion due to a gasoline leak is excluded.

D. The barrier test is much more easily implemented than is the pendulum test. The proposed rule calls for the weight of "test device and supporting structure [to be] equal to the weight of the tested vehicle." (S5.2.3) In addition, the test device must be continuously readjusted for height (S6.2 & S6.2). The barrier test requires no weight or height adjustments.

E.   The difference in the accuracy of measuring speed between the pendulum and the barrier test is negligible.

F.   The barrier test has been in existence for many years, hence much more data is available.

II.   <u>ADDITIONAL SAFETY CHECKS</u>.   Under the proposed rule, only lamps and reflecting devices (S4.2), latching systems (S4.3), fuel and cooling systems (S4.4), and exhaust systems (S4.5) must be unimpaired following the impact. The rule should also require that other systems and features which are vital to the safe operation of the vehicle be able to withstand the test impact without damage, if the Bureau's stated goal of protecting safety systems is to be realized.   The Bureau's listing should also include:

A.   Brakes
B.   Steering mechanism
C.   Free-turning radius of tires
D.   Internal engine parts
E.   Engine mounts
F.   Drive train
G.   Air conditioner
H.   Transmission
I.   Tires
J.   Bumper systems

In each of the above A-J, damage to any of these items might not hamper a vehicle's mobility at slow speeds, but could present major safety problems at higher speeds. If, for example, a latent defect in the steering mechanism develops following a low speed crash, this might result in total steering loss at higher speeds.

A vehicle involved in a low speed crash which is sub-sequently immobilized in this manner after traveling at higher speeds is in itself a safety hazard to all other vehicles on the roadway.

Debris left on the roadway following an accident is also a safety hazard for any other car that comes along. For this reason the rule should also insure that the following items be unimpaired following the test:

A.   Windshield
B.   Side and rear windows

    C.   Chrome grill and sheet metal
    D.   Hubcaps
    E.   Any other trim which may come loose and fall off
the car during the test.

As it is proposed, the rule does not contain any provision that the test vehicle be capable of mobility following the test. The car should have to be driven away from
the test site under its own power as the final part of the
test itself.

III. <u>BUMPER MISMATCH</u>. The proposed rule also seeks "to
reduce the frequency of override or underride in higher
speed collisions." (S1). ". . . In higher speed collisions the tendency of a bumper to override another . . .
creates hazards for vehicle occupants. Vehicles with
interlocked bumpers block traffic and expose their
occupants to considerable danger, particularly if they
attempt to get out to unlock the bumpers." (49 CFR Part
571; Dockets No. 1-9 and 1-10, Notice 3) The rule would
require that all bumpers be installed with their centerline at a height between 14 and 20 inches in order to
prevent such bumper mismatch in a collision.

Nevertheless, in a collision involving two different
model automobiles, each meeting the proposed standard, the
top of one bumper may strike the bottom of the other,
effectively diminishing the bumpers' efficiency, even at
the proposed five m-p-h speed. While the test procedure
requires impact at the 20 inch height, this mismatch is
possible because the rule does not specify any minimum
bumper width. Theoretically, a one-inch-wide bumper installed at the 20 inch height could pass the test, but
would certainly present a safety hazard on the road.
Neither does the rule require that the bumper have a flat
surface extending the entire width of the car's front and
rear. A flat surface would prevent interlocking of bumpers
due to ornamental protrusions.

The Bureau should adopt more exacting standards to
prevent bumper mismatch. If the Bureau has the authority
--as it indicates it does--to specify performance standards requiring that the bumper center be between 14 and 20
inches above the narrow this range to a point. Only with
a standard height and a minimum width will bumper mismatch
be avoided. The government has recognized the need for
uniform bumper heights. Former GSA standards provided
that bumper centerlines be between 17-18 inches off the

ground, and have a minimum width of 10 inches. These
standards were discontinued in reliance on DOT's issuing
similar standards pertaining to bumper height, in accordance with the government policy of establishing consistent government and national standards.

IV. SPEED. The rule proposes that the impact speed be
5 m-p-h (a pendulum moving at 7 1/3 feet per second (S4)).
"The proposed standard is expected to provide a basis for
future standards dealing with the absorption of energy at
higher speeds." (Notice 3, supra) If the government can
set this speed, it can set a higher speed. The Bureau
should speed up its time-table, and require that vehicles
be able to withstand rigid barrier impacts at speeds up to
7 1/2 m-p-h. This is now technologically possible. A
bill sponsored by Sen. Abraham Ribicoff, D-Conn., would
require that cars built after January 1, 1973, be able to
withstand 10 m-p-h front and rear end crashes without
damage. And a Florida law now requires that cars built
after January 1, 1973, be able to withstand a 5 m-p-h
impact without damage, and cars built after January 1,
1975, be able to stand up to impacts of 10 m-p-h.

The greatest number of automobile accidents which
present physical danger to the motorists and passengers
occur at speeds in excess of 5 m-p-h. It is therefore
necessary to set the highest crash standards which are
technologically and economically feasible.

V. PASSENGER SAFETY. The Bureau has only dealt indirectly
with passenger safety, giving no consideration to the G
forces on the passengers resulting directly from the
crash impact. A bumper meeting the Bureau's standards
could have a reverse safety factor at higher speeds,
thereby forcing the passengers to suffer a greater G force
impact than with current bumpers. To avoid this contin-
gency, a standard maximum relationship between the frame
force and the speed should be adopted (see Figure I).
This has been realized by systems which have been proposed to the Bureau and can be found in Dockets 1-9, 1-10.

VI. BUMPER RESILIENCY. Most bumpers today are solidly
mounted to the automobile chassis, and the proposed standards would allow this practice to continue. While these
non-resilient bumpers may satisfy the requirements of the
low speed crash tests, they transmit much of the crash
force to the frame of the car and to its occupants. At
higher speeds they serve only to aggravate an accident as
they fold into the car body.

While some automakers claim that the folding metal
serves to absorb the crash energy and thus protect the
passenger, we feel that the bumper should serve as the
first line of defense, and the frame as the second.

We recommend that the rule require that automobiles
be equipped with resilient bumpers, which would absorb
impact energy by their own compression into the bumper
mountings. This bumper should be capable of energy
absorption in multiple crashes, it should be maintenance
free, and should be unimpaired following the test impact.
(The Menasco bumper, which works with a piston device, is
an example of what is available.) This type of a bumper
would pass all the requirements for low speed tests, and
would, in addition, cushion the impact at greater speeds,
quite possibly saving passengers from serious harm.

VII. PEDESTRIAN SAFETY. The Bureau has given no consideration to the issue of pedestrian safety. This is a
paramount question. There is a serious problem of sharp
protrusions on the front of vehicles, which present a
grave danger to pedestrians. Upon impact, the bumper
must not serve to sweep the pedestrian under the vehicle.
The Bureau should amend its statement of purpose (Notice
3, supra) to include this and to establish a standard to
achieve this purpose.

VIII. COST & AESTHETICS. It is already well established
that automobile safety equipment costs money. Certainly
such devices as seat belts, head restraints, padded dash-
boards, and safety glass for windshields cost a great
deal. And admittedly these costs are carried by the consumer. However, the insurance industry can be expected to
reduce premiums as automobiles become less brittle,
thereby lessening this burden.

Functional design must take precedence over "fine
art," in the design of modern automobiles. But this does
not mean that cars need not be beautiful--only that there
must be a purpose for that beauty. Some of the bumpers
we've seen, which meet our proposed standard, are quite
attractive and quite indistinguishable from current bumper
styles, except in function.

IX. STANDING. Since the enactment of the National
Traffic and Motor Vehicle Safety Act of 1966 the automotive
industry has had a great influence on its interpretation

and application, while the consumer has taken a back seat.
The proposed rule's inadequacy reflects this situation.
As a result SMASH (Students Mobilizing on Auto Safety
Hazards) was organized to intervene in these proceedings,
and represent the interest of consumers which have thus
far been neglected. SMASH is composed of five law
students, who study at George Washington University Law
School in Washington, D.C. Its membership includes:
Edward M. Basile (2023 "N" Street, NW, Washington, DC);
Fred Conway (1225 13th Street, NW, Washington, DC);
Brian Corcoran (1401 "N" Street, NW, Washington, DC);
Martin Gold (2400 Virginia Avenue, NW, Washington, DC);
Dennis S. Kahane (2508 "I" Street, NW, Washington, DC).

/s/ Edward M. Basile

/s/ Fred Conway

/s/ Brian Corcoran

/s/ Martin Gold

/s/ Dennis S. Kahane

FRAME FORCE v. IMPACT VELOCITY

RIGID BARRIER COLLISIONS

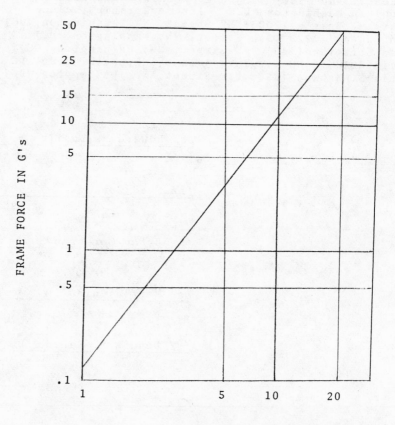

FIGURE 1

Consumer Groups Dealing with NHTSA

Center for Auto Safety
P.O. Box 7250 Ben Franklin Station
Washington, DC 20044

    This non-profit organization monitors activities of
the Safety Administration and concentrates its efforts
on improving vehicle design. Access to the Center's
extensive collection of literature and statistics is
available to anyone. The Center also maintains a file
of over 30,000 complaint letters it has received from
disgruntled owners of defective automobiles.

The Insurance Institute for Highway Safety
Watergate Office Building
Washington, DC 20037

    Supported by members of the insurance industry, this
non-profit organization "carries out research, communications, and grant-in-aid programs to find and apply
ways to reduce losses from highway crashes." The Institute produced a study on the high cost of repairs to
vehicles in low speed crashes.

Physicians for Automotive Safety
50 Union Avenue
Irvington, NJ 07111

    This group has been especially concerned with the
protection of children in vehicle crashes. They have
evaluated manufacturer and safety administrator efforts
protecting children in crashes.

Cleveland Auto Safety Research Center
Case Main Building Room 102
10900 Euclid Avenue
Cleveland, OH 44106

    This student-run organization assists vehicle owners
whose requests to manufacturers have been denied and
where claims are too small to interest lawyers. The
Center also analyzes and identifies trends of abuse in
the auto industry.

Highway Action Coalition
1346 Connecticut Avenue, N.W.
Washington, DC 20036

    This group's primary interest is in the use of high-
way trust fund money for other modes of transportation.
They publish a newsletter called <u>The Concrete Opposition</u>.

Industry Representatives Concerned with NHTSA

American Association of Motor Vehicle Administrators
1828 L Street, N.W.
Washington, DC 20036

American Transit Association
815 Connecticut Avenue, N.W.
Washington, DC 20006 (intra-city urban transportation)

American Trucking Association, Inc.
1616 P Street, N.W.
Washington, DC 20036 (trucking industry)

Motor Vehicle Manufacturers' Association
320 New Center Building   1619 Mass. Ave., N.W.
Detroit, Michigan 48202   Washington, DC 20036
                               (11 manufacturers)

Highway Users' Federation for Safety and Mobility
1776 Massachusetts Avenue, N.W.
Washington, DC 20036

National Association of Motor Bus Owners
1025 Connecticut Avenue, N.W.
Washington, DC 20036 (460 inter-city carriers)

National Automobile Dealers Association
2000 K Street, N.W.
Washington, DC 20006

The Rubber Manufacturers' Association
1346 Connecticut Avenue, N.W.
Washington, DC 20036 (200 rubber companies)

The Tire Industry Safety Council
766 National Press Building
Washington, DC 20004 (18 tire manufacturers)

Truck, Body and Equipment Association
1012 - 14th Street, N.W.
Washington, DC 20005

CHAPTER 14

THE INTERNAL
REVENUE SERVICE

> *Taxation without representation is tyranny.*
> —James Otis,
> *Argument on ... Writs of Assistance,*
> *1769*

Taxpayers spend over $1.4 billion to fund the Internal Revenue Service (IRS). In return, the IRS extracts from taxpayers some $210 billion in taxes to support government operations. (We will use fiscal year [FY] 1972 figures except where otherwise indicated.) The IRS has extensive powers it applies to taxpayers not voluntarily paying their lawful share. It is important that the public participate in IRS policy decisions to ensure that these powers are not misused. This chapter will describe the IRS and methods of overcoming IRS resistance to public scrutiny and participation.

Scope of the IRS

The IRS processes some 112 million tax returns annually—one for about every two people in the United States. Almost 76 million are returns from individuals, who pay $109 billion in federal income taxes. IRS handles 22 million payroll tax returns, with $44 billion in employment taxes. Corporations file about 1.9 million tax returns and pay IRS some $35 billion in federal income taxes. Finally, IRS collects some $17 billion in excise taxes and $5 billion in estate taxes. Of the $210 billion collected altogether, IRS refunds about $19 billion for overpayments.

One of the agency's major jobs is correcting taxpayer arithmetic. It checks about 90 percent of the individual tax returns for mathematical accuracy, and finds errors in about one of every twenty returns. But it doesn't do this just to be helpful; of the 4 million returns that require correction, 2 million result in payment of additional tax of about $239 million, while 1.6 million result in a tax decrease of $119 million. The raison d'être of the IRS is to take money from taxpayers, not refund it.

One of the main jobs of the Service is explaining to people how they can figure out what they owe. Part of this is done through IRS publications. Before the April filing deadline, news releases are sent to 1,500 daily and 6,000 weekly newspapers. But a lot of us still don't quite get it, and about 28 million taxpayers either phone or visit the IRS offices for help on their returns. Unfortunately, in FY 1972 the agency provided only 350 man-years (out of more than 69,000 employees) to help us out.

IRS taxpayer assistance is not always of the highest caliber. In April 1972, *Wall Street Journal* reporter Tom Herman visited five different IRS offices for tax advice. Each time he presented the same tax information, but when Mr. Herman was finished, he found that each of the five IRS offices had given him a different tax opinion! One calculated he was due a $484 refund, while another figured a refund of only $177. The offices couldn't even agree on the correct number of forms to fill out!

The IRS does more than just collect individual income taxes. It also picks up employment taxes (F.I.C.A., R.R. Retirement, and F.U.T.A.),* excise taxes, estate and gift taxes, fiduciary taxes, and corporate taxes, and processes a large number of information returns filed by organizations that do not pay taxes (such as exempt nonprofit organizations) and declarations of tax estimation.

Auditing returns and going after tax delinquents is a major IRS function. In FY 1972, 1.7 million audits were conducted after discrepancies were discovered in the seven service centers in the United States. (There are now ten such centers.) Over 2.1 million delinquent accounts were closed that year, yielding $2.2 billion. There are indications that complications in the tax law are troubling IRS. In FY 1971 IRS conducted audit examinations of only 1.7 percent of individual income tax returns —the third consecutive year that this enforcement activity declined. At the same time, IRS found underpayment of taxes at an all-time high. According to the service, taxpayers didn't pay $3.4 billion they owed in taxes! Taxpayers with complicated returns had the worst record. IRS found that $2.1 billion of the total was due from taxpayers each of whom owed $100,000 or more. Large corporations were among the

---

*Federal Income Contribution Act, Railroad Retirement, and Federal Unemployment Tax Act.

major offenders. In FY 1971 IRS recommended additional tax and penalties of over a billion dollars against corporations with assets of over $250 million.

The agency maintains a pervasive intelligence machinery, and cooperates with other agencies in "strike forces" to undertake investigations of organized crime suspects. It also investigates some elaborate schemes to evade taxes through obscure financial transactions between corporate affiliates and subsidiaries with related directorships. About 9,000 tax fraud cases are investigated every year. Of these, about 1,800 are turned over to the Justice Department with a recommendation for prosecution.

In addition to its seven regional offices, ten service centers, fifty-eight district offices, and 900 local offices, the IRS reaches into foreign countries. The Office of International Operations is merely an extension of offices in the United States for the convenience of the IRS and taxpayers abroad. The Foreign Tax Assistance Staff has nothing to do with our own tax collection system, but provides technical advisors and trainers to fifty-eight other countries to help them collect their own taxes.

The Public and the IRS

Any government agency benefits from public observation. When exposed to the spotlight of publicity, an agency will improve its decisions to withstand the test. This is especially true with an agency like the IRS, which for so long has avoided public observation.

Even while denying public access, the IRS is very sensitive to its public relations image. In 1970 IRS Commissioner Randolph Thrower wrote to all assistant commissioners:

> During recent months, I have become increasingly aware of the urgent need for everyone within the Revenue Service to be conscious of the public relations aspects of our actions. . . .This should include full consideration of the public impact of our operating decisions.
>
> I am well aware that we will never predict public or press reaction with 100 percent accuracy. However, when it is possible to make such predictions, the Public Information Division should be consulted to insure our full consideration of all public affairs implications. It is important that we consider the public relations aspect as well as legal aspects of our decisions. . . .

Commissioner Thrower even ordered that all Revenue Rulings be screened by the Director of the Public Information Division (PID) before publication. In a 1971 memorandum to Treasury Secretary John Connally, Thrower wrote:

> If, on the basis of a public relations issue, our PID Director expresses a serious concern which is not satisfied, the matter will come to my personal attention before publication. . . .
>
> While we are operating under a rather strict commitment to the Tax Committees of Congress to publish our precedent rulings, we do recognize the importance of having these written with a view to their public relations impact, and will continue to remain sensitive to these considerations.

Citizens should make use of the tool of full press coverage of important issues in dealing with this agency, which is so sensitive to its public image.

Philip and Susan Long are two taxpayers who are putting the spotlight on IRS decisions. In November 1969 the agency audited the Longs and their two real estate development companies and assessed a deficiency.

The Longs decided to fight. They paid for a series of advertisements in the *Washington Post,* called "Life under the IRS." The ads kept the public abreast of their David-and-Goliath struggle with IRS. In the course of their case, from audit through the various conferences, the Longs became concerned with the fairness of IRS procedures. When IRS officials refused to reveal statistics and documents relating to agency practices, the Longs took the IRS to court under the Freedom of Information Act (FOIA).

So far, the Longs have filed over one hundred FOIA requests. They recently set a precedent in one case, *Long v. IRS* [CA273-7102, U.S. District Court for the Western District of Washington at Seattle]. The Longs sought access to IRS manuals, including the rules for IRS settlement of tax cases. Philip Long contended that "horse trading" was an improper way for the agency to settle tax cases; either the money was due or not. In their successful suit, the Longs finally obtained access.

Another aggrieved group came to join the fight to open IRS to public examination. This was *Freedom,* the publication of the Church of Scientology. Working with the Longs, *Freedom* published some of the most important documents obtained from the IRS. These included IRS guidelines for disclosure of information to the public, IRS treatment of "sensitive cases," and guidelines for IRS settlements of disputes in appellate conference.

Citizens concerned with these and related topics should write for a copy of *The IRS Papers* to *Freedom*, 2005 W. 9 Street, Los Angeles, California 90006. The Longs have many additional volumes of IRS documents. If you want to find out more about them, or offer suggestions or information, write: Philip and Susan Long, 4885 Lakehurst Lane, Bellevue, Washington 98006. (See also the excellent summary of the Long's IRS documents in *The Wall Street Journal*, 5 February 1973, p. 1.)

Reuben Lenske was another taxpayer with objection to IRS treatment. After winning his case in court, Lenske turned to another tool of citizen action: the Congressional hearing. In 1968 Lenske appeared before Senator Edward Long's (D-Mo.) Subcommittee on Administrative Practice and Procedure. Senator Long then summoned high IRS officials to explain their conduct and general procedures. The Senator also urged IRS consideration of procedures which more carefully respected taxpayer rights.

Many taxpayers have found their Congressman or Senator a useful source of information about IRS. Congress must approve the IRS budget each year, so the agency is careful to respond to Congressional inquiries. Citizens who are refused information by IRS can often succeed by having their Representative ask for the same material. There is one caution: IRS often tries to have the Congressman keep the information secret from other citizens. Try to get your Congressman to agree not to suppress information this way.

In 1972 attorneys of the Tax Reform Research Group (TRRG) used another approach. They appeared before the Senate Appropriations Subcommittee responsible for the IRS budget. Chairman Joseph Montoya heard their request for information and offered to use his powerful office to obtain IRS response. The IRS quickly and extensively answered the thirty-five detailed questions posed by the reform group. Senator Montoya then had the questions and answers published as a part of the Appropriations Subcommittee hearing record. Not only was important information obtained, but in a form which stands now as an IRS public statement! Again in 1973, the TRRG appeared before the Montoya committee. They and other witnesses called upon IRS to consider the rights of average taxpayers. Much new information on IRS practices and procedures was generated, including statements by present and former IRS commissioners and officials that taxpayers' rights were often overlooked in the agency's zealous quest for more revenues. The committee posed twenty one new questions to IRS and received answers ranging from informative to incomplete and deceptive. The 1973 Montoya hearings are an excellent record of IRS practices and of the abuses to which average taxpayers are subjected at the hands of the IRS.

The combination of increasing Congressional interest in the IRS and active citizen use of the FOIA is beginning to open the agency to public scrutiny. Increasing numbers of news stories are published as a result of the newly revealed information. As each new citizen or group becomes active, the movement snowballs. The situation today is far from the closed IRS system of even a few years ago. More progress can be expected in the near future with greater citizenship participation. Appendix 14-B (p. 823) lists some national groups working on tax reform.

History of the IRS

Income taxes aren't necessarily inevitable. The founding fathers didn't contemplate their use except in special circumstances. Madison's notes on the Constitutional Convention indicated that most of the delegates thought enough taxes would be derived from import and export duties. But internal revenue laws were in effect from 1791 to 1802 to retire the Revolutionary War debt, and after their repeal in 1802 they were re-enacted from 1813 to 1817 to pay for the War of 1812. In 1862 Congress again enacted internal revenue laws to pay for the Civil War, and at that time established a permanent internal revenue system. On 1 July of that year Congress established the office of Commissioner of Internal Revenue. The first Commissioner of Internal Revenue took office on 17 July 1862.

In 1913 the Sixteenth Amendment to the Constitution was ratified, over-ruling the Supreme Court's decision in *Pollock* v. *Farmers' Loan & Trust Co.* [2 U.S. 429] that an income tax was unconstitutional, and allowing Congress for the first time to levy taxes on individuals and corporations. From 1913 to 1951 the basic organization of the IRS remained largely unchanged, although tax collections increased from $344 million to $50 billion and the number of employees increased from 4,000 to 57,000.

In 1952 Congress passed a reorganization plan to modernize the structure of the IRS. Political appointments were abolished for positions below the Commissioner, and the administration was decentralized. The agency was reorganized into departments according to its functions—operations, administration, technical, planning, and inspection. In 1953 the number of regions was cut from seventeen to nine, and a data processing department was added. During the 1960s the regions were gradually reduced to seven, and the Alcohol and Tobacco Tax Division was changed to Alcohol, Tobacco, and Firearms Division, after passage of the Gun Control Act of 1968. In 1972 the Division was separated from IRS and established as a separate bureau in the Treasury Department. See Appendix 14-A (p. 821) for a current organization chart of the IRS.

Income taxation was born to pay for wars, and it grows on armed conflict. In World War I revenues went from $512 million in 1916 to $4.6 billion in 1921. A similar rise in tax revenue occurred during World War II, when tax receipts increased from $5 billion in 1939 to over $40 billion in 1946. Although the number of IRS employees more than tripled during World War I (from 4,000 to 17,000) and nearly tripled again in World War II (from 22,000 in 1939 to 59,000 in 1946), since that time the work force has increased by only 10,000, to a total of 69,700 employees. The reason is not peace but computers. The change to automatic data processing in the 1950s arrested the operating costs of the agency and eased the mind-boggling task of processing millions of tax returns. The IRS now maintains ten data processing service centers throughout the country. Data from taxpayers' returns are tabulated and fed into a computer, through a scanning machine, to be recorded on magnetic tape. The tapes, containing about 15,000 returns per reel, are then sent to the National Computer Center in Martinsburg, Virginia, where they are recorded on a master file before being returned to the regional offices. From the master file IRS checks taxpayers through their social security numbers to determine if they have reported all of their income, whether husbands and wives filing separately are claiming the same exemptions, whether tax is owed from past years, and whether any taxpayers are getting two refunds by filing two tax returns.

Congress and the Code,
Taxpayers, and the Rules

In 1916 the Internal Revenue Code numbered sixteen pages; today it has 1,600 pages of regulations. The tax laws now include special subsidies for oil depletion, charitable deductions, capital gains, accelerated depreciation for real estate and business machinery, and much more. Along with each new subsidy added to the tax laws, the IRS—as part of its responsibility for tax administration— must become expert in yet another area of social policy. IRS must decide whether a certain processed mineral qualifies for depletion benefits, whether a particular organization qualifies for tax exemption as a charity, or whether certain complicated corporate transactions qualify for capital gains treatment. The question is whether the tax collecting agency can perform properly the roles of administrator of so many diverse public subsidy programs. Many IRS decisions have become the subject of much controversy. For example, in 1962 General Electric and a number of other companies were indicted for violating the Sherman Act by conspiring to fix prices and submitting rigged bids to governmental agencies. The major companies pleaded guilty on the main charges. After these violations of the criminal law were established, 1,800 civil suits were brought against the companies to recover damages resulting from the unfair trade practices. Many of the suits were consolidated into a huge lawsuit which cost the companies millions of dollars in damage payments. The companies wrote to the IRS and obtained a ruling that allowed them to deduct these costs from their income tax. In effect the companies were allowed by the IRS to pass half the cost of penalties resulting from their crimes onto the government (and eventually to other taxpayers) in the form of tax deductions [Staff of Joint Comm. on Internal Revenue Taxation, 89th Cong., 1st Sess., Staff Study of Income Tax Treatment of Treble Damage Payments under the Anti-Trust Laws, 121-22 (Comm. Print, 1965)]. For most taxpayers fines and penalties are not deductible, but the offending companies were able to use their sophisticated legal resources to convince the IRS that the treble damage penalty was not a penalty at all, but merely an ordinary and necessary cost of doing business.

Congress took action and cured this specific problem by the Tax Reform Act of 1969, but it serves as an example of how business interests can bring powerful resources to bear in order to obtain favorable treatment in the IRS administrative process. In general, the interest of ordinary taxpayers is not given the same careful treatment because there are too few citizens who are informed of the available administrative procedures and who have the time and financial resources to use those procedures. This introduction to the procedures is a first step in redressing the balance.

Rules (more specifically, regulations and Revenue Rulings) are made by the IRS because Congress didn't provide all the answers in the Internal Revenue Code. At the top of the hierarchy of tax law is the Internal Revenue Code as passed by Congress. One step below that are the Internal Revenue Regulations which implement the Code, now numbering almost 4,500 pages in length. For example, the Internal Revenue Code allows businesses to deduct depreciation of their assets from gross income; the IRS adopts regulations spelling out what forms of "depreciation" (such as "straight-line" or "declining balance") are acceptable. In effect, Congress has delegated to the IRS the power to fill in the details of the tax laws. Specifically, proposed regulations are issued under authority contained in Section 7805 of the Internal Revenue Code of 1954 [68A Stat. 917; 26 U.S.C. 7805]. The process is subject to the requirements of the Administrative Procedure Act (for a description of the APA see Chapter 4). Regulations are published in the Code of Federal Regulations (C.F.R.).

Revenue Rulings are a step below the regulations, which they interpret, and provide guidance to taxpayers in situations not covered by the regulations. For example, the Code allows depreciation of an asset, the regulations provide for a "straight-line" method of depreciation, but the taxpayer wants to know whether his widgets are depreciable over a five-year life span or a ten-year life span. He asks the IRS, which issues a ruling on the question. Revenue Rulings are not issued according to the requirements of the APA. They are responses to letters of inquiry submitted by taxpayers to obtain rulings on specific situations. There are two kinds of Rulings: the "private letter" rulings (about which more will be said later) and the Revenue Rulings published in the *Internal Revenue Bulletin.*

Several other types of statements issued by the IRS also provide technical tax information. These are not considered "law" themselves, but are merely statements of IRS policy and positions in relation to the law. "Determination letters" and "information letters" are two such statements. "Determination letters" are similar to private letter rulings, but aren't as important. Like the letter rulings, they are issued in response to an inquiry by an individual or an organization, and relate to a specific situation; unlike a letter ruling, they are issued by the district director and are based on principles and previously announced precedents of the national office. They are issued only where the question has been clearly decided by statutes, court decisions, or regulations published in the *Internal Revenue Bulletin.* "Information letters," which can be issued by either the district or the national office, merely point out to the taxpayer a well-settled interpretation or principle of tax law.

They are different from determination letters and letter rulings in that they are not applied to a specific fact situation.

The IRS also publishes Technical Information Releases and News Releases. Technical Information Releases used to be News Releases on complicated subjects. Now they are reports on new developments that are considered too technical to be of interest to newspapermen and general readers; they may contain anything from tax information to the number of illegal distilleries seized in a year. Besides these releases, the IRS publishes Statistical Information Releases and about sixty pamphlets such as *Your Federal Income Tax* and *Tax Benefits for Older Americans.*

Tax regulations are thought up in a lot of places, but they are all introduced into the rule making machinery by the Office of the Assistant Secretary for Tax Policy in the Department of the Treasury. One source of new regulations is the White House. The President, working with the Council of Economic Advisors, may decide on a new tax regulation to heat up or slow down the economy; or, in preparation of the National Budget by the Office of Management and Budget (OMB), a tax regulation to provide revenue for increased expenditures may be proposed. The President may also seek a tax regulation favorable to a constituency which he feels deserves a tax break or two. Other sources for proposed tax regulations are Congress and the IRS itself. Proposals from the IRS are usually for regulations to settle an area of disagreement in tax law.

The proposed regulation starts from the Office of the Assistant Treasury Secretary for Tax Policy in the form of an order to the Legislation and Regulations Division of the IRS to draft a regulation. The division draws on reports of Congressional committee hearings of the House Ways and Means Committee, the Senate Finance Committee, and the Joint Committee on Taxation concerning provisions of the Internal Revenue Code relevant to the proposed regulation. Once it is drafted, the regulation is returned to the Treasury Department. If the Treasury Department approves the draft of the proposed regulation, it is signed by the Secretary of the Treasury and sent to the *Federal Register* for publication as a Notice of Proposed Rule Making (NPRM).

The NPRM, required by the APA, includes the text of the proposed rule and an invitation to the public to submit written comments and request an opportunity to comment orally at a public hearing. If, within thirty days of publication, no one submits written comments or a written request to make oral comment at a public hearing, there will be no public hearing and the regulation will generally go into effect as proposed. The regulations describing procedures for IRS rule making are found in the C.F.R., Title 26, Part 601, Section 601.601. Under those regulations comments upon a proposed regulation are in most cases publicly available for inspection by anyone. A person submitting comments may request in writing that a portion of the comment be kept secret, but that will be allowed only if the person establishes that the particular portion is exempt from disclosure under one of the nine exceptions to the Freedom of Information Act. (See p. 720.) This is a change from the IRS's prior practice which, until 30 April 1973, permitted confidential treatment simply on the request of the person submitting the comment.

If you decide to submit written comments with a request to make oral comments at a public hearing, send your comments and requests to the Commissioner of Internal Revenue, Attention: CC:LR:T, Washington, D.C. 20224 (five copies are preferred, but not required). Include an outline of the topics to be discussed at the hearing, with the time to be devoted to each topic. The IRS will then prepare an agenda with the order of presentation for oral comments and the time allotted for each presentation. Usually ten minutes will be allotted to each person making oral comments. After written comments and a request for a hearing are received, the IRS schedules a hearing and a Notice of Public Hearing for Proposed Rule Making is published in the *Federal Register,* indicating the time, place, and date of the hearing. Traditionally, IRS has been willing to schedule hearings when requested by business taxpayers. It remains to be seen whether IRS will respond as easily to public interest requests for hearings.

At the hearing, you are limited to discussing matters relating to written comments which have already been submitted and to questions and answers in connection with the written comments. Your oral presentation cannot be just a restatement of your written commentary. You should be prepared to answer questions not only on the topics listed in your outline, but also in connection with written comments submitted by others. Copies of all nonconfidential written comments are available either before or at the hearing on request. But the request should be made within thirty days after publication of the Notice of Public Hearing in the *Federal Register,* and you must agree to pay copying costs of 10 cents per page. Copies of the written comment are also available to those who request them after the thirty-day period "as soon as they are available" [26 C.F.R. 601.601(a) (3) (ii)] —not necessarily by the time of the hearing.

The regulations provide for transcripts of hearings "to the extent re-

sources permit" [26 C.F.R. 601.601(a) (3) (vi)], but the IRS is not required to have a transcript made. Under the terms of Section 11 of the
recently adopted Federal Advisory Committee Act, Pub. L. 92-463
5 U.S.C. App. I, 6 October 1972, agencies shall make available to any
person, at actual cost of duplication, copies of transcripts of agency
proceedings. This cost should range between 7 and 20 cents per page.
Before the enactment of this Act, transcripts were available only through
private reporting services at much higher rates. If transcripts have been
made they are now available directly from the IRS at a cost-related fee.

The hearings must be conducted according to the minimum standards
of conduct relating to conflicts of interest and rules of conduct (set
forth in 5 C.F.R. Part 735-20 to Part 735-30). Those provisions prohibit any employee of the Treasury Department from:

1. Using public office for private gain.
2. Giving preferential treatment to any person.
3. Impeding government efficiency or economy.
4. Losing complete independence or impartiality.
5. Making a government decision outside official channels.
6. Affecting adversely the confidence of the public in the integrity
   of the government.

The regulations provide that additional comments may be heard, even
though application was not timely, to the extent that time permits.
After the hearing is over, the proposed regulation may be redrafted.
The regulation is then published in final form in the *Federal Register* as
a Treasury Decision.

The procedural rules for submitting a petition to change a regulation
or issue a new one are at 26 C.F.R. 601:601 (c). Identify the section or
sections of the Code which are involved, and if your petition is to
amend or repeal a regulation, include the text of the regulation. (If
your petition is to amend a regulation, the text in its amended form
should also be included.) The reason for the change should be written
clearly and concisely, stating the situation involved, your arguments for
the change, the legal basis for the change, and relevant legal authorities
to support such a change. Again, five copies are preferred. Such petitions are supposed to be given careful consideration, and you will be
advised of the action taken. Include true copies of any relevant documents. All material will be kept in the IRS files and will not be returned, so no original documents or exhibits should be submitted. Send

your petition to the Commissioner of Internal Revenue, Attention: CC:LR:T, Washington, D.C. 20224.

Revenue Rulings, a second kind of rule making, are begun when taxpayers (usually corporate) write to the IRS for a private letter ruling interpreting the tax law. The rulings program has developed because of the taxpayer's need to know in advance of filing whether he has a tax liability in a situation not covered by the regulations. The taxpayer writes to the Office of the Assistant Commissioner (Technical) to explain his situation and request a ruling. That office then issues a ruling after considering the matter in either its Income Tax Division or the Miscellaneous and Special Tax Division. Procedural regulations for rulings are at 26 C.F.R. 601.201.

There are two parts to the rulings program: private letter rulings and Revenue Rulings. The private letter rulings are in direct response to taxpayer inquiries. There are over 30,000 of them every year. Private letter rulings are sent to the inquiring taxpayer, and are not published. A private letter ruling contains a statement of the relevant facts, applicable law, and conclusions, with authorities in support of the conclusions.

In effect, the private letter ruling is a luxurious free taxpayer service provided by IRS. In FY 1971 IRS spent 339,000 professional man-hours on 32,300 unpublished rulings, an average of 10.5 hours each. Since the average taxpayer remains uninformed about the rulings service, this program tends to benefit those wealthy enough to retain private tax counsel.

There is another serious defect in the program. The *Internal Revenue Bulletin* states: "Unpublished rulings will not be relied on, used, or cited as precedents by Service personnel in the disposition of other cases." In effect, this means that the Service can rule favorably for one taxpayer but unfavorably for another in identical circumstances. Since the rulings are secret, the taxpayer with an unfavorable ruling may never know that his competitor has a secret edge. A taxpayer reform group, Tax Analysts and Advocates, has won a lawsuit, under the FOIA, to force publication of all rulings. The federal government has appealed. Congress could also require by specific legislation that those rulings be made public. Publication is essential if all taxpayers are to be treated fairly.

Presently, only about 300 rulings are selected for publication as Revenue Rulings in the *Internal Revenue Bulletin*, after research by the Interpretative Division of the Chief Counsel's Office. Identifying names and facts are deleted from Revenue Rulings. Their purpose is to provide a more general rule, and careful consideration is given to possible fact situations which might fall within the scope of the ruling. Distinctions and limitations are added to the opinion to make it applicable to other cases having similar facts. Rulings are regarded as important statements of IRS position by the courts, and IRS employees are required to follow them as precedent.

From 1919 to 1953 rulings were published in different series relating to the different areas of federal taxes, such as Appeals and Review Memorandums (A.R.M.), Estate and Gift Tax (E.T.), General Counsel Memorandums (G.C.M.), Income Tax (I.T.), Pension Trust Service (P.S.), Sales Tax (S.T.), Solicitor's Opinions (Sol. Op.), and Office Decisions (O.D.). Since 1953, all rulings published in the *Bulletin* have been termed Revenue Rulings (Rev. Rul.) regardless of the area of tax law concerned.

A request for a private letter ruling (sent to Commissioner of Internal Revenue, Attention: T:PS:T, Washington, D.C., 20224) must contain a complete statement of facts relating to the transaction. This includes the name, address, and taxpayer account numbers of all interested parties; the district office where each of the interested parties files his return; a complete statement of the business reasons for the transactions; and true copies of all contracts, wills, deeds, agreements, or other documents involved in the transaction. Requests for rulings or determination letters should be submitted in duplicate if:

1. The request is for a ruling for tax exempt organization status.
2. More than one issue is presented in the request.
3. A closing agreement (described below) is requested.

Form 1023 is used for requesting rulings on tax exempt or organization status. The request must contain a statement whether, to the best of your knowledge, the identical question is being considered by any field office of the IRS in connection with an active examination or audit of a tax return already filed.

Your arguments for the ruling must be explained and supported. The request must be signed by you or by your representative, who must be an attorney, a Certified Public Accountant (CPA), or one of the 10,000 enrolled agents qualified by examination to practice before the IRS. If the request for a ruling is deficient, the IRS is required to acknowledge the request and point out the requirements which have not been met.

It's not all done in writing, though. You can have an oral discussion if you ask for it in writing [Revenue Procedure 62-28, 1962-2 *Cumulative Bulletin* 496]. The IRS will set a time and place for the conference —usually far enough in advance to give IRS personnel an opportunity to study the points at issue. Under 26 C.F.R. 601.502 the conference must be attended either by the taxpayer or by his qualified representative, usually an attorney or CPA with power of attorney. The person making a request is entitled to one conference at the national office; it usually will be held at the branch level in the Tax Rulings Division attended by someone who has authority to act for the branch chief.

Once the ruling is issued (usually within ninety days, although there is no time limit in the statute or regulations), the person who made the request may protest. The protest must be considered by an informal board established for this purpose by the Assistant Commissioner (Technical). All protests, whether or not there is a conference, will be considered by the board. The board will then notify the Income Tax Division of the results of its consideration of the protest. This procedure can be invoked by a written request directed to the Assistant Commissioner (Technical).

Although private letter rulings are supposed to be isolated and confidential transactions between a taxpayer and his tax collector, they constitute a secret body of precedent for IRS personnel and tax attorneys who regularly participate in the process. Certainly those rulings that are selected for publication (with identifying details removed) in the *Bulletin* are relied on and deferred to. But there is scant provision at present for public access to either the private letter ruling program or the process of selecting certain rulings to be published as Revenue Rulings in the *Internal Revenue Bulletin*. This policy of secrecy is being challenged through both FOIA litigation and Congressional activity. The names of those who obtain private letter rulings are considered by the IRS to be exempt from public disclosure under the FOIA. However, the texts of the rulings should be obtainable with identifying names and facts deleted.

Only a fraction of those who request IRS records such as rulings, handbooks, and memos under the FOIA succeed. There are three major obstacles frustrating those who seek the rulings. First, the FOIA exempts information made privileged by other statutes, such as that covered by Section 6103 of the Internal Revenue Code (relating to publicity of returns and disclosure of information on persons filing income tax returns), or by Section 7313 (relating to unauthorized disclosure of confidential information), and 18 U.S.C. 1905 (generally relating to disclosure of confidential information). Second, a request for a ruling must identify the ruling specifically, and it is extremely difficult to identify a ruling that one has not seen. Third, the financial costs often present practical barriers. The IRS charges $3.50 per hour to find the material and delete identifying details, and, once it is found, charges 10 cents per page to copy it.

Requests for rulings are usually denied on the basis of statutes protecting confidential material. Requests for parts of the *Audit Manual, Offers in Compromise Handbook,* and revenue agents' reports and memos have been denied on the theory that they are privileged interagency memos. The courts, most notably the Sixth Circuit Court of Appeals in *Hawkes* v. *IRS* 467 F. 2d 787 (1972), have refused to accept IRS claims of confidentiality and some information, such as agent's manuals, are now available. In *Shakespeare Company* v. *U.S.* [389 F. 2d 772 (1968)], a taxpayer demanded production of certain private letter rulings relevant to his excise tax claim, relying partly on the FOIA. The Court of Claims reversed the decision of the trial court, which had ordered the agency to produce the documents. The reversal was based on the fact that the request did not identify specific rulings. The court said: "We can find nothing in the above act which would entitle this plaintiff to engage in a hunt for something which might aid it in this action any more than it could within the subpoena or discovery processes."

Private letter rulings aren't usually available, and Revenue Rulings in the *Bulletin* are not promulgated in accordance with the requirements of the APA. The IRS position is that Revenue Rulings are always interpretative, and interpretative rules are expressly exempt from the procedural requirements of the APA, as opposed to regulations, substantive rules, or legislative rules which create law-implementing statutes. For a good discussion of the rulings issue, see Reid, "Public Access to IRS Rulings," 41 *George Washington L. Rev.* 23 (1972).

A closing agreement is a negotiated settlement between the Commissioner of Internal Revenue and a taxpayer about specific issues or tax liability for a certain period. It may apply to a tax period already ended or to a future period [26 C.F.R. 301.7121 and 26 C.F.R. 601. 202]. Agreements for the future must provide that the agreement is subject to any change in the law after the date of the agreement. All closing agreements must be based on private letter rulings.

A closing agreement may be the price a taxpayer pays for a private letter ruling, since regulations allow the government to "require the taxpayer to enter into a closing agreement as a condition to the issuance of a ruling." Compromises are also authorized by the Internal Revenue Code under Section 7122, with procedures at 26 C.F.R. 301.7122. They are used mostly in cases in which it is unlikely that the taxes owed can ever be collected.

Audits, Appeals, and Taxpayers

The IRS is unable to enforce all of the tax laws against every taxpayer with an improper return. Rather, the agency must allocate its man-power to do the most fair and efficient job possible.

As a result of their discoveries under the FOIA, Philip and Susan Long have found that although the IRS audits a larger percentage of big corporations, it allocates proportionally fewer man-hours to large corporations than to small ones. This is despite the fact that audits of large corporations bring the government many more dollars per man-hour than audits of smaller companies.

In FY 1971 field audits by IRS agents of all individual and business taxpayers netted an average of $132 per IRS man-hour. Audits of non-business returns of less than $10,000 averaged $108 per IRS man-hour, while audits of nonbusiness returns of $50,000 and over averaged $351 per man-hour. Business returns showed the same pattern. Audits of business returns under $10,000 brought $68 per IRS man-hour, while audits of business returns over $30,000 averaged $161 per man-hour.

These dismaying facts led IRS Commissioner Johnnie Walters to speak out angrily against "flouting of the law" by large corporations and their "dabbling in tax avoidance and evasion schemes." But the IRS remains uncooperative in releasing the detailed statistics documenting such charges. What is known is that fewer than a half dozen IRS audi-tors work on even the largest corporations' tax returns—an impossible task to perform with even minimal thoroughness, given the complexity and international operations of these giant companies.

After the IRS audits a taxpayer, it may assess a "deficiency"—the amount of taxes it claims the taxpayer still owes. The taxpayer can either pay or fight. If he fights, the dispute goes through a district "conference" and an appellate "conference" within IRS. At each level the IRS generally tries to settle the case with a compromise. IRS may also offer a compromise if the taxpayer threatens to take the case to court. In this way IRS settles over 90 percent of contested cases out of court.

According to the statistics, compromise settlements increasingly favor the taxpayer, the longer he fights his case. In FY 1972 IRS district offices settled, on the average, for 42 cents of each dollar originally claimed by the auditing agent. At the next level, the appellate division settled for 35 cents on the dollar.

Unfortunately, IRS settlements favor wealthier taxpayers. In FY 1972 the appellate division settled small cases—in the $1 to $999 range—for 67 cents on the dollar. In big cases, where IRS originally claimed $1 million or more was owed, the appellate division settled for an average of 34 cents on the dollar.

Many of these figures first came to light when the Longs obtained previously secret IRS documents. In an extensive front page story on 5 February 1973, *The Wall Street Journal* published much of the Long's data. Among the reasons for the discrimination in favor of the rich, according to the article, is: "The rich are more likely to have knowledgeable and tenacious tax lawyers and accountants." The Long's data also indicate substantial favorable settlements for taxpayers willing to fight in court.

Once the taxpayer stops contesting his case, IRS moves to collect the taxes it claims are owed. Sometimes IRS is very rough. An elderly accountant in Mountain View, California, owed back taxes because of heavy medical expenses for his wife. In 1971 the couple arranged a repayment schedule with one IRS official. Before the final due date another agent seized the family car, golf clubs which had been in the trunk, and the watch off the taxpayer's wrist. Then IRS published a large advertisement in the local paper, cartooning the elderly taxpayer as a man wearing only a barrel and a necktie, and announcing auction of the seized property.

The IRS later officially apologized for the embarrassing advertisement. But letters to Senator Joseph Montoya of the Senate Appropriations Subcommittee indicate that a number of taxpayers have been excessively harassed during the collection process. One small businessman complained of an IRS lien against his bank account even though the back taxes had already been paid.

In the *Washington Post* of 12 December 1970, a former IRS Revenue Officer, with six years' service, wrote:

> The threat to execute a levy becomes the threat to take a man's job. . . . .Perhaps half of all cases I handled involved the disadvan-

taged poor: uneducated and unskilled blacks and Puerto Ricans to whom the loss of a job is a major disaster. . . .There is not the slightest doubt in my mind that I have driven men to commit robberies. . .in order to meet my monthly collection quota.

In theory, the levy power is needed as a final weapon against people who refuse to pay their taxes. But every Revenue Officer knows that the most typical use of the levy is against people who want to pay off a tax delinquency in monthly installments, but at a rate insufficient to meet the office quota. I've often had to execute levies against people who did not know they owed a back tax, because audit notices were sent to a wrong address, as well as many whose tax cases were still under adjudication.

As the *Post* observed in an editorial the same day:

> The decision to levy upon an entire pay check is left to the revenue officer. He is not required to conduct a hearing, and there is no established machinery for appeal from his ruling.
>
> Under the best of circumstances this is an extremely arbitrary method of dealing with citizens. When collection quotas for the revenue officers are added to the equation, the possibilities of abuse are substantially multiplied. Diligence in the collection of taxes is both desirable and necessary, but it should not go to the point of driving citizens into desperation—much less into crime. An investigation appears to be in order as the basis for revision of the law or the IRS regulations.

The excessive discretion of IRS officers, combined with only limited public glimpses at abuses of collection powers, again highlights the need for active public observation of our powerful tax collection agency.

The IRS and You

With increasing numbers of successful FOIA suits, the picture of the IRS is being clarified. The pattern of concentration on smaller taxpayers and favoring of the large taxpayer has already emerged. It is time for citizen action to improve the fairness—and efficiency—of these IRS operations so long shrouded in secrecy. It is time for regulatory proposals to the IRS. Should the agency balk, Congress may become interested in remedial legislation.

Benjamin Franklin was wrong about the inevitability of taxes, and thousands of very wealthy Americans prove it every year by legally avoiding much of their personal income tax liability. This has been an introduction to the administrative procedures responsible for much of that avoidance. Many of these rulings are private, and a first step would be to bring this secret body of law into the open. Other regulations are arrived at publicly, but they are so grey and technical that it takes a keen eye on the *Federal Register* to be aware of their meaning and to register an opinion. The procedures for appealing an individual tax case through the bureaucracy and then to the courts deserve careful study. Tax justice should not depend on the money you can afford for an attorney. If you become involved in a dispute with the IRS, remember the FOIA and other citizen actions. On the other hand, you will do much better if you work to improve IRS procedures before the agent knocks on your door. Prevention of abuses or injustice is the objective of citizen action on these procedures and policies.

Organization Chart of the Internal Revenue Service

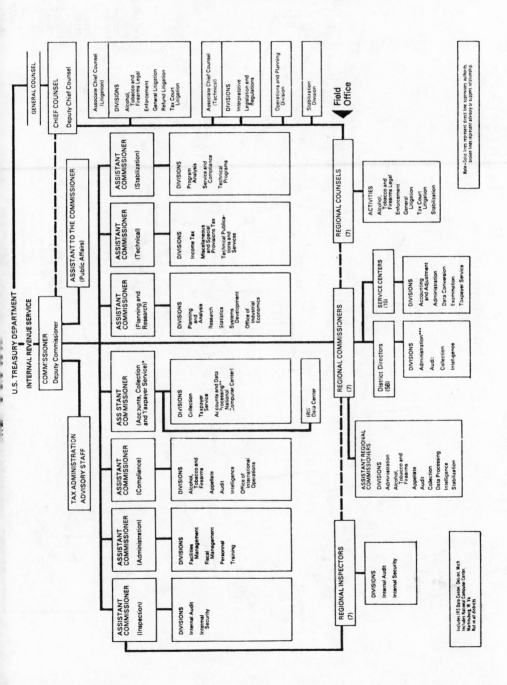

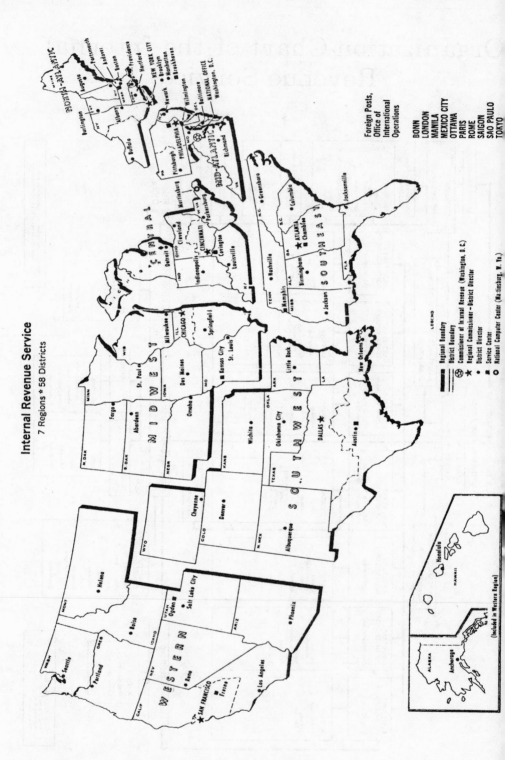

Internal Revenue Service

7 Regions ☆ 58 Districts

NORTH-ATLANTIC — Burlington, VT; Buffalo, NY; Albany, NY; Augusta; Portsmouth; Andover; Boston; Providence; Hartford; NEW YORK CITY; Brooklyn; Manhattan; Brookhaven; Newark; Wilmington

MID-ATLANTIC — PHILADELPHIA; Pittsburgh; Baltimore; Washington, D.C.; NATIONAL OFFICE; Richmond; Martinsburg; Parkersburg

CENTRAL — Detroit; Cleveland; CINCINNATI; Covington; Indianapolis; Louisville; Greensboro; Columbia

SOUTHEAST — Nashville; Memphis; Birmingham; ATLANTA; Chamblee; Jackson; Jacksonville

MIDWEST — Fargo; Aberdeen; St. Paul; Milwaukee; CHICAGO; Springfield; Des Moines; Omaha; Kansas City; St. Louis

SOUTHWEST — Wichita; Oklahoma City; Cheyenne; Denver; Albuquerque; DALLAS; Austin; Little Rock; New Orleans

WESTERN — Seattle; Portland; Helena; Boise; Salt Lake City; Ogden; Reno; SAN FRANCISCO; Fresno; Los Angeles; Phoenix

Honolulu, HAWAII; Anchorage, ALASKA (Included in Western Region)

LEGEND
- ⊕ Commissioner of Internal Revenue (Washington, D.C.)
- ★ Regional Commissioner – District Director
- ● District Director
- ■ Service Center
- ○ National Computer Center (Martinsburg, W. Va.)
- ▬ Regional Boundary
- — District Boundary

Foreign Posts, Office of International Operations

BONN
LONDON
MANILA
MEXICO CITY
OTTAWA
PARIS
ROME
SAIGON
SAO PAULO
TOKYO

National Groups Working on Tax Reform

Tax Reform Research Group
P.O.Box 14198
Washington, DC 20044

    The Tax Reform Research Group, associated with Ralph
Nader's Public Citizen, Inc., studies income tax and
property tax reform.   It publishes the newspaper <u>People</u>
<u>& Taxes</u>. (Subscriptions are $4.00 for ten issues a year.)
Write to the above address to subscribe or for other tax
action information.

Robert Loitz
P.O.Box 3518
Akron, OH 44310

    The one-man tax reform campaign of Robert Loitz has
grown into a nationwide petition drive.   For copies of
his tax reform petition and other tax information write
to the above address.

Taxation With Representation
2369 North Taylor Street
Arlington, VA 22207

    This group issues a monthly newsletter and publishes
technical tax reform proposals of attorneys, economists,
and accountants.   Membership is $15.00 annually and
includes subscription to the newsletter and free copies of
the reform proposals.

Tax Analysts and Advocates
732 17th Street, N.W.
Washington, DC 20006

    This group includes a public interest law firm which
specializes in tax reform and a group of economists and
attorneys who prepare current analyses of tax bills in
Congress.   The group publishes a weekly newsletter, "Tax
Notes."

Tax Action Campaign
1921 Pennsylvania Avenue, N.W.
Washington, DC 20006

   Former U.S. Senator Fred Harris established this
group to promote Federal income tax reform through citizen
action.   Write to them for background tax information and
details of tax reform activities in your community.

Bicentennial T.E.A. Party
1307 Sansom Street
Philadelphia, PA 19107

   The T.E.A. Party plans a series of public events
highlighting the need for tax reform and commemorating
the 200th anniversary of the Boston Tea Party.

Common Cause
2100 M Street, N.W.
Washington, DC 20036

   Common Cause is a national membership organization
(dues are $15.00 annually) which lobbies for open Con-
gressional procedures, publicized campaign contributions,
and other reforms important to the quality of our tax
laws.

CHAPTER 15

THE ENVIRONMENTAL
PROTECTION AGENCY
AND AIR POLLUTION

> *... in 1971, not one grain of dust, not one liter of gaseous pollution has yet been removed from the atmosphere of this Nation as a direct result of the 1967 air legislation.*
> —William Ruckelshaus, Former Administrator of the Environmental Protection Agency, speech to National Press Club, Washington, D.C., 12 January 1971

There was more legislation—the Clean Air Act Amendments of 1970. Something was needed, because the muck in the air not only wasn't being removed—it was increasing. In 1969, the latest year for which comprehensive statistics are available, there were 281.1 million tons of measured pollutants dumped into the air—a 3.2 percent increase over 1968. But, as the 1967 efforts demonstrated, legislation alone won't be enough to stop the poisoning of the air. It will take vigorous and sustained effort by a "breathers' lobby," working on the Environmental Protection Agency (EPA), in order to stop the steady displacement of our atmosphere with pollutants.

EPA Regulatory Activities

Before getting into the details of how EPA works and doesn't work on air pollution, you should know that EPA has other things to do, too. EPA is one of the babies of the administrative agencies, since it was only formed in the fall of 1970. It is an agency in the executive branch, as opposed to the relatively independent regulatory commissions such as the Federal Power Commission or the Federal Trade Commission. That means that it is much more susceptible to direction from and through the White House. But it may also be less prone to the bureaucratic ossification and co-optation that sets in so easily in the independent commissions. The Presidential reorganization plan that formed the EPA was designed to take most of the programs concerned with environmental protection which were scattered throughout the executive branch and consolidate them in one place. These are the regulatory activities that were collected, and their former administrative homes:

1. Air pollution: the National Air Pollution Control Administration was transferred from the Department of Health, Education, and Welfare.
2. Water pollution: the Federal Water Quality Administration was transferred from the Department of Interior.
3. Pesticides: programs were transferred from the Department of Interior, the Department of Agriculture, and the Department of Health, Education, and Welfare.
4. Solid waste: the Bureau of Solid Waste Management was transferred from the Department of Health, Education, and Welfare.
5. Radiation: regulatory responsibilities were transferred from the Atomic Energy Commission, the Federal Radiation Council, and the Bureau of Radiological Health in the Department of Health, Education, and Welfare.
6. Ecological systems study: transferred from the Council on Environmental Quality.

The Council on Environmental Quality (CEQ) is separate from the EPA, and advises the President on environmental programs generally. This chapter is concerned exclusively with what you can do about air pollution. This is not because other EPA functions are less important, but some of them, such as water pollution control, are likely to be changed drastically in the near future by recently or soon to be enacted legislation; for an introduction such as this book provides, it seems appropriate to focus on the fundamental and inescapable subject of air.

Controlling Air Pollution

In talking about air pollution, some mention of elementary chemical terms is also inescapable. The text will keep it as simple as possible. The 281.2 million tons of pollutants referred to in the first paragraph only counted pollutants that are monitored on a relatively systematic basis: hydrocarbons (HC), sulfur oxides (SO_x), carbon monoxide (CO) Nitrogen oxides (NO_x), and particulates. There is no monitoring, so far, of some of the most deadly pollutants, such as fluorides and lead. Appendix 15-A (p. 857) is a glossary of some commonly used technical terms.

Transportation—primarily the automobile's internal combustion engine—contributed slightly more than one-half to the total air pollution by tonnage. Other major sources, such as fuel combustion from stationary sources (primarily public utilities) and industrial processes, contributed about 30 percent, solid waste disposal was responsible for slightly under 5 percent, and the balance came from "miscellaneous" sources [*Environmental Quality,* Third Annual Report of Council on Environmental Quality, August 1972, p. 6 (hereinafter cited as 1972 CEQ Report)].

On a bad day air pollution can kill you immediately, if you're very young or old, or have emphysema, or one of a number of other conditions. Deadly "temperature inversions" from London to Donora, Pennsylvania, have shown that. If you're tough and healthy it will only make you sick and take some years off the end of your life. For example, if you are a New Yorker who stopped smoking to avoid cancer, you're only partially free, because you're still inhaling more benzo-a-pyrene (a carcinogenic hydrocarbon in cigarette smoke) than you would from smoking a pack of cigarettes a day.

Health injuries that already have been identified as being related to air pollution include respiratory ailments, such as lung cancer, emphysema, and bronchitis; cardiovascular diseases; cancer not connected to the lung; and potential birth defects (John Esposito, *Vanishing Air,* New York: Grossman Publishers, 1970). Such injuries cost money as well as causing pain and anguish. The CEQ suggests that, based on 1963 data, a 50 percent reduction in air pollution in major urban areas would lower the costs of health damage by $2.08 billion annually [*Environmental Quality,* Second Annual Report of Council on Environmental Quality, August 1971, p. 106 (hereinafter cited as 1971 CEQ Report)].

The EPA estimates that the total economic cost of air pollution in terms of human mortality and morbidity is about $6 billion annually, and that the annual cost in terms of damage to vegetation and property values, as well as health, is about $16 billion annually—or $80 for each person in the United States. But that is not all. As the CEQ says:

> In all probability, the estimates of cost will be even higher when the impact on aesthetic and other values are calculated, when the cost of discomfort from illness is considered, and when the damage can be more precisely traced to pollutants. Also, the estimates may increase as more is known about the damages of long-term exposure to very low levels of any one pollutant or many in combination. It must be emphasized, however, that these cost estimates only crudely approximate the damages from air pollution. [1971 CEQ Report, p. 107]

You pay these costs and breathe the effluents without any choice; frequently you don't even know about it, since the most deadly pollutants are the ones you don't see or smell.

These are really expenses of industry which are being passed on to you. Since you are paying some of their bills, it seems fair to ask what industry is paying. Using their own figures, which have not always deserved maximum credibility, in 1970 $1.34 billion was invested in air pollution control equipment. The EPA estimates that private investment in air pollution control equipment necessary to meet current and projected standards for the 1970-1975 period will be about $22.1 billion [1971 CEQ Report, p. 115]—a spending rate about four times what industry presently claims to be investing. That kind of expenditure is not going to be made by industry because of exhortation or conscience. The smell of pollution is still the smell of money for American business. That is a fundamental point to keep in mind. Your goal is to make it cheaper—and maybe more comfortable—for industry to clean up than to pollute.

The Clean Air Act [42 U.S.C. 1857 *et seq.* (hereinafter cited by section of the Act)] leaves a great deal to be desired. But before it was amended by the Clean Air Amendments of 1970 [Pub. L. No. 91-604, 31 December 1970], the Clean Air Act was an environmental disaster, as indicated by the quotation opening this chapter. If you read it, and you should (get a copy from the Senate Public Works Committee, Room 4202, New Senate Office Building, Washington, D.C., 20510), it will impress you with its equivocation, its opportunities for delay, and its questionable efficacy. But it and the National Environmental Policy Act [42 U.S.C. 4321 *et seq.*] are the only federal statutes available on air pollution. For a description of how the 1970 amendments were passed, and some stronger alternatives, see *Earth Tool Kit,* edited by Environmental Action Committee (New York: Pocket Books, 1971, pp. 329-334).

The federal government first officially recognized that there was an air pollution problem in 1955. That year Congress enacted legislation authorizing the federal government to conduct research and provide technical assistance to states for control of air pollution. The 1963 Clean Air Act established a program to provide grants to assist states in creating and maintaining pollution control agencies. It also provided a mechanism for direct federal action against interstate air pollution problems. A cumbersome and protracted abatement procedure gave the federal government power to require interstate polluters to reduce or halt their emissions. In 1970 that procedure was repealed for any pollutant covered by ambient air standards, although recommendations and orders issued for other pollutants before 1970 are still in effect. In 1965 a step was taken toward bringing under control the largest single source of air pollution, the automobile. The Clean Air Act amendments of that year authorized mandatory emission standards for motor vehicles beginning with the 1968 model year. In 1967 the Air Quality Act (actually a series of amendments to the Clean Air Act) was adopted. The largely useless provisions of that law are of little practical importance now in view of the 1970 amendments.

The earlier legislation is sometimes justified as having been necessary for gaining "insight" and "experience"—euphemisms for learning that those legislative gestures didn't work. Now we are essentially starting from scratch with the Clean Air Act Amendments of 1970. The new law is weak, but at this point there is nothing to do but try to make it work. One of the major reasons for earlier failures was the absence of citizen militance about enforcement. Inordinate discretion placed in the hands of administrators, together with failure of citizen surveillance, are an invitation for special interests to do what they do best—delay and obfuscate. The 1970 Clean Air Amendments won't be any better than their predecessors unless there is concerted effort by citizens throughout the entire process of their enforcement.

Air pollution control is a complex matter, technically and legally, but in one sense the problem is painfully simple: Identify the source of pollution and prescribe a method for reducing ("abating") it. But that is not the way things are done. Control technology in many fields is still behind what it would be if industry were willing to invest the money required for its development. And the law is a maze, with twists and dead ends reflecting the pressures placed upon legislators not to do what should have been done. The purpose of this section is to guide you through that statutory maze.

You will have to deal with people as much as with words on paper. To help you get to the right ones quickly, an organization chart of EPA is contained in Appendix 15-B (p. 860). Call these people directly whenever you have a problem which falls within their jurisdiction. The best way to stay informed about proposed EPA actions is to read the *Federal Register* regularly (see p. 26 for information on how to get it). Proposed actions are usually announced there, with a period during which you can submit comments. EPA publishes a free Citizens' Bulletin that contains summaries of major EPA actions, future hearings, and pending rule making. Any citizen can be put on the mailing list by writing the Office of Public Affairs, Environmental Protection Agency, Washington, D.C. 20460. Several of the national conservation and environmental protection organizations print informative newsletters (see Appendix 18-B, p. 904). Commercial newsletters, which frankly specialize in inside and advance information, are invaluable but expensive tools. Two of the best are *Air and Water News* ($145 per year—Trends Publishing Co., 807 New Center Bldg., Detroit, Mich. 48202) and the *Environmental Health Newsletter* ($60 per year— Gershon Fishbein, Publisher, 1097 National Press Building, Washington, D.C. 20004).

The answers to your questions aren't all in the EPA. Section 101 of the Clean Air Act states that ". . . the prevention and control of air pollution at its source is the primary responsibility of States and local governments. . . ." Throughout the Act there is an explicit and implicit assumption that enforcement will be a cooperative effort by local, state, and federal agencies. This means that information and assistance not available from an agency at one level of government may be available from one of the others. It also means that your rights under local law are in large part dictated by federal statutes and regulations. For instance, Section 114 of the Act requires that virtually all information collected by EPA or a state agency from individual sources be available to the public, unless the Administrator of EPA has made a specific finding that the information is entitled to protection as a trade secret. Even trade secret information can be made publicly available if relevant to a proceeding under the Act. EPA may not exempt emission data from public access under any circumstances. This is a federal right of public access which over-rides any state decisions that information be kept confidential. So whenever you are denied assistance or information by a state or local agency, it may be useful to make it clear that you are asserting a right under the federal statute, and that you are prepared to go to EPA, or to court, for assistance.

Stationary sources of pollution, such as factories, make better targets for your efforts than the moving ones (automobiles). The first step is to find out in what "air quality control region" the pollution source is located. Under Section 107 of the Act EPA designates part of a state or states as an "air quality control region," composed of areas that have a common air pollution problem because of geographic characteristics, weather, or patterns of population and industry. But you won't find any signs saying you are entering the Eastern Washington-Northern Idaho Interstate Air Quality Control Region. The regions are only supposed to make cooperation easier between other governmental units, and have no political power. The laws and rules for dealing with the common problem are determined by state, local, and federal governments. Because you deal with all the government units in an area, some of them, such as the New York-New Jersey-Connecticut (Metropolitan Areas) air quality control region, will make your job more difficult. All of the air quality control regions in the country have now been designated by EPA, and your first step is to find out which one you are in.

Call or write your state pollution control agency or your EPA regional office for a description of the boundaries and for information about the pollution problems of your region. Documents called Consultation Reports are available for some major regions, although the consultation report approach has been dropped and no more will be prepared. Informal descriptions and consultation reports will describe industrial and pollution problems, with maps showing pollution concentrations at various points in the region.

Examine the information to determine the boundaries of your region. Look for the major pollution sources likely to affect the quality of air in your community. If your region does not contain a major pollution source, it may be affected by another abatement plan, and you may want to contact clean air groups in the other region to coordinate your efforts. Or you may want to petition your state governor and the EPA administrator to redesignate the region in a more logical manner.

Ask your regional EPA office and the environmental or public health departments of local universities to tell you the major sources of pollution (by name) and the results of emission inventories (listed by pollutants). Also ask for the annual reports of ambient pollution levels in the region for the last several years. These levels should be expressed in the same terms as the national ambient air quality standards (described later).

Section 108 of the Act requires EPA to publish Air Quality Criteria Reports for pollutants to be controlled. These are important documents which survey most of the important studies conducted on these pollutants. They are, in effect, the federal government's definitive statement on the adverse health effects of exposure to these pollutants. Currently there are six Criteria Reports—for particulate matter, sulfur oxides, carbon monoxide, hydrocarbons, nitrogen oxides, and photochemical oxidants. Simplified versions of the Reports, called "Summary and Conclusions," are available free of charge from EPA's Office of Public Affairs.

Simultaneous with issuance of criteria documents, EPA issues corresponding Control Techniques Reports which survey the methods available to reduce the levels of the pollutants. Both the Control Techniques Reports and the Air Quality Criteria Reports are available from the Government Printing Office (G.P.O.) for $1 to $1.50 per copy. It is important to get these reports and study them closely for two reasons. First, before a pollutant can become a candidate for control (that is, before a national ambient air quality standard can be issued), a Criteria Report must have been issued by EPA. Under Section 108(a) of the Act, the Administrator has an obligation to issue a criteria report for any pollutant which in his judgment has an adverse effect on health. Pressure must be kept on EPA to keep issuing these reports on a systematic basis. If you are concerned about a pollutant for which no Criteria Report has been issued, and which is not being controlled as a "hazardous substance" (see below), you should write directly to the Administrator.

The second reason for studying the Criteria Report is that, unless your state decides to be more severe, the standard limiting a pollutant will be the national ambient air quality standard. Section 116 of the law specifically gives states the power to set and enforce ambient air standards which are more strict than national ambient air quality standards. Study the Criteria Report and talk to experts about new knowledge in the field (remember that the reports have not been regularly updated). You may decide that your region should adopt a standard tougher than the national standard.

The Control Techniques documents will be important tools in the most critical element in the process—the development and enforcement of plans to implement the standards in your region. The Control

Technique Reports survey methods available to bring about a reduction in levels of pollutants, such as process changes, control equipment, and fuel substitution. They will be useful texts when studying implementation plans, but remember that they are only for general information. It will take more digging when you get to specific problems and control techniques.

Under Section 109 of the Act, the Administrator is required to issue national primary and secondary ambient air quality standards for a pollutant within ninety days after a Criteria Report has been published for it. An ambient air standard basically sets maximum limits on a pollutant in the air around you, as opposed to maximum emission standards for a pollutant as it is produced at the source. Unless a state decides to set and enforce more stringent standards, under the authority stated in Section 116 of the Act, the national ambient air quality standards become the standards in your region.

Ambient air quality standards are supposed to be based on the conclusions of the Criteria Reports, with the addition of a safety margin. The primary standards are based on judgments by the Administrator as to what minimal standards are adequate to protect public health, and they are supposed to be achieved within three years after a plan for implementation is approved.

Secondary national ambient air quality standards are based on the Administrator's judgment as to the levels necessary to protect what the law calls "the public welfare"—essentially levels at which effects on vegetation have been observed. The law does not specify a time within which the secondary levels have to be achieved, but only says that it must be "reasonable." See Appendix 15-C (p. 861) for primary and secondary ambient air quality standards.

The national primary and secondary ambient air quality standards for the six pollutants which have been the subject of Criteria Reports are in Part 50 of Title 40 of the Code of Federal Regulations (hereinafter cited as 40 C.F.R. 50) (Title 40 of the C.F.R. contains all except the most recent regulations. It was revised on 1 January 1973. This is an absolute must for any environmentally concerned citizen and is available for $1.75 from the G.P.O.) It is technical, but it is included so that readers with the technical expertise can understand the methods of sampling and measurement of the standards. Legally, there is nothing to keep the standards from being changed whenever new knowledge about dangers of a pollutant are learned. But in practice it will probably take considerable effort to get them changed.

Ambient air quality standards are only goals. They are technical descriptions of what clean (or at least cleaner) air should be. But to be effective they must be translated into specific control strategies. That is what a state's implementation plan is for. As you may suspect, an implementation plan is a complicated mass of documents. But it is critical for you to be aware of its main elements. One of the most important opportunities for citizen access in formulating an implementation plan is the public hearing.

Section 110(a)(1) of the Act requires each state to submit—within nine months after the adoption of national standards—a plan for the implementation and maintenance of those primary and secondary ambient air quality standards within the state. The law also requires that public hearings be held on the implementation plan after reasonable public notice. EPA regulations [40 C.F.R. 51.4] issued under this provision of the law define a "reasonable" period as at least thirty days prior to the hearing. They also require that notice be given to the public in the form of prominent advertisements announcing the dates and places of the hearings, "and the availability of the principal portions of the proposed plan including, as a minimum, all rules and regulations which are proposed to be included in such plan, for public inspection in at least one location in each region to which the plan will apply." The state is also required to maintain a record of the hearings which must at least contain a list of the witnesses and the text of each presentation. Whether you testify for or against a plan, make sure you are well prepared for the hearing. This is a checklist to use in preparing for hearings.

1. Will the plan be available at several places in the region, or just in one place?
2. Will the hearing on the plan for your region be held at a convenient place within the region, or at the state capitol?
3. Will the hearing cover only the plan for your region or will there be one plenary hearing for all plans affecting the state? (Ideally, each region should have its own hearing followed by a general hearing to consider the combined effect of such plans. Of course, this question doesn't apply if your state contains only one region.)
4. Will separate hearings be held on the implementation plan for each pollutant or will the plans for all six be considered together?
5. Are the hearings scheduled at a convenient time? (Industry lobbyists are available from nine to five on weekdays, while you probably are not. Evening and weekend hearings are better.)

6. What are the ground rules for the hearings, such as time allotments for witnesses and opportunities to ask questions? You don't have to be an expert on administrative law to get a sense of whether or not the procedures are fair.
7. How will witnesses be scheduled? (Some companies like to get on early, when press and television are present. Others prefer not to appear at all, but just submit their testimony for the record. Decide for yourself who the participants in a fair hearing should be and what a reasonable schedule of witnesses should look like.)

If you follow through on many of the suggestions in the checklist, you are likely to be told that you are delaying the process of developing an implementation plan. It is true that public participation takes time, but all too often "administrative convenience" and "expedience" have resulted in minimal or illusory control.

State implementation plans must be submitted to EPA for approval, and EPA has the power to disapprove all or part of a plan and issue a substitute. Under Section 110(a)(1) of the Act, a state must submit an implementation plan within nine months after a national standard is promulgated. (Six standards have been promulgated as of this writing and the states must submit plans indicating what they will do to control all six. As new standards are issued for additional pollutants, the states will have to adopt additional measures—once again after public hearings—to bring those pollutants under control.) Within four months after a plan is submitted by a state, EPA is required by Section 110(a)(2) to either approve or disapprove it.

Under Section 110(c), EPA must promulgate all or part of its own plan for the state if the state fails to submit a plan, or if EPA determines that the state's plan is inadequate, or if the state fails to revise the plan in accordance with EPA instructions within sixty days. Whenever it becomes necessary for EPA to promulgate a plan or a portion of a plan, it must be done within six months of the date when the states were required to submit plans. As of January 1973, EPA had approved implementation plans submitted by twenty-four states. For the remaining twenty-six states, EPA has proposed and/or finally promulgated implementation plans.

In two recent lawsuits against EPA, portions of the approved implementation plans have been held invalid. In *Sierra Club* v. *Ruckelshaus*, Civil Action No. 1031-72, the District Court for the District of Columbia held, and the Court of Appeals affirmed, that EPA could not approve an implementation plan unless it contained provisions guarding against deterioration of existing levels of air quality which were already better than the standards. By a 4-4 decision without opinion, the Supreme Court effectively upheld the lower courts. EPA is now requiring all state implementation plans to be revised to prevent significant deterioration of ambient air levels already purer than the standards. In *Natural Resources Defense Council* v. *EPA,* the Court of Appeals for the District of Columbia ordered EPA to rescind its decision allowing seventeen states (Alabama, Arizona, California, Colorado, Indiana, Kansas, Maryland, Massachusetts, Minnesota, Missouri, New Jersey, New York, Ohio, Pennsylvania, Texas, Utah, and Washington) an additional two years (until May 1977) to come into compliance. Revised implementation plans including transportation controls had to be submitted to EPA by 15 April 1973. In addition, the court ordered EPA to review all state implementation plans to ensure that they contain sufficient provisions to guarantee maintenance of the standards beyond 31 May 1975.

Because the process of developing an implementation plan is so complex, and because so many states lack the expertise—or will—to do an effective job, EPA has issued guidelines entitled "Requirements for Preparation, Adoption and Submittal of Implementation Plans." The proposed rules were first announced in the *Federal Register* in April 1971. After receipt of comments, EPA drafted a revised and improved "June version." The final regulations were announced in August, but there had been a lot of maneuvering between April and August. The proposed guidelines were reviewed by the President's Office of Management and Budget (OMB). Review of proposed regulations by other federal agencies is one of the little-known but critically important functions of OMB. This review function is justified on the ground that it "coordinates" government regulations and does not make substantive changes in policy. Therefore, OMB has never felt compelled to make its proceedings public—much less involve the public in the process.

The result is an object lesson in how things get done, or, as in this case, undone, behind the scenes in Washington. The Department of Commerce, the traditional and statutory spokesman for business in the federal government, objected strenuously to certain sections of the proposed guidelines, and the final guidelines announced in August reflected this pressure. Some useful and effective provisions, such as a requirement to use motor vehicle inspections, were deleted entirely; in other cases small word changes colored the effect of the final rules so that health considerations became less important than they were in the earlier versions. Instead, "economic considerations" have been given greater importance [Hearings on Implementation of the Clean Air Act Amendments of 1970 Before the Senate Public Works Comm., 92nd Cong., 2d Sess. 1972, Part 1].

But remember that these guidelines were to set out *minimum* requirements for state plans. The fact that the minimum requirements were minimized even further by secret pressure doesn't mean that your state can't follow the guidelines drafted in June. The EPA can reject a plan because it does too little, but a plan cannot be rejected because it is too effective, the Department of Commerce and OMB notwithstanding. The following discussion of implementation plan requirements will indicate some of the areas where the stronger proposed guidelines ought to be used. But you should examine both sets of guidelines very closely, particularly since the final guidelines will be relied on by your opponents. The next few pages state some of the questions you should ask as you study your implementation plan. Unless otherwise indicated, Section number references apply to the final guidelines.

What are the priorities set for your region? 40 C.F.R. 51.3 establishes a system of classification for regions to reflect the severity of concentrations by particular pollutants. For sulfur oxides and particulates, a region is classified as Priority I, II, or III. For carbon monoxide, photochemical oxidants, nitrogen dioxide, and hydrocarbons regions are classified as either Priority I or III. In short, there is no across-the-board priority category, and a region may be Priority I with respect to one pollutant and Priority II or III with respect to others. The reason for the priority ranking system is explained this way:

> The requirements of this part vary according to the classification of each region, in order that the time and resources to be expended in developing the plan for that region, as well as the substantive content of the plan will be commensurate with the complexity of the air pollution problem.

In other words, the plan should give more attention and stricter controls to high-priority pollutants.

Do the priority rankings make sense for your region? In answering this question, note that under the original guidelines (Section 420.02) Priority I classifications were more stringent for some pollutants. They were changed in the final guidelines from twenty-one milligrams per cubic meter to fifty-five micrograms per cubic meter for carbon monoxide; from 100 micrograms per cubic meter (the primary standard) to

110 micrograms per cubic meter for nitrogen oxide; and from 170 to 195 micrograms per cubic meter for photochemical oxidants.

Does the plan contain a "nondegradation" clause? This is essentially a commitment that in places where the quality of the air is better than the national standards, pollution levels will not be permitted to increase up to the level of the national standards. Under *Sierra Club* v. *Ruckelshaus* discussed above, it must contain such a provision.

Have you considered the need for standards stricter than the national ambient air quality standards? Section 116 of the Clean Air Act clearly preserves this right for the states. Raise this question at implementation plan hearings, even if there is little hope for success at that point. It can lay the groundwork for a later call for your governor to propose stronger standards and to amend the implementation plan accordingly.

Does the plan contain the legal authority required by the EPA? 40 C.F.R. 51.11 lists six functions for which the state must have sufficient legal authority:

1. To adopt emission standards sufficient to assure attainment and maintenance of the national standards.
2. To enforce applicable laws, regulations, and standards, and to seek injunctive relief.
3. To abate pollution in emergency episodes comparable to the power given the federal government by Section 303 of the Clean Air Act (see 40 C.F.R. 51.16 and Appendix L of the final guidelines).
4. To prevent construction, modification, or operation of any stationary source of pollution where the attainment or maintenance of the national standard will be prevented.
5. To obtain any information and make any inspections or tests necessary to determine whether a source is complying with the law.
6. To require owners or operators of stationary sources to monitor their own emissions and report them, and to make this data public.

Does the plan establish a state-wide permit system and land use controls for stationary sources? Does it set up a motor vehicle inspection program and impose controls on transportation? The proposed April rules (Section 420.11, items 4 and 7) would have made these elements a mandatory part of an acceptable implementation plan, but the requirements were either eliminated or de-emphasized in the final guidelines, leaving it up to the individual states to impose them.

The original guidelines would have required that a state employ what is probably the most efficient method of determining that new plants and modifications to existing plants comply with emission limitations—state-wide permit programs. Briefly, under such a system the owner of a projected plant or one to be modified would apply for a permit, in much the same way that he now applies for a building permit. The application process would make it easier for the state to receive information on projected processes and emissions, and permits would be granted only under conditions consistent with the region's implementation plan. The final guidelines do not make permit programs mandatory, although 40 C.F.R. 51.18 does require the state to review new sources and modifications—without indicating how.

Land use controls and motor vehicle inspection systems are still mentioned in the final guidelines, but they are no longer mandatory. The guidelines only say that where these approaches are adopted the state shall indicate its timetable for obtaining the legal authority to carry out these measures.

What are the core elements of the plan's control strategy? The June version of the guidelines contained Appendix B, which was a model set of fairly comprehensive air pollution control regulations. Appendix B was described in the proposed guidelines as being the basis, although not necessarily the entire answer, for an adequate control program. As a result of OMB machinations, Appendix B was "recast" in the final guidelines as a series of recommendations. Nevertheless, the original Appendix B provides a model for the core of the control strategy in fairly clear statutory language that could be adopted almost verbatim by your state. The original Appendix B provides a model for such important elements as:

1. A permit system for new construction or modification of existing plants.
2. Monitoring, records, and reporting by sources of pollution.
3. Sampling and testing methods.
4. Reporting malfunctions of air pollution control equipment.
5. A procedure for determining the existence of and dealing with air pollution emergency episodes.
6. Compliance schedules.
7. Specified emission control levels for all pollutants covered by national standards.

The regulations covering your region should be evaluated against the June version of Appendix B.

What are the other elements of the control strategy? Several of these, such as land use controls, a motor vehicle inspection program, and transportation controls, have been mentioned earlier. The June guidelines (Section 420.14) were more specific about transportation controls as a means of reducing automotive pollutants (carbon monoxide, hydrocarbons, photochemical oxidants, and nitrogen oxides). The final guidelines are, at best, vague about transportation controls. But the list from the earlier guidelines is useful:

1. Controls requiring the installation of emission control devices on motor vehicles in use. (Standards for new vehicles are prescribed only by the federal government, and by the State of California for cars sold in that state.)
2. Controls requiring that motor vehicle fleets, both governmental and commercial, convert to low emission fuels such as liquefied natural gas or liquefied petroleum gas.
3. Controls to reduce traffic, particularly in rush hours, such as commuter taxes, gasoline rationing, parking limitations, staggered work hours, or restrictions on motor vehicle idling time.
4. Expansion or promotion of the use of mass transportation facilities through measures such as increases in frequency, convenience, and passenger-carrying capacity of mass transportation systems; subsidization of the costs of operating such systems; and providing special bus lanes on major streets and highways.

The Natural Resources Defense Council has issued a *Citizens' Guide to Transportation Control Strategies Under the Clean Air Act,* which is available by writing to them at 36 West 44 Street, New York, N.Y. 10036. In prescribing additional requirements for the California (Los Angeles) implementation plan, former EPA Administrator Ruckelshaus required motor vehicle gasoline rationing, retrofitting of used motor vehicles, conversion of fleet vehicles to liquid petroleum or natural gas, vehicle inspections, and controls on evaporative emissions at gasoline stations and other supply sources [38 *Fed. Reg.* 2194 (1973)].

What does the compliance schedule look like? 40 C.F.R. 51.15 takes into account the fact that an effective plan must contain legally enforceable compliance schedules so that rules and regulations on the books do not become hypothetical. Compliance schedules may be submitted to the EPA after submission of the implementation plan itself. The reason for this delay is to give the states time to negotiate specific compliance with each of the major sources of pollution in the region. Therefore, while the compliance schedule may not be available when the implementation plan is at the public hearing stage, the state's plans for negotiation should be. Make sure the worst sources of pollution are the first on the list for compliance negotiation.

If a primary standard is involved, compliance is not supposed to take more than three years—unless an extension is granted. The guidelines require that whenever compliance will take more than eighteen months, the compliance schedule must indicate periodic progress toward total compliance during that period. In other words, if a facility is given twenty-four months to come into compliance, it may not continue on a pollution-as-usual basis for the first twenty months and then install the necessary control equipment during the final four months. Progress toward compliance must be in regular stages throughout the twenty-four month period.

It is not clear from the guidelines whether the compliance schedules or reports on progress toward meeting the compliance schedules must be made public. You should insist that they be, and that the state guarantee its commitment to make them public by stating so in its rules and regulations.

There are several surveillance and reporting requirements of which you should be aware in order to monitor the progress of an implementation plan:

1. 40 C.F.R. 51.17 requires the plan to provide for an air quality surveillance system which would be operational within two years of the plan's approval. The section contains details regarding the number and, in certain cases, the placement of monitoring equipment. A latter-day Archimedes would tell you that he can give you any quality of air you want if you let him choose the location of the monitoring equipment. Get an expert technical opinion on the appropriate location of monitoring equipment in your region. It is not clear from this section whether this data must be made public, but you should make sure that it is.

2. 40 C.F.R. 51.19 requires each plan to provide for regular reporting and monitoring of emissions by the sources themselves. 40 C.F.R. 51.10 requires that all data concerning emissions from specific sources be correlated with applicable emission limitations or other measures. It is clear from the guidelines that this

information must be publicly available. Get it.

3. 40 C.F.R. 51.7 requires that the states submit quarterly and semiannual reports to EPA "on air quality . . . in a manner which shall be prescribed by the Administrator." The format for these reports is based on existing air pollution monitoring forms [38 *Fed. Reg.* 3083 (1973)]. Since the reports include mostly emission data, 114(c) of the Clean Air Act should require disclosure. Persuade your local officials to commit themselves to a policy of making their reports to EPA public.

You should be aware of the various procedures for revising the implementation plan and for extending guidelines. According to 40 C.F.R. 51.6, plans will have to be revised from time to time to account for changes such as new national air quality standards, improved technology, new emission taxes, or a finding by the Administrator of EPA that the plan is inadequate. In order for revisions to be adopted, the revised plan must be resubmitted to public hearings and then approved by the Administrator. Make sure that no revised plan is submitted to EPA without prior notice and public hearings.

40 C.F.R. 30 (Subpart C) of the guidelines sets out the provisions for three different kinds of extensions:

1. A two-year extension of the time that a Priority I region in a state must comply with the national primary air quality standard.
2. An eighteen-month extension of the deadline for submitting that portion of an implementation plan for any national secondary air quality standard.
3. A one-year postponement of a plan's control strategy applicable to certain specified sources of pollution.

Read the guidelines carefully to understand the specific conditions that must be met before the Administrator of EPA can grant such extensions.

According to Section 113 of the Act, the federal government may enforce an implementation plan, a new source performance standard, or a hazardous substance standard through orders or injunctions if a state fails to do the job properly. Citizen groups have the right to feed any information they discover concerning violations directly to the Administrator. After a party has been notified of his violation, he is subject to fines of up to $25,000 per day and up to one year in jail if he knowingly does not comply. For a second conviction, the violator is subject to fines up to $50,000 per day of violation or up to two years in prison, or both.

Section 105 of the Act sets up an elaborate program of federal grants to initiate and maintain state air pollution control agencies, and many states would have no programs at all today if it were not for Section 105. It is natural to think that an agency doing a poor job would improve with more money. But it is worth considering that more money might just mean more of a poor job. The law states that the Administrator must have assurances that the state is capable of developing a comprehensive air pollution program, and one of the requirements of the implementation plan is a fairly detailed report from the state agency indicating its capability to enforce the plan. In addition, every contract for a grant between EPA and a state contains goals which the state agency must achieve in order to be eligible for continued funding. Little real attention is paid to these conditions in the law or the contracts. But if your state agency is doing poorly for reasons that have more to do with ineptitude than poverty, consider bringing it to the attention of the Administrator, perhaps through a legal action asking him not to send good money after bad to useless state agencies. Regional directors routinely send evaluations of state programs to EPA national headquarters. Get copies of these as a first step in evaluating your agency's performance.

You can't have much impact on the way EPA sets national emission standards for automobiles, but you can play an important role in seeing to it that standards are used. Section 202 of the Act presents a novel legal approach to environmental problems. It contains a deadline for a specified reduction in auto emission levels. In 1970 Congress determined that one of the problems in reducing automotive emissions was that leaving it to administrators to set the standards didn't work. The standards set under this discretionary power were not only lax, but also poorly enforced.

Section 202 requires that the hydrocarbons and carbon monoxide standards for 1975 model year cars be set at levels 90 percent below the levels set for 1970. The levels applicable to 1975 model year cars are 3.1 grams per vehicle mile of carbon monoxide and 0.41 grams per vehicle mile for hydrocarbons [40 C.F.R. 85.21]. These numbers are not literally 90 percent reductions below the standards for 1970. The reason for this, according to EPA, is that a new test procedure for determining compliance (*Federal Register*, 2 July 1971) will be used after 1972. Therefore, what EPA claimed to do was to work out an "equivalency" for the 1970 standard based on the new test, and then reduce this equivalency by 90 percent.

The Natural Resources Defense Council filed suit in the District Court for the District of Columbia to require EPA to set more stringent standards. The court dismissed the suit by finding the setting of the new standards "to be a reasonable exercise of the discretion necessary to correlate a fixed directive of the statute with evolving test procedures in a new technological area of governmental regulation" [Memorandum Opinion and Order at 2, *Natural Resources Defense Council* v. *Ruckelshaus,* Civil Action No. 2598-71 (5 May 1972)]. As a result, people in major urban areas will have to resort to transportation controls such as have been proposed for Los Angeles to make up for the increased emissions from motor vehicles. In any event, the 1975 standard will, if properly enforced, bring about a substantial reduction in these automotive pollutants.

Section 202 also requires that the 1976 standard for oxides of nitrogen be 90 percent below the average emissions of this pollutant in 1970 vehicles. There was no 1970 standard for oxides of nitrogen to use as a base, so "actual" levels are used (*Federal Register*, 21 January 1970). The NO_x standard for 1976 is 0.4 grams per mile [40 C.F.R. 85.21].

Predictably, the auto industry has resisted these controls, arguing that Section 202 attempts the impossible feat of legislating technology. The industry says that control systems are not presently available and that it is highly questionable whether they can be developed in time for mass production in 1975 and 1976. EPA's answer has been that it has little choice under the statute but to prescribe the 90 percent reductions that Congress ordered. (Remember that the 90 percent reduction is the questionable result of the changed test procedure.) The stakes in this argument are high. While the law (Section 205) contains provisions for fairly stiff fines, this is not what the automakers are worried about. Section 203 of the law says that new automobiles which do not meet the standards cannot be sold in interstate commerce. In simple terms, this means that if the automakers cannot meet the standards, they cannot sell cars.

In May 1972 EPA discovered that the Ford Motor Company had conducted unallowed maintenance during required testing procedures on 1973 cars so that they emitted fewer pollutants than they otherwise would have. Ford was allowed to ship 1973 models to their dealerships when new initial testing indicated that emission standards would be met. Ford only had to run limited 50,000-mile durability tests before the cars could be sold. An EPA request to the Justice Department that criminal charges be brought against the responsible Ford officials was rejected but the Justice Department imposed fines totaling seven million dollars on Ford Motor Company for the violations.

Ford Motor Company is not alone in attempts to circumvent the emission standards. In January 1973 EPA ordered American Motors, Chrysler, Ford, and General Motors to remove "defeat devices" from all 1973 vehicles manufactured after 15 March 1973. The devices would cut out portions of the emission control systems under conditions not tested by EPA but encountered during the course of normal driving. Of course EPA gave these manufacturers a tremendous concession when it quietly refused to order the manufacturers to recall already sold 1973 vehicles for removal of the devices.

What impact can you have on the enforcement of the law as it relates to automobiles? There are a number of areas where interested citizens and citizen groups can have some impact.

The auto industry has an enormous stake in perpetuating the Internal Combustion Engine (ICE). It claims to have examined and to be continuing to examine possible alternatives. Yet not until forced to reveal research and development expenditures under threat of subpoena in the May 1972 suspension proceedings would the auto industry release even the most rudimentary information concerning the amount of money being spent on such alternatives—a very small sum compared to resources available. (The amount of money General Motors claims to spend on *all* auto pollution research—most of it related to perpetuation of the ICE—is about one-half its annual advertising budget). There is no reason why such detailed disclosure should not be part of a state's implementation plan. At the same time, the federal government is spending paltry sums (about $25 million) to examine the feasibility of alternatives on its own. Even so, it has no program to develop working prototypes of alternative vehicles. Even if alternatives to the ICE cannot be developed in time for the 1975-1976 deadlines, they will be needed later. Those years of anticipated changes will not bring about the end of the auto pollution problem. Much more must be done during the latter half of the 1970s. The 1971 CEQ Report makes this clear; ". . . in the long run, if the number of cars on the road continues to increase at the present rate, even the effect of these controls eventually could be negated—unless something else is done" [1971 CEQ Report, p. 213]. The development of alternative prototypes is within the capabilities of both the federal government and larger state governments.

One small opportunity for the federal government to keep informed

WORKING ON THE SYSTEM

about possible alternatives to the ICE is the Federal Clean Car Incentive Program (FCCIP). Developers lease prototype vehicles to the federal government for evaluation. When a prototype passes emission and performance tests, ten to one hundred additional vehicles may be purchased for further testing. If satisfactory emission and performance levels are maintained, the auto is then eligible for certification as a low pollution vehicle.

Section 212 of the Act creates a Low Emission Vehicle Certification Board which has the power to substitute for conventional autos those which have been certified by the EPA as low emission vehicles. Certified cars chosen by the board will be purchased for the federal government's own use at premium prices up to twice what it would normally pay for conventional vehicles. Your state plan can include procedures which follow the federal government's efforts in this area. The state could require that low emission vehicles be purchased for official use and also that large fleets, such as taxicabs, employ only low emission vehicles certified under the federal program. Information about the FCCIP and the low emissions purchase program may be obtained from EPA's Office of Air Programs, (FCCIP), 2565 Plymouth Road, Ann Arbor, Michigan 48105.

Many advances in automotive technology which have become standard parts of today's automobile were developed by lone inventors and small companies. The same promise holds true for automotive emissions control, since the lone inventor and small company do not have the same investment in the ICE as the established giants. The programs described above are very halting first steps toward providing some incentives for the breakthroughs that will be needed in this field. These programs require substantial initial investment with little assistance available from the federal government until the prototypes can be delivered for testing.

For the inventor who has an idea but no capital, EPA has no program for systematically evaluating the hundreds, perhaps thousands of ideas offered to it. The lone inventor should not give up, however. Continued requests could result in the creation of such a program. Ideas and requests for government assistance should be brought to the attention of Dr. Stanley Greenfield, EPA's Assistant Administrator for Research and Monitoring. Copies of this correspondence and additional requests for assistance should be sent to your members of Congress.

Dealing with the "three basic" automotive pollutants will not necessarily remove all of the health problems associated with automotive emissions. There are several other automotive pollutants which are not being dealt with effectively. For example, lead is toxic, and 96 percent of the lead particulate matter found in the atmosphere results from gasoline-leaded fuels. The federal government is presently quibbling over the effects of "low-level, prolonged exposure"—dosages not large enough to kill you on the spot, but which many scientists believe are dangerous over a period of time. There is no technological reason for lead to be in gasoline. The issue is essentially economic: Manufacturers find it cheaper to get gasolines up to needed octane levels by adding lead rather than by improving their refining techniques.

Other automotive pollutants such as particulate matters, including asbestos from brake linings and organic particles from tires as well as exhaust gas particles, aldehydes and other carbonyl compounds, and nitrogen compounds other than nitrogen oxides (e.g., ammonia), are all emitted from the automobile. EPA's investigation into the effects of exposure to these chemicals is minimal, and plans for control are non-existent.

It is important to remember that Section 209 of the Act only keeps the states from establishing emission standards for *new* motor vehicles. The rule of thumb is that it takes about ten years for something close to a complete turnover in our national supply of automobiles. There were no national controls until 1968, and almost everything which has been done until now can be discounted because of the poor reliability of the so-called control systems. Your state can make a valuable contribution toward solving the problem by requiring, as part of its implementation plan, the retrofitting of all used motor vehicles with effective emission control devices when such devices become available. (Some automobile companies claim to have developed such devices, but their effectiveness is still unknown.) Indeed, the guidelines for implementation plans, which were substantially amended after OMB pressure, suggested this as one form of transportation controls (Section 420.14).

An adequate public response to the air pollution problem cannot be developed until we depart from the absurdly primitive methods we have chosen to move people around our nation and our cities. The nation now has about 100 million automobiles, or a separate transportation system for almost every two people in the country. At the same time, it cannot boast of a single mass transit system which is not inconvenient, costly, or dehumanizing. (A potential exception, it is hoped, will be San Francisco's Bay Area Rapid Transit System.) To a great extent we can thank the auto manufacturers and others who benefit from roads for this gross imbalance. Truckers, road builders, cement and asphalt manufacturers, oil companies, and automobile drivers' associations all have linked arms with the auto industry to see that more than $21 billion is spent annually on highway construction.

The main instrumentality for perpetuating this distortion of rational priorities is the federal government's Highway Trust Fund. The Fund—the brainchild of former Congressman Fallon of Maryland and the road lobby—is designed to assure that specially earmarked funds will always be available for concrete swaths. Taxes collected on gasoline, tires, and automobile accessories are segregated from the general revenues for this purpose. So while more than $4 billion comes out of this Fund each year to assist in the massive job of paving over the nation, the federal government in 1972 spent less than $400 million (or less than the auto industry's advertising budget) for mass transit. You can learn more about what you can do to improve mass transit by communicating with The Highway Action Coalition, Room 731, 1346 Connecticut Avenue, N.W., Washington, D.C. 20036 (202-833-1845).

What can be done about lead and other dangerous additives to gasoline? Section 211 of the Act gives EPA power to require that all additives to gasoline be registered; it may also require the manufacturer to conduct tests on the health effects of such additives. This section also empowers EPA to ban the use of any additive which the Administrator determines to be a danger to the public health or welfare, or which will impair the operation of any emission control device. This second basis for banning an additive may eventually lead to the removal of lead. Among the devices which auto manufacturers are testing in order to meet the 1975-1976 deadlines is one called a catalytic converter. It has been found that the lead in gasoline very quickly impairs the operation of the converter, so that it does not do the job it should to reduce other emissions. Since most 1975 cars will be equipped with catalytic converters, EPA has ordered gasoline distributors to provide at least one grade of lead-free gasoline (less than 0.05 gram per gallon) by 1 July 1974 at each service station [38 *Fed. Reg.* 1254]. If the auto industry decides to go entirely with catalytic converters after 1975, then all lead gasoline will necessarily be banned by the time pre-1975 cars are phased out (about 1984).

In the meantime, EPA continues to study the health effects of lead. (Adverse health effects are the alternative justification for banning the additive.) On 10 January 1973 EPA proposed a phasedown of lead in gasoline, beginning with 2.0 grams per gallon on 1 January 1975 and reducing to 1.25 grams per gallon after 1 January 1978 [38 *Fed. Reg.* 1258]. Because this represented at least a one-year delay in reduction of gasoline lead levels, thirteen environmental organizations, including the Natural Resources Defense Council, Center for Science in the Public Interest, Environmental Action, Environmental Policy Center, Friends of the Earth, and the Highway Action Coalition, filed suit in federal court in the District of Columbia to eliminate the delay. The section of the law which prevents the states from setting emission standards does not cover fuel additives, and a number of campaigns to remove lead from gasoline have been launched around the country to remove lead on a state-by-state or city-by-city basis.

New York City, for example, has passed a law which would require total removal of lead from gasoline by January 1974. While this is not the most efficient way of dealing with a national problem, a similar campaign could take place in your state or city if enough citizens see lead as a serious health hazard. Two environmental groups have called for a deliberate national phaseout program for lead. The Center for Science in the Public Interest and the Environmental Defense Fund filed a joint petition before EPA in November 1971 asking, among other things, for a minimal 20 percent annual reduction in lead, the posting of octane ratings, and the removal of all lead from gasolines by 1976. The petition was subsequently denied.

Where to Get Information

Be sure that you have all the technical and legal information that you need to present an intelligent and strong case at hearings or in meetings with company or agency officials. It is important to master the elementary technical jargon so that such things as major sources of pollution, emission levels, hazardous pollutants, and so on, are familiar to you. These are some of the sources to check in your self-education.

Start with the glossary (Appendix 15-A, p. 857) and the environmental bibliography (Appendix 18-A, p. 900) to become familiar with terms, major sources, and main health effects of air pollution. Your reading list should include John Esposito, *Vanishing Air* (New York: Bantam Books and Grossman Publishers, 1970), *A Citizen's Guide to Clean Air* (put out by the Conservation Foundation), *Air Pollution Primer* (by the National Tuberculosis and Respiratory Disease Association), and the Natural Resources Defense Council's manual, *Action for Clean Air*. You might also write for "Urban Environmental Pollution—Literature Search #70-50," a list of citations discussing pollutants (in the urban setting) that are health hazards. Write the Literature Search Program, National Library of Medicine, 8600 Rockville Pike, Bethesda, Maryland 20014.

Newsletters published by environmental groups will keep you up-to-date on what is happening in the area of air pollution. Consult the list of groups that have such newsletters in Appendix 18-B (p. 904). Write for the monthly *EPA Citizens' Bulletin,* and the booklets *Don't Leave It All To The Experts* and *Citizen Action Can Get Results,* from the Office of Public Affairs, Environmental Protection Agency, Washington, D.C. 20460.

Contact local universities and conservation groups for help with technical questions. Try to get local scientists, physicians, engineers, law students, and lawyers involved in environmental efforts. See Chapter 18 for more suggestions on how to get technical and legal assistance. EPA has technical experts who can testify at hearings or serve as witnesses in lawsuits if they are subpoenaed. Call or write the Office of Air Programs of your regional EPA office to find out the names of regional experts who can testify.

The Office of Public Affairs in both the regional and federal EPA offices can provide assistance to citizen groups. If you want to complain about a violation of the Clear Air Act, and you are not getting any satisfaction from your state agency, contact your regional Office of Public Affairs as a first step in starting through the bureaucracy. The Office of Public Affairs can also provide you with information on community workshops being held as part of the federal Citizens' Action for Clean Air project to inform citizens about the Clean Air Act and national air quality standards. If the workshop has already been held in your area, contact the local contracted organization to see if it has written materials available for distribution.

EPA sponsors courses on air pollution which you can take, either as a formal program of study or on an occasional basis to acquaint yourself with the problems. They range in length from one day to six weeks. For a bulletin of current orientation courses and university training programs, write to Office of Manpower Development, Environmental Protection Agency, Research Triangle Park, North Carolina 27711.

EPA has also developed an air pollution training course, consisting of twelve cassette tapes and workbooks, which can be loaned to organizations for up to three weeks. The training course materials are available free of charge. Write to George Ziener, Chief, Instructional Development Section, Institute for Air Pollution Training, Environmental

Protection Agency, Research Triangle Park, North Carolina 27711. Ask for Air Pollution Orientation Course #422A.

The Natural Resources Defense Council is in the process of preparing other booklets similar to their manual on implementation plan hearings. Write to them (the address is in Appendix 18-B, p. 904) and ask for the names and release dates of new publications.

If you are interested in the more scientific and technical aspects of air pollution, there is a limited supply of a resource manual published by the Scientists' Institute for Public Information. *Selected Air Pollution Topics: A Citizen's Resource* can be obtained by writing to SIPI (address in Appendix 18-B, p. 904).

EPA has available a wide range of general publications on the environment; free materials can be obtained by writing to Office of Public Inquiries and Publications, Environmental Protection Agency, Washington, D.C. 20460. The Publications Office does not handle technical information, but can supply free general materials on air and water pollution, and also information on other topics, such as public service announcements and career choices in pollution control. For EPA technical publications, write to Office of Air Programs, Office of Technical Information and Publications, Environmental Protection Agency, P.O. Box 12055, Research Triangle Park, North Carolina 27711.

This office also has an Air Pollution Technical Information Center (APTIC), which provides a monthly abstracting service of papers and reports at a cost of $22 per year. Over 1,000 journals are screened monthly, and about 800 articles are added every month to the information system. APTIC also does individual literature searches on specific technical questions. Lists of citations or abstracts are sent out in response to such queries. For information on literature searches, write to the Research Triangle (above address) or call 919-549-8411, Ext. 2135.

The Department of Commerce has the National Technical Information Service (NTIS), a clearing house for scientific information relating to air pollution. A list of available publications can be obtained by writing or calling (at 703-321-8543) the National Technical Information Service, Department of Commerce, 5285 Port Royal Road, Springfield, Virginia 22151. NTIS will also do literature searches for $25 each. Write to the above address for more information on services available.

Transcripts of Congressional hearings are valuable informational documents and will provide you with names of people to contact for additional information. Check your library for copies of hearings or request them from the Senate Subcommittee on Air and Water Pollution, Committee on Public Works, Publications Desk, #4204 New Senate Office Building, Washington, D.C. 20510. The Committee has Parts 1-3 of the 1972 Hearings on the Implementation of the Clean Air Amendments of 1970 and Parts 3, 4, and 5 of the 1970 Clean Air Act hearings available free of charge. Parts 1 and 2 of the 1970 hearings can be ordered at a nominal cost from the G.P.O. (See Chapter 2 on how to order material from the G.P.O.)

Other Remedies:
Law Beyond the Clean Air Act

Sooner or later you will probably have to talk about going to court (or actually go) in order to be effective in fighting air pollution. The scope of "environmental law," while it has a long way to go, has been expanding rapidly over the last several years. This brief introduction is not designed to enable a nonlawyer to bring his own lawsuit. But legal actions are an important adjunct to citizen participation and you should have a working knowledge of some of the relevant theories. Chapters 2 and 4 offer a more detailed introduction to legal materials and some of the doctrines of administrative law that you are likely to encounter.

Recent developments in the law have, for the most part, been in two general areas—defining new environmental rights and bringing up-to-date such ancient common law doctrines as trespass and nuisance. A good source book is Norman J. Landau and Paul D. Rheingold, *The Environmental Law Handbook* (New York: Ballantine Books, Inc., 1971).

Broadly speaking, the law of *negligence* attempts to strike a balance between one person's (or company's) freedom to act and another person's right not to get hurt by that action. It defines that balance in particular situations by determining whether the actor was carrying out his "duty of care." When he does not, in the opinion of the judge or jury, carry out that duty reasonably, he must pay the person he hurt. A lot of old negligence cases would now be referred to as pollution cases—oldtimers tended to talk about "noxious fumes" and the like. One of the major problems for the person who sues—in addition to the always thorny problem of showing actual damage—is convincing the court that the defendant's action is unreasonable as the general community would define that word. Very often these cases get into complicated questions of what kind of control technology is generally used and whether there is a duty to employ the latest available technology even if that is not what other polluters are doing in similar situations.

Trespass, legally, essentially means what it means in everyday language—entering onto another's land. Courts moved slowly from the concept of entry by a person to "entry" by visible substances, and then, finally recognizing the atomic theory, "entry" by nonvisible substances—such as odors and even odorless, colorless gases (such as CO—carbon monoxide) which may cause harm. A trespass requires some intention on the part of the entering party, not just an unreasonable (negligent) act. However, you don't have to show an intent to do damage, and it is possible to prove intent if the trespasser continues his activities after he has been put on notice of the damage he is causing. Historically, there are advantages to suing for a trespass. Since the law is always harder on intentional wrongdoing, you may collect punitive damages as well as compensatory (actual) damages. Punitive damages are like court-determined fines awarded to the plaintiff, with the size depending on the wealth of the defendant. The idea is to make it so unprofitable for the defendant to continue his intentional damage that he will stop, and ideally the whole business will serve as an example to others.

Properly speaking, *nuisance* is not a "legal theory," but more of a way for a court to look at the damage caused by the defendant and attempt to decide what to do about it. There are intentional and un-intentional (i.e., negligent) nuisances, as well as public and private nuisances. The problems of proof and the damages available are not very different from negligence or trespass. But nuisance is an important tool in the environmentalist's kit if he wants to do more than collect damages. If he wants the court to order the polluter to stop, he usually must sue on the basis of a nuisance.

In many jurisdictions you can, theoretically at least, bring an action (mandamus) to make a public official do his job, or you can try to sue him for damages resulting from his failure to abate pollution. The problem with these suits is described in more detail in Chapter 4, pages 65-84. The fundamental barrier is that courts will not listen to such suits if the official has "discretion" about whether or not to act. Unless it is crystal clear that he *must* perform an act, the courts will not order him to perform it or award damages to people who have suffered because of his nonperformance.

The law of *product liability* has progressed to the point where you are not required to be the purchaser of the product that injures you in order to sue. If the manufacturer could reasonably expect that you would be affected by his product, you have a claim against the manufacturer, if you can show damages. The injuries resulting from noxious automobile fumes are demonstrable, and it probably is only a matter of time and lawsuits until automobile manufacturers are held liable for them.

A *shareholder* has the right to sue his company to prevent it from doing anything which may harm the value of the stock. Corporations which continue to pollute run the risk of spending enormous sums on complicated litigation, fines, and damage suits. Conceivably, a shareholder could force his company to take steps to stop polluting before the law catches it and makes it pay.

Some lawyers believe that *a constitutional right to a clean environment* can be found in the First, Ninth, or Fourteenth Amendments to the Constitution. Certainly the exercise of constitutional rights is made more difficult in a blanket of smog. These constitutional theories have been argued in some successful pollution suits, but a court has never squarely ruled on constitutional arguments as the sole basis for a suit. Some states, such as Michigan, have recently passed statutes or amended their state constitutions to provide either a statutory or constitutional right to a clean and healthful environment. Such provisions provide a citizen the right to sue where private or public action is endangering his or her right to a healthful environment. You should check your state's constitution and laws to determine whether you have such a statutory or constitutional right. If not, you should petition to have it amended to provide this right.

Section 304 of the *Clean Air Act* gives "any person" the right to bring suit against any private polluter or governmental body which is allegedly in violation of an emission standard or any order issued by EPA. An action may also be commenced against EPA where there is an alleged failure to perform a nondiscretionary act or duty required by law. Except where you allege a violation involving a hazardous pollutant, you must give sixty days notice to EPA, the polluter, and the state in which the polluter is located. The purpose of the notice provision is to give EPA an opportunity to correct the violation. The action may only be brought to enforce the standard or order, not for damages, but bringing an action under this section doesn't mean you can't bring a separate action for damages, or join both actions. The court, where it deems it appropriate, may award any party to the suit costs and reasonable attorney's fees.

Section 307 gives the rules for challenging any standard—except the 1975-1976 auto emission standards under Section 202(b)—or any action with regard to an implementation plan. The action must be brought within thirty days of the date of approval of the action in question unless the grounds for the case arise after the thirty days expire.

The National Environmental Policy Act, which has been on the books since late 1969, tells all federal agencies to consider the impact on the environment of any conceivable major action—for example, grant making, licenses, permits, regulations, and policy declarations. The agencies are required to write these considerations in the form of Environmental Impact ("102") Statements. These are filed for review with the CEQ, which submits them to other agencies for comment. Under Section 309 of the Clean Air Act, EPA must comment.

The statements are supposed to indicate in detailed fashion how the agency has considered the environmental impact of its actions. The most important requirement is that, where adverse environmental impact has been found, the agency must state whether more environmentally acceptable substitute actions have been considered. The internal effect of these statements on the agencies is as yet unclear. However, the statements have formed the basis for a number of successful suits charging that the requirements of the Act have not been carried out and that the failure resulted in federal actions with unsound environmental consequences.

The importance of the law is not limited to direct pollution by the federal government. Many major polluting activities by private companies or state governments are conducted with some complicity on the part of the federal government. For instance, major decisions having to do with power plant siting are made by the Atomic Energy Commission and the Federal Power Commission (see Chapters 8 and 9), and the proliferation of polluting automobiles would not have happened without the Federal Highway Trust Fund.

A Last Gasp

The problem of air pollution is one of the most subtle and pervasive
products of our collective misfeasance. Except during occasional temperature inversions that trap pollutants in a metropolitan area, it is not
manifested in attacks of stinging eyes and choking breath for most of
us. Even in those dramatic emergencies it strikes mostly at the weak and
the sick, the very young and the very old. Because of this it is sometimes thought of by many as a matter of secondary concern. As the
United Papermakers and Paperworkers Union put it, speaking of both
air and water pollutants: "The primary objections to paper and pulp
mill emissions and discharges involve nuisance and esthetic factors, not
health hazards." Out of a sense of *machismo* and warped urban pride,
some city dwellers even seem to feel that the ability to carry on in a
foul atmosphere is an index of hardiness. And of course the attitude
persists, as the Papermakers statement probably reflects, that the smell
of air pollution is the "smell of the payroll."

It is easy to become accustomed to foul air when there is no opportunity to breathe air that is clean. It is difficult to perceive as a threat
something as insidious as the pollutants that slowly poison and dull
consciousness, with the real impact implicit in the rise of pulmonary
disorders, or the real effects of property damage due to continual,
largely invisible, airborne erosion. It takes a drastic revision of our perspective to realize that the atmosphere is a shallow and exhaustible
envelope, that the air we use is not free. This chapter is intended to
assist in reclaiming the atmosphere and developing new ways to clean
the air.

Glossary*

AIR: so-called pure air is a mixture of gases containing about 78 percent nitrogen; 21 percent oxygen; less than 1 percent of carbon dioxide, argon, and other inert gases; and varying amounts of water vapor.

AIR POLLUTION: man-made contamination of the atmosphere, beyond that which is natural and excluding the narrowly occupational, such as the contaminated air that miners or asbestos workers breathe.

AIR QUALITY CONTROL REGION: as the federal government uses the term, an area where two or more communities--either in the same or different states--share a common air pollution problem.

AIR QUALITY CRITERIA: as the federal government uses the term, the varying amounts of pollution and lengths of exposure at which specific adverse effects to health and welfare take place.

AIR QUALITY STANDARD: as the federal government uses the term, the prescribed level of a pollutant that cannot be legally exceeded during a specified time in a specified geographical area.

--Primary standard: set at levels which (based on the Criteria Documents) are adequate to protect human health.

--Secondary standard: set at levels which (based on the Criteria Documents) are adequate to protect "welfare"--things other than health, such as plants, livestock, buildings.

BRONCHIAL ASTHMA: abnormal responsiveness of the air passages to certain substances. An attack consists of a widespread narrowing of the bronchioles by muscle spasm, swelling of the mucous membrane, or thickening and increase of mucous secretions, accompanied by wheezing, gasping, and sometimes coughing.

CANCER: an abnormal, potentially unlimited, disorderly new cell growth.

---

*Adapted from Air Pollution Primer of the National Tuberculosis and Respiratory Disease Association, 1969.

CARBON MONOXIDE: a colorless, odorless, very toxic gas
    produced by any process that involves the incomplete
    combustion of carbon-containing substances. One of
    the major air pollutants, it is primarily emitted
    through the exhaust of gasoline-powered vehicles.

EMISSION INVENTORY: a list of primary air pollutants
    emitted into a given community's atmosphere, in
    amounts (commonly tons) per day, by type of source.
    The emission inventory is basic to the establishment
    of emission standards.

EMISSION STANDARD: the maximum amount of a pollutant that
    is permitted to be discharged from a single polluting
    source; e.g., the number of pounds of fly ash per
    cubic foot of air that may be emitted from a coal-
    fire boiler.

EMPHYSEMA (PULMONARY):   an anatomic change in the lungs
    characterized by a breakdown of the walls of the
    alveoli which can become enlarged, lose their re-
    silience, and disintegrate.

FLUORIDES: gaseous or solid compounds containing fluorine,
    emitted into the air from a number of industrial
    processes; fluorides are a major cause of vegetation
    and--indirectly--livestock damage.

FLY ASH: the particulate impurities resulting from the
    burning of coal and other material, which are ex-
    hausted into the air from stacks.

INTERNAL COMBUSTION ENGINE: an engine in which both the
    heat energy and the ensuing mechanical energy are
    produced inside the engine proper.

INVERSION: the phenomenon of a layer of cool air trapped
    by a layer of warmer air above it so that the bottom
    layer cannot rise. A special problem in polluted
    areas because the contaminating substances cannot be
    dispersed.

NITROGEN OXIDES: gases formed in great part from atmos-
    pheric nitrogen and oxygen when combustion takes
    place under conditions of high temperatures and high
    pressure; e.g., in internal combustion engines;
    considered major air pollutants.

OZONE: a pungent, colorless, toxic gas. As a product of
    the photochemical process, it is a major air
    pollutant.

PARTICULATE: a particle of solid or liquid matter.

PHOTOCHEMICAL PROCESS: the chemical changes brought about
    by the radiant energy of the sun acting upon various
    polluting substances. The products are known as
    photochemical smog.

RINGELMANN CHART: actually a series of charts, numbered
    from 0 to 5, that simulate various smoke densities,
    by presenting different percentages of black. A
    Ringelmann No. 1 is equivalent to 20% black; a
    Ringelmann No. 5, to 100%. They are used for
    measuring the opacity of smoke arising from stacks
    and other sources, by matching with the actual
    effluent the various numbers or densities, indica-
    ted by the charts. Ringelmann numbers are sometimes
    used in setting emission standards.

STACK: a smokestack; a vertical pipe or flue designed to
    exhaust gases and any particulate matter suspended
    therein.

SULFUR OXIDES: pungent, colorless gases formed primarily
    by the combustion of fossil fuels; considered major
    air pollutants; sulfur oxides may damage the res-
    piratory tract as well as vegetation.

Organization Chart of the Environmental Protection Agency

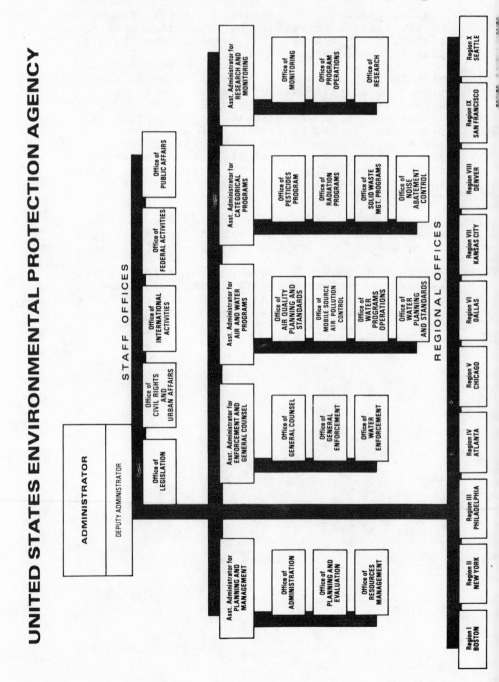

UNITED STATES ENVIRONMENTAL PROTECTION AGENCY

ADMINISTRATOR

DEPUTY ADMINISTRATOR

STAFF OFFICES

Office of LEGISLATION

Office of CIVIL RIGHTS AND URBAN AFFAIRS

Office of INTERNATIONAL ACTIVITIES

Office of FEDERAL ACTIVITIES

Office of PUBLIC AFFAIRS

Asst. Administrator for PLANNING AND MANAGEMENT

Office of ADMINISTRATION

Office of PLANNING AND EVALUATION

Office of RESOURCES MANAGEMENT

Asst. Administrator for ENFORCEMENT AND GENERAL COUNSEL

Office of GENERAL COUNSEL

Office of GENERAL ENFORCEMENT

Office of WATER ENFORCEMENT

Asst. Administrator for AIR AND WATER PROGRAMS

Office of AIR QUALITY PLANNING AND STANDARDS

Office of MOBILE SOURCE AIR POLLUTION CONTROL

Office of WATER PROGRAMS OPERATIONS

Office of WATER PLANNING AND STANDARDS

Asst. Administrator for CATEGORICAL PROGRAMS

Office of PESTICIDES PROGRAM

Office of RADIATION PROGRAMS

Office of SOLID WASTE MGT. PROGRAMS

Office of NOISE ABATEMENT CONTROL

Asst. Administrator for RESEARCH AND MONITORING

Office of MONITORING

Office of PROGRAM OPERATIONS

Office of RESEARCH

REGIONAL OFFICES

Region I BOSTON | Region II NEW YORK | Region III PHILADELPHIA | Region IV ATLANTA | Region V CHICAGO | Region VI DALLAS | Region VII KANSAS CITY | Region VIII DENVER | Region IX SAN FRANCISCO | Region X SEATTLE

National Primary and Secondary Ambient Air Quality Standards

Pollutant	Primary standard	Secondary standard
Sulfur oxides	80 ug/m³ (0.03 ppm)-annual arithmetic mean 365 ug/m³ (0.14 ppm)-maximum 24 hour concentration	60 ug/m³ (0.02 ppm) annual arithmetic mean 260 ug/m³ (0.1 ppm) maximum 24 hour concentration 1300 ug/m³ (0.5 ppm) maximum 3 hr. concentration
Particulate matter	75 ug/m³-annual geometric mean 260 ug/m³-maximum 24 hour concentration	60 ug/m³-annual geometric mean 150 ug/m³-maximum 24 hour concentration
Photochemical oxidants	160 ug/m³ (0.08 ppm)-maximum 1 hour concentration	Same as primary
Hydrocarbons	160 ug/m³ (0.24 ppm)-maximum 3 hour concentration (6-9 A.M.)	Same as primary
Nitrogen dioxide	100 ug/m³ (0.05 ppm)-annual arithmetic mean	Same as primary
Carbon monoxide	10 milligrams/m³ (9 ppm)-maximum 8 hr. concentration 40 milligrams/m³ (35 ppm)-maximum one hour concentration	Same as primary

--ug/m³=microgram per cubic meter.
--reference temperature: 25°C; 760 mm Hg.

CHAPTER 16

THE OCCUPATIONAL SAFETY AND HEALTH ADMINISTRATION

The Problem

Statistics alone will never fully describe the magnitude of the occupational health and safety problem in this country. Workers continuously battle noise, chemicals, heat, gases, radiation, and dusts on their jobs with little knowledge of the harmful consequences of such pollutants on their bodies. Such workers who seek aid from noncompany physicians are seldom able to identify the toxic substances with which they work, thus weakening the chances for accurate diagnosis of any occupationally caused diseases. Company doctors, on the other hand, may reflect their corporate consciousness by failing to provide candid diagnoses of illness, or by overlooking the known adverse health effects of certain industrial processes.

The combination of honest failure to associate illnesses with toxic substances being handled at work and of purposeful camouflage of such associations by companies and physicians has led to a gross under-reporting of the number of workers who die every year from diseases caused by their jobs. Historically, attention has been focused solely on the estimated 14,500 deaths from on-the-job injuries. A recent federal report, however, offers a more realistic picture of the situation. It estimates that 100,000 workers die every year from acute or chronic exposures to environmental insults on the job, resulting in such diseases as lung cancer, bladder cancer, asbestos-related disease, byssinosis, berylliosis, coalworkers' pneumoconiosis, and emphysema.

The Occupational Safety and Health Act

Although knowledge of such occupational illnesses and trauma caused public outcries as long ago as the turn of the century, no comprehensive federal action to end the industrial carnage was taken until 1970. To replace the relatively ineffective programs at the state level—where business interests easily dominate—Congress passed a strong federal law (Pub. L. 91-596) stating that its purpose was to

> assure so far as possible every working man and woman in the Nation safe and healthful working conditions and to preserve our human resources.

The Occupational Safety and Health Act, which went into effect on 28 April 1971, covers a workforce of approximately 60 million people —excluding federal, state, and local government employees or those employees whose working conditions are specifically protected by other federal health and safety laws.

Section 5 of the Act states that each employer has the general duty to furnish a place of employment "free from recognized hazards that are causing, or are likely to cause, death or serious physical harm to his employees." In addition, employees have the right to file complaints if they believe standards promulgated under the Act are being violated.

Administration of the Act is vested in the Department of Labor's Occupational Safety and Health Administration (OSHA), whose responsibility it is to promulgate, revise, and enforce occupational safety and health standards. Implementation of the Act by the Department of Labor, however, has often consisted of a series of roadblocks set up to frustrate workers' attempts to correct hazards rather than to ensure their health and safety.

OSHA has compliance officers responsible for inspecting the nation's 5 million workplaces for violations of standards. But it has only about 500 inspectors—an average of one inspector for every 10,000 establishments, or for every 120,000 employees. Moreover, the majority of compliance officers has received no training in industrial hygiene and are therefore unable to ascertain whether or not the amount of a particular toxic substance exceeds the air concentration value set by law.

Responsibility for research and evaluation of occupational diseases lies with the National Institute of Occupational Safety and Health (NIOSH), which is part of the Department of Health, Education, and Welfare.

Both agencies are hampered by severe budgetary constraints, and only a fraction of what the agencies request is actually appropriated to them. Combined, their total budget for fiscal 1974 is less than $96 million—divided in such a way that NIOSH receives only $26 million.

Due to the enormity of its task, OSHA has set priorities on five target health hazards (carbon monoxide, lead, asbestos, silica, and cotton dust) and on five target industries which have high accidental injury rates. These target industries and health hazards, coupled with fatality cases and employee complaints, are the top priorities for inspections. In fact, random unannounced general industry inspections of the workplace comprised less than 50 percent of the 14,452 inspections in 1971.

In the face of the stringent budgets under which both agencies operate, and the frequent political pressures under which they both have been observed to act, there is a need for very close citizen surveillance to assure administrative compliance with Congress' declared purpose in enacting this legislation. The rest of this chapter will focus on ways for citizens and workers to keep a watchful eye over the occupational safety and health enforcement process and eliminate many weaknesses in its implementation.

Citizen-Worker Surveillance:
The Role of Individual Employees

The Occupational Safety and Health Act has many deficiencies (including inadequate penalties and delays in standard setting and appeals procedures), but it does afford workers tools with which to generate pressure for correction of hazards in the workplace. In order to employ these tools effectively, employees must familiarize themselves with their rights under the Act and determine which standards or regulations are applicable to their particular jobs. In addition, workers must educate themselves with respect to the effects of harmful substances on their bodies so that companies cannot mystify them with technical and medical information which they could in fact understand.

The occupational health standards listed in the following table illustrate the various forms in which standards for environmental contaminants appear (all are averages over an eight-hour day):

Asbestos	5	fibers per cubic centimeter
Benzene	10	parts per million
Carbon monoxide	50	parts per million
Lead	0.2	milligrams per cubic meter
Noise	90	decibels

For example, a violation of the Occupational Safety and Health Act exists if the average amount of carbon monoxide in the air exceeds fifty parts per million over an eight-hour working day.

Of the thousands of dangerous substances used in the workplace, standards have been set for only 450. While these standards are frequently outdated and woefully inadequate, the tempo at which the Department of Labor is attempting to revise them or to promulgate new standards is incredibly slow. Despite the grave dangers present in many workplaces, the Department of Labor had revised only one health standard—asbestos—a year and a half after passage of the Act. No other action has been taken with respect to the grave health hazards found in many workplaces today. (The complete set of occupational safety and health standards can be obtained by requesting the 18 October 1972 standards package from your regional office of the Occupational Safety and Health Administration [see Appendix 16-A, p. 875] or by sending 20 cents to the Superintendent of Documents, G.P.O., Washington, D.C. 20402).

The importance of familiarity with the standards is found in Section 8(f)(1) of the Act, which states:

> Any employees or representative of employees who believe that a violation of a safety or health standard exists that threatens physical harm, or that an imminent danger exists, may request an inspection by giving notice to the Secretary [of Labor] or his authorized representative of such violation or danger.

A form is provided by the Department of Labor for such complaints and requests of inspection. The employee should send the completed form to the appropriate area office, the address of which can be obtained from the regional office of the Department of Labor (see Appendix 16-A, p. 875). Each employee filing a complaint should be sure to indicate in Question 9 of the form whether or not his or her name should be withheld from the employer.

A model format to use when requesting an inspection is as follows:

Some 280 persons are employed in the production and maintenance unit of this plant. They are continually exposed to hazards to their health as a result of the failure of the employer to maintain safe, clean, and sanitary conditions in their place of employment. Specifically, (1) waste cans are not cleaned frequently enough to maintain sanitary conditions; (2) toilet facilities are not clean; (3) towels are not provided at lavatories; (4) washing facilities are not clean; (5) drinking fountains are not clean; (6) no separate space is provided for having lunch—employees are required to eat at their jobs where they are exposed to toxic cotton dust and dust from trash cans; (7) cotton dust exposure exceeds permissible limit set in Section 1910.93; and (8) noise exposure exceeds permissible limit set in Section 1910.95 of the Occupational Safety and Health Regulations.

While this specific complaint was filled out by a union official as an employee representative, *any worker can file a complaint.* This is a particularly important piece of information for the 42 million unorganized workers in the nation's workforce. The difficulties and frustrations encountered by unions experienced at filing complaints and dealing with the Department of Labor, however, indicate that nonunionized employees—especially those in very small shops—might consult experienced union leaders or a labor attorney before attempting to use the law.

Based on the experience of OSHA's first two years, workers should have no illusions about rapid or broad changes in their working environment, or guarantees that their workplaces will be made safe and healthful. Nevertheless, some changes can be effected by constant vigilance over the Act's implementation—and over employers' attempts to subvert the intent of the law. Some useful reference materials are noted in Appendix 16-C (p. 878).

Some rights under the Act are:

1. Observing industry monitoring of the workplace and access to findings.
2. Filing complaints with the Department of Labor.
3. Requesting hazard evaluations to be done by NIOSH when working with a substance or process thought to be dangerous (write to NIOSH, 5600 Fishers Lane, Rockville, Maryland 20852, for the form).
4. Accompanying the OSHA inspector on a walkaround inspec-

tion of the workplace (to insure that the inspector sees *all*
work areas).
5. Monitoring the employer's compliance with the Act to be sure
that he (a) posts the required summary of illnesses and injuries
[OSHA 102], (b) posts all citations for violations of the Act,
and (c) informs employees about all hazardous exposures.

Some areas for worker input and public participation are:

1. Asking the Occupational Health and Safety Review Commission* for reductions in time periods allowed to employers for
abatement of violations.
2. Participating in hearings on temporary or permanent variance
requests by local employers who allege that they need additional time for compliance, or that they want a permanent
exemption from the standard. (If employers request a temporary variance, workers must be notified and can request a hearing; a hearing is required for permanent variance requests.
Workers can participate in either hearing.)
3. Participating in the standards setting area by commenting on
proposed rule making procedures or on requests for information published in the *Federal Register*.
4. Appearing as witnesses at hearings on state occupational safety
and health plans proposed to replace the federal Occupational
Safety and Health Act.

The Role of Local Unions

Management has the ability to keep workers ignorant about the hazards
they face on the job and about provisions of the law which workers can
use to combat these hazards. Workers who do not know names of the
toxic chemicals with which they are working, nor (or) the possible adverse
health effects of the substances, cannot effectively utilize the federal
law. Even to be able to file complaints, workers must at least know
how to recognize and monitor the hazards in their workplace.

Physicians, scientists, students, and lawyers may provide local unions

---

*The Occupational Safety and Health Review Commission is an independent quasi-judicial
agency which has the authority to review all contested citations issued by the Department of
Labor.

with resources for monitoring the implementation of the Occupational Safety and Health Act. A model for an educational program has been developed by the Scientists Committee for Occupational Health in conjunction with the Oil, Chemical, and Atomic Workers Union (OCAW). This group of scientists and doctors has been teaching shop stewards and other union members from chemical and cosmetic factories and oil refineries about hazards they face and the means for measuring and preventing them. Weekly sessions cover the chemical and physical hazards found on their jobs, with explanations of their effects on workers' bodies.

Once hazards are recognized, workers can ask for a hazard evaluation from NIOSH, or can file a complaint for violation of a standard and request a Department of Labor inspection. Members of OCAW employed at a chlor-alkali plant in West Virginia called in both of these agencies when their health was endangered by excessive exposure to mercury in 1971. For additional evidence the union called upon an outside volunteer physician to analyze employees' urine samples for mercury levels. Their union complaint resulted in the first citation issued under the Occupational Safety and Health Act and in a $1,000 fine to Allied Chemical for

> airborne concentrations of mercury which significantly exceed levels generally accepted to be safe levels of such concentrations. . . . This condition constitutes a recognized hazard that is causing or is likely to cause death or serious physical harm to employees.

Although the fine was merely one-tenth of the $10,000 allowable under the Act, workers report that the action they instituted resulted in at least some discernible improvement in working conditions.

Local unions, in combination with public interest groups, have also cooperated in publishing pamphlets describing the hazards on their jobs and their successful attempts at monitoring and combating these hazards. Two examples of such joint local union-public interest group pamphlets are *Asbestos—The Hazards of Sprayed Fireproofing*, published through the cooperation of Local #34, Asbestos Workers Union, and the Minnesota Public Interest Research Group, and *Fighting Noise*, published in cooperation with Local #6, Newspaper Web Pressmen, Washington, D.C., the Health Research Group, and Urban Planning Aid, Inc. (addresses in Appendix 16-B, p. 877). These manuals can serve as strategy models for members of other unions working to solve occupational health problems in their workplaces.

Ineffective enforcement of occupational safety and health programs at the state level was one of the main reasons for passage of the federal law in 1970. The law, however, contains provisions for allowing the states to regain their lost control over enforcement activities. A state may reassume responsibility for developing and enforcing job safety and health standards if it submits to the Department of Labor a plan which is "as effective as" the federal law.

As of 29 December 1972, states whose plans had not been approved by the Labor Department were pre-empted under the Occupational Safety and Health Act from enforcing state standards. Since only plans for South Carolina, Montana, and Oregon had been approved by that date, the federal government became solely responsible for enforcing health and safety standards in all other states.

The Department of Labor is committed to surrendering its control over job safety and health to the states. In line with this policy, the Secretary of Labor has been willing to approve state plans in spite of failures to meet the criteria requiring plans to be "as effective as" the federal law. Experience with the South Carolina plan indicates that the federal enforcement effort must be maintained until a state adequately demonstrates that its plan will in fact function as effectively as the federal statute and standards.

The South Carolina plan was the first to be submitted to the Department of Labor. In July 1972 hearings were held at the state level at which both labor and industry leaders testified. Textile union leaders, in criticizing the plan, said that the state's proposed funds could not even cover the asbestos and cotton dust standards that are target health hazards under the federal law, and which could affect the health of the 139,000 textile workers employed in the state. Other union leaders testified that the state statute did not deal with toxic materials, that opportunity for employee walkaround with inspectors was not provided, and that there was no provision for entry of inspectors without delay.

Despite strong public interest objections, the plan was approved by OSHA. In an effort to reverse this unauthorized approval of the South Carolina plan, the South Carolina Labor Council, AFL-CIO, and Local 382 of the International Brotherhood of Electrical Workers in early 1973 sued the state and OSHA to enjoin the state from enforcing its plan, alleging eighteen points where South Carolina's plan failed to be as effective as the federal law.

Recognizing the Department of Labor's policy to approve plans without careful scrutiny as to their effectiveness, state and local labor unions as well as public interest groups should demand public hearings on those plans which have not yet been approved, and should maintain surveillance over the standards setting, enforcement, and budget allocations in those states where plans have already been approved.

The Role of International Unions

To have an effective safety and health program and to use the law effectively, unions need to collect data about the health of their members and the hazards to which they are exposed. This can be done on a short-term basis—by calling on noncompany physicians, scientists, and industrial hygienists to evaluate medical records of members or hazards in industry—or by developing long-term studies to show the morbidity and mortality experiences of union members.

The United Rubber Workers Union, for example, has undertaken a major in-depth in-plant environmental health study to be performed by the Harvard and North Carolina Schools of Public Health and the major rubber and tire companies. The large rubber companies are setting aside 0.5 cents per hour worked per employee as part of the tripartite agreement. The program, which will include industrial hygiene, toxicology, and medical and epidemiologic studies, is the first of its kind to be won as part of a collective bargaining agreement. In the future information from the study could be used by rubber workers to obtain the safe and healthful workplaces required by the Occupational Safety and Health Act.

Local unions must be kept abreast of developments under the Act because they are often in the best position to offer firsthand testimony on in-plant pollution. OCAW and the Washington-based Health Research Group, for example, filed a petition with the Department of Labor requesting a temporary emergency standard for ten cancer-causing chemicals (carcinogens) used in the workplace. Thirty days for public comment were allowed. Unfortunately, industrial lobbyists paid to keep up with such rule making procedures may be the only other organizations to offer comments. Some workers suffering with cancer from on-the-job exposures to carcinogenic and toxic substances may never even know of the opportunity to present the Department of Labor with their occupational experience. International union newsletters could inform readers not only about work hazards but also about proposed rule making procedures in which workers can participate. This type of public participation is increasingly important in order to counteract the combined attempt by government and industry to consider the short-range economic effects, rather than the immediate and long-range health effects of standards.

Individuals or unions can ask for new standards by submitting petitions to the Department of Labor (for example, the OCAW-Health Research Group carcinogen petition), or they can request hearings on new standards which have been proposed. They can also challenge the validity of a standard that has been promulgated by seeking judicial review of the Department of Labor's action. Such review has been sought by the AFL-CIO with regard to the asbestos standard promulgated by the Department of Labor on 7 June 1972. The standard had been lowered from twelve fibers to five fibers per cubic centimeter by the Department of Labor in December 1971. NIOSH had thereafter recommended that the standard be lowered even further—to two fibers per cubic centimeter by 1974. At the hearing on the proposed asbestos standard, physicians testified that *any* inhalation of asbestos fibers was life-threatening and that a standard no greater than two fibers should go into effect immediately. This widely used substance has been proven to cause asbestosis (scarring of the lung) and frequently results in lung cancer twenty to thirty years after inhalation.

With these facts and medical conclusions in hand, the Department of Labor proceeded to promulgate a final standard giving industry *four years*—until 1976—to comply with the two-fiber standard, providing further evidence that the Department is concerned with economic convenience rather than workers' health in setting standards.

Another potential role of international unions in this area would be to generate opposition among local members against amendments to the federal law which threaten to weaken it—such as those amendments introduced to eliminate from coverage of the Act workers in establishments with fewer than fifteen employees.

The Future

At the same time that safety standards for chemicals and other toxic substances are being widely violated in the workplace, and new non-regulated chemicals are introduced each day, industry and government would have us believe that great strides are being made toward increased worker protection. In light of the actual epidemic proportions of the occupational health problem in this country, citizen-worker surveillance over activities in this area must increase in the future.

The combination of stringent budgets for occupational safety and health programs, reduced enforcement capabilities, and the concern over false "cost-effectiveness" of governmental programs, may result in relegating worker health and safety to a very low priority during the next few years. In addition, the size of fines meted out by regulatory agencies for violation of standards most often makes it cheaper for industries to pollute the in-plant environment than to clean it up. For these reasons, labor unions must devote greater resources and staff personnel (full-time members or consultants) to health. In addition, unionized workers should consider the entire range of occupational exposures encountered in the workplace for settlement by collective bargaining. Some of the important areas which can effectively change occupational safety and health policy are:

1. Formation of a safety committee composed of union and management members and a chairman chosen by the union and management in alternating months.
2. Specific arbitration clause for health and safety grievances.
3. Mandatory pay for union members who represent labor during inspections ("walkaround" pay).
4. Specific clauses governing work conditions (for example, noise, ventilation, dust).
5. Surveillance and monitoring of employee exposure to occupational hazards and notifying employees of results.
6. Labeling of the contents of all substances used according to chemical name.
7. Posting of occupational hazard notices in the workplace.

At the state level citizens and workers should maintain continuous surveillance if a state reassumes enforcement activities, particularly since developmental plans are subject to review by the Department of Labor for three years after approval. In states where an occupational safety and health plan contains legislation not yet acted upon by the state legislature, public interest and labor organizations should apply pressure to strengthen the provisions, since a plan "more effective" than the federal law will not be subject to rejection by the Secretary of Labor.

At the federal level, citizens should press for changes in the Occupational Safety and Health Review Commission so that a worker can appeal a case in which the Department of Labor refuses to issue a citation for an alleged violation, rather than merely being allowed to appeal the time allowed for abatement of the violation. Additional citizen support should be generated for more rational federal standards and requirements for workmen's compensation, so that those workers who have been and continue to be exposed to in-plant pollution will at least receive monetary benefits for diseases which develop in the future.

The passage of the Occupational Safety and Health Act has accelerated the struggle for health and survival on the job, but the first two years of its "enforcement" have made workers realize that it is nothing more than a legal framework for action which they must initiate. In order to move into the future and make the law more meaningful, citizen-workers must increase awareness of the physical, chemical, and mental assaults on workers, and use the law to preserve this country's most valuable resource.

Regional Offices of the Occupational Safety and Health Administration

Write to your Regional Administrator for information on standards or to request an inspection:

Connecticut   REGION I
Maine
Massachusetts   18 Oliver Street
New Hampshire   Boston, Mass. 02110
Rhode Island   617/223-6712
Vermont

New Jersey   REGION II
New York
Puerto Rico   1515 Broadway
Virgin Islands   (1 Astor Plaza)
                New York, N.Y.   10001
                212/971-5941

Delaware   REGION III
Maryland
Pennsylvania   Penn Square Building
Virginia   Room 623
West Virginia   Juniper and Filbert Streets
                Philadelphia, Pa. 19107
                215/597-4102

Alabama   REGION IV
Florida
Georgia   1375 Peachtree Street, N.E.
Kentucky   Suite 587
Mississippi   Atlanta, Ga.   30309
North Carolina   404/526-3573
South Carolina
Tennessee

Illinois   REGION V
Indiana
Minnesota   300 S. Wacker Drive
Michigan   Room 1201
Ohio   Chicago, Ill. 60606
Wisconsin   312/353-4716

NATIONAL OFFICE

Assistant Secretary of Labor
Department of Labor
14th & Constitution Avenue, N.W.
Washington, D.C. 20210
202/961-2554

Arkansas   REGION VI
Louisiana
New Mexico   7th Floor Texaco Building
Oklahoma   1512 Commerce Street
Texas   Dallas, Tex.   75201
                214/749-2477

Iowa   REGION VII
Kansas
Missouri   Waltower Building
Nebraska   823 Walnut Street
                Kansas City, Mo.   64106
                816/374-5249

Colorado   REGION VIII
Montana
North Dakota   1961 Stout Street
South Dakota   Box 3588
Utah   Denver, Colo.   80225
Wyoming   303/837-3883

Arizona   REGION IX
California
Hawaii   10353 Federal Building
Nevada   450 Golden Gate Avenue
                Box 36017
                San Francisco, California   94102
                415/556-0584

Alaska   REGION X
Idaho
Oregon   506 Second Avenue
Washington   1808 Smith Tower Building
                Seattle, Wash.   98104
                202/442-5930

Where to Get Assistance

The following groups are able to assist individual workers or local unions with problems in the occupational health area, although many are under-staffed and may not be able to handle all cases which come to their attention. Interested citizens or workers can also seek advice from public interest or environmental groups, and from students in medicine, law, engineering or the sciences.

Calumet Environmental and Occupational Health
    Committee
5305 Hohman, Suite 505
Hammond, IN

Connecticut Occupational Safety and Health
    Project
P.O.Box 780
New Haven, CT 06503

Health Research Group
2000 P Street, N.W.
Suite 708
Washington, DC 20036

Medical Committee for Human Rights
2253 West Taylor Street
Chicago, IL 60612

Minnesota Public Interest Research Group
3036 University Avenue, S.E.
Minneapolis, MN 55414

National Health and Environmental Law
    Program
2477 Law Building
405 Hilgard Avenue
Los Angeles, CA 90024

Scientists Committee for Occupational Health
5-C Barrett Drive
Kendall Park, NJ 08824

Urban Planning Aid Industrial Health and Safety
    Project
639 Massachusetts Avenue
Cambridge, MA 02139

Useful Reference Materials

Bernardo Ramazzini, Diseases of Workers (New York:
    Hafner, 1964. Translated from the Latin text De
    Morbis Artificum of 1713)

Donald Hunter, The Diseases of Occupations (London: The
    English Universities Press, Ltd., 1969)

Frank Wallick, The American Worker: An Endangered Species
    (New York: Ballantine, 1972)

International Labor Office, Encyclopedia of Occupational
    Health and Safety (Geneva: ILO Press, 1971)

Mary-Win O'Brien and Joseph Page, Bitter Wages (New York:
    Grossman Publishers, 1973)

Medical Committee for Human Rights, Health Hazards in the
    Workplace (Chicago: Medical Committee for Human
    Rights, 1972)

Occupational Diseases: A Guide to their Recognition,
    U.S. Department of Health, Education and Welfare,
    Public Health Service Publication No. 1097 (Wash-
    ington: Government Printing Office, 1966)

Paul Brodeur, Asbestos and Enzymes (New York: Ballan-
    tine, 1971)

Ray Davidson, Peril on the Job (Washington: Public
    Affairs Press, 1970)

Urban Planning Aid, A Unionist's Guide to the Occupational
    Safety and Health Act of 1970; How to Inspect Your
    Workplace; How to Improve Health and Safety Con-
    ditions; A Resource List for Health and Safety
    Problems; Noise and Your Job (Boston: Urban Plan-
    ning Aid, 1971, 1972)

Newsletters

Bureau of National Affairs (Washington, D.C.): Occupa-
    tional Safety and Health Reporter

Commerce Clearing House, Inc. (Chicago): Employment
    Safety and Health Guide

Gershon Fishbein (Washington, D.C.): Occupational
    Safety and Health Letter

The Law

Public Law 91-596. Occupational Safety and Health Act
     of 1970 (GPO, 1970) Can be ordered from the
     Superintendent of Documents, GPO, Washington, D.C.
     20402

     Annotated text: Commerce Clearinghouse, Occupational
     Safety and Health Act of 1970: Law and Explanation
     (1971)

Occupational Safety and Health Administration, U.S.
     Department of Labor, Compliance Operations Manual
     (OSHA #2006, GPO, 1972)

CHAPTER 17

THE CONSUMER PRODUCT SAFETY COMMISSION

On 27 October 1972 President Nixon signed Public Law 92-573, the Consumer Product Safety Act of 1972. This legislation, which with certain exceptions became effective on 26 December 1972, created an independent regulatory commission to be known as the Consumer Product Safety Commission (CPSC), with broad authority to regulate the safety of consumer products. In addition to the new authority provided, the CPSC will also be administering and enforcing the Federal Hazardous Substances Act, the Poison Prevention Packaging Act, and the Flammable Fabrics Act, statutes formerly administered and enforced by the Food and Drug Administration (FDA), the Federal Trade Commission (FTC), and the Department of Commerce.

While the ultimate effectiveness of the new Commission of course depends on the commissioners appointed by the President and on the level of appropriations provided, the Act does contain a number of innovative provisions which can be used by consumers and consumer organizations to help insure that the CPSC fulfills the purposes of the Act—to protect the public against unreasonable risks of injury associated with consumer products.

The newly appointed chairman of the Commission is Richard O. Simpson, who will serve for three years. The vice-chairman, Barbara A. Hackman Franklin, has been appointed to a seven-year term. Constance E. Newman and Lawrence M. Kushner will serve six- and four-year terms respectively. The fifth member, R. David Pittle, will serve for five years.

These provisions are as follows:

1. *Section 7(b)—Proceedings to Develop Consumer Product Safety Standards*

Under Section 7(b), the Commission's *Federal Register* notice for a proceeding to develop a consumer product safety standard must include an invitation for any person, within thirty days after date of publication of the notice, to "offer to develop the consumer product safety standard." The CPSC is generally required to accept one or more offers if it determines that the offerer is technically competent, is likely to develop an appropriate standard within the period specified in the invitation, and will comply with Commission regulations requiring proposed standards to be supported by test data, opportunity for participation by interested parties in development, open records on all phases of the development, and access to financial records if the CPSC contributes to development of the standard.

This provision, unique in federal safety legislation, opens up an opportunity for independent testing groups, consumer organizations with access to testing expertise, and university groups to "become offerers," and thereby break the grip of business-dominated voluntary standards groups such as the American National Standards Institute (ANSI) and American Standards and Testing Materials (ASTM) on the standards setting process. Such groups should take advantage of Section 7(c)(2), which authorizes the CPSC to contribute to the offerer's cost in developing a proposed standard.

2. *Section 10—Commission Responsibility—Petition for Consumer Product Safety Rule*

Section 10(a) authorizes interested persons, including consumers or consumer organizations, to petition the commission to commence a proceeding for the issuance, amendment, or revocation of a consumer product safety rule (i.e., a consumer product safety standard or a rule declaring a consumer product a banned hazardous product). The petition must set forth facts claimed to establish the necessity of the rule, and a brief description of the substance of the rule. The CPSC is authorized to hold a public hearing or conduct such investigation or proceeding as appropriate, and is required within 120 days after the petition is filed to either grant or deny it. If granted, the CPSC is required to commence rule making procedures promptly; if denied, it must publish in the *Federal Register* the reasons for denial. Finally, if the petition is denied, Section 10(e) authorizes the petitioner to commence a federal district court action to compel the Commission to initiate a proceeding to take the action requested. If the preponderance of the evidence in such a *de novo* proceeding shows that the consumer product presents an unreasonable risk, and that the Commission's failure to initiate rule making unreasonably exposes petitioner or other consumers to a risk of injury presented by the consumer product, the court is required to order the CPSC to initiate rule making. Section 10(e), however, applies only with respect to petitions filed more than three years after enactment of the Act. Thus, although for three years consumers will be limited to petitioning to issue a rule, the Act does nevertheless provide a specific procedure for consumers to bring particular consumer products hazards to the attention of the CPSC.

3. *Section 15—Formal Hearings on Substantial Product Hazards*

Under Section 15, interested persons, including consumers and consumer organizations, are given an opportunity for a formal trial-type hearing on the issue of whether a product presents a substantial product hazard (defined as a failure to comply with an applicable product safety rule or a defect which creates a substantial risk of injury to the public) and on the appropriate remedy—notification, repair, replacement, or refund. While a formal trial-type hearing requires extensive resources and expertise, the issues involved may well deserve such an effort.

4. *Section 23(a)—Suits for Damages by Persons Injured*

Section 23(a) provides that any person who shall sustain injury by reason of any knowing (including willful) violation of a consumer product safety rule, or any other rule or order issued by the CPSC, may sue in any district court of the United States, any persons who knowingly (including willfully) violated any such rule or order, subject to the provisions of 28 U.S.C. 1331 as to the amount in controversy ($10,000), and shall recover damages sustained, and the cost of suit, including a reasonable attorney's fee, if considered appropriate in the discretion of the court. This remedy is stated to be in addition to and not in lieu of any other remedies provided by common law or under federal or state law.

5. *Section 24—Private Enforcement of Product Safety Rules and of Section 15 Orders*

Section 24 authorizes interested persons to bring an action in federal district court to enforce a consumer product safety rule or an order under Section 15 (Notification and Repair, Replacement or Refund), and to obtain appropriate injunctive relief. Interested persons may elect, by a demand for such relief in the complaint, to recover reasonable attorney's fees, in which case the court shall award the costs of suit, including a reasonable attorney's fee, to the prevailing party. This section cannot be used, however, if the same alleged violation is the subject of a pending civil or criminal action by the United States under the Act.

This section should be useful primarily to consumer groups as a prod to governmental enforcement of product safety rules.

6. *Section 27—Public Hearings*

Section 27(a) authorizes the CPSC to conduct a hearing or other inquiry necessary or appropriate to its functions anywhere in the United States. Consumer groups should urge the Commission to utilize this section as a means of focusing public attention on particular product hazards, and should prepare themselves to participate in such hearings held in their locality.

CHAPTER 18

ORGANIZING AND OTHER PROBLEMS
Keeping Going

> As soon as several of the inhabitants of the United States have taken up an opinion or a feeling which they wish to promote in the world, they look out for mutual assistance; and as soon as they have found each other out, they combine. From that moment they are no longer isolated men, but a power seen from afar, whose actions serve for an example, and whose language is listened to.
>
> —Alexis de Tocqueville, "Of the Use Which Americans Make of Public Associations in Civil Life," *Democracy in America, Vol. IX,* 1840

Organizing

The most important single thing to remember in putting together a consumer organization is that most people will work hardest and longest for a goal that will affect them personally and which they think they can achieve. This qualification presents two major obstacles which are even more formidable in organizing to work on federal agencies: one is a matter of understanding, and the other of will. The connection between the federal government and everyday experiences such as food and air is not obvious. The causal relationship must be explained and illustrated. Even if the relationship is understood, the attitude that "you can't fight city hall" becomes a massive barrier to action in the face of the biggest "city hall" of all. The achievements of others in dealing with Washington, some of which are described in this book, can serve to illustrate that entrenched and unresponsive power can be forced to respond. But the attitude should serve as a warning in choosing goals—make them as specific and achievable as possible. Victories follow on each other, even when they are small.

Frequently, the first step will be to convince people that they are being affected personally by decisions of federal agencies. Sometimes it takes exposure to or description of something other than the "standard brands" of services or products being supplied before an average citizen realizes that there is a possible alternative. For example, he may not be aware that a polluted river was clean enough to swim in a few years before, and could be made that way again, and he may have forgotten what unpolluted air is like, or not connect the air he breathes with his constant cough.

Expressing a common grievance is the first step in forming an organization to work for a common goal. There are probably many people in your community who feel as you do about a grievance, but your common concern will not become shared, and the grievance will not become an issue, until someone speaks out. There may already be a citizen organization working actively for the same goal which you have just formulated in your own mind. The first step is usually the hardest, in fact as well as in conventional wisdom. But remember that inertia is the tendency both of a resting body to remain at rest, and of a body in motion to keep moving.

Once you have spoken to a few other people who share your concern, it is time to make or find an organization with which to work. No community is without organization, and it can save much time and energy if an organization which is already established in the community can be mobilized to deal with your problem. Look around for organizations and institutions to which people already owe a degree of loyalty, and which may provide a framework through which members can deal with a regulatory agency. Schools, churches, unions, social clubs, professional societies, and conservation groups all have potential as a basis on which to build. The existence of several organizations which are already concerned makes it much easier to form a coalition around a particular issue, rather than starting from scratch in competition with existing structures.

If there is no existing organization, or, more likely, if the issue requires formation of an ad hoc coalition of existing institutions, the next step is to call a meeting. To a certain extent this constitutes a leap of faith, but don't make it any more hazardous than it has to be. A first meeting which is attended only by families of the organizers can end a campaign. Try to set an attendance goal of the minimum number of people necessary to get the project off the ground, then get promises to attend from at least a third more. Mount a publicity campaign well in advance of the meeting, using mailing lists, leaflets, and announcements at meetings of other organizations. Remember to use all of the communications media in the community for this first step. Utilize radio, television, and newspaper public service announcements. If the treasury can afford it, use paid ads. Organize the meeting around some attraction which goes beyond speeches by the organizers. Outside speakers could be such an attraction, or documentary films, such as those available from the University of Indiana film library of documentaries [Indiana University Audio-Visual Center, Bloomington, Indiana]. The *Source Catalog on Communications* is an excellent compilation of books and organizations concerned with all kinds of communication, and it is only $1.50 from SOURCE, P.O. Box 21066, Washington, D.C. 20009 (202-387-1145). Another useful book is by the O.M. Collective, *The Organizer's Manual* (New York: Bantam Books, 1971, $1.25).

Go into the meeting with a fairly detailed plan of how the campaign should be organized, but don't be married to that idea to the extent of rejecting other plans which can accomplish the same end. One basic decision to be made is the legal status of the organization. This is closely linked to the fundamental problem of getting enough money to keep the organization alive and functioning. One type of organization would be a nonprofit corporation which qualifies under 26 U.S.C. 501(c)(3) of the Internal Revenue Code as an educational or charitable institution. Contributions to such an organization are tax deductible, and the income is tax exempt. *Action for a Change* by Ralph Nader and Donald Ross (New York: Grossman Publishers, 1972, $1.65) is a detailed guide to forming a specific kind of organization—student-financed Public Interest Research Groups. It contains a discussion of the tax status of public interest groups.

If there are no local consumer groups already in existence, a pamphlet entitled *Forming Consumer Organizations* may be useful. Copies of this can be obtained by writing the President's Committee on Consumer Interests, Washington, D.C., 20506. In addition to guidelines to forming consumer organizations, this booklet contains useful information in its index of national consumer organizations. (See Appendix 18-B, p. 904, for a list of some of them.) It also has a roster of state and local consumer organizations, with mailing addresses of local offices. Appendix 18-C (p. 910) also supplies this information.

If your efforts are directed at federal agencies, you may want to establish liaison with public interest groups located in Washington. Several of these groups have already been described in the chapters

discussing their particular areas. Appendix 18-D (p. 931) is a list
of some public interest legal groups. While most of them have specialized fields, and all are very busy, they may be able to give you some
assistance or refer you to someone who can. Another method of getting
a voice in the Capitol is to work through the national office of your own
organization. Unions, professional associations, and all kinds of interest
groups have Washington offices. Write to them, let them know how you
feel, and ask for their assistance.

Getting Help

Effective participation in federal regulatory proceedings often requires
considerable technical expertise. Unfortunately, it is often expensive to
obtain such expertise—and often difficult to find witnesses outside the
regulated industry. The Center for Science in the Public Interest is using
a computer to match people who need technical assistance with experts
who can provide it. Forms for either requesting help or offering it are
in Appendix 18-E (p. 935). Consumers Union (CU) is also in the
process of compiling a list of professionals who are available to help
consumer action programs. People who have indicated their willingness
to participate in consumer programs are indexed both by profession and
by state. The Washington office of CU acts as a liaison between consumer groups in need of professional witnesses and these experts. No
copies of the complete listing are given out or sold, but consumer
groups in need of expert assistance can be referred to such professionals
by writing Consumers Union, 1714 Massachusetts Avenue, N.W., Washington, D.C. 20036. Make your request for professional assistance as
specific as possible and include an acknowledgment that names furnished will not be used for any commercial or partisan political purposes.
    Once you have solved the problem of obtaining experts of your own
to counter the expensive expertise retained by industry, there is still a
problem of how to use expertise most efficiently. If you are testifying
at a hearing, use your witness not just to present your position on
direct examination, but also draw on his knowledge during cross-
examination of the other side's witnesses. A technique which might
prove useful is suggested by a provision in the Atomic Energy Commission's Rules of Practice. This provides for lay interrogators in technical areas, and, in effect, allows the interrogator to conduct the cross-
examination of technical witnesses [10 C.F.R. 2.733]. An application

for an order permitting such interrogators in technical proceedings before other agencies might prove successful and useful.

Another technique is to enlist the support of other federal agencies which are supposed to be advancing your particular interest. For example, the Environmental Protection Agency has intervened in a Federal Power Commission hydroelectric licensing proceeding to see that environmental consequences are adequately considered. Other agencies, such as the Equal Employment Opportunity Commission, may at least give a sympathetic ear. One example of what such assistance can mean is the provision in many agency rules that a hearing transcript be available without charge on request by another federal agency.

Some of the suggestions in this book can be carried out by individuals working alone, but most will require several people working together. How you organize people to work together can be as varied as the people and their goals, but the five-person unit described here is one way to proceed.

The minimum number of five people allows one person to be responsible for each of the basic general tools. One should be a lawyer or a person with some legal training or interest to insure that each legal detail of the regulatory process is followed, and that the best advantage is taken of the Freedom of Information Act (FOIA). A second person, designated as a liaison with administrative agency staff members (particularly those close to the group's geographic area of activity), will become particularly knowledgeable about the agency's complaint process. A third person should be designated to coordinate the collection, evaluation, and dissemination of product information obtained from the marketplace, including regular correspondence with similar groups in the community and throughout the country. A fourth person should be responsible for maintaining a surveillance and evaluation program on the agency's information activities to insure that they are accurate, complete, understandable, and useful. The fifth person should coordinate the group's efforts, seeing that the product and public information data gathered gets to the proper individuals for relay to the agency, and, outside the organization, that complaints are made, papers filed, and contacts with agency officials maintained, including routine observation of expert advisory committees. If each of these people spends between five and ten hours a week on his or her assigned tasks, this relatively small group could have a surprisingly large influence. If many such groups were developed across the country, they could conceivably change the entire direction of federal administrative agencies.

It is important to remember that the tasks are not complex; they require only an informed use of common sense, some interest in the area, and a systematic and sustained effort. The jobs for members are described more fully in the following paragraphs.

1. The legal specialist should be a lawyer, a law student, or someone with capable interest in the law. The legal work that must be done for the group is not especially difficult. Reading statutes and following steps laid out in the appropriate sections of the Code of Federal Regulations will usually fulfill the necessary legal requirements. The specific area of concern for the person assuming the legal responsibilities of the group should be the details of the regulation-issuing process and the FOIA. The legal procedures required to comment on regulations and to obtain information were supposedly designed to be carried out by individual private citizens who do not have formal legal training. Following those procedures will at least establish a record of good faith attempts, and if they are frustrated they may show that, under current conditions, change is not possible, and thus pave the way for improved procedures.

The search for a person to deal with legal problems might prove difficult, but there are usually young lawyers and law students willing to contribute time to public interest causes. Local bar associations, legal aid committees, legal services offices, and any other groups or individuals expressing concern for the public interest are potential sources for an attorney who might be willing to give five to ten hours a week. Law students are usually quite capable of doing the legal work necessary for such a group. If none of these approaches turns up a lawyer or law student, then any reasonably alert individual who is interested in the law and willing to spend some time can learn the necessary legal procedures.

2. The person within the group performing agency liaison must assume the responsibility for maintaining and coordinating communication between the group and agency officials in the area. He should set up periodic meetings, visits, and communications with administrative officials in order to develop a relationship between the group and the agency. This person should come to know the structure and complaint procedures of the agency as well as the agency personnel know them.

It is through this liaison that the group communicates its interests, displeasures, and compliments to the agency, and also convinces the agency of the breadth and depth of its interest. Convincing the agency of the reality of a group's concern is the first step in building credibility, both with the agency and the public. The bureaucracy tends to embrace and favor those who understand its language. Learning to translate consumer concerns into the language of the agency is an important part of learning to influence the agency.

3. In order for the group's communications to be substantive, the group must establish procedures for collecting, evaluating, and disseminating data such as information on products being sold. One individual in the group should assume the responsibility for working out a program for gathering and using this information. Individual methods will vary from area to area, but there are some general procedures that can be adopted for group use.

For agencies dealing with consumer products, such as the Food and Drug Administration or the Federal Trade Commission, part of such a program involves routine monitoring of the markets where members and others shop. This means taking a few extra minutes each shopping trip to check labels, practices, and quality of products in food and drug stores to discover any practices which should be changed. Routinely gathering information about product quality, safety, labeling and advertising should become a regular part of the group members' routines. (A manual on how to conduct a pricing survey can be obtained by sending $5 to the Center for Study of Responsive Law, P.O. Box 19367, Washington, D.C. 20036.)

In addition, there should be an organized effort to gather information from people who are not members of the group. You could establish and publicize a telephone number to be called or address to be written with food and drug purchase complaints. Gathering this information and transmitting it to the agency in some cohesive format is a task to be organized by careful planning by one member of the group.

4. A fourth person should handle both the public information activities of the group and surveillance of the public information of the agency. The first job requires meeting with the various representatives of the news media in the community and explaining the purpose of the group, and then being sure that they are all kept informed of current group activities. Informing the public of your action is a prime responsibility of the group. When something is happening that is important to a large segment of the community, the news media will usually report it. Appendix 11-C (p. 662) is a sample press release. Remember that a press release is a factual account which can be printed as a news story. (Providing thoroughly researched background information to overworked, deadline-pressured reporters in a timely fashion may prevent a one-sided story based only on the official line.)

The second part of the public information task involves routine reading and evaluation of the agency's public information material, especially for accuracy and relevance. This means getting all agency press releases and other public information regularly, reading them, and then notifying the agency of any errors of omission and commission. In addition, the person in charge of public information may prepare material that the group feels might be useful for the agency to issue.

It is this person who maintains contact with other similar groups in the community or across the country, which means performing the task usually assigned to a corresponding secretary. That job is a lineal descendant of the correspondence committees of the American Revolution, which met to receive and send to committees in other parts of the country letters describing the revolutionary activities taking place in each area. In the organized consumer group the individual in charge of public information should have the responsibility of finding out what other groups may be developing, either in his own area or in other places which might have had similar experiences, as well as communicating the group's own experiences as widely as possible.

5. Someone must insure that members of the group are working together and not at cross purposes. The coordinator makes arrangements for periodic meetings, maintains the files, and sees to it that communication within the group is maintained. Depending on how you want to organize your group, the coordinator may assume varying degrees of direction and authority. He may be an acknowledged leader who makes all important decisions for the group, or he may be a facilitator for the efforts of all the members.

Be prepared for a few problems in the group. Since none of you will be in it for the money, there will be a natural tendency for people to seek satisfaction from the work in other ways, such as exercise of power in and outside the group, or the public attention frequently focused on the coordinator or the public information representative. Beware of what has been described as "the shoals of personal piques, ego problems, envy, megalomania, resentment, deception, and other frailties" [Nader and Ross, *Action for a Change* (New York: Grossman Publishers, 1972), p. 11]. They are distributed among all people, and the nonprofit nature of your effort is no guarantee against them. Be as honest with yourselves about responsibility, responsiveness, and authority within your group as you are in your other efforts, and occasionally check your principles against your actions.

Money is another problem that can defeat good intentions. Often people who want to organize groups for action on public issues flounder because they feel that they must raise money before they can act. But it is possible to develop a small, organized consumer unit as described here without raising much money. If the homes of participants are used for meetings, storage space, and places to work out of, there is no need to rent an office. The minor costs for magazine subscriptions or some other initial outlay can also be accepted on an individual basis by the members. Of course a lack of money will limit the activities of the group. But a lot can be done just with individual effort. As the group has initial (and perhaps minor) success using its own donated services, it can build a reputation and even a following. Then it is time to consider raising funds for other projects.

Once a reputation is formed on the basis of achievement, a possible method of financing is to develop a general membership in the community served by the group. This will involve developing mechanisms for sharing the decision making with the general membership, which will provide money through dues. Another modest source of income is to use the group's accumulated information and research to prepare and sell a mimeographed information letter to the general community. Usually such an effort, if done well, can more than pay for itself. These are a few examples of the types of activities that can be undertaken when the group decides to grow. All of them are based on the ability of the group to stick successfully to its task of continuous organized effort on an agency for a period of at least a year.

Proposals for Change

The proposals for citizen access in this book requiring legal assistance were not included in order to stir up business for lawyers; if anything, they should serve as reminders of jobs lawyers could do for public good instead of their own financial welfare. They were included because most opportunities for public access involve procedures which are basically adversarial: the agency involved makes some decision after hearing arguments for different solutions to a problem. These arguments may be presented through informal conferences, written comments submitted after publication of a proposal, or in the course of a full-scale hearing, but the process nearly always involves legal advocacy. The administrative process simply does not mean that wise and disinterested men in administrative agencies consider unbiased data about problems and then make rulings which they think will best serve the public interest. It is not an aspersion on the integrity of people in administrative agencies to say that their decisions are often influenced by persuasive advocacy. The solution is not just to appoint better regulators and give them the resources they need; it is to devise a structure that will recognize the fundamentally adversarial nature of the administrative process and provide for advocacy for all the affected interests on something approaching a basis of equality. The cost of legal representation in administrative hearings, and the candid admission by many specialized firms, such as those in communications law, that they feel it would be a conflict of interest to represent both commercial clients and public groups, should make it clear that the availability of advocates for industry can hardly be compared with the available advocacy for the undifferentiated interests of the general public.

It is because of this fundamental disparity of advocacy that periodic proposals for restructuring bureaucracies are only of secondary importance. It probably would be better for the Atomic Energy Commission (AEC) to be split in half, with some different agency responsible for regulating the safety of nuclear technology; it would be a definite improvement to have a rational system for making decisions about allocation and development of power instead of scattering the responsibilities at random throughout the government. But these proposals and others, such as those of the Ash Commission (*A New Regulatory Framework,* available for $1 from the Government Printing Office), would merely change the name and some minor rules of the game, while leaving it as one-sided as ever. The subgovernment of agency personnel and the regulated industry, with their intermediaries of Washington lawyers and trade press, would adjust to the new titles and structures with little trouble. A more fundamental change is necessary for representation of consumers as well as producers.

Providing effective advocacy for the unrepresented takes, first of all, organization by and of them. This book provides some of the information necessary for that effort. But it is not enough to assume that an organization of parents or television viewers can have an equal voice with the financial, legal, and technical resources of children's clothing manufacturers or television networks. That assumption was set forth in classic form in December 1971 when the Administrative Conference of the United States debated a modest proposal for public participation in administrative proceedings. The Conference is a permanent advisory organization of agency representatives and administrative lawyers who meet annually to make recommendations on improving the administrative process. It has about eighty members, and has been described as the "Supreme Soviet of the Federal Bureaucracy." The Conference was considering a recommendation that agencies consider, among other things, encouraging *pro bono publico* legal representation of public interest groups in agency proceedings, and payment of some expenses for such groups. The ten-man governing council of the Conference had voted against adoption of the proposal, and one of the council members explained their position by saying that there was a difference between having *equality* of opportunity to participate in administrative proceedings, and *encouraging* people to participate. The council, he continued, was in favor of equality, but encouragement was another matter. It didn't take long for one member of the Conference to comment that the "equality" which the council had in mind was reminiscent of Anatole France's aphorism: "The law, in its majestic equality, forbids the rich as well as the poor to sleep under bridges, to beg in the streets, and to steal bread."

But the council had its way. As debate went on, it turned increasingly into a series of self-serving statements by representatives of the various agencies, who took the floor to tell how much they had done to make it easier for the public to be heard. Those testimonials, plus warnings that public participation would only serve to encourage the lunatic fringe and that reimbursement of expenses would turn Lone Rangers into bounty hunters (the day after a *Washington Post* headline characterized Ralph Nader as the "Lone Ranger" of the consumer movement), persuaded the Conference that an abstract endorsement of public participation was enough. The modest recommendation for experimentation, with some devices to make such participation a reality, was defeated by voice vote. Since then the Conference's rejection has been cited in at least one court ruling against public interest groups. It was quite a change from the Conference's 1969 Report, which had encouraged agencies to employ a staff to act as "People's Counsel" in proceedings affecting the poor. But that proposal was adopted in 1968, when the memory of the "Poor People's Campaign," camped by the Lincoln Memorial and making daily trips to the doors of the bureaucracy, was still fresh.

The major objections voiced by the Conference were that the pace of administrative proceedings would be delayed by public participants, and that such participation would cost money. The first objection carries with it the assumption that administrative proceedings are presently carried out with some speed to be maintained at the cost of shutting out people who are the subjects of the process, and it ignores the most basic industry tactic of delaying inevitable agency actions as long as possible. The argument of cost is potent for taxpayers only if it is not kept in perspective. First, recall that the expense to which industry goes in order to insure its own representation is considered by both industry and the government as a cost of doing business. Thus, the astronomical legal expenses, such as those reported by railroads to the Interstate Commerce Commission, are included in the "rate base" which is passed on to consumers, and are deductible in computing taxable income. Second, consider that the proposal called for experimentation with compensation for a few minor expenses of participation in administrative proceedings. Former Federal Communications (FCC) Commissioner Nicholas Johnson once tried to put the cost of the entire administration of the federal government in perspective:

> If you take the Federal budget, $200 billion, roughly, and take all of the expenses associated with the judicial branch of the Government, all of the salaries and the travel expense, the publishing, and the courthouse, and so forth, and put that on one line; all the money associated with the legislative branch of the Government, the salaries of the Senators and Congressmen and their staff, and this [New Senate Office] building, and travel, and printing of the Congressional Record, all of that, and put it on another line. Take all of the budget of all of the independent regulatory Commissions, every dime spent on them totally, put them on a third line. Take the salary expenses for most of the executive branch agencies with the exception of defense and a couple of others, put them on the fourth line. Total that. That total is one-half of one percent of the Federal budget. I mean, you could become anarchist and abolish the whole Government, and you would never see it on April 15 on your income tax return. [Hearings before the Subcommittee on Administrative Practice and Procedures, Committee on the Judiciary, United States Senate, 91st Cong., 2d Sess. on S. 3434 and S. 2544, 21 July 1970]

He went on to describe where some of the other 99.5 percent went: in subsidies to merchant shipping ($700 million annually), oil import quotas ($6 billion per year), and $10 billion per year to the ten largest Department of Defense contractors.

Most agencies have ample authority to pay for legal representation of consumer groups that would otherwise be unable to appear before them. The statutory authority of the ICC is one example of this unused method for hearing more than the industry side of things. Unfortunately, agencies have been reluctant to do more than grudgingly concede that consumer groups have a right to participate. The standard agency response to attempts by such groups to participate has shifted from outright refusal (for which the FCC and others have been reprimanded by the courts) to allowing participation without alleviating the costs of such participation. For example, the FCC has refused to allow a broadcast licensee to reimburse a public interest group for legal expenses as part of a negotiated settlement agreement. The Department of Justice opposed the Commission's refusal, and in its brief on appeal to the courts the Department commented:

> No citizens' groups could properly prepare and handle a petition to deny before the Commission without lawyers to counsel them: professional and specialized assistance is essential. This need is especially acute in the case of those economic and social groups most likely to be the victims of inadequate service.

The FTC was less decisive when requested to reimburse some minor expenses incurred by a group of law students who had intervened in a proceeding. Instead of refusing outright, former Chairman Kirkpatrick of the FTC passed the buck by formally asking the Comptroller General to advise whether the Commission had authority to make such a payment. The Comptroller General heads the General Accounting Office (GAO), which is an arm of Congress charged with checking up on agency expenditures. If the members of the Administrative Conference were concerned about the speed of administrative proceedings, they should have considered the GAO's deliberate speed in handling the FTC's question. The request was sent by the FTC in March 1971. In the summer of that year several members of Congress, including Senators Percy and Kennedy, wrote letters to the Comptroller General urging him to rule on the FTC's question. The reply to inquiries was that the GAO was "giving this matter detailed and thorough consideration."

More than a year after former Chairman Kirkpatrick's request, the GAO officially declared that "appropriated funds of the Commission would be available to assure proper case preparation" of indigent intervenors. Even so, the Commission, which had already ruled that the student group was indigent and that they were responsible spokesmen "for substantial issues of law or fact which would not otherwise be properly raised or argued," voted three to two (without discussion) to deny the students' motion for reimbursement. However, Commissioner Dixon changed his vote before the decision was publicly announced, so that on 3 November 1972 the Commission ordered that the expenses be paid.

The GAO is not the only agency that has trouble getting around to matters that would facilitate public participation in administrative proceedings. In the fall of 1970 a proposal called the Model Rules for Citizen Participation in Administrative Proceedings was submitted by a coalition of consumer groups to all of the administrative agencies. The text of the Model Rules was reprinted in the Congressional Record, one of a very few places where the proposal was printed for the public to see. It was submitted to twenty-one chairmen of independent regulatory agencies and to twelve executive agencies, as well as being sent to the White House for possible promulgation as an executive order; at almost all of the agencies the Model Rules suffered the fate that is the fundamental barrier to the use of rule making petitions as a means of public participation: the petition was ignored. Only two of the thirty-three agencies that received the petition treated it as a proposal for rule making and assigned docket numbers. Six others replied that they had received the petition, but took no other action. The others did not even acknowledge receipt. Perhaps they are, like the GAO with the FTC's question, giving the matter "detailed and thorough consideration," but it seems likely that the proposal is destined for oblivion in agency file cabinets.

Several bills have been introduced in Congress attempting to establish an independent consumer advocate to speak for consumers before all of the agencies. The Consumer Protection Agency Bill of 1972 was finally killed after being worked over and gutted by an intensive industry and White House lobbying campaign. When, and in what shape, the idea of an independent consumer advocate will emerge from Congress is still in question. But the idea of public participation is as persistent as representative government, and it cannot be defeated by a single lobbying campaign or bureaucratic indifference. Rather than being a mere faddish notion, as many agency officials and members of Congress seem to feel, it is as fundamental as the urge to have some say in the decisions that affect your life. It starts, on the federal level, with the realization that decisions made by apparently remote and impenetrable federal agencies affect our lives in fundamental ways. It takes shape when people act on these realizations and begin to learn what those agencies are and how the system loosely called "the administrative process" works. It continues when people engaged in such efforts learn from the experience of others and begin to take steps of their own to work on that system and make it respond. This book is one step in that process.

The Environmental Bookshelf

The Environmental Bookshelf

Legal References

Sidney Edelman, The Law of Air Pollution Control (Dayton,
    Ohio: Professional Books Service, 1971)

John Esposito, "Air and Water Pollution: What To Do
    While Waiting for Washington," Harvard Civil
    Liberties--Civil Rights Law Review, Vol. 5, No. 1,
    January 1970

Gladwin Hill, "The Politics of Air Pollution: Public
    Interest and Pressure Groups," 10 Arizona Law
    Review 37

Norman J. Landau and Paul D. Rheingold, The Environmental
    Law Handbook (New York: Ballantine/Friends of the
    Earth, 1970)

Leonard Miller and Doyle Borchers, "Private Lawsuits and
    Air Pollution Control," American Bar Association
    Journal, May 1970, Vol. 56

Joseph Saz, Defending the Environment (New York: Alfred
    Knopf, 1971)

The Environmental Law Digest: Primer for the Practice
    of Law. Reprinted from the Environmental Law Report-
    er, Vol. 1, No. 1, January 1971. ($1.00 from the
    Environmental Law Institute, 1346 Connecticut
    Avenue, N.W., Washington, DC 20036)

Environmental Law Reporter. Published by the Environ-
    mental Law Institute (address above). Subscriptions
    for cumulative looseleaf monthly are $50.00/year

Environmental Law. Northwestern School of Law--Lewis
    and Clark College. Vol. 1, Spring 1970, No. 1
    (Published at 10015 S.W. Terwilliger Blvd., Port-
    land, OR 97219, $3.00 per issue)

Legal Control of the Environment - The Fourth (1972).
    Available from the Practising Law Institute, 1133
    Avenue of the Americas, New York, NY 10036. $20.00

"Qui Tam Actions and the 1899 Refuse Act: Citizen Law-
    suits Against the Polluters of the Nation's Water-
    ways." Pamphlet available from the Subcommittee
    on Conservation and Natural Resources of the House
    Committee on Government Operations

Arnold W. Reitze, Environmental Law, Volumes One and Two
    (Washington, DC: North American International, 1972)

Richard M. Hall, Robert Stover and Jeff Tauber, Citizen
    Action Handbook: The Refuse Act Permit Program
    (New York: Natural Resources Defense Council, 36
    W. 44th Street, New York, NY 10036) Free

"Challenge of the Environment: A Primer on EPA's Statu-
    tory Authority" (Environmental Protection Agency,
    Washington, DC 20460) Free

General Environmental Books

"The Quest for Environmental Quality," Federal and State
    Action, 1969-1970, Annotated Bibliography. Advisory
    Commission on Intergovernmental Relations, Washington,
    DC 20575, April 1971. (For sale by the Superintendent
    of Documents, U.S. Government Printing Office, Wash-
    ington, DC 20402, $.35)

J. Clarence Davies III, The Politics of Pollution (New
    York: Pegasus, 1970)

Environmental Quality, Third Annual Report of the Council
    on Environmental Quality, August 1972 (Available
    free from the Council, 722 Jackson Place, N.W., Wash-
    ington, DC 20006)

"A Citizen's Guide to Clean Air," A Manual for Citizen
    Action, 1972 (Available from Conservation Foun-
    dation, 1717 Massachusetts Avenue, N.W., Washington,
    DC 20036) Free

"Action for Clean Air," A Manual for Citizen Partici-
    pation in State Implementation Plan Proceedings,
    1971. (Write to the National Resources Defense
    Council, 36 W. 44th Street, New York, NY 10036) Free

John Esposito, Vanishing Air, The Nader Task Force Report
    on Air Pollution (New York: Grossman, Bantam Books,
    1970)

Helen Leavitt, Superhighway-Superhoax (New York: Ballantine, 1970)

Barry Commoner, The Closing Circle (New York: Bantam Books, 1972)

Rene DuBos, A God Within (New York: Scribner, 1972)

Rene DuBos, Only One Earth (New York: Ballantine, 1973)

Edward Hessler, A Bibliographic Essay. Department of Ecology and Behavioral Biology. (Bell Museum of Natural History, University of Minnesota, Minneapolis, MN 55455)

T. Brown, Oil On Ice (San Francisco: Sierra Club Battlebook, 1971)

Kathy and Peter Montague, Mercury (San Francisco: Sierra Club Battlebook, 1971)

Thomas Whiteside, The Withering Rain: America's Herbicidal Policy (New York: Dutton, 1971)

Richard Saltonstall, Jr., Your Environment and What You Can Do About It (New York: Walker, 1970)

Paul Ehrlich, The Population Bomb (New York: Ballantine/Sierra Club, 1968)

James Ridgeway, The Politics of Ecology (New York: Dutton, 1971)

Garrett DeBell, Ed., Environmental Handbook (New York: Ballantine/Friends of the Earth, 1970)

Garrett DeBell, Ed., Voters' Guide to Environmental Politics (New York: Ballantine, 1970)

Sam Love, Ed., Earth Tool Kit (New York: Pocket Books, 1971)

John G. Mitchell and C. L. Stallings, Eds., Ecotactics (New York: Pocket Books, 1970)

Conservation Directory (Washington, DC: National Wildlife Federation, 1412 16th St., N.W.)

Paul Swatek, The Users' Guide to Protection of the Envi-
     ronment (New York: Ballantine, 1970)

Air Pollution Primer. National TB and Respiratory Dis-
     ease Association. (Available from Metropolitan
     Washington Coalition for Clean Air, 1714 Massachu-
     setts Avenue, N.W., Washington, DC 20036, $.50)

Air Pollution. Air Pollution Workbook. Water Pollu-
     tion. Pesticides. (All available from Scientists
     Institute for Public Information, 30 East 68th
     Street, New York, NY 10021)

Wesley Marx, The Frail Ocean (New York: Ballantine, 1970)

James Fallows, The Water Lords, The Nader Task Force
     Report on the Savannah River (New York: Grossman,
     1971; Bantam, 1972)

David Zwick with Marcy Benstock, Water Wasteland, The
     Nader Task Force Report on Water Pollution (New
     York: Grossman, 1971; Bantam, 1972)

Rachel Carson, Silent Spring (New York: Fawcett/Crest,
     1970)

F. Graham, Jr., Since Silent Spring (New York: Fawcett/
     Crest, 1970)

Harrison Wellford, Sowing the Wind, The Nader Task Force
     Report on the U.S.D.A. (New York: Grossman, 1972;
     Bantam, 1973)

Groups That Can Help

Below are listed some of the many national
organizations working in the public interest,
in addition to those listed in the individual
chapters.

Center for Concerned
    Engineering
1224 DuPont Circle Bldg.
Washington, DC 20036
202/659 1126

Small research organiza-
tion doing analyses of
product hazards, including
transportation and build-
ing fields.

Center for Law and Social
    Policy
1751 N Street, N.W.
Washington, DC 20036
202/872 0670

Research and legal organization working on national
and international economic
issues (export, import
policies). Also, rights
of mentally handicapped.
Issues docket of activi-
ties four times a year.
Free

Center for Science in the
    Public Interest
1779 Church Street, N.W.
Washington, DC 20036
202/332 6000

Organization of scientists
offering advice on strip-
mining, highways, fuels
and fuel additives. Con-
tributors receive monthly
newsletter. Evaluating
Highway Environmental Im-
pacts available for $3.00

Citizen Action Group
2000 P Street, N.W.
Washington, DC 20036
202/833 9704

Gives aid, in form of ad-
vice and training, on how
to organize public interest
action groups, how to un-
dertake projects for reform.
Aim is to increase velocity
of exchange between local
groups and public interest
advocates in Washington.

Common Cause
2100 M Street, N.W.
Washington, DC 20036
202/833 1200

Membership/lobbying organization. Provides members with information on selected political and legislative issues.

"Common Cause Report From Washington," monthly to all members. Membership $15/year.

Conservation Foundation
1717 Massachusetts Ave., N.W.
Washington, DC 20036
202/265 8882

Conducts research, education and information programs to stimulate public and private decision-making and action to improve quality of environment.

Corporate Accountability
    Research Group
1832 M Street, N.W.
Washington, DC 20036
202/833 3931

Small group of lawyers, one economist, organized to investigate antitrust legislation, enforcement, and degree of corporate economic concentration. Group lobbies, participates in congressional hearings. Drafting legislation to require federal chartering of giant corporations.

Corporate Information
    Center
475 Riverside Drive
New York, NY 10027
212/870 2294

An office of National Council of Churches. Provides church constituency with information on issues of corporate social responsibility. Goal is to influence church community on investment practices.

Newsletter, list of publications available on request.

Council on Economic
    Priorities
456 Greenwich Street
New York, NY 10013
212/431 4770

Disseminates information on practices of U.S. corporations in four areas: minority employment, effect on environment, defense production and foreign investments. Publishes bi-monthly <u>Economic Priorities Report</u>, in-depth studies.

Subscriptions $10/student, $25/individual, $350/corporation.

Environmental Defense Fund 162 Old Town Road East Setauket, L.I.,NY 11733 516/751 5191	Serves as legal action arm for scientific community. Currently has 80 cases on docket. 36,000 members.
1525 18th Street, N.W. Washington, DC 20036 202/833 1484	EDF Newsletter issues four times a year. Membership $10, students $5.
Environmental Policy Center 324 C Street, S.E. Washington, DC 20003 202/547 6500	Formed in 1972 by Washington environmental lobbyists whose work had influenced Clean Air Act of 1970, fights against SST, Everglades jetport, Cross-Florida Barge Canal. Serves as Washington base for local and regional citizens' groups. Non-membership.
Environmental Action 1346 Connecticut Ave.,N.W. Washington, DC 20036 202/833 1845	Lobbying organization, specializing in air and water pollution legislation. Organized Earth Day in 1970. "Environmental Action," bi-weekly newsletter, $7.50 per year. <u>Earth Tool Kit</u> - see Appendix 18-A (in this book).
Friends of the Earth 72 Jane Street New York, NY 10014 212/675 5911	Membership/lobbying organization. Will offer specific advice on energy problems, strip-mining, sulfur tax, predator control, the Everglades.
620 C Street, S.E. Washington, DC 20005 202/543 4312	"Not Man Apart"--monthly

newsletter published with
League of Conservation
Voters and John Muir Insti-
tute. $15/year membership.
Non-member subscription
rate $5/year.

Izaak Walton League of
America
1800 N. Kent Street
Arlington, VA 22209
703/528 1818

Membership organization.
Can furnish speakers, literature, and films on conservation. Advice on water
pollution problems.

"Outdoor America"--monthly
newsletter to members.
$10/year.

League of Women Voters of
the United States
1730 M Street, N.W.
Washington, DC 20036
202/296 1770

Membership organization.
Leagues in every state.
Promotes political responsibility through informed
and active participation in
government.

National Parks and Con-
servation Association
1701 18th Street, N.W.
Washington, DC 20009
202/265 2717

Private. Has reference
library open to public. Can
offer information and assistance on problems and their
solutions in national parks
and over-all environment.
Publication list available.

Natural Resources Defense
Council
36 West 44th Street
New York, NY 10036
212/869 0150

1700 N Street, N.W.
Washington, DC 20036
202/783 5710

Environmental law group.
Advises local and regional
groups on applicable legislation and means of enforcement. When expedient, represents these groups in
court. Projects include
suit to halt ConEd proposed
construction at Storm King;
suit banning N.Y. State
from dumping waste into Vermont's Lake Champlain.

National Wildlife Federation
1412 16th Street, N.W.
Washington, DC 20036
202/483 1550

Membership organization.
Staff can offer advice on
environmental problems.
List of publications available. Reference library
open to public.

Conservation Directory,
compiled annually, is ex-
cellent listing of local,
state, and national con-
servation groups. $2.00

EQ Index--annual synopsis
of pollution problems.

Nature Conservancy
1800 N. Kent Street
Arlington, VA 22209
703/524 3151

Membership organization
involved almost solely
with acquiring ecologically
valuable land for preser-
vation.

Nature Conservancy News,
quarterly. Membership
$10/year.

Project on Corporate
      Responsibility
1525 18th Street, N.W.
Washington, DC 20036
202/387 3210

Initially organized to
conduct Campaign GM, group
sponsored shareholder proposals to ten major corporations in 1972. Filed petitions asking SEC to make
corporations accountable
for their social impact.
Newsletter is gratis to
shareholders who support
Project's work.

Resources for the Future
1755 Massachusetts Ave.,N.W.
Washington, DC 20036
202/462 4400

Private corporation founded
in 1952, funded largely by
Ford Foundation, to study
natural resources and ramifications of their use.
Newsletter, substantive
Annual Report, and list of
in-depth publications are
free.

Retired Professional Action
    Group
2000 P Street, N.W.
Washington, DC 20036
202/785 3266

Research and advocacy on
problems of wide social
concern such as land sale
abuses, discrimination in
employment, conditions in
nursing homes.

Scientists' Institute for
    Public Information
30 East 68th Street
New York, NY 10021
212/249 3200

Provides objective infor-
mation on public policy
issues affecting environ-
ment. Local committees
help in finding expert witnesses for hearings.
Worked with Natural Re-
sources Defense Council on
technical aspects of air
pollution. List of pub-
lications and local com-
mittees available.

Sierra Club
1050 Mills Tower
San Francisco, CA 94104
415/981 8634

Education and legislative
activities in conservation
and environmental areas.
Local chapters have vari-
ety of services--speakers,
"hot line" for environmental problems, and recrea-
tional activities.

Sierra Club Legal Defense
    Fund
311 California Street
San Francisco, CA 94104
415/398 1411

"Sierra Club Bulletin"--
monthly magazine to mem-
bers. Membership fees vary.

Wilderness Society
729 15th Street, N.W.
Washington, DC 20005
202/347 4132

Educational organization
aimed at helping groups to
preserve wilderness. Act
as consultants to local
groups when wilderness
areas come up for review
by Interior Department.

Directory of State and Local Government and Non-Government Consumer Groups

Prepared by Consumer Federation
of America, Inc.
February   1973
Price $1.00

Non-Government Groups

Alabama

Alabama Consumers Association
1018 S. 18th St.
Birmingham, AL 35205

Alaska

Kenai Peninsula Consumers Council
Box 2940
Kenai, AK 99611

Arizona

Arizona Consumers Council
6840 Camino de Michael St.
Tucson, AZ 85718   (chapters in Flagstaff, Phoenix,
Tucson)

Arkansas

Arkansas Consumer Research
314 Chester St.
Little Rock, AR 72201

California

Consumer Federation of California
911 13th St.
Modesto, CA 95354

--Orange County and city of Los Angeles
Los Angeles and Orange Counties Chapter, CFC
621 S. Virgil
Los Angeles, CA 90005

--city of Beverly Hills
American Consumers Council
9270 Wilshire Blvd, Suite 208
Beverly Hills, CA 90212

Čalifornia cont'd.

San Francisco Consumer Action
2209 Van Ness Avenue
San Francisco, CA 94109

Connecticut

Connecticut Consumer Association, Inc.
425 College St.
New Haven, CT 06511

District of Columbia

D.C. Citywide Consumer Council
745 50th St., N.E.
Washington, DC 20019

Consumer Help Center
714 21st St., N.W.
Washington, DC 20006

Anacostia Consumer Help Center
2906 Martin Luther King Ave., S.E.
Washington, DC 20032

Ayuda (Spanish-speaking center)
2436 1/4 .18th St., N.W.
Washington, DC 20009

Neighborhood Consumer Information Center
3005 Georgia Ave., N.W.
Washington, DC 20001

Florida

Florida Consumers Federation
c/o Lillian Mohr
Florida State University
Tallahassee, FL 32306

Georgia

Georgia Consumer Council
Box 311 - Morris Brown College
Atlanta, GA 30314

Idaho

Idaho Consumer Affairs, Inc.
817 West Franklin St.
Boise, ID 83701

Illinois

    Consumer Federation of Illinois
    53 West Jackson Blvd., Room 1625
    Chicago, IL 60604

    National Consumers United
    1043 Chicago Ave.
    Evanston, IL 60602

Indiana

    Consumers Association of Indiana, Inc.
    1000 N. Madison Ave.
    Greenwood, IN 46142

Iowa

    Iowa Consumers League
    200 Walker, Suite A
    Des Moines, Iowa 50317

Kansas

    Consumer United Program
    8410 West Highway 54
    Wichita, KS 67209

        --city of Kansas City
    Kansas City Consumer Association
    7720 West 61st St.
    Shawnee Mission, KS 66202

Kentucky

    Consumers Association of Kentucky, Inc.
    2440 Eastway Dr.
    Lexington, KY 40508

Louisiana

    Louisiana Consumers' League
    P.O.Box 1332
    Baton Rouge, LA 70821

    5301 Camp St.
    New Orleans, LA

Maryland

    Maryland Consumers Association, Inc.
    10202 Lariston Lane
    Silver Spring, MD 20903

    P.O.Box 143
    Annapolis, MD 21404

Massachusetts

    Association of Massachusetts Consumers
    c/o Boston College
    Chestnut Hill, MA 02167

Michigan

    Consumer Alliance of Michigan
    P.O.Box 1051-A
    Detroit, MI 48232

    Consumer Action Center
    115 1/2 East Liberty St.
    Ann Arbor, MI 48107

        --city of Detroit
    Consumer Research Advisory Council
    9000 East Jefferson St., Apt. 4-5
    Detroit, MI 48214

    3127 East Canfield
    Detroit, MI 48207

        --city of Grand Rapids
    Southwest Consumer Services Center
    400 Franklin S.W.
    Grand Rapids, MI 49503

Minnesota

    Minnesota Consumers League
    P.O.Box 3063
    St. Paul, MN 55101

    1671 S. Victoria Rd.
    St. Paul, MN 55118

Mississippi

    Mississippi Consumer Association
    1601 Terrace Rd.
    Cleveland, MS 38732

Missouri

    Missouri Association of Consumers
    805 Edgewood
    Columbia, MO 65201

    St. Louis Consumer Federation
    7526 Byron Ave.
    St. Louis, MO 63105

Montana

> Montana Consumers Affairs Council, Inc.
> P.O.Box 417
> Helena, MT 59601
>
> P.O.Box 1501
> Great Falls, MT 59401

Nevada

> Consumers League of Nevada
> 1663 La Jolla Ave.
> Las Vegas, NV 89109

New Jersey

> Consumers League of New Jersey
> 20 Church St.
> Montclair, NJ 07042

New Mexico

> Albuquerque Consumer Federation
> Box 5219
> Sandia Base, NM 87115

New York

> New York Consumer Assembly
> 465 Grand St.
> New York, NY 10002
>
> Consumer Association of New York
> 109 Heather Drive
> Rochester, NY 14625
>
> Consumer Council of the Genessee Valley, Inc.
> P.O.Box 3949 - Brighton Station
> Rochester, NY 14610
>
> Metropolitan New York Consumer Council
> 1710 Broadway
> New York, NY 10019

North Carolina

> North Carolina Consumers Council, Inc.
> P.O.Box 1982
> Raleigh, NC 27602

Ohio

Consumers League of Ohio
940 Engineers Bldg.
Cleveland, OH 44114

Ohio Consumers Association
83 Deland Avenue
Columbus, OH 43214

Consumer Conference of Greater Cincinnati
318 Terrace Ave.
Cincinnati, OH 45220

Consumer Protection Association
118 St. Clair Ave.
Cleveland, OH 44114

Oregon

Oregon Consumers League
732 Southwest Third Ave.
Portland, OR 97204

Pennsylvania

Pennsylvania League for Consumer Protection
P.O.Box 948
Harrisburg, PA 17108

Consumers Education and Protective Association
6048 Ogontz Ave.
Philadelphia, PA 19141

Philadelphia Area Consumer Organization
2200 Locust St.
Philadelphia, PA 19103

Alliance for Consumer Protection
P.O.Box 1354
Pittsburgh, PA 15221

Bucks County Consumer Organization
Route 1
Newtown, PA 18940

Rhode Island

Rhode Island Consumers' League
c/o Urban League of Rhode Island
131 Washington St.
Providence, RI 02903

South Dakota

South Dakota Consumers League
P.O.Box 72
Brookings, SD 57006

Tennessee

Tennessee Consumer Alliance
P.O.Box 12352, Acklen Station
Nashville, TN 37312

Knoxville Area Chapter, TCA
P.O.Box 10712
Knoxville, TN 37919

Texas

Texas Consumer Association
P.O.Box 13191
Austin, TX 78711

Utah

League of Utah Consumers
444 S. 2nd St., W.
Salt Lake City, UT 84101

Virginia

Virginia Citizens Consumers Council
P.O.Box 3103
Alexandria, VA 22302

Washington

Washington Committee on Consumer Interests
2700 First Ave., Room 206
Seattle, WA 98121

West Virginia

Consumer Association of West Virginia
707 Forestry Tower
Morgantown, WV 26506

Wisconsin

Wisconsin Consumers League
7017 Dorchester Lane
Greendale, WI 53129

Green Bay Wisconsin Consumers League Chapter
P.O.Box 3731
Green Bay, WI 54303

Wisconsin cont'd.

Dane County Consumers League
626 Constitution Lane
Madison, WI 53711

The Greater Milwaukee Consumer League
9722 Watertown Plank Rd.
Milwaukee, WI 53266

Wyoming

Consumer United Program
863 South Spruce St.
Casper, Wyoming 82601

Government Agencies

Alabama

Asst. Attorney General for Consumer Protection
State Administration Bldg.
Montgomery, AL 36104

Alaska

Attorney General of Alaska
Pouch "K", State Capitol
Juneau, AK 99801

Arizona

Asst. Attorney General in Charge Consumer Fraud
    Division
159 State Capitol Bldg.
Phoenix, AZ 85007

Arkansas

Director, Consumer Protection Division
Office of Attorney General, Justice Bldg.
Little Rock, AR 72201

California

Sr. Asst. Attorney General in Charge,
    Consumer Protection Unit
600 State Bldg.
Los Angeles, CA 90012

Director, Dept. of Consumer Affairs
1010 N St.
Sacramento, CA 95814

<u>California</u> cont'd.

      --Humbolt County
Dept. of Weights and Measures and Consumer Affairs
P.O.Box 3757
Eureka, CA 95501

      --Santa Clara County
Dept. of Weights and Measures and Consumer Affairs
Division of Consumer Affairs
409 Matthew St.
Santa Clara, CA 95050

      --Ventura County
Dept. of Weights and Measures
Division of Consumer Affairs
608 El Rio Drive
Oxnard, CA 93030

      --city of Los Angeles
Chairman, Los Angeles Consumer Protection Committee
107 S. Broadway
Los Angeles, CA 90012

      --city of San Francisco
Chairman, Bay Area Consumer Protection
      Coordinating Committee
c/o Department of Justice
6000 State Bldg.
San Francisco, CA 94102

<u>Colorado</u>

      Asst. Attorney General, Office of Consumer Affairs
503 Farmers Union Bldg.
1575 Sherman St.
Denver, CO 80203

<u>Connecticut</u>

      Asst. Attorney General, Consumer Fraud Division
Capitol Annex, 30 Trinity St.
Hartford, CT 06115

      Commissioner, Dept. of Consumer Protection
State Office Bldg.
Hartford, CT 06115

      Director, Consumer Frauds Division
State Office Bldg.
Hartford, CT 06115

Delaware

Deputy Attorney General
Consumer Protection Division
1206 King St.
Wilmington, DE 19801

Director, Division of Consumer Affairs
704 Delaware Ave.
Wilmington, DE 19801

District of Columbia

City Hall Complaint Center
District Bldg. - First Floor, Room 7
14th St. & Pennsylvania Ave., N.W.
Washington, DC 20004

United Planning Organization
1021 - 14th St., N.W.
Washington, DC 20005

Neighborhood Legal Services
666 - 11th St., N.W.
Washington, DC 20001

Florida

Attorney General of Florida
State Capitol
Tallahassee, FL 32304

Director, Division of Consumer Affairs
Florida Dept. of Agric. & Consumer Services
Center Bldg.
Tallahassee, FL 32304

        --Dade County
Director, Consumer Protection Division
1351 N.W. 12th St.
Miami, FL 33125

Asst. State Attorney and Chief
Consumer Fraud Division
Metropolitan Dade County Justice Bldg.
1351 N.W. 12th St.
Miami, FL 33125

Consumer Affairs Officer
Division of Consumer Affairs
Dept. of Public Safety
220 East Bay St.
Jacksonville, FL 32202

        --city of St. Petersburg
Director of Consumer Affairs
264 First Avenue, N.
St. Petersburg, FL 33701

Georgia

        Program Director
        Georgia Consumer Services Program
        15 Peachtree St., Room 909
        Atlanta, GA 30303

                --city of Atlanta
        Consumer Affairs Specialist
        Community Relations Commission
        Memorial Drive Annex Bldg.
        121 Memorial Dr., SW
        Atlanta, GA 30303

Hawaii

        Director of Consumer Protection
        Office of the Governor
        P.O.Box 3767
        Honolulu, HI 96811

Idaho

        Asst. Attorney General in Charge
        Consumer Protection Division
        State Capitol
        Boise, ID 83707

Illinois
        Asst. Attorney General and Chief
        Consumer Fraud Section
        134 N. LaSalle St., Room 204
        Chicago, IL 60602

                --city of Chicago
        Dept. of Consumer Sales & Weights and Measures
        City Hall, 121 N. LaSalle St.
        Chicago, IL 60602

        Chicago Consumer Protection Committee
        U.S. Courthouse & Federal Office Bldg.
        Room 486 - 219 S. Dearborn St.
        Chicago, IL 60604

Indiana

        Director, Office of Consumer Protection
        219 State House
        Indianapolis, IN 46204

        Director, Consumer Advisory Council
        c/o Indiana Dept. of Commerce
        336 State House
        Indianapolis, IN 46204

<u>Indiana</u> cont'd.

        --city of Indianapolis
Dept. of Public Safety & Consumer Protection
Room 2542 City-County Bldg.
Indianapolis, IN 46204

<u>Iowa</u>

        Asst. Attorney General and Chief
Consumer Protection Division
20 East 13th Court
Des Moines, IA 50319

<u>Kansas</u>

        Asst. Attorney General in Charge
Consumer Protection Division
State House
Topeka, KS 66612

        --Sedgwick County
Deputy County Attorney and Director
Consumer Protection Division
Court House
Wichita, KS 67203

<u>Kentucky</u>

        Asst. Attorney General, Consumer Protection Division
State Capitol
Frankfort, KY 40601

        Chairman, Citizens' Commission for Consumer
            Protection
State Capitol
Frankfort, KY 40601

        --city of Louisville
Division of Weights and Measures & Consumer Affairs
Metropolitan Sewer District Bldg.
Louisville, KY 40202

<u>Louisiana</u>

        Director, Consumer Affairs and Promotion Office
Dept. of Agriculture
P.O.Box 44302, Capitol Station
Baton Rouge, LA 70804

        --city of New Orleans
New Orleans Consumer Protection Committee
1000 Masonic Temple Bldg.
333 St. Charles St.
New Orleans, LA 70130

<u>Louisiana</u>   cont'd.

    Office of Consumer Affairs
    City Hall - Room 8E06
    New Orleans, LA 70112

<u>Maine</u>

    Asst. Attorney General
    Consumer Protection Division
    State House
    Augusta, ME 04330

<u>Maryland</u>

    Asst. Attorney General and Chief
    Consumer Protection Division
    1200 One Charles Center
    Baltimore, MD 21201

        --Montgomery County
    Office of Consumer Affairs
    County Office Bldg.
    Rockville, MD 20850

        --Prince Georges County
    Consumer Protection Division
    Prince Georges County Court House
    Upper Marlboro, MD 20870

<u>Massachusetts</u>

    Chief, Consumer Protection Division
    State House
    Boston, MA 02133

    Secretary, Executive Office of Consumer Affairs
    State Office Bldg, Room 905
    100 Cambridge St.
    Boston, MA 02202

    Executive Secretary, Massachusetts Consumers' Council
    100 Cambridge St.
    Boston, MA 02202

        --city of Boston
    Boston Metro. Consumer Protection Commission
    c/o Federal Trade Commission
    J.F. Kennedy Federal Bldg. - Government Center
    Boston, MA 02203

Michigan

Asst. Attorney General in Charge
Consumer Protection
Law Building
Lansing, MI 48902

Special Asst. to the Governor for Consumer Affairs
c/o Department of Licensing
1033 S. Washington St.
Lansing, MI 48910

Chairman, Michigan Consumer Council
525 Hollister Building
Lansing, MI 48933

    --city of Detroit
Director, Interagency Consumer Commission
Office of the Mayor, City Hall
Detroit, MI 48226

Detroit Consumer Protection Coordinating Committee
c/o Law Building
Lansing, MI 48902

Minnesota

Special Asst. Attorney General for Consumer
    Protection
102 State Capitol
St. Paul, MN 55101

Director, Office of Consumer Services
Dept. of Commerce, Room 230
State Office Building
St. Paul, MN 55101

Mississippi

Asst. Attorney General, Consumer Protection Division
State Capitol
Jackson, MS 39201

Missouri

Asst. Attorney General, Consumer Protection Division
Supreme Court Building
Jefferson City, MO 65101

    --city of St. Louis
Office of Consumer Affairs
3511 Lindell Blvd.
St. Louis, MO 63103

Montana

Attorney General
The Capitol
Helena, MT 59601

Admin. Asst. to Governor
The Capitol
Helena, MT 59601

--Silver Bow County
Consumer Protection Division
Office of County Attorney
155 W. Granite St.
Butte, MT 59701

Nebraska

Consumer Affairs, Department of Agriculture
Box 4844
Lincoln, NE 68509

Nevada

Director, Consumer Affairs Division
Department of Commerce
South Fall St., Room 315
Carson City, NV 89701

New Hampshire

Attorney General
State House Annex
Concord, NH 03301

New Jersey

Director, Division of Consumer Affairs
1100 Raymond Blvd.
Newark, NJ 07102

--Camden County
Director, Camden County Office of Consumer Affairs
Commerce Building, Room 606
One Broadway
Camden, NJ 08101

New Mexico

Director, Consumer Protection Division
Supreme Court Building, Box 2246
Santa Fe, NM 87501

New York

Asst. Attorney General in Charge
Consumer Frauds and Protection Bureau
80 Centre St.
New York, NY 10013

Chairman, Consumer Protection Board
380 Madison Ave.
New York, NY 10017

--Nassau County
Commissioner, Office of Consumer Affairs
160 Old Country Road
Mineola, NY 11501

--Orange County
Director, Dept. of Weights & Measures and
        Consumer Affairs
Goshen, NY 10924

--Rensselaer County
Sealer, Dept. of Weights & Measures and
        Consumer Affairs
399 Whiteview Road
Troy, NY 12180

--Rockland County
Sealer-Coordinator, Office of Consumer Protection
County Office Building
New Hempsted Rd.
New City, NY 10956

--Westchester County
Sealer, Div. of Weights & Measures and
        Consumer Affairs
38 Brockway Place
White Plains, NY 10601

--city of Long Beach, Long Island
Director, Consumer Affairs
City Hall
Long Beach, Long Island, New York 11561

Commissioner, Dept. of Consumer Affairs
80 Lafayette St.
New York, NY 10013

--city of Schenectady
Sealer, Bureau of Weights & Measures and
        Consumer Protection
City Hall
Schenectady, NY 12305

New York cont'd.

    --city of Yonkers
Consumer Protection Officer
Office of Consumer Protection
City Hall, 138 S. Broadway
Yonkers, NY 10701

North Carolina

Consumer Protection Division
P.O.Box 629
Raleigh, NC 27602

North Dakota

Asst. Attorney General, Consumer Protection Division
The Capitol
Bismarck, NC 58501

Ohio

Consumer Protection Division
Dept. of Commerce - State of Ohio
275 East State St.
Columbus, OH 43215

    --city of Columbus
City Sealer of Weights & Measures
City Hall
Columbus, OH 43215

Oklahoma

Administrator, Dept. of Consumer Affairs
Lincoln Office Plaza, Suite 74
4545 Lincoln Blvd.
Oklahoma City, OK 73105

Oregon

Chief Counsel, Consumer Protection Division
555 State Office Building
Portland, OR 97201

Administrator, Consumer Services Division
Oregon Dept. of Commerce
Salem, OR 97310

    --Multnomah County
Director, Metropolitan Consumer Protection Agency
Multnomah County Court House, Room 600
Portland, OR 97204

Pennsylvania

Director, Bureau of Consumer Protection
Pennsylvania Dept. of Justice
2-4 N. Market Square
Harrisburg, PA 17101

Coordinator, Office of Consumer Affairs
Department of Agriculture
2301 N. Cameron St.
Harrisburg, PA 17120

--Allegheny County
Director, Allegheny County Bureau of Consumer
      Protection
209 Jones Law Building Annex
Pittsburgh, PA 15219

--Lackawanna County
Director, Department of Transportation,
      Environmental and Consumer Affairs
8th Floor News Building
Scranton, PA 18503

--city of Philadelphia
Director, Consumer Services
City Hall, Room 210
Philadelphia, PA 19106

Philadelphia Consumer Protection Committee
53 Long Lane
Upper Darby, PA 19082

Rhode Island

Chief Asst. of Consumer Affairs
Providence County Court House
Providence, RI 02903

Rhode Island Consumers' Council
365 Broadway
Providence, RI 02902

South Carolina

Attorney General
State Capitol
Columbia, SC 29201

South Dakota

Office of Consumer Affairs
State Capitol
PIerre, SD 57501

Tennessee

    Attorney General
    State Capitol
    Nashville, TN 37219

Texas

    Asst. Attorney General and Chief
    Antitrust and Consumer Protection Division
    Capitol Station, P.O.Box 12548
    Austin, TX 78711

    Commissioner, Office of Consumer Credit
    1011 San Jacinto Blvd./P.O.Box 2107
    Austin, TX 78767

Utah

    Asst. Attorney General for Consumer Protection
    State Capitol
    Salt Lake City, UT 84114

    Administrator of Consumer Credit
    403 State Capitol
    Salt Lake City, UT 84114

Vermont

    Asst. Attorney General in Charge
    Consumer Protection Bureau
    94 Church St.
    Burlington, VT 05401

    Family Economics and Home Management Dept.
    Room 210, Terrill Hall
    University of Vermont
    Burlington, VT 05401

Virginia

    Special Asst. to the Governor on
        Minority Groups and Consumer Affairs
    Office of the Governor
    Richmond, VA 23219

    Administrator, Consumer Affairs
    Department of Agriculture and Commerce
    8th St. Office Building
    Richmond, VA 23219

<u>Virginia</u> cont'd.

>   --Arlington County
> Consumer Protection Commission
> Arlington County Court House
> Arlington, VA 22201
>
>   --Fairfax County
> Fairfax County Consumer Protection and Public
>   Utilities Commission
> 4100 Chain Bridge Road
> Fairfax, VA 22030
>
>   --northern Virginia (regional)
> Consumer Affairs Office
> Suite 300, 7309 Arlington Blvd.
> Falls Church, VA 22042
>
>   --city of Virginia Beach
> Consumer Protection Officer
> Bureau of Consumer Protection
> Inspections Division, City Hall
> Virginia Beach, VA 23456

<u>Washington</u>

> Deputy Attorney General and Chief
> Consumer Protection and Antitrust Division
> 1266 Dexter Horton Building
> Seattle, WA 98104
>
>   --city of Seattle
> Coordinator, City of Seattle Consumer
>   Protection Office
> 500 Municipal Building
> Seattle, WA 98104

<u>West Virginia</u>

> Attorney General of West Virginia
> The Capitol
> Charleston, WV 25305
>
> Director, Consumer Protection Division
> West Virginia Department of Labor
> 100 Washington St., E.
> Charleston, WV 25305

<u>Wisconsin</u>

> Consumer Affairs Coordinator
> Department of Justice
> Madison, WI 53702
>
> Director, Bureau of Consumer Protection
> 801 W. Badger Road
> Madison, WI 53713

Wyoming

>State Examiner and Administrator
>Consumer Credit Code
>State Supreme Court Building
>Cheyenne, WY 82001

Commonwealth of Puerto Rico

>Director, Consumer Services Administration
>P.O.Box 13934
>Santurce, PR 00908

Virgin Islands

>Director, Consumer Services Administration
>P.O.Box 831, Charlotte Amalie
>St. Thomas, VI 00801

>Deputy Director, Consumer Services Administration
>Vitraco Mall, Christiansted
>St. Croix, VI 00820

Legal Assistance for Environmental Cases

The following is a partial list of lawyers who handle environmental cases or who can offer advice on environmental litigation. Those who specialize in the nuclear power area are marked with an asterisk. The best source for additional names--or for determining what types of environmental cases lawyers have handled--is the Environmental Law Digest (see Appendix 18-A in this book).

Fred Anderson   202/659 8037
Environmental Law Institute
1346 Connecticut Avenue, N.W.
Washington, DC 20036

Richard Arnold   501/773 3187
507 Hickory
Texarkana, Arkansas 75501

Thomas Arnold*   617/742 5400
131 State Street
Boston, Massachusetts 02109

Malcolm Baldwin   202/265 8882
Conservation Foundation
1717 Massachusetts Avenue, N.W.
Washington, DC 20036

Townsend Belser, Jr.*   803/253 9453
1213 Lady Street
Columbia, South Carolina 29201

Berlin, Roisman and Kessler*   202/833 9070
1712 N Street, N.W.
Washington, DC 20036

Ted Carlstrom   415/327 1900
151 University Avenue
Palo Alto, California 94301

Myron Cherry*   312/222 9350
1 IBM Plaza
Chicago, Illinois 60611

Bernard S. Cohen   703/836 2121
110 N. Royal Street
Alexandria, Virginia 22313

David Comey*   312/641 5570
Business Men in the Public Interest
109 North Dearborn Street
Chicago, Illinois 60602

Roger Diamond   213/454 1351
15415 Sunset Boulevard
Pacific Palisades, California 90272

William Dobrovir   202/293 1544
2005 L Street, N.W.
Washington, DC 20036

Hope Eastman   202/483 3830
American Civil Liberties Union
1424 16th Street, N.W.
Washington, DC 20036

Luke Fontana*   504/525 0028
824 Esplanade Avenue
New Orleans, Louisiana 70160

Robert Gnaizda   415 441 8850
Anthony Kline*
Public Advocates, Inc.
433 Turk Street
San Francisco, California 94102

Charles Halpern   202/872 0670
Center for Law and Social Policy
1751 N Street, N.W.
Washington, DC 20036

Stafford Keegin   415/397 4600
1 Maritime Plaza
San Francisco, California 94111

Norman Landau   212/962 7545
233 Broadway
New York, New York 10007

Irving Like*   516/669 3000
200 West Main Street
Babylon, New York 11702

Angus Macbeth*   212/869 0150
David Schoenbrod*
Natural Resources Defense Council
36 West 44th Street
New York, New York 10036

Thomas Maloney, Jr.   201/623 1980
570 Broad Street
Newark, New Jersey 07102

Richard Marshall   915/533 6919
S.W. National Bank Building
P.O. Drawer 888
El Paso, Texas 79945

James Moorman   415/398 1411
Sierra Club Legal Defense Fund
311 California Street
San Francisco, California 94104

David Pesonen*   415/392 1320
Fremont Building
341 Market Street
San Francisco, California 94105

Paul Rheingold   212/986 3036
99 Park Avenue
New York, New York 10016

David Sive   212/421 2150
425 Park Avenue
New York, New York 10016

Spaeth, Blase, Valentine & Kline   415/327 6700
400 Channing
Palo Alto, California 94301

Gus Speth*   202/783 5710
Natural Resources Defense Council
1710 N Street, N.W.
Washington, DC 20036

Howard Vogel*   612/333 3481
814 Flower Exchange Building
Minneapolis, Minnesota 55415

Donald S. Willner   503/228 6611
Corbett Building
Portland, Oregon 97201

John S. Winder   202/785 2444
Metropolitan Washington Coalition
        for Clean Air
1714 Massachusetts Avenue, N.W.
Washington, DC 20036

Citizen Assistance Forms

CITIZEN ASSISTANCE FORM

Center for Science in the Public Interest
1779 Church Street, N.W.
Washington, D.C. 20036
(202) 232 2534

The Center for Science in the Public Interest, a non-profit, tax-exempt organization, is computer-matching citizens who need help on consumer and environmental problems with scientists (natural and social) and engineers who wish to contribute their expertise.

If you need technical assistance for a problem you are working on, complete this form and send it to the Center. You will hear from us soon.

Donations (tax-deductible) are the only means of supporting this service--your contribution will help us help you.

NAME_____

ADDRESS_____ZIP_____

AFFILIATION_____

HOW MUCH TIME WILL THIS TAKE (approx.)?_____

CAN YOU PAY EXPENSES?_____

WE NEED HELP ON:

_____air pollution
_____water pollution
_____noise pollution
_____solid waste problems
_____radiation
_____toxic substances
_____land use
_____mining (coal, oil, etc.)
_____energy problems
_____use of natural resources
_____pesticides or herbicides
_____product safety
_____cosmetics
_____wilderness preservation

_____drug quality and testing
_____food and food additives
_____worker health and safety
_____deceptive advertising
_____property taxes
_____poverty issues
_____historic site
      preservation
_____transportation (mass
      transit, highways)
_____recycling wastes
_____soil pollution
_____urban planning
_____other (describe below)

TYPE OF HELP NEEDED:

____library research   ____working with legislators
____laboratory research   ____evaluating toxicological
____teaching   data
____writing or editing   ____investigating government
____lecturing   agencies
____preparing environmental impact statements

BRIEF DESCRIPTION OF PROBLEM (use reverse side)

SCIENCE IN THE PUBLIC INTEREST INFORMATION FORM

Center for Science in the Public Interest
1779 Church Street, N.W.
Washington, D.C. 20036
(202) 232 2534

Consumer and environmental problems facing our society urgently need citizen-oriented scientific and engineering input. You can help. The Center for Science in the Public Interest, a non-profit, tax-exempt organization, is computer-matching citizens who need help with scientists--both natural and social--and engineers who wish to contribute their expertise to the public interest.

Please fill out the form below and send it to the Center. Donations (tax-deductible) are the only means of supporting this service so please give some financial help.

NAME_____

ADDRESS_____ZIP_____

AFFILIATION_____

FIELD OF SPECIALIZATION_____

HOW MUCH TIME PER MONTH CAN YOU CONTRIBUTE?_____

DO YOU REQUIRE COMPENSATION?_____

AREAS OF SPECIAL INTEREST: (check as many as you wish)

_____ air pollution   _____ packaging
_____ water pollution   _____ food and food additives
_____ noise pollution   _____ consumer chemical products
_____ solid waste problems   _____ worker health and safety
_____ radiation   _____ deceptive advertising
_____ toxic substances   _____ property taxes
_____ land use   _____ public works disruption
_____ mining (coal, oil, etc.)   of communities
_____ energy problems   _____ poverty issues
_____ use of natural resources   _____ historic site
_____ pesticides or herbicides   preservation
_____ product safety   _____ transportation (mass
_____ cosmetics   transit, highways)
_____ wilderness preservation   _____ recycling wastes
_____ drug quality and testing   _____ soil pollution
_____ urban planning   _____ social responsibility of
                                             scientists

TYPE OF WORK DESIRED:

_____library research   _____working with legislators
_____working with legal groups   _____lecturing
_____writing or editing   _____working with citizen
_____teaching   organizations
_____organizing in professional   _____evaluating toxicological
          societies   data
_____laboratory research   _____investigating government
_____preparing environmental   agencies
          impact statements

Glossary

ABA	American Bar Association
ACAP	Aviation Consumer Action Project
ACT	Action for Children's Television
ACT	Americans for Charter Travel
AEC	Atomic Energy Commission
AHA	American Heart Association
AHCCP	Ad Hoc Committee on Consumer Protection
ALPA	Air Line Pilots Association
ALTA	Association of Local Transport Airlines
AMA	American Medical Association
AMS	Agricultural Marketing Service
Amtrak	National Rail Passenger Corporation
ANPRM	Advance Notice of Proposed Rule Making
ANSI	American National Standards Institute
APA	Administrative Procedure Act
APTIC	Air Pollution Technical Information Center
ASTA	American Society of Travel Agents
ASTM	American Standards and Testing Materials
ATA	Air Transport Association of America
ATA	American Trucking Associations, Inc.
AT&T	American Telephone and Telegraph
B&O	Baltimore and Ohio Railroad
CAB	Civil Aeronautics Board
CATV	Cable Television
CCH	Commerce Clearing House
CEQ	Council on Environmental Quality
C.F.R.	Code of Federal Regulations
CNI	Coalition of National Intervenors
CPA	Certified Public Accountant
CPSC	Consumer Product Safety Commission
CRLA	California Rural Legal Assistance Fund
CU	Consumers Union
DOT	Department of Transportation
ECCS	Emergency Core Cooling System
EEOC	Equal Employment Opportunity Commission
EPA	Environmental Protection Agency
EPNG	El Paso Natural Gas
FAA	Federal Aviation Administration
FCC	Federal Communications Commission
FCCIP	Federal Clean Car Incentive Program
FDA	Food and Drug Administration
F.I.C.A.	Federal Insurance Contribution Act
FOIA	Freedom of Information Act
FPC	Federal Power Commission
F.R.	Federal Reporter
F. 2d	Federal Reporter, Second Series

F. Supp.	Federal Supplement
FTC	Federal Trade Commission
F.U.T.A.	Federal Unemployment Tax Act
FY	Fiscal Year
GAO	General Accounting Office
G.P.O.	Government Printing Office
GRAS	Generally Recognized as Safe
HEW	Department of Health, Education, and Welfare
IATA	International Air Transport Association
ICC	Interstate Commerce Commission
ICE	Internal Combustion Engine
IOU	Investor-Owned Utility
IRS	Internal Revenue Service
JCAE	Joint Committee on Atomic Energy
LABEL	Law Students Association for Buyers' Education and Labeling
L. Ed.	Lawyers' Edition (Supreme Court Reports)
MCA	Maximum Credible Accident
MHA	Maximum Hypothetical Accident
NAACP	National Association for the Advancement of Colored People
NAB	National Association of Broadcasters
NACA	National Agricultural Chemical Association
NACA	National Air Carrier Association
NAMBO	National Association of Motor Bus Owners
NARP	National Association of Railroad Passengers
NARUC	National Association of Regulatory Utility Commissioners
NEPA	National Environmental Policy Act
NERC	National Electric Reliability Council
NHTSA	National Highway Traffic Safety Administration
NIH	National Institutes of Health
NIOSH	National Institute of Occupational Safety and Health
NPRM	Notice of Proposed Rule Making
NRDC	National Resources Defense Council
NS	Nuclear Ship
NTIS	National Technical Information Service
OCAW	Oil, Chemical, and Atomic Workers Union
OMB	Office of Management and Budget
OSHA	Occupational Safety and Health Administration
PJM	Pennsylvania, New Jersey, Maryland Power Intersection
POWER	People Organized to Win Effective Regulation
REA	Rural Electrification Administration
Rev. Rul.	Revenue Ruling
SAE	Society of Automotive Engineers
SAME	Students Against Misleading Enterprise
SAPP	Sodium Acid Pyrophosphate
SMASH	Students Mobilizing on Auto Safety Hazards
SOUP	Students Opposed to Unfair Practices
STATES	Safety Through Action to Enlist Support
STATIC	Student Task-force Against Telecommunications Information Concealment
TVA	Tennessee Valley Authority
U.S.C.	United States Code
U.S.C. Ann.	United States Code Annotated
USDA	United States Department of Agriculture
U.S.	United States Supreme Court Reports
YOUTHS	Youth Organizations United Toward Highway Safety

INDEX

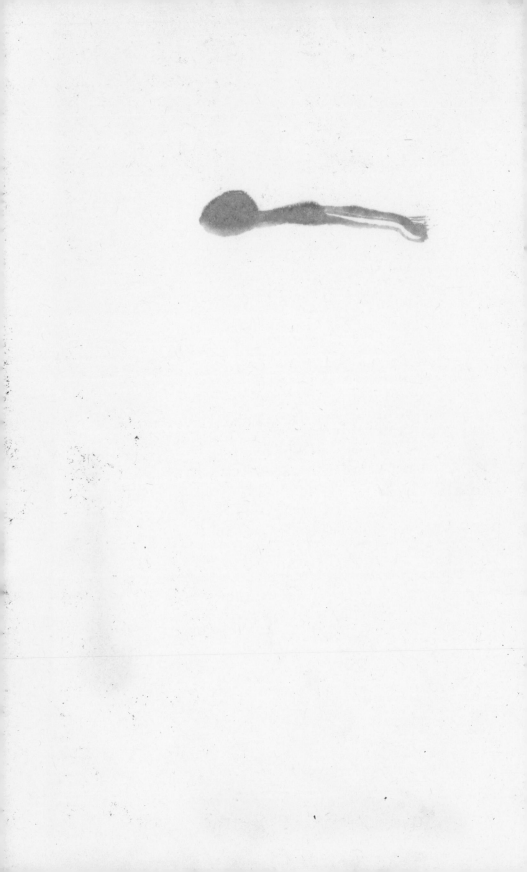